BEGINNER'S GUIDE TO

STAINED & DECORATIVE GLASS

BEGINNER'S GUIDE TO

STAINED & DECORATIVE GLASS

Oriel Hicks

Sterling Publishing Co., Inc.
New York

Creative director: Sarah King
Editor: Clare Haworth-Maden
Project editor: Judith Millidge
Designer: 2H Design

Library of Congress Cataloging-in-Publication Data Available

10   9   8   7   6   5   4   3   2   1

Published in 2002 by Sterling Publishing Company, Inc.
387 Park Avenue South, New York, N.Y. 10016

This book was designed and produced by
D&S Books
Cottage Meadow, Bocombe, Parkham
Bideford, Devon, EX39 5PH

Distributed in Canada by Sterling Publishing
C/o Canadian Manda Group,
One Atlantic Avenue, Suite 105
Toronto, Ontario, Canada M6K 3E7

Every effort has been made to ensure that all the information in this book is accurate.
however, due to differing conditions, tools, and individual skills, the publisher cannot
be responsible for any injuries, losses, and other damages which may result from the
use of the information in this book.

Printed in Singapore

Sterling ISBN 0-8069-9351-0

Contents

Introduction

It is not known exactly when glassmaking first started, but it was almost certainly at least four thousand years ago. The technique was probably invented accidentally by the Egyptians or the Phoenicians, when firing clay pots in the sand; glass beads would form from the silica and other chemicals around it in the sand. Glass was then regarded as a very precious commodity, on a par with gold.

It was another two thousand years at least, in about the first century B.C., that a method of glassblowing was invented along the Eastern Mediterranean coast, and eventually the Romans were able to make the highly prized sheet glass, which was sometimes used in their houses. The glass was rarely completely clear, and the glassblowers soon realized that the color of glass produced depended on what kind of wood was used in the furnace, because the chemical composition of the different types of potash varied. They then began to experiment, adding oxides of different metals and other chemicals to create different hues and depths of color.

Star of the Sea, *St. Mary's Catholic Church, Isles of Scilly. Designed and made by the author.*

Stained-glass Windows

The oldest stained-glass window is in Augsburg, Germany, and dates from about A.D. 1000. Windows were probably being made in various parts of Europe for at least a century before this, however. Stained glass was used in churches to illustrate stories from the Bible at a time when most of the congregation was illiterate. Some of the finest, and most famous, stained glass is in the cathedral of Chartres in France, which was made during the twelfth and thirteenth centuries. Stained glass became very popular all over Europe, and most cathedrals and churches, right down to the smallest, had some stained glass in them.

Tragically, during the seventeenth century in England, much of this beautiful glass was ripped out and destroyed because it was considered idolatrous. The windows dating from before that time that are still in existence are those that monks had the foresight to remove and hide in crypts or graveyards until it was safe to reinstate them. Because stained glass was used solely for churches, its production subsequently ceased, and the recipes for many colors were lost forever. By the end of the seventeenth century, a new kind of glass had become popular in churches. It was not stained, but clear glass that had been painted with colored enamels and then fired. Although the technique was permanent, the color was superficial and didn't have the depth and vibrancy of stained glass.

This technique continued to be used until the later part of the nineteenth century, when William Morris, a founding member of the Arts and Crafts Movement, along with the artists and designers Dante Gabriel Rossetti and Edward Burne-Jones, demanded the making of real stained glass for their windows. At around this time, too, the native New Yorker, Louis Comfort Tiffany, was working with stained glass in the United States. Since white was added to it to make it semiopalescent, the glass that he used was not as transparent. This type of glass, which is still made today, is usually called Tiffany glass. With its soft, flowing lines and romantic subjects, the style of these artists' stained glass was typical of the time.

St. Christopher & St. Mary's, Church of England Church, Isles of Scilly.

Stained-glass window in the author's house.

Dalles de Verre

During the two world wars of the twentieth century, many churches and cathedrals were either destroyed or had their windows blown out. The glass in the windows of some modern churches and cathedrals is often a new type of glass called *dalles de verre*, which requires a completely different method of creation. Instead of being blown into sheets, molten glass is poured into molds to form small slabs about 2.5 centimeters (1 inch) thick. When cold, these slabs are removed from their molds and chipped to size and shape with a chisel-edged hammer so that the edges are faceted. The design must be kept very simple, mainly using colored squares, triangles, and oblongs. The colored glass for each section of the design is laid out on the floor on a bed of sand and reinforced resin or concrete is then poured between the slabs of glass and left to set. The large section thus formed is used as a building block, which, with other blocks, forms a window that acts as a wall. The crown of England's Liverpool Cathedral was made in this way, as was the beautiful window at Buckfast Abbey in Devon, also in England, where there is still a workshop run by monks who design and make this kind of stained-glass window.

As occurred during the nineteenth century, the end of the twentieth century saw a big revival in the popularity of stained glass, which is now commonly used in public buildings like libraries and courts and in the offices of multinational companies. Today it is also a popular craft that is practiced by many people.

Different view of the stained-glass window.

CHAPTER 1
Materials and Equipment

Glass is made by melting silica (sand) with potash and soda at a temperature of about 1300°C (2372°F). In true stained glass, the color is added at this stage by mixing in various oxides of metals and rare earths. Copper oxide will give you green glass, for example, while cobalt oxide will give you blue, and antimony results in various shades of red and deep amber. The most expensive color is cranberry pink, which is made by adding small quantities of 9 carat gold and copper to obtain the beautiful pink color.

Today, stained glass can be made either by the original method of blowing glass, when it is called antique glass, or by a machine process. In both cases, the color is added in the same way by using oxides.

Opalescent blue/green glass.

Types of Glass

In the mouth-blown, antique method, a ball of molten glass is taken from the crucible and blown into a cylinder, called a muff. This is cooled and the cylinder is then cut down one side, reheated, and opened out to form a flat sheet. It has striations, reams, and bubbles in it, which give it movement and life. It is often not completely flat, and because the thickness varies across the sheet, the depth of color changes. This type of glass, which is called a pot color, as the color is added in the crucible, is used in church windows and restoration work. Sometimes two or more colors are used in the same sheet of glass; this is called reamy. Another type of antique glass is called flash glass, which is made by using clear glass and "flashing" molten glass of a different color onto one surface. This is used for cut or acid-etched glass, where the colored layer is removed with either a grinding wheel or hydrofluoric acid. The Victorians used a lot of this type of glass in their doors and windows.

Glass can also be poured onto a bed of sand and rolled flat. This gives it definite "right" and "wrong" sides, as one surface will pick up the texture of the sand. Machine-made glass is poured between two rollers, one of which may be slightly textured to give the glass an obscured finish.

Tiffany glass is made by adding small amounts of white glass to colored glass, which results in a slight wispy appearance and brings out the color without the need for backlighting. If more white is added, the finished sheet will be more opalescent, which means that although nothing is visible through it, light will still penetrate the glass, making it glow. Tiffany glass is therefore useful for lampshades, clock faces, and photo frames, in other words, objects that are intended to be looked at rather than through. The layers of white in the colored glass can be seen on the cut edge of the sheet, rather like the lettering that runs through the type of candy sold at English seaside resorts which is known as rock. Another type of opalescent glass is iridescent glass. This is made by taking a sheet of colored opalescent glass and painting one side with a luster. The glass is then fired at a lower temperature than that at which the glass melts, making the luster permanent and giving the glass the attractive appearance of mother of pearl or oil on water.

Interestingly, glass is technically a viscous, not a solid, substance. If a sheet of glass is left in an upright position in a church window for centuries, for example, it will become thicker at the lower edge than at the upper, because gravity has caused the glass to flow downward. Also, if a sheet of glass is scored but not broken, the score line will eventually close, or heal, over. Although it remains visible, it will not subsequently break along this line.

Iridescent glass.

Glass Paints

The glass paints referred to here are not the traditional types found on church windows, which are only used for shading real stained glass to give the details of faces, hands, and robes, for inscriptions, and so on. The paints that have been used for the projects in this book are instead colored lacquers that are applied to one surface of a sheet of clear glass and are then left to dry through exposure to the air rather than fired in a kiln.

These paints can be bought at art and craft stores and are sold in a range of colors. Their base can be either water, white spirit, or cellulose thinners, the latter being the most highly toxic, but also the most color-fast (the others tend to fade in strong sunlight after a year or two). An outline relief is used to contain the glass paint in their different areas of color. This is a type of black, gold, or silver acrylic paste that is sold in a tube with a long nozzle. After application, it is left to dry for a couple of hours before the glass paint is used.

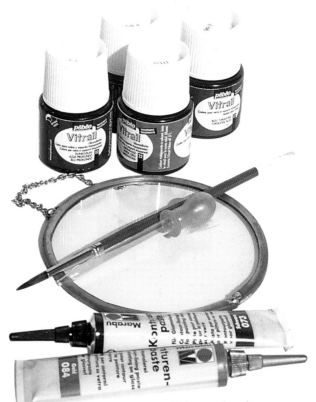

Paints and outline.

Etching Paste

Although a type of opalescent white glass paint applied to glass will give the appearance of an etched texture, true etching on glass is always done using an etching paste containing hydrofluoric acid. This will etch only about 8 microns into the glass and will therefore not affect the strength of toughened glass (an important consideration if it is to be used for a panel in a door, for instance).

Hydrofluoric acid is a very dangerous substance and must be used with great care. It is imperative that rubber gloves are worn at all times and that work is carried out either in a very well ventilated area or preferably outside. In addition, brushes and tools used for etching should, for the sake of safety, not be used for any other purpose.

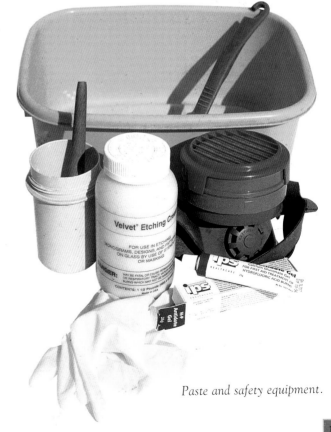

Paste and safety equipment.

Glasscutters

Various glasscutters and a jar of white spirit with a sponge.

The earliest windows were cut using a hot metal rod to crack the glass by means of differential expansion, in the same way that plunging a hot wine glass into cold water will break it. Very intricate shapes could be cut in this way, usually by the monks who made the windows, but it was an extremely time-consuming method. Later, when it was discovered that a diamond was harder than glass, the glass was scored with this stone, breaking the surface tension. The glass was then cracked by the application of force underneath the cut.

Nowadays, a wheeled cutter made of steel or tungsten carbide is usually used to create the score line. Although a tungsten-carbide cutter is considerably more expensive than a steel cutter, it is a good investment because a lot less pressure is needed to make the score line and the wheel will also last much longer. A pistol-grip tungsten cutter is also available, which is useful if you do not have enough strength in your hands to use a traditional cutter. Cutters are lubricated by means of white spirit or a thin machine oil within the shaft, which keeps the cutting wheel permanently oiled through a wick or gravity feed. If a steel-wheeled cutter, or one without a reservoir, is used, the wheel must always be lubricated with thin oil before a score line is made in the glass. For this purpose, it is a good idea to have a small jar to hand containing a piece of sponge soaked in white spirit to wipe away excess oil.

Different-sized pairs of breaking pliers, a straight edge, and a carborundum stone.

Other Tools Used in Glasscutting

It is sometimes necessary to cut a long, straight line across a sheet of glass. This is more easily achieved with the use of a straight edge, when you would place the cutter against the top edge and then pull it toward you. The straight edge should have a nonslip strip on the under side and must be thick enough to ensure that the glasscutter does not jump onto it, instead remaining alongside it while you are cutting.

Cut-run pliers, which are a bit like tilebreakers, can be useful if you are a nervous of breaking the glass. They do exactly as their name indicates and replace the hands when breaking glass by gripping it on each side of the score line and applying pressure underneath it, causing the glass to break cleanly.

If you are confident enough to break the glass with your hands, however, when cutting a very narrow piece of glass it will still be necessary to hold it with a pair of breaking pliers in order to get a sufficient grip. Breaking pliers are wide-nosed pliers that meet only at their tips, which means that the glass is not damaged as they close. The straight end of the pliers is used to grip the glass parallel to the score line at the near edge of the cut, bending and thus breaking the glass much as a finger and thumb would.

Copper Foil

Originally, only lead came was used for making window panels. Nowadays, however, it is more common to use copper foil for small, indoor panels and giftware. The foil, which comes on a reel, is available in different widths. One side is adhesive, enabling it to stick to the glass, and this adhesive side is covered in backing paper so that it runs off the reel more easily. The foil can either be backed with a transparent adhesive, or, if it is to be used with clear glass (in a terrarium, for instance), with black adhesive, which will prevent the copper color being visible; in addition, silver-backed foil can be used on mirrored glass for the same reason.

Copper foil.

Foilwork accessories.

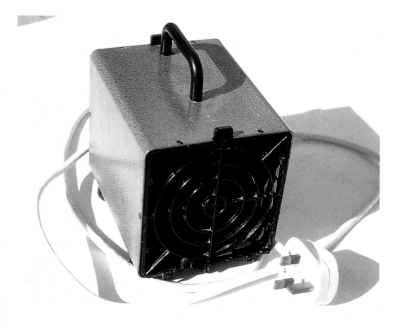

Accessories for Foilwork

Although foil can be applied directly to the glass edge by hand, this is a fiddly process. It is much easier to use a handfoiler, which centers the copper foil on the edge of the glass and removes the backing paper as it goes along.

More intricate foiling tools are also available, which often work well with large pieces of glass, but not so efficiently with small ones. Some also crimp the foil around the piece of glass. If you are using a handfoiler, you could also invest in a separate tool called a handcrimper, but your fingers are often just as efficient.

Copper foil is put around the glass in order to take solder and is not actually seen on the finished object. Before solder is applied to the foil, however, the foil must be fluxed. Flux is an oil, and if the foil does not adhere to the glass thoroughly, the flux will seep underneath it and lift it off. Once the copper foil has been crimped to the glass edge, it must therefore be pressed down firmly with a small tool called a fid.

As well as being an oil, flux is acidic. Its main function is to deoxidize the copper foil prior to soldering and to make the solder flow. Because the flux burns away once the soldering iron is applied, a fume trap, which draws the fumes away from the area being soldered, is a highly recommended piece of equipment. You could also use small fan, but this is more likely to cool the soldering iron.

A fume trap.

Lead Came

Lead is a soft substance, which will bend around very tight curves if necessary. It has been used to join pieces of glass together for as long as stained-glass windows have been made. It comes in lengths of approximately 2 meters (6 ½ feet) and in various widths. It is "H"-shaped in section, with a channel on each side to take the pieces of glass. The crosspiece of the "H" section is called the heart, and the top and bottom, which are the parts seen when looking at a window, are each called the leaf.

When it is first cut, lead is a very shiny metal, but it soon oxidizes to become a dull gray color and continues to oxidize right the way through the lead, which is why many cathedrals have a stained-glass workshop on the premises to restore their windows (unless it is broken, the glass will last almost indefinitely, but, depending on the quality of the air in the location, the windows have to be removed, taken apart, and the lead replaced every fifty to a hundred years).

Lead is so soft that it will rub off on your hands. Because it is a poisonous substance that can be absorbed through the skin and, when soldering, through inhalation, it is advisable to wear rubber gloves or a good barrier cream when using lead came and a mask when rubbing it down with a wire brush prior to soldering.

Lead came.

Leadworking tools.

Tools for Leadwork

The lead came should be cut with a sharp lead knife. Being a metal, the lead will blunt even the sharpest knife fairly quickly, so an oilstone is useful to keep the edge on it.

Because lead is such a soft substance, it often becomes damaged in transit and must then be straightened before use. To do this, one end of the lead came is gripped in a lead vise or cleat attached to a workbench, while the other is held with a pair of pliers, enabling the lead to be stretched for quite a distance. This process not only straightens the lead, but makes it stiffer and easier to work with.

If there are crimps in the lead, or the channel is not wide enough to take the piece of glass, the channel can be widened using either a fid or a tool designed to do a number of different tasks, perhaps unsurprisingly called a Nova all-purpose tool. Some people use a tool called a lathekin instead, or else an oyster knife, but these can be difficult to obtain. You could always make your own, however, or adapt a similar tool.

15

The Grinder

Although a grinder is probably the most expensive piece of equipment that you will have to buy, you will soon discover what an invaluable tool it is for getting rid of all of those little blips and bits that you couldn't remove with the glasscutter. Bear in mind, though, that when you start to grind a piece of glass, the edge that you are pushing against may still be rough enough to cut you. Once it has been ground, however, you won't cut your fingers when you come to do the foiling and the pieces will also fit together perfectly.

The grinder's grinding wheel is embedded with diamond grit, which is kept wet with a sponge that sits adjacent to it, in a reservoir of water below the top plate. By pushing a piece of glass against this turning wheel and then moving it from side to side, you can obtain a lovely smooth edge.

Many models incorporate a glass safety shield that sits between you and your work, preventing the powdered glass and water from splashing into your eyes, but if your grinder does not have a safety shield, ensure that you wear goggles. It is also vitally important that you keep the water in the reservoir well topped up, as powdered glass is a severe health hazard. Finally, clean out the wet, ground glass in the reservoir at regular intervals to avoid clogging the mechanism.

A glass grinder. The wheel is embedded with diamond grit.

The Soldering Iron

Soldering irons can either be electric or run off butane gas. An electric one should be a minimum of 75 watts, as the bit has to be large and heavy-duty enough to hold a great deal of heat, otherwise it will grind to a halt halfway down when you are soldering a long "bead" of solder. It is also advisable to opt for an iron-clad copper bit rather than a simple straight one, because the copper will be eaten away at the tip.

The gas soldering iron has a flame jet which plays on the copper bit which sits at a right angle to the handle. It is a much more expensive option than an electric soldering iron, and is usually only used for large-scale leaded-light work.

Whichever type you choose, ensure that your soldering iron has some kind of stand, as it will become very hot and will scorch anything that it is placed on. When using it, be careful not to touch any part of it except the handle, and do not let the flex (or anything else) drag across the iron, as the iron will quickly melt the flex down to the bare wires.

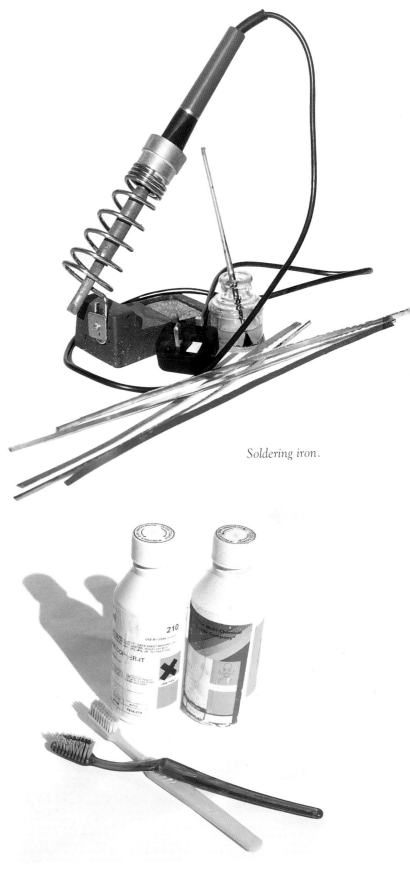

Soldering iron.

Solder

The solder that is nowadays used for copper foilwork is known as "F grade." This is a fifty-fifty mix of lead and tin which has a very low melting point, making it flow well. It is perfectly adequate for leaded-light work, although a blow-pipe-grade solder, 40 percent tin and 60 percent lead, is often used for this.

Although you can buy solder with a flux core, it should never be used for stained-glass work. This is because although the flux helps the solder to flow, it also prevents it from sticking to the glass when it has been painted on beforehand.

Patina

A patina is a chemical that reacts with the solder to give it a different-colored finish. Copper sulfate will do this by coating the solder with a thin layer of copper. If other chemicals are added as well, they will leave a dark or antique finish.

Patina.

Safety First!

It is essential to have a good first-aid kit, which should include such items as plasters, tweezers for removing glass splinters, an eyewash, a spray for treating burns instantly (although ten minutes under a running cold faucet will do the same thing) and an antidote gel for hydrofluoric acid.

Rubber gloves are useful for many tasks, and are essential when you are working with acid. A dust mask, or preferably a gas mask suitable for use with acid, should be used if you are etching inside. Goggles, or protective glasses, and a rubber or PVC apron are also good ideas.

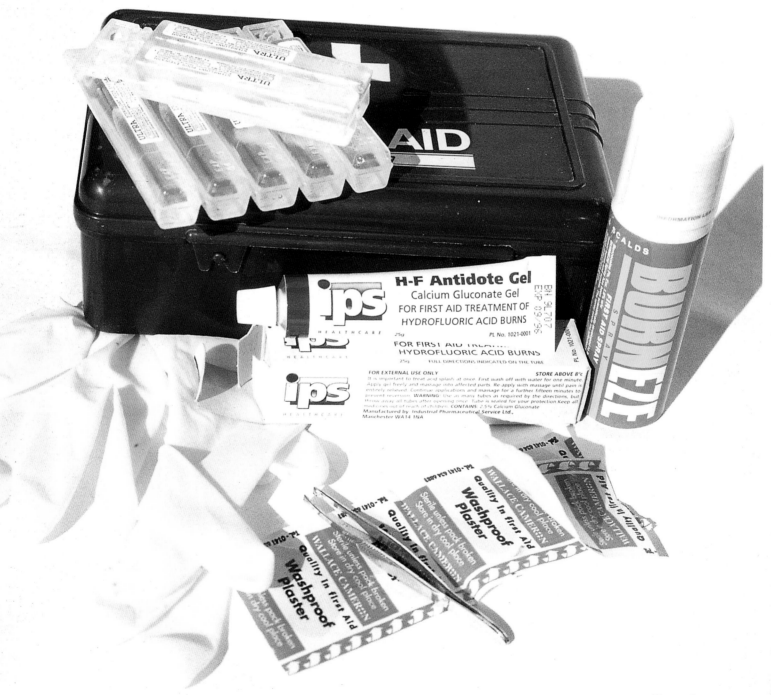

First-aid equipment.

CHAPTER 2
Starting Out

You'll soon discover that the greater the line of curvature on a piece of glass, the harder it is to cut, and right angles are definitely out. Even if you manage to cut an internal right angle into a piece of glass, it will be structurally unsound and will crack and break when the first vibration hits it. This is one reason to keep your design simple.

In addition, very small pieces of glass are both difficult to foil and are almost certain to be dropped and lost in the pile of the carpet. Working with very long, thin pieces of glass is also not to be recommended as their delicate points will often break off at the cutting stage. Remember, too, that there should be as much contact between the pieces of glass as possible, and that pieces that are joined by just one small point will bend and break away from each other quite quickly.

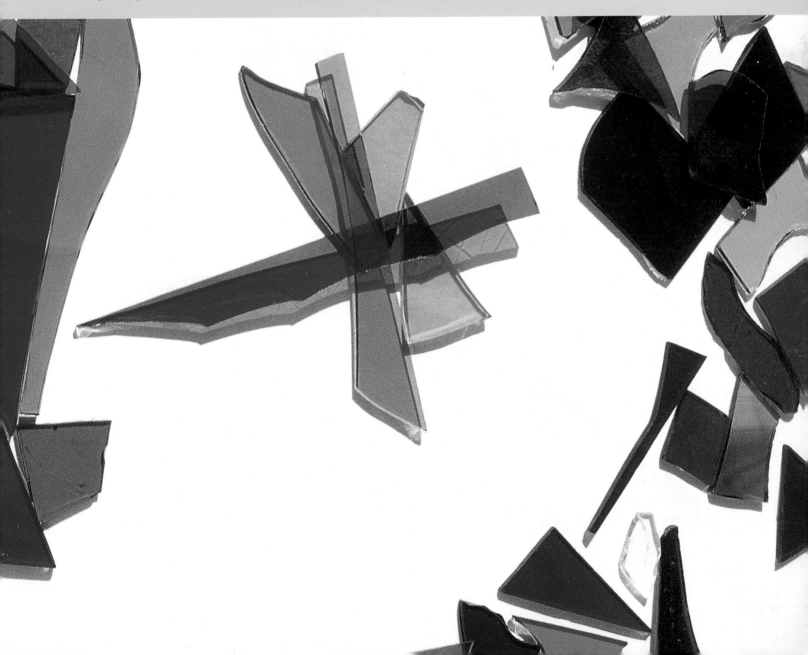

Planning Your Design

Fig. 1.

Fig. 2.

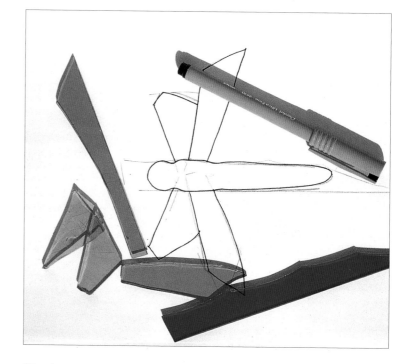

Fig. 3.

Fig. 4.

Look for pictures or photographs of things that you would like to make, for instance, a flower or a fish. Try to simplify the basic shape to as few pieces as possible, rather like making a caricature of a human face. Pick out only the characteristics that give the object its identity and disregard the rest (Fig. 1).

It is often both easy and fun to create designs from pieces of glass in your cullet box. ("Cullet" is the generic term for small pieces of glass offcuts.) Rather than throwing them away, this is a good way of using up offcuts (Fig. 2).

Ideas for subjects will often suggest themselves if you play around with different pieces of glass for long enough (Fig. 3).

I tipped out the contents of my cullet box and sorted through the pieces until the shape of a dragonfly suggested itself (Fig. 4). Tomorrow it could be a sailing boat, and the day after that a simple flower.

You will probably only need to trim off a bit here and a piece there to create a design that hadn't occurred to you before you started (Fig. 5). Your design may also take on a life of its own while you are working on it, as in the case of my dragonfly.

Having trimmed the pieces, I decided that the design would be improved by placing the larger wing above the smaller one. It was not too late to change it, so I reground the pieces slightly so that they fitted snugly against both the body and each other (Fig. 6). You'll probably agree that this was an improvement on the original idea (Fig. 7).

Fig. 5.

Fig. 6.

Fig. 7.

How to Cut Glass

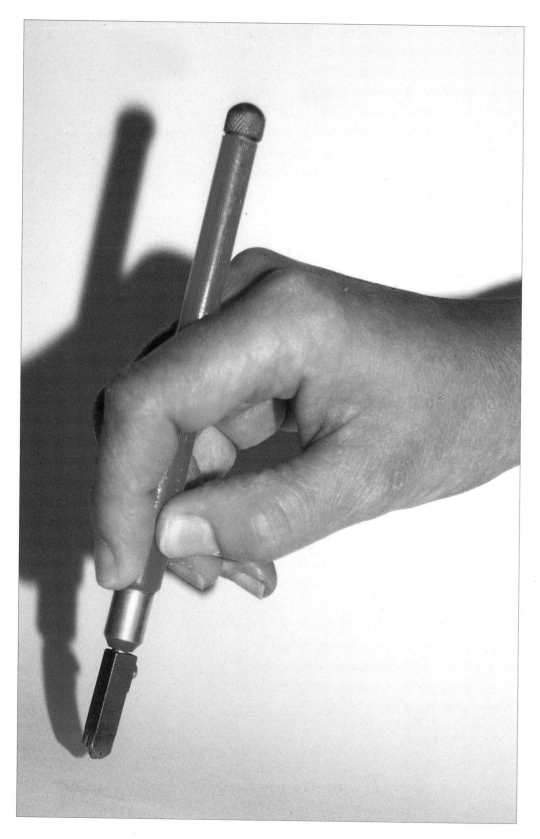

The glasscutter must be held in an upright position and the wheel must be rolled (Fig. 8). This may sound obvious, but it is amazing how many people try to drag the wheel sideways across the glass, making a sound that sets your teeth on edge (the wheel does not need to be very much out of true to produce this effect).

If you are using a standard-shaped glasscutter rather than a pistol-grip one, you should ideally hold it between your first and second fingers and not between your first finger and thumb, as if you were holding a pencil. This ensures that the glasscutter is kept in an upright position and, being securely held, cannot wobble. If you are using a steel-wheeled cutter that has to be dipped in white spirit, hold it with your index finger resting on the fingerpad at the front. If you are using an oil-filled cutter, make sure that the little screw on the head of the cutter is facing toward you, which is the most comfortable way to hold it.

The little square notches at the back of glasscutters were traditionally used for grozing, or chewing off, bits of glass that did not come off cleanly when the glass was cut. Nowadays we usually use specially designed breaking, or grozing, pliers.

If you are cutting a large sheet of glass against a straight edge for the first time,

Fig. 8.

Fig. 9.

put the glasscutter at the far side of the sheet and pull it toward you. If you are cutting small pieces of glass to a pattern for a suncatcher, however, it is easier to see the line that you are cutting if you push the glasscutter, which prevents your hand from obscuring the line that you are cutting to. Before moving on to the next stage, I recommend that you practice the following method until you get it right. (It doesn't matter how many score lines you make in an old piece of glass, as your local glass merchant will have boxes full of cullet should you need it.)

Holding the glasscutter securely, place the wheel as close to the near edge of the glass as you can without it slipping off. First push the glasscutter downward into the glass, so that pressure is applied right from the beginning of the cut, and then push it away from you to the far edge of the glass (Fig. 9). Do not stop along the way: you must make one continuous line. You should hear a sound as the wheel bites into the surface of the glass and moves all the way across. If you don't hear this sound being made all the way,

don't try to improve the cut line by going over it again, as this will only make matters worse. Remember that what you are trying to do is to break the surface tension of the glass, and that because glass is technically a viscous liquid, it is less likely to break in the right place if you make more than one score line. Going over the same line again will also considerably reduce your glasscutter's life expectancy.

If you find that you produce no sound at all when you are pushing the glasscutter across the glass, you may need to use your other hand to push down on the top of the glasscutter to put more pressure on it. Although successful glasscutting has more to do with having the knack rather than applying brute force, it is often helpful to start with brute force and then to work toward developing that knack at a later stage. To cut a curved line, use the same procedure as you would for scoring a straight line.

When you have made a score line that sounds as if it has taken all

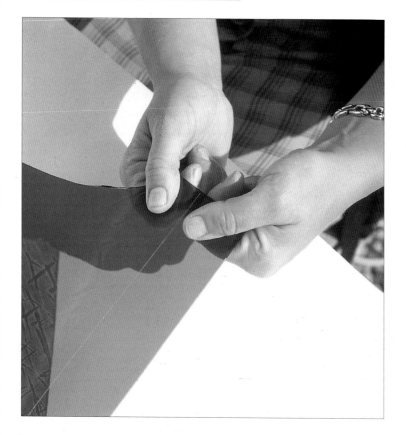

Fig. 10.

the way across the glass, put down your glasscutter and, with your knuckles and thumbs together, parallel to each side of the cut, grip the glass at the near edge (Fig. 10). The glass should be facing away from you, so that any chips do not fly into your face. Now roll your knuckles apart to break the glass (Fig. 11). The technique and amount of force needed are similar to those used when breaking a piece of chocolate off a candy bar. Many people do not feel confident about doing this, but if you keep your hands together as you carry out the maneuver, it should not be possible to be cut by the glass. If, however, your hands are apart, the glass may slip and cut you across the back of the knuckles.

After the score has been made, it is sometimes necessary to tap it underneath the glass to start the breaking process, especially on a curved score line. Do this with the other end of the glasscutter, which has a metal knob on it, and hold it in the same position as you would for cutting, but upside down (Fig. 12). Aim to use a pincer movement, like a crab's, holding your thumb on top of the glass while you tap the score line from underneath with the knob. The advantage of tapping the cut like this is that if the glass suddenly breaks you will be holding the piece that comes off, rather than it falling on the work surface and possibly breaking.

Fig. 11.

Fig. 12.

Fig. 13.

If you find it difficult to hit the glass sharply enough to crack it in this way, an easier method is to turn the scored glass upside down, placing it on enough layers of newspaper to provide a yielding surface, and then to tap it gently (Fig. 13). Much less force is required to crack the glass in this way, so err on the side of caution and tap gently more than once in order to avoid ending up with a pile of fragments. Don't forget to turn the glass around again, so that the score line is on the upper side, before trying to break it. Once you have tapped the cut and started the break successfully, it is then possible to hold it with your hands, as for the straight-line cut, and then to bend it apart. You will see the glass tearing along the line until it breaks in two.

Alternatively, if it is a very small piece of glass, or you are nervous about breaking it, you could use breaking pliers. Place the edge of the pliers parallel to the cut line and then bend the glass apart (Fig. 14). Remember that glass that has been cut on the curve often has a nasty under-cut edge and can therefore be much more dangerous to handle than a straight-edged piece.

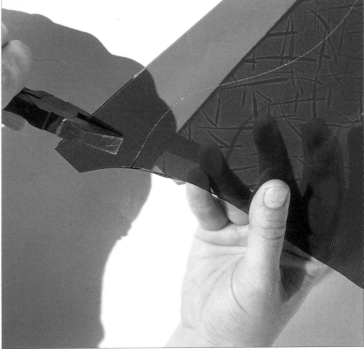

Fig. 14.

Fig. 15.

It is advisable to remove this under-cut edge immediately, before you cut yourself, using either the grinder, wet carborundum stone, or another piece of glass scraped along the edge (Fig. 15). To cut some of the larger straight-sided pieces for the terrarium and lampshade, you will need to use a straight edge (this technique is covered in the mosaic mirror project (see page 65).

For some of the projects in this book, you will need to use a bottle with the top cut off. Although you can buy a bottlecutter, this will only cut a straight line around a round bottle. If you want to cut an irregularly-shaped bottle or an undulating line – which is more interesting – you can only do this with a handheld glasscutter.

Using a pen, first mark the line on the bottle (Fig. 16). Then, placing your fingers against the bottle to stop the glasscutter skidding, score a line around the bottle along the pen line, making sure that the end of your line meets the original point (Fig. 17).

Fig. 16.

Fig. 17.

Holding the bottle over a plastic bowl or basin, pour boiling water over the cut, taking care not to scald your fingers (Fig. 18). When it has been thoroughly heated, run the cut under a cold faucet immediately. If the faucet runs too slowly, the cut won't break, while if it runs too fast, the cut will crack right around and sometimes down the bottle, too. Only by trial and error will you discover the exact speed of flow needed.

When you get it right, the bottle will crack all the way round and you can then lift off the top, which will make a slight popping sound, leaving a clean edge (Fig. 19). This now only needs to be neatened with the grinder or be given a light dusting with a wet carborundum stone (Fig. 20).

Because it is embedded with diamond grit, the wheel on the grinder is very expensive, so the more accurately you cut your glass on your first attempt, the less often you will have to use the grinder and the longer the wheel will last. The wheel is, however, very useful for removing sharp edges and grinding pieces to fit exactly where required. After the pieces of glass have been ground, and before they are foiled, they must be washed in boiling water, which, contrary to popular belief, will not crack the glass. While they are still hot, carefully remove them from the water, place them on some newspaper, and dry them with a paper towel. This will remove any fingermarks, residual powdered glass, and white spirit left by the glasscutter, rendering the pieces of glass grease-free and ready for foiling.

Fig. 18.

Fig. 19.

Fig. 20.

Foiling

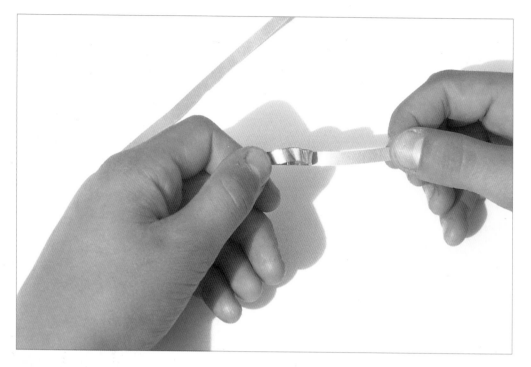

To thread the handfoiler, take a reel of copper foil, separate the foil from its backing paper to a length of about 2.5 centimeters (1 inch) and then curl the backing paper downward, away from the foil, using your thumbnail (Fig. 21).

If you look at a spare length of backing paper, you will notice that the side that lay against the adhesive is shiny and that the other side has a mat finish. If you take the mat side, the copper foil will adhere to it, making a little "leader" that will not stick to the handfoiler as you thread it (Fig. 22). It is almost impossible, and very frustrating, to try to thread the foil without this leader attached, as the foil will stick to everything it touches.

Fig. 21.

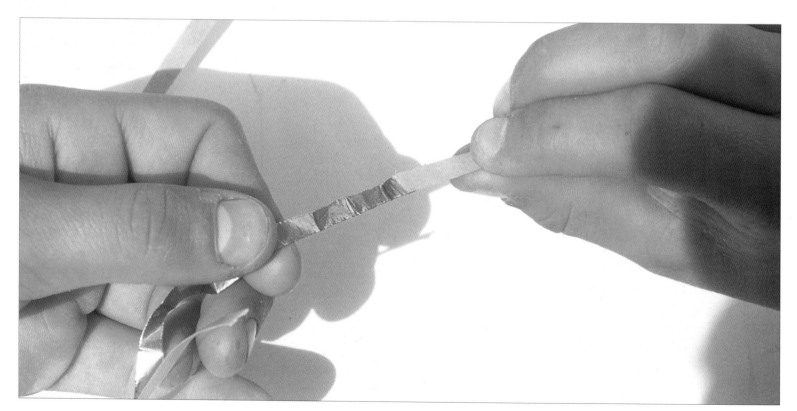

Fig. 22.

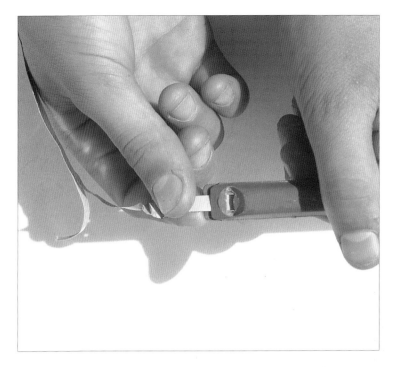

Thread both the backing paper and the foil – with its leader – through the tiny slot at the back of the handfoiler, with the copper side uppermost (Fig. 23).

As the backing paper goes through the slot, it should almost immediately emerge from another slot underneath the foiler. The copper foil itself, however, along with its leader, should continue up the shaft of the foiler (Fig. 25), coming out at the top end beneath a little roller .

Pull the leader through and cut it off. Your handfoiler has now been threaded (Fig. 26).

When holding the foiler, be careful not to touch the foil as it travels up the shaft of the tool, as it will then adhere to the foiler and won't emerge from the top. Pull about 60 to 90 centimeters

Fig. 23.

Fig. 24.

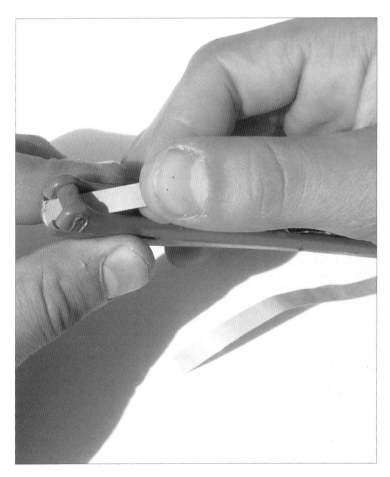

Fig. 25.

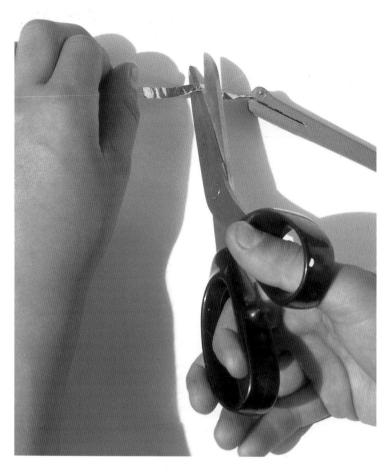

Fig. 26.

(2 or 3 feet) of slack from the roll before starting work. If there is not sufficient slack, the foil is likely to twist and snag before entering the foiler, thus jamming it.

If you take the foiler in your hand and turn it upside down, so that the adhesive side of the foil is facing you, you will notice a channel in the back of the foiler, which is about the same width as the thickness of your glass. Take the piece of glass to be foiled and place it in this channel, which is designed to center the foil on the edge of the glass, with an equal amount of overlap on each side. As you pull the glass through the channel, the little roller at the top of the foiler will then push the copper foil onto the edge (Fig.27). (It usually works much better if the foiler is held still and the piece of glass is moved round rather than the other way around.)

Although the foiler is designed to remove the backing paper from the foil, it often doesn't, and if the paper rides up inside the handle of the tool, it may be necessary to keep pulling it back down, otherwise the foil will emerge from under the roller with the backing paper still attached, which means that it can't adhere to the glass.

When you have gone right round the glass and have returned to your starting point, overlap the first bit of copper foil by about 1.25 centimeters ($\frac{1}{2}$ inch) and then break or cut the foil (Fig. 28). Using your finger and thumb, crimp the free edges of the foil over the edges of the glass.

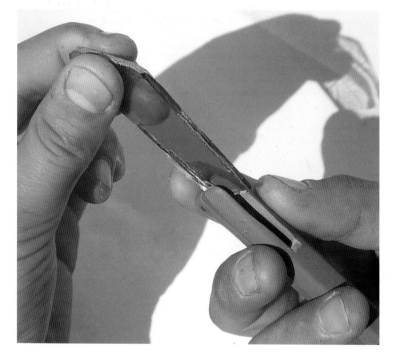

Fig. 27.

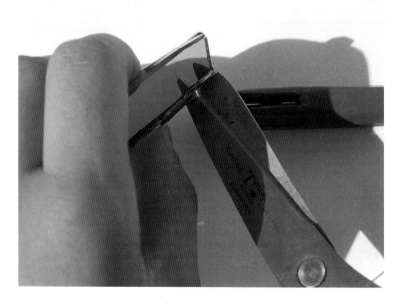

Fig. 28.

Fig. 29.

Always push slightly inward, toward the middle of the piece of glass, as it is quite easy to cut yourself on the foil if you're not careful. On corners, first tuck in one side and then overlap it with the adjacent side to leave a neat finish (Fig. 29).

Using a fid, go round the edge of each piece of glass, flattening the copper foil on both sides and ensuring that it has adhered securely to the glass so that the flux will not seep out later (Fig. 30). If a crackling sound seems to coming from the foil as you use the fid, it indicates that it has not stuck properly and must be peeled off, washed, and dried thoroughly and then replaced to prevent your work from falling apart later on.

Once you have foiled all of the pieces for your item, place them on a board ready for soldering.

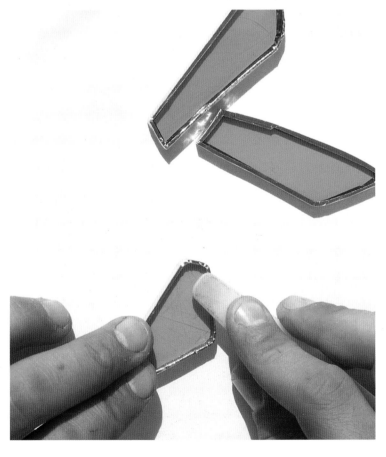

Fig. 30.

Soldering

Fig. 31.

Fig. 32.

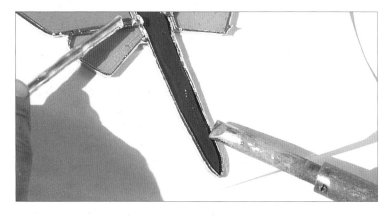

Fig. 33.

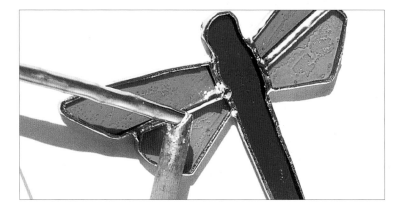

Fig. 34.

Your work must now be fluxed before it can be soldered. You will find a little – preferably spill-proof – jar for the flux useful, as well as an old, small paintbrush. Pour a little safety flux into the jar and then, using the brush, flux generously over all of the copper foil, also going a little way onto the glass (Fig. 31). Not only will this make the solder adhere to the copper foil securely, but it will also ensure that the solder does not stick to the glass, instead rolling off it. Because many people forget to flux their work on the second side if they leave it till later, it is probably best to flux both sides at this stage.

Place all of the pieces of glass for your suncatcher in their correct positions and then carefully drop a little bead of solder onto as many points on your work as is necessary to hold it together (Fig. 32). Try not to touch the work with the soldering iron, because the slightest movement may knock the pieces out of position while the solder is setting. Once the cardinal points have been attached, your pieces will be held together to form a unified item.

You now have to "tin" the perimeter of your work, that is, apply a thin coating of solder to it. Wipe the hot soldering-iron bit across the end of the stick of solder and stroke it down the work's foiled edge (Fig. 33).

Once you have coated the perimeter foil, you then have to build up the piece's internal joints with thicker beads of solder – a good exercise in hand-eye coordination.

Tipping the soldering iron on its edge, so that only the corner of the bit touches the work and the flat face is facing toward you, try to melt just sufficient solder onto this plate and then trickle it off the bottom point onto your joint, keeping the edge of the bit in contact with the foil (Fig. 34). Try to maintain a consistent speed and to form a raised bead of solder that is not so flat that you can see the form of the foil beneath it, but not so thick that it is lumpy and uneven. The glass should not crack, firstly because the copper foil, which is a good conductor, will dissipate the heat very quickly, and, secondly, because since you are soldering on the edge of the glass, it has room to expand. (If you were to touch the middle of a piece of glass with a hot soldering iron for any length of time, it would probably crack

You will only run a neat bead of solder after a great deal of practice, so don't become discouraged at this stage if you're not satisfied with the neatness of your bead (and you almost certainly won't be at first). Don't try prodding or dabbing it with a hot soldering iron. This will only make matters worse, as you will melt a small area of the solder, which, as you pull the iron away, will form a peak and set as a sharp point. If you want to redo it, flux the bead again and run the iron down the whole length of it without using any more solder (there will almost certainly be sufficient on the joint already).

A reasonable length of the bead should be melted at any one time as you are working on it, enabling the solder to find its own level in its liquid state before setting to ensure a smooth, even bead. If you move the iron too fast, the bead will melt on the top surface only, leaving leave a rough, uneven line of solder with dragmarks in it. If you move the iron too slowly, on the other hand, especially on a three-dimensional piece of work, the solder will disappear down the little crack in the middle, never to be seen again. Only time, patience, and practice will help you to overcome these problems. Don't worry at this stage about any excess solder on the outer edge of the work: this will be melted in at a later stage.

Once you have soldered all of the joints on one side of your work, turn it over. Ensure that all of the copper has been well fluxed on the reverse side and then repeat the tinning process around the edge, also building up the beads on the internal joints.

You now need to finish the outer edge of the work. It is advisable to pick up the work with a paper towel at this stage, as it will have become fairly hot. Keeping your hand well covered with the paper towel, hold your suncatcher vertically to flux the outside edge. (The paper towel should prevent your hand from being scalded if any solder drips or splashes onto it.) If your suncatcher has any straight edges, start with these, as they are easier to work on than curved edges. There may either be enough solder on the outer edge already, in which case it only needs to be redistributed, or you may need to add a little more. The solder on the outer edge should be as thick as you can make it without it actually dripping off. You should not be able to see the square edges of the glass under the foil. Because the foil is very thin, the more solder you can add to it, the stronger the edge will become.

Melt the solder along this edge with the corner, not the flat, of the bit (Fig. 35). This will lay the solder onto the work rather than scraping it off. The edge that you are soldering must be kept completely horizontal to the workbench, because, in its molten state, the solder will run with gravity, and any tilt from the horizontal will cause it to run off the foil. This is hard enough to do on a straight edge, but when you have a curve – either convex or concave – it is ten times more so. If you don't think that you already have enough solder on the edge, it is often helpful to place little buttons of solder along it, which will as reservoirs that you can pick up with the iron as you pass.

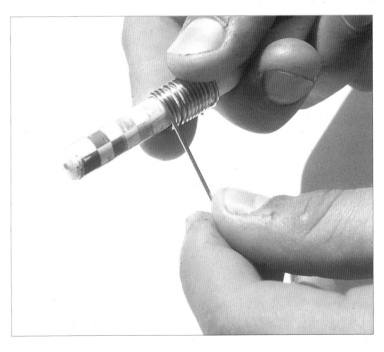

Fig. 35.

Fig. 36.

Fig. 37.

Fig. 38.

Flux the curved edge and melt the solder along it using one smooth, continuous movement. It is much easier to hold the soldering iron still and to move the suncatcher slowly, rather than the other way round, making sure that the part that you are soldering is kept horizontal at all times. This will ensure that the solder will have set before you turn the work to an angle at which it would otherwise drip. (If you get it wrong, you will realize why covering your hand with a paper towel was a good idea.)

When soldering, you may sometimes find that there is a bit of solder which, no matter what you do, refuses to lie flat when the soldering iron leaves it. In such cases, dab a little flux onto the solder (which, true to the Latin origins of the word, will make the solder "flow"), reapply the iron, and you should then find that it behaves itself perfectly. Another problem that you may encounter is melting the stick of solder onto your piece in error, where it then sets before you can remove it, leaving your prized artwork looking like a lollipop. If this happens to you, don't panic and pull at it, which, along with the solder, would remove the copper foil. Because it got there by being melted, melt it again by touching your soldering iron against it, and you should then find that it comes away easily.

To hang your work, you will need a small copper ring, which you can easily make by stripping the outer sheath from some electrical flex with a sharp craft knife to reveal the copper wire underneath. (You will find the flex easier to strip if you place it in a basin and pour boiling water over it.) A length of copper wire can then be wound around a pencil or pen and the rings clipped off one at a time as you need them (Fig. 36). For the suncatcher, take one of these copper rings, and, holding it with a small pair of long-nosed pliers, first flux the two open ends of the ring and then melt a small bead of solder onto them to join them (Fig. 37).

Find the suncatcher's balance point by carefully holding it up between your finger and thumb until it hangs straight (remember that the flux is oily and your work may drop or break). Where your finger and thumb meet is the balance point to which you should attach the ring. (It is now advisable to abut your work against something immovable, otherwise you may end up chasing it around the board.) Apply some more flux to the balance point, as well as to the ring, and then, holding the ring firmly with the pliers, place it against the edge of the suncatcher and touch it with the hot soldering iron until it fuses to the edge.

Gently wash off the flux with a little liquid detergent mixed with plenty of hot water and then dry the suncatcher with paper towels. It can now be hung in a sunny window, where it will catch the light and throw colors around the room (Fig. 38). The solder will eventually become dull, but if you prefer it to remain shiny, you can polish it with a metal-cleaning preparation. If, on the other hand, you prefer the solder coppered or darkened, paint it with the appropriate patina, which will react with the solder and coat it with a copper or black finish.

CHAPTER 3
Glass Painting

Vase or Night-light Holder

This is a very simple technique, which anyone who has done marbling on paper will recognize, using the principle that spirit floats on water and does not mix with it. Different shapes and sizes of receptacles will suggest different uses. A tall, narrow bottle, for example, would make an unusual candleholder, while if you cut it below the neck, you have a handy-sized vase. You could also dip a mixing basin to make an attractive fruit bowl or perhaps provide a container for a display of floating candles.

Equipment and Materials

clean 4 liter (1 gallon) ice-cream box
or similar
2 or 3 different-colored, spirit-based
glass paints
clear jam jar or bottle with the top
cut off (see page 26)
newspaper
white spirit
paper towels

1. Fill the ice-cream box about three-quarters full of cold water. (Bear in mind that the jar or bottle will be dipped in the water and will therefore will displace some of it, so it is advisable to test how much water will be displaced before adding the glass paint.) Add a small amount of one or two colors (and a maximum of three) of glass paint, pouring it gently onto the surface of the water.

2. Gently move the colored paints around so that they create a marbled effect on the surface of the water.

37

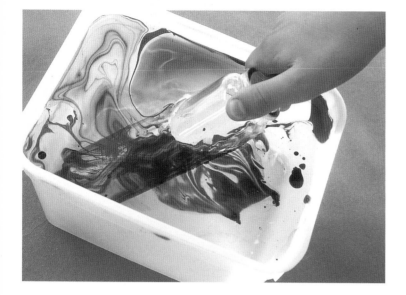

3. Make sure that the jam jar or bottle is dry, and then dip it slowly into the water up to its neck, but not so far that water enters the jar.

4. Lift out the jar or bottle. As you remove it from the water, your first layer of paint will be coated with a second, producing interesting patterns of overlapping colors. You will probably find that bold swirls of color work better than overmixed ones.

5. Place the jar or bottle on some clean, dry newspaper and allow it to dry naturally for at least 24 hours. Do not touch the paint while it is drying, to avoid dislodging or smudging it.

6. Depending on the height and size of the vessel that you dipped, you can use it either as a vase or a night-light holder. In a later chapter we will be dealing with acid-etching glass (see page 54), which gives it an opaque finish. If the glass-painting technique is used on an acid-etched jar, it will give out a glow without the candle being visible.

Painted Roundel

A roundel is a circle of glass that has a protective edge of lead. Any simple design can be painted onto it to brighten up a window that doesn't look out over much of a view. I have given you a choice of a seahorse or a poppy design to get you started. A painted glass roundel is intended to look like real stained glass, with thick, black lines around it. Don't be tempted to try to make it look like watercolor painting. Go for the bold, rather than subtle, approach. Most makes of glass paint do not include a white because white is simply an absence of color, so if you want an element of your design to appear white, don't paint it. The darker the color you paint around it, the lighter this area will seem.

Equipment and Materials
template (see pages 122 and 123)
pencil
paper
1 plain-glass roundel (obtainable from good craft stores), 10 centimeters (4 inches) or 17.5 centimeters (7 inches) in diameter
paper towels for cleaning
methylated spirits
outline-relief paste in the color of your choice
sharp craft knife
3 or 4 different-colored glass paints
paintbrushes
white spirit, cellulose thinner, or water for cleaning, depending on the base of your glass paint

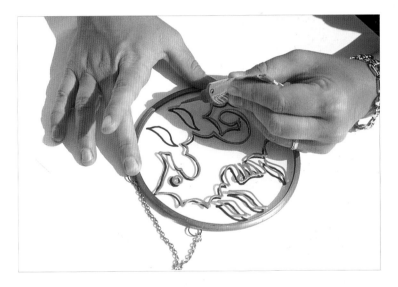

1. If you are working to your own design, firstly place the roundel on a piece of paper and draw around it with a pencil. Next, draw an inner circle, so that you have allowed for the width of the lead around the edge. Keep the design fairly simple, as the outline relief will leave quite a thick line. Remember that the raised relief acts as a barrier between colors, so each area must be completely contained by the outline, otherwise colors will flow into each other and may blur the design. Clean the glass roundel thoroughly, using some paper towels and methylated spirits.

2. Place the roundel on your design and, using the outline relief, carefully trace the design onto the glass. The neatest way to do this is to squeeze a tiny amount of the relief paste from the tube's long nozzle and then to lift it away from the glass a little, so that it lays the paste on the glass from above. This technique is rather like frosting a cake, and will leave a much smoother line than if the nozzle is in contact with the glass. When you near the end of the line that you are tracing, stop putting pressure on the tube and lower the last residue onto the glass, so that the nozzle touches the surface of the glass again as you reach the end of the line.

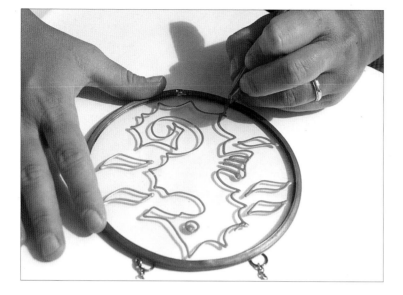

3. Now set the roundel aside in a warm, dry place where it will not be disturbed, as the outline relief is liable to smudge for some time after it has been applied. When the outline relief is completely dry, neaten up any mistakes. Using a sharp craft knife, carefully trim away any blobs or overruns and then peel them off, taking care not to dislodge the parts that you want to keep.

4. Depending on the type of your design, begin painting either in the middle and then work outward, or at the top, working down to the bottom. Either way, you are less likely to smudge the areas that you have already painted as you are working. If you have used outline relief, the glass paint can be laid on fairly thickly, as it will not go beyond the barrier.

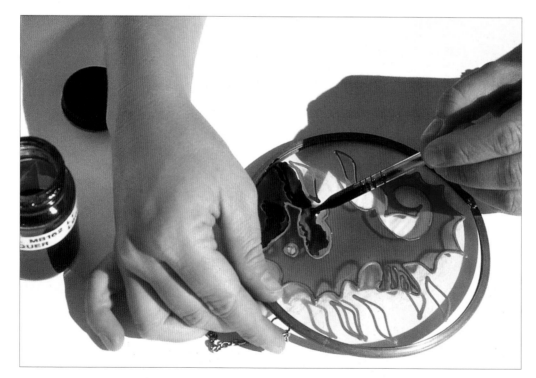

5. It is also possible, as I have done, to lay the paint on using a medicine dropper, which should leave a more even finish because the paint will find its own level. If you have used a black pen, however, you will not be able to lay the paint on so thickly, as it will run over the black line into the next color. Although you may find that your brushstrokes are visible, if you use them creatively, you can make them work to your advantage. If you are painting sea, for instance, you can make the brushstrokes look like little waves. If you are painting a dolphin, you can start the brushstroke at its nose, and sweep down to its tail.

When you have finished, leave the roundel to dry flat, preferably in a dust-free environment, as any particles that are in the air will soon settle on the paint and will cement themselves irrevocably to it. It is safest to leave the roundel for 24 hours before hanging it, especially if the glass paint is particularly thick.

In the case of young children, or people whose hands are not very steady, it may be easier to use a black poster pen, which creates an opaque line. Because it isn't raised, it will not act as a barrier, however, and you will have to be slightly more careful when applying the glass paints. While the pen line takes only take a minute or so to dry, the outline relief requires a couple of hours to be on the safe side.

Greetings Cards

Although this is technically not a stained-glass project, more of a stained-acetate one, because it uses glass paints, it makes an interesting and simple project. Once you have mastered the technique, you will think of many occasions on which a card could be sent that had never occurred to you before. The cards will be treasured by their recipients, too, who may tape them to a window.

Equipment and Materials
template (see page 121)
A4-sized sheet of transparent acetate
(the type used for overhead
projectors is ideal)
cutting board
sharp craft knife
outline relief
colored glass paints of your choice
A4-sized white card
sharp pencil
double-sided sticky tape or photo
mounts
silver or gold pen

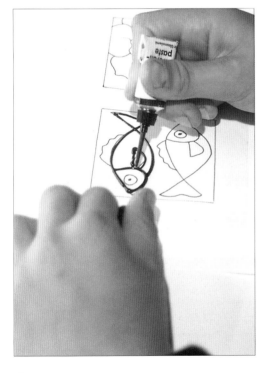

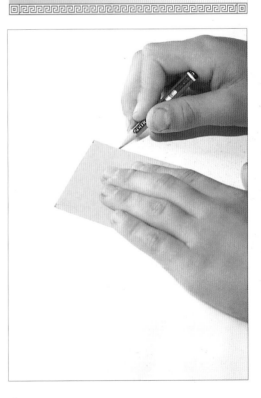

1. Take the sheet of acetate and cut it into six by firstly bisecting it lengthwise and then cutting each of these sections into three equal pieces. Place a piece of film over one of the templates in this book (you may find it helpful to tack it gently into position so that it does not move). Trace the outline with the outline relief and leave it to dry.

2. Using several different colors, fill each area of the design with glass paint and leave them to dry.

3. Fold the white card in half, with the shorter sides together. Then fold the card in half the other way, to form a standing card shape. (All of the designs that I have given you are suitable for a vertical format, but you could also design your own card for a horizontal format.) Cut a narrow piece of acetate to leave room for your message below, and remember that if you want a side-opening card in this format, the first fold of the card must be made with the long sides together.

4. Cut a template the same size as your design and place it just above the center on the front of the card, thereby leaving a larger margin at the bottom for your message. Draw around this square. Unfold the card, place it on the cutting board, and using the craft knife, cut out the square.

5. Refold the card and, using a sharp pencil, mark the corners on the lower sheet, so that you will know where to position your acetate.

6. Neatly write your message ("Happy birthday," "Congratulations," or whatever is relevant to the occasion). It is easier to position the message centrally when the card is folded. If it ends up being a little off-center, however, fill the space with a small motif – a star, for instance.

7. Unfold the card again. Using the penciled corners drawn earlier as a guide, stick down your design with either double-sided sticky tape or photo mounts.

8. I have given you enough designs to cover nearly every eventuality, but I am sure that you can come up with plenty of your own. Remember to keep them uncomplicated and bold, which is not only simpler, but also has greater impact.

Painted Glass Bowl

Applying outline relief and glass paint to a curved surface is much more difficult than applying them to a flat one, as gravity plays a part. As you work around the bowl, it also becomes much easier accidentally to smudge the far side of the work. It is therefore best to complete one section at a time. Patience is essential for this project, and the saying "More haste, less speed" is certainly true in this case. If you smudge either the outline relief or the paint, there is little alternative but to wipe it off and start all over again.

Equipment and Materials
template (page 119)
white paper
pencil
1 medium-sized Pyrex mixing bowl or the bottom half of a pickled-onion jar or similar (see page 26)
masking tape (optional)
ice-cream box filled with screwed-up newspaper
methylated spirits
cleaning cloth
outline relief
4 or 5 different-colored glass paints
water
white spirit or cellulose thinner for cleaning, depending on the glass-paint base
paintbrushes

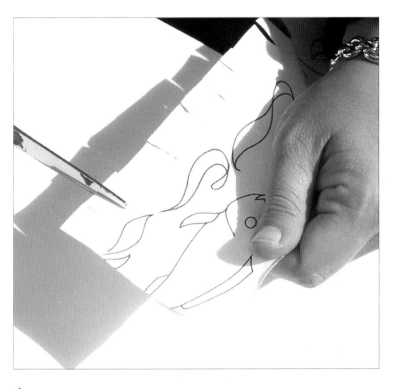

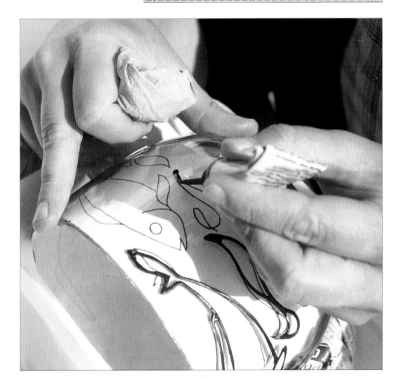

1. Cut a strip of white paper whose width is equal to the depth of the bowl and whose length equals the circumference of the inside of the bowl. Draw your design onto the paper, making sure that the ends of your design meet up to form a continuous frieze. It may help to tape your design to the inside of the bowl so that it doesn't move while you are tracing it with the outline relief.

2. Place the bowl in the newspaper-filled ice-cream box, which will act as a support, and hold the bowl on its side. Using the outline relief, start tracing your design onto the glass, holding the nozzle fractionally above the glass as you work. To avoid smudging your work as you go round, when you have traced approximately a quarter of your design, leave it to dry before continuing with the next section.

3. Now you can begin to use the glass paints. Remember that you should paint only a section at a time, otherwise gravity will cause the paints to leak over the outline-relief barrier and to run into the next section. The paint must at least be tacky before you move the bowl around to start the next section.

4. You will need to curb your impatience in order not to ruin your work. The wait will be worth it, however, as you will end up with a beautiful bowl that you could fill with potpourri or sea shells to grace any bathroom.

CHAPTER 4
Glass Etching

Named Mirror Tile

Equipment and Materials
template (page 118)
sheet of sticky-back plastic
1 15.25, 23, or 30.5 centimeter (6, 9,
or 12 inch)
square mirror tile
small, sharp craft knife or scalpel
soft cloth
soft and sharp pencils
computer printout of the designated
name and small motif(s)
sticky tape
white spirit
newspaper
rubber gloves
etching paste
chunky, hogshair paintbrush and
plastic container to hold it
lots of fresh water
old plastic basin and brush
sodium bicarbonate
paper towels

Because etching paste contains hydrofluoric acid, which is a very dangerous substance, the etching stage of this process must be carried out in a well-ventilated area, preferably outside, or using a fume-extractor fan. I have chosen to create my design on a 23 centimeter (9 inch) mirror tile, which you can buy in packs, from do-it-yourself stores.

A computer is very useful for creating the lettering for the mirror. Type the name of the person to whom you wish to give the mirror and select a font that is simple, bold, and will be easy to cut (remember that you have to do this freehand, using a small craft knife). It's also nice to incorporate a small motif. I have included two that you can use or, alternatively, you could design your own. Remember, though, to keep it simple.

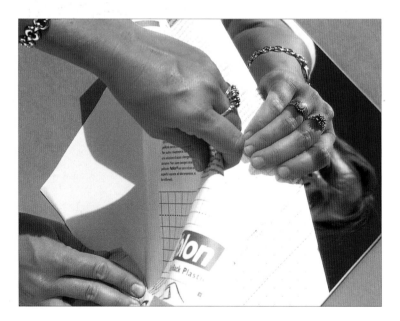

1. You will need to cover the mirror with sticky-backed plastic, which the acid won't react with. Using a sharp craft knife, cut a piece of plastic approximately 1.25 centimetres (¹/₂ inch) larger all round than your tile. Peel back one corner of the plastic and stick it to the mirror so that it overlaps the edge.

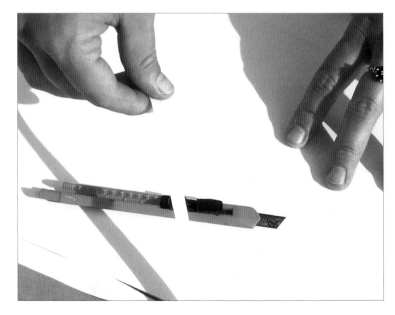

2. Carefully peel off the rest of the backing paper, rubbing it down with a soft cloth held in your other hand as you work from corner to corner to smooth out any bubbles that may have become trapped between the plastic and the surface of the mirror. Carefully trim back the plastic to the edge of the glass.

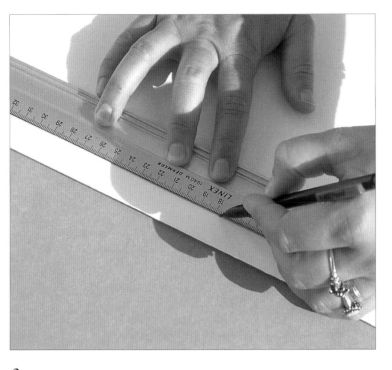

3. Draw a horizontal pencil line approximately 2.5 centimeters (1 inch) above the bottom of the mirror. This is the line that your lettering will sit on. If you have chosen a font whose letters have very long tails, however, you may need to draw the line slightly farther away from the edge of the mirror.

4. Turn the computer printout upside down and rub over the back of it with a soft pencil until it has become completely blackened. Turn the printout around again and, using sticky tape, stick it to the plastic covering, ensuring that the lettering sits on the pencil line and is parallel with the edge of the mirror.

5. Using a sharp pencil, carefully trace the outlines of the letters, which should appear as marks on the plastic. Do the same with the motif, positioning it just beyond the point at which the lettering stops, or at the top corner if there is insufficient room.

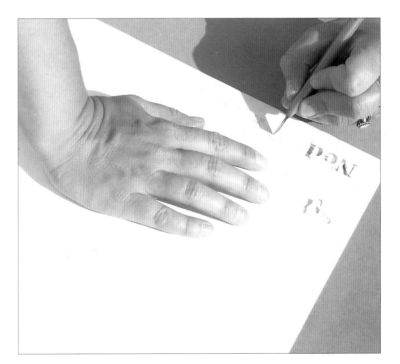

6. Using a sharp craft knife or scalpel, cut this line through the plastic and carefully peel off the letters and motif. Small patches of adhesive may be left on the surface of the glass, which you should carefully clean off with a little white spirit and a soft cloth.

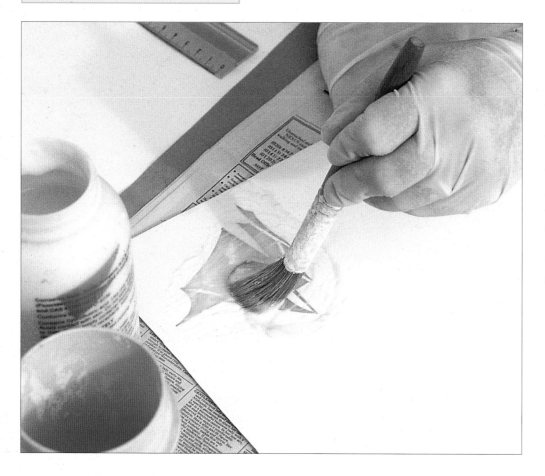

7. Place the mirror on some newspaper in a well-ventilated place, put on the rubber gloves, remove the lid from the jar of etching paste, and, using the hogshair paintbrush, carefully lay the paste onto the exposed areas of mirror fairly thickly. Replace lid on the jar immediately. Once all of the exposed areas have been covered, keep the paste moving by swirling it around gently with the brush to avoid the etched texture becoming patchy. This should be done at regular intervals over the next 10 to 15 minutes, by which time the paste should have etched the mirror sufficiently.

8. Using a plastic-bristled brush, wash the etching paste off the mirror in a plastic basin filled with lots of fresh water, nullify any residual acidity with sodium bicarbonate, and then discard the water – preferably down an outside drain. Once you have removed all traces of the etching paste, check the edges and back of your mirror to ensure that none remains. It is now safe to remove your rubber gloves.

Carefully peel off the sticky-back plastic, and, using a soft cloth and some white spirit, polish the mirror tile to remove any residual adhesive. These tiles usually come with a set of sticky pads to fix them to walls (the only surface to which they will not adhere is a washable wallpaper). Mirrors etched with names and dates make ideal presents with an individual touch for baptisms, weddings, or birthdays.

Ned 19 August 2000

House Name

This rather subtle-looking technique will add a touch of distinction to the most humble dwelling. If your house doesn't have a name, enlarge the numbers given in the previous project and use them instead. You could even include your family name. I have designed an ivy motif to decorate the edge, but if you prefer to create your own design, so much the better.

Equipment and Materials
sheet of sticky-back plastic
20.3 x 30.5 centimeter x 3 millimeter
(8 x 12 x ⅛ inch) clear glass
small, sharp craft knife or scalpel
soft cloth
soft and sharp pencils
computer printout of the designated
name or number and small motif(s)
sticky tape
white spirit
newspaper
rubber gloves
etching paste
chunky, hogshair paintbrush and
plastic container to hold it
lots of fresh water
old plastic basin and brush
sodium bicarbonate
wooden frame for the glass

1. Cut and apply the sticky-backed plastic to the clear glass as described on page 45, ensuring that there are no bubbles between the plastic and glass.

2. Transfer the name or number of your house, as well as your chosen motif, and cut out the characters with a sharp craft knife.

3. (Right) Carry out the etching process exactly as before (see page 50), remembering to wear rubber gloves. When washing off the etching paste, be careful not to let any acid-contaminated water come into contact with the back of the glass, as this will cause a slight milkiness if it is left for any length of time (even when it is very diluted, the acid will still etch glass).

4. (Below) Once you have removed the sticky-back plastic and have cleaned the piece of glass, mount it in a wooden frame and hang in a window next to your front door.

If this project has left you feeling adventurous, you may be able to replace an existing glass door panel using this technique. Remember, however, that glass for doors must be toughened. Measure the size of the panel right into the rebate and then deduct 3 millimeters (¹/₈ inch) from the horizontal and vertical measurements, which should give you the correct size of glass required. If you ask a professional glazier to cut the glass to size for you, it will be sent away to be toughened by heat treatment. The acid will not eat sufficiently deeply into the top surface of the toughened glass to weaken it, making this method of decoration perfectly safe. The etching process must, of course, be carried out before the glass is inserted into the aperture.

Decorated Glass Jar

Acid-etching texture on glass will partially obscure anything behind it, making it an ideal way of hiding flower stems in a vase. Your artwork will also be displayed better against a dark background, such as foliage. If you stand your vase in strong sunlight when it is empty, the etch will appear very white and the little boats will seem to be racing each other.

Equipment and Materials

template (page 125)
sheet of sticky-back plastic
a jar or bottle that has been cut in half
small, sharp craft knife or scalpel
soft cloth
Blu-tack (optional)
straight edge
soft and sharp pencils
a template of the design (optional)
sticky tape
white spirit
newspaper
rubber gloves
etching paste
chunky, hogshair paintbrush and plastic container to hold it
old plastic basin and brush
lots of fresh water
sodium bicarbonate

1. Cut a piece of sticky-backed plastic high enough to cover the jar or bottle and long enough to surround it with an overlap of about 1.25 centimeters (¹/₂ inch). Peel back a corner of the backing paper and stick it to the jar or bottle, carefully peeling off the rest as you smooth the plastic over the jar or bottle until you have covered it and the plastic overlaps.

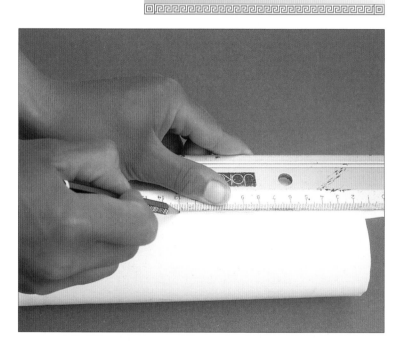

2. Place the jar or bottle on its side and secure it in some way (ideally with Blu-tack) to prevent it from rolling. Using a straight edge, draw a vertical straight line down the length of the jar or bottle, roughly in the middle of the overlapped section of plastic.

3. Using a sharp knife, score down this line, cutting through both pieces of plastic.

4. Remove the top strip of plastic that has been exposed and then peel back the other side and remove the offcut below that. When the two edges are replaced, they should meet to form a perfect straight line.

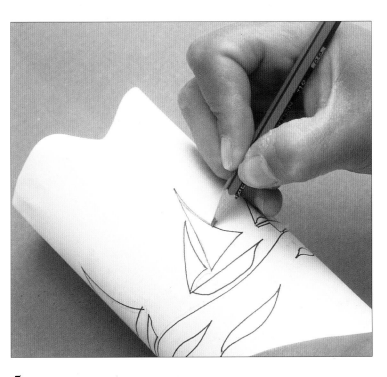

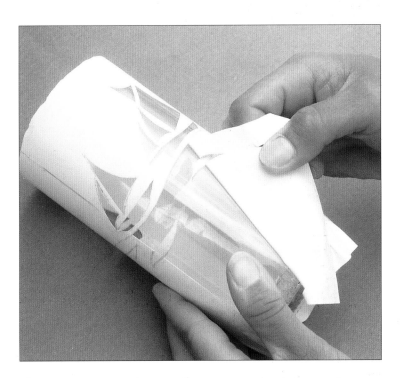

5. Draw or trace your design onto the jar or bottle, ensuring that the design forms a continuous frieze.

6. Cut the outlines of the design with a sharp knife and peel off any areas that you want to etch. (Really concentrate while you are doing this, otherwise you may find that you have peeled off the wrong areas.)

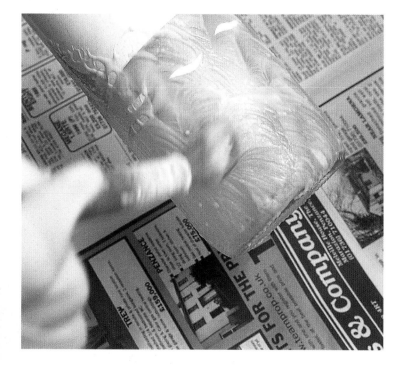

7. Place the jar or bottle on plenty of newspaper in a well-ventilated area. Wearing rubber gloves, place one hand inside the jar or bottle so that you can grip and move it without touching the outside. Start laying the etching paste onto the exposed areas of the glass with the hogshair brush, and once you have applied it all, move it around at regular intervals so that the etched texture does not become patchy.

8. After about 15 minutes, fill the plastic basin with plenty of fresh water and wash off the etching paste with the plastic-bristled brush, discarding the water in a safe manner when you have finished.

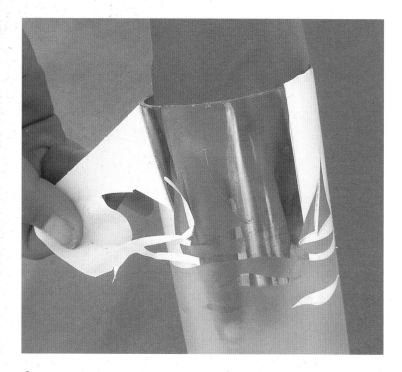

9. Thoroughly rinse the jar or bottle again before removing your rubber gloves. Peel off the sticky-back plastic.

10. The etched texture on this vase will show up best in strong sunlight, so in order to display it to its best advantage, place it on a sunny windowsill.

Decorative Mirror Tile With Adhesive Lead

This is more of a wall decoration than a mirror. It looks effective, but doesn't actually leave much space to admire oneself in, although, with luck, your friends will be admiring your handiwork rather than themselves.

Equipment and Materials

sheet of sticky-back plastic
30.5 centimeter (12 inch) square
mirror tile
small, sharp craft knife
soft cloth or paper towels
soft and sharp pencils
a template of the design
sticky tape
white spirit
newspaper
rubber gloves
etching paste
chunky, hogshair paintbrush and
plastic container to hold it
old plastic basin and brush
lots of fresh water
sodium bicarbonate
adhesive lead strip
sharp pair of scissors
fid
scalpel
small, soft shoebrush or old
toothbrush
graphite grate polish

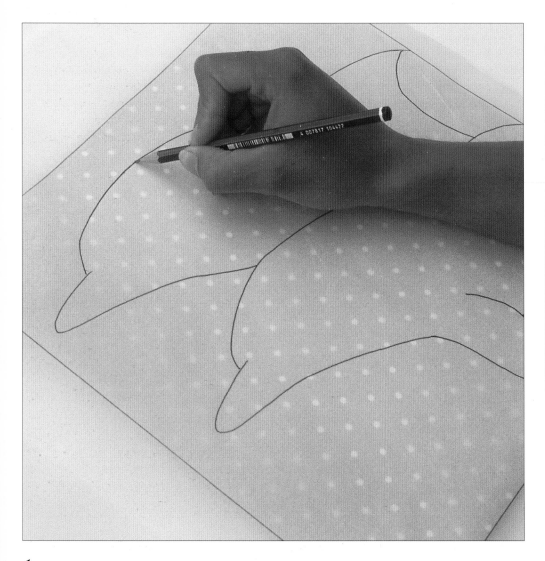

1. Apply the sticky-back plastic to the mirror tile, allowing an overlap of approximately 1.25 centimeters (¹/₂ inch) all round. Trim the plastic to the size of the mirror. Trace the design to be etched onto the plastic and cut through the outline with a sharp knife.

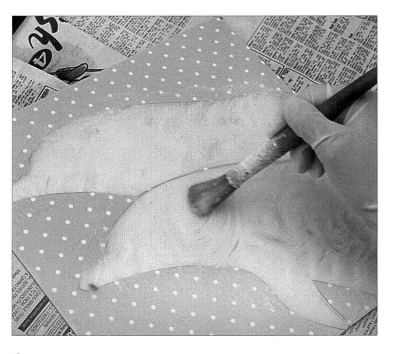

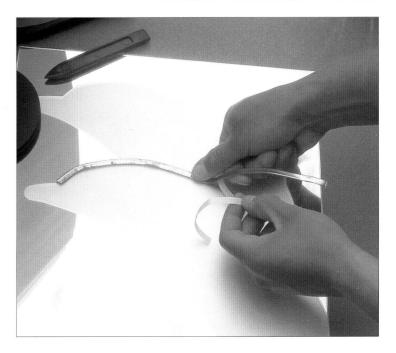

2. Peel off the plastic and prepare the area for etching. Apply the etching paste in the usual manner, ensuring that you always keep it moving, as the larger the area to be etched, the more likely it is to appear patchy when you have finished. After 15 minutes, wash off the etching paste, using plenty of water. Dry the mirror tile thoroughly and remove the sticky-back plastic.

3. Measure a length of adhesive lead, which will reach from the forehead of the dolphin to the tip of its back fin, adding a little extra to be on the safe side, before cutting it with scissors. Peel off the backing paper and lay the lead strip onto the mirror, easing it gently around the curves as you go. Trim off the excess lead and, using a fid, press it onto the mirror.

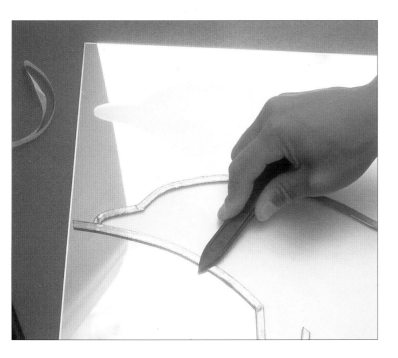

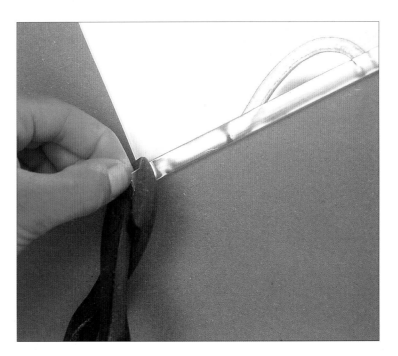

4. Cut the next length of adhesive lead so that it is long enough to reach from the dolphin's forehead to the end of its snout, cutting the adhesive lead to an angle that will abut the first piece. Now repeat the process outlined in step 3. Continue in this way until you have outlined both dolphins with the adhesive lead.

5. Apply a further strip of adhesive lead around the perimeter of the mirror so that the edges are completely hidden. This will make the tile look as though it has been framed.

6. Cut a piece of sticky-back plastic large enough to cover the etched area of the top dolphin and then stick it down.

7. Using your fingernail or a blunt pencil, press hard against the edge of the lead so that the plastic is sufficiently indented to act as a cutting guide.

8. Using a scalpel, cut around the outside.

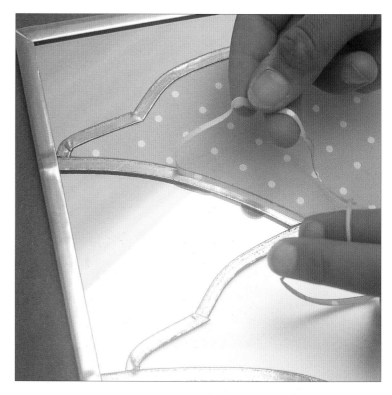

9. Peel off any excess plastic.

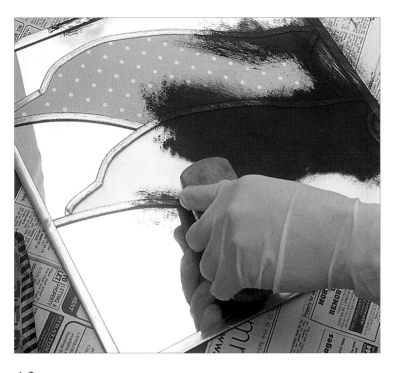

10. Using a shoebrush or an old toothbrush, apply enough grate polish to the lead and the etched area of the second dolphin to cover them. Working in a circular motion, keep rubbing the polish with the brush until it has been absorbed into the surface of the lead and etched mirror.

11. Give it 4 or 5 minutes, and then, using a soft cloth, paper towels or another clean, soft brush, polish the blackened areas thoroughly to bring out the shine of the graphite.

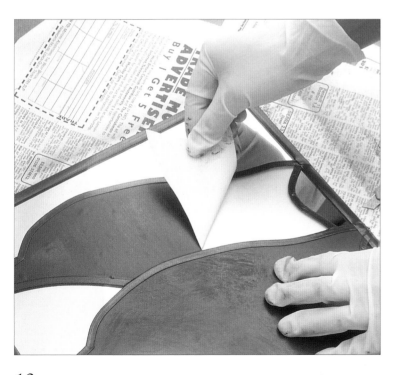

12. Carefully remove the plastic, taking care not to get any of the polish on the white, etched area, as it is difficult to clean off (if you do, however, remove it with white spirit). Because grate polish is oil-based, it may come off on your hands for a few days after application, so leave it to dry for a couple of days before mounting it.

13. The mirror tile can be attached to the wall with the double-sided adhesive pads that the manufacturer usually supplies with it.

CHAPTER 5
Glass Cutting

Mosaic Mirror

This mosaic-framed mirror does not require foiling and consists of straight-edged pieces, so it is an ideal first project for glass cutting. Unlike true mosaic tesserae, which can be cut with a clipperlike tool, stained-glass tesserae must be cut with an ordinary glasscutter to avoid them shattering and covering you with dangerous shards. It is also easier to design an item that includes larger pieces of glass, which are more manageable.

Equipment and Materials

saw
dust mask
1 piece M.D.F. or chipboard for an eventual size 40.6 centimeters (16 inches) square
3 pieces opalescent glass of different colors
glasscutter
pencil
straight edge
stiff card
scissors
breaking pliers
carborundum stone or grinder
1 mirror tile 30.5 centimeters (12 inches) square
tile cement and spreader
piece of thin paper
flat board
cloths for cleaning
grout (optional)
fine sandpaper
bradawl
2 screw eyes
chain or cord for hanging

1. Wearing a dusk mask and using a saw, cut a piece of M.D.F. or chipboard 40.6 centimeters (16 inches) square to accommodate the mirror and mosaic tiles around it.

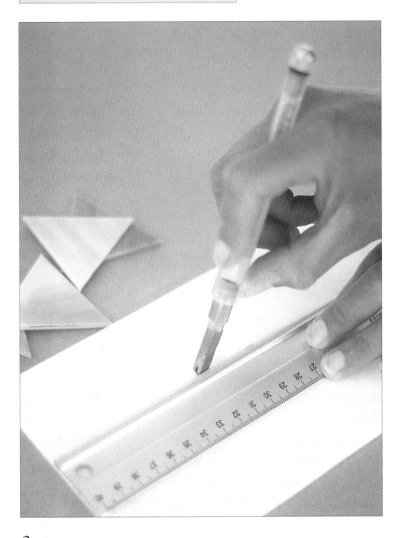

2. Equilateral triangles of colored glass are used to make the design for the frame. The easiest way to cut these is, using a glasscutter, first to cut a strip of glass 5 centimeters (2 inches) wide from a sheet of colored glass. Having chosen green, white, and blue, I cut two strips of white glass approximately 35.5 centimeters (14 inches) long, and one each of green and blue glass of the same length.

You will find it helpful to draw a line on the glass to guide you and to cut the glass using a straight edge. When the wheel of the glasscutter is positioned on the line, the straight edge should be about 3 millimeters (1/8 inch) away from it to accommodate the width of the glasscutter's head. Place the glasscutter at the far edge of the glass and then, holding the straight edge firmly, pull the glasscutter toward you to the near side of the glass. (If you are using an oil-filled glasscutter, you will notice that the head appears to wobble – this is to prevent the glasscutter from wandering away from the straight edge when you are cutting the glass. If you are using an ordinary glasscutter, you will have to take care that this does not happen.)

3. Using the drawing in this book, make a template from stiff card and cut it out. Place the template on the glass and draw around it to mark the outlines of each of the tesserae. The individual triangles can be scored either freehand or against a straight edge, whichever you find the easiest. Once you have scored it, break off each tessera triangle with either your hands or breaking pliers. You will need to cut 20 white triangles, 12 blue, and 12 green triangles. You will also need to cut four white tesserae to a different shape, as given in this book.

If all of these tesserae break cleanly, you will have to do very little to them, but if they have sharp or uneven edges, you will have to rub them down gently with a wet carborundum stone, or, if you have one, a grinder.

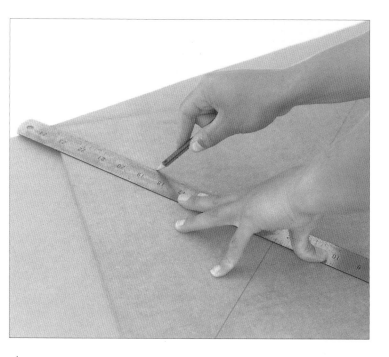

4. To center the mirror tile on the M.D.F. or chipboard, using a straight edge and pencil, draw diagonal lines across the board from each corner so that they cross in the middle. The diagonals should intersect the corners of the mirror tile when it is placed in the right position. Ensure that the mirror tile and glass tesserae are clean and grease-free.

5. Place a good-sized dollop of tile cement in the middle of the M.D.F. or chipboard and spread it out using the spreader that should have been supplied with the cement.

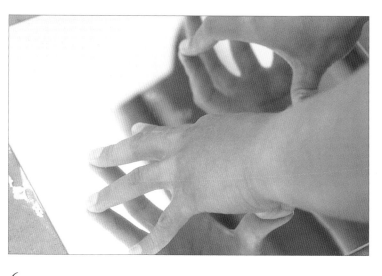

6. Press the mirror tile firmly into the cement, ensuring that its corners line up with the diagonals. The cement should ooze out from under the edges of the mirror tile.

7. Apply more cement around the edge of the mirror tile and then arrange the tesserae on it, starting with the white triangles, which should fit exactly along the edge of the mirror. Now position the colored triangles between the white triangles. The last tiles to be positioned are the corner pieces. The cement should ooze up between the tesserae a little.

   To ensure that the tiles are level, place a piece of thin paper over the whole mirror and a flat board on top of that. Press down on the board gently and evenly to level the tiles and prevent any sharp edges from sticking up.

8. Remove the board and peel off the paper carefully before gently wiping off any excess cement from the surface of the mirror and tesserae. Leave the cement to set for the time indicated by the manufacturer.

When the cement is dry, polish the mirror to remove any residue before applying more cement or grout to any gaps between the tesserae. Leave the grout for 15 minutes and then wipe the work clean.

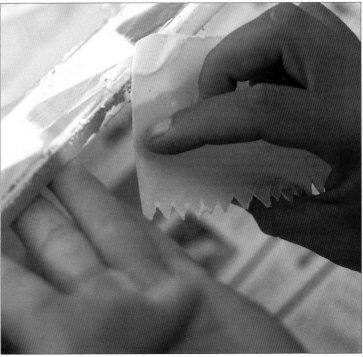

9. To dull any sharp edges around the perimeter, coat the edges of the mirror with a generous layer of cement or grout and then leave it to dry.

10. When your work is dry, gently rub it down with some fine sandpaper.

Turn the mirror over and measure two points an equal distance from the top on each side. Use a bradawl to mark these points with a small hole and attach a screw eye to each hole. String a chain or cord through the screw eyes to hang the mirror.

Twig or Driftwood Mobile

When buying stained glass, it is often possible to obtain offcuts, which are sold by weight. For this mobile, I have made all of the pieces a regular shape, but different sizes. If you prefer, however, you could opt for completely different shapes or use untrimmed offcuts. By hanging the individual pieces close together, different colors will be obtained where they overlap. The glass is tougher than you might expect, and unless a force 8 gale is forecast, the mobile should be safe to leave outside. The mobile can either be displayed as a purely decoratively ornament, or, if it is hung outside or in an open window, can serve as a wind chime.

Equipment and Materials
4 or 5 different-colored glass offcuts
glasscutter
breaking pliers
grinder or carborundum stone
plain copper foil
foiler
soldering board
flux
soldering iron
solder
paper towels
4 or 5 small copper rings
G-cramp
piece of driftwood or decoratively shaped twig
workbench
drill with a small-sized bit
length of nylon fishing line

1. If you are intending to cut your glass offcuts to shape, the easiest way to do this is to place each piece of glass on the pattern and then to trim it by hand using a glasscutter and breaking pliers.

2. It is best to remove any rough edges on the glass with a grinder, so that when you foil them you won't cut either your fingers or the copper foil. (A carborundum stone will do the same job, but will take much longer.) Wash all of the glass pieces in very hot water and ensure that they are thoroughly dry.

3. Having made sure that your hands are clean, grease-free, and dry, apply the copper foil to each piece of glass in turn (see page 31).

4. When you have foiled all of the pieces of glass, place them on a soldering board, flux them liberally, and tin around the edges. Turn each over, flux the other side, and repeat the tinning process.

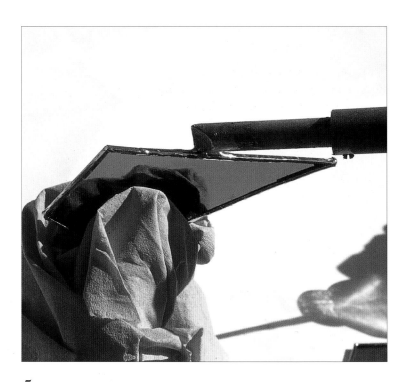

5. Apply more solder to the outer edges of each piece of glass. (Remember to protect your hand with a paper towel when you are holding the glass.) To strengthen the finished piece, lay on as much solder as you can without it running or dripping off.

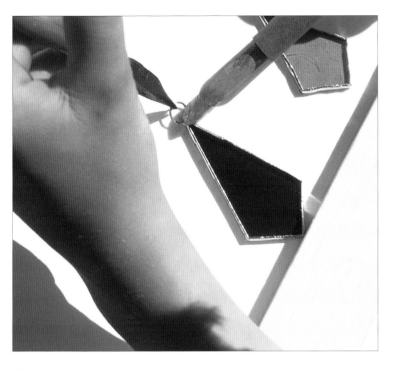

6. When you have obscured the copper foil on all of the pieces, and have applied sufficient solder to enable you to round off all of the square edges, attach a copper ring to the top of each shape. Thoroughly wash and dry each piece.

7. Using a G-clamp, secure the piece of driftwood or twig to a workbench. With a small-diameter drill bit, drill a line of holes. The space of the gaps between the holes will depend on the size of your glass pieces, as well as the amount of overlap required. Drill another hole at each end of the top edge of the driftwood or twig from which to suspend your mobile.

8. Using nylon fishing line cut to the required lengths, hang each piece of glass from the driftwood or twig at slightly different heights. Make a hanging loop through the top two holes with the same type of line.

Fish Suncatcher

These simple little fish look very jolly when hung in a bathroom window. You could also make batches of different-colored fish into a mobile and hang them in direct sunlight, causing their colors to flicker all around the room.

Equipment and Materials
2 or 3 colors of transparent glass
glasscutter
breaking pliers
grinder or carborundum stone
plain copper foil
foiler
soldering board
flux
soldering iron
solder
paper towel
1 copper ring
black glass paint and fine brush or
permanent paint marker

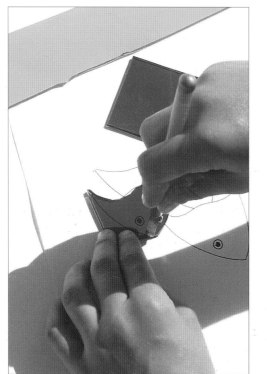

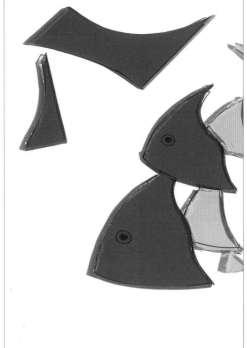

1. Using a glasscutter and breaking pliers, cut four pieces of glass and then trim them by hand.

2. Grind, wash, and foil all of the pieces. Arrange them together on the soldering board and flux them. Ensure that all of the pieces are in their exact positions before tack-soldering them together.

3. Once you have tacked them together, tin around the outer edges of the pieces with a small amount of solder. Now build up the bead between the body of each fish and its tail, as well as the joints between the two fishes. Turn the work over and repeat the process on the other side, not forgetting to flux it.

4. Holding the suncatcher upright, flux the tinned edges and lay some solder along them, keeping each horizontal. Because some of the edges are curved and the molten solder will run off them, you may find this more difficult than for the mobile. It is therefore easier to hold the soldering iron still in one hand, while carefully tilting the suncatcher with the other. This will keep the edge of the suncatcher that is directly below the soldering iron horizontal.

5. Don't forget to solder the exposed edges of the little triangle between the two fishes, as well as the outside edges.

6. To find the point of balance from which to suspend the fish, pick it up between your finger and thumb (take care, however, because it will now be hot and oily). When it is hanging in a good vertical position, you are holding the point of balance.

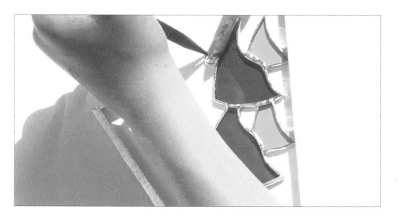

7. Fix the copper ring to the point of balance and then wash and dry the suncatcher.

8. Place the suncatcher on the pattern in this book, and then, using either black glass paint and a fine brush or permanent paint marker, trace the eye onto the glass.

Your work of art is now ready to be displayed.

Sailboat on a Stand

Instead of hanging in the window, this little sailboat is designed to stand on the windowsill. You could also make it from opalescent, rather than transparent, glass and display it in a cabinet. Once you have got the hang of this very simple version, you could design some more elaborate craft with different sail patterns to create your own miniature fleet.

Equipment and Materials
template (page 118)
2 or 3 pieces different-colored transparent glass
glasscutter
breaking pliers
card
fine pen
1 piece opalescent glass
grinder or carborundum stone
($^7/_{32}$ inch) and ($^1/_4$ inch) copper foil
foiler
soldering board
flux
soldering iron
solder
about 20 centimeters (8 inches) copper wire
small pair of pliers
paper towel
ice-cream box or similar filled with screwed-up newspaper
black glass paint and fine brush (optional)

1. First cut out the glass pieces for the transparent parts of the boat, using the design given in this book. You will need to make a template out of card to draw around when cutting out the base, as you will not be able see the outline of the pattern through the opalescent glass. Outline the pattern pieces on the opaque glass using a fine pen, and then cut it in the same way as the transparent glass. (You may find that opalescent glass is harder to cut because the white substance that makes the glass opaque also makes it harder. In addition, when you come to break the glass after having scored it, while you can see that the score line has cracked on transparent glass, you can't on opaque glass, and will either have to trust your senses, or, after a little practice, judge whether or not it has cracked by the tone that it made while you were scoring it.)

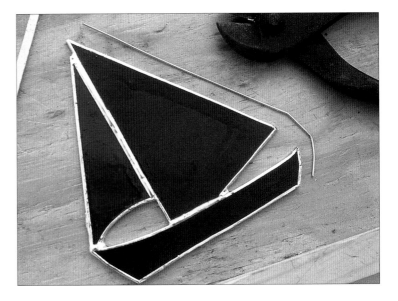

2. Grind, wash, and then dry the five pieces of glass before foiling them. For both the hull and sails, the $^7/_{32}$ inch foil is sufficient. Because it is a three-dimensional object, however, it is safer to use a slightly wider foil around the base pieces, and I recommend $^1/_4$ inch foil. Place the three transparent pieces of the boat on the soldering board and flux them generously. Tack the pieces together.

3. Cut a length of copper wire long enough to reach from the top of the large sail to the bottom of the hull. You will need to make two slight bends in the wire with some small pliers: one where it leaves the sail and one where it joins the top of the stern to follow the angle of the edge. Now flux the wire and tack-solder it to the outside foil of these two pieces.

4. Using slightly more solder on the edges incorporating the wire, tin around the shape. Now build up the bead down the mast and along where the sail meets the hull. Turn the boat over, flux the other side, and repeat the process.

When you come to build up the solder around the outside edge, lay it over both the copper wire and the foil to make the outside of this edge appear as though it has just been soldered rather more thickly. Although it conveniently happens to look like a rigging rope, the wire is there to brace the boat, which is slightly weak at the point between the sail and hull, and the straight line may weaken and bend with constant handling.

5. Once you have completed the two-dimensional shape of the boat, turn it upside down and place it on the newspaper in the ice-cream box. (This will help to support the boat, leaving both of your hands free to tack on the base pieces.) Flux the bottom of the boat again, as well as the foil on the base pieces. Tack the first base piece to the bottom of the boat, making sure that the pointed end faces the bow of the boat (otherwise the boat will appear to be sailing backward). It should be tacked corner edge to corner edge so that the pieces do not overlap.

6. Turn the box around and tack on the second base piece, again edge to edge. A "U"-shaped channel will be left between the two base pieces, with the bottom of the boat's hull as the bottom of the channel. Carefully remove the boat from the box and stand it on its base, the right way up.

7. Flux the copper foil in the right angle made between the boat and the base and then lay a little bead of solder along this angle, from one end of the hull to the other. Repeat the process on the other side of the boat and then fill the gap between the two halves of the base behind the hull with solder.

8. Turn the boat upside down and return it to the newspaper-filled box. Now fill the channel with solder. This time the solder bead must be left as flat as possible, and not raised, otherwise the boat will wobble when it is placed on a flat surface.

9. Flux the outer edges of the base, and then, holding the boat by its sail, lay solder along these straight edges to finish off your work.

10. Carefully wash and dry the boat. If you like, you could paint a registration number on the sail using black glass paint and a fine brush. Your little craft is now ready for launching on a sunny windowsill.

Holly Wreath

With a candle in the center, this wreath would make an ideal table decoration for Christmas. You could also hang it from a securely attached doorhook. With a little imagination, you could adapt the design to create a fruit or floral garland, or maybe even one incorporating swimming fish. Have a doodle: you may surprise yourself!

Equipment and Materials
template (page 119)
green glass
orange or red glass (you could use orange or red glass nuggets for the berries)
glasscutter
breaking pliers
grinder
(³/₈ inch) plain copper foil
foiler
soldering board
flux
soldering iron
solder
paper towel
copper wire
large marker pen or (³/₄ inch) dowel

1. Cut a strip of green glass 3 centimeters (about 1¹/₂ inches) wide and about 60 centimeters (24 inches) long and a strip of orange or red glass 2 centimeters (about ³/₄ inch) by 12 centimeters (4³/₄ inches).

2. Using the leaf template given in this book, draw the holly leaves onto the strip of green glass, turning over the template after you have completed each (by doing this, the leaves will interlock, leaving little waste). This should give you six half-leaves facing one way and six facing the other.

3. Cut the orange glass into pieces 2 centimeters (³/₄ inch) square, as shown on the template. Using breaking pliers, score and clip off the corners of each, so that you are left with octagons.

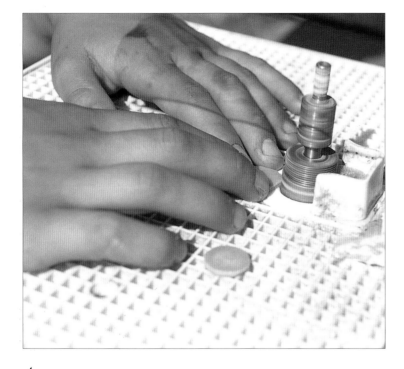

4. Using a grinder, round off the points of the octagons to form circles, and also neaten up the leaves.

5. Wash all of the glass pieces in boiling water and dry them. Now foil the pieces with (¹/₂ inch) copper foil. Pair up the sets of half-leaves so that the right-hand side is offset slightly forward from the left-hand side. This will enable you to key up the leaves more easily when you are making the wreath.

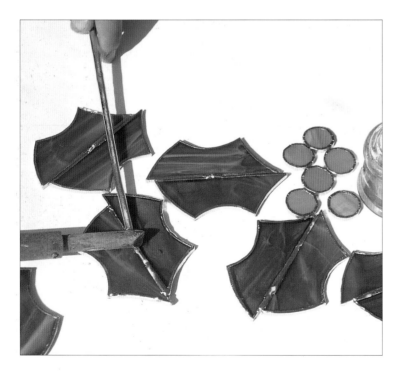

6. Tack-solder the halves together to make up the individual leaves.

7. Solder both of the sides and all of the edges of the leaves. Tin and build up a solder bead on the berries (these are very small, so take care not to burn your fingers on the soldering iron).

8. Arrange the leaves in a circle, as shown, and tack-solder them together.

9. Tack-solder the berries onto the central spine of each leaf, in the position shown.

10. Holding the wreath vertical, tack-solder the berries at other points to ensure that they are secure. Turn the wreath upside down and touch up the tack points on the under side.

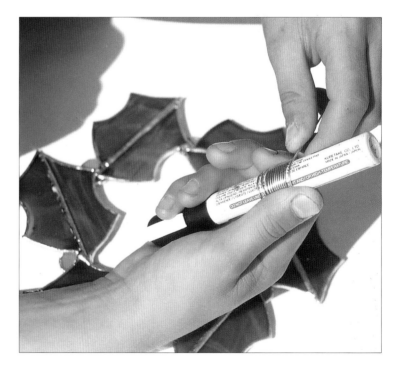

11. Wind a length of copper wire around a large marker pen or 1.9 centimeter (³/₄ inch) dowel 13 or 14 times.

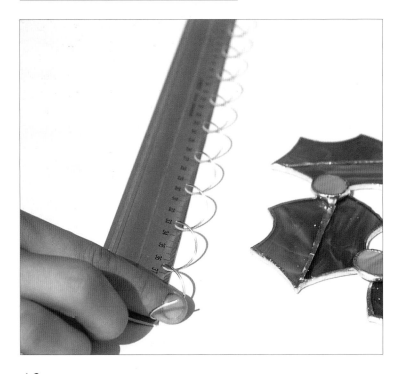

12. Remove the pen or dowel, and, holding the ends of the wire, pull them outward until 12 revolutions stretch to a length of 46 centimeters (about 18 inches).

13. Form the wire into a circle and overlap the ends so that you have a loop of wire that consists of these 12 revolutions. Cut off the excess wire as shown.

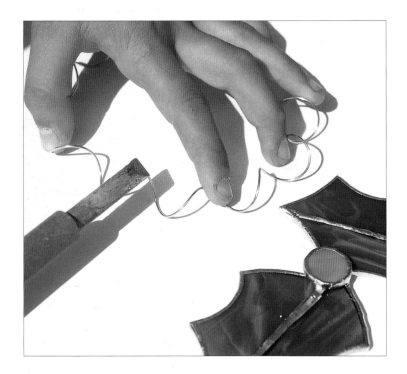

14. Flux and solder the ends together.

15. Place the wire circle on the base of the wreath. There should be two revolutions per leaf, so tack every alternate revolution to the same position on a leaf. The wire circle will act as a stand if you want to use the wreath as a centerpiece and is also secure enough to hang from a door as a garland.

Terrarium

This terrarium is more complicated to construct than a two-dimensional object because there is no base board to retain the solder, which means that it tends to trickle between the joints. It may therefore be necessary to stuff the terrarium with screwed-up newspaper or to stick some masking tape to the back of the joints while you are soldering them. Three-dimensional projects have a habit of collecting more solder on the board beneath the work in progress than on the work itself, so it is fortunate that the solder can be melted and used again.

Equipment and Materials
template (page 124)
3 different colors opalescent glass
3 millimeter (¹/₈ inch) clear glass
3 millimeter (¹/₈ inch)
mirror glass
stiff card
glasscutter
breaking pliers
grinder
22 millimeter (⁷/₈ inch) copper,
black-, and silver-backed foil
foiler
straight edge
soldering board
flux
soldering iron
solder
paper towel
large container filled with
screwed-up newspaper
or blocks of wood
masking tape
copper wire

1. Cut out all of the pieces of glass according to the pattern in this book. In the case of the opaque glass, transfer the pattern to stiff card, place the card on the glass, and draw around it. Now foil the pieces of glass. When foiling the transparent pieces, use black-backed foil rather than ordinary copper foil, as the adhesive side of the foil will be visible through the glass and will appear coppered when the solder is applied to the joints. For the same reason, use silver-backed foil for the mirrored backplate. Next, make up the individual flat panels of the terrarium. Lay the individual pieces of the first panel together, with their sides lined up against a straight edge, and tack-solder them together at two points on each joint.

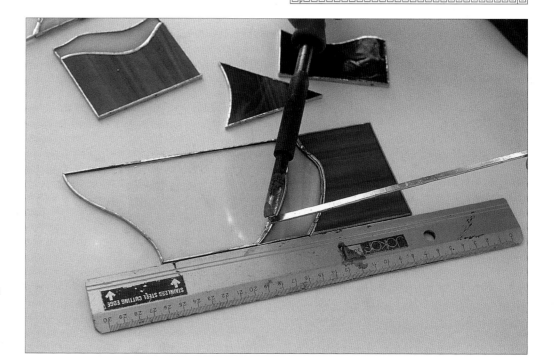

2. Tin around the outer edge of the whole panel, then build up beads of solder along the lines where you first tacked. Simply tin any pieces that will not be tacked to others, such as the mirrored backplate and base.

3. After tinning them, carefully hold the mirrored backplate and base together, corner to corner, and then tack-solder them.

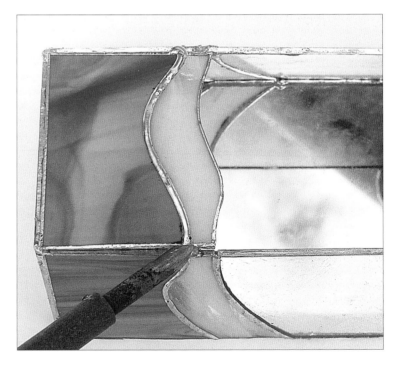

4. Turn these two pieces on their sides, so that a right angle is facing you, making it easier to tack-solder the side panel to both the back panel and the base panel in the same way. (You may need to support it slightly so that it doesn't tip forward.) Turn your work over, and tack-solder the other side panel.

5. Lay your work onto its mirrored backplate and then tack the upper and lower front panels to the sides and base, ensuring that the top corners of the upper panel meet the corners of the side pieces accurately.

6. Tack-solder the colored roof panel to both the top front panel and the mirrored back panel and then tack-solder the triangular side panels into the corners. If your cutting has been accurate, everything should fit together, but it is possible that there will be gaps between the panels through which the solder will drip. Bearing in mind that the solder is liquid when it is molten, each of these joints should now be soldered horizontally, with each side sloping downward at an equal angle and the top joint level. You can do this either by supporting your work with a fairly large box filled with screwed-up newspaper or by using blocks of wood to support it at various angles while you are soldering each joint. If they are accessible, it is helpful to cover the inside joints with masking tape or to stuff screwed-up newspaper into the terrarium, as it will not be easy to remove any drops of solder that have leaked through should they have fallen on, and stuck to, an internal soldered joint.

7. Before soldering the joints between the small top triangles and the mirrored backplate, you need to insert a length of copper wire into the channel of this joint and embed it well with solder. Cut a length of copper wire long enough to embed it at least 2.5 centimeters (1 inch) into the channel on each side and then create a loop above it to hang the terrarium from. Now tack-solder one end of the wire into the channel created by the backplate and the side triangle. Bend the wire into an arc above it, and then tack-solder the other end into the channel on the opposite side.

8. When you have soldered this bead, the wire should be set well enough into the solder to prevent the foil from pulling away from the glass due to the weight of the terrarium and its contents.

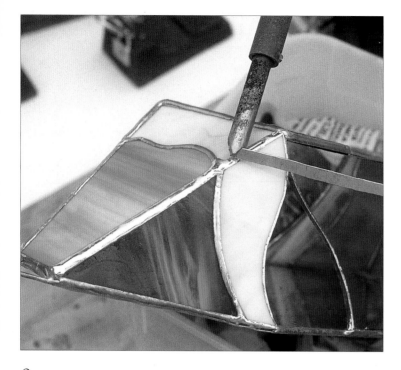

9. Check to make sure that you haven't forgotten to solder any joints.

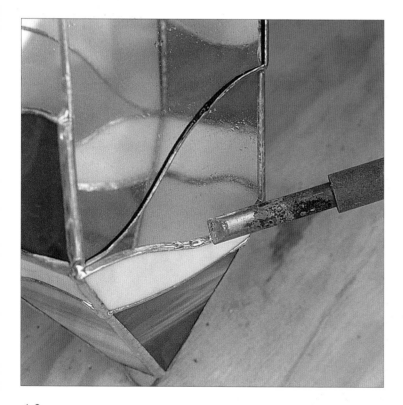

10. Carefully wash and dry your terrarium. You could now fill it with a thin layer of grit, plenty of soil, and some suitable plants, such as ivy, tradescantia, and other small, trailing plants. It is not suitable for cut flowers in standing water, however, as the joints between the foil and the glass are not 100 percent watertight.

Lampshade

I have kept the design and construction of this lampshade simple for two reasons. Firstly, I think that much American-made glass is so attractive that it seems a shame to cut it into such small pieces that its beauty is lost. Secondly, a form over which to create the shade is required for many of the very intricate designs, which you may use only once and which will add to the overall cost of your lamp. The only support needed for this simple, six-sided shade is a couple of different-sized offcuts of timber and a box of screwed-up newspaper. The lampshade is suitable for hanging from the ceiling or for a small bedside or standard lamp.

Equipment and Materials
template (page 120)
3 different-colored pieces of opalescent glass
glasscutter
breaking pliers
grinder
waterproof marker pen
22 millimeter ($7/_{32}$ inch) copper foil
foiler
straight edge
soldering board
flux
soldering iron
solder
paper towel
large container filled with screwed-up newspaper or board with a batten right angle
vase cap
masking tape (optional)
patina (optional)
either a lampbase and brass fittings (finial, harp, bulbholder, three-core flex, and plug) or brass fittings for a hanging shade (2.5 centimeter (1 inch) threaded tube, hanging ring, chain, ceiling rose with hook, bulbholder, and three-core flex)

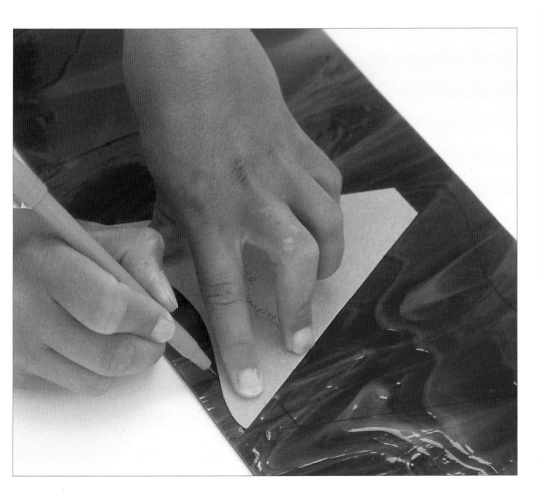

1. Using the pattern in this book, cut the 18 pieces of glass needed for the shade, 6 shapes from each piece of colored glass.

2. The most effective, and least wasteful, way to cut the largest pieces of glass for the main body of the lampshade is to interlock them, one facing upward and one facing downward.

3. The individual panel pieces must fit together snugly, so when you are grinding them to fit each other, it is helpful to number the three pieces of each side with a waterproof marker pen, so that when you make up each panel you can be certain that the pieces you ground to fit are the same pieces that you are soldering together.

4. Once you have ground and washed all of the pieces, foil them with (⁷/₃₂ inch) copper foil. Now tack-solder the individual pieces together to make up six separate panels, each consisting of three pieces. Use a straight edge to align the pieces.

5. Build up a bead of solder between these pieces on both sides. Now lightly tin around the edge of each panel, making sure that there are not too many overruns of solder on the outside edges which would prevent the panels from fitting together closely.

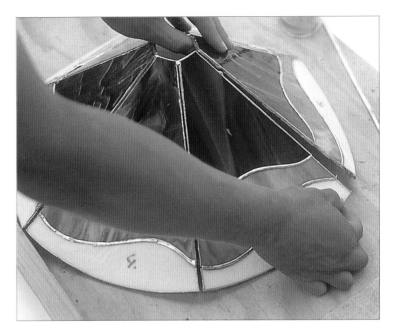

6. These individual panels should now be tack-soldered together. There are several ways of doing this. I find that working on a board with a batten right angle in one corner, against which the bottom edge of the pieces can be supported, is the easiest. However, you may find it better either to lay the first panel flat, right side down, and then to tack-solder the second panel onto it from the inside, or else to support it in a box of rolled-up newspaper.

7. Whichever you prefer, you must ensure that you tack-solder the top corners of each panel accurately, so that when you come to fit the last panel, it lines up with the first one snugly.

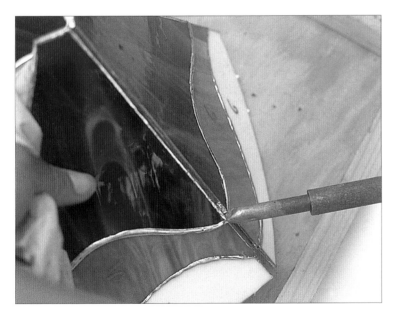

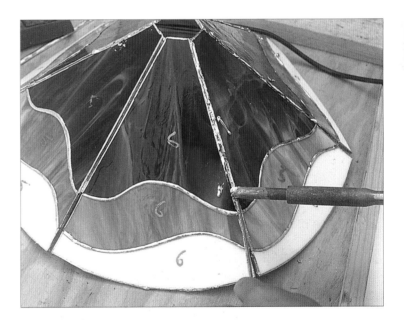

8. You must also tack-solder each panel near the bottom to hold the structure rigid, making sure that there is as little a gap as possible between the panels. Because the weight of the glass is considerable, if you are not gentle enough when doing this, it is quite easy to pull the copper foil away from the sections while you are tack-soldering them together. If this should happen to you, wash and dry all of the pieces thoroughly before foiling over the section that you have pulled away.

9. Once you have tack-soldered all of the pieces in place, run a little solder down the "V"-shaped channel between each joint to strengthen it temporarily. This doesn't have to be neat, as you will be soldering a proper bead over it later, but it will help to hold the shape of the shade at this stage.

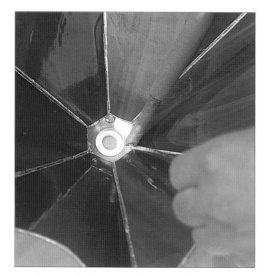

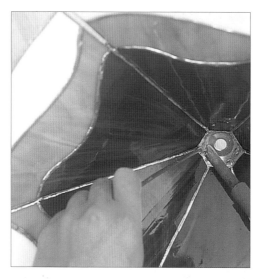

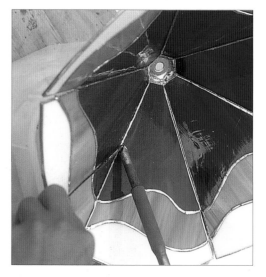

10. Invert the lampshade and place it on a hard surface with a vase cap positioned under the small hexagonal opening at the top of the shade. (The cap must be centrally positioned over this opening, and it is easier to judge the accuracy of the positioning when it is this way up.)

11. To make sure that it remains in position, drop a little tack of solder onto every other joint where it makes contact with the vase cap, and then fill in this area with a more generous amount of solder, so that the vase cap is securely sealed to the top of the lampshade. This will hold all of your pieces together in a stable hexagon while you are carrying out the rest of the soldering.

12. Build up each of the inside joints with solder. Although the solder does not need to be proud, enough should be applied to support each joint.

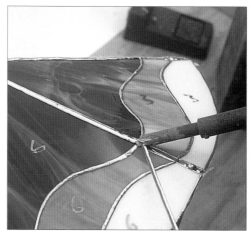

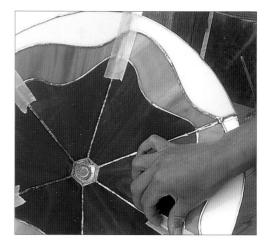

13. Turn the lampshade the right way up and support it by whatever method you find easiest, ensuring that the joint to be soldered is level.

14. Start to build up the external joints. Each of these must be exactly horizontal to the base board, otherwise the solder will either run off or blob at one end. If your cutting is not 100 percent accurate – and it rarely is – you must somehow prevent the solder from trickling through.

15. You could stick some masking tape to the inside of each joint to support the inside bead of solder that you have already applied. However, because the tape will not stick to a fluxed surface, you must gently wash and dry the lampshade thoroughly to ensure the adhesion of the tape.

You may need to go over each bead more than once because small bubbles will appear at the points where the flux boils with the heat of the iron, leaving an uneven surface.

16. The outside beads of solder must also adhere to the vase cap to prevent it from pulling away from the foil around the top of the shade because of the weight of the glass. Remember that flux will help the solder to run and to make a smooth bead (but it will also sometimes spit, so make sure that you either keep it well away from your eyes or wear goggles).

17. When you have soldered all of the joints to your satisfaction, build up the foil on the lower rim of the shade with solder. Because this is a curved edge, it is easiest to leave little reservoirs of solder drops along this edge before you make a start.

18. Flux the edge and then, with the corner in contact with the foil, run the soldering iron along it, turning the shade with your other hand so that the section that you are soldering is horizontal, thus preventing the solder from running off. Remember that using the flat face of the iron will remove the solder rather than lay it on. Remove the masking tape and touch up the inside joints where some solder may have dripped through.

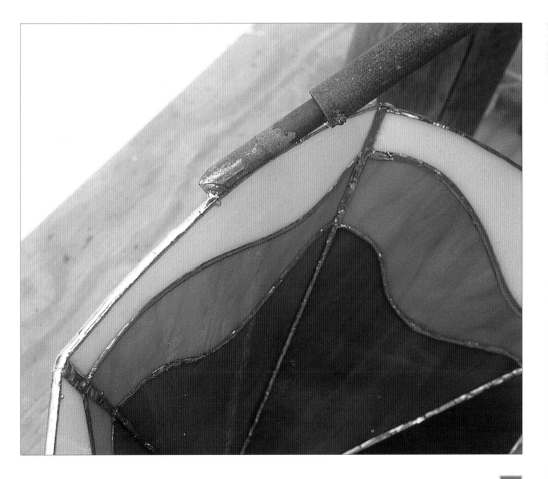

If you do not like the effect of the silver solder, you can modify it at this stage with a patina, which will give either a coppered effect or darken it. Wash and dry your finished lampshade. It can now be attached to a lampbase or hung.

19. Before attaching the lampshade to a lampbase, you will
need a harp, which has a small screw at the top which fits
through the hole in the vase cap. A finial is then screwed into
the harp to hold the shade steady. The base of the harp, which is
detachable from the sides, must be placed below the bulbholder.
All fittings must be of brass, not plastic, and the lamp will require
a three-core flex, which is earthed. You should be able to buy
brass lampbases with the correct fittings from most stores that
stock stained glass. You can also use a wooden base if a brass
fitting is screwed to the top to take the bulbholder.

For a hanging shade, the bulbholder must be screwed into a short
length of threaded tube, which is then pushed through the hole
in the vase cap and screwed into a brass hanging ring. The
lampshade can then be hung at your preferred height from a
length of chain suspended from a brass ceiling rose with a hook.
The flex must be threaded through the chain so that it does not
bear the weight of the lamp, which would be dangerous. Finally,
check all of the wiring in the plug and bulbholder before
switching on the power, otherwise your lamp may not be the only
thing to light up!

*Right: Clockwise from top: lampbase, bulbholder, finial, vase
cap, ceiling rose with chain, four- and three-legged spiders,
hanging ring, and harp.*

CHAPTER 6
Advanced Projects

Tiffany-style Painted Lampshade

This project makes use of most of the techniques in this book: acid-etching, painting, and cutting. It's very eco-friendly, as you can use one old jar to create a beautiful new object. It is probably the cheapest way to acquire a Tiffany-style lampshade.

Equipment and Materials
template (page 119)
large glass jar
fine pen
boiling water
glasscutter
grinder
acid-etching equipment (see page 11)
box filled with screwed-up newspaper
outline-relief paste
sharp craft knife
glass paints
paint brushes or a medicine dropper
cotton buds and white spirit (if the outline relief is gold and the glass paints are spirit-based)
four-legged spider
hacksaw
lamp base
lamp base and brass fittings (finial, 12.7 centimeter (5 inch) harp, bulbholder, three-core flex, and plug)

1. The first stage of this project is the most difficult. Fill the large glass jar with water to reach the top of the shoulder, just below the screw top. Using a fine pen, mark the water level on the glass. This is your score-line guide. Carefully score along the line. (It is not very easy at this angle, as the glasscutter wheel is inclined to slip.) Pour boiling water over the score line, being careful not to scald yourself (the water will trickle back down the under side of the jar when it is held at this angle). Hold the score line under a running cold faucet and turn the vessel until the glass cracks along the score line. Pull off the top section and discard it.

2. The second cut is made lower down the bottle. Decide how deep you want the lampshade to be, bearing in mind that it has to obscure a 12.7 centimeter (5 inch) harp. The cut does not have to be a straight line, and I have made mine an undulating one.

3. Draw this line on the jar with a pen, pour boiling water over the score line, and then run the jar under a cold faucet until the score line cracks.

4. Grind the edges of the top and bottom cuts.

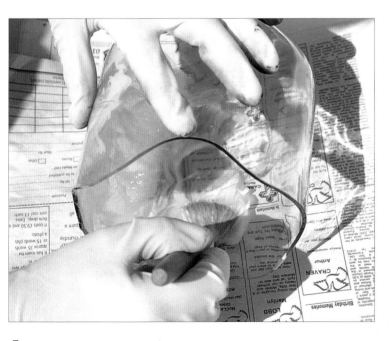

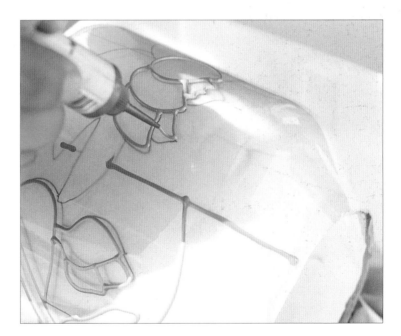

5. Using all of the recommended safety equipment (see page 11), acid-etch the inside of the lampshade. Remember to keep the acid moving to ensure a smooth and even finish. The reason for etching the inside, and not the outside, of the jar is so that when you apply the glass paint, the etched texture will not "fill in" and become transparent again, revealing the lamp fittings.

6. Wash and dry the lampshade thoroughly. Cut around the paper pattern and snip into the small nicks marked along the bottom edge. Because these tabs overlap each other, they will ensure that the pattern fits into the shoulder of the lampshade. Place the lampshade in the box of screwed-up newspaper. Using the outline relief, trace the design onto it. Remember to let each section dry thoroughly before moving the shade around to the next part, otherwise you will smudge the outline relief.

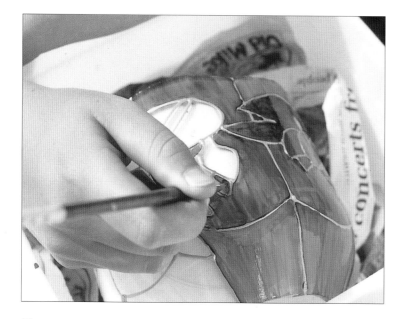

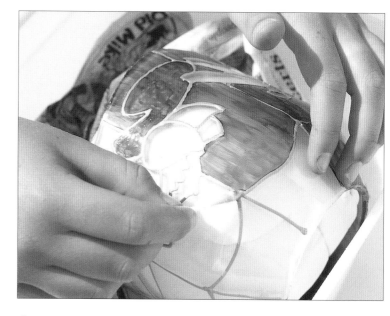

7. Once the outline relief is dry, trim off any unsightly overruns with a sharp craft knife. You can now start painting. Although it is quite difficult to keep the paint even and not leave brushstrokes, your technique will improve with practice. (You may find it easier to use a medicine dropper.) Be careful not to use too much paint, however, because since you are working on a curved surface the paint will bleed over the outline relief. Paint the whole shade, except the wings of the dragonfly, which will appear white.

8. If you are using a gold outline, as I have done (rather than black), you may need to clean the paint off it as you work. Wipe the top of the outline relief carefully with a cotton bud dipped in white spirit (assuming you are using spirit-based paint). Don't make the cotton bud too wet, as you don't want white spirit to flood into your paint and leave a pale area. An even easier way, although it's rather a cheat, is to finish painting the whole shade and then to go over the outline very carefully with a gold pen.

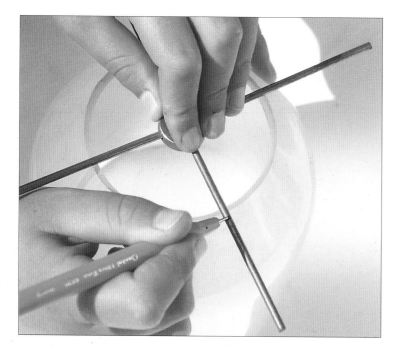

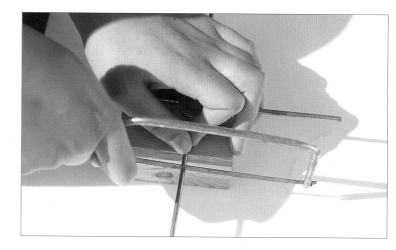

10. Using a hacksaw, cut the legs to length.

Wire up the lampbase and fit a plug. Make sure that you use three-core flex (i.e., with an earth wire). Some lampbases have a threaded fitting on which to screw the bulbholder, but if yours does not, fit a short length of threaded tube into the base. Remember to place the harp over this before you fit and wire the bulbholder. At the top of the harp is a threaded spigot. Place the spider over this and screw on the finial, tightening it to hold it in position. Your Tiffany-style lampshade can now be placed so that it rests on the spider's legs.

9. Position the spider across the top of the lampshade so that the hole in it is centered with the hole in the top of the shade. Using a pen, mark a point approximately 6 millimeters (¼ inch) more than the width of the top of the lampshade on the spider's legs.

Chalice

This dramatic-looking object can be used for flower arrangements, as a sports trophy, or even as a bacchanalian fruit bowl. By cutting the bottle at a certain height and making the neck into the base, most bottles can be converted into some sort of trophy, and the proportions of this brandy bottle work exceptionally well. However, to paraphrase Mrs. Beeton, "First, drink your brandy!"

Equipment and Materials
bottle, preferably a brandy bottle
glasscutting equipment (see page 27)
boiling water
sheet of copper foil
sharp craft knife
(⅝ inch) copper foil
fid
at least 12 glass nuggets
(⅜ inch) copper foil
paper
black pen
soldering equipment
approximately 15 inches copper wire
long-nosed pliers
copper-sulfate patina
paintbrush

1. Using the technique of filling the bottle with water to just below the shoulder to ensure a straight line, mark a score line on the bottle.

2. Score and cut the bottle, using the boiling/cold-water method to separate the top and bottom (see pages 26 to 27).

3. Grind the rough edges and then wash and dry both parts of the bottle.

4. Cut a circle of copper foil approximately 6.5 centimeters (2 ½ inches) larger all round than the base of the bottle. Now cut a length of foil to go around the top of the neck, which should be 6 millimeters (¼ inch) longer than the circumference of the neck and about 7.6 centimeters (3 inches) wide; if the neck of the bottle is tapered, ideally it should also be slightly curved.

5. Now cover the top edge of the chalice with 1.4 centimeter (⅝ inch) copper foil. Measure a length that is sufficient to go around the perimeter, to which you have added an overlap of about 1.25 centimeters (¼ inch). Peel the backing paper from the first couple of centimeters or inch of foil and place it against the outside top edge, so that less than a third of the width adheres to the edge. (Remember to leave enough to cover the horizontal plane and to overlap slightly onto the inside edge.) Continue foiling around the edge in this manner until you have overlapped the point where you started.

6. Carefully crimp the foil inward until it covers the top edge and then crimp it again so that the remainder is on the inside. Using a fid, ensure that the foil has adhered well to all of these surfaces.

7. Wash and then foil the nuggets at this stage, too. How many you foil is up to you: do you want your chalice to be well encrusted or more subtly decorated? Use the 9 millimeter (³/₈ inch) foil for this job, and again ensure that the foil overlaps and that it has adhered to the surface well.

8. Peel off the backing paper from the foil circle and position the chalice's cup section in the middle of the sticky side. Turn the chalice upside down and press the copper foil into the dip in the center of the base, pressing it down well with a fid. Cut the foil in several places from the edge to the point at which it has adhered to the bottle.

9. Fold down the individual sections and stick them to the bottle so that they overlap each other. If necessary, and using a sharp craft knife, trim the top edge of the foil on the bottle so that you have a continuous top edge that is pleasing to the eye.

10. Peel off the backing paper from the neck section of copper foil and stick it to the bottle, ensuring that there is a good overlap at the top of the neck so that the foil goes down inside it slightly. This will ensure good adhesion when you are soldering the two halves together.

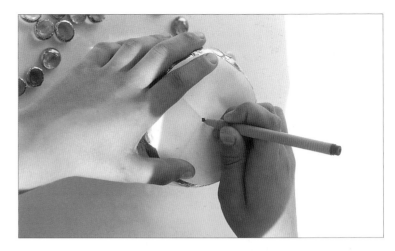

11. Make sure that all of the copper foil adheres to the glass well and that there are no air bubbles. Should you find one, pierce it with a craft knife and then press it flat.

12. You will now need to attach the base of the goblet to the cup. It must be centrally positioned, and the easiest way to find the center of the cup is to take a circle of paper the same size as the base, fold it in half, in half again, and then to unfold it and place it on the base. Make a hole in the center of the paper where the two folds intersect. When the top of the base is placed upside down over it, you can see this spot by looking through the original neck of the bottle. It is much easier to align the point in the center of this small circle.

13. Flux and tack-solder the base to the cup. Cut three pieces of copper wire approximately 10 centimeters (4 inches) long and bend each one in the middle to make a right angle. Position the lengths of copper wire so that they are aligned with both the neck of the bottle and the base of the cup and, using a pair of long-nosed pliers, add more angles to match the profile of the bottle's neck.

14. Ensure that the copper wires are evenly spaced around the neck and then tack-solder each one into position.

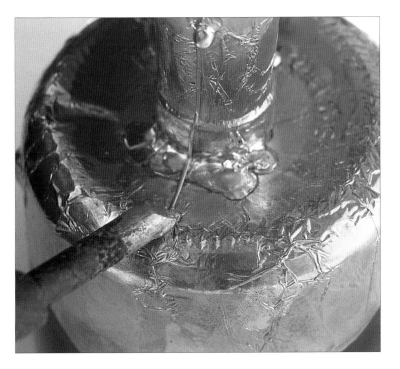

15. Cover the whole foil area in solder, encasing the strengthening wires until they have been obscured.

16. Because it is never possible to make the surface of the solder smooth, I have applied it spot by spot. This ensures that there is a sufficiently thick layer of solder and also gives it a hammered effect.

17. Flux the foil around the top edge of the chalice and apply a generous layer to the outer, inner, and top surfaces. You may need to flux and melt the solder again to obtain a smooth finish. If so, move the soldering iron slowly enough to allow all of the solder in one area at a time to melt, otherwise it will drag and leave a sharp, uneven surface.

18. Flux and tin the copper foil around each of the nuggets.

19. How you group the nuggets on the chalice is up to you, but it is advisable to tack-solder them first, in case you later change your mind. Once you are happy with your arrangement, build up the solder around each nugget until no gap is left under which the patina could later seep.

20. Wash the chalice thoroughly, paint it with copper-sulfate patina, and then wash it again. The patina will give the effect of hammered copper set with jewels – a piece worthy of King Arthur.

Leaded Light

We now turn to the traditional method of making stained-glass windows. Leaded lights have a framework of pure lead, which is sold in cames approximately 2 meters ($6\frac{1}{2}$ feet) long. The lead is "H"-shaped in section, and the pieces of glass slot into the channels on either side. Only the joints at which these cames meet are soldered.

this project shows a simple bird motif, which you could frame and hang, although a weather-proof leaded light would normally be fitted into an existing window frame. Once you have completed this practice window, you may be tempted to design your own panel to fit an aperture in your home. If so, keep your design simple and recognize your glasscutting limitations. Although lead is more forgiving when it comes to hiding bad glasscutting than copper foil, it will not hide every mistake, and you don't want the rain coming through your finished window.

Unlike making a panel using the foil technique, a gap has to be left between the pieces of glass when you are cutting them in order to accommodate the heart of the lead in the finished panel. Because this heart is 1.2 millimeters (about $\frac{1}{16}$ inch) wide, this thickness of line must be used when you are drawing out the design from which you will cut your glass. The more accurately you cut the glass, the more easily the pieces of your panel will fit together.

Equipment and Materials

3 different-colored pieces of transparent glass
glasscutting tools (see pages 12 to 13)
permanent marker pen
grinder
M.D.F. board or plywood to make a glazing board
2 wooden battens 5 x 2.5 centimeters (2 x 1 inch)
dust mask
screws and screwdriver
1 came 12 millimeter ($\frac{5}{8}$ inch) flat lead
2 cames 7 millimeter ($\frac{3}{8}$ inch) oval lead
rubber gloves or barrier cream
cleat or lead clamp
workbench
pliers
lead knife
fid or oyster knife
masking tape
hammer
horseshoe nails
small brass wire brush
tallow candle
soldering iron
solder
leaded-light cement
small scrubbing brush or vegetable brush
sawdust
soft- to medium-bristle brush
grate polish
2 soft shoebrushes

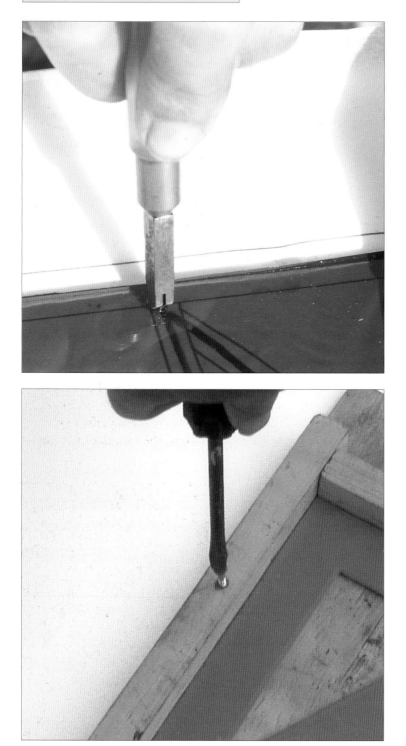

1. Lay each colored sheet of glass on the cut-line drawing and cut it to the exact size of the white area, leaving the black outline uncovered. The pieces are numbered on the cut-line drawing, and each time you cut a piece of glass, write its number on it with a permanent marker pen and cross off the corresponding number on the drawing. This will help you to keep track of the pieces that you have cut and will also enable you to identify where they fit in the design. Although this technique is not that crucial for a window of this limited scale, if you are making a large window consisting of 30 or 40 pieces, you will be faced with a frustrating jigsaw puzzle if you have not numbered your pieces. Once you have cut all of the pieces of glass, position them on the cut-line drawing to check that the gaps between the pieces are regular and as close to the 1.2 millimeter (about 1/16 inch) width as possible. Grind any rough edges or pieces that you have not quite cut to the correct shape and then wash them.

2. Before creating the window panel, you will need to make a glazing board on which to work. To make up this board, use a piece of plywood or M.D.F. board cut at least 10 centimeters (about 4 inches) larger all round than your window design. (Remember to wear a dust mask when cutting the board.) Screw down two pieces of wooden batten to form an exact right angle in one corner. This will hold the panel square and give a firm edge against which to push when you are seating the pieces of glass into the lead-came channels.

Two types of lead came are used in this panel. The one used for the panel's outside edge is 12 millimeter ($^5/_8$ inch) flat lead, while the one used for the internal leadwork is 7 millimeter ($^3/_8$ inch) oval lead. The sections of these lead types are slightly different: the flat lead has a leaf that is of an even thickness right across it, while the leaf of the oval lead is thicker in the middle and thinner at the outer edge, preventing it from crimping when it is being bent around curves. You must stretch the lead before using it in order to straighten out any crimps that may have formed in transit and to make it more rigid and easier to work with. It will also lengthen it.

Lead is poisonous and can be absorbed through the skin, so before working with it you must either wear rubber gloves (although because they are not very tough they are not ideal) or rub a good-quality barrier cream on your hands.

3. To stretch the lead, place one end of the came into a cleat or clamp attached to the side of your workbench.

4. Hold the other end firmly with a pair of pliers and stretch the lead using a continuous, even tension until it will not comfortably stretch any farther. Using the lead knife, remove the damaged ends of the flat lead came by positioning the lead knife vertically across the came's top leaf and applying pressure using a rocking motion. The knife should now cut through the came without crushing the heart or flattening the leaf, thus retaining the original "H"-section.

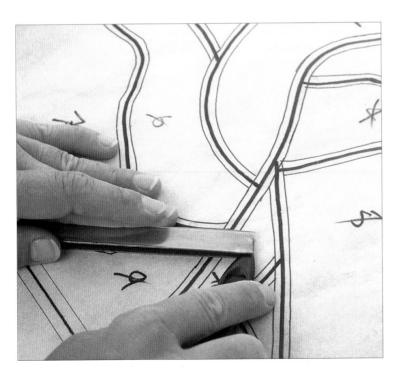

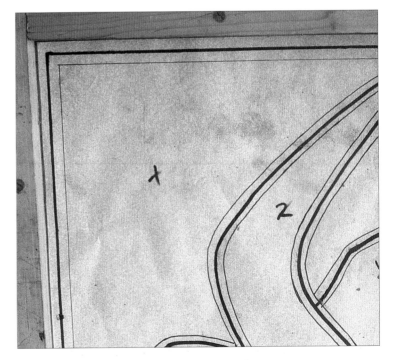

5. You may need to open up the channel again with a fid or oyster knife.

6. Trim off the excess paper on two consecutive sides of your drawing up to the thin, outer line. Position it on the glazing board so that the trimmed corner fits snugly into the right angle made by the battens and stick it down with masking tape. This will act as your guide when you are making the window.

7. Cut a length off the flat lead came to fit the first side of the window panel on the pattern and a second length to fit in the corner at a right angle to it.

8. Fit your first piece of glass into the corner, ensuring that you have seated it securely into the channels of both lead cames. The outer edges of this piece of glass should line up with the thick, black "heart" line on the drawing.

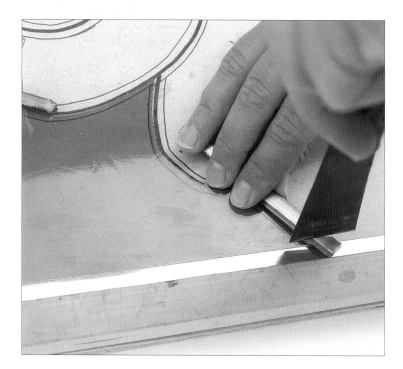

9. Cut a piece of oval lead came slightly longer than that needed for the first lead (marked 1), estimating the angle at which it needs to be cut so that it abuts the edge lead exactly.

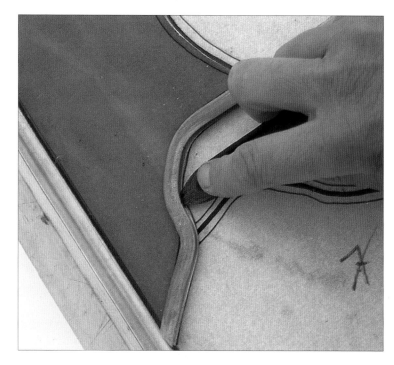

10. Ease the came on to the edge of the glass, using a fid to make sure that it has been well seated into all of the indentations.

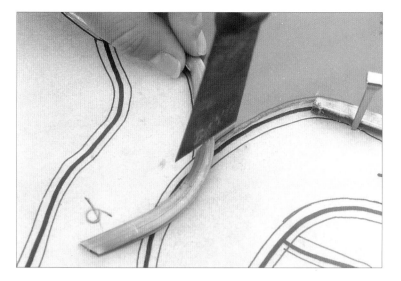

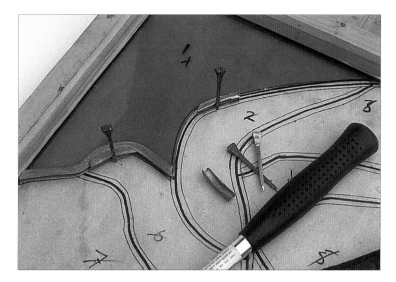

11. Mark where you need to cut the other end by drawing the sharp edge of the lead knife across the surface of the came at the angle required to abut the next piece of lead. You will see from the drawing where this next piece of lead should go, and because the leaf of the next came will overlap the glass slightly, you must cut your first lead slightly short of the edge of the glass. Cut the lead as described previously, using a slight rocking motion.

12. You will need to hammer a horseshoe nail into the base board adjacent to this piece of glass to hold it and its edge lead in position and prevent it from moving. Because the nail is made of steel, it may damage either the edge of the glass, which is brittle, or the lead, which is soft. Create a buffer to prevent this happening by positioning a small lead-came offcut between the nail and the glass or lead.

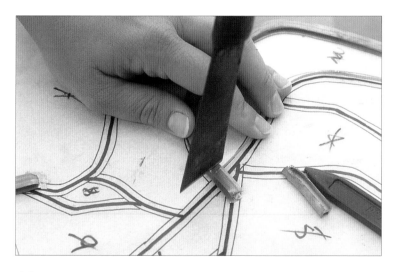

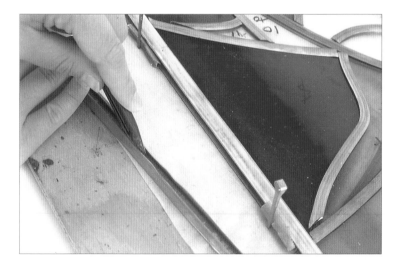

13. Cut a second piece of lead, again slightly longer than required, and trim it at a sharply acute angle where it will abut the other edge lead. Place it securely on the glass, ensuring that it is well seated into the indentation where the wing will fit. Trim the lead slightly so that it will abut its next partner neatly.

The third came will need to be much longer, as it reaches almost from one side of the panel to the other. Take the second piece of glass, the gray wing, and position it in the panel, making sure that it is well seated into the lead cames, and hold it in place with a horseshoe nail and lead buffer.

14. Continue in this manner, inserting a piece of glass and then a lead came in the order in which they are numbered, until finished.

When all 12 pieces of glass are in place, they should be within the parameters of the drawing. You may need to grind a little off some pieces in order to ensure a close fit, but do not grind the glass before you are sure that this is necessary. All of the outside pieces should now be held in position with horseshoe nails and lead buffers against their open edges. Cut two lengths of flat lead came for the final two sides of the panel. Once the third piece is in place, trim the last one exactly to size. Make sure that the outer edge of the glass is securely seated into the lead came and then secure it with horseshoe nails and lead buffers. Give the nails and buffers an extra-hard tap, as they will need to be very secure when you are soldering the panel.

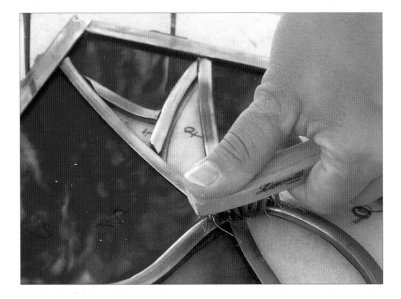

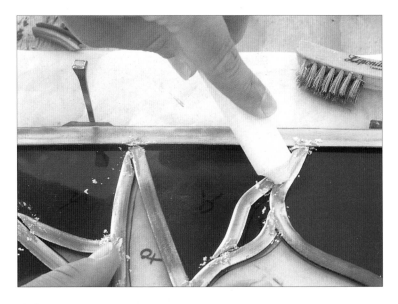

15. Before you solder the joints of the panel, you will need to remove any trace of lead oxide from the cames, otherwise the solder will not adhere to the lead properly. (Although the lead may look very shiny, it will harbor more oxide than is visible to the eye.) Using a brass wire brush (brass, unlike steel, will not scratch the glass), and wearing a dust mask, polish each joint in turn, brushing in two or three different directions, until they are as clean as possible. The only joint that you cannot clean at this point is the inaccessible one in the angle of the two battens.

16. Now flux the joints with a tallow candle to enable them to take the solder, rubbing a generous amount of tallow over each joint. Heat up the soldering iron. Because the melting temperature of lead is very close to that of solder, 50 percent of solder being lead, it is advisable to solder some practice pieces first to avoid burning holes in the came.

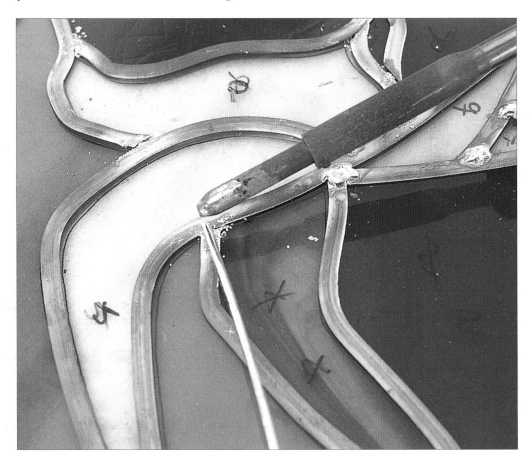

17. When you feel sufficiently confident to start on the panel, solder three corner joints to hold it together. Hold the stick of solder onto the joint and melt off just enough to give a rounded bead that holds the two cames together. If it is not perfect the first time, add a little more flux and try again. Remember not to leave the soldering iron on the joint for too long: it is better to solder the joint twice using a small amount of solder than to try to remove the solder if you have used too much. You may find it necessary to reapply tallow to the joint several times, especially if the lead is not new.

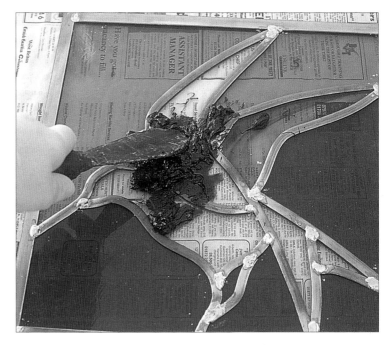

18. Solder all of the joints and then carefully check that you have not missed any. Remove the horseshoe nails and gently pull the panel away from the corner battens. Clean the last corner joint with the wire brush and then finish off this final connection with tallow and solder. Repeat the wire-brushing, fluxing, and soldering operations on the reverse side.

19. Although your window is now complete, it is not weather-proof, so all of the gaps between the lead and the glass must be filled with leaded-light cement. (This substance is similar to linseed-oil putty, except that it has a thinner consistency and contains black coloring so that it is not visible beneath the lead in the finished window.)

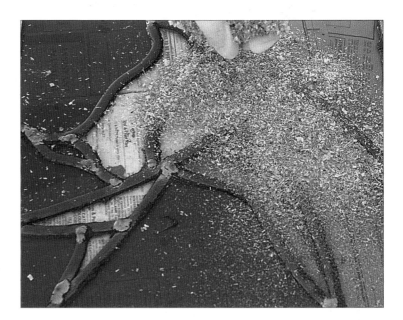

20. The easiest way to apply the cement is to mix it well, lay dollops of it over your panel, and then, using a scrubbing brush or vegetable brush, scrub over the panel, pushing the cement under the leaf of the lead with the bristles and using a circular movement to go around each piece of glass to fill any gaps. Turn the panel over and repeat this procedure.

21. Remove any excess cement from the glass by first sprinkling it with fine sawdust, which will draw the oil from the cement.

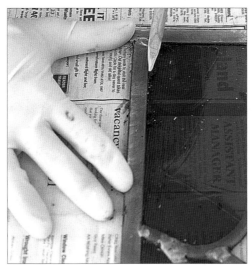

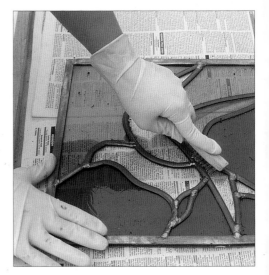

22. Then, with a soft- to medium-bristle brush, and using a circular motion, scrub the window until all of the excess cement has been absorbed by the sawdust. Sweep the sawdust off the window.

23. There will be some excess cement in areas close to the lead. Leave the window to dry for about 24 hours. Then take a sharpened stick or fid and carefully move it around the perimeter of each piece of glass, cutting away any residual cement as you go. This should be "cheesy" enough to come off without dragging the wet cement from under the leaf of the lead.

24. Go over the panel again with the brass wire brush to remove any cement that may still be stuck to the lead or joints, as well as any residual tallow. Leave the panel to dry for about a week – longer if it's large. Remember that if the panel is moved before the cement has set properly, the seal between the cement and the lead may be broken, making it less weather-proof.

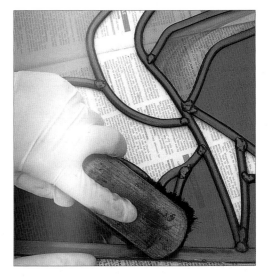

25. To enhance the appearance of the lead, apply grate polish to it with a soft shoebrush. (It is easiest to apply the grate polish to the bristles of the brush before rubbing the brush over the window.)

26. Leave the grate polish to dry for a few minutes and then polish it off with a clean, soft shoebrush.

27. Not only will this give a more professional finish to your work, it will also dull the bright silver of the solder and the parts of the lead that were wire-brushed.

The polish may come off on your hands before it has dried properly, so leave it for a day or two. If your panel is to be set into an existing aperture, make it the same size as the glass that is already in the aperture and then remove the existing glass and insert it. Secure your new panel with pins and putty, or wood beading.

Ideas for Further Projects

Detail of copper tie on saddle bar.

Detail of the Star of the Sea *window, showing a traditional glass-painting technique.*

You are now armed with the knowledge necessary to make any window up to about 50 centimeters (20 inches) high that you care to design. Note that windows larger than this will need extra support in the form of "saddle bars," bars of lead-covered steel or phosphor-bronze that are set into the surrounding window frame. The panel is literally tied onto these saddle bars with copper wires that have been soldered onto the panel's lead cames before being pulled tight around the saddle bars and twist-tied. (If you look closely at any church window, you will see saddle bars set all the way up at intervals of 38 to 50 centimeters (15 to 20 inches).)

Traditional stained-glass windows also include details like faces, hands, and folds of robes that have been painted onto the colored glass with special glass paint. This is not the same type of glass paint that we have used in this book, but a shading paint which simply obscures the light. Its main constituents are iron oxide and powdered glass, which are mixed with water and a trace of gum arabic to help the paint temporarily to adhere to the surface of the glass. Once the glass paint has been applied, it is fired in a special kiln to a temperature of 680°C (1256°F). During the firing process, the powdered glass in the paint melts and permanently fuses the iron oxide to the surface of the stained glass. The technique has remained almost unchanged for at least a thousand years. I have not covered this method of glasspainting in detail, as the cost of the specialized kiln required puts it out of the reach of most hobbyists. From a layout point of view, it is probably more formidable to design a panel using lead lines only, as you are constricted by what is possible to cut in glass.

In this book, I have tried to include projects that range from the very simple to the challenging. They are designed to follow on from each other as your ability improves, so that you need only take a small step at a time.

Most of the ideas can be adapted to suit your imagination and ability. The acid-etched mirrors, for instance, can be customized to make lovely presents for baptisms or weddings. If you enlarge the numerals that I have supplied, you could fashion your house number, rather than a name, in glass. In addition, there are many more objects than just boats that would benefit from a stand. And by using glass paints on a drinking goblet, you could make a wonderful night-light holder. The list of possibilities is endless – all you need is a little imagination. I hope that this book will act as a springboard for your creativity, but beware: glass can be an addictive substance!

Glossary

Antique glass: mouth-blown, rather than machine-made, glass. Not necessarily old glass.

Bead: a line of solder that has been built up until it is rounded and smooth.

Breaking pliers: specialist pliers that meet only at the tip in order to hold and break glass without damaging the edge.

Carborundum stone: a whetstone used for sharpening the lead knife and for taking dangerous edges off cut glass (it must be used wet for this).

Cleat: a device that is clamped to a fixed point, like a workbench, which will grip one end of the lead came when stretching it.

Crimp: to bend the copper foil over the edge of the glass and press it flat.

Cullet: offcuts of glass.

Dalles de verre: slabs of thick stained glass used in some modern windows.

Etching paste: hydrofluoric-acid-based paste that leaves a permanent obscured texture on the glass.

Fid: a small tool used for flattening copper foil onto glass, also for widening the channel of lead came prior to fitting the glass into it.

Finial: a decorative "button" that screws onto the top of a harp to finish it off and holds a shade steady on a lampbase.

Flash glass: clear glass which has a colored layer fused onto one side which can be cut through or etched with hydrofluoric acid.

Flux: a liquid or paste substance that cleans oxide off copper or lead and helps the solder to flow more evenly.

Foiler: usually a handheld tool used for applying copper foil to the edges of the glass.

Glazing board: a wooden board, with battens of timber fixed at a right angle in one corner, against which to work when glazing a leaded light.

Grate polish: a proprietary preparation made from oil and graphite used for blackening lead came in a finished window.

Harp: a two-piece structure that fits onto a lampbase, encompasses the bulb, and holds the lampshade secure.

Heart: lead came is made in an "H" section; the heart is the center bar, which has a channel on each side to take pieces of glass.

Lead-light cement: cement similar to linseed-oil putty, but containing more oil, making it easier to apply. It is colored black so that it is not noticeable under the lead.

Leaf: the top and bottom sections of lead came, visible in the finished window.

M.D.F. board: medium-density fiberboard, a reconstituted board similar to chipboard, but finer grained.

Outline relief: an acrylic paste applied from a tube through a nozzle that acts as a barrier to glass paint.

Patina: a substance, usually copper-sulfate-based, which reacts with solder, causing it to turn a copper or dark color.

Reamy: streaks of color and texture found in mouth-blown antique glass, occasionally reproduced in machine-made glass.

Spider: a small brass ring with three or four prongs attached, which is used for supporting a large lampshade by soldering the prongs into the soldered beads on the inside.

Suncatcher: a small, free-form shape made from stained glass that hangs in a window.

Template: a shape cut from card, used to draw around on opaque glass.

Tessera (plural, tesserae): a piece of glass or stone used for making mosaics.

Tiffany glass: colored glass which is obscured by the addition of white glass at the making stage.

Tin: to coat copper foil thinly with solder before building up a thicker bead.

Toughened glass: ordinary, machine-made glass, which, once cut to size, is heat-treated to strengthen it. It cannot be cut again, as it would explode into tiny cubes.

Templates

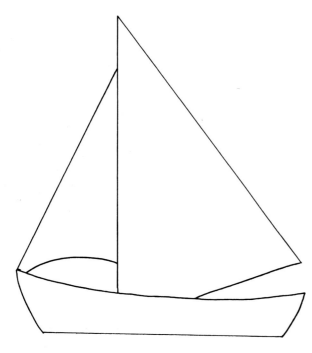

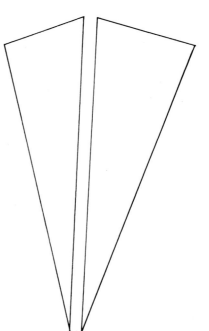

Sailboat on a stand. Copy or trace and increase by 142%.

Named mirror tile. Copy or trace and use actual size.

Alternative mirror-tile design.

Tiffany-style painted lampshade. Copy or trace and increase by 200%.

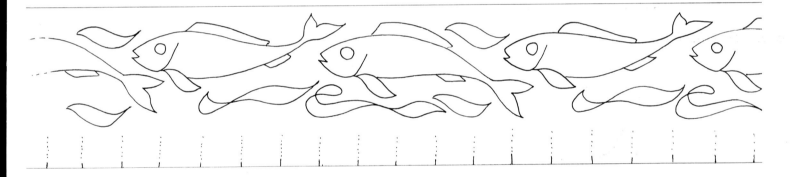

Painted glass bowl. Copy or trace and increase by 200%.

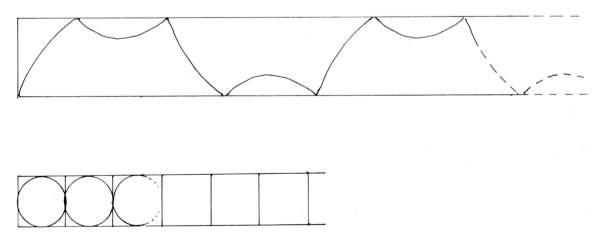

Holy wreath – leaves and berries. Copy or trace and use actual size.

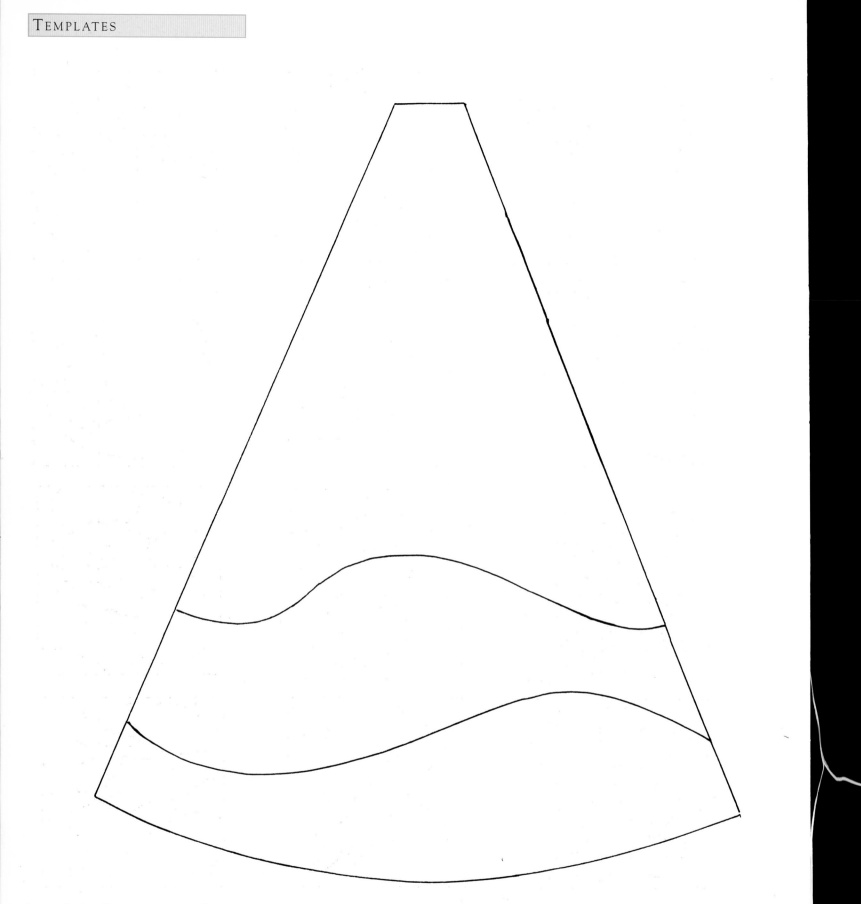

Lampshade. Copy or trace and use actual size.

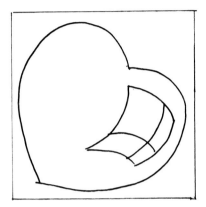

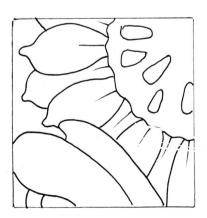

Greetings-card designs. Copy or trace and increase by 142%.

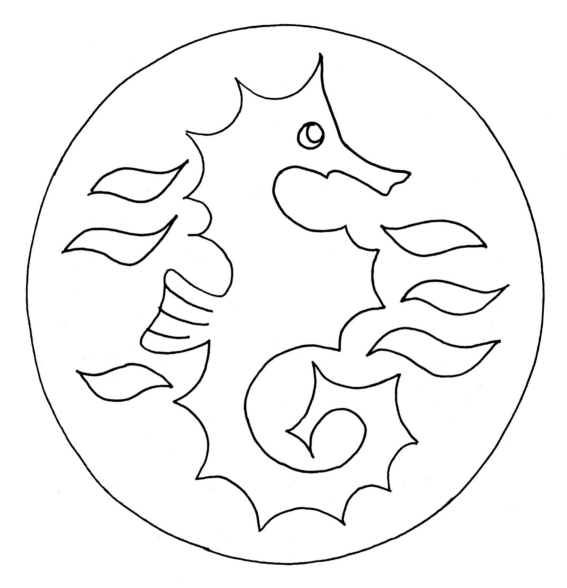

Painted roundel. Copy or trace and use actual size.

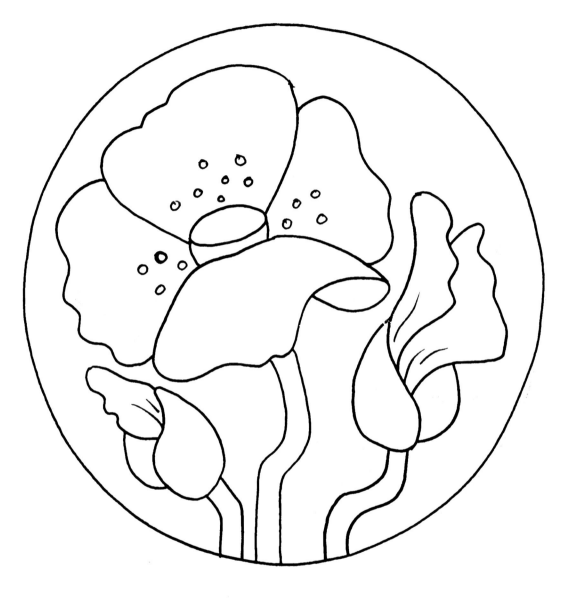

Alteranative painted roundel. Copy or trace and use actual size.

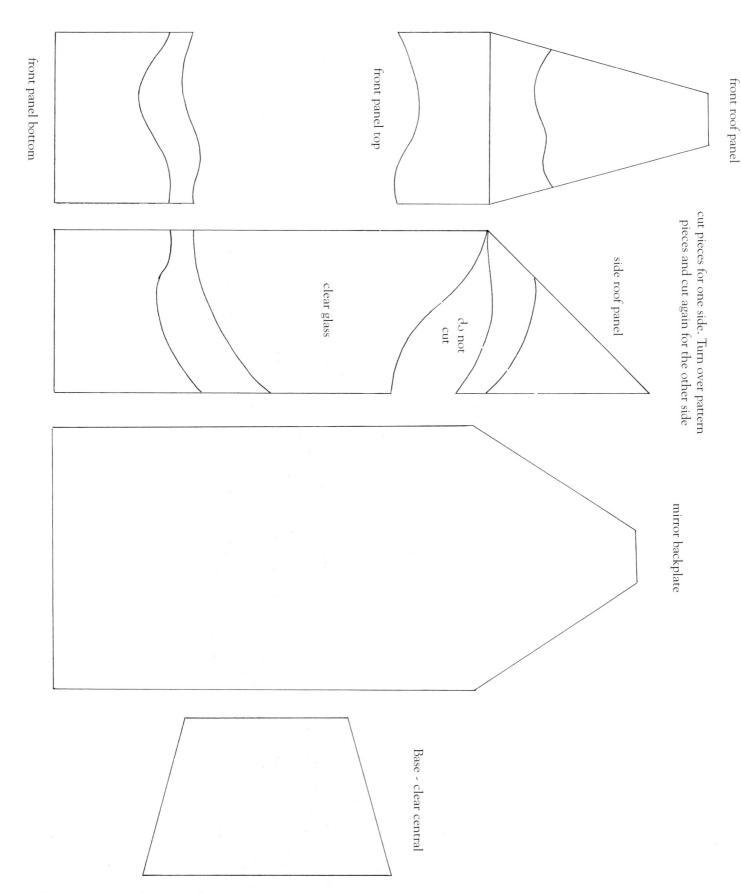

front roof panel

front panel top

front panel bottom

cut pieces for one side. Turn over pattern
pieces and cut again for the other side

side roof panel

do not
cut

clear glass

mirror backplate

Base - clear central

Terrarium. Copy or trace and increase by 200%.

100%.

Index

Supervision Today!

Seventh Edition

Supervision Today!

Stephen P. Robbins

San Diego State University
San Diego, California

David A. DeCenzo

Coastal Carolina University
Conway, South Carolina

Robert M. Wolter

Indiana University Purdue University Indianapolis (IUPUI)
Indianapolis, Indiana

PEARSON

Boston   Columbus   Indianapolis   New York   San Francisco   Upper Saddle River
Amsterdam   Cape Town   Dubai   London   Madrid   Milan   Munich   Paris   Montreal   Toronto
Delhi   Mexico City   Sao Paulo   Sydney   Hong Kong   Seoul   Singapore   Taipei   Tokyo

Editorial Director: Vernon Anthony
Senior Acquisitions Editor: Gary Bauer
Editorial Assistant: Tanika Henderson
Director of Marketing: David Gesell
Marketing Manager: Stacey Martinez
Senior Marketing Coordinator: Alicia Wozniak
Senior Marketing Assistant: Les Roberts
Project Manager: Holly Shufeldt
Manager, Visual Research: Mike Lackey
Image Research and Permission Coordinator: Sarah Peavey
Senior Art Director: Jayne Conte
Cover Designer: Karen Salzbach
Cover Photo: Superstock
Full-Service Project Management and Composition: Moganambigai Sundaramurthy, Integra Software Services, Pvt. Ltd.
Printer/Binder: Courier
Cover Printer: Lehigh-Phoenix Color Corp.

Credits and acknowledgments borrowed from other sources and reproduced, with permission, in this textbook appear on appropriate page within text (or on page 475).

Many of the designations by manufacturers and seller to distinguish their products are claimed as trademarks. Where those designations appear in this book, and the publisher was aware of a trademark claim, the designations have been printed in initial caps or all caps.

Library of Congress Cataloging-in-Publication Data

Robbins, Stephen P
   Supervision today! / Stephen P. Robbins, David A. DeCenzo, Robert M. Wolter.—7th ed.
    p. cm.
   ISBN-13: 978-0-13-278403-0
   ISBN-10: 0-13-278403-3
   1. Supervision of employees. I. DeCenzo, David A. II. Wolter, Robert M. III. Title.
HF5549.12.R628 2013
658.3'02—dc23   2011042907

10 9 8 7 6 5 4 3 2 1

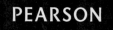

ISBN 10:   0-13-278403-3
ISBN 13: 978-0-13-278403-0

Brief Contents

Contents

part **2**   Planning, Organizing, Staffing, Controlling, and Decision Making   57

CHAPTER 5

part 3   Motivating, Leading, Communicating, and Developing   197

part 4   Appraisal, Safety, Negotiation, Change, and Labor Relations   305

Preface

Welcome to the seventh edition of *Supervision Today!* We continue to present this book in a way that our users have found useful. Many of you helped make the previous editions of this book a resounding success. In this edition, we continue that trend and make your reading experience even better.

In our quest to make this the most complete supervision text currently available, we've taken into account feedback from our readers. We continue to present a book that focuses on the basic elements of supervision—one that covers the essential and traditional concepts in effectively supervising employees; that has a strong applied, practical, and skill focus; and that is user friendly. This new edition continues to be rich in instructional aids and experiential opportunities. Let's highlight some of these elements: specifically, the basis for the content, the new features, and the "student-friendly" approach of this edition.

Foundations of the Seventh Edition

Most of us understand concepts better when we can relate them to our everyday lives. In this edition we help you build an understanding of supervising through real-life concepts, examples, and practice. We believe that when you have an opportunity to apply what you are learning—in an educational setting that encourages risk taking— you will perform more effectively on the job. Moreover, in the process you will build your supervisory skills portfolio!

We recognize that the supervisor's job continues its rate of dramatic change. Supervisors are working with a more diverse workforce in terms of race, gender, and ethnic background. Supervisors' jobs are constantly affected by technological changes, a more competitive marketplace, and corporate restructuring and workflow redesign. Despite all of these changes, supervisors still need to understand the traditional elements of directing the work of others and the specific skills required: goal setting, budgeting, scheduling, delegating, interviewing, negotiating, handling grievances, counseling employees, and evaluating employees' performance.

A good supervision text must address both traditional and contemporary issues. We believe we've done this by focusing on relevant issues and by including lots of examples and visual stimuli to make concepts come alive. The full-color design format captures visually the reality and the excitement of the supervisor's job. We've also spent years developing a writing style that has been called "lively, conversational, and interesting." That's just another way of saying that you should be able to understand what we're saying and feel as though we're actually in front of you giving a lecture. Of course, only you can judge this text's readability. We ask you to read a few pages at random. We think you'll find the writing style both informative and lively.

What's New for the Seventh Edition?

We have been very pleased with the response to the previous edition of the textbook. Reviewers and current adopters tell us that the content is solid and that the skill-building exercises work well in the classroom. For the seventh edition we have concentrated on refining the presentation and addressing the evolving roles that supervisors are asked to embrace in today's workplace. Significant additions to the seventh edition include the following:

- Contingent workforces
- Balanced scorecard

- Entrepreneurship
- Overcoming layoff survivor sickness
- Employee theft
- Work–Life balance
- Coaching
- IM and texting issues and guidelines
- Assimilating immigrant workers into the culture
- Workplace violence
- Creating a disciplinary paper trail
- Suggestions for developing a successful career

Key Features of the Seventh Edition

Before you start a journey, it's valuable to know where you're headed so you can minimize detours. The same holds true in reading a text. To make learning more efficient, we continue to include the following features.

CHAPTER OUTCOMES   Each chapter opens with a list of outcomes that describe what you will be able to do after reading the chapter. These outcomes are designed to focus your attention on the major issues in each chapter. Each outcome is a key learning element.

KEY CONCEPTS   Each chapter contains a list of the key concepts addressed in the chapter. These terms represent critical comprehension areas. And through the Key Concept Crossword you can get feedback on how well you've understood the key concepts.

RESPONDING TO A SUPERVISORY DILEMMA   These interesting chapter-opening stories focus on an issue regarding a topic that will be discussed in the chapter. Although they have value, these vignettes are often overlooked. To address this problem, and to focus heavily on supervisory issues, all of our opening vignettes are posed as situational dilemmas. No matter where you may work as a supervisor, at some point in your career you will be faced with a difficult issue—one that goes beyond simply following the law. These opening vignettes are designed to encourage you to think about what you may face and to begin to develop a plan of action for handling workplace dilemmas. For this edition 50 percent of the opening vignettes are new, offering a contemporary view of workplace dilemmas.

MARGIN NOTES   Key concepts identified at the beginning of each chapter are set boldface when they first appear in the chapter. The margin note defines the term for quick reference.

NEWS FLASH!   Because of the popularity of these vignettes in previous editions, we continue to include them in this new edition. Each vignette presents an issue that highlights a distinction between traditional and contemporary supervisory roles. For this edition each chapter contains a news flash item specific to the topics included in the chapter.

SOMETHING TO THINK ABOUT   Supervisors make many decisions every day. Some decisions present clear-cut answers based on legal and company rules and regulations. Other resolutions may not be so obvious. You need to evaluate and think through a number of variables in order to develop an answer or course of action. These sections are excellent class discussion starters and for this edition are included in each chapter to focus on the presented topics.

FOCUS ON COMPREHENSION We continue to present our second-level headings in the form of questions. Each of these questions was carefully written to reinforce understanding of very specific information. After reading a chapter (or a section), you should be able to return to these headings and answer the question. If you can't answer a question or are unsure of your response, you'll know exactly what sections you need to reread or review, or where to place more of your effort. All in all, this format provides a self-check on your reading comprehension.

COMPREHENSION CHECK This is a quick "Are-you-understanding-what-you're-reading?" feature. In each chapter there are two Comprehension Checks with objective questions (which are answered at the end of the chapter) that offer quick feedback on whether you've understood what you've read. If you have problems answering these questions correctly, you should reread those sections before moving on to new material in the book. Of course, not every element of the chapter's material can be tested—nor can simply answering these questions correctly guarantee comprehension. But answering these questions correctly can indicate that you are making progress and that learning has taken place.

THINKING CRITICALLY Critical thinking is also an important outcome. Several years ago, training organizations began taking a hard look at themselves. Typically, they found that their programs needed to expand language-based skills, knowledge, and abilities across the curriculum. What outcomes did this achieve? In essence, it indicated the need for all training programs to cover the basic skill areas of communication, critical thinking, computer technology, globalization, diversity, and ethics and values.

This edition of *Supervision Today!* continues this feature to help you acquire these key skills by upgrading levels of thinking from knowledge to comprehension and, finally, to application. We convey relevant supervisory knowledge, give you an opportunity to reinforce your comprehension, and demonstrate how you can apply the concepts.

END-OF-CHAPTER FEATURES: A SKILL-FOCUSED APPROACH

Today it's not enough simply to know about supervision; you need skills to succeed in your supervisory efforts. So we've maintained our skill component in the Enhancing Understanding and Developing Your Supervisory Skills sections at the end of each chapter, which include the following features:

- Summary
- Comprehension Questions
- Key Concept Crossword
- Getting to Know Yourself
- Building a Team
- A step-by-step description of how to develop your skills in the area that is discussed in that chapter
- Two case studies

These features are designed to help you build analytical, diagnostic, team-building, investigative, Internet, and writing skills. We address these skill areas in several ways. For example, we include experiential exercises to develop team-building skills; cases to build diagnostic, analytical, and decision-making skills; suggested topical writing assignments to enhance writing skills; and Web activities to develop Internet research skills.

SUMMARY Just as chapter outcomes clarify where you are going, chapter summaries remind you where you've been. Each chapter of this book concludes with a concise summary organized around the opening learning outcomes.

COMPREHENSION: REVIEW AND DISCUSSION QUESTIONS   These questions reinforce chapter content. If you have read and understood the content of a chapter, you should be able to answer the review questions, which are drawn directly from the material in the chapter. The discussion questions, on the other hand, tend to go beyond comprehension of chapter content. They're designed to foster higher-order thinking skills. The discussion questions enable you to demonstrate that you not only know the facts in the chapter but can also use those facts to deal with more complex issues.

KEY CONCEPT CROSSWORD   Crossword puzzles using the key concepts from each chapter provide another way to reinforce comprehension on a level, and in a way, that you may enjoy.

GETTING TO KNOW YOURSELF   Before you can effectively supervise others, you must understand your current strengths as well as areas in need of development. To assist in this learning process, we encourage you to complete these self-assessments from the Prentice Hall Self-Assessment Library 3.4.

EXPERIENTIAL EXERCISES   These exercises give you an opportunity to work as a team, learning and practicing the supervisory skills introduced in the chapter. By combining your new knowledge and natural talents, you will be able to practice a supervisory activity and assess your own progress.

INTERNET: WEB ACTIVITIES   This feature gives you an opportunity to use the Internet as an investigative/informational tool.

CHAPTER TOPIC HOW-TO FOCUS   This section begins with step-by-step instructions on how to develop a skill directly related to a topic addressed in the chapter.

COMMUNICATING EFFECTIVELY   In this feature, suggested writing projects help you develop writing skills. Projects can also become presentations to reinforce verbal and presentation skills.

THINKING CRITICALLY: CASE ANALYSES   Each chapter concludes with two case studies designed to make you think critically as you make decisions regarding a supervisory issue. These cases enable you to apply your knowledge to solve problems faced by supervisors. For this edition 25 percent of the cases have been replaced and updated with new topical situations dealing with current workplace issues.

Supplemental Materials

FOR THE STUDENT

MyBizSkillsKit contains a wealth of study aids, illustrated case simulations, and access to the Golden Personality Type Profiler Assessment. An access code to MybBizSkillsKit can be value-packaged with the textbook or purchased online. It includes the following:

> **BizSkills Illustrated Business Simulation Cases** present students with workplace situations where they have to make the call. These illustrated case applications contain built-in feedback and scoring and can feed a gradebook, if desired.

> **The Golden Personality Type Profiler.** This popular personality assessment, similar to the full Myers-Briggs assessment program, but oriented toward workplace behavioral assessment, provides students with information about fundamental personality dimensions. It takes about 15–20 minutes to complete, and students receive an easy-to-use and practical feedback report based on their results. This tool helps students improve their self-knowledge and ability to work effectively with others by providing students with feedback on their leadership and organizational

strengths, communication and teamwork preferences, motivation and learning style, and opportunities for personal growth.

Test-prep Quizzes for each chapter, including true/false, multiple choice, and short essay questions; all questions include immediate feedback.

Web Exercises for each chapter

Web Links to useful online resources

MySearchLab® gives students access to EBSCO's ContentSelect Research Database. MySearchLab also includes a plagiarism tutorial, citation tutorial, and tools to help improve student writing including Longman Online Handbook of Writing. Preview at www.mysearchlab.com.

Supervision Today! Textbook can be value-packaged with MyBizSkillsKit for Supervision Student Access Code. Order: ISBN (0-13-296461-9)

A stand-alone MyBizSkillsKit Student Access Code can also be ordered online at wwww.mypearsonstore.com.

Also available separately:

SELF-ASSESSMENT LIBRARY 3.4 ONLINE ACCESS PACKAGED WITH EVERY BOOK   SAL is a unique learning tool that allows students to assess their knowledge, beliefs, feelings, and actions in regard to a wide range of personal skills, abilities, and interests. SAL 3.4 contains 67 research-based self-scoring exercises that generate immediate individual analysis for the student. SAL 3.4 Online Access is packaged at no additional cost with each book. A print version is also available. Additional Online Access Codes and printed copies of SAL 3.4 are available for purchase from www.prenhall.com. Features of this release include the following:

- 18 additional research-based instruments
- Save feature allows students to create an assessment portfolio easily
- The in-depth Instructor's Manual guides instructors in interpreting class results, thereby facilitating greater classroom discussion.

FOR THE INSTRUCTOR

INSTRUCTOR MATERIALS AVAILABLE ONLINE   The Instructor's Manual, PowerPoint Lecture Slides, and Test Generator are available online for download. To access supplementary materials online, instructors need to request an instructor access code. Go to www.pearsonhighered.com/irc, where you can register for an instructor access code. Within 48 hours of registering you will receive a confirming e-mail including an instructor access code. Once you have received your code, locate your text in the online catalog and click on the Instructor Resources button on the left side of the catalog product page. Select a supplement and a log-in page will appear. Once you have logged in, you can access instructor material for all Prentice Hall textbooks.

THE INSTRUCTOR'S MANUAL   includes a suggested course syllabus, sample exam, lecture index, lecture outlines, solutions to review and discussion questions, suggested answers to *Thinking Critically* case studies, additional activities, chapter tests, and midterm and final exams.

POWERPOINT LECTURE SLIDES   Slides provide detailed lecture notes, including key figures from the book, to guide classroom discussion.

TEST GENERATOR   The Test Generator is a testing program that lets instructors view and edit test bank questions, create tests, and print or post them online in a variety of formats.

JWA VIDEO OFFER   This offer gives you the opportunity to select Emmy-award-winning videos from the JWA library. Videos address all kinds of training issues related to supervision. Complimentary copies are available upon adoption. Contact your Prentice Hall sales representative for details.

COURSECONNECT SUPERVISION ONLINE COURSE: CONVENIENCE, SIMPLICITY, SUCCESS Looking for robust online course content to reinforce and enhance your student learning? We have the solution: CourseConnect! CourseConnect courses contain customizable modules of content mapped to major learning outcomes. Each learning object contains interactive tutorials, rich media, discussion questions, MP3 downloadable lectures, assessments, and interactive activities that address different learning styles. When you buy a CourseConnect course, you purchase a complete package that provides you with detailed documentation you can use for your accreditation reviews. CourseConnect courses can be delivered in any commercial platform such as WebCT, BlackBoard, Angel, Moodle, or eCollege platforms. For more information contact your Prentice Hall representative or call 800-635-1579.

Acknowledgments

Writing a textbook is often the work of a number of people whose names generally never appear on the cover. Yet, without their help and assistance, a project like this would never come to fruition. We'd like to recognize some special people who gave so unselfishly to making this book a reality.

We want to thank the users of previous editions and students who provided a number of suggestions for this revision. Special thanks to the reviewers of the fifth edition: Linda McGurn, Johnson County Community College, William Milz, Northeast Wisconsin Technical College, Andy C. Saucedo, NMSU Dona Ana Community College, and Joe Wright. And to the reviewers of the sixth edition: Valeria Truitt, Craven Community College; Martha A. Hunt, New Hampshire Technical Institute; Jacquelyn Blakely, Tri County Technical College; George Cleaver, Manatee Community College; Robert D. Lewallen, Iowa Western Community College; Eva M. Smith, Spartanburg Technical College; Dr. Thomas W. Lloyd, Westmoreland County Community College; and Jerry L. Thomas, Arapahoe Community College.

To all of our reviewers, please know that we take your comments and feedback seriously. We review each comment and see how it might be incorporated into the text. Unfortunately, in a few instances, although the comments and suggestions were absolutely on target, sometimes adding specific information isn't feasible. That's not to say that we discounted what you said, but we had to balance the focus of the book with the feedback given.

Finally, we'd like to add personal notes.

From Steve's corner: To my wife, Laura Ospanik. Laura continues to be a phenomenal source of ideas and support. For that I am grateful.

From Dave's corner: I want to give special thanks to my family, who give me the encouragement and support to do my job. Each of you is special to me in that you continue to bring love and warmth into my life. Terri, Mark, Meredith, Gabriella, and Natalie, thank you. You continue to make me proud to be part of your lives.

From Rob's corner: I want to thank my wife, and best friend, Sheila, for encouraging and supporting me in my work on the seventh edition of *Supervision Today!* I am grateful for the opportunity to be part of this learning endeavor.

An Invitation

Now that we've explained the ideas behind the text, we'd like to extend an open invitation. If you'd like to give us some feedback, we encourage you to write. Send your correspondence to Dave DeCenzo at E. Craig Wall, Sr. College, Coastal Carolina University, P.O. Box 269154, Conway, SC 29528-6054. Dave is also available via e-mail at ddecenzo@coastal.edu

We hope you enjoy reading this book as much as we enjoyed preparing it for you.

Steve Robbins
Dave DeCenzo
Rob Wolter

Defining Supervision and Supervisory Challenges

Part 1 introduces you to the world of work and the functions of a supervisor. Emphasis in this section is placed on supervisory roles and the skills needed to be successful in today's ever-changing work environment. Supervisory positions are also being influenced by a number of environmental factors. What these factors are and how they affect the supervisory function are discussed.

CHAPTER 1

Supervision Definitions

Key Concepts

After completing this chapter, you will be able to define these supervisory terms:

- conceptual competence
- controlling
- effectiveness
- efficiency
- first-level managers
- interpersonal competence
- leading
- management
- management functions
- middle managers
- operative employees
- organization
- organizing
- planning
- political competence
- process
- skill
- supervisors
- supervisory competencies
- technical competence
- top management

Chapter Outcomes

After reading this chapter, you will be able to:

1. Explain the difference among supervisors, middle managers, and top management.
2. Define *supervisor*.
3. Identify the four functions in the management process.
4. Explain why the supervisor's role is considered ambiguous.
5. Describe the four essential supervisory competencies.
6. Identify the elements that are necessary to be successful as a supervisor.

Responding to a Supervisory Dilemma

Organizations are changing, but are organizations changing their traditional structures? By and large, the answer is yes, traditional organizational structures are still evident today. However, some organizations, to appeal to potential employees, are changing the traditional organizational structure. One such company is Google. According to *Fortune* magazine (http://money.cnn.com/magazines/fortune/bestcompanies/2011/index.html), Google ranks in the top five best places to work and has ranked so for five consecutive years. What makes this organization so different from others? Why are employees flocking to organizations such as Google?

The traditional organizational pyramid has operative employees at the bottom of the triangle, supervisors above them, middle managers above supervisors, and top management above all (see Exhibit 1-1). This structure is a vertical approach to management where the decision making is done at the top and orders are sent down to the operational employees at the bottom of the organizational hierarchy. Operative employees do not have much say in the organization's operations.

Google uses a cross-functional organizational structure combined with a unique philosophy. Their cross-functional organizational structure is more of a team approach to management and is structured horizontally. According to Google.com (http://www.google.com/intl/en/corporate/), they purposively maintain a small-company feel, believing every employee is a hands-on contributor and everyone is an equally important part of Google's success. Google's benefits package also plays a major part in attracting employees. Google states that, from employee retirement funds to their free lunch and dinner program, they strive to offer customizable programs that suit the needs of each of their employees. What more could an employee want?

Which organizational structure do you think works best and why? Do you think the vertical structure works better in some cases whereas the horizontal structure works better in others? Would you prefer a more relaxed working environment or do you prefer something more structured?

This book is about the millions of supervisors working in today's dynamic organizations and the jobs they do in helping their organizations reach their goals. This book will introduce you to the challenging activities and the rapidly changing world of supervision today!

Organizations and Their Levels

organization

A systematic grouping of people brought together to accomplish some specific purpose.

Supervisors work in places called organizations. Before we identify who supervisors are and what they do, it's important to clarify what we mean by the term *organization*. An organization is a systematic grouping of people brought together to accomplish some specific purpose. Your college or university is an organization. So are supermarkets, charitable agencies, churches, neighborhood gas stations, the Indianapolis Colts football team, Nokia Corporation, the Australian Dental Association, and Cedars-Sinai Hospital. These are all organizations because each comprises specific common characteristics.

WHAT COMMON CHARACTERISTICS DO ALL ORGANIZATIONS HAVE?

All organizations, regardless of their size or focus, share three common characteristics. First, every organization has a purpose. The distinct purpose of an organization is typically expressed in terms of a goal or set of goals that the organization hopes to accomplish. Second, each organization is composed of people. It takes people to establish the purpose as well as to perform a variety of activities to make the goal a reality. Third, all organizations develop a systematic structure that defines the various roles of members and that often sets limits on their work behaviors. This may include creating rules and regulations, giving some members supervisory responsibility over other members, forming work teams, or writing job descriptions so that organizational members know their responsibilities.

Although organizations and their structures vary widely, often adapting to the environment in which the organization operates, in most traditional organizations, we can show an organization's structure as a pyramid containing four general categories (see Exhibit 1-1).

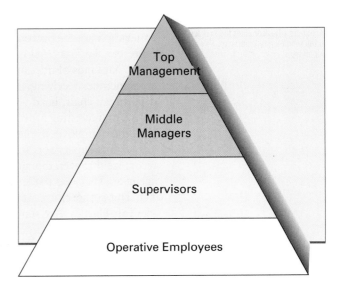

Exhibit 1-1
Levels in the traditional organizational pyramid.

WHAT ARE THE ORGANIZATIONAL LEVELS?

Generally speaking, organizations can be divided into four distinct levels: operative employees, supervisors, middle managers, and top management. Let's briefly look at each level.

The base level in the pyramid is occupied by operative employees. These employees physically produce an organization's goods and services by working on specific tasks. The counter clerk at Burger King, the claims adjuster at Progressive Insurance, the assembly-line worker at the Toyota auto plant, and the UPS representative who delivers your packages are examples of operative employees. This category may also include many professional positions: doctors, lawyers, accountants, engineers, and information technology specialists. The common feature these operative workers share is that they generally don't manage or oversee the work of any other employee.

Now turn your attention to the top two levels in Exhibit 1-1. These are traditional management positions. Top management is a group of people responsible for establishing the organization's overall objectives and developing the policies to achieve those objectives. Titles of typical top management positions in business firms include chair of the board, chief executive officer, president, and senior vice president. Among nonprofit organizations, top management may have such titles as museum director, superintendent of schools, or governor of a state. Middle managers include all employees below the top management level who manage other managers. These individuals are responsible for establishing and meeting specific goals in their particular department or unit. Their goals, however, are not established in isolation. Instead, the objectives set by top management provide specific direction to middle managers regarding what they are expected to achieve. Ideally, if each middle manager meets his or her goals, the entire organization meets its objectives. Examples of job titles held by middle managers include vice president of finance, director of sales, division manager, group manager, district manager, unit manager, or high school principal.

Let's again return to Exhibit 1-1. The only category that we haven't described is supervisors. Like top and middle managers, supervisors are also part of an organization's management team. What makes them unique is that they oversee the work of operative employees. Supervisors, then, are the only managers who don't manage

operative employees
Employees who physically produce an organization's goods and services by working on specific tasks.

top management
A group of people responsible for establishing an organization's overall objectives and developing the policies to achieve those objectives.

middle managers
All employees below the top management level who manage other managers and are responsible for establishing and meeting specific departmental or unit goals set by top management.

supervisors
Part of an organization's management team, supervisors oversee the work of operative employees and are the only managers who don't manage other managers. *See also* first-level managers.

first-level managers
Managers who represent the first level in the management hierarchy. *See also* supervisors.

other managers. Another way to think of supervisors is as first-level managers. That is, counting from the bottom of the traditional pyramid-shaped organization, supervisors represent the first level in the management hierarchy.

What kinds of titles are likely to tell you that someone is a supervisor? Though names are sometimes deceiving, people with job titles such as assistant manager, department head, department chair, head coach, foreman, or team leader are typically in supervisory positions. An interesting aspect of supervisors' jobs is that they may engage in operating tasks with their employees. The counter clerk at Burger King may also be the shift supervisor. The claims supervisor at Progressive may also process claim forms. It is important to recognize that even though they perform operative tasks, supervisors are still part of management. That was made clear in 1947, when the U.S. Congress passed the Taft-Hartley Act. This act specifically excluded supervisors from the definition of *employee*. Moreover, the Taft-Hartley Act stated that any person who can "hire, suspend, transfer, lay off, recall, promote, discharge, assign, reward, or discipline other employees while using independent judgment is a supervisor." Because first-level managers usually have this authority, the fact that they also engage in the same kind of work that their employees perform in no way changes their management status. In reality, they are still expected to perform the duties and responsibilities associated with the management process.

The Management Process

management
The process of getting things done, effectively and efficiently, through and with other people.

process
The primary activities supervisors perform.

efficiency
Doing a task right; also refers to the relationship between inputs and outputs.

effectiveness
Doing the right task; goal attainment.

Just as organizations have common characteristics, so, too, do managers at all levels of the organization. Although their titles vary widely, there are several common elements to their jobs—regardless of whether the supervisor is a head nurse in the Heart Center unit of the Washington Hospital Center who oversees a staff of eleven critical-care specialists, or the chief executive officer of the 82,000-plus-member Exxon Corporation. In this section, we look at these commonalities as we discuss the management process and what managers do.

WHAT IS MANAGEMENT?

The term management refers to the process of getting things done, effectively and efficiently, through and with other people. Several terms of this definition warrant some discussion: *process*, *efficiently*, and *effectively*.

The term process in the definition of management represents the primary activities that supervisors perform. We call these the management functions. The next section describes these functions.

Efficiency means doing the task right and refers to the relationship between inputs and outputs. If you get more output for a given input, you have increased efficiency. You also increase efficiency when you get the same output with fewer resources. Because supervisors deal with input resources that are scarce—money, people, equipment—they are concerned with efficient use of these resources. Consequently, supervisors must be concerned with minimizing resource costs.

Although minimizing resource costs is important, it isn't enough simply to be efficient. A supervisor must also be concerned with completing activities. We call this effectiveness. Effectiveness means doing the right task. In an organization, this translates into goal attainment. Exhibit 1-2 shows how efficiency and effectiveness are interrelated. The need for efficiency has a profound effect on the level of effectiveness.

Means: Efficiency — Resource Usage — Low Waste → High Attainment — Goals

Ends: Effectiveness — Goal Attainment

Exhibit 1-2
Efficiency versus effectiveness.

It's easier to be effective if you ignore efficiency. For instance, you could produce more sophisticated and higher-quality products if you disregard labor and material input costs—yet that would more than likely create serious financial problems. Consequently, being a good supervisor means being concerned with both attaining goals (effectiveness) and doing so as efficiently as possible.

WHAT ARE THE FOUR MANAGEMENT FUNCTIONS?

In the early part of the twentieth century, a French industrialist named Henri Fayol wrote that all managers perform five management functions: They plan, organize, command, coordinate, and control.[1] In the mid-1950s, two professors at UCLA used the functions of planning, organizing, staffing, directing, and controlling as the framework for their management textbook.[2] Most management textbooks continue to be organized around management functions, though these have generally been condensed to the basic four: planning, organizing, leading, and controlling (see Exhibit 1-3).

Because organizations exist to achieve some purpose, someone has to define that purpose and the means for its achievement. A manager is that someone. The planning function encompasses defining an organization's goals, establishing an overall strategy for achieving these goals, and developing a comprehensive hierarchy of plans to integrate and coordinate activities. Setting goals keeps the work to be done in its proper focus and helps organizational members keep their attention on what is most important.

Managers also have to divide work into manageable components and coordinate results to achieve objectives. This is the organizing function. It includes determining which tasks will be done, who will do them, how the tasks will be grouped, who will report to whom, and when decisions will be made.

We know that every organization contains people and that part of a manager's job is to direct and coordinate the activities of these people. Performing this activity is referred to as the leading function of management. When managers motivate employees, direct the activities of others, select the most effective communication channel, or resolve conflicts among members, they're engaging in leading.

The final function managers perform is controlling. After the goals are set, the plans formulated, the structural arrangements determined, and the people hired, trained, and motivated, something may still go amiss. To ensure that things are going as they should, a manager must monitor the organization's performance. Actual performance must be compared with the previously set goals. If there are any significant deviations, it's the manager's responsibility to get the organization back on track. This process of monitoring, comparing, and correcting constitutes the controlling function.

management functions
Planning, organizing, leading, and controlling.

planning
Defining an organization's goals, establishing an overall strategy for achieving these goals, and developing a comprehensive hierarchy of plans to integrate and coordinate activities.

organizing
Arranging and grouping jobs, allocating resources, and assigning work so that activities can be accomplished as planned; determining which tasks are to be done, who is to do them, how the tasks are to be grouped, who reports to whom, and when decisions are to be made.

leading
Motivating employees, directing activities of others, selecting the most effective communication channel, and resolving conflicts among members.

controlling
Monitoring an organization's performance and comparing performance with previously set goals. If significant deviations exist, getting the organization back on track.

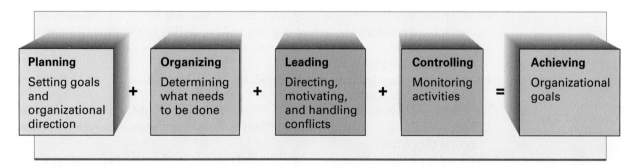

Exhibit 1-3
Management functions.

---

[1]H. Fayol, *Industrial and General Administration* (Paris: Dunod, 1916).
[2]H. Koontz and C. O'Donnell, *Principles of Management: An Analysis of Managerial Functions* (New York: McGraw-Hill, 1955).

DO MANAGEMENT FUNCTIONS DIFFER BY ORGANIZATIONAL LEVELS?

A manager's level in an organization affects how these management functions are performed. A supervisor in the sales department at Black & Decker won't do the same kind of planning as Black & Decker's president. That's because although all managers perform the four management functions, there are important differences relating to their level. Typically, top management focuses on long-term strategic planning such as determining what overall business a company should be in. Supervisors focus on short-term, tactical planning such as scheduling departmental workloads for the next month. Similarly, top management is concerned with structuring the overall organization, whereas supervisors focus on structuring the jobs of individuals and workgroups.

Changing Expectations of Supervisors

Seventy years ago, if you had asked a group of top executives what they thought a supervisor's job was, you would have gotten a fairly standard answer. They would describe a man (which it was likely to be back then) who forcefully made decisions, told employees what to do, closely watched over those employees to make sure they did as they were told, disciplined them when they broke the rules, and fired those that didn't "shape up." Supervisors were the bosses "on the operating floor," and their job was to keep the employees in line and get the work out.

If you ask top executives that same question today, you'll find a few who still hold to the supervisor-as-boss perspective. But you'll also hear executives describe today's supervisor using terms such as *trainer, adviser, mentor, facilitator,* or *coach.* In this section, we look at some of these changing expectations of supervisory managers.

WHAT ROLES DO SUPERVISORS PLAY?

The supervisor's job is unique in that it bridges the management ranks with the operating employees. No one else in the organization can make that claim. Yet because of this uniqueness, supervisors have an ambiguous role. Each of the following offers a different viewpoint of the supervisor's role:[3]

Key person: Supervisors serve as the critical communication link in the organization's chain of authority. They are like the hub of a wheel around which all operating activities revolve.

Person in the middle: Because they are "neither fish nor fowl," supervisors must interact and reconcile the opposing forces and competing expectations from higher management and workers. If unresolved, this conflicting role can create frustration and stress for supervisors.

Just another worker: Some people, particularly upper-level managers, see supervisors as "just another worker," rather than as management. This is reinforced when their decision-making authority is limited, when they're excluded from participating in upper-level decisions, and when they perform operating tasks alongside the same people they supervise.

Behavioral specialist: Consistent with the belief that one of the most important abilities needed by supervisors is strong interpersonal skills, they are looked at as behavioral specialists. To succeed in their jobs, supervisors must be able to understand the varied needs of their staff and be able to listen, motivate, and lead.

---

[3]Based on J. Newstrom and K. Davis, *Organizational Behavior: Human Behavior at Work*, 9th ed. (New York: McGraw-Hill, 1993), 239.

Although each of these four role descriptions has some truth to it, each also offers a slanted view of the supervisor's job. Our point is that different people hold different perceptions of this job, which can create ambiguity and conflicts for today's supervisor.

Comprehension Check 1-1

1. All of the following except one are characteristics of all organizations. Which one is not a characteristic?
   a. Purpose
   b. Profit
   c. People
   d. Structure

2. The term *process* in the definition of management refers to
   a. the primary activities supervisors perform on their jobs
   b. the transformation of raw materials into goods
   c. the relationship between doing a task correctly and doing the correct task
   d. the means of goal attainment

3. The management function that involves monitoring activities to ensure that targets are being met is called
   a. planning
   b. organizing
   c. leading
   d. controlling

4. A key person in a supervisory role is someone who
   a. interacts with opposing forces to reconcile differences
   b. serves as the critical communication link in the organization
   c. is just another worker
   d. has a strong ability to listen and understand what is being said

ARE SUPERVISORS MORE IMPORTANT IN TODAY'S ORGANIZATIONS?

Regardless of what people think and the different role perceptions they hold, a case can be built that the supervisor's job will continue to become increasingly important and complex in the future. Why? We can provide at least three reasons.

First, organizations are implementing significant change and quality programs to cut costs and increase productivity. Examples of these programs include continuous quality improvements, the introduction of work teams, group bonus plans, flexible work hours, and accident-prevention and stress-reduction programs. These programs tend to focus on the work activities of operating employees. As a result, supervisors have become increasingly important because they typically assume responsibility for introducing and implementing these change efforts at the operations level.

Second, organizations are making extensive cutbacks in their number of employees. Boeing, General Motors, United Airlines, Motorola, IBM, and American Express are just a few of the major companies that have cut anywhere from 1,000 to 50,000 jobs. Organizations are particularly thinning their ranks among middle managers and staff-support personnel. "Lean and mean" continues to be a major theme for the best corporations. The implications of these cutbacks for supervisors are clear. Fewer middle managers will mean that supervisors will have more people directly reporting to them. Moreover, many tasks previously performed by people in support units—such as work design, process flow, scheduling, and quality control—will be reassigned to

Like athletic coaches, today's supervisors need to get their employees "ready for the game" and cheer them on to success.

supervisors and their employees. The net effect will be significantly expanded responsibilities for supervisors.

Finally, employee training is becoming more important than ever as organizations seek to improve productivity. New employees—many of whom are poorly prepared for work or have language or communication deficiencies— require basic training in reading, writing, and mathematics. Changes in jobs brought about by computers, automation, and other technological advances require additional skills training among current employees to prevent their skills from becoming obsolete. Supervisors will carry the primary burden for identifying these skill deficiencies, designing appropriate training programs, and in some cases even providing the training itself.

DOES A SUPERVISOR NEED TO BE A COACH?

Today's supervisors are far less likely to be able to do all aspects of their employees' jobs. Supervisors need to know what their employees are doing, but they are not necessarily expected to be as skilled at specific job tasks as each employee. Moreover, employees don't need an authority figure to tell them what to do or to "keep them in line." Instead, they may need a coach who can listen to, guide, train, and assist them. In their coaching role, supervisors are expected to ensure that their employees have the resources they need to do a first-class job. They must also develop their employees, clarify responsibilities and goals, motivate employees to higher levels of performance, and represent their workgroup's interests within the organization.

Transition from Employee to Supervisor

It wasn't easy making the move from being one of the quality-control specialists in the department to being the supervisor. On Friday I had been one of them. The next Monday I became their boss. Suddenly, people that I had joked around and socialized with for years were distancing themselves from me. I could see that they were apprehensive. They weren't sure, now, if I could be trusted. I didn't think our relationship was going to be much different. Hey, we were friends. We went out together every Friday after work. But I'm management now. I still think I'm like them, part of the group. But they don't see me that way. Even when I join them for drinks, it's not like it used to be. They have their guard up now. It's been a hard adjustment for me.

These comments from an individual promoted to quality-control supervisor at Monsanto capture the dilemma many new supervisors face when they're promoted from the ranks.

It's important to reflect for a moment on what this step of becoming a supervisor really means. For many in the workforce, becoming a supervisor is a major turning point in their career. It's a time when one becomes responsible not only for one's own work but also for the work of others. It's a time when authority is given to someone; and that authority can be used in a variety of ways. It's a time of added responsibility and accountability to the organization—when one becomes part of the management team.

Although for many this is an exciting time, being a supervisor can present challenges. Meeting goals, making appropriate decisions, supervising employees, and being the communication vehicle for information that needs to get to employees all present activities and events that can be complex and troublesome. But they can also be very rewarding when one has the skills and competencies to be an effective supervisor.

In this section, we look at the primary roads people take to becoming supervisors and the challenges they face in mastering a new identity.

WHERE DO SUPERVISORS COME FROM?

Many new supervisors are promoted from within the ranks of their current employers. The second major source of supervisory personnel is new college graduates. Occasionally, employees from other organizations are hired to become first-line supervisors; however, this is increasingly rare because if employers have an open supervisory position, they often prefer to fill it with someone they know and who knows the organization. That favors promoting from within.

Employers tend to promote operative employees to first-line management jobs for several reasons. Employees know how the operations function. They understand how things are done in the organization. They typically know the people they'll be supervising. Another advantage is that the organization knows a lot about the candidate. When management promotes "one of its own" into a supervisory position, it minimizes risk. When hiring from the outside, management must rely on limited information provided by previous employers. By promoting from within, management can draw on its full history with a candidate. Finally, and very important, promoting from within acts as an employee motivator by providing an incentive for employees to work hard and excel.

Supervisors must understand that supervising employees today is dramatically different from in the past. Today a supervisor must act as a coach rather than as a taskmaster. This translates into being aware of employees' needs and being willing to let them do their jobs, giving support wherever it is needed.

What criteria does management tend to use in deciding who to promote into first-line managerial positions? Employees with good work records and an interest in management tend to be favored. Ironically, not all "good" operative employees make good supervisors. The reason is that people with strong technical skills don't necessarily have the skills needed to manage others. Organizations that successfully promote from the ranks select employees with adequate technical skills and provide them with supervisory training early in their new assignments.

Recent college graduates provide the other primary source of candidates for supervisory positions. Two-year and four-year college programs in supervision and management provide a basic foundation for preparing for the supervisor's job. With additional organizational training, many new college graduates are equipped to step into first-line management.

IS THE TRANSITION TO SUPERVISOR DIFFICULT?

Moving from one middle-management job to another or from a middle-management position to one in top management rarely creates the anxiety that comes when one moves from being an employee to being a supervisor. It's a lot like being a parent. If you already have three kids, the addition of one more isn't too big a deal. Why? It's because you already know quite a bit about parenting—and you've been through it before. The challenge lies in the transition from being childless to being a parent for the first time. The same applies here. The challenge is unique when one moves into first-line management; it is unlike anything managers will encounter later in their rise up the organizational ladder.[4]

---

[4]See, for example, R. D. Ramsey, "So You've Been Promoted or Changed Jobs. Now What?" *Supervision,* November 1998, 6–8.

A previous study of what nineteen new supervisors experienced in their first year on the job helps us to better understand what it's like to become a first-line manager.[5] Fourteen men and five women participated in this study. All worked in sales or marketing. However, what they experienced would seem relevant to anyone making the employee–supervisor transition.

Even though these new supervisors had worked in their respective organizations as salespeople for an average of six years, their expectations of a supervisory position were incomplete and simplistic. They didn't appreciate the full range of demands that would be made on them. Each had previously been a star salesperson. They were promoted, in large part, as a reward for their good performance. But "good performance" for a salesperson and "good performance" for a supervisor are very different—and few of these new supervisors understood that. Ironically, their previous successes in sales may actually have made their transition to management harder. Because of their strong technical expertise and high motivation, they depended on their supervisors less than the average salesperson for support and guidance. When they became supervisors and suddenly had to deal with low-performing and unmotivated employees, they weren't prepared for it.

The nineteen new supervisors actually encountered a number of surprises. We briefly summarize the major ones because they capture the essence of what many supervisors encounter as they attempt to master their new identity.

Their initial view of the manager as "boss" was incorrect: Before taking their supervisory jobs, these managers-to-be talked about the power they would have and of being in control. As one put it, "Now I'll be the one calling the shots." After a month, they spoke of being a "troubleshooter," a "juggler," and a "quick-change artist." All emphasized solving problems, making decisions, helping others, and providing resources as their primary responsibilities. They no longer conceived of their jobs as being "the boss."

They were unprepared for the demands and ambiguities they would face: In their first week, these supervisors were surprised by the unrelenting workload and pace of being a manager. On a typical day, they had to work on many problems simultaneously and were met with constant interruptions.

Technical expertise was no longer the primary determinant of success or failure: The supervisors were used to excelling by performing specific technical tasks and being individual contributors, not by acquiring managerial competence and getting things done through others. It took four to six months on the job for most to come to grips with the fact that they now would be judged by their ability to motivate others to high performance.

A supervisor's job comes with administrative duties: These supervisors found that routine communication activities such as paperwork and exchange of information were time consuming and interfered with their autonomy.

They weren't prepared for the "people challenges" of their new jobs: The supervisors unanimously asserted that the most demanding skills they had to learn in their first year dealt with managing people. They expressed being particularly uncomfortable in counseling employees and providing leadership. As one stated, "I hadn't realized...how hard it is to motivate people or develop them or deal with their personal problems."

Given this and similar issues that arise when one becomes a supervisor, what does it take to be an effective supervisor? What competencies or general categories of skills are needed? Are these the same, regardless of one's level in the organization? We answer these questions in the next section.

---

[5]This section is based on L. A. Hill, *Becoming a Manager: Mastery of New Identity* (Boston, MA: Harvard Business School Press, 1992).

DO YOU REALLY WANT TO BE A SUPERVISOR?

The fact that you're learning about supervision indicates you're interested in understanding how to supervise people. What is it about supervising people that excites you? Is it the fact that you can help an organization achieve its goals? Is it the challenge of supervising others—directing their work—that interests you? Is it the fact that supervision may lead to a management position and hopes of climbing the career ladder? Whatever your reasons, you need a clear picture of what lies ahead.

Supervisory positions are not easy. Even if you've been a superstar as an employee, this is no guarantee that you'll succeed as a supervisor. The fact that you are capable of doing excellent work is a big plus, but there are many other factors to consider. You need to recognize that supervising others may mean longer work hours. You're often on the job before your employees and leave after they do. Supervising can literally be a twenty-four-hours-a-day, seven-days-a-week job. Now, that's not to be interpreted as being on the job every hour of every day. But when you accept the responsibility of supervising others, you really never can "get away" from the job. Things happen, and you'll be expected to deal with them—no matter when they happen or where you are. It's not unheard of to get a call while you're on vacation, if problems arise. Organizational policy may require peers and subordinates to contact you via cell phone or wireless handheld device in the event of any unforeseen event. How was someone in the organization able to contact you during your getaway? You are probably required by organizational policy to provide emergency contact information and to call in periodically to see how things are going.

You also need to recognize that, as a supervisor, you may have a seemingly endless pile of paperwork to complete. Although organizations are continually working to eliminate much of their paperwork, a lot remains. This may include employee work schedules, production cost estimates, inventory documentation, or budget and payroll matters.

Another matter of importance that you should consider is the effect the supervisor's job may have on your pay! In some organizations, a raise in your base pay when you become a supervisor may not translate into higher annual earnings. How so? Consider that, as a supervisor, you are generally no longer eligible for overtime pay or commission. Instead, you may get compensatory (comp) time (time off). When you are an operative employee, your organization is legally required to pay you a premium rate (typically time-and-a-half) for overtime work. That may not be true when you become a supervisor. If you get a $6,000 raise when you become a supervisor, but earned $6,500 last year in overtime, you're actually earning less as a supervisor. This is something that you'll need to discuss with your organization before making your decision to become a supervisor.

What are the previous paragraphs really saying? They're telling you to think about why you want to supervise. Managing others can be rewarding. The excitement is real—and so are the headaches. You need to understand exactly what your motives are for becoming a supervisor—and what trade-offs you're willing to make to become the best supervisor you can be.

Supervisory Competencies

More than thirty years ago, Professor Robert Katz began a process of identifying essential supervisory competencies.[6] What Katz and others have found is that successful supervisors must possess four critical competencies: technical, interpersonal, conceptual, and political competencies. They are as relevant today as when Katz originally described them.

supervisory competencies
Conceptual, interpersonal, technical, and political competencies.

---

[6] R. L. Katz, "Skills of an Effective Administrator," *Harvard Business Review*, September–October 1974, 90–102; and B. Humphrey and J. Stokes, "The 21st Century Supervisor," *HR Magazine*, May 2000, 185–192.

Something to Think About (and promote class discussion)

BECOMING A SUPERVISOR

Becoming a supervisor is a challenging opportunity. Some individuals look forward to "taking the helm" of a crew of workers, whereas others are put into this situation with little advance notice—or training. As you consider going into a supervisory position—or making yourself a more effective supervisor than you are today—think about the following two areas.

1. List five reasons why you want to be a supervisor.

I enjoy helping others

I am good at it & enjoy it.

I like directing people (people & time mngment)

challenging

Helping complete goals

2. Identify five potential problems or difficulties that you may encounter when you become a supervisor.

WHAT IS TECHNICAL COMPETENCE?

Top management is composed of generalists. The activities that consume top managers—strategic planning, developing the organization's overall structure and culture, maintaining relations with major customers and bankers, marketing the product, and the like—are essentially generic in nature. The technical demands of top management jobs tend to be related to knowledge of the industry and a general understanding of the organization's processes and products. This isn't true for managers at other levels.

Most supervisors manage within areas of specialized knowledge: the vice president of human resources, the director of computer systems, the regional sales manager, and the supervisor of health claims. These supervisors require technical competence—the ability to apply specialized knowledge or expertise. It's difficult, if not impossible, to supervise employees with specialized skills effectively if you don't have an adequate understanding of the technical aspects of their jobs. Although the supervisor need not be able to perform certain technical skills, understanding what each worker does is part of every supervisor's job. For example, the task of scheduling work flow requires technical competence to determine what needs to be done.

technical competence
The ability to apply specialized knowledge or expertise.

News Flash!

THE SUPERVISOR'S ROLE IN MODERN ORGANIZATIONS

For years the role of the working or front-line supervisor has been considered by many organizations to be little more than a stepping-stone into management. Business and management schools devoted their attention primarily to teaching principles and theories applicable to upper management. Many professors figured their graduates would hold down beginning supervisory roles for a short period and then move into something more challenging. How things have changed!

Today's organizations are complex. Some of the complexity is due in part to the following:

- A more culturally diverse workforce than ever before.
- Molding a productive team out of a mix of full-timers, part-timers, "temps," and contract workers.
- Implementation of quality and productivity programs such as ISO certification and six sigma, JIT and lean manufacturing, and organizing work using self-directed teams.
- Enforcing the ever-growing number of employment laws pertaining to hiring and dismissal, anti-discrimination, sexual harassment, disability accommodation, workplace violence, Family and Medical Leave Act of 1993 (FMLA), Occupational Safety and Health Administration (OSHA), Health Insurance Portability and Accountability Act (HIPAA) of 1996, worker's compensation, overtime, and ergonomics.
- Globalization and international competition, downsizing, outsourcing, and flattening of the organizational structure by removing levels of management.

The Good News for Supervisors

To meet all the challenges inherent in the complexity of modern organizations, the role of the front-line supervisor has changed dramatically. This is great news for someone aspiring to become a front-line supervisor because, while challenging, these changes present tremendous career and growth opportunities.

1. *The stature of the front-line supervisor has been elevated.* Instead of being a bit player at the bottom rung of the management ladder, the supervisor has become a key position.

The obvious reason is that many middle- and upper-level management positions have been eliminated. Organizations are "flattening" their organizational hierarchy. There are fewer middle- and upper-level managers in flat organizations. The flat organizational structure means that more authority, power, and responsibility are being delegated to lower-level managerial positions. The talent and skill of the supervisor in a flat organization is a major factor to its success.

2. *Empowerment of the supervisor's job is ongoing.* Some of the "power" previously held by those whose jobs have been eliminated will be delegated to the supervisors they used to supervise. This shift means that the line supervisor or "team leader" of the past can take a more positive stance. She or he can submit new suggestions with more freedom and more influence. In short, the line supervisor will play a bigger role in the total management team. Upper management (those left) will have to listen more and react to what they hear.

3. *Supervisors have more autonomy.* With fewer directives to follow, fewer inspections from those above, and fewer people to please, supervisors have the power and responsibility to run their departments or "teams" more like the owner of a small business might do. Supervisors will be encouraged to operate with more authority while also being held accountable.

4. *Supervisors receive more advanced training.* As upper management shifts additional responsibilities to their front-line supervisors, they will provide more training to help them succeed. In addition, more supervisors will appoint assistants and prepare them for temporary "takeover" roles when they are absent. In other words, front-line supervisors will move closer to those upper-management leaders who remain with the firm and whose roles, in turn, will be expanded.

5. *Supervisors derive tremendous personal benefits from their role in today's business culture.* For example:

- Effective supervisors will be easier to spot and will be "first call" on promotional possibilities.

(continued)

Continued

- Women who excel as front-line supervisors will discover that the so-called glass ceiling is less likely to affect them.
- The challenges of front-line supervision provide a great training ground and preparation for upper-management positions.
- Supervision offers the opportunity to engage in meaningful and challenging work that will enhance one's self-respect and the respect from others.
- Supervisors will receive more immediate positive reinforcement of their contribution to organizational success as a result of

leading their employees through collaborative and team-based approaches than was possible through former top-down management methods.
- Supervisors will have greater opportunities to engage in continuous learning, which is a top motivator.

Source: C. Goodwin and D. B. Griffith. "The Supervisor's Role and Responsibility in the Modern Organization," *Supervisor's Survival Kit,* 11th ed. (Upper Saddle River, NJ: Pearson—Prentice Hall, 2006), 32–34.

HOW DO INTERPERSONAL COMPETENCIES HELP?

interpersonal competence
The ability to work with, understand, communicate with, and motivate other people, both individually and in groups.

The ability to work well with people, understand their needs, communicate well, and motivate others—both individually and in groups—constitutes interpersonal competence. Many people are technically proficient but interpersonally incompetent. They might be poor listeners, be unconcerned with the needs of others, or have difficulty dealing with conflicts. Supervisors get things done through other people. They must have good interpersonal skills to communicate, motivate, negotiate, delegate, and resolve conflicts.

WHAT IS CONCEPTUAL COMPETENCE?

conceptual competence
The mental ability to analyze and diagnose complex situations.

Conceptual competence is the mental ability to analyze and diagnose complex situations. Strong conceptual abilities allow a supervisor to see that the organization is a complex system of many interrelated parts and that the organization itself is part of a larger system that includes the organization's industry, the community, and the nation's economy. This gives the supervisor a broad perspective and contributes to creative problem solving. On a more practical level, strong conceptual abilities help managers make good decisions.

WHY MUST ONE HAVE POLITICAL COMPETENCE?

political competence
A supervisor's ability to enhance his or her power, build a power base, and establish the "right" connections in the organization.

Political competence is the supervisor's ability to enhance his or her power, build a power base, and establish the "right" connections in the organization. Supervisors engage in politics when they attempt to influence the advantages and disadvantages of a situation. It goes beyond normal work activities. Whenever two or more people come together for some purpose, each has some idea of what should occur. If one person tries to influence the situation such that it benefits him or her more than the others, or keeps others from gaining some advantage, politics is "being played." But not all political behavior is negative. It doesn't have to involve manipulating a series of events, complaining about fellow supervisors, or sabotaging the work or reputation of another to further one's career. There's a fine line between appropriate political behavior and negative politics. We come back to organizational politics in Chapter 14.

HOW DO COMPETENCIES SHIFT BY MANAGERIAL LEVEL?

Although supervisors need to possess all the four competencies, the importance of each competency in any manager's job varies with the individual's level in the organization. As Exhibit 1-4 illustrates, (1) technical competence declines in importance as individuals rise in the organization; (2) interpersonal competencies are a constant for success, regardless of level in the organization; and (3) conceptual and political competencies increase in importance as managerial responsibility rises.

Technical abilities typically have the greatest relevance for first-level managers. This is true for two reasons. First, many supervisors perform technical work as well as managerial work. In contrast to other levels of management, the distinction between individual contributor and first-line manager is often blurred. Second, supervisors spend more time on training and developing their employees than do other managers. This requires them to have a greater technical knowledge of their employees' jobs than that needed by middle- and top-level managers. There is overwhelming evidence that interpersonal abilities are critical at all levels of management. This shouldn't come as a shock because we know that managers get things done through other people. Supervisors are particularly in need of interpersonal competencies because they spend so much of their time in leading-function activities. When we talked with dozens of practicing supervisors, the one common viewpoint they shared was the importance of people skills to the successful achievement of their units' objectives.

The importance of conceptual competence increases as managers move up in the organization. This is because of the types of problems managers encounter and the decisions they make at higher levels. Generally speaking, the higher a manager rises in an organization, the more the problems he or she faces tend to be complex, ambiguous, and ill defined. These problems require custom-made solutions. In contrast, supervisors

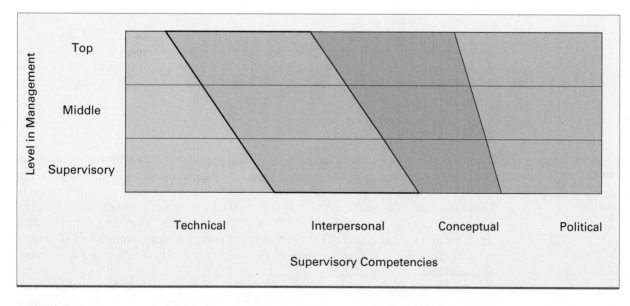

Exhibit 1-4

How competency demands vary at different levels of management.

generally have more straightforward, familiar, and easily defined problems, which lend themselves to more routine decision making. Ill-structured problems and custom-made solutions make greater conceptual demands on managers than do structured problems and routine decision making.

Finally, the higher one climbs in the organization's hierarchy, the more critical political competence becomes. Because resource-allocation decisions are made at higher levels in an organization, middle and top managers are "fighting" for their piece of the organizational pie. Their need to develop alliances, support one project over another, or influence certain situations involves higher-level political skills. But don't interpret this as implying that politics are less important for supervisors. Because so much of the supervisor's job is well defined, they need strong political skills to get their unit's work completed and to survive.

From Concepts to Skills

Knowledge about a subject is important, but just as important is whether you can do anything with that knowledge. Can you put your knowledge into practice? Just as you wouldn't want a surgeon who had never operated on anyone taking a knife to you, or to fly on an aircraft with a pilot who's never flown, it's not enough for you to just know about supervision. You should be able to actually supervise! You can learn to be an effective supervisor! No one is born with supervisory skills, although some people have a head start.

It's true that supervision comes easier to some people than to others. Individuals who are fortunate enough to have parents, relatives, or friends who supervise employees have role models to emulate and give them insights into what the job entails. Similarly, individuals whose parents helped them set realistic goals, provided positive feedback, encouraged autonomy, practiced open communication, and fostered the development of a strong self-concept have learned behaviors that will help them as supervisors. Also, those who have had the fortune to work for a good supervisor have a role model to imitate. However, those without these advantages can improve their supervisory abilities.

This book will help you to be an effective supervisor by focusing on both conceptual knowledge and practical skills. In a succeeding chapter, for example, we discuss the importance of planning to a supervisor's success and show how setting goals is a key part of planning. Then, we present specific techniques for helping employees set goals and provide you with an opportunity to practice and develop your goal-setting skills.

WHAT IS A SKILL?

skill
The ability to demonstrate a system and sequence of behavior that is functionally related to attaining a performance goal.

A skill is the ability to demonstrate a system and sequence of behavior that is functionally related to attaining a performance goal.[7] No single action constitutes a skill. For example, the ability to write clear communications is a skill. People who have this skill know the particular sequence of actions to take to propose a project or summarize a report. They can separate primary from secondary ideas. They can organize their thoughts in a logical manner. They can simplify complex ideas. None of these actions is by itself a skill. A skill is a system of behavior that can be applied in a wide range of situations.

Which key skills are related to supervisory effectiveness? Although there is no unanimous agreement among teachers and trainers of supervision, certain skills have

---

[7]R. E. Boyatzis, *The Competent Manager: A Model for Effective Performance* (New York: Wiley, 1982), 33.

surfaced as being more important than others. Exhibit 1-5 lists key supervisory skills, organized as they are presented in this text. In aggregate, they form the competency base for effective supervision.

WHAT ELSE IS CRITICAL FOR ME TO KNOW ABOUT SUPERVISING?

By now you may be somewhat amazed by what a supervisor has to do and the skills he or she must have to succeed in an organization, but you should consider several other elements. Specifically, what personal issues should you address? Let's look at these.

One of the first things you'll need to do is to recognize that you are part of management as a supervisor. This means that you support the organization and the wishes of management above you. Although you might disagree with those wishes, as a supervisor, you must be loyal to the organization. You must also develop a means of gaining respect from your employees, as well as your peers and boss. If you're going to be effective as a supervisor, you'll need to develop their trust and build credibility with them. One means of doing this is to keep your skills and competencies up-to-date. You must continue your education, not only because it helps you, but also because it sets an example for your employees. It communicates that learning matters.

You'll also have to understand what legitimate power you have been given by the organization because you direct the activities of others. This legitimate power is your authority to act and expect others to follow your directions. Yet ruling with an iron fist may not work. Accordingly, you'll need to know when to assert your authority and how to get things done without resorting to "Because I told you so." In the latter case, you need to develop interpersonal skills that help you influence others. This is particularly true when dealing with organizational members whom you don't supervise.

Finally, you'll need to recognize that organizational members are different—not only in their talents, but as individuals. You'll need to be sensitive to their needs, tolerate and even celebrate their differences, and be empathetic to them as individuals. Success, in part, begins with understanding what being flexible means.

Throughout this text, we address each of these areas. For instance, in the next chapter, we introduce you to the diversity of the workforce and what that may mean for you. In Chapter 9, we introduce trust and credibility and their role in your leadership effectiveness.

Related to Planning and Control
- Goal setting
- Budgeting
- Creative problem solving
- Developing control charts

Related to Organizing, Staffing, and Employee Development
- Empowering others
- Interviewing
- Providing feedback
- Coaching

Related to Stimulating Individual and Group Performance
- Designing motivating jobs
- Projecting charisma
- Listening
- Conducting a group meeting

Related to Coping with Workplace Dynamics
- Negotiation
- Stress reduction
- Counseling
- Disciplining
- Handling grievances

Exhibit 1-5
Key supervisory skills.

Comprehension Check 1-2

5. *True or false?*   The transition from middle manager to top-level manager creates about as much anxiety as going from worker to supervisor.

6. Which one of the following is an interpersonal competency?
   a. Specialized knowledge
   b. Motivating others
   c. Analyzing skills
   d. Enhancing one's power base

7. A _____ is the ability to demonstrate a system and sequence of behavior that is functionally related to attaining a performance goal.
   a. planning effort
   b. political competency
   c. skill
   d. successful planner

8. Which one of the following items does not relate to stimulating individual and group performance?
   a. Listening
   b. Conducting group meetings
   c. Interviewing
   d. Projecting charisma

Enhancing Understanding

SUMMARY

After reading this chapter, I can:

1. **Explain the difference among supervisors, middle managers, and top management.** Whereas all are part of the managerial ranks, they differ by their level in the organization. Supervisors are first-level managers—they manage operative employees. Middle managers encompass all managers from those who manage supervisors up to those in the vice presidential ranks. Top management is composed of the highest-level managers—those responsible for establishing the organization's overall objectives and developing the policies to achieve those objectives.

2. **Define** *supervisor.* A supervisor is a first-level manager who oversees the work of operative or nonmanagement employees.

3. **Identify the four functions in the management process.** Planning, organizing, leading, and controlling make up the management process. Planning involves establishing the overall strategy and setting goals. Organizing involves arranging and grouping jobs, allocating resources, and assigning work so that activities can be accomplished as planned. Leading involves motivating employees, directing the activities of others, communicating properly, and resolving conflict among organizational members. Controlling involves monitoring the organization's performance and comparing it with previously set goals.

4. **Explain why the supervisor's role is considered ambiguous.** A supervisor is (1) a key person (a critical communication link in the organization); (2) a person in the middle (interacting and reconciling opposing forces and competing expectations); (3) just another worker (decision-making authority is limited, and supervisors may perform operating tasks alongside the same people they supervise); and (4) a behavioral specialist (able to listen, motivate, and lead).

5. **Describe the four essential supervisory competencies.** The four essential supervisory competencies are technical, interpersonal, conceptual, and political competence. Technical competence reflects one's ability to apply specialized knowledge or expertise. Interpersonal competence is the ability to work with, understand, and communicate with others both individually and in groups. Conceptual competence is one's mental ability to analyze and diagnose complex situations. Political competence is the ability to enhance one's power by building a power base and establishing the right connections in the organization.

6. **Identify the elements that are necessary to be successful as a supervisor.** Several elements are necessary to become a successful supervisor, including understanding that you're part of the management team, handling legitimate power properly, and recognizing differences in employees.

COMPREHENSION: Review and Discussion Questions

1. What differentiates supervisory positions from all other levels of management?

2. Is the owner–manager of a small store with three employees an operative employee, a supervisor, or a top manager? Explain.

3. What specific tasks are common to all managers, regardless of their level in the organization?

4. Contrast time spent on management functions by supervisors versus top management.

5. "The best rank-and-file employees should be promoted to supervisors." Do you agree or disagree with this statement? Explain.

6. Why is conceptual competence more important for top managers than it is for first-level supervisors?

7. A supervisor is both "a key person" and "just another worker." Explain this phenomenon.

KEY CONCEPT CROSSWORD

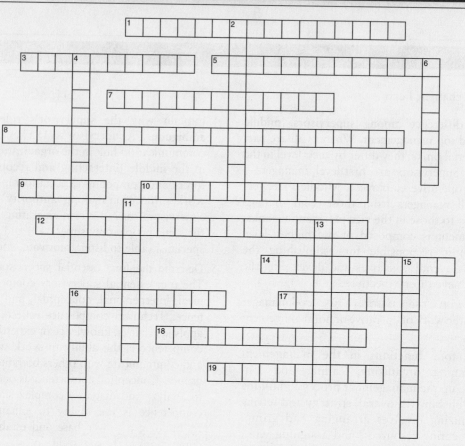

ACROSS

1. people who manage other managers
3. competency in the ability to analyze and diagnose complex situations
5. competency in the ability to work with and communicate with others
7. people responsible for establishing an organization's overall goals
8. conceptual, interpersonal, technical, and political
9. the ability to demonstrate a behavior related to attaining a performance goal
10. doing the right task
12. planning, organizing, leading and controlling
14. first-line managers
16. competency in the ability to enhance one's power
17. defining an organization's goals
18. the systematic grouping of people to accomplish a specific purpose
19. doing a task right

DOWN

2. the process of getting things done, effectively and efficiently through and with people
4. monitoring activities
6. motivating employees
11. competency in the ability to apply specialized knowledge or expertise
13. an employee who physically produces goods and services
15. arranging and grouping jobs
16. the primary activities supervisors perform

ANSWERS TO COMPREHENSION CHECKS

Comprehension Check 1-1

1. b   2. a   3. d   4. b

Comprehension Check 1-2

5. False   6. b   7. c   8. c

Developing Your Supervisory Skills

GETTING TO KNOW YOURSELF

Before you can effectively supervise others, you must understand your present strengths and areas in need of development. To assist in this learning process, we encourage you to complete the following self-assessments from the Prentice Hall Self-Assessment Library 3.4.

1. How Motivated Am I to Manage? (III. B. 4.)

2. What's My Basic Personality? (I. A. 1.)

3. What's My Jungian 16-Type Personality? (I. A. 2.)

4. What's My Emotional Intelligence Score? (I. E. 1.)

After you complete the assessment, we suggest you retain the results and store them as part of your "portfolio of learning about yourself."

BUILDING A TEAM

➤ An Experiential Exercise: Sharing and Receiving Information

When you begin a new course, do you have specific expectations of what you want from the class? You probably do, but how often do you communicate them to the instructor?[8] This information is important to both of you. As a supervisor, you will need to become accustomed to sharing and receiving information about your expectations and the expectations of others. You can begin by defining your expectations for this course. First, take out a piece of paper and place your name at the top. Then, respond to the following questions:

1. What do I want from this course? Why?

2. Why are these things important to me?

3. How does this course fit into my career plans?

4. What is my greatest challenge in taking this class?

When you have finished answering these questions, pair up with another class member (preferably someone you do not already know) and exchange papers. Get to know each other (using the information on these sheets as a starting point). Prepare an introduction of your partner, and share your partner's responses to the four questions with the class and your instructor.

➤ Internet: Web Activity

Go to http://www.pearsonhighered.com/robbins/. Find *Supervision Today!* 7th Ed. and click Companion Website.

MENTORING OTHERS

A mentor is someone in the organization, usually more experienced and in a higher-level position, who sponsors or supports another employee or student (frequently called a protégé). A mentor can teach, guide, and encourage the protégé as that person is socialized to the culture of the organization. Some organizations have formal mentoring programs, but even if your organization does not, mentoring is an important supervisory skill for you to develop. Increasingly, students are asked to participate in providing service to the community by mentoring K through twelve students, as well as college-level peers. Check with your program or department chair to determine whether mentoring opportunities are available within your school or community.

---

[8]The idea for this exercise came from B. Goza, "Graffiti Needs Assessment Involving Students in the First Class Session," *Journal of Management Education* 17, no. 1 (February 1993), 99–106.

STEPS IN PRACTICING THE SKILL

STEP 1: Communicate honestly and openly with your protégé. If your protégé is going to learn from you and benefit from your experience, you're going to have to be open and honest as you talk about what you've done. Bring up the failures as well as the successes. Remember that mentoring is a learning process, and for learning to take place, you're going to have to be open and honest in "telling it like it is."

STEP 2: Encourage honest and open communication from your protégé. You need to know as the mentor what your protégé hopes to gain from this relationship. You should encourage the protégé to ask for information and to be specific about what he or she wants to gain.

STEP 3: Treat the relationship with the protégé as a learning opportunity. Don't pretend to have all the answers and all the knowledge. But do share what you've learned through your experiences. And in your conversations and interactions with your protégé, you may be able to learn as much from that person as he or she does from you. So, be open to listening to what your protégé is saying.

STEP 4: Take the time to get to know your protégé. As a mentor, you should be willing to take the time to get to know your protégé and his or her interests. If you're not willing to spend extra time, you should probably not embark on a mentoring relationship.

➤ Communicating Effectively

1. **Develop a three- to four-page response to the following question:** Are supervisors in a no-win situation in an organization? Present both sides of the argument and include supporting data. Conclude your discussion by defending and supporting one of the two arguments you've presented.

THINKING CRITICALLY

➤ Case 1-A: Transition to Supervisor

Tristan came in on the ground floor in his company and had excelled in his position for several years when he was promoted to a supervisory position. He was excited about the increased responsibility and money, and he also enjoyed the status and respect that came with the new title.

Tristan's position was to supervise a new production department at a new plant site of his small regional company. In preparation he was ordered to attend a two-week supervisor's training program at headquarters. As he expected, the training was focused on HR concerns, customer satisfaction issues, and corporate quality production expectations. Because the new location was intended to showcase the company's strength in quality manufacturing, he was allowed to recruit his own team from among the company's statewide employee pool. Several seasoned workers, acquainted with him as a result of his time with the company, expressed interest in the startup department.

Lauren was hired as the departmental administrative assistant and William was hired as the new line foreman. Tristan was elated and felt that things were moving ahead quickly enough for his superiors to be pleased with the progress he was making. He continued to fill the necessary positions. Within a month the department was ready to get going. Everyone was excited, attitudes were positive, and he was looking forward to the inaugural production run.

Tristan had never held a supervisory position before, yet he knew Lauren and William were both strong employees with great work ethic. He was certain everyone he selected possessed a similar work ethic and was driven to succeed. However, this quickly proved erroneous, and when it became obvious the hoped-for production quality was nonexistent, everything became a dismal failure at once. The department failed to produce at the expected quality level, and turmoil among the employees was widespread. During the nearly two years he was supervisor, Tristan was never able to earn the respect of his employees or experience the success in production quality envisioned by the company.

In reality, many first-time supervisors earn their position by simply doing well at their job; however, without proper training, in both supervision and leadership, disappointing outcomes like Tristan's are more common than you would imagine. Just because an employee is good, or even great, it does not mean he or she will be a great supervisor.

RESPONDING TO THE CASE

1. If you envision transitioning into a supervisory position, what can you do to ensure you don't end up like Tristan?

2. What supervisory competencies should you work to develop? Why?

➤ Case 1-B: Leading the A-Team

Karen Simmons is a day supervisor for a local Lube-Thru lube shop in Sioux City, Iowa. Karen is responsible for twelve employees. Her job responsibilities include planning the daily activities of these employees, certifying that all work has been done properly, and handling all money transactions. When Karen is not "supervising," she serves as an under-hood A-team crew member. In this capacity, she checks a variety of fluids, adds fluids as necessary, and inspects such things as the air filter, fuel filter, and the car's lights. Frequently, as supervisor, she has to move an employee from one task to another during the day—sometimes to complete a job and other times to perform specialized tasks. For instance, only two of her employees are certified to handle transmission servicing.

Karen is in contact with her boss, owner Jill Ingalls, on a daily basis at the close of business. She discusses with her boss how many cars were serviced that day, what services were performed, and the amount of money that is being deposited. Karen keeps Jill informed on the status of inventories and what orders need to be placed. She also keeps Jill apprised of all customer or employee issues that arise.

3. Which of the four management functions do you believe most supervisors need help with? Why do you think this is the case?

4. The role of supervisor can be considered a first step toward management. What are the benefits and potential disadvantages of pursuing a management career?

Because of the service nature of this business, it's imperative that employees arrive at work on time and complete their work quickly. Karen knows that the key to this business is a happy workforce that, in turn, satisfies customers. Accordingly, she takes special care to make sure her employees are enjoying their work, and she keeps them apprised of changes that may affect them. Occasionally, Karen "springs" for an after-work pizza party just to say thanks to her employees for doing a good job.

RESPONDING TO THE CASE

1. List as many of Karen's responsibilities as you recall. Prioritize the list. Explain why you placed certain items at the top of the list and others at the bottom.

2. Describe the supervisory functions that Karen performs. Do you believe some functions are more important than others are? Explain.

3. How can Karen avoid problems she might encounter supervising her employees while still pleasing her boss? What can she do to foster good relationships with her boss? With her employees?

Supervision Challenges

Key Concepts

After completing this chapter, you will be able to define these supervisory terms:

- baby boomers
- code of ethics
- collectivism
- continuous improvement
- cultural environments
- cyberloafing
- downsizing
- e-business
- e-commerce
- ethics
- individualism
- *kaizen*

- parochialism
- power distance
- quality of life
- quantity of life
- social obligation
- social responsibility
- social responsiveness
- technology
- telecommuting
- uncertainty avoidance
- workforce diversity
- work process engineering

Chapter Outcomes

After reading this chapter, you will be able to:

1. Explain how globalization affects supervisors.

2. Describe how technology is changing the supervisor's job.

3. Explain the concept of e-business and e-commerce.

4. Identify the significant changes that have occurred in the composition of the workforce.

5. Explain why corporations downsize.

6. Understand the concept of continuous improvement and identify its goals.

7. Describe why supervisors must be able to "thrive on chaos."

8. Define *ethics*.

Responding to a Supervisory Dilemma

Technology is any equipment, tool, or operating method designed to make work more efficient. Technology is making it possible to better serve customers in many industries. Technology in the workplace has enormous benefits, but it can also have downsides.

Employees have always been susceptible to distractions at work, and the Internet has only broadened these distractions. Workers admit to spending over two hours wasting their time at work, with almost half of that time spent online. Some employees have access to social media websites like Facebook and Twitter and spend company time looking at what their friends are doing. Shopping on websites such as Amazon and writing blogs are all serious timewasters while on the job. Some companies have blocked such websites so that employees are not allowed to use these sites while at work. However, with the use of smart phones employees can just as easily view Facebook and other sites while at their desk. The biggest shopping day, the day after Thanksgiving, is called Black Friday. Now there is a new term for the Monday following Thanksgiving— Cyber Monday. Employees return to work following the holiday and do their shopping while at work. Hours of employee time and company money are spent doing everything but work.

There are two conflicting perspectives regarding surfing the Internet while at work: (1) that time wasted costs employers billions of dollars and (2) that occasional diversions from the work are necessary to refresh workers and to stimulate their creativity, thus actually boosting the employer's "bottom line."* As a supervisor, combating Web surfing or cyberloafing can be a difficult task. While the supervisor could make the job more interesting, provide breaks to use the Internet, and establish clear guidelines for employee's Internet usage, employees will, most likely, still go online at their own discretion.

Do you think surfing the Internet is a timewaster resulting in loss of money, or is it necessary for employees to remain focused? Do you use company time to go online for personal use? How much time do you spend going online at work? Do you think the key to keeping employees off of the Internet is to block popular social media websites? Do you feel that it would prevent employees from wasting work hours? As a supervisor what would your approach be to employees that are caught using Facebook and Twitter on company time?

---

*S. Opperman, " 'Surfin' USA'—Accessing the Net at Work and Other Time-Wasting Activities—Are They a Cost or a Benefit to Your Agency," *FedSmith*, July 11, 2007, www.fedsmith.com/article/1298 (accessed February 15, 2011).

It has been said often that the only thing that remains constant in our lives is change. Most people would undoubtedly agree that this statement is true. Supervisors must always be prepared for changing events that may have a significant effect on their lives. Changing events have always helped shape the interactions between supervisors and their employees, and undoubtedly will continue to do so. Some of the more recent changes include global market competitiveness, technology and e-business enhancements, workforce diversity, continuous-improvement programs, downsizing, and the issue of ethics. Let's look at how these changes are affecting supervisors in organizations.

Global Competitiveness

Many North American companies grew large and powerful following World War II because they faced modest competition from around the world. For instance, in the 1950s and 1960s, General Motors (GM) became the world's largest and most profitable corporation. Was it because GM efficiently produced first-rate products that were carefully matched to the needs of auto consumers? Maybe in part; however, GM's success was more a result of the fact that its only major competition came from two other relatively less-efficient American producers—Ford and Chrysler. Now, look at General Motors today. It has drastically reduced costs, improved quality, and cut the time it takes from designing a car to having it in dealer showrooms. Did GM make these changes voluntarily? Absolutely not! It was forced to do this to meet changing global competition. Ford and Chrysler significantly improved their quality, developed innovative products such as the minivan, and began selling imported cars under their brand names. Ford and Chrysler also forged ahead in their global presence through a series of international acquisitions. Ford went global by purchasing Jaguar in 1990, Volvo in 1999, and Land Rover in 2000. However, because of global competitiveness and an economic turnaround, Ford sold Jaguar and Land Rover to Indian auto manufacturer Tata Motors in 2008. Chrysler went global by acquiring Maserati in 1987, selling it in 1993, and then merging with Daimler-Benz in 1998 to form DaimlerChrysler. However, the alliance was short lived, and economic uncertainty resulted in the 2007 sale of Chrysler to Cerberus Capital Management, where it was known as Chrysler LLC. In April 2009 Chrysler LLC declared bankruptcy, and on June 10, 2009, it emerged as Chrysler Group LLC from a Chapter 11 reorganization bankruptcy. It was sold to the Italian automaker Fiat, whose current stake in Chrysler is 30 percent. Chrysler's current (2011) owners other than Fiat are the UAW retiree health care trust fund (59.2 percent), the U.S. government (8.6 percent), and the Canadian and Ontario governments (2.2 percent).[1] Meanwhile, aggressive competition from foreign companies such as Honda, Toyota, Nissan, and BMW has been increasing pressure on GM to continue to change if it is going to survive.

IS THERE SUCH A THING AS "BUY AMERICAN"?

The GM example illustrates that organizations are no longer constrained by national borders. Consider, for instance, that McDonald's sells hamburgers in China and KFC sells chicken in China. Exxon, Coca-Cola, AFLAC, and Walmart are American companies that receive significant portions of their income from foreign operations.[2] Honda, BMW, Mitsubishi, Mercedes-Benz, Subaru, Nissan, and Hyundai all have plants in the United States. Parts for Ford vehicles come from all over the world: Mexico (seats, windshields, and fuel tanks), Japan (shock absorbers), Spain (electronic engine controls), Germany (antilock brake systems), and England (key axle parts).

It is important to point out that although organizations have become increasingly global in their perspectives and have accepted the reality that national borders no longer define corporations, some in the public have been slower to accept this fact. Some people feel that the sale of foreign products takes jobs from Americans. The cry often is "Buy American." The irony is that many so-called foreign products are made in the United States. For example, Michelin, a French company, sells tires made in the United States. The message from this example should be obvious: A company's national origin is no longer a very good gauge of where it does business or the nationality of its employees (see "Something to Think About: Who Owns What?"). Such companies as Honda and Samsung employ thousands of people in the United States. At the same time, such firms as Coca-Cola, Exxon, and Citicorp employ thousands in places such

---

[1]Fred Meier, *USA Today*, April 12, 2011, http://content.usatoday.com/communities/driveon/post/2011/04/fiat-given-another-5-by-feds-now-owns-30-of-chrysler/1 (accessed May 9, 2011).

[2]L. M. Cacace and R. K. Tucksmith, "Global 500," *Fortune*, July 26, 2004, F1–F4.

as India, Hong Kong, and the United Kingdom. So, phrases such as "Buy American" represent old stereotypes that fail to reflect the changing global village.

HOW DOES GLOBALIZATION AFFECT SUPERVISORS?

A boundaryless world introduces new challenges for supervisors. These range from how supervisors view people from foreign lands to how they develop an understanding of these immigrating employees' cultures. A specific challenge for supervisors is to recognize the differences that might exist and find ways to make their interactions with all employees more effective. One of the first issues to deal with, then, is the perception of "foreigners."

Americans in general have previously held a rather parochial view of the world. Parochialism means that we see things solely through our own eyes and from our uniquely American perspective. This translates into "We believe what we do is best." Americans often do not recognize that other people have valid, though different, ways of thinking and doing things. Parochialism causes Americans to view their practices as being better than practices in other cultures. Obviously, we know that cannot be the case. However, changing this perception first requires us to understand different cultures and their environments.

All countries have different cultural environments—values, morals, customs, and laws. Although cultural issues are much more involved than this and go beyond the scope of this book, we will look at some basic cultural issues that supervisors need to understand. For example, in the United States we have laws that guard against discriminatory hiring and employment practices. Similar laws do not exist in all other countries. Understanding cultural environments, then, is critical to the success of supervising others in the global village.

One of the better-known studies about cultural environments was done by researcher Geert Hofstede.[3] Hofstede analyzed various aspects of different countries' cultures and found that a country's culture has a major effect on employees' work-related values and attitudes. By analyzing various dimensions, Hofstede developed a framework for understanding cultural differences. Countries that share similar cultures are represented in Exhibit 2-1.

Hofstede's findings group countries according to such cultural variables as status differences, societal uncertainty, and assertiveness. These variables indicate a country's means of dealing with its people and how the people see themselves. For example, in an individualistic society, people are primarily concerned with their own family. On the contrary, in a collective society (the opposite of individualistic), people care for all individuals who are part of their group. The United States is a strongly individualistic society. Therefore, an American supervisor may have difficulties relating to people from Pacific Rim countries, where collectivism dominates, unless he or she is aware of this cultural difference.

When working with people from different cultures, we informally learn the differences that exist between their culture and ours. Many companies also provide formal training in this area. Supervisors learn that they must be flexible and adaptable in their dealings with employees. Recognizing differences in employees' backgrounds and customs fosters appreciation and even celebration of those differences (see "News Flash! The Cultural Variables").

parochialism
Seeing things solely through one's own eyes and from one's own perspective; believing that one's own way is the best.

cultural environments
Values, morals, customs, and laws of countries.

Latin American	Argentina
	Chile
	Colombia
	Mexico
	Peru
	Venezuela
Anglo-American	Australia
	Canada
	Ireland
	New Zealand
	South Africa
	United Kingdom
	United States
Central European	Austria
	Germany
	Switzerland
Latin European	Belgium
	France
	Italy
	Portugal
	Spain
Nordic	Denmark
	Finland
	Norway
	Sweden

Exhibit 2-1

Countries with similar cultural characteristics.

Source: Adapted from S. Ronen and A. Kranut, "Similarities among Countries Based on Employee Work Values and Attitudes," *Columbia Journal of World Business.* (Summer 1977), 94.

---

[3]G. Hofstede, *Cultural Consequences: International Differences in Work-Related Values* (Beverly Hills, CA: Sage, 1990).

Something to Think About (and promote class discussion)

WHO OWNS WHAT?

One way to grasp the changing nature of the global environment is to consider the country of ownership for some familiar products and companies. You might be surprised to find that many name-brand products you thought were made by U.S. companies aren't so. Take the following quiz. Correct answers are listed at the end of the chapter; however, because the international world of business is so dynamic you may wish to explore online resources to determine whether there have been any ownership changes.

1. The parent company of Braun household appliances (electric shavers, coffee makers) is located in
   - a. Switzerland
   - b. Germany
   - c. the United States
   - d. Japan

2. Bic Corporation (pen maker) is
   - a. Japanese
   - b. British
   - c. American (U.S.)
   - d. French

3. The company that makes Häagen-Dazs ice cream is located in
   - a. Germany
   - b. Great Britain
   - c. Switzerland
   - d. the United States

4. RCA television sets are produced by a company based in
   - a. France
   - b. the United States
   - c. China
   - d. Taiwan

5. The firm that owns Green Giant (vegetables) is located in
   - a. the United States
   - b. Canada
   - c. Great Britain
   - d. Italy

6. The owners of the Godiva chocolate company are located in
   - a. the United States
   - b. Switzerland
   - c. Turkey
   - d. Sweden

7. The company that produces Vaseline is
   - a. American
   - b. Dutch/British
   - c. German
   - d. French

8. Wrangler jeans are made by a company headquartered in
   - a. Japan
   - b. Taiwan
   - c. Great Britain
   - d. the United States

9. The company that owns Holiday Inn is based in
   - a. Saudi Arabia
   - b. France
   - c. the United States
   - d. Great Britain

10. Tropicana orange juice is made by a company that is headquartered in
    - a. Mexico
    - b. Canada
    - c. the United States
    - d. Japan

Technology Enhancements

Change, newness, uncertainty—what do they mean for tomorrow's supervisors? Although making predictions can be viewed as an exercise in futility, evidence supports the idea that supervisors need to concern themselves with change. The key to success, if it can be narrowed down to one statement, is this: Be prepared to make adjustments. Opportunities will abound for those prepared to accept and deal with the information age. Realize that as little as thirty years ago, almost no one had a fax machine, cellular phone, or personal digital assistant. Computers were still too large to fit on desks. *E-mail*, *modem*, and *Internet* weren't everyday words spoken by the general public. Home security typically involved having a large dog. Sophisticated gadgetry was pretty much left to the action-packed movies!

Today, information technology, supported by advances in the silicon chip, has altered a supervisor's life forever. Electronic communications, optical character and voice recognition, and storage and retrieval databases, among other technologies, are significantly influencing how information is created, stored, and used.

News Flash!

THE CULTURAL VARIABLES

To date, the most valuable framework to help managers better understand differences between national cultures has been developed by Geert Hofstede.* He surveyed more than 116,000 employees in forty countries, all of whom worked for IBM. What did he find? Hofstede found that supervisors and employees vary in four dimensions of national culture: (1) individualism versus collectivism; (2) power distance; (3) uncertainty avoidance; and (4) quantity versus quality of life.†

Individualism refers to a loosely knit social framework in which people are supposed to look after their own interests and those of their immediate family. This is made possible because of the large amount of freedom that such a society allows individuals. Its opposite is collectivism, which is characterized by a tight social framework. People expect others in groups to which they belong (e.g., a family or an organization) to look after them and protect them when they are in trouble. In exchange for this, they feel they owe absolute allegiance to the group.

Power distance is a measure of the extent to which a society accepts the fact that power in institutions and organizations is distributed unequally. A high-power-distance society accepts wide differences in power in organizations. Employees show a great deal of respect for those in authority. Titles, rank, and status carry a lot of weight. In contrast, a low-power-distance society plays down inequalities as much as possible. Supervisors still have authority, but employees are not fearful or in awe of the boss.

A society that is high in uncertainty avoidance is characterized by an increased level of anxiety among its people, which manifests itself in greater nervousness, stress, and aggressiveness. Because people feel threatened by uncertainty and ambiguity in these societies, mechanisms are created to provide security and reduce risk. Their organizations are likely to have more formal rules, there is less tolerance for deviant ideas and behaviors, and members strive to believe in absolute truths. Not surprisingly, in organizations in countries with high uncertainty avoidance, employees demonstrate relatively low job mobility, and lifetime employment is a widely practiced policy.

Quantity versus quality of life, like individualism and collectivism, represents a dichotomy. Some cultures emphasize the quantity of life, and value things such as assertiveness and the acquisition of money and material goods. Other cultures emphasize the quality of life, placing importance on relationships and showing sensitivity and concern for the welfare of others.

With which cultures are U.S. supervisors likely to best fit? Which are likely to create the biggest adjustment problems? All we have to do is identify those countries that are most and least like the United States on the four dimensions. The United States is strongly individualistic, but low on power distance. This same pattern is exhibited by Great Britain, Australia, Canada, the Netherlands, and New Zealand. Those least similar to the United States on these dimensions are Venezuela, Colombia, Pakistan, Singapore, and the Philippines.

The United States scores low on uncertainty avoidance and high on quantity of life. This same pattern is shown by Ireland, Great Britain, Canada, New Zealand, Australia, India, and South Africa. Those least similar to the United States on these dimensions are Chile and Portugal.

The study supports what many suspected: that the American supervisor transferred to London, Toronto, Melbourne, or a similar Anglo city would have to make the fewest adjustments. The study further identifies the countries in which culture shock—a feeling of confusion, disorientation, and emotional upheaval caused by being immersed in a new culture—is likely to be the greatest, resulting in the need to radically modify the American supervisory style.

*G. Hofstede, *Cultural Consequences: International Differences in Work-Related Values* (Beverly Hills, CA: Sage, 1990).
†Hofstede called this last dimension *masculinity versus femininity*. We changed it because of the strong gender reference in Hofstede's choice of terms.

Equally important are the constantly evolving skills and competencies supervisors must possess. Those who embrace knowledge and continuously learn new skills will be the ones who survive in the high-tech world. Imagine needing information on how well your unit is meeting production standards. Forty years ago, obtaining that information might have taken as long as a month. Today, a few keystrokes on the keyboard of the computer on your desk can get you that same information almost instantaneously!

In the past three decades, American companies such as General Electric, Walmart, and 3M have witnessed automated offices, robotics in manufacturing, computer-assisted-design software, integrated circuits, microprocessors, and electronic meetings. These technologies combined have made these organizations more productive and, in some cases, helped them to create and maintain a competitive advantage.

WHAT IS TECHNOLOGY?

Technology is any equipment, tool, or operating method designed to make work more efficient. Technological advances involve integrating technology with any process for changing inputs (raw materials) into outputs (goods and services). In decades past, most processing operations were performed by human labor. Technology has made it possible to enhance most production processes by replacing human labor with sophisticated electronic and computer equipment. An example is the assembly operation at Chrysler Group LLC, which relies heavily on robotics. These robots perform repetitive tasks—such as spot welding and painting—much faster than humans can. In addition, the robots aren't subject to the health problems caused by exposure to chemicals or other hazardous materials.

The use of technology goes far beyond application to mass-production manufacturing processes. Technology is making it possible to serve customers better in many industries. The banking industry, for instance, has replaced thousands of bank tellers by installing ATMs and electronic bill-paying systems—often at locations that are more convenient to the customer. At Merillat Industries, part of Masco Cabinetry, in Michigan, housing cabinets can be custom made using more than 63,000 configurations at a fraction of the cost of special-made cabinets, and in a much shorter time.[4]

Technological advancements are also used to provide better, more useful information. Cars built today, for example, have a built-in computer circuit that a technician can plug into to diagnose problems with the automobile—saving countless diagnostic hours for a mechanic. Many automobiles have systems that permit the driver to map his or her location and receive accurate, on-the-spot directions to the driver's destination.

HOW DOES TECHNOLOGY CHANGE THE SUPERVISOR'S JOB?

Few jobs today are unaffected by advances in computer technology. Whether it is automated robotics on the production floor, computer-aided design in the engineering department, or automated accounting systems, new technologies are changing the supervisor's job.

Although technology has had a positive effect on internal operations within organizations, how, specifically, has it changed the supervisor's job? To answer that question, we need only look at how the typical office is set up. Organizations today have become integrated communications centers. By linking computers, telephones, fax machines, copiers, printers, and the like, supervisors can get more complete information more quickly than ever before. With that information, supervisors can better formulate plans, make faster decisions, more clearly define the jobs that workers need to perform, and monitor work activities on an as-they-happen basis. In essence, technology today has enhanced supervisors' ability to perform their jobs.

Technology is also changing where a supervisor's work is performed. Historically in organizations, the supervisor's work site was located close to the operations site. As a result, employees were in close proximity to their bosses. A supervisor could observe how the work was being done, as well as easily communicate with employees face-to-face. Through the advent of technological advancements, supervisors are now able to supervise employees in remote locations. Face-to-face interaction has decreased dramatically. Work, for many, occurs where their computers are. Telecommuting capabilities—linkage of a remote worker's computer and modem with those of coworkers and management at an office—have made it possible for employees to be located anywhere in the global village.

individualism
A view holding the individual above the group with the expectation that individuals will stand up for themselves and choose their own affiliations rather than blindly obeying external forces of politics, society, and economic issues. This view stresses independence over interdependence.

collectivism
A view holding that the group above the individual in terms of politics, society, and economic issues trumps the claim of any individual. This view stresses interdependence over independence.

power distance
Extent to which the less-powerful members of institutions and organizations expect and accept the idea that power is distributed unequally. Belief in small power distance results in expectance of power relations that are more consultative or democratic, with people relating to one another more as equals regardless of formal positions. Belief in large power distance results in the less powerful accepting power relations that are more autocratic and paternalistic, wherein subordinates acknowledge the power of others based simply on their position in certain formal, hierarchical positions.

uncertainty avoidance
The extent to which members of a society attempt to cope with anxiety by minimizing ambiguity. Cultures with high uncertainty avoidance prefer rules and structured circumstances, whereas low uncertainty avoidance cultures operate effectively in the absence of clear-cut rules, policies, and procedures.

quantity of life
Belief that values competitiveness, assertiveness, ambition, and the accumulation of wealth and material possessions.

quality of life
Belief that places more value on relationships and overall worth of one's life in society.

technology
Any equipment, tool, or operating method designed to make work more efficient.

telecommuting
Linking a worker's remote computer and modem with those of coworkers and management at an office.

---

[4]R. Bourke, "Configuring No Two Alike," *Computer-Aided Design*, November–December 2001, 38.

Communicating effectively with individuals in remote locations and ensuring that their performance objectives are being met are some of the supervisor's new challenges.

E-Business at Work

College faculty are fond of saying that "the world of organizations is changing" and "the only thing constant is change." There is no better evidence of these statements than the change in business brought about by the Internet. This section highlights how computers and the Internet are reshaping supervisory practices. To begin this discussion, let's take a look at what we mean by e-businesses and what's unique about them.

WHAT IS AN E-BUSINESS?

e-commerce
The online buying and selling of products or services.

e-business
A comprehensive term describing the way an organization does its work by using electronic linkages with its key constituents to achieve its goals efficiently and effectively.

Two terms that seem to cause considerable confusion need to be clarified: *e-commerce* and *e-business*.[5] The term e-commerce is becoming the standard label to describe the online buying and selling of products or services. It encompasses presenting products on websites and filling orders. The vast majority of articles and media attention given to using the Internet in business are directed at online shopping—marketing and selling goods and services over the Internet. When you hear about the tremendous number of people shopping on the Internet, and how businesses set up websites where they can sell goods, conduct transactions, get paid, and fulfill orders, you're hearing about

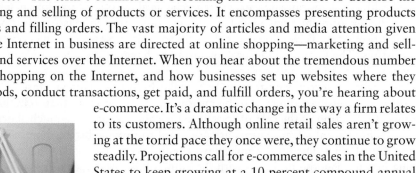

e-commerce. It's a dramatic change in the way a firm relates to its customers. Although online retail sales aren't growing at the torrid pace they once were, they continue to grow steadily. Projections call for e-commerce sales in the United States to keep growing at a 10 percent compound annual growth rate through 2014! Online retail sales for 2010 in the United States are expected to be nearly $250 billion, up from $155 billion in 2009. In 2009, online retail sales were up 11 percent, compared to 2.5 percent for all retail sales.[6] You should be aware, however, that 90 percent of e-commerce sales are business-to-business transactions. The vast majority of e-commerce sales are of products such as Intel chip sales to Dell or Goodyear sales to Ford rather than to consumers like you and me buying computers or sweaters for personal consumption.

In contrast, e-business refers to the full breadth of activities included in a successful Internet-based enterprise. As such, e-commerce is a subset of e-business. E-business includes developing strategies for running Internet-based companies, improving communication with suppliers and customers, collaborating with partners to electronically coordinate design and production, identifying a different kind of leader to run a "virtual" business, finding skilled people to build and operate intranets and websites, and running the "back room" or the administrative side. E-business includes creating new markets and customers, but it's also concerned with finding optimal ways to combine computers, the Web, and applications software.

Telecommuting means an employee can do work from nearly anywhere—as long as the work gets completed in a timely fashion.

[5]E. Strout, "Launching an E-Business: A Survival Guide," *Sales and Marketing Management*, July 2000, 90–92.

[6]ForresterResearch Inc., cited in "Forrester Forecast: Online Retail Sales Will Grow To $250 Billion By 2014," *TechCrunch*, Erick Schonfeld, March 8, 2010, http://techcrunch.com/2010/03/08/forrester-forecast-online-retail-sales-will-grow-to-250-billion-by-2014/ (accessed May 10, 2011).

An e-business uses the Internet (a worldwide network of interconnected computers), intranets (an organization's private network—see Exhibit 2-2), and extranets (an extended intranet accessible only to selected employees and authorized outsiders) to open up an organization's communication channels, making it possible to integrate and share information and allowing customers, suppliers, employees, and others to communicate with and through the organization on a real-time basis.

Now that you have a better understanding of what an e-business is, let's turn our attention to some of the implications e-business will have for supervisors.

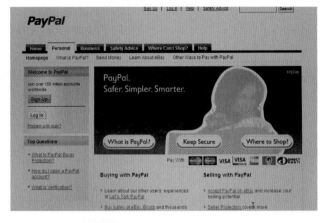

Exhibit 2-2
An example of an intranet.

WHAT CHANGES CAN SUPERVISORS EXPECT FROM E-BUSINESS?

Alan Naumann, head of Calico Commerce, expressed a view widely held by e-business supervisors: "Despite all our focus on speed, we consciously slow down for one thing: hiring people...it's the one aspect of business today in which the cost of mistakes is greater than the advantage of acting in real time." Recruiting good people is particularly challenging for supervisors in e-businesses. These jobs require a unique brand of technical and professional people. The employees have to be smart and able to survive in the demanding cultures of e-business firms. However, people who understand e-business are in short supply and tend to have high mobility.[7] This makes it difficult for supervisors to recruit effectively.

Once applicants have been identified, supervisors in e-businesses need to carefully screen final candidates to ensure that they fit well into the organization's culture. E-businesses tend to have common cultural characteristics: an informal workplace, team spirit, intense pressures to complete projects quickly and on time, and a 24×7 (twenty-four hours a day, seven days a week) work mentality. Selection tools such as tests, interviews, and references need to "select out" people that aren't team players and can't handle ambiguity and stress.

Motivating employees in an e-business also poses a challenge to today's supervisors. Employees in e-businesses are more susceptible to distractions that can undermine their work effort and reduce their productivity. In addition, technical and professional employees in e-businesses often have skills that make them very marketable, and many realize their employers' dependence on these skills. As a result, employees in e-businesses frequently have different compensation expectations than do their peers in more traditional organizations and will cope with a variety of distractions that may not be evident in traditional businesses.

Employees have always been susceptible to distractions at work such as interruptions by colleagues or personal phone calls. The Internet, however, has significantly broadened these distractions to include surfing the Net, playing online games, stock trading, shopping at work, and searching for other jobs online. Recent estimates indicate that a good portion of lost worker productivity is caused by cyberloafing. In an online survey, American workers admitted to wasting more than 2.09 hours per day, with surfing the Internet accounting for 44.7 percent of that time. If the work itself isn't interesting or creates excessive stress, employees are likely to be motivated to do something else. If employees have easy access to the Internet, that "something else" is increasingly using the Net as a diversion. However, because cell phones, BlackBerrys, and Internet access make many employees as productive at home as at work, the off-hours activity may more than make up for non-work-related pursuits at the office.[8]

cyberloafing
Lost productivity time as a result of an employee using the Internet at work for personal reasons.

---

[7]"E-Commerce: Online Recruiting—Notable Websites," *Fortune*, Winter 2001, 224.

[8]S. Oppermann, " 'Surfin' USA'—Accessing the Net at Work and Other Time-Wasting Activities—Are They a Cost or Benefit to Your Agency?" *FedSmith*, July 11, 2007, www.fedsmith.com/article/1298/ (accessed May 9, 2008).

The solution to this problem for supervisors includes making jobs interesting to employees, providing formal breaks to overcome monotony, and establishing clear guidelines so that employees know what online behaviors are expected. Many supervisors are also installing Web-monitoring software to assist in this matter—although doing so may have an effect on employee morale. Supervisors in e-businesses will also have to make faster decisions and maintain their flexibility. Supervisors in any organization never have all the data they want when making decisions. But the problem is much worse in e-businesses. Their world is moving fast and the competition is intense. Supervisors in e-businesses often see themselves as sprinters and their contemporaries in offline businesses as long-distance runners. Their rapidly speeded-up working environment makes waiting for more and more data to make a decision simply ineffective in an e-business. In addition to speed, supervisors in e-businesses need high flexibility. They have to be able to roll with the ups and downs. They need to be able to redirect their employees when they find that something doesn't work. They have to encourage experimentation.

Finally, e-businesses are rewriting the rules of communication. Because they're designed around comprehensive, integrated information networks, traditional communication channels of going through the "chain of command" no longer constrain communication. E-businesses allow, even encourage, individuals to communicate directly without going through channels. Employees can communicate instantly anytime, with anyone, anywhere, and their supervisors may not know what is being said. As such, how communication flows has changed dramatically, making obsolete or revising interpersonal communication concepts such as the distinction between formal and informal networks, nonverbal communication, and filtering. They also are redefining how activities such as meetings, negotiations, supervision, and "water cooler" talks are conducted.

Comprehension Check 2-1

1. *Parochialism* refers to
   a. one's religion
   b. seeing things through one's own eyes
   c. having values and morals
   d. placing importance on the quality of life

2. Allowing workers to work at remote sites and have them linked to the organization through some form of technology is called
   a. outsourcing
   b. global management
   c. telecommuting
   d. all of the above

3. _____ refers to the full breadth of activities included in a successful Internet-based enterprise.
   a. E-business
   b. E-commerce
   c. Telecommuting
   d. None of the above

4. Lost productivity time as a result of employees using the Internet for personal rather than work matters is called
   a. electronic commerce
   b. telecommuting
   c. employee theft
   d. cyberloafing

Working in a Diverse Organization

Half a century ago, workers and their needs were strikingly alike. In the 1950s, for example, the U.S. workforce consisted primarily of white males, many of whom came from the same neighborhoods or towns, were employed in manufacturing, and had wives who stayed at home tending to the family's two-plus children. Today's workforce is far more diverse, and it will continue to change.

WHAT IS WORKFORCE DIVERSITY?

The single most important human resource issue in organizations today may be adapting organizational policies and practices in light of increasing workforce diversity. This diverse workforce is made up of males, females, whites, blacks, Hispanics, Asians, Native Americans, people with disabilities, homosexuals, straights, and the elderly. Some excellent predictors are available to indicate exactly what the composition of this workforce will look like in the future. In 1990, there were approximately 125 million people in the U.S. workforce. According to the U.S. Department of Labor, the U.S. labor force is projected to increase by 12.6 million from 2008 to 2018 and reach nearly 167 million in 2018. With an increase in the number of immigrants, the U.S. population is expected to increase its size and composition. Increasing rapidly, by 2018, Hispanics are expected to have 29 million in the labor force. Asians will grow to reach more than 9 million workers by 2018. The black labor force is projected to surpass 20 million in 2018.[9] What is important is the makeup of those new workers. Minorities and women will make up a significantly larger share of the workforce. As a result, companies and their supervisors must ensure that their motivational programs and techniques are appropriate for such diverse groups of people.

workforce diversity
The composition of the workforce to include men, women, whites, blacks, Hispanics, Asians, Native Americans, people with disabilities, people with diverse sexual preferences, the elderly, and so on.

HOW DOES DIVERSITY AFFECT SUPERVISORS?

The implications of workforce diversity for supervisors are widespread. Employees don't set aside their cultural values and lifestyle preferences when they come to work. Therefore, supervisors must remake organizations to accommodate these different lifestyles, family needs, and work styles. They must be flexible enough in their supervisory style to seek the involvement of all employees and be aware of the fact that all employees are differently motivated in terms of what they want and need from work. Awareness of the diversity of the employee pool requires a broad range of new policies and practices. A few examples will make this point. Work schedules will need to be more flexible to accommodate single parents, working parents, and couples maintaining commuter relationships (living in different locations). Companies will need to explore the possibilities of providing child care and elder care so that employees may be better able to give full attention to their work. Benefits programs may need to be redesigned and individualized to reflect more varied needs. Career-planning programs may need to be reassessed to deal with employees who are less willing to relocate for broadened job experience or promotions. All employees will need training so that they can learn to understand and appreciate people who are different from themselves. And, of course, supervisors will need to rethink their motivation techniques to respond to a widening range of employee needs.

In addition to the diversity brought about by such factors as lifestyle, gender, nationality, and race, supervisors must be aware of the potential effect brought about by the baby boomers. You've probably heard a lot about the baby boomers. This group

baby boomers
The largest group in the workforce; they are regarded as the career climbers—at the right place at the right time. Mature workers view them as unrealistic in their views and workaholics.

---

[9]M. Toossi, "Employment Outlook: 2008–18 Labor Force Projections to 2018: Older Workers Staying More Active," *Monthly Labor Review* 132, no. 11 (November 2009), http://www.bls.gov/opub/mlr/2009/11/mlr200911.pdf (accessed May 10, 2011).

typically includes individuals born between 1946 and 1964. The reason you hear so much about them is that there are so many of them. Through every stage of their life (going to elementary school, teenage years, climbing the career ladder, etc.), they've had an enormous effect on the U.S. economy because of their sheer numbers. And as they enter their retirement years, they may have one final effect on supervisors. How so? Again, their sheer numbers play a role.

Many of these baby boomers hold very skilled positions in organizations. Although not typically as computer proficient as individuals entering the workforce today, their skills in mathematics, the sciences, skilled trades, and the like are outstanding. When an employee group such as this retires en masse, their departure will leave gaping skill-level holes in organizations. Clearly, this has the potential to create a labor shortage—making it much more difficult for supervisors to recruit and to direct the job activities needed to accomplish organizational goals.

Irrespective of age, employees today are trying to balance work and home life. The typical employee in the 1960s or 1970s showed up at the workplace Monday through Friday and did his or her job in eight- or nine-hour chunks of time. The workplace and hours were clearly specified. That's no longer true for a large segment of today's workforce. Employees are increasingly complaining that the line between work and nonwork time has become blurred, creating personal conflicts and stress.[10]

A number of forces have contributed to blurring the lines between work and personal lives. First, the creation of global organizations means their world never sleeps. At any time and on any day, for instance, thousands of Chrysler Group LLC employees are working somewhere. The need to consult with colleagues or customers eight or ten time zones away means that many employees of global firms are on call twenty-four hours a day. Second, communication technology allows employees to do their work at home, in their car, or on the beach in Tahiti. This lets many people in technical and professional jobs do their work any time and from any place.[11] Third, organizations are asking employees to put in longer hours. It's not unusual for employees to work more than forty-five hours a week, and some work much more than fifty. Finally, fewer families have only a single breadwinner. Today's married employee is typically part of a dual-career couple.[12] This makes it increasingly difficult for married employees to find the time to fulfill commitments to home, spouse, children, parents, and friends.

Employees are increasingly recognizing that work is squeezing out their personal lives, and they're not happy about it. For example, recent studies suggest that employees want jobs that give them flexibility in their work schedules so that they can better manage work–life conflicts.[13] In addition, the next generation of employees is likely to have similar concerns.[14] A majority of college and university students say that attaining a balance between personal life and work is a primary career goal. They want "a life" as well as a job! Organizations that don't help their people achieve a work–life balance will find it increasingly hard to attract and retain the most capable and motivated employees.[15] Generational differences often surface as a cause for

---

[10]See, for example, P. Cappelli, J. Constantine, and C. Chadwick, "It Pays to Value Family: Work and Family Trade-Offs Reconsidered," *Industrial Relations*, April 2000, 175–198; M. A. Verespej, "Balancing Act," *Industry Week*, May 15, 2000, 81–85; and R. C. Barnett and D. T. Hall, "How to Use Reduced Hours to Win the War for Talent," *Organizational Dynamics*, March 2001, 42.

[11]See, for instance, L. Belkin, "From Dress-Down Friday to Dress-Down Life," *New York Times*, June 22, 2003, 1; and E. Tahminicioglu, "By Telecommuting, the Disabled Get a Key to the Office, and a Job," *New York Times*, July 20, 2003, 1.

[12]M. Conlin, "The New Debate over Working Moms," *BusinessWeek*, November 18, 2000, 102–103.

[13]"The New World of Work: Flexibility Is the Watchword," *BusinessWeek*, January 10, 2000, 36.

[14]See, for example, "U.S. Employers Polish Image to Woo a Demanding New Generation," *Manpower Argus*, February 2000, 2.

[15]L. L. Martins, K. B. Eddleston, and J. F. Veiga, "Moderators of the Relationship between Work–Family Conflict and Career Satisfaction," *Academy of Management Journal* (May 2002), 399–409.

Baby Boomers (1946–1964)	Generation X (1965–1980)	Generation Y (1981–2002) Millennials
Uses technology as a necessary tool, but not obsessed with technology for its own sake	Techno-savvy	Techno-savvy, and even questions the value of standard IT technique such as e-mail, with a preference for communications on a Web site
Appreciates hierarchy	Dislike hierarchy	Dislikes hierarchy, prefers participation
Tolerates teams but values independent work	Teamwork very important	Teamwork very important
Strong career orientation	Strives for work–life balance but will work long hours for now, prefers flexible work schedule	Strives for work–life balance and may object to work interfering with personal life; expects flexible work schedule
More loyalty to organization	Loyalty to own career and profession	Loyalty to own career and profession and feels entitled to career goals
Favors diplomacy and tact	Candid in conversation	Quite direct in conversation
Seeks long-term employment	Will accept long-term employment if situation is right	Looks towards each company as a stepping stone to better job in another company
Believes that issues should be formally discussed	Believes that feedback can be administered informally and welcomes feedback	Believes that feedback can be given informally, even on the fly, and craves feedback
Somewhat willing to accept orders and suggestions	Often questions why things should be done in a certain way	Frequently asks why things should be done in a certain way, and asks a lot of questions
Willing to take initiative to establish starting and completion dates for projects	Slight preference for a manager to provide structure about project dates	Prefers structure on dates and other activities based on childhood of structures activities
Regards rewards as a positive consequence of good preformance and seniority	Expects frequent rewards	Feels strong sense of entitlement to rewards, including promotions
Will multitask in front of work associates when it seems necessary	Feels comfortable in multitasking while interacting with work associates	Assumes that multitasking, including listening to music on earphones while dealing with work associates, is acceptable behavior

Note: Disagreement exists about which age brackets fit baby boomers, Generation X, and Generation Y, with both professional publicatons and dictionaries showing slight differences.

Sources: The majority of ideas in this table are from Robers McGarvey, "The Coming of Gen X Bosses," *Entrepreneur*, November 1999, pp. 60–64; Gregg Hammill, "Mixing and Managing Four Generations of Employees," *FDU Magazine Online*, Winter/Spring 2005, p. 5; Sommer Kehrli and Trudy Sopp, "Managing Generation Y: Stop Resisting and Start Embracing the Challenges Generation Y Brings to the Workplace," *HR Magazine*, May 2006, pp. 113–119; Ron Alop, *The Trophy Kids Grow Up: How the Millennial Generaion Is Shaking Up the Workplace* (San Francisco, CA: Jossey-Bass/Wiley, 2008); Alsop,: "Schools, Recruiters Try to Define Traits for Future Students," *Wall Street Journal*, February 4, 2006, p. B6; Kathyryn Tyler, "Generation Gaps: Millennials May Be Out of Touch with the Basics of Workplace Behavior," *HR Magazine*, January 2008, pp. 69–72.

Exhibit 2-3

Value stereotypes for several generations of workers.

tension in the workplace and can become a concern for the supervisor. "Exhibit 2-3 identifies the massive group stereotypes associated with the different age groups in the workforce."

Changing How Business Operates

Where supervisors work today is changing. Whereas in the past, big business dominated the American scene, that's not necessarily the case today. More growth has occurred in small and medium-sized companies during the past decade, and these businesses have been able to be more customer responsive. Nonetheless, big business is not throwing in the towel. Instead, to be more like their smaller counterparts, large businesses have been making some significant changes. The most obvious of these are downsizing, continuous-improvement programs, and work process engineering. Let's look at each of these and discuss how they will affect you on the job.

WHY ARE ORGANIZATIONS DOING MORE WITH LESS?

downsizing
A reduction in workforce and reshaping of operations to create "lean and mean" organizations. The goals of organizational downsizing are greater efficiency and reduced costs.

American companies have been working to become "lean and mean" organizations. As a result of deregulation in certain industries (e.g., the airlines), foreign competition, mergers, and takeovers, organizations have cut employees from their payrolls. In fact, by the end of the twentieth century, almost all Fortune five hundred companies—such as Sears, General Electric, American Airlines, and IBM—had cut staff and reshaped their operations. In business terms, this action is called downsizing.[16]

Organizations downsized to accomplish two primary goals: to create greater efficiency and to reduce costs. In many cases this meant that they reduced the number of workers employed by the organization. This included employees at all levels, including supervisors. Organizations did not do this because it was fun for them. Many were forced into this action. Why? The world around them changed!

To deal effectively with factors in a rapidly changing business environment, such as increased global competition, companies had to become more flexible about how work got done. Formal work rules that dominated bureaucracies didn't permit changes to occur fast enough. There were just too many people involved in making decisions—and in their implementation. In addition, workers in the organizations may not have had the necessary skills to adapt to the changes in their jobs. In some cases, the organization had not planned ahead, or had not spent the money years ago, to ensure that employee skills would be up-to-date. As a result, someone outside the organization had to be hired to do the work. Companies believed that it was sometimes cheaper to continue to do the work outside than it was to train and pay for a full-time employee. Thus, along with downsizing for flexibility's sake came a realization that costs should be significantly cut by downsizing full-time staff resources.

However, downsizing didn't achieve its goals in all cases. Downsizing efforts sometimes took their toll on workers and the potential financial gains they were supposed to achieve. Several studies have indicated that more than two-thirds of all companies that downsized had problems with employee morale, and those remaining in the organization mistrusted management. Moreover, companies that downsized experienced a higher incident rating of employees filing disability claims.

WHY THE EMPHASIS ON CONTINUOUS-IMPROVEMENT PROGRAMS?

continuous improvement
Activities in an organization that enhance processes that result in the improved quality of goods and services produced.

A quality revolution continues to take place in both the private and the public sectors. The generic term that has evolved to describe this revolution is continuous improvement.[17] The revolution was inspired by a small group of quality experts—individuals such as Joseph Juran (1904–2008) and W. Edwards Deming (1900–1993). Today, many of these individuals' original beliefs have been expanded into a philosophy of organizational life that is driven by customer needs and expectations (see Exhibit 2-4). Importantly, however, continuous-improvement programs expand the term *customer* beyond the

---

[16]*Downsizing* may also be referred to as *restructuring, reduction in force*, or *rightsizing*.

[17]In some cases, continuous-improvement programs may be grouped under a concept called *total quality management* (TQM).

traditional definition to include everyone involved with the organization, either internally or externally—encompassing employees and suppliers as well as the people who buy the organization's products or services. The objective is to create an organization committed to continuous improvement, or as the Japanese call it, kaizen.[18]

Although continuous-improvement plans have been criticized by some for overpromising and underperforming, their overall record is good. Varian Associates, Inc., a maker of scientific equipment, used continuous-improvement programs in its semiconductor unit to cut the time it took to put out new designs by fourteen days. Another Varian unit, which makes vacuum systems for computer clean rooms, boosted on-time delivery from 42 to 92 percent through continuous-improvement methods. Globe Metallurgical, Inc., a small Ohio metal producer, credits continuous-improvement programs with helping it become 50 percent more productive. And the significant improvements made over the past decade in the quality of cars produced by GM, Ford, and Chrysler Group LLC can be directly traced to the implementation of total quality management methods.

1. **Focus on the customer.** The customer includes not only outsiders who buy the organization's products or services, but also internal customers (such as shipping or accounts payable personnel) who interact with and serve others in the organization.

2. **Seek continuous improvement.** This is a commitment to never being satisfied. "Very good" is not enough. Quality can always be improved.

3. **Improve the quality of everything the organization does.** Continuous improvement uses a very broad definition of quality. It relates not only to the final product but also to how the organization handles deliveries, how rapidly it responds to complaints, how politely the phones are answered, and the like.

4. **Measure accurately.** Continuous improvement uses statistical techniques to measure every critical variable in the organization's operations. These are compared against standards or benchmarks to identify problems, trace them to their roots, and eliminate their causes.

5. **Involve employees.** Continuous improvement involves the people on the line in the improvement process. Teams are widely used in continuous-improvement programs for finding and solving problems.

Exhibit 2-4
The foundations of continuous improvement.

HOW DOES WORK PROCESS ENGINEERING DIFFER FROM CONTINUOUS IMPROVEMENT?

Although implementing continuous-improvement methods is a positive start in many organizations, these methods generally focus on incremental change. Such action—a constant and permanent search to make things better—is intuitively appealing. Many organizations, however, operate in an environment of rapid and dynamic change. As the elements around them change ever so quickly, a continuous-improvement process may keep them behind the times.

The problem with a focus on continuous improvement is that it can provide a false sense of security. It may make organizational members feel as if they are actively doing something positive, which is somewhat true. Unfortunately, ongoing incremental change can avoid facing up to the possibility that what the organization may really need is radical or quantum change, referred to as work process engineering.[19] Continuous change may also make employees feel as if they are taking progressive action while, at the same time, avoiding having to implement quantum changes that will threaten certain aspects of organizational life. The incremental approach of continuous improvement, then, may be today's version of rearranging the deck chairs on the *Titanic*. It is imperative in today's business environment that all organizational members consider the challenge that work process engineering may have on their organizational processes. Why? Because work process engineering can lead to major organizational gains in cost- or time-cutting, or improved service, as well as help an organization prepare to meet the challenges that technology changes foster.

kaizen
Japanese term for an organization committed to continuous improvement.

work process engineering
Radical or quantum change in an organization.

---

[18]"Winning with *Kaizen*," *IIE Solutions*, April 2002, 10.

[19]M. Budman, "Jim Champy Puts His 'X' on Reengineering," *Across the Board*, March–April 2002, 15–16.

WHAT ARE THE SUPERVISORY IMPLICATIONS OF DOWNSIZING, CONTINGENT WORKFORCES, CONTINUOUS-IMPROVEMENT PROGRAMS, AND WORK PROCESS ENGINEERING?

Although downsizing, contingent workforces, continuous-improvement programs, and work process engineering are activities that are frequently initiated at the top management levels of an organization, they do have an effect on supervisors. Supervisors are often heavily involved in implementing the changes. They must be prepared to deal with the organizational issues these changes bring about. Let's look at some of the implications.

Downsizing and Supervisors When an organization downsizes, the most obvious effect is that people lose their jobs. Therefore, a supervisor can expect certain things to occur. Employees—both those let go and the ones that remain—may get angry. Both sets of employees may perceive that the organization no longer cares about them. Even though the downsizing decision is made at higher levels of management, the supervisor may receive the brunt of this resentment. In some cases, the supervisor may have participated in deciding which individuals to let go and which ones to keep, based on the organization's goals. After downsizing, employees who remain may be less loyal to the company.

An important challenge for supervisors is motivating a workforce that feels less secure in their jobs and less committed to their employers. Corporate employees used to believe that their employers would reward their loyalty and good work with job security, generous benefits, and pay increases. By downsizing, companies have begun to discard traditional policies on job security, seniority, and compensation. These changes have resulted in a sharp decline in employee loyalty. As corporations have shown less commitment to employees, employees have shown less commitment to them. This affects the supervisor's ability to motivate employees and maintain high productivity.

Downsizing may also cause increased competition among a supervisor's employees. If decisions are made to eliminate jobs based on a performance criterion, employees may be less likely to help one another. It may become every employee for himself or herself. Such behavior can defeat the team that a supervisor has built.

Finally, downsizing may foster issues for the survivors. Unless the work processes have been revamped, major tasks of jobs that were cut may still be required. Usually that means increased workloads for the remaining employees. This can lead to longer workdays, creating conflicts for employees between their work and personal lives. It can also lead to greater anxiety, more stress on the job, and increased absenteeism. For the supervisor, these too can dramatically affect work unit productivity.

Contingent Workforces "Companies want a workforce they can switch on and off as needed."[20] Although this quote may shock you, the truth is that the labor force already has begun shifting away from traditional full-time jobs toward a contingent workforce—part-time, temporary, and contract workers who are available for hire on an as-needed basis. In today's economy, many organizations have responded by converting full-time permanent jobs into contingent jobs. It's predicted that by the end of the next decade the number of contingent employees will have grown to about 40 percent of the workforce. (It's at 30 percent today.)[21] In fact, one compensation and benefits expert says that "a growing number of workers will need to structure their careers around this model."[22] That's likely to include you!

What are the implications for supervisors and organizations? Since contingent employees are not "employees" in the traditional sense of the word, supervising them has its own set of challenges and expectations. Supervisors must recognize that because contingent workers lack the stability and security of permanent employees, they may not identify with the organization or be as committed or motivated. Supervisors may

---

[20]J. Revell, C. Bigda, and D. Rosato, "The Rise of Freelance Nation," *CNNMoney.com*, June 12, 2009.
[21]Ibid.
[22]Ibid.

need to treat contingent workers differently in terms of practices and policies. However, with good communication and leadership, an organization's contingent employees can be just as valuable a resource to an organization as permanent employees are. Today's supervisors must recognize that it will be their responsibility to motivate their entire workforce, full-time and contingent, and to build their commitment to doing good work!

Continuous-Improvement Programs and Supervisors Each supervisor must clearly define what quality means to the jobs in his or her unit. This needs to be communicated to every staff member. Each individual must then exert the needed effort to move toward perfection. Supervisors and their employees must recognize that failing to do so could lead to unsatisfied customers taking their purchasing power to competitors; should that happen, jobs in the unit might be in jeopardy.

The premise of continuous improvement can generate a positive outcome for supervisors and employees. Everyone involved may now have input into how work is best done. The foundation of continuous improvement is built on the participation of the people closest to the work. As such, continuous improvement can eliminate many of the bottlenecks that have hampered work efforts in the past. Continuous-improvement programs can help create more-satisfying jobs—for both the supervisor and his or her employees.

Work Process Engineering and Supervisors If you accept the premise that work process engineering will change how businesses operate, it stands to reason that supervisors, too, will be directly affected. First of all, work process engineering may leave some supervisors and employees confused and angry. When processes are restructured, some longtime work relationships are severed.

Although work process engineering has its skeptics, it can generate some benefits for supervisors. It may mean that they have an opportunity to learn new skills. They may now work with the latest technology, supervise work teams, or have more decision-making authority. These same skills may keep them marketable and help them move to another organization, should that time ever come. Finally, as these changes sweep across corporate America, supervisors may see changes in how they are paid. Under a work-process-engineered work arrangement, supervisors and their employees may be in a better position to be compensated for the work they do and receive bonuses and incentives when they excel.

Employee Loyalty and Engagement Supervisors have generally viewed employee loyalty as necessary for decreasing turnover and achieving organizational stability. Problems develop when marginal employees cannot or will not leave the organization, instead exhibiting loyalty by remaining on the job. Employee loyalty is not the ultimate measure of effectiveness and should be balanced by workforce engagement in meaningful work. Supervisors must diligently strive to improve those practices leading to workforce engagement by identifying strategic issues, core human resources (HR) processes, and operational components inherent in the organization.[23]

Thriving on Chaos

As a student, which of the following scenarios do you find more appealing?

Scenario 1: Semesters are fifteen weeks long. Faculty members are required to provide, on the first day of each class, a course syllabus that specifies daily assignments, exact dates of examinations, and the precise percentage weights that various class activities count toward the final grade. College rules require instructors to hold

[23]S. Hundley, F. Jacobs, and M. Drizin, *Workforce Engagement: Strategies to Attract, Motivate, and Retain Talent* (Scottsdale, AZ: WorldatWork Press, 2007).

classes only at the time specified in the class schedule. These rules also require instructors to grade assignments and return the results within one week from the time they're turned in.

Scenario 2: Courses vary in length. When you sign up for a course, you don't know how long it will last. It might go for two weeks or thirty weeks. Furthermore, the instructor can end a course any time he or she wants, with no prior warning. The length of a class also changes each time it meets. Sometimes it lasts twenty minutes; other times it runs for three hours. Scheduling of the next class meeting is done by the instructor at the end of each class. Oh yes, the exams are all unannounced, so you have to be ready for a test at any time; instructors rarely provide you with any significant feedback on the results of those exams.

If you're like most people, you chose Scenario 1. Why? Because it provides security through predictability, you know what to expect, and you can plan for it. It may, therefore, be disheartening for you to learn that the supervisor's world—including the supervisor's job—increasingly looks a lot more like Scenario 2 than Scenario 1.

We propose that tomorrow's successful supervisors will be those who have learned to thrive on chaos. They will confront an environment in which change is taking place at an unprecedented rate. New competitors spring up overnight; old ones disappear through mergers, acquisitions, new technologies, or failure to keep up with the changing marketplace. Downsized organizations mean fewer workers to complete the necessary work. Constant innovations in computer and telecommunications technologies make communications instantaneous. These factors, combined with the globalization of product and financial markets, have created chaos. As a result, many traditional business strategies—created for a world that was far more stable and predictable—no longer apply.

Successful supervisors must change, too. They must be able to make sense out of a situation in which everything appears futile. Supervisors must be able to turn disasters into opportunities. To do so, they must be more flexible in their styles, smarter in how they work, quicker in making decisions, more efficient in managing scarce resources, better at satisfying the customer, and more confident in enacting massive and revolutionary changes. As management writer Tom Peters captured this concept in one of his best-selling books, "Today's supervisors must be able to thrive on change and uncertainty."[24]

From Chaos to Crisis

Although supervisors today must be able to deal with the chaos surrounding them, managing in a crisis takes on a different proportion in a supervisor's work life. A supervisor must be alert to the warning signs of a unit in trouble. Some signals may include potential performance declines, budget deficiencies, unnecessary and cumbersome policies, fear of conflict and taking risks, tolerance of work incompetence, and poor communications within the department.

Another perspective on recognizing performance declines revolves around the "boiled frog phenomenon,"[25] a classic psychological response experiment. In one case, a living frog is dropped into a boiling pan of water, reacts instantly, and jumps out of the pan. But the second frog, a live frog that's dropped into a pan of mild water that is gradually heated to the boiling point, fails to react and dies. A supervisor may be particularly vulnerable to the boiled frog phenomenon because he or she may not recognize the "water heating up"—that is, the subtly declining situation. When changes

---

[24]T. Peters, *Thriving on Chaos: Handbook for a Management Revolution* (New York: Knopf, 1987).

[25]P. Strozniak, "Averting Disaster," *Industry Week*, February 12, 2001, 11–12.

in performance are gradual, a serious response may never be triggered or may not be triggered until it is too late to do anything about the situation. So, what does the boiled frog phenomenon teach us? It tells us that supervisors need to be alert to the signals that something is amiss in the department, and not wait until the situation reaches the crisis (boiling) point.

Although most crises in organizations don't go from problem to crisis overnight, traumatic events do occur.[26] The April 20, 2010, explosion of *Deepwater Horizon*, which drilled on the BP-operated Macondo Prospect, is a clear example. So, what can organizations and supervisors do?

One of the key components in handling a disaster is to have a plan in place. This may include having disaster recovery plans—which may include duplicate and backup systems, emergency work sites, and telecommuting options.[27] Although these are important, one aspect appears to have the consensus of the experts in this arena—supervisory support for employees and their families.[28] Good communications during these disasters becomes paramount to help employees understand what is happening. Supervisors must be able to let employees talk about their feelings and allow them to grieve, if needed. Supervisors must also recognize that stress may be rampant in some employees, and some may become depressed and need additional assistance. In such situations there are no manuals to rely on; rather, such times require supervisors to be kind, sensitive, and empathetic. And they must do this at a time when they, too, may be experiencing the same emotional "crises" as their employees!

There's no doubt that trying times require drastic measures. And although the hope is that events like those we witnessed on April 20, 2010, will never happen again, traumatic events in an organization may occur at any time. Those organizations and supervisors that anticipate such catastrophes and have disaster plans in place will be one step ahead in minimizing the effects of the aftermath.

The Good and Profitable Organization

Every organization has one simple goal: It wants to survive. Survival may take on different forms, though. For many it means being profitable, whereas for others it means generating enough money to continue the work for the good of society. The former often raises many questions. Can an organization operate in a manner that allows it to do the "right" thing and still make money? Although the answer is yes, the news headlines are filled with stories about organizations that may not operate in a manner that seems appropriate. For instance, if tobacco companies know that nicotine leads to serious health problems, should they have withdrawn cigarettes from the market decades ago? Should U.S. companies manufacturing products in Mexico adhere to U.S. environmental and safety laws when Mexico doesn't require them—even when it's been shown that some birth defects in Brownsville, Texas, are a function of pollution coming across the gulf from Mexico? Regardless of our feelings on such issues, we really can't condemn such organizations. In most cases, after all, they are obeying the law—and that's all that is required of them! We frequently assume that as long as businesses obey the law, they have a right to do whatever is necessary to ensure survival. We take this as a given. However, many organizations today are implementing policies and practices that focus on socially responsible behavior. Let's look at this phenomenon.

---

[26]"What Companies Can Do in Traumatic Times," *BusinessWeek*, October 8, 2001, 92.

[27]L. Copeland, C. Sliwa, and M. Hamblen, "Companies Urged to Revisit Disaster Recovery Plans," *Computerworld*, October 15, 2001, 7.

[28]See, for example, J. Brandt, "Survivors Need Your Solace," *Chief Executive*, October 2001, 12; and H. Paster, "Manager's Journal: Be Prepared," *Wall Street Journal*, September 24, 2001, A-24.

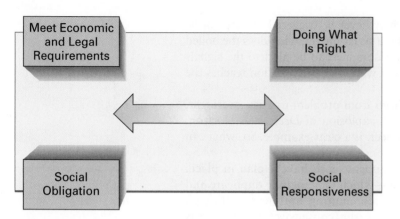

Exhibit 2-5
Social obligation versus social responsiveness.

social responsibility
An obligation that organizations have to pursue long-term goals that are good for society.

social obligation
The foundation of a business's social involvement. An organization's social obligation is fulfilled when it meets its economic and legal responsibilities.

social responsiveness
A process guided by social norms that requires businesses to determine what is right or wrong and thus seek fundamental truths; an attempt to do those things that make society better and not to do those things that could make it worse.

WHAT IS A SOCIALLY RESPONSIBLE ORGANIZATION?

Social responsibility is an obligation that organizations have to society. It means going beyond the law and profit making. Social responsibility tries to align organizational long-term goals with what is good for society. *Society* in this context refers to such groups as an organization's employees, its customers, and the environment in which it operates.

We can understand social responsibility better if we compare it with two similar concepts: social obligation and social responsiveness (see Exhibit 2-5).[29] Social obligation is the foundation of a business's social involvement. A business has fulfilled its social obligation when it meets its economic and legal responsibilities and no more. It does the minimum that the law requires. In contrast to social obligation, both social responsibility and social responsiveness go beyond merely meeting basic economic and legal standards. Social responsiveness adds a moral obligation to do those things that make society better and not to do those that could make it worse. Social responsiveness, then, requires business to determine what is right or wrong and thus seek fundamental truths. Societal norms guide this process. Let's look at these two in an example to make them clearer.

When a company meets pollution control standards established by the federal government or doesn't discriminate against employees on the basis of their race in a promotion decision, the organization is fulfilling its social obligation—and nothing more. Various laws say that employers may not pollute or be biased against certain groups, and this company is abiding by those laws. However, when a company packages its products in recycled paper or provides health care insurance for an unmarried employee's significant other, this firm is being socially responsive. How so? Although pressure may be coming from a number of societal groups, such businesses are providing something society desires—without having to be told to do so by law!

It's often easy for us to sit back and talk about a company being socially responsible, but what about when "they" become "us"? Socially responsible behavior for individuals brings the matter a little closer to home!

HOW DO WE ACT RESPONSIBLY?

Many people believe that our society is currently suffering a moral crisis. Behaviors that were once thought reprehensible—lying, cheating, misrepresenting, covering up mistakes—have become, in many people's eyes, common business practices. Products that can cause harm to their users remain on the market. Males in one large organization have been alleged to have sexually harassed their female counterparts.

How about in business—and more specifically the job of supervisor? What kinds of questionable issues might a supervisor face? Here are a few general questions related to supervisory actions: Should you tell the truth all the time? Is it right to bend the rules to your company's advantage whenever you can? Does anything go, as long as you don't get caught? Now consider a couple of specific cases: Is it proper for one of your salespeople to offer a bribe to a purchasing agent as an inducement to buy? Is it wrong to use the company telephone for personal long-distance calls?

---

[29]W. Acar, K. E. Aupprele, and R. M. Lowry, "An Empirical Exploration of Measures of Social Responsibility Across the Spectrum of Organizational Types," *International Journal of Organizational Analysis* (January 2001), 26–57.

Supervisors face many dilemmas. Situations exist in which they're required to define right and wrong conduct. Because of their comments and behavior, supervisors are a primary source for conveying an organization's climate. For most employees, their supervisor is the only contact they have with management. As such, management's standards are interpreted by employees through the actions of their supervisor. If supervisors take company supplies home, cheat on their expense accounts, or engage in similar practices, they set a tone in their workgroups that is likely to undermine all the efforts by top management to create a corporate climate of high-principled standards. In large companies such as American Express and Exxon, supervisors have codes of conduct to guide them as to what constitutes acceptable and unacceptable practices. These are often formal documents that state an organization's primary values and the ethical rules it expects employees to follow.

As organizations apply increased pressure on supervisors and employees to cut costs and increase productivity, ethical dilemmas are almost certain to increase. By what they say and do, supervisors contribute toward setting their organization's standards. This is illustrated in comments from a supervisor in a midwestern police department:

> I tell my people that gratuities, in any form, are wrong. Take meals, for example. A restaurant might offer my people half-price meals because, they say, they like police officers. I believe there's a hidden agenda in everything. The reason they're giving you half-price meals is because they want police officers and their vehicles there. Crooks aren't going to hit it. But basically they're buying our services for half the cost of a hamburger. If you have to arrest that restaurant manager, I guarantee you, he's going to come back and say, "Well, you eat at my restaurant at half price." What I tell my people is, "If I find out, we're going to have problems with it." I recommend to my people that, if it's the restaurant's policy to give half off the bill to officers, pay the additional amount in the tip. If it's a $4 hamburger and they charge you $2, put down a $3 tip.

What individuals like this supervisor want from their employees is for them to act ethically. What exactly is this thing we call ethics?

WHAT IS ETHICS?

Ethics commonly refers to the rules or principles that define right and wrong conduct. People who lack a strong moral character are much less likely to do the wrong things if they are constrained by rules, policies, job descriptions, or strong cultural norms that frown on such behaviors. Conversely, very moral people can be corrupted by an organization and its culture that permit or encourage unethical practices. Consider an ethical situation alluded to previously—that of a purchasing agent taking a bribe. Taking a monetary bribe, we believe, is something almost everyone would consider unethical behavior. That's because it could also be an illegal activity. But what if the "bribe" is not as visible as money—or doesn't exist at all? For example, suppose you are the supervisor of the purchasing department for a medium-sized hospital. You have several vendors who are making their best sales pitch to you in an effort to get your business. Vendor 1 makes his presentation to you, and leaves with you quite an attractive price list—given the large quantities you may be buying. Vendor 2 makes a similar presentation, and her company's prices are comparable. But she also invites you and your friend to attend an upcoming sporting event—tickets you wanted to get but couldn't because they were sold out. Do you go to the event with this vendor? Do you think it is okay to do so? After all, it's a game. Furthermore, even if her company does get your business, their prices are, in fact, in line with the competing vendor.

This example illustrates how ambiguity about what is ethical can be a problem for employees. Codes of ethics (formal documents that state an organization's primary values and ethical rules it expects employees to follow) are an increasingly popular response for reducing that ambiguity. It has been suggested that codes be specific enough to guide employees in what they're supposed to do. Unfortunately, you may not have

ethics
Rules or principles that define right and wrong conduct.

code of ethics
A formal document that states an organization's primary values and the ethical rules it expects employees to follow.

How ethical will employees be? That's a difficult question to answer. However, if the behavior of their supervisor is ethical, there is a stronger likelihood that these employees will follow suit. Accordingly, the role a supervisor plays in establishing ethical behavior in a department is critical.

such a policy to fall back on. In that case, you are going to have to respond in a way that you feel is appropriate—and deal with the consequences. Let's look at this more closely.

Suppose you are asked by your boss to fix prices with competitors and, at the same time, steal technology from the same groups you are colluding with. Your boss knows that in so doing, your organization can create an unbeatable market for its products and possibly run your competitors out of business. Also, if you do these things, you'll be rewarded hand-somely—in fact, you may be put in charge of the operation.[30] What are your options? One option is to do what your boss has asked. After all, he's the boss, and he can make your life great or miserable. However, if you go to such extremes as price fixing or stealing trade secrets, you might be criminally liable. You, not the manager, may face the charges. Even though you did it for the good of your organization, realize that the boss may not protect you if you get caught. In essence, your career may be tarnished.

Another option is to talk to your boss and register your displeasure with being asked to do this deed. It's doubtful that the request will be withdrawn, but at least you can state your position. You may also refuse to do what you've been asked to do. Of course, this refusal could create problems for you. You may feel that you need to go to organizational members in positions of higher authority. You may find that they are willing to help you, but you cannot always count on that happening. Yet another option is to give the impression that you'll do what your boss asked, but never carry out the request. You might make up excuses that prices couldn't be fixed because other companies wouldn't agree to go along. In such an instance, you're hoping that the manager will "buy" your excuse, or simply forget to follow up on the request. Again, it's a risk you may be willing to take. Another downside to this option is that you are still committing an unethical act—lying to your boss.

Assuming that your boss continues to press you, you'll have another choice available to you. This, however, is the most extreme. If the request clearly goes against your beliefs, and you cannot get any help from individuals in the organization, you may have to think about quitting, or even going outside the organization to report what is happening. Sure, there are disadvantages to doing so, but at least you may have the comfort of knowing you've done the right thing. In situations involving ethics, it's impossible to predict what you'll face. It helps if you prepare ahead of time and anticipate how you will handle ethical dilemmas (see "Guidelines for Acting Ethically" on page 54–55). The more you do to prepare, the easier it will be when and if that day arrives and you're asked to do something that "goes against your grain."

---

[30]This example is adapted from M. Whitcare, "My Life as a Corporate Mole for the FBI," *Fortune*, September 4, 1995, 52–62.

Comprehension Check 2-2

5. The composition of the workforce that includes people from all walks of life is called

   a. supply of labor
   b. human resource inventory
   c. workforce diversity
   d. the global village

6. When an organization is reducing its workforce and reshaping its operations to create a leaner organization, this process is called

   a. planning
   b. organizing
   c. efficient operations
   d. downsizing

7. Which of the following terms is best associated with the term *continuous improvement*?

   a. *kaizen*
   b. downsizing
   c. restructuring
   d. total quality management

8. A set of principles that define right and wrong behavior for organizational members is called

   a. social responsibility
   b. corporate governance
   c. ethics
   d. all of the above

Enhancing Understanding

SUMMARY

After reading this chapter, I can:

1. **Explain how globalization affects supervisors.** Globalization affects supervisors in many ways. The key factor is recognizing differences that exist among people from various cultures and understanding how these differences may block effective communications.

2. **Describe how technology is changing the supervisor's job.** Technology is changing the supervisor's job in several ways. Supervisors have immediate access to information that helps them make decisions. Technological advancements assist supervisors who have employees in remote locations, reducing the need for face-to-face interaction with these individuals. On the other hand, effectively communicating with individuals in remote locations, as well as ensuring that performance objectives are being met, will become a major challenge for supervisors.

3. **Explain the concept of e-business and e-commerce.** The term *e-commerce* is becoming the standard label to describe the online buying and selling of products or services and refers to any sales activity involving electronic business. It involves using the Internet to conduct business transactions. E-business, on the other hand, involves the full breadth of activities in a successful Internet-based enterprise. It includes developing strategies for running the business, improving communications with suppliers and customers, collaborating with partners to electronically coordinate design and production, identifying a different kind of leader to run a virtual business, finding skilled people to build and operate intranets and websites, and running the back room or the administrative side.

4. **Identify the significant changes that have occurred in the composition of the workforce.** Compared to sixty years ago, when the workforce consisted primarily of white males, the workforce has become more diverse and will continue in this direction. Changing population demographics, globalization of businesses, and passage of federal legislation that prohibits employment discrimination have contributed to this change. The changing workforce means that supervisors interact with people who are diverse in terms of gender, race, ethnicity, physical ability, sexual orientation, and age—all of whom have different lifestyles, family needs, and work styles. The most

significant implication for supervisors is the requirement of sensitivity to the differences in each individual. That means they must shift their philosophy from treating everyone alike to recognizing differences and responding to these differences in ways that will ensure employee retention and greater productivity.

5. **Explain why corporations downsize.** Corporate downsizing has occurred in response to global competition. It is an attempt by companies to become more responsive to customers and more efficient in their operations. The supervisory effect is twofold. First, supervisors must ensure that their skills and those of their employees are kept up-to-date. Employees whose skills become obsolete are more likely to be candidates for downsizing. Second, those who keep their jobs will more than likely be doing the work of two or three people. This situation can create frustration, anxiety, and less motivation.

6. **Understand the concept of continuous improvement and identify its goals.** Continuous-improvement programs expand the term *customer* beyond the traditional definition to include everyone involved with the organization, either internally or externally. This encompasses employees and suppliers as well as the people who buy the organization's products or services. The objective is to create an organization committed to continuous improvement—always looking to be better and to provide a better, higher-quality product or service. The five primary goals of continuous improvement are (1) focus on the customer, (2) seek continuous improvement, (3) improve the quality of everything the organization does, (4) measure accurately, and (5) involve employees.

7. **Describe why supervisors must be able to thrive on chaos.** Supervisors work in environments in which change is taking place at an unprecedented rate. They must be more flexible in their styles, smarter in how they work, quicker in making decisions, more efficient in handling scarce resources, better at satisfying the customer, and more confident in enacting massive and revolutionary changes. Supervisors must also be prepared for and sensitive to employee needs in the event of a traumatic occurrence in an organization. This sensitivity comes in the form of listening to

employees, recognizing the stress they are experiencing, and providing them help, as needed.

8. **Define** *ethics.* Ethics refers to rules or principles that define right or wrong conduct. In an organization, these rules or principles may be defined in a written code of ethics—a formal document that states an organization's primary values and ethical rules it expects employees to follow.

COMPREHENSION: Review and Discussion Questions

1. Do you believe that globalization has had the effect of making U.S. organizations more responsive to their customers? Explain.

2. "Technology improvements sometimes hinder supervisory effectiveness." Do you agree or disagree? Support your position.

3. What supervisory effects does e-business have for supervisors?

4. What is workforce diversity, and what challenges does it create for supervisors?

5. What advice would you give to a friend who doesn't understand downsizing but knows that her company is going to be laying off employees in about three months?

6. Describe the difference between continuous-improvement programs and work process engineering.

7. How can learning to manage chaos better prepare supervisors for their jobs in the next decade?

8. Can organizations be socially responsible and still be profitable? If you think so, cite some examples of companies you believe fit this profile and describe what they are doing.

9. Is it ethical to cheat on an exam if you know that it will not affect another student's grade and you are guaranteed that you won't get caught? Why or why not?

10. Identify the characteristics and behaviors of what you would consider an ethical supervisor.

KEY CONCEPT CROSSWORD

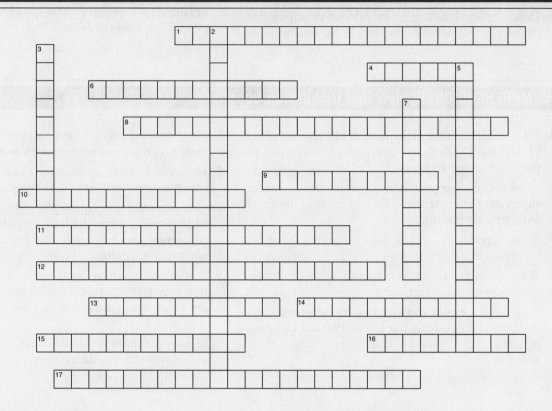

ACROSS

1. an obligation that organizations have to pursue long-term goals that are good for society
4. rules that define right or wrong conduct
6. formal document that states an organization's primary values that it expects employees to follow
8. radical or quantum change in the organization
9. reduction in the workforce
10. linking a worker's remote computer with the office
11. composition of the workforce that reflects the varied backgrounds of workers
12. an organizational process guided by social norms
13. the largest group in the workforce who were born between 1946 and 1964
14. seeing things from one's own perspective
15. lost productivity as a result of an employee using the Internet at work for personal reasons
16. doing work by using electronic linkages with key constituents
17. activities that enhance processes designed to improve the quality of the goods and services produced

DOWN

2. values, morals, customs, and laws of a country
3. any transaction that occurs when data are processed and transmitted over the Internet
5. an organization's fulfillment when it meets its economic and legal responsibilities
7. any high-tech equipment, tools, or operating methods that are designed to make work more efficient

ANSWERS TO COMPREHENSION CHECKS

Comprehension Check 2-1

1. b   2. c   3. a   4. d

Comprehension Check 2-2

5. c   6. d   7. a   8. c

ANSWERS TO SOMETHING TO THINK ABOUT (and promote class discussion)

1. C Braun is a wholly owned subsidiary of U.S.-based Procter & Gamble.

2. D Societe Bic SA owns the company.

3. C Häagen-Dazs is owned by General Mills, and in the United States and Canada, the brand is used under license by Nestlé, a multinational packaged food company founded and headquartered in Vevey, Switzerland.

4. C Previously owned by Thomson, RCA television brand was sold to TCL, a Chinese electronics manufacturer headquartered in Huizhou of Guangdong province, southern China, in 2003.

5. A General Mills owns Green Giant.

6. C Godiva had been a subsidiary of Campbell Soup Company in the United States since 1966. However, Campbell sold Godiva to Istanbul, Turkey-based Yildiz Holding A.S. on March 18, 2008, for $850 million.

7. B Vaseline is produced by Unilever, a multinational corporation, formed of Anglo-Dutch parentage, that is a dual-listed company consisting of Unilever NV in Rotterdam and Unilever PLC in London.

8. D The Wrangler brand is owned by the VF Corporation, an American apparel corporation that is the world's largest clothing company, with headquarters in Greensboro, North Carolina.

9. D Holiday Inn Hotels and Resorts is part of the InterContinental Hotels Group family of brands with global headquarters in the United Kingdom.

10. C Tropicana Products, an American-based company, was founded in Bradenton, Florida, in 1947 by Anthony T. Rossi. Since 1998, it has been owned by PepsiCo, Inc., headquartered in Purchase, New York.

Developing Your Supervisory Skills

GETTING TO KNOW YOURSELF

Before you can effectively supervise others, you must understand your present strengths and areas in need of development. To assist in this learning process, we encourage you to complete the following self-assessments from the Prentice Hall Self-Assessment Library 3.4.

1. Am I Likely to Become an Entrepreneur? (I. E. 4.)
2. Am I Well Suited for a Career as a Global Manager? (III. B. 5.)

3. What Are My Attitudes toward Workplace Diversity? (I. B. 4.)
4. How Do My Ethics Rate? (I. D. 2.)
5. How Committed Am I to My Organization? (III. B. 2.)

After you complete the assessments, we suggest you retain the results and store them as part of your "portfolio of learning about yourself."

BUILDING A TEAM

➤ An Experiential Exercise: Working with Diversity

In today's workforce, several generations coexist. There are the baby boomers (born between 1946 and 1964); Generation X (born between 1965 and 1977); and Generation Y (born in 1978 and after). Each group has its own focus and holds different values. Form three groups based on these age brackets. Group 1 will include the baby boomers; Group 2, Generation X; and Group 3, Generation Y. Refer to exhibit 2-3 on page 39 to help guide your discussion.

STEP 1: Discuss your feelings about all three groups. To help frame your responses, use the following questions.

  a. What do you believe each group
    1. values in life?
    2. wants from their job?
    3. expects from their supervisor?

b. Now, identify two characteristics that best describe each group.

STEP 2

a. Each group will share its responses to the four questions in Step 1 with the entire class.
b. What similarities and what differences exist between the views of the groups? Do these differences reflect how you see people differently? Discuss your responses.
c. Are the characteristics of your age bracket more positive for yourself than the characteristics you listed for the other two groups? What does this tell you about the perceptions of diverse workers?

➤ Internet: Web Activity

Go to http://www.pearsonhighered.com/robbins/. Find *Supervision Today!* 7th Ed. and click Companion Website.

GUIDELINES FOR ACTING ETHICALLY

Making ethical choices can often be difficult for supervisors. Obeying the law is mandatory, but acting ethically goes beyond mere compliance with the law. It means acting responsibly in "gray" areas where rules of right or wrong are ambiguous. What can you do to enhance your supervisory abilities in acting ethically? We offer some guidelines.

STEPS IN PRACTICING THE SKILL

STEP 1: Know your organization's policy on ethics. Company policies on ethics, if they exist, describe what the organization perceives as ethical behavior and what it expects you to do. This policy will help you clarify what is permissible for you to do—the managerial discretion you have. It will become your code of ethics to follow.

STEP 2: Understand the ethics policy. Just having the policy in your hand does not guarantee that it will achieve what it is intended to do. You need to fully understand it. Ethical behavior is rarely a cut-and-dried process. With the help of the policy as a guiding light, you will have a basis from which to decide ethical issues in the organization. Even if a policy doesn't exist, there are several steps you can take when confronted with a difficult situation.

STEP 3: Think before you act. Ask yourself, why are you doing what you're about to do? What led to the problem? What is your true intention in taking some action? Is it for a valid reason, or are there ulterior motives behind it—such as demonstrating organizational loyalty? Will your action injure someone? Can you disclose to your manager or your family what you're going to do? Remember, it's your behavior that will be seen in your actions. You need to make sure that you are not doing something that will jeopardize your role as a manager, your organization, or your reputation.

STEP 4: Ask yourself "what-if" questions. When you think ahead about why you're doing something,

you should also be asking yourself "what-if" questions. For example, the following questions may help you shape your actions: What if you make the wrong decision—what will happen to you? To your job? What if your actions are described, in detail, on the local news or in the newspaper? Would it bother or embarrass you or those around you? What if you get caught doing something unethical? Are you prepared to deal with the consequences?

STEP 5: Seek opinions from others. If you must do something major, and you're uncertain about it, ask for advice from other managers. Maybe they've been in a similar situation and can give you the benefit of their experiences. If not, maybe they can just listen and act as a sounding board for you.

STEP 6: Do what you truly believe is right. You have a conscience and you are responsible for your behavior. Whatever you do, if you truly believe it is the right action to take, what others say (or what the proverbial "Monday morning quarterbacks" say) is immaterial. You need to be true to your own internal ethical standards. Ask yourself, can you live with what you've done?

➤ Communicating Effectively

1. Provide a two- to three-page write-up on an e-commerce business (e.g., Barnes & Noble or Gap) and the effect e-commerce is having on the operation of the business. Emphasize the way the business has had to change to become an e-commerce business and the benefits that have accrued. End your paper with a discussion on the effect e-commerce has had on supervisors in this business.

2. Faced with a traumatic crisis, supervisors may be required to take some drastic measures. Identify one organization that has experienced a catastrophe. Discuss the nature of the tragedy and what the organization did to assist the affected employees.

THINKING CRITICALLY

➤ Case 2-A: Self-Service Banking

Kelly Jenkins has been with First Union National Bank of North Carolina for six years. When Kelly started working at First Union National, she was in high school and worked as a drive-in teller during the summer months. Kelly joined First Union National for a number of reasons. First, she was offered a job. More important, the bank would pay for her college courses—as long as she worked at least twenty hours per week. Working her way through college, she has made many friends with both employees and customers. In fact, many of her customers know her so well, they ask for her when they bank at First Union National.

Kelly has taken every opportunity for training that the bank has offered. Whenever a new process was implemented or a new technology was installed at the bank, Kelly was one of the first to sign up for training classes. Additionally, she has carried fifteen credit hours each semester to ensure that she would achieve her goal of graduating with a degree in economics in four years. Kelly has so impressed the bank officials that she has been offered the opportunity to enter into the bank's branch management program. Surprisingly, shortly after graduating from college, she has accepted a similar position with a competing bank at a comparable salary. In retrospect, this was the bank Kelly wanted to work for all along, but it didn't offer college tuition reimbursement.

Now in her new position, Kelly has inadvertently let her boss know that she has material she collected while an employee at First Union National. He has let her know that he is interested in seeing it. The information concerns the direction in which First Union National is moving over the next five years. In fact, one piece of data in the information packet Kelly has provided indicated that First Union National is establishing plans to offer several unique and innovative electronic banking services. Hearing this, top management at Kelly's bank has decided to forge ahead immediately with services similar to those First Union National is planning to offer. Kelly's bank simply does not want to lose its competitive position.

➤ Case 2-B: Ethical Considerations

A major computer parts manufacturer has decided to open a plant in a medium-sized city in the southeast that has been especially hard hit with job losses in the textile field. The new company will receive substantial incentives in the form of free land, tax relief, and generous training allowances from local and state government. Hiring for the new operation has been announced and will include high-tech positions, supervisory positions, and a few technical positions. The published pay rates for these positions appear to be at or near the top of the local range for comparable jobs.

Marilyn is an experienced supervisor with one of the remaining textile plants in the area. She has received some literature in the mail explaining the mission of the new company and alerting the community to its need to fill a number of positions, including supervisor positions. An employment application for the new company was enclosed with the materials.

At lunch and on breaks, Marilyn has heard her crew talking about the opportunities at the computer manufacturing company. She has been told that several of her

RESPONDING TO THE CASE

1. Do you believe it is unethical for Kelly to join First Union National Bank solely because the bank will pay for her education? Support your position.

2. In the case, Kelly inadvertently lets her new employer know she has information about some First Union National plans. Is it ethical for this employer to request that information and use it in an attempt to beat First Union National to the market with new electronic banking services? Why or why not?

3. Would your response to Question 2 change if you knew that Kelly was hired because she was known to have been privy to such information and this was a way to obtain it? Explain. If this is the case, would Kelly be acting ethically in providing the requested information? Defend your position.

people plan to fill out applications for the new company. In the last week, a representative from the new company left a message on her home phone saying that she would like to invite Marilyn to visit the company and interview for a supervisor's position. Marilyn is in a quandary about several issues.

RESPONDING TO THE CASE

1. What is Marilyn's responsibility to her present employer regarding her knowledge that several employees are planning to seek positions with the new company?

2. How should Marilyn reply to the recruiter who is asking her to come in for an interview? Does this constitute an ethical decision for her?

3. Is it ethical for one company to receive funds to move into an area when other companies struggle to keep jobs from going offshore or from being lost to automation?

Planning, Organizing, Staffing, Controlling, and Decision Making

The foundation of supervision is effectively planning the work to be done; properly grouping work activities and employees; hiring the people who possess the proper skills, knowledge, and abilities to do those jobs; and monitoring the activities of the work being done. In Part 2, we discuss the major elements that facilitate establishing and attaining organizational and departmental goals. Once goals are established, employees must be properly grouped to support those goals. Then, after determining what work is to be done, supervisors must find qualified job candidates, develop them, and keep their skills up-to-date. With plans, structures, and employees in place, supervisors must design and implement controls that will ensure that goals are met. Each area of planning, organizing, staffing, and controlling requires a high level of decision-making and problem-solving skills. Thus, we examine these crucial supervisory skills as well.

Planning and Goal Setting

Key Concepts

After completing this chapter, you will be able to define these supervisory terms:

- activities
- balanced scorecard
- benchmarking
- budget
- business plan
- critical path
- entrepreneurial
- entrepreneurship
- events
- Gantt chart
- goal setting
- intermediate-term plan
- ISO 9000 series
- long-term plan

- PERT chart
- policies
- procedure
- productivity
- program
- rule
- scheduling
- short-term plan
- single-use plan
- six sigma
- standing plan
- strategic planning
- tactical planning

Chapter Outcomes

After reading this chapter, you will be able to:

1. Define *productivity*.
2. Describe how plans should link from the top to the bottom of an organization.
3. Identify what is meant by the terms *benchmarking*, *ISO 9000 series*, and *six sigma*.
4. Contrast policies and rules.
5. Describe the Gantt chart.
6. Explain the information needed to create a PERT chart.
7. Describe the four ingredients common to goal-setting programs.
8. Define *entrepreneurship* and explain how it affects supervision.

Responding to a Supervisory Dilemma

Supervisors often find themselves faced with similar situations, and standing plans help them to deal with them in a procedurally consistent fashion. Organizations typically have maternity leave policies and procedures in place for supervisors to help them deal with the temporary loss of a valuable employee. Top management will define the policies to allow the organization to operate within the limits of the law. If the organization has determined that it will allow flexible maternity leave for its employees, the supervisor may be in charge of organizing a replacement worker to ensure that work continues during the absence. Maternity leave is usually created from a variety of benefits that include sick leave, vacation, holiday time, personal days, short-term disability, and unpaid family leave time.

Surprisingly, women reporting workplace discrimination due to pregnancy is on the rise even as birthrates decline. "Employment lawyers say that, in many cases, employers are simply making honest mistakes as they try to understand a variety of federal and state laws governing issues such as pregnancy discrimination and family leave. And they say it's easy to overlook the very real costs of pregnancy to small employers, who may see productivity suffer significantly when women take time off after having a baby. But pregnant women claim they've been unfairly fired, denied promotions and in some cases urged to terminate pregnancies in order to keep their jobs."*

The Equal Opportunity Employment Commission (EEOC) filed a suit against Denham Springs Publishing Company for violation of federal law after firing an employee because she was pregnant. In the press release, EEOC states that Denham "discharged Jayme Fraught Jones due to her pregnancy instead of allowing her to take maternity leave. Jones began working for Denham Springs Publishing in May 2005 as the special programs coordinator for the Livingston Parish News. In December 2005, Jones became the sales and marketing director for the newly acquired Antiques Gazette. In October 2006, Jones began inquiring about the company's maternity leave policy because it was unwritten. Despite Jones' repeated requests for information, her supervisor, Lauren Katz, the sales and marketing director of the Livingston Parish News, refused to tell her what maternity leave was available... Prior to her requests for maternity leave, Jones had no disciplinary action, she received a salary increase with increased responsibility, and within days of her discharge, she received a large bonus for generating increased revenue. Jones was terminated because she was pregnant and they did not want to provide her with any maternity leave."[†]

Imagine you are a supervisor and one of your female employees has just told you that she is pregnant and will be taking maternity leave. Can you demand medical notes from a pregnant woman's doctor concerning her work status? Can you reassign female employees to lower-paying positions because of pregnancy? Can you forbid a pregnant employee from continuing to work if she wants to and is physically capable of doing all tasks associated with the work? Can you refuse to adjust workloads for a pregnant employee if you do so for a worker who is not pregnant but claims some other disability or mitigating circumstance? Paying close attention to maternity leave laws such as the Pregnancy Discrimination Act of 1978 and the Family and Medical Leave Act of 1993 that protect the rights of the pregnant mother will allow your organization to plan for and be better prepared to answer these questions and handle situations as they arise. The bottom line is that you should treat your pregnant employees no differently than you would any other employees.

---

*S. Armour, "Pregnant workers report growing discrimination," *USA TODAY*, February 17, 2005, http://www.usatoday.com/money/workplace/2005-02-16-pregnancy-bias-usat_x.htm (accessed May 11, 2011).

[†]U.S. Equal Employment Opportunity Commission, "Denham Springs Publishing Company Sued by EEOC for Pregnancy Discrimination," Press Release, September 15, 2010, http://www.eeoc.gov/eeoc/newsroom/release/9-15-10e.cfm (accessed May 11, 2011).

As mentioned in Chapter 1, planning encompasses defining an organization's objectives or goals, establishing the overall strategy for achieving those goals, and developing a comprehensive hierarchy of functions to integrate and coordinate activities. For our purposes, we treat the terms *objectives* and *goals* as interchangeable. Each is meant to convey some desired outcome that an organization, department, workgroup, or individual seeks to achieve.

What Is Formal Planning?

Does planning require that goals, strategies, and plans be written down? Ideally, they should be, but they often aren't. In formal planning, specific goals are formulated, committed to writing, and made available to other organization members. Additionally, specific action programs exist in formal planning to define the path for the achievement of each goal.

Many supervisors engage in informal planning. They have plans in their heads, but nothing is written down, and there is little or no sharing of these plans with others. This probably occurs most often in small businesses where the owner-supervisor has a vision of where he or she wants to go and how to get there. In this chapter, when we use the term *planning*, we refer to the formal variety. Formal planning is most often required for an organization to be productive (see "News Flash! The Downsides of Planning").

Productivity

In almost any discussion of performance in an organization, the focus will eventually turn to the topic of productivity. Productivity, in essence, becomes the name of the game! This could refer to producing a product, such as computer chips, or providing a service, such as fixing a computer's hard drive when it has a problem. Yet in a number of organizations—especially those that provide services—defining productivity can be very difficult. In some cases, it becomes a perceived, if not a real, impossibility. In today's organizations, supervisors must be able to determine what constitutes productivity.

productivity
Output per labor hour, best expressed by the formula Productivity = Output/ (Labor + Capital + Materials). Productivity measures can be applied to the individual, the group, and the total organization.

WHAT IS PRODUCTIVITY?

In its simplest form, productivity can be expressed in the following ratio:

$$\text{Productivity} = \frac{\text{Output}}{\text{Labor} + \text{Capital} + \text{Materials}}$$

Output per labor hour is perhaps the most common partial measure of productivity. Industrial engineers, who conduct time-and-motion studies in factories, largely focus on generating increases in labor productivity. The U.S. Navy ARIES biodiesel plant, an Automated Real-time, Remote, Integrated Energy System, located at Naval Base Ventura County, is an example of increasing productivity by substituting capital (i.e., machinery and equipment) for labor. Materials productivity is concerned with increasing the efficient use of material inputs and supplies. A meat-packing plant, as an illustrative case, improves its materials productivity when it finds additional uses for by-products that were previously treated as waste.

Productivity can also be applied at three different levels—the individual, the group, and the total organization. Word-processing software, fax machines, and e-mail have made administrative assistants more productive by allowing them to generate more output during their workdays. The use of teams has increased the productivity of many workgroups at companies such as Coors Brewing and Aetna Life. Southwest Airlines

News Flash!

THE DOWNSIDES OF PLANNING

Formalized planning became very popular in the 1960s. And, for the most part, it still is popular today! It makes sense to establish some direction. After all, as the Cheshire Cat said to Alice in *Alice in Wonderland*, the way you ought to go "depends a good deal on where you want to get to." But critics have begun to challenge some of the basic assumptions underlying planning. Let's look at the major arguments that have been offered against formal planning.

- **Planning may create rigidity.** Formal planning efforts can lock an organization into specific goals to be achieved within specific timetables. When these objectives were set, the assumption may have been made that the environment wouldn't change during the time period the objectives cover. If that assumption is faulty, supervisors who follow a plan may have trouble. Rather than remaining flexible—and possibly scrapping the plan—supervisors who continue to do the things required to achieve the original objectives may not be able to cope with the changed environment. Forcing a course of action when the environment is fluid can be a recipe for disaster.

- **Plans can't be developed for a dynamic environment.** As we just mentioned, most organizations today face dynamic change in their environments. If a basic assumption of making plans—that the environment won't change—is faulty, then how can one make plans at all? We have described today's business environment as chaotic. By definition, that means random and unpredictable. Dealing with chaos and turning disasters into opportunities require flexibility. And that may mean not being tied to formal plans.

- **Formal plans can't replace intuition and creativity.** Successful organizations are typically the result of someone's vision. But these visions tend to become formalized as they evolve. Formal planning efforts typically include a thorough

investigation of the organization's capabilities and opportunities and an analysis that reduces the vision to a routine event. That can spell disaster for an organization. For instance, the rapid rise of Apple Computer in the late 1970s and throughout the 1980s was attributed, in part, to the creativity and anticorporate attitudes of one of its cofounders, Steven Jobs. But as the company grew, Jobs felt a need for more formalized management—something he was uncomfortable performing. He hired a CEO, who ultimately ousted Jobs from his own company. With Jobs's departure came increased organizational formality—the same thing Jobs despised so much because it hampered creativity. By 1996, this one-time leader of its industry had lost much of its creativity and was struggling for survival. Jobs returned to Apple that same year and began working to turn the organization around.

- **Planning focuses supervisors' attention on today's competition, not on tomorrow's survival.** Formal planning reinforces success, which may lead to failure. We have been taught that success breeds success. That has been an American "tradition." After all, if it's not broken, don't fix it. Right? Well, maybe not! Success may, in fact, breed failure in an uncertain environment. It is hard to change or discard successful plans—leaving the comfort of what works for the anxiety of the unknown. Successful plans, however, may provide a false sense of security—generating more confidence in the formal plans than they deserve. Supervisors often won't deliberately face that unknown until they are forced to do so by changes in the environment. But by then, it may be too late!

Sources: H. Mintzberg, *The Rise and Fall of Strategic Planning* (New York: Free Press, 1994); K. Rebello and P. Burrows, "The Fall of an American Icon," *BusinessWeek*, February 5, 1996, 34–42; and D. Miller, "The Architecture of Simplicity," *Academy of Management Review* 18, no. 1 (January 1993), 116–138.

is a more productive organization overall than rivals such as American Airlines or U.S. Airways because Southwest's cost per available seat-mile is 30–60 percent lower than that of these competitors.

Productivity has become a major goal in virtually every organization. By *productivity*, we mean the overall output of goods and services produced divided by the inputs needed to generate that output. For countries, high productivity can lead to economic growth and development. Employees can receive higher wages, and company profits can increase without causing inflation. For individual organizations, increased productivity lowers costs and allows firms to offer more competitive prices.

Increasing productivity is key to global competitiveness. Organizations that hope to succeed globally are looking for ways to improve productivity. Because productivity is a composite of people and operations variables, to improve productivity, managers must focus on both. W. Edwards Deming, a management consultant and quality expert, believed that supervisors, not workers, were the primary source of increased productivity. Deming's fourteen points for improving an organization's productivity reveal his understanding of the interplay between people and operations. High productivity can't come solely from good "people management." The truly effective organization maximizes productivity by successfully integrating people into the overall operations system.

WHY IS PRODUCTIVITY IMPORTANT TO THE UNITED STATES?

In recent years, American productivity, as calculated by the federal government, was stagnant and at times decreasing. As little as twenty-five years ago, the United States ranked eighth or ninth in terms of productivity for industrialized nations. Is that an accurate depiction of what is happening in the United States today? "The most recent figures from the United States Department of Labor reveal that manufacturing labor productivity decreased in 2009 in 12 of the 19 economies compared by the Bureau of Labor Statistics. However, the United States had the largest productivity increase, 7.7 percent, and Japan had the steepest productivity decline, –11.4 percent."[1] By all accounts, it appears that U.S. productivity is rising. America has once again regained the top spot among industrialized nations. Much of this rise, however, has been attributed to downsizing and work process engineering efforts in the early 1990s. By reducing inefficiencies, focusing heavily on quality, and introducing technological improvements, companies have maintained or even increased production—all the while employing fewer workers. American companies are also increasing productivity by becoming more quality and customer oriented. The industries in which the United States is doing exceptionally well in relation to other industrialized nations are depicted in Exhibit 3-1.

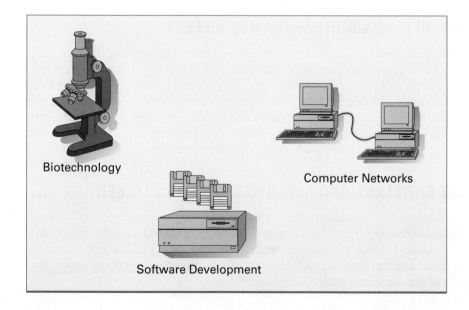

Exhibit 3-1

Industries in which the United States is a major producer in the world market.

[1]United States Department of Labor, Bureau of Labor Statistics "International Comparisons of Manufacturing Productivity and Unit Labor Cost Trends, 2009," *Economic News Release*, December 21, 2010, http://www.bls.gov/news.release/prod4.nr0.htm (accessed May 11, 2011).

What does all this fuss about productivity mean? In essence, having increased productivity makes the U.S. economy stronger. All economic indicators typically revolve around how much U.S. industries produce and sell—both at home and in the global village. Accordingly, when an industrialized nation such as the United States has a strong productivity base, it creates jobs, enhances its production dominance among industrialized nations, encourages job security for employees, and affords research and development efforts to continue finding ways to further productivity gains.

Planning and Level in the Organization

All supervisors, irrespective of their level in the organization, should plan. But the type of planning they do tends to vary with their level in the organization, and the planning they do will differ in several ways. In the discussion that follows, we look at plans in terms of their breadth and their time frames.

WHAT IS THE BREADTH OF PLANNING?

strategic planning
Organizational planning that includes the establishment of overall goals and positioning an organization's products or services against the competition.

The best way to describe planning is to look at it in two parts: strategic and tactical. Strategic planning covers the entire organization; it includes establishing overall goals and positioning the organization's products or services against the competition. Walmart's strategy, for instance, is to build large stores in rural areas, offer an extensive selection of merchandise, provide the lowest prices, and then draw consumers from the many surrounding small towns.

tactical planning
Organizational planning that provides specific details on how overall goals are to be achieved.

Tactical planning covers the specific details on how overall goals are to be achieved. The Walmart store manager in Fayetteville, Arkansas, is engaged in tactical planning when developing a quarterly expense budget or making out weekly employee work schedules.

For the most part, strategic planning is done by top-level managers; a supervisor's time is more likely devoted to tactical planning. Both are important for an organization's success, but they are different in that one focuses on the big picture, while the other emphasizes the specifics within that big picture.

HOW DO PLANNING TIME FRAMES DIFFER?

short-term plan
A plan that covers a period of less than one year.

intermediate-term plan
A plan that covers a period of one to five years.

long-term plan
A plan that covers a period in excess of five years.

Planning often occurs in three time frames—short term, intermediate term, and long term. Short-term plans are less than one year in length. Intermediate-term plans cover from one to five years. Long-term plans cover a period of more than five years. A supervisor's planning horizon tends to emphasize the short term: preparing plans for the next month, week, or day. People in middle-level managerial jobs, such as regional sales directors, typically focus on one–five-year plans. Long-term planning tends to be done by the top executives, such as vice presidents and above.

HOW ARE PLANS AND SUPERVISORY LEVELS LINKED?

It is important to remember that effective planning is integrated and coordinated throughout the organization. Long-term strategic planning sets the direction for all other planning. Once top management has defined the organization's overall strategy and goals and the general plan for getting there, then, in descending order, the other levels of the organization develop plans.

Exhibit 3-2 illustrates this linking of plans from the top to the bottom of an organization. The president, vice president, and other senior executives define the organization's overall strategy. Then upper-middle managers, such as regional

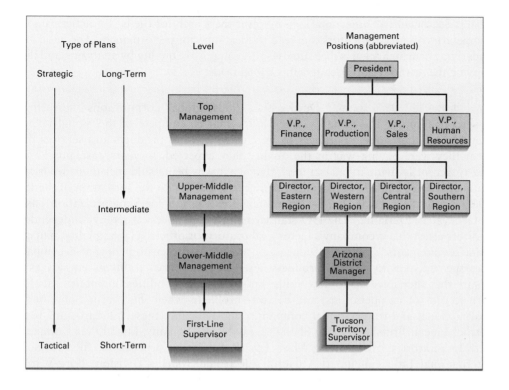

Exhibit 3-2
Planning and levels in the organization.

sales directors, formulate their plans. This continues down to first-line supervisors. Ideally, these plans will be coordinated through joint participation. In the case shown in Exhibit 3-2, for instance, the Tucson territory supervisor would participate with other territory supervisors in providing information and ideas to the Arizona district manager as she formulates plans for her entire district. If planning is properly linked, the successful achievement of all the territory managers' goals should result in the Arizona district manager achieving her goals. If all the district managers meet their goals, this should lead to the successful attainment of the regional sales manager's goals, and so on up each level in the organization.

CAN CONTINUOUS-IMPROVEMENT PROGRAMS BE A HELP IN PLANNING?

An increasing number of organizations are applying quality practices as a way to build a competitive advantage.[2] As we discussed in the last chapter, to the degree that an organization can satisfy a customer's need for quality, it can also differentiate itself from the competition and attract and hold a loyal customer base. Moreover, constant improvement in the quality and reliability of an organization's products or services can result in a competitive advantage others cannot steal. Product innovations, for example, offer little opportunity for sustained competitive advantage. Why? Because usually they can be quickly copied by rivals. But incremental improvement is something that becomes an integrated part of an organization's operations and can develop into a considerable cumulative advantage.

In addition to continuous-improvement programs, three other quality elements can be useful in planning. These are benchmarking, ISO 9000 series, and six sigma. Let's briefly look at each of these.

---

[2]F. K. Wang and W. Lee, "Learning Curve Analysis in Total Productive Maintenance," *Omega*, December 2001, 491–499.

benchmarking
The search for the best practices among competitors or noncompetitors that lead to their superior performance.

ISO 9000 series
Standards designed by the International Organization for Standardization that reflect a process whereby independent auditors attest that a company's factory, laboratory, or office has met quality management standards.

What Is Benchmarking? Benchmarking involves the search for the best practices among competitors or noncompetitors that lead to their superior performance.[3] The basic idea underlying benchmarking is that supervisors can improve quality by analyzing and then copying the methods of the leaders in various fields.

What Is the ISO 9000 Series? During the 1980s, global corporations increasingly pushed to improve their quality. They knew that to compete in the global village, they had to offer some assurances to purchasers of their products and services that what they were buying was of the quality they expected. In years past, purchasers had to accept individual "guarantees" that what was being sold met their needs and standards. That individual guarantee changed in 1987, with the formation of the ISO 9000 series, designed by the International Organization for Standardization based in Geneva, Switzerland.[4] The ISO standards reflect a process whereby "independent auditors attest that a company's factory, laboratory, or office has met quality management requirements."[5] These standards, once met, assure customers that a company uses specific steps to test the products it sells; continuously trains its employees to ensure that they have up-to-date skills, knowledge, and abilities; maintains satisfactory records of its operations; and corrects problems when they occur. Some of the multinational and transnational companies that have met these standards are Texas Petrochemical; British Airways; Shanghai-Foxboro Company, Ltd.; Braas Company; Betz Laboratories; Hong Kong Mass Transit Railway Corporation; BP Chemicals International Ltd.; Cincinnati Milacron Electronic Systems Division; Borg-Warner Automotive; and Taiwan Synthetic Rubber Corporation.

A company that obtains an ISO certification can boast that it has met stringent international quality standards and is one of a select group of companies worldwide to achieve that designation. Certification can offer more than just a competitive advantage; it also permits entry into some markets not otherwise accessible. For example, one hundred sixty-three nations have adopted the ISO standards. Uncertified organizations attempting to do business in those countries may be unable to compete successfully against certified companies. Many customers in the global village want to see the certification, and it becomes a dominant customer need. And in 1997, ISO 14000 went into effect. Companies achieving this certification will have demonstrated that they are environmentally responsible.

How Can Attaining Six Sigma Signify Quality? Wander around organizations such as General Electric, Middle River Aircraft, and Eastman Kodak, and you are likely to find green and black belts. Karate classes? Hardly. These green and black belts signify individuals trained in six sigma processes.[6]

Six sigma is a philosophy and measurement process developed in the 1980s at Motorola. The premise behind six sigma is to "design, measure, analyze, and

[3]E. Jossi, "Take a Peek Inside," *HR Magazine*, June 2002, 46–52; and R. A. Martins, "Continuous Improvement Strategies and Production Competitive Criteria: Some Findings in Brazilian Industries," *Total Quality Management* 12, no. 3 (May 2001), 281–291.

[4]See, for example, J. P. Wilson, M. A. T. Walsh, and K. L. Needy, "An Examination of the Economic Benefits of ISO 9000 and the Baldrige Award to Manufacturing Firms," *Engineering Management Journal* 15, no. 4 (December 2003), 3–5; and International Organization for Standardization, "ISO 9000 Essentials," 2011, http://www.iso.org/iso/iso_catalogue/management_and_leadership_standards/quality_management/iso_9000_essentials.htm (accessed October 14, 2011).

[5]T. B. Schoenrock, "ISO 9000: 2000 Gives Competitive Edge," *Quality Progress*, May 2002, 107.

[6]"Green Belt Training Starts February 4: Other Courses On-Line," *Quality Progress*, February 2002, 13; J. M. Lucas, "The Essential Six Sigma," *Quality Progress*, January 2002, 27–31; and D. Treichler, R. Carmichael, A. Kusmanoff, J. Lewis, and G. Berthiez, "Design for Six Sigma: 15 Lessons Learned," *Quality Progress*, January 2002, 33.

- Select the critical-to-quality characteristics.
- Define the required performance standards.
- Validate the measurement system, methods, and procedures.
- Establish the current processes capability.
- Define upper and lower performance limits.
- Identify sources of variation.
- Screen potential causes of variation to identify the vital few variables needing control.
- Discover the variation relationship for the vital variables.
- Establish operating tolerances on each of the vital variables.
- Validate the measurement system's ability to produce repeatable data.
- Determine the capability of the process to control the vital variables.
- Implement statistical process control on the vital variables.

Exhibit 3-3
Six sigma—twelve process steps.
Source: *Cited in D. Harrold and F. J. Bartos, "Optimize Existing Processes to Achieve Six Sigma Capability," reprinted with permission from* Control Engineering, March 1998, 87, © *Reed Business Information. www.controleng.com, http://m.controleng.com/index. php?id=2819&tx_ttnews [tt_news]= 18806&cHash=6296d5b090 (accessed date October 14, 2011)*

control the input side of a production process."[7] That is, rather than measuring the quality of a product after it is produced, six sigma attempts to "design in" quality as the product is being made (see Exhibit 3-3). It uses statistical models, coupled with specific quality tools, high levels of rigor, and know-how in understanding how to improve processes.

How effective is six sigma at ensuring quality? Let's answer that by posing a question. In your opinion, is 99.9 percent effective enough? That may depend, but consider this: At 99.9 percent effectiveness, twelve babies would be given to the wrong parents each day, 22,000 checks would be deducted from the incorrect checking accounts each hour, and two planes a day would fail to land safely at Chicago's O'Hare International Airport.[8] That's definitely not what anyone intends. Accordingly, six sigma is designed to decrease defects to fewer than four per million items produced. That's a significant improvement considering that just a decade ago, three sigma was a fairly standard objective by most organizations, but one that results in more than 66,000 defects per million.

six sigma
A philosophy and measurement process that attempts to "design in" quality as a product is being made.

Key Planning Guides

Once an organization's strategy and overall goals are in place, supervision in the company will design additional plans to help guide decision makers. Some of these will be standing plans that, once designed, can be used over and over again by managers faced with recurring activities. Others will be single-use plans, which are detailed courses of action used once or only occasionally to deal with problems that don't occur repeatedly. In this section, we review the popular types of each.

WHAT ARE STANDING PLANS?

Standing plans allow supervisors to save time by handling similar situations in a predetermined and consistent manner. For example, when a supervisor has an employee who increasingly fails to show up for work, the problem can be handled more efficiently and consistently if a discipline procedure has been established in advance. Let's review the three major types of standing plans: policies, procedures, and rules.

standing plan
A plan that can be used over and over again by managers faced with recurring situations.

---

[7]T. Aeppel, "Career Journal: Nicknamed 'Nag,' She's Just Doing Her Job," *Wall Street Journal*, May 14, 2002, B-1.
[8]For another view on this topic, see "Why You Can Safely Ignore Six Sigma," *Fortune*, January 22, 2001, 140.

policies
Broad guidelines for supervisory action.

Policies "We promote from within wherever possible." "Do whatever it takes to satisfy the customer." "Our employees should be paid competitive wages." These three statements are examples of policies—that is, broad guidelines for supervisory action. Typically established by top management, they define the limits within which supervisors must stay as they make decisions.

Supervisors rarely make policies. Rather, they interpret and apply them. Within the parameters that policies set, supervisors must use their judgment. For instance, the company policy that "our employees should be paid competitive wages" doesn't tell a supervisor what to pay a new employee. However, if the going hourly rate in the community for this specific job is in the $16.20–$19.50 range, the company policy would clarify that offering a starting hourly rate of either $14.75 or $26.00 is not acceptable.

Procedures Suppose a purchasing supervisor receives a request from the engineering department for five computer-assisted-design workstations. The purchasing supervisor checks to see whether the requisition has been properly filled out and approved. If not, she sends the requisition back with a note explaining what is deficient. When the request is complete, the approximate costs are estimated. If the total exceeds $15,000, which they do in this case, three bids must be obtained. If the total had been $15,000 or less, only one vendor would need to have been identified and the order could have been placed.

procedure
A standardized way of responding to repetitive problems; a definition of the limits within which supervisors must stay as decisions are made.

The previous series of steps for responding to a recurring problem is an example of a procedure. Where procedures exist, supervisors only have to identify the problem. Once the problem is clear, so is the procedure to handle it. In contrast to policies, procedures are more specific; like policies, they provide consistency. By defining the steps that are to be taken and the order in which they are to be done, procedures provide a standardized way of responding to repetitive problems.

Supervisors follow procedures set by higher levels of management and also create their own procedures for their staff to follow. As conditions change and new problems surface that tend to recur, supervisors develop standardized procedures for handling them. When the service department of a local Chevrolet dealership began accepting debit cards for payment, the department's supervisor had to create a procedure for processing such transactions, and then carefully train all the service agents and cashiers in how to handle such a transaction.

rule
An explicit statement that tells employees what they ought or ought not to do.

Rules A rule is an explicit statement that tells an employee what he or she ought or ought not to do. Rules are frequently used by supervisors to confront a recurring problem because they are simple to follow and ensure consistency. In the previous example, the $15,000 cutoff rule simplifies the purchasing supervisor's decision about when to use multiple bids. Similarly, rules about lateness and absenteeism permit supervisors to make discipline decisions rapidly and with a high degree of fairness.

single-use plan
A detailed course of action used once or only occasionally to deal with a problem that doesn't occur repeatedly.

WHAT ARE SINGLE-USE PLANS?

In contrast to the previous discussions of standing plans, single-use plans are designed for a specific activity or time period. The most popular types of these plans are programs, budgets, and schedules.

When you see a sign like this one, what does it mean to you? Is it a suggestion? A general guideline? No! It's a statement of what you must do or not do. Accordingly, we call such "signs" rules.

Programs Mike Arnold got the news at a meeting on Monday morning. His company—American Airlines—was going to lay off a thousand employees. As the baggage-handling supervisor for American's Dallas hub, he was told to put together a reorganization plan that would allow his department to operate effectively with as many as 20 percent fewer workers. What Mike developed was a program—a single-use set of plans for a specific major undertaking within the organization's overall goals. It included a list of the most expendable employees, plans for new equipment, plans for redesigning the handling area, and suggested options for jobs that could be potentially combined.

All supervisors develop programs. A major program—such as building a new manufacturing plant or merging two companies and consolidating their headquarters' staff—will tend to be designed and overseen by top management. It may extend over several years and may even require its own set of policies and procedures. Supervisors also frequently have to create programs for their departments. Some examples include the departmental reorganization at American Airlines, mentioned previously; creation of a comprehensive ad campaign by an advertising account supervisor for a new client; or development by a regional sales supervisor for Hallmark of a training program to teach her staff a new phone-activated, computerized inventory system. Note the common thread through all these examples: They are nonrecurring undertakings that require a set of integrated plans to accomplish their objectives.

program
A single-use set of plans for a specific major undertaking within an organization's overall goals. Programs may be designed and overseen by top management or supervisors.

Budgets Budgets are numerical plans. They typically express anticipated results in dollar terms for a specific time period. For example, a department may budget $30,000 this year for employee computer training. Budgets may also be calculated in nondollar terms—for example, employee hours, capacity utilization, or units of production. Budgets may cover daily, weekly, monthly, quarterly, semiannual, or annual periods.

budget
A numerical plan that expresses anticipated results in dollar terms for a specific time period; used as a planning guide as well as a control device.

Comprehension Check 3-1

1. Planning that covers the entire organization in establishing the overall goals is called
   a. tactical planning
   b. long-term planning
   c. strategic planning
   d. organizational planning

2. When a company searches for the best practices among competitors, this is called
   a. strategic planning
   b. benchmarking
   c. work process engineering
   d. all of the above

3. The philosophy and measurement process that attempts to "design in" quality is called
   a. six sigma
   b. benchmarking
   c. work process engineering
   d. *kaizen*

4. A broad guideline that defines limits within which supervisors must stay is called a
   a. procedure
   b. rule
   c. policy
   d. code of ethics

Budgets are covered here as part of the planning process. However, they are also control devices. The preparation of a budget involves planning because it gives direction. The creation of a budget tells what activities are important and how resources should be allocated to each activity. A budget becomes a control mechanism when it provides standards against which resource consumption can be measured and compared.

Department Expense Budget
Calendar Year 2013

ITEM	QUARTER			
	1st	2nd	3rd	4th
Salaries/Fixed	$33,600	$33,600	$33,600	$33,600
Salaries/Variable	3,000	5,000	3,000	10,000
Performance Bonuses				12,000
Office Supplies	800	800	800	800
Photocopying	1,000	1,000	1,000	1,000
Telephone	2,500	2,500	2,500	2,500
Mail	800	800	800	800
Travel	2,500	1,000	1,000	1,000
Employee Development	600	600	600	600
Total Quarterly Expenses	$44,800	$45,300	$43,300	$62,300

Exhibit 3-4

Department expense budget.

If there is one type of plan in which almost every manager at any level gets involved, it's the budget. Supervisors typically prepare their department's expense budget and submit it to the manager at the next higher level for review and approval (see Exhibit 3-4). Supervisors may also, depending on their needs, create budgets for employee work hours, revenue forecasts, or capital expenditures such as machinery and equipment. Once approved by higher management, these budgets set specific standards for supervisors and their departmental personnel to achieve.

Schedules If you were to observe a group of supervisors or department managers for a few days, you would see them regularly detailing what activities have to be done, the order in which the activities are to be done, who is to do each, and when the activities are to be completed. These supervisors are performing an activity called scheduling.

Two popular scheduling techniques that can help you prioritize activities and complete work on time are the Gantt chart and the PERT chart. The Gantt chart was developed early in the twentieth century by an industrial engineer named Henry Gantt. The idea was inherently simple but has proved extremely helpful in scheduling work activities. The Gantt chart is essentially a bar graph with time on the horizontal axis and activities to be scheduled on the vertical axis. The bars show output, both planned and actual, over a period of time. The Gantt chart visually shows when tasks are supposed to be done and compares that to the actual progress on each. As stated, it is a simple but important device that allows managers to detail easily what has yet to be done to complete a job or project and to assess whether it is ahead, behind, or on schedule.

Exhibit 3-5 depicts a simplified Gantt chart that was developed for producing a book by a supervisor in the production department of a publishing firm. Time is expressed in months across the top of the chart. The major activities are listed down the left side. The planning comes in deciding what activities need to be done to get the book finished, the order in which they need to be done, and the time that should be allocated to each activity. Where a box sits within a time frame reflects its planned sequence. The shading represents actual progress. The chart also becomes a control device when the supervisor looks for deviations from the plan.

Gantt charts are helpful as long as the activities being scheduled are few in number and independent of each other. But what if a supervisor had to plan a large project such as reorganizing a department, launching a cost-reduction campaign, or installing a major piece of new equipment? Such projects often require coordinating hundreds

scheduling

Detailed planning of activities to be done, the order in which they are to be done, who is to do each activity, and when the activities are to be completed.

Gantt chart

A bar chart with time on the horizontal axis and activities to be scheduled on the vertical axis; shows when tasks are supposed to be done and compares actual progress on each task.

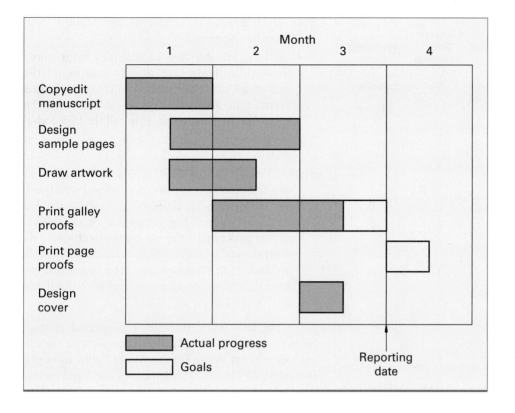

Exhibit 3-5
A sample Gantt chart.

of activities, some of which must be done simultaneously and some of which cannot begin until other activities have been completed. If you're constructing a building, for example, you obviously can't start erecting walls until the foundation is poured. How, then, can you schedule such a complex project? You could use a Program Evaluation and Review Technique (PERT) chart.

A **PERT chart** is a diagram that depicts the sequence of activities needed to complete a project and the time or costs associated with each activity. The PERT chart was originally developed in the late 1950s for coordinating the more than 3,000 contractors and agencies working on the Polaris submarine weapon system. This project was incredibly complicated, with hundreds of thousands of activities that had to be coordinated. PERT is reported to have cut two years off the completion date for the Polaris project.

A PERT chart can be a valuable tool in the hands of a supervisor. With a PERT chart, a supervisor must think through what has to be done, determine which events depend on one another, and identify potential trouble spots. A PERT chart makes it easy to compare what effect alternative actions will have on scheduling and costs. Thus, PERT allows supervisors to monitor a project's progress, identify possible bottlenecks, and shift resources as necessary to keep the project on schedule.

To understand how to construct a PERT chart, you need to know three terms: events, activities, and critical path. Let's define these terms, outline the steps in the PERT process, and then work through an example.

Events are endpoints that represent the completion of major activities. **Activities** represent the time or resources required to progress from one event to another. The **critical path** is the longest or most time-consuming sequence of events and activities in a PERT chart. Developing a PERT chart requires the supervisor to identify all key activities needed to complete a project, rank them in order of dependence, and estimate each activity's completion time. This can be translated into five specific steps:

STEP 1: Identify every significant activity that must be achieved for a project to be completed. The accomplishment of each activity results in a set of events or outcomes.

PERT chart
A diagram that depicts the sequence of activities needed to complete a project and the time or costs associated with each activity.

events
Endpoints that represent completion of major activities.

activities
The time or resources required to progress from one event to another.

critical path
The longest or most time-consuming sequence of events and activities in a PERT chart.

Event	Description	Expected Time (in weeks)	Preceding Event
A	Approve design	8	None
B	Get construction permits	4	None
C	Take bids on new furnace and its installation	6	A
D	Order new furnace and equipment	1	C
E	Remove old furnace	2	B
F	Prepare site	3	E
G	Install new furnace	2	D, F
H	Test new furnace	1	G
I	Train workers to handle new furnace	2	G
J	Final inspection by company and city officials	2	H
K	Bring furnace on-line into production flow	1	I, J

Exhibit 3-6

Data for the furnace modernization project.

STEP 2: Determine the order in which these events must be completed.

STEP 3: Diagram the flow of activities from start to finish, identifying each activity and its relationship to all other activities. Use circles to indicate events and arrows to represent activities. This results in the diagram that we call the PERT chart.

STEP 4: Compute a time estimate for completing each activity.

STEP 5: Finally, using a PERT chart that contains time estimates for each activity, determine a schedule for the start and finish dates of each activity and for the entire project. Any delays that occur along the critical path require the most attention because they delay the entire project. That is, the critical path has no slack in it; therefore, any delay along that path immediately translates into a delay in the final deadline for the completed project.

Now let's work through a simplified example. Suppose you're the production supervisor in the casting department at the Benson Metal Fabricators plant in eastern Michigan. You have proposed and received approval from corporate management to replace one of three massive furnaces with a new, state-of-the-art electronic furnace. This project will seriously disrupt the operations in your department, so you want to complete it as quickly and as smoothly as possible. You have carefully dissected the entire project into activities and events. Exhibit 3-6 outlines the major events in the furnace modernization project and your estimate of the expected time required to complete each activity. Exhibit 3-7 depicts the PERT chart based on the data in Exhibit 3-6. Your PERT chart tells you that if everything goes as planned, it will take twenty-one weeks to complete the modernization program. This is calculated by tracing the chart's critical path: Start-A-C-D-G-H-J-K-Finish. Any delay in completing the events along this path will delay the completion of the entire project. For example, if it took six weeks instead of four to get construction permits (activity B), this would have no effect on the final completion date. Why? Because Start-B + B-E + E-F + F-G equals only eleven weeks, while Start-A + A-C + C-D + D-G equals seventeen weeks. However, if you wanted to cut the twenty-one-week time frame, you would give attention to those activities along the critical path that could be speeded up.

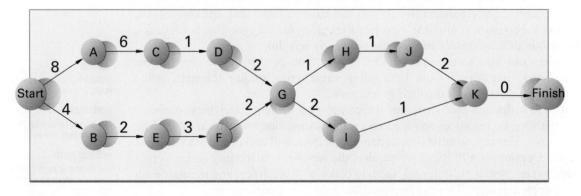

Exhibit 3-7

PERT chart for the furnace modernization project.

Something to Think About (and promote class discussion)

FROM THE PAST TO THE PRESENT

Management by objectives (MBO) is not new. The concept goes back over fifty years when Peter Drucker first popularized the term in his 1954 book *The Practice of Management*.* Its appeal lies in its emphasis on converting overall objectives into specific objectives for organizational units and individual members.

MBO makes goals operational by a process in which they cascade down through the organization. The organization's overall objectives are translated into specific objectives for each succeeding level—division, departmental, individual—in the organization. The result is a hierarchy that links objectives at one level to those at the next level. For the individual employee, MBO provides specific personal performance objectives. If all the individuals achieve their goals, then the unit's goals will be attained. Likewise, if all the units attain their goals, then the divisional goals will be met until ultimately the organization's overall goals will become a reality.

Does MBO work? Assessing the effectiveness of MBO is a complex task. But goal-setting research can give us some answers. For instance, research has shown that specific, difficult-to-achieve goals produce a higher level of output than do no goals or generalized goals such as "do your best." Also, feedback favorably affects performance because it lets a person know whether his or her level of effort is sufficient or needs to be increased. These findings are consistent with MBO's emphasis on specific goals and feedback. What about participation, though, since MBO strongly advocates that goals be set participatively? Research comparing participatively set goals with assigned goals has not shown any strong or consistent relationship to performance. One critical factor in the success of any MBO program, however, is top management commitment to the process. When top managers had a high commitment to MBO and were personally involved in its implementation, productivity gains were higher than if this commitment was lacking.

---

*"From the Past to the Present" box based on P. F. Drucker, *The Practice of Management* (New York: Harper & Row, 1954); J. F. Castellano and H. A. Roehm, "The Problem with Managing by Objectives and Results," *Quality Progress* 34, no. 3 (March 2001), 39–46; J. Loehr and T. Schwartz, "The Making of a Corporate Athlete," *Harvard Business Review* (January 2001), 120–128; A. J. Vogl, "Drucker, of Course," *Across the Board* (November–December 2000), 1. For information on goals and goal setting, see, for example, E. A. Locke, "Toward a Theory of Task Motivation and Incentives," *Organizational Behavior and Human Performance* 3, no. 2 (May 1968), 157–189; E. A. Locke, K. N. Shaw, L. M. Saari, and G. P. Latham, "Goal Setting and Task Performance: 1969–1980," *Psychological Bulletin* (July 1981), 12–52; E. A. Locke and G. P. Latham, *A Theory of Goal Setting and Task Performance* (Upper Saddle River, NJ: Prentice Hall, 1990); P. Ward and M. Carnes, "Effects of Posting Self-Set Goals on Collegiate Football Players' Skill Execution During Practice and Games," *Journal of Applied Behavioral Analysis* 35, no. 1 (Spring 2002), 1–12; D. W. Ray, "Productivity and Profitability," *Executive Excellence* (October 2001), 14; D. Archer, "Evaluating Your Managed System," *CMA Management* (January 2000), 12–14; and C. Antoni, "Management by Objectives: An Effective Tool for Teamwork," *International Journal of Human Resource Management* 16, no. 2, (February 2005), 174–184. For information on participation in goal setting, see, for example, T. D. Ludwig and E. S. Geller, "Intervening to Improve the Safety of Delivery Drivers: A Systematic Behavioral Approach," *Journal of Organizational Behavior Management* 24, no. 1 (April 4, 2000), 11–24; P. Latham and L. M. Saari, "The Effects of Holding Goal Difficulty Constant on Assigned and Participatively Set Goals," *Academy of Management Journal* 22, no. 1 (March 1979), 163–168; M. Erez, P. C. Earley, and C. L. Hulin, "The Impact of Participation on Goal Acceptance and Performance: A Two Step Model," *Academy of Management Journal* 28, no. 1 (March 1985), 50–66; and G. P. Latham, M. Erez, and E. A. Locke, "Resolving Scientific Disputes by the Joint Design of Crucial Experiments by the Antagonists: Application to the Erez Latham Dispute Regarding Participation in Goal Setting," *Journal of Applied Psychology* 73, no. 4 (November 1988), 753–772. For information on effectiveness of MBO, see, for example, F. Dahlsten, A. Styhre, and M. Williander, "The Unintended Consequences of Management by Objectives: The Volume Growth Target at Volvo Cars," *Leadership & Organization Development Journal* 26, no. 7 (July 2005), 529–541; J. R. Crow, "Crashing with the Nose Up: Building a Cooperative Work Environment," *Journal for Quality and Participation* 25, no. 1 (Spring 2002), 45–50; and E. C. Hollensbe and J. P. Guthrie, "Group Pay-for-Performance Plans: The Role of Spontaneous Goal Setting," *Academy of Management Review* 25, no. 4 (October 2000), 864–872.

Goal Setting

goal setting
A system by which employees jointly determine specific performance goals with their supervisors. Progress toward goals is periodically reviewed, and rewards are allocated on the basis of this progress.

Many supervisors are helping their employees set performance goals in an effort to achieve departmental and organizational goals. One means of doing this is through a process called goal setting, which is the next generation of the management practice called management by objectives (MBO). In this system, employees jointly determine specific performance goals with their supervisors. Progress toward goals is periodically reviewed, and rewards are allocated on the basis of this progress. Rather than using goals to control, goal setting uses them to motivate people.

Goal setting makes objectives operational by devising a process by which they cascade down through the organization. The organization's overall goals are translated into specific goals for each succeeding level (e.g., divisional, departmental, individual) in the organization. Because lower-unit managers jointly participate in setting their own goals, goal setting works from the bottom up as well as from the top down. The result is a hierarchy that links goals at one level to those at the next level. That's not how organizational members did things in the past.

HOW WERE GOALS SET IN YEARS PAST?

The traditional role of goals in organizations was one of control imposed by top management. The president of a manufacturing firm would typically tell the production vice president what he expected manufacturing costs to be for the coming year. The president would tell the marketing vice president what level she should expect sales to reach for the coming year. The plant manager would tell her maintenance supervisor how much his departmental budget would be. Then, at some later point, performance would be evaluated to determine whether the assigned goals had been achieved.

The central theme in traditional goal setting was that goals were set at the top, and then were broken down into subgoals for each level in the organization. It was a one-way process: The top imposed its standards on everyone below. This traditional perspective assumed that top management knew what was best because only it could see the "big picture."

In addition to being imposed from above, traditional goal setting was often largely nonoperational. If top management defined the organization's goals in broad terms such as achieving "sufficient profits" or "market leadership," these ambiguities had to be turned into specifics as the goals filtered down through the organization. At each level, managers would supply their own meaning to the goals. Specificity was achieved by each manager applying his or her own set of interpretations and biases. As shown in Exhibit 3-8, the result was that goals lost clarity and unity as they made their way down from the top.

WHAT IS THE KEY TO MAKING GOAL SETTING EFFECTIVE?

There are four ingredients common to goal-setting programs: goal specificity, participation, time limits, and performance feedback. Let's look at each of these.

Goal Specificity Goals should be specific statements of expected accomplishments. It's not adequate, for example, merely to state a desire to cut costs, improve service, or increase quality. Such desires have to be converted into tangible goals that can be measured and evaluated. To cut departmental costs by 7 percent, to improve service

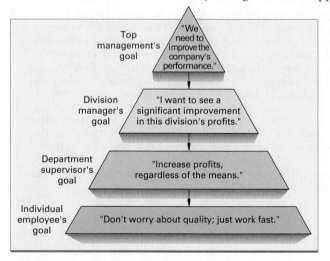

Exhibit 3-8
What may happen in traditional goal setting.

by ensuring that all telephone orders are processed within twenty-four hours of receipt, or to increase quality by keeping returns to less than 1 percent of sales are examples of specific goals.

Participation In goal setting the goals are not unilaterally set by the boss and assigned to employees, as was characteristic of traditional goal setting. Instead, goal setting replaces these imposed goals with jointly determined goals. Together, the supervisor and employee choose the goals and agree on how they will be achieved and evaluated (see the section titled "Goal Setting" earlier in this chapter).

Time Limits Each goal has a concise time period in which it is to be completed. Typically, the time period is three months, six months, or a year. So, everyone has not only specific goals, but also a specific time period in which to accomplish them.

Performance Feedback The final ingredient in a goal-setting program is feedback on performance. Goal setting seeks to give continuous feedback on progress toward goals. Ideally, this is accomplished by providing ongoing feedback to individuals so that they can monitor and correct their own actions. This is supplemented by periodic formal appraisal meetings in which supervisors and employees can review progress toward goals and further feedback can be provided.

WHY MIGHT GOAL SETTING WORK FOR YOU?

There are several reasons why goal setting works, and why it can help you be a more effective supervisor. First, it gives both you and your employees clarity and direction in your jobs. Your employees will know what's important to you in their jobs—and the specific outcomes by which their performance will be judged. Second, goal setting increases your employees' involvement, commitment, and motivation. They'll feel more empowered because they will have the freedom to choose the means for achieving their goals. That is, it's the goals that are important to you. How they do it is not the focal point. Additionally, providing regular feedback on their performance and tying rewards to the achievement of objectives act to stimulate employee motivation. Finally, goal setting can minimize the politics in performance appraisals and reward allocations. Subjective factors—such as an employee's effort and attitude, or your prejudices—are replaced by objective measures of performance and rewards based on that performance.

SELF-FULFILLING PROPHECY FOR YOUR FOLLOWERS

Behave in a positive fashion when setting goals with your employees. Research indicates that effective supervisors behave in a way that leads to superior employee performance, but unfortunately supervisors are better at communicating low expectations than they are at communicating high expectations.

Consider that every supervisor has expectations of their subordinates. Supervisors communicate positive and negative expectations consciously and unconsciously; subordinates are effective at picking up on the expectations of their supervisor, and subordinates' behavior is generally consistent with the perceived expectations of their supervisor. So, even if it requires some acting, behave as though you believe in the overwhelming greatness and ability of your subordinates and let them rise to their perception of your expectations![9]

---

[9]J. S. Livingston, "Pygmalion in Management," *Harvard Business Review* 66, no. 5 (September–October 1988), 121–130; and "TAU Researchers Examine 'Great Expectations' in the Workplace," American Friends of Tel Aviv University, April 29, 2008, www.aftau.org/site/News2?page=NewsArticle&id=6927 (accessed May 14, 2008).

BALANCED SCORECARD: THE NATURAL EVOLUTION OF GOAL SETTING?

Balanced Scorecard

A strategic planning and management system used to translate and align business activities to the vision statement of a business after review of the company's financial processes, customer processes, internal processes, and innovation/growth processes.

The balanced scorecard approach is a way to evaluate organizational performance from more than just the financial perspective.[10] A balanced scorecard typically looks at four areas that contribute to a company's performance: financial, customer, internal processes, and people/innovation/growth assets. According to this approach, supervisors should develop goals in each of the four areas and then measure whether the goals are being met.

Although a balanced scorecard makes sense, supervisors will tend to focus on areas that drive their organization's success and use scorecards that reflect those strategies.[11] For example, if strategies are customer centered, then the customer area is likely to get more attention than the other three areas. Yet, you can't focus on measuring only one performance area because others are affected as well. For instance, at IBM Global Services in Houston, supervisors developed a scorecard around an overriding strategy of customer satisfaction. However, the other areas (financial, internal processes, and people/innovation/growth) support that central strategy. The division manager described it as follows, "The internal processes part of our business is directly related to responding to our customers in a timely manner, and the learning and innovation aspect is critical for us since what we're selling our customers above all is our expertise. Of course, how successful we are with those things will affect our financial component."[12]

A Special Case of Planning: The Entrepreneurial Supervisor

You have heard the story dozens of times. With only an idea, a few hundred dollars, and use of the family garage, someone starts what eventually becomes a multi-billion-dollar global corporation. Formal planning often carries a "big business" bias. It implies a formality that fits well with large, established organizations that have abundant resources. But the primary interest of many students is not in managing large and established organizations. That desire, coupled with changes in technology, the economy, and social conditions such as two-income families, has fostered an increase in entrepreneurial startup companies. Like the "Google Guys" Larry Page and Sergey Brin, Hotmail founders Jack Smith and Sabeer Bhatia, Groupon creator Andrew Maso, or Jack Dorsey of Twitter, they are excited about the idea of starting their own business from scratch—an action that is called entrepreneurship.

Entrepreneurial

Willing to use initiative and take risks in order to make a profit.

WHAT IS ENTREPRENEURSHIP?

entrepreneurship

The process of initiating a business venture, organizing the necessary resources, and assuming the risks and rewards.

Entrepreneurship is the process of starting new businesses, generally in response to opportunities. Many people think that entrepreneurial ventures and small businesses are the same, but they're not. Entrepreneurs create entrepreneurial ventures—organizations

---

[10]R. S. Kaplan and D. P. Norton, "How to Implement a New Strategy Without Disrupting Your Organization," *Harvard Business Review* (March 2006), 100–109; L. Bassi and D. McMurrer, "Developing Measurement Systems for Managers in the Knowledge Era," *Organizational Dynamics* (May 2005), 185–196; G. M. J. DeKoning, "Making the Balanced Scorecard Work (Part 2)," *Gallup Brain*, August 12, 2004, http://gmj.gallup.com/content/12571/making-balanced-scorecard-work-part. aspx (accessed October 14, 2011); G. J. J. DeKoning, "Making the Balanced Scorecard Work (Part 1)," *Gallup Brain*, July 8, 2004, http://gmj.gallup.com/content/12208/making-balanced-scorecard-work-part.aspx (accessed October 14, 2011); K. Graham, "Balanced Scorecard," *New Zealand Management* (March 2003), 32–34; K. Ellis, "A Ticket to Ride: Balanced Scorecard," *Training* (April 2001), 50; and T. Leahy, "Tailoring the Balanced Scorecard," *Business Finance* (August 2000), 53–56.
[11]Leahy, "Tailoring the Balanced Scorecard."
[12]Ibid.

that pursue new opportunities, are characterized by innovative practices, and have growth and profitability as their main goals. Even though entrepreneurial ventures may start small, they pursue growth, and entrepreneurship itself is growing. "According to the 'Kauffman Index of Entrepreneurial Activity,' a leading indicator of new business creation in the United States, 0.34 percent of American adults created a business per month in 2010, or 565,000 new businesses, a rate that remained consistent with 2009 and represents the highest level of entrepreneurship over the past decade and a half. In contrast, however, the quarterly employer firm rate has dropped from 0.13 percent in 2007 to 0.10 percent in 2010."[13]

However, as many entrepreneurs (successful and not-so-successful) would attest, being an entrepreneur isn't easy. According to a new study by the Small Business Administration, two-thirds of new employer establishments survive at least two years, and 44 percent survive at least four years.[14] These results were similar for different industries, but the interesting thing is that entrepreneurial venture survival rates are about the same in economic expansions and recessions.

In comparison to entrepreneurial ventures, a small business is an independent business having fewer than five hundred employees that doesn't necessarily engage in any new or innovative practices and that has relatively little impact on its industry. Any small business isn't necessarily entrepreneurial because it's small and some new small firms may grow, but many remain small businesses, by choice or by default. It is important not to confuse supervising in a small business with entrepreneurship. Why? Because not all small-business supervisors are entrepreneurs. Many do not innovate. A great many supervisors in small businesses are merely scaled-down versions of the conservative, conforming bureaucrats who staff many large corporations and public agencies. Those who do act like entrepreneurs—creating the intensity and entrepreneurial spirit—in larger organizations are sometimes called *intrapreneurs*.[15] However, in such organizations, intrapreneurs do not have the autonomy to do what they want, and neither do they deal with the amount of risk entrepreneurs do. However, their efforts to be bold and creative, while not always having the financial independence, do go a long way in helping advance their careers.

DO ENTREPRENEURS POSSESS SIMILAR CHARACTERISTICS?

One of the most researched topics in entrepreneurship has been the search to determine what, if any, psychological characteristics entrepreneurs have in common. A number of common characteristics have been found, and one list of personality characteristics included the following: high level of motivation, abundance of self-confidence, ability to be involved for the long term, high energy level, persistent problem solver, high degree of initiative, ability to set goals, and moderate risk-taker. Another list of characteristics of "successful" entrepreneurs included high energy level, great persistence, resourcefulness, the desire and ability to be self-directed, and relatively high need for autonomy. Another development in defining entrepreneurial personality characteristics was the proactive personality scale to predict an individual's likelihood of pursuing entrepreneurial ventures. The proactive personality is a personality trait describing

[13]R. Weitekamp and B. Pruitt, " 'Jobless Entrepreneurship' Tarnishes Steady Rate of U.S. Startup Activity, Kauffman Study Shows," *Kauffman Foundation*, March 7, 2011, http://www.kauffman.org/newsroom/jobless-entrepreneurship-tarnishes-steady-rate-of-us-startup-activity.aspx (accessed May 12, 2011).

[14]A. E. Knaup, "Survival and Longevity in the Business Employment Dynamics Database," *Monthly Labor Review Online* 128, no. 5 (May 2005), 50–56, http://www.bls.gov/opub/mlr/2005/05/ressum.pdf (accessed May 12, 2011).

[15]J. S. Hornsby, D. E. Kuratko, and S. A. Zahara, "Middle Managers' Perception of the Internal Environment for Corporate Entrepreneurship: Assessing a Measurement Scale," *Journal of Business Venturing* 17, no. 2 (May 2002), 253–273; and E. Batten, "Out of the Blue and into the Black," *Harvard Business Review* (April 2002), 112–119.

those individuals who are more prone to take actions to influence their environment—that is, they're more proactive.[16]

The research allows us to draw a general description of entrepreneurs. They tend to be independent types who prefer to be personally responsible for solving problems, for setting goals, and for reaching those goals by their own efforts. They plan extensively and the most important thing that an entrepreneur does in planning the venture is developing a business plan—a written document that summarizes a business opportunity and defines and articulates how the identified opportunity is to be seized and exploited. A written business plan can range from basic to thorough. The most basic type of business plan would simply include an executive summary, sort of a mini–business plan that's no longer than two pages. A synopsis-type plan is a little more involved. It's been described as an "executive summary on steroids." In addition to the executive summary, it includes a business proposal that explains why the idea is relevant to potential investors. A summary business plan includes an executive summary and a page or so of explanation of each of the key components of a business plan. A full business plan is the traditional business plan. Finally, an operational business plan is the most detailed (fifty or more pages) since it's used by ventures that are already operating with an existing strategy.[17]

Entrepreneurs also value independence and particularly do not like being controlled by others. They are not afraid of taking chances, but they are not wild risk takers. That is, entrepreneurs prefer to take calculated risks where they feel that they can control the outcome.

The evidence on entrepreneurial personalities leads us to several conclusions. First, people with this personality makeup are not likely to be contented, productive employees in the typical large corporation or government agency. The rules, regulations, and controls that these bureaucracies impose on their members frustrate entrepreneurs. Second, the challenges and conditions inherent in starting one's own business mesh well with the entrepreneurial personality. Starting a new venture, which they control, appeals to their willingness to take risks and determine their own destinies. But because entrepreneurs believe that their future is fully in their own hands, the risk they perceive as moderate is often seen as high by nonentrepreneurs. Finally, the cultural context in which individuals were raised will have an effect. For instance, in the former East Germany, where the cultural environment exhibits high power distance and high uncertainty avoidance (see the discussion of Geert Hofstede in Chapter 2), many of the associated entrepreneurial characteristics—such as initiative and risk taking—are lacking.

HOW DO ENTREPRENEURS COMPARE WITH TRADITIONAL SUPERVISORS?

Exhibit 3-9 summarizes some key differences between entrepreneurs and traditional supervisors. Whereas the latter tend to be custodial, entrepreneurs actively seek change by exploiting opportunities. When searching for these opportunities, entrepreneurs often put their personal financial security at risk. The hierarchy in large organizations typically insulates traditional supervisors from these financial wagers and rewards them for minimizing risks and avoiding failures.

business plan

A document that identifies the business founder's vision and describes the strategy and operations of that business.

---

[16]S. Robbins, D. Decenzo, and M. Coulter, *Fundamentals of Management* (Upper Saddle River, NJ: Prentice Hall, 2011).

[17]Ibid.

	Traditional Supervisors	**Entrepreneurs/Intrapreneurs**
Primary motivation	Promotion and other traditional corporate rewards such as office, staff, and power	Independence, opportunity to create, financial gain
Time orientation	Achievement of short-term goals	Achievement of five- to ten-year growth of business
Activity	Delegation and supervision	Direct involvement
Risk propensity	Low	Moderate
View toward failures and mistakes	Avoidance	Acceptance

Exhibit 3-9

Comparison of entrepreneurs and traditional supervisors.

Source: *Adapted from* Intrapreneuring *by G. Pinchot, 1985, New York: Harper & Row.*

Comprehension Check **3-2**

5. A diagram that depicts the sequence of activities needed to complete a project and the time or costs associated with each activity is called a
   a. Gantt chart
   b. PERT chart
   c. load chart
   d. critical path chart

6. The longest length of time it takes to complete a project in the shortest amount of time is called the
   a. PERT chart analysis
   b. Gantt chart perspective
   c. activity analysis
   d. critical path

7. The following descriptors are consistent with which type of person: bold, innovative, taking initiatives, and risk-taking?
   a. Top managers
   b. Entrepreneurs
   c. First-line supervisors
   d. Charismatic leaders

8. A document that identifies the vision of the organization and describes the goals and operations of the business is called a
   a. business plan
   b. strategic plan
   c. tactical plan
   d. code of ethics

Enhancing Understanding

SUMMARY

After reading this chapter, I can:

1. Define *productivity*. In its simplest form, productivity can be expressed in terms of the following ratio: outputs divided by labor plus capital, plus materials. Productivity can also be calculated for three different areas: the individual, a workgroup, and the total organization.

2. **Describe how plans should link from the top to the bottom of an organization.** Long-term strategic plans are typically set by top management. Then, each succeeding level down the organization develops its plans. Plans at each level should help to accomplish those for the level above and give direction for the level below.

3. Identify what is meant by the terms *benchmarking, ISO 9000 series, and six sigma. Benchmarking* is a term that reflects the search for best practices among competitors or noncompetitors that lead to the identification and implementation of enhanced performance. The *ISO 9000 series*, designed by the International Organization for Standardization, reflects a process whereby independent auditors attest that a company's factory, laboratory, or office has met certain quality standards. *Six sigma* is a philosophy and measurement process that attempts to "design in" quality as a product is being made.

4. **Contrast policies and rules.** Policies and rules are both standing plans. Policies are broad statements that leave room for supervisory discretion. Rules, on the other hand, are explicit statements that tell supervisors what they can and cannot do. Rules do not allow supervisory discretion.

5. **Describe the Gantt chart.** The Gantt chart is a simple scheduling device. It is a bar graph with time on the horizontal axis and activities on the vertical axis. It shows planned and actual activities, and it allows supervisors to easily identify the status of a job or project.

6. **Explain the information needed to create a PERT chart.** To create a PERT chart, you need to identify all key activities needed to complete a project, their order of dependence, and an estimate of each activity's completion time.

7. **Describe the four ingredients common to goal-setting programs.** Goal setting is a system in which specific performance goals are jointly determined by employees and their supervisors. Progress toward attaining goals is periodically reviewed, and rewards are allocated on the basis of the progress. The four ingredients common to goal-setting programs are goal specificity, participation, time limits, and performance feedback.

8. **Define *entrepreneurship* and explain how it affects supervision.** Entrepreneurship is the process of initiating a business venture, organizing the necessary resources, and assuming the risks and rewards in making things happen. Entrepreneurs approach planning by first seeking out opportunities that they can exploit, and then working to make things happen. Traditional supervisors often approach planning by first determining the availability of their resources, and then taking what action they can.

COMPREHENSION: Review and Discussion Questions

1. Why is productivity so important to organizations and their members?

2. Contrast the planning top managers do with that done by supervisors.

3. Under what circumstances are short-term plans preferred? Under what circumstances are specific plans preferred?

4. Why do companies benchmark their operations with other organizations in their industry?

5. Do you believe that obtaining certifications such as six sigma or ISO 9000 really helps an organization compete? Discuss your position.

6. Explain how budgets are both a planning and a control device.

7. How might you use a Gantt chart to schedule a group term paper for a college class?

8. What are the implications of the critical path for PERT analysis?

9. Why has goal setting proved so popular in organizations?

10. What differentiates a traditional supervisor in a small business from an entrepreneurial supervisor? An intrapreneur?

KEY CONCEPT CROSSWORD

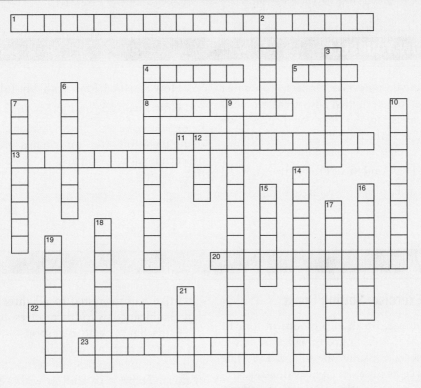

ACROSS

1. a system by which employees jointly determine specific performance goals with their supervisors
4. a numerical plan
5. a diagram that depicts the sequencing of activities needed to complete a project
8. a plan used to deal with a problem once
11. the longest or most time-consuming sequence of events in a PERT chart
13. the time or resources required to progress from one event to another
20. the search for best practices
22. a plan that can be used over and over again
23. output per labor hour

DOWN

2. endpoints that represent completion of major activities
3. a set of plans for a specific major undertaking
4. the document that explains the business founder's vision and describes the strategy and operations of that business
6. a measurement process attempting to design in quality
7. a type of planning that establishes the overall goals and positioning of the organization
9. the process of initiating a business venture
10. detailed planning of activities to be done in the order in which they are to be done
12. an explicit statement that tells employees what they can and cannot do
14. a plan that covers a period from one to five years
15. broad guidelines for supervisory actions
16. a type of planning that provides specific details on how overall goals will be met
17. a plan that covers a period of less than one year
18. a standardized way of responding to repetitive problems
19. a plan that covers a period in excess of five years
21. a bar chart with time on one axis and activities on the other

ANSWERS TO COMPREHENSION CHECKS

Comprehension Check 3-1

1. c   2. b   3. a   4. c

Comprehension Check 3-2

5. b   6. d   7. b   8. a

Developing Your Supervisory Skills

GETTING TO KNOW YOURSELF

Before you can effectively supervise others, you must understand your present strengths and areas in need of development. To assist in this learning process, we encourage you to complete the following self-assessments from the Prentice Hall Self-Assessment Library 3.4.

1. What Time of the Day Am I Most Productive? (I. E. 2.)

2. How Good Am I at Personal Planning? (I. E. 3.)

3. How Satisfied Am I with My Job? (I. B. 3.)

4. How Involved Am I in My Job? (I. B. 2.)

After you complete the assessment, we suggest that you retain the results and store them as part of your "portfolio of learning about yourself."

BUILDING A TEAM

➤ An Experiential Exercise: Setting Goals

This is a role-play exercise. Break into groups of four to six students. One student in each group will assume the role of Chris, and one will assume the role of Lee. The other students will serve as observers and evaluators.

Michael Brooks has recently been promoted to the position of branch supervisor at one of the largest branches of Myer Company, a plumbing supply chain in the Midwest. His staff includes three project leaders who report directly to him, and another fifteen or so employees who work on these projects. One of these project leaders is responsible for directing the nine warehouse employees, while the other two direct showroom sales and the administrative functions, respectively. Mike reports to the owner.

Mike has suggested to all three project leaders that they establish goals for themselves and their employees.

Chris Smith, who is responsible for the warehouse, has set up a meeting with the most senior employee, Lee Brannigan, to begin the goal-setting process. The objective of this exercise is to end up with a set of goals for Lee. They might address issues such as prompt attention to customer needs, showing courtesy to customers, keeping proper inventory levels, and enhancing job skills.

This exercise should take no more than fifteen minutes. Afterward, the observers from each group should discuss with the entire class how their goal-setting session went. Focus specifically on the steps presented in the next section, "Setting Goals," and any problems that surfaced.

➤ Internet: Web Activity

Go to http://www.pearsonhighered.com/robbins/. Find *Supervision Today!* 7th Ed. and click Companion Website.

SETTING GOALS

We want to take the basic concepts of goal setting and turn them into specific goal-setting skills that you can apply on the job. Effective goal-setting skills can be condensed into eight specific behaviors. When you follow all eight, you will have mastered the skill of goal setting.

STEPS IN PRACTICING THE SKILL

STEP 1: Identify an employee's key job tasks. Goal setting begins with defining what you want your employees to accomplish. The best source for this information is each employee's up-to-date job description, if one is available. It details what tasks an employee is expected to perform, how these tasks are to be done, what outcomes the employee is responsible for achieving, and the like.

STEP 2: Establish specific and challenging goals for each task. This is self-explanatory. We should add that, if possible, these goals should be made public. When employees' goals are made public—announced in a group or posted for others to see—employees seem to be more highly committed to them.

STEP 3: Specify deadlines for each goal. Again, as previously discussed, goals should include a specific time limit for accomplishment.

STEP 4: Allow the employee to participate actively. Employees are less likely to question or resist a process in which they actively participate rather than one that is imposed upon them from above.

STEP 5: Prioritize goals. When someone is given more than one goal, it is important to rank the goals in order of importance. The purpose of this step is to encourage the employee to take action and expend effort on each goal in proportion to its importance.

STEP 6: Rate goals for difficulty and importance. Goal setting should not encourage people to choose easy goals to ensure success. So, goal setting needs to take into account the difficulty of the goals selected and whether individuals are emphasizing the right goals. When these ratings are combined with the actual level of goal achievement, you will have a more comprehensive assessment of overall goal performance. This procedure gives credit to individuals for trying difficult goals even if they don't fully achieve them.

STEP 7: Build in feedback mechanisms to assess goal progress. Ideally, feedback on goal progress should be self-generated rather than provided externally. When an employee is able to monitor his or her own progress, the feedback is less threatening and less likely to be perceived as part of a management control system.

STEP 8: Commit rewards contingent on goal attainment. Offering money, promotions, recognition, time off, or similar rewards to employees contingent on goal achievement is a powerful means to increase goal commitment. When the going gets tough on the road toward meeting a goal, people are prone to ask themselves, What's in it for me? Linking rewards to the achievement of goals helps employees answer this question.

▶ Communicating Effectively

1. "Supervisors that fail to plan formally are planning to fail." Do you agree or disagree with the statement? Explain your position.

2. Under what circumstances do you believe goal setting would be most useful to you as an employee? As a supervisor? Explain your position for both situations.

THINKING CRITICALLY

▶ Case 3-A: Establishing Plans

The Mailing Place is a full-service direct-mail company with many clients in the home services industry. Companies such as the Rug Doctor, House Maids, and Handyman Inc. use the Mailing Place to send out targeted direct-mail pieces to homes that typically use these types of services. Jill Akers started with the Mailing Place when she was a college student and in four years has progressed to the position of evening supervisor. Her responsibilities include assembling the materials for an order; planning for labor to fold, stuff, and run the PCs used to produce labels; and ensuring that orders have the proper postage. There are four full-time workers in her area, and some large orders will require as many as ten temporary positions. The Mailing Place is paid based on the number of pieces mailed

and receives a sizable bonus when their customers acquire new business.

Jill's boss has come to her and asked for her assistance with a new line of work for the company. The new work is to produce personalized mailings for mortgage and banking companies in support of their call center operations. The new clients will give the Mailing Place a listing of the contacts made in a day. The Mailing Place will assemble materials to be mailed within twenty-four hours. Jill's boss thinks the night shift should handle this work to ensure the type of rapid fulfillment the banks are requiring. Jill is supposed to come up with a plan to incorporate this work into her area.

The night shift at the Mailing Place is currently working from 5 p.m. to 4 a.m., four days a week. Each employee needs about one week of on-the-job training to become efficient on all the machines and the PC programs. The labor cost is the major component of the Mailing Place's expenses, and controlling labor is a key to its success. The new line of work will start in about a month, and after three months the new volume is expected to be equal to their present level of work. Jill's boss is hopeful that with the increased volume the operation will become more productive.

RESPONDING TO THE CASE

1. List and describe the planning elements that Jill needs to consider in preparing for this new line of work.

2. Describe two options for handling the staffing levels for this new line of work. What issues and complications are likely to surface with the new amount of work for Jill's department?

3. How would you suggest using schedules and budgets in the planning process for the Mailing Place?

➤ Case 3-B: When Proper Procedure is not Followed

"You are so out of here!" Cindy could hardly believe the words she heard coming from the mouth of Sonja, the new corporate assistant property manager for the Desirable Apartment Company. After all, Sonja had barely been working as long as Cindy, and Cliff, the corporate property manager himself, was sitting right next to Sonja hardly saying a word. Cindy knew coming into the organization, as the wife of one of the members of the executive committee, Larry, that she could not expect to be treated any differently than anyone else, but this was way out of hand.

As soon as Cindy left the property, Sonja and Cliff quickly reported the situation to Lamarr, the vice president of corporate assets, and their immediate supervisor. After hearing the story, Lamarr walked in to the office of the vice president of Human Resource Development, Heather, and said, "You are not going to believe what just happened out at the Builtwell property with Larry's wife Cindy." He went on to tell her the entire story as he understood it.

Heather was a thoughtful seasoned veteran of HR and knew the company inside and out. She knew this incident had the potential to shake the company to its core because of the close relationship of all the members of the executive committee. This company was built on a strong foundation of family values, and she could see the potential disruption from firing the wife of an executive. She immediately contacted Cindy to hear her side of the story and give her the opportunity to describe what happened that day.

Cliff spent the evening trying to figure out what had gone wrong during the meeting with Cindy. What had started out to be a simple meeting to discuss sales expectations for Cindy in her role as leasing agent had quickly gone from bad to worse as Sonja attempted to assert herself during the meeting. Sonja had recently been hired into her new position and was eager to have an impact on the company... "boy was she ever," he thought with

remorse. He worked late into the evening crafting an explanatory e-mail to Heather, trying to explain why company protocol had not been followed during the dismissal and why he, as Sonja's supervisor, had not intervened.

After reading Cliff's e-mail late that night, Heather sent a response to Lamarr that was apparently never received. Early the next morning she sent a follow-up e-mail, saying that, "It does not appear that you received my e-mail from this morning, so this is my 2nd attempt, in response to Cliff's e-mail last night, to offer my viewpoint on the situation."

Heather went on to state, "I also spent last evening trying to digest the current events. I hope that Sonja can eventually succeed in exhibiting leadership that represents the Desirable Apartment culture. I listened to both points of view of what happened. I heard examples of how Cindy was poorly treated by the Builtwell staff, and I listened to management's description of Cindy's behavior. I think everyone is viewing the situation through their particular filter, and it is challenging to piece it together. I do not think that the Builtwell on-site manager, Jill, is totally innocent in this situation, either."

"I would like to believe it was not Sonja's intention to have Cindy terminated. However, Sonja and Jill had a conversation before the meeting, and Jill asked if she should sit in. I believe this set the tone for the later meeting with Cindy. I am also left wondering about Jill's reply to the Builtwell property maintenance manager when he asked where Cindy was that day. Jill replied, 'Cindy is no longer with the company.' Jill had the perception Cindy was terminated... and I have to wonder, why?"

Talking with Lamarr in his office later the next day, trying to wrap up the situation, Heather told him she had been doing damage control, "I spoke to Larry, and although still upset, he is focused and moving forward." As Heather was leaving, she looked Lamarr in the eye and said, "In the end, I am left with what must have been the feeling of the Butler team after the final game of the 2011 NCAA game, 'What the heck just happened?' "

RESPONDING TO THE CASE

1. Outline the specific steps Cliff should have taken with Sonja prior to their meeting with Cindy to ensure the meeting went smoothly with no surprises.

2. As supervisor, what should Cliff have done when it became apparent Sonja was overstepping her authority during the meeting with Cindy?

3. What steps do you believe Heather should take with Sonja? With Cliff? With Cindy?

4

Organizing

Key Concepts

After completing this chapter, you will be able to define these supervisory terms:

- authority
- boundaryless organization
- centralization
- chain of command
- customer departmentalization
- decentralization
- delegation
- departmentalization
- divisional structure
- empowerment
- functional authority
- functional departmentalization
- functional structure
- geographic departmentalization

- job description
- learning organization
- line authority
- matrix
- process departmentalization
- product departmentalization
- responsibility
- simple structure
- span of control
- staff authority
- team-based structure
- unity of command
- work specialization

Chapter Outcomes

After reading this chapter, you will be able to:

1. Define *organizing*.
2. Describe why work specialization should increase economic efficiency.
3. Explain how the span of control affects an organization's structure.
4. Contrast line and staff authority.
5. Explain why organizations are becoming increasingly decentralized.
6. Describe how flatter organizational structures can be beneficial to the organization.
7. Explain the concept of a learning organization and how it influences organizational designs and supervisors.
8. Discuss the value of job descriptions.
9. Identify the four-step process of delegation.

Responding to a Supervisory Dilemma

Throughout the years a number of surveys have indicated that significant differences exist between the values, attitudes, and beliefs that supervisors personally hold and those they encounter in the workplace. And these differences are not simply a U.S. phenomenon. Supervisors around the world, in such places as the Pacific Rim, Europe, and India, are all facing the same predicaments. That is, should they follow orders that go against their own values and beliefs?

Consider the following scenarios:

- Your boss instructs you to shred all correspondence regarding a specific account you've worked on. You are not told why, only that you are to shred everything in the file. Would you shred the documents?

- Your boss indicates that one of your employees must be terminated. The employee happens to be someone of the opposite sex from your boss. You have heard rumors about your boss and this person, but you know nothing specifically about the two of them. Would you just fire your employee because your boss said so? Would it make a difference if you were told that if you didn't fire the person, it would be considered an indication of your lack of supervisory ability and you'd be fired?

- Your boss instructs you to tell whomever may call you about her whereabouts that you were working with your boss last evening and didn't leave the office until well after 8 p.m. Would you support your boss's request when the call came?

- Your boss asks you to bring coffee to his desk every morning. Would you?

- Your boss asks you to redo some statistical sampling because the first batch sampled failed. To discard the product would be cost ineffective. She tells you (with a strong wink) that she wants you to sample again to see if this time the product passes. Do you sample again and give the results your boss is hinting at?

- Your boss asks you to submit a cost figure for a proposal that he is certain is the winning bid. You've heard rumors that your boss has an inside track on this proposal because one of his closest friends is on the proposal review committee in the other organization. Do you go with the cost figure given to you?

- Your boss asks you to donate $100 to a political candidate who happens to be her relative. This candidate is not someone you support politically or philosophically. Your boss wants 100 percent participation in her department. Do you make the contribution?

- Your boss asks you to buy a $50 raffle ticket to win a new sports car in support of a school one of his children attends. Would you buy the raffle ticket?

In any of the preceding scenarios, how would you react? Would you do what is asked or ordered? Why or why not?

In the 1920s and 1930s, as organizations got bigger and more formal, supervisors felt a need to provide more coordination of activities and tighter control over operations. Early business researchers argued that formal bureaucracies would best serve the company. That belief held for more than seven decades. As such, bureaucratic structures flourished. However, by the 1980s, the world began to change drastically. The global marketplace, rapid technological advancements, diversity in the workforce, and socioeconomic conditions made these formal bureaucracies inefficient for many businesses. Consequently, since the late 1980s many organizations have restructured to be more customer and market oriented and to increase productivity.

It is critical today for an organization to have the right structure. Although setting up the organization's structure is typically done by top management in an organization (or the owner/entrepreneur in a small/startup business), it is important for all organizational members to understand how these structures work. Why? Because you'll understand your job better if you know why you're "arranged" as you are. For example, how many people can you effectively supervise? When do you have authority to make a decision, and when is it merely advice that you're providing? What tasks can you delegate to others? Will you supervise employees who produce a specific product? Will your department exist to serve a particular customer, a geographic region, or some combination of these? You'll see how to find the answers to questions such as these in this chapter. We look at the traditional components that go into developing an organization's structure, discuss the various ways that employees may be grouped, and look at how organizational structures change over time.

What Is Organizing?

Organizing is arranging and grouping jobs, allocating resources, and assigning work in a department so that activities can be accomplished as planned. As previously mentioned, the top management team in an organization typically establishes the overall organization structure. They determine, for instance, how many levels there will be from the top of the organization to the bottom, and the extent to which lower-level managers will have to follow formal rules and procedures in carrying out their jobs. In large U.S. corporations, it's not unusual to have five to eight levels from top to bottom; hundreds of departments; and dozens of manuals (e.g., manuals on purchasing, human resources, accounting, engineering, maintenance, sales) that define procedures, rules, and policies within departments. Once the overall structure is in place, supervisors need to organize their individual departments. In this chapter, we show you how to do that.

Keep in mind that our discussion here concerns the formal arrangement of jobs and groups of jobs. These are defined by management. In addition, individuals and groups will develop informal alliances that are neither formally structured nor organizationally determined. Almost all employees in all organizations form these informal arrangements to meet their needs for social contact.

Basic Organizing Concepts

Every organization—large and small, for-profit and not-for-profit, and so on—has a structure. Some of them, such as Toyota and IBM, have a more formalized structure. Others, such as many entrepreneurial ventures, have a less formalized and very simple structure. So, what makes up this "thing" we work in? Let's look at what we call the organization structure.

The early writers in management developed a number of basic organizing principles that continue to offer valuable guidance to supervisors today: work specialization, span of control, chain of command, authority and responsibility, centralization versus decentralization, and departmentalization.

WHAT IS WORK SPECIALIZATION?

Work specialization means that rather than an entire job being done by one individual, it is broken down into a number of steps that are each completed by a separate individual. In essence, individuals specialize in doing part of an activity rather than the entire activity. Assembly-line production, in which each worker does the same standardized task over and over again, is an example of work specialization.

work specialization
The process of breaking down a job into a number of steps, with each step being completed by a different individual.

Until recently, designers of organizations have taken as an irrefutable law that increases in work specialization lead to increases in economic efficiencies. In most organizations, some tasks require highly developed skills; others can be performed by the untrained. If all workers were engaged in each step of, say, an organization's manufacturing process, all would have to have the skills necessary to perform the most demanding and the least demanding tasks. The result would be that, except when performing the most highly skilled or highly sophisticated tasks, employees would be working below their skill level. Because skilled workers are paid more than unskilled workers and their wages tend to reflect their higher level of skill, it is an inefficient use of resources to pay highly skilled workers to do easy tasks.

Today, supervisors understand that although work specialization provides economic efficiencies, it is not an unending source of increased productivity. There is a point at which the problems of work specialization surface—boredom, fatigue, stress, low productivity, poor quality, increased absenteeism, and high turnover. Contemporary supervisors still use the work specialization concept in designing jobs. At the same time, they recognize that in an expanding number of situations, productivity, quality, and employee motivation can be increased by giving employees a variety of activities to do, allowing them to do a whole and complete piece of work, and putting them together into teams.

WHAT IS THE SPAN OF CONTROL?

span of control
The number of employees a supervisor can efficiently and effectively direct.

It is not very efficient for a supervisor to direct only one or two employees. Conversely, it's pretty obvious that the best of supervisors would be overwhelmed if he or she had to directly oversee several hundred people. This, then, brings up the span of control question: How many employees can a supervisor direct efficiently and effectively?

There is, unfortunately, no universal answer. For most supervisors, the optimal number is probably somewhere between five and thirty. Where, within that range, the exact span should be depends on a number of factors. How experienced and competent is the supervisor? The greater his or her abilities are, the more employees he or she can handle. What level of training and experience do employees have? The greater their abilities are, the fewer demands they'll make on their supervisor; thus, a supervisor can directly oversee more employees. How complex are the employees' activities? The more difficult the employees' jobs, the more narrow the span of control. How many different types of jobs are under the supervisor's direction? The more varied the jobs, the more narrow the span. How extensive are the department's formal rules and regulations? Supervisors can direct more people when employees can find solutions to their problems in organizational manuals rather than having to go to their immediate boss.

An important trend has been taking place in organizations. Spans of control have expanded almost universally (see Exhibit 4-1). The reason is that this is a way for an organization to reduce costs. For example, by doubling the span size, you cut the number of supervisors needed in half. This, remember, is one of the basic premises of downsizing. Of course, this move to wider spans may not be effectively carried out without modifications in work assignments and improvements in skill levels. To make wider spans work, organizations may need to spend more on supervisory and employee training. They may also be able to redesign jobs around teams so that individuals can help each other solve problems without needing to go to their manager.

Something else important is taking place in organizations that involves a supervisor's span of control: the increased use of telecommuting (see "Something to Think About (and promote class discussion): Return to Yesteryear" later in this chapter). Telecommuting, e-commuting, e-work, telework, working at home (WAH), or working from home (WFH) allows employees to do their work at home (or anywhere they can find to log in) on a computer linked to the office. Currently, several million employees in the United States are telecommuting. WorldatWork,

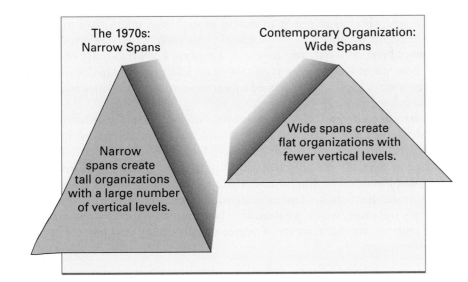

Exhibit 4-1
Contrasting spans of control.

a global human resources association, tells us that "the number of Americans who worked from home or remotely at least one day per month for their employer ('employee telecommuters') increased from approximately 12.4 million in 2006 to 17.2 million in 2008, according to the random-digit dialed (RDD) telephone survey conducted by The Dieringer Research Group with funding from WorldatWork. The rise in the number of telecommuters represents a two-year increase of 39 percent, and an increase of 74 percent since 2005. In 2005, the number of employees allowed to work from home or remotely at least one day per month by their employer was approximately 9.9 million."[1]

The big plus in telecommuting is that it gives employees more flexibility. It frees them from the constraints of commuting and fixed hours and increases opportunities for meeting family responsibilities. For supervisors, telecommuting means supervising individuals they rarely see. Where it is being used, supervisors usually have a fairly wide span of control. This is because telecommuters tend to be skilled professionals and clerical employees—computer programmers, marketing specialists, financial analysts, and administrative support personnel—who typically make minimal demands on their supervisors. Additionally, because the supervisor's computer and the employee's computer are typically networked, supervisors often are able to communicate with telecommuters as well as or better than they can with employees who are physically in their offices.

WHAT IS THE CHAIN OF COMMAND?

For many years the chain-of-command concept was a cornerstone of organizational design. Although it has far less importance today, contemporary supervisors still need to consider its implications when deciding how best to structure their organization.

The chain of command is the continuous line of authority that extends from upper organizational levels to the lowest levels and clarifies who reports to whom. It helps employees answer questions such as, "Whom do I go to if I have a problem?" or "To whom am I ultimately responsible?" Such questions led early management writers to the conclusion that an employee should have one and only one supervisor to whom he or she is directly responsible.

chain of command
The continuous line of authority in an organization.

---

[1]WorldatWork, "Telework Trendlines 2009," February 2009, data from The Dieringer Research Group Inc., http://www.worldatwork.org/waw/adimLink?id=31115 (accessed May 22, 2011).

unity of command

A principle that states that an employee should have one and only one supervisor to whom he or she is directly responsible.

An employee who has to report to two or more bosses might have to cope with conflicting demands or priorities.[2] Accordingly, the early writers believed that each employee should report to only one manager, a concept known as unity of command. In those rare instances when the unity of command had to be violated, early management workers always explicitly designated a clear separation of activities and a supervisor responsible for each.

The unity of command was logical when organizations were comparatively simple. Under some circumstances it is still sound advice and organizations continue to adhere to it. But technology, for instance, has enabled information access in an organization that was once accessible only to top managers. Moreover, with computers, employees can communicate with anyone else in the organization without going through the formal communication channels—the chain of command. As such, there are instances, which we introduce later in this chapter, when strict adherence to the unity of command creates a degree of inflexibility that hinders an organization's performance.

WHAT IS AUTHORITY?

authority

Rights inherent in a supervisory position to give orders and expect those orders to be obeyed.

Authority refers to rights inherent in a supervisory position to give orders and expect the orders to be obeyed. Each supervisory position has specific rights that incumbents acquire from their position's rank or title. Authority, therefore, relates to one's position within an organization and ignores the personal characteristics of the individual supervisor. People follow individuals in authority not because they like or respect them but because of the rights inherent in their position (see "News Flash! Obeying Authority").

line authority

The authority that entitles a supervisor to direct the work of his or her employees and to make certain decisions without consulting others.

There are three different types of authority relations: line, staff, and functional (see Exhibit 4-2). The most straightforward and easiest to understand is line authority. This is the authority that gives the supervisor the right to direct the work of his or her employees and make certain decisions without consulting others.

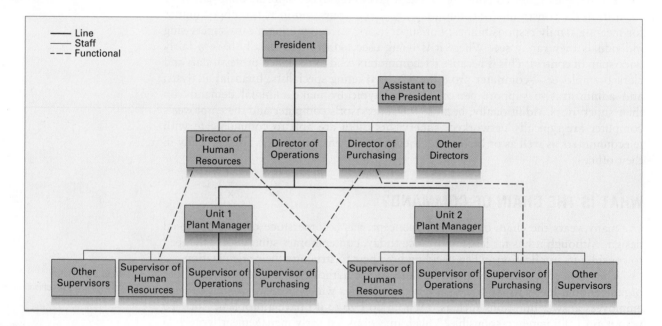

Exhibit 4-2

Organization chart depicting line, staff, and functional authority relationships.

---

[2]R. Preston, "Inside Out," *Management Today*, September 2001, 37; and R. D. Clarke, "Over Their Heads," *Black Enterprise*, December 2000, 79.

Staff authority supports line authority by advising, servicing, and assisting, but it is typically limited. For example, the assistant to the science department head at a university has staff authority. She acts as an extension of the department head. She can give advice and suggestions, but they needn't be obeyed. However, she may be given the authority to act for the department head. In such cases, she gives directives under the line authority of her boss. For instance, she might issue a memo and sign it "Joan Wilson for R. L. Dalton." In this instance, Wilson is acting only as an extension of Dalton. Staff authority allows Dalton to get more things done by having an assistant who can act on his behalf.

A third type of authority, functional authority, represents rights over individuals outside one's own direct areas of responsibility. For example, it is not unusual for a supervisor in a manufacturing plant to find that his or her immediate boss has line authority over him or her but that someone in corporate headquarters has functional authority over some of his or her activities and decisions. The supervisor in charge of the purchasing department at an Allison Transmission, Inc., plant in Chennai, India,

staff authority
A limited authority that supports line authority by advising, servicing, and assisting.

functional authority
Control over individuals outside one's own direct areas of responsibility.

News Flash!

OBEYING AUTHORITY

Do people do what they are told—and not question those in a position of authority? Years ago in most businesses, that was a standard of operating. For many supervisors, this is what they expected—if not demanded! But just how far would someone go in obeying orders? Probably the best indication of an answer to this was a research project conducted years ago by a social psychologist at Yale University.

Subjects were placed in the role of a teacher in a learning experiment and told by the experimenter to administer a shock to a learner each time that learner made a mistake. The question was, would the subjects follow the commands of the experimenter? Would their willingness to comply decrease as the intensity of the shock was increased? To test these questions, the researcher hired a set of subjects. Each was led to believe that the experiment was to investigate the effect of punishment on memory. Their job was to act as teachers and administer punishment whenever the learner made a mistake on a learning test. Punishment in this case was administered by electric shock. The subject sat in front of a shock generator with thirty levels of shock, beginning at zero and progressing in 15-volt increments to a high of 450 volts. The range of these positions was from "slight shock" at 15 volts to "danger: severe shock" at 450 volts. To add realism to the experiment, the subjects received a sample shock of 45 volts and saw the learner strapped in an electric chair in an adjacent room. Of course, the learner was an actor, and the electric shocks were phony—but the subjects didn't know this.

The subjects were instructed to shock the learner each time he or she made a mistake.

Subsequent mistakes would result in an increase in shock intensity. Throughout the experiment, the subject got verbal feedback from the learner. At 75 volts, the learner began to grunt and moan; at 150 volts, he demanded to be released from the experiment; at 180 volts he cried out that he could no longer stand the pain; and at 300 volts, he insisted he be let out because of a heart condition. After 300 volts, the learner did not respond to further questions.

Most subjects protested and, fearful that they might kill the learner if the increased shocks were to bring on a heart attack, insisted they could not go on. But the experimenter responded by saying that they had to, that was their job. The majority of the subjects dissented, but dissension isn't synonymous with disobedience. Sixty-two percent of the subjects increased the shock level to the maximum of 450 volts. The average level of shock administered by the remaining 38 percent was nearly 370 volts—more than enough to kill even the strongest human!

What can we conclude from this experiment? Well, one obvious conclusion is that authority is a potent source of getting people to do things. Subjects in the experiment administered levels of shock far above that which they wanted to do. They did it because they were told they had to and despite the fact that they could have voluntarily walked out of the room anytime they wanted.

Source: Based on S. Milgram, *Obedience to Authority* (New York: Harper & Row, 1974).

Something to Think About (and promote class discussion)

RETURN TO YESTERYEAR

One hundred fifty years ago in U.S. history, it was not uncommon for workers to perform their craft out of their homes. In fact, most workers performed some tasks, produced a finished product, and took it to a market to sell. But the Industrial Revolution changed all that. Large manufacturing companies drew workers away from rural areas and into the cities. Along with this movement came the traditional job—one that required employees to show up at the company's facility and spend their eight- to twelve-hour workday—and developed the need for someone—the supervisor—to keep the workers working.

As time went on and the urban gave way to the suburban, there developed a strong commuting mentality in workers and businesses. The expectation was that businesses located according to some strategic imperative and workers would find their way to the workplace on their own. The automobile industry flourished, and mass transit largely disappeared in many locations throughout the country. Today, the paradigm of work being inexorably linked to commuting is undergoing a major reframing as organizations and their employees react to the high prices of fuel in a global economy.

Initially viewed as an opportunity for organizations to take advantage of increased connectivity between home and office, while reducing costs associated with underused office space, the concept of telecommuting or the broader term of *telework** is now being viewed as the ethical solution for organizations intent on reducing their carbon footprint. Additionally, in the aftermath of catastrophic events such as 9/11, Hurricane Katrina, the 2008 earthquake in China, the 2010 BP Oil Deepwater Horizon drilling rig explosion, and the 2011 earthquake and tsunami in Japan, organizations are increasingly aware of the need to maintain business continuity for customers, employees, and shareholders.

Downsizing and work process engineering have resulted in the wholesale disappearance of traditional jobs. When you factor in technological changes and the widespread acceptance and use of computers, modems, personal digital assistants (PDAs), wireless technologies, fax machines, and cell phones, the concept of workers reporting to a centralized location does not make sense. Existing telework capabilities make it possible for employees to be located anywhere on the globe, and employers no longer have to consider locating a business near its workforce. For example, if an insurance company in Idaho finds that it is having problems attracting qualified local applicants for its claims-processing jobs, and a pool of qualified workers is available in Colorado Springs, the company doesn't need to establish a facility in Colorado. Instead, the company can provide these employees with computer equipment and appropriate ancillaries; the work can be done hundreds of miles away, and then transmitted to the "home" office.

Teleworking also offers an opportunity for a business in a high-labor-cost area to have its work done in an area where lower wages prevail. Take the publisher in New York City that finds that manuscript editing costs have skyrocketed. By having that work done by a qualified editor in Parkton, West Virginia, the publisher could reduce labor costs. Likewise, not having to provide office space in the city to this editor, given the cost per square foot of real estate in the area, adds to the cost savings.

Decentralized work sites also offer opportunities that may meet the needs of the diversified workforce. Those who have family responsibilities, such as child care, or those who have disabilities may prefer to work in their homes, rather than travel to the organization's facility. Teleworking, then, provides the flexibility in work scheduling that many members of the diversified workforce desire.

With the increasing move to retirement by baby boomers, and the subsequent influx of Generation Y into the workplace, flexibility in working conditions continues to be a prime recruitment tool for many organizations. Teleworking has the potential to provide a better work–life balance for those to choose to work from home, thereby holding promise for increases in productivity and worker satisfaction. Working from home may also benefit the community by reducing traffic, exhaust emissions, and U.S. dependence on foreign oil.

Finally, there's some incentive from government agencies for companies to consider these alternative work arrangements. For example, the federal government, in its effort to address environmental

---

*J. M. Niles, *Managing Telework: Options for Managing the Virtual Workforce* (New York: John Wiley & Sons, 1998); and The Telework Coalition, "What Is the Difference between Telework and Telecommuting?" http://www.telcoa.org/id193.htm (accessed May 14, 2011).

concerns in the United States, may make state highway funds contingent on the state's ability to reduce traffic congestion in heavily populated areas. One means of achieving that goal is for businesses to receive some incentive, such as a tax break, for implementing decentralized work sites. In a similar fashion, state departments of labor may also provide an incentive to businesses to relocate their work activities from more affluent communities to economically depressed areas.

As a supervisor, however, you'll bear the brunt of the change. You'll be expected to keep in contact with your offsite employees. You'll have to monitor their work and evaluate what they have done. Teleworking is clearly changing the supervisor's job description—or is it? What do you think about teleworking and its impact on corporate America?

is responsible to that plant's manager and the corporate director of purchasing at the company's head office in Indianapolis, Indiana.

Why, you might wonder, would the organization create positions of functional authority? After all, it breaks the unity-of-command principle by having people report to two bosses. The answer is that it can create efficiencies by permitting specialization of skills and improved coordination. Its major problem is overlapping relationships. This is typically resolved by clearly designating to an individual which activities his or her line boss has authority over and which activities are under the direction of someone else with functional authority. To follow up our purchasing example, the director in Indianapolis, Indiana, might have functional authority to specify corporation-wide purchasing policies on forms to be used and common procedures to be followed. All other aspects of the purchasing supervisor's job would be under the authority of the plant manager.

How Do Authority and Responsibility Differ? Supervisory jobs come with authority. They also come with responsibility. Supervisors are responsible for achieving their unit's goals, keeping costs within budget, following organizational policies, and motivating their employees. Authority without responsibility creates opportunities for abuse. For instance, if the supervisor isn't held responsible for motivating employees, he or she may become inclined to make excessive demands on an employee, resulting in that employee being injured on the job. Conversely, responsibility without authority creates frustration and the feeling of powerlessness. If you're held responsible for your territory's sales performance, you should have the authority to hire, reward, discipline, and fire the salespeople who work for you.

responsibility
Supervisory obligations such as achieving a unit's goals, keeping costs within budget, following organizational policies, and motivating employees.

Why Must Authority and Responsibility Be Equal? The previous analysis suggests the importance of equating authority and responsibility. When top management creates organizational units such as divisions, regions, territories, and departments—and allocates supervisory personnel to each with specific goals and responsibilities—it must also give these supervisors enough authority to successfully carry out those responsibilities. The more ambitious and far reaching the goals a supervisor undertakes, the more authority he or she needs to be given.

WHERE ARE DECISIONS MADE?

One of the questions that needs to be answered in the organizing function is, "At what level are decisions made?" Centralization is a function of how much decision-making authority is pushed down to lower levels in the organization. Centralization–decentralization, however, is not an either-or concept. Rather, it's a degree phenomenon. By that we mean that no organization is completely centralized or completely decentralized. Few, if any, organizations could effectively function if all their decisions were made by a select

centralization
Decision-making responsibility in the hands of top management.

decentralization
The pushing down of decision-making authority to those closest to the problems.

few people (centralization) or if all decisions were pushed down to the level closest to the problems (decentralization). Let's look, then, at how the early management writers viewed centralization, as well as at how it exists today.

Early management writers proposed that centralization in an organization depended on the situation.[3] Their objective was the optimal and efficient use of employees. Traditional organizations were structured in a pyramid, with power and authority concentrated near the top of the organization. Given this structure, historically, centralized decisions were the most prominent. But organizations today have become more complex and are responding to dynamic changes in their environments. As such, many believe that decisions need to be made by the individuals closest to the problems— regardless of their organizational level. In fact, the trend over the past three decades has been movement toward more decentralization in organizations.

Today, more than any time in recent years, supervisors and operatives are being actively included in the decision-making process. As many organizations have cut costs and streamlined their organizational design to respond better to customer needs, they have pushed decision-making authority down to the lowest levels in the organization. In this way, those people most familiar with a problem—and often those closest to it—are able to quickly size it up and solve it.

WHAT ARE THE FIVE WAYS TO DEPARTMENTALIZE?

Early management writers argued that activities in the organization should be specialized and grouped into departments. Work specialization creates specialists who need coordination. This coordination is facilitated by putting specialists together in departments under the direction of a manager. Creation of these departments is typically based on the work functions being performed, the product or service being offered, the target customer or client, the geographic territory being covered, or the process being used to turn inputs into outputs. No single method of departmentalization was advocated by the early writers. The method or methods used should reflect the grouping that would best contribute to the attainment of the organization's objectives and the goals of individual units.

departmentalization
Grouping departments based on work functions, product or service, target customer or client, geographic territory, or the process used to turn inputs into outputs.

functional departmentalization
Grouping activities into independent units based on functions performed.

How Are Activities Grouped? One of the most popular ways to group activities is by functions performed, or functional departmentalization. A supervisor might find his or her plant separated into work units—such as engineering, accounting, information systems, human resources, and purchasing (see Exhibit 4-3). Functional departmentalization can be used in all types of organizations. Only the functions change to

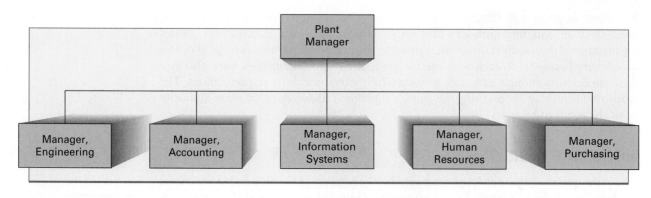

Exhibit 4-3
Functional departmentalization.

---

[3]H. Fayol, *General and Industrial Management*, C. Storrs, trans. (London: Pitman Publishing, 1949), 19–42.

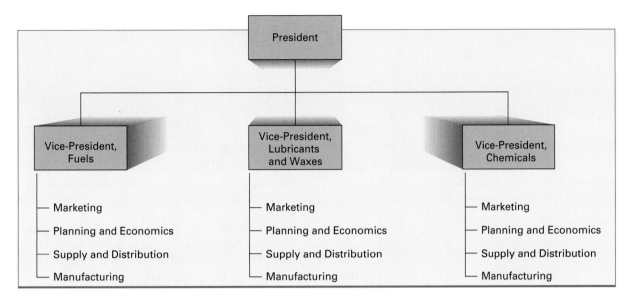

reflect the organization's objectives and activities. A hospital might have departments devoted to research, patient care, accounting, and so forth. A professional indoor soccer franchise might have departments labeled player personnel, ticket sales, and travel and accommodations.

Exhibit 4-4 illustrates the product departmentalization method used at Bombardier Ltd., a Canadian company. Each major product area in the corporation is placed under the authority of a senior manager who is a specialist in, and is responsible for, everything having to do with his or her product line. Another company that uses product departmentalization is L.A. Gear. Its structure is based on its varied product lines, which include women's footwear, men's footwear, and apparel and accessories. If an organization's activities were service related, rather than product related—as are those of Bombardier and L.A. Gear—each service would be autonomously grouped. For instance, an accounting firm would have departments for taxes, management consulting, auditing, and the like. In such a case, each department offers a common array of services under the direction of a product or service supervisor.

The particular type of customer the organization seeks to reach can also be used to group employees. The sales activities in an office supply firm, for instance, can be broken down into five departments to serve government, military, corporate, small business, and nonprofit customers (see Exhibit 4-5). A large law office can segment its

product departmentalization
Grouping activities into independent units based on problems or issues relating to a product.

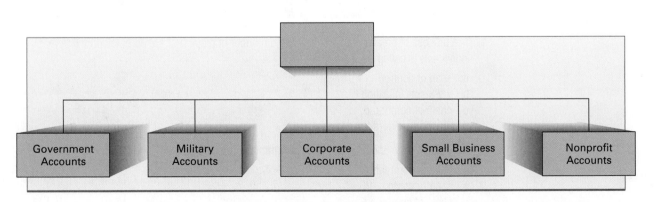

Exhibit 4-5
Customer departmentalization.

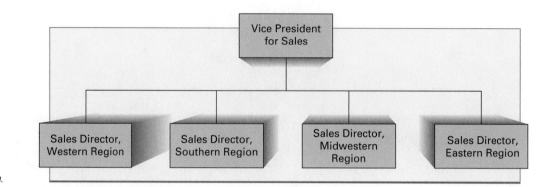

Exhibit 4-6
Geographic departmentalization.

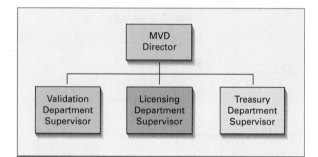

Exhibit 4-7
Process departmentalization.

customer departmentalization
Grouping activities around common customer categories.

geographic departmentalization
Grouping activities into independent units based on geography or territory.

process departmentalization
Grouping activities around a process; this method provides a basis for the homogeneous categorizing of activities.

staff on the basis of individual clients served. The assumption underlying customer departmentalization is that customers in each department have a common set of problems and needs that can best be met by having specialists for each.

Another way to departmentalize is on the basis of geography or territory—geographic departmentalization. The sales function might have western, southern, midwestern, and eastern regions (see Exhibit 4-6). A large school district might have six high schools to provide for each of the major geographic territories within the district. If an organization's customers are scattered over a large geographic area, this form of departmentalization can be valuable. For instance, Coca-Cola's organizational structure reflects the company's operations in two broad geographic areas—the North American business sector and the international business sector (which includes East, South Asia and Pacific Rim Group, North Asia, Eurasia and Middle East Group, and the Africa, European Union, and Latin America Groups).

The final form of departmentalization is called process departmentalization, which groups activities on the basis of work or customer flow. Exhibit 4-7 represents an example of process departmentalization by depicting the various departments in a motor vehicle department. If you have ever been to a state motor vehicle office to get a driver's license, you probably went through several departments before receiving your license. In some states, applicants go through three steps, each handled by a separate department: (1) validation, by the motor vehicle division; (2) processing, by the licensing department; and (3) payment collection, by the treasury department.

Comprehension Check 4-1

1. The process of breaking down a job into a number of steps that are completed by different individuals is called

    a. span of control
    b. work specialization
    c. chain of command
    d. workforce diversity

2. Reporting to one and only one boss is commonly referred to as

    a. unity of command
    b. span of control
    c. chain of command
    d. none of the above

3. The control a supervisor has over individuals outside his or her own direct area is called
   a. responsibility
   b. power
   c. centralization
   d. functional authority

4. Which of the following is *not* one of the ways an organization can group its employees?
   a. Functional departmentalization
   b. Product departmentalization
   c. Service departmentalization
   d. Customer departmentalization

From Departmentalization to Structure

Most large organizations continue to use most or all of the departmental groups suggested by the early management writers. Black & Decker, for instance, organizes each of its divisions along functional lines, its manufacturing units around processes, its sales around geographic regions, and its sales regions around customer groupings. But a recent trend needs to be mentioned. That is, rigid departmentalization is being complemented by the use of teams that cross over traditional departmental lines.

Today's competitive environment has refocused the attention of management to its customers. To better monitor the needs of customers and to be able to respond to changes in those needs, many organizations have given greater emphasis to customer departmentalization. We are also seeing a great deal more use of teams today as a device for accomplishing organizational objectives. Nearly all Fortune 500 firms are using teams.[4] As tasks have become more complex and diverse skills are needed to accomplish those tasks, management has increasingly introduced the use of teams and task forces.

So, what types of organization designs exist in companies such as Toshiba, Liz Claiborne, Hershey Foods, and Sun Life Assurance Company of Canada? Let's look at the various types of organization designs that you might see in contemporary organizations.

A SIMPLE STRUCTURE

Most organizations start as an entrepreneurial venture with a simple structure. This organization design reflects the owner as president, with all employees reporting directly to him or her.

A simple structure is defined more by what it is not than by what it is. It is not an elaborate structure. If you see an organization that appears to have almost no structure, it is probably of the simple variety. By that we mean that work specialization is low, few rules govern the operations, and authority is centralized in a single person—the owner. The simple structure is a "flat" organization; it usually has only two or three vertical levels, a loose body of empowered employees in whom the decision-making authority is centralized.

The simple structure is most widely used in smaller businesses in which the supervisor and the owner are often the same person. The strengths of the simple structure

simple structure
A nonelaborate structure, low in complexity, with little formalization, and with authority centralized in a single person; a "flat" organization with only two or three levels.

---

[4]E. Kelly, "Keys to Effective Virtual Global Teams," *Academy of Management Executive* 15, no. 2 (May 2001), 132–133; and D. Ancona, H. Bresman, and K. Kaeufer, "The Comparative Advantage of X-Team," *Sloan Management Review* 43, no. 3 (Spring 2002), 33–39.

should be obvious. It is fast, flexible, and inexpensive to maintain, and accountability is clear. One major weakness is that it is effective only in small organizations. It becomes increasingly inadequate as an organization grows because its few policies or rules to guide operations and its high centralization result in information overload at the top. As size increases, decision making becomes slower and can eventually come to a standstill as the single executive tries to continue making all the decisions. If the structure is not changed and adapted to its size, the firm is likely to lose momentum and eventually fail. The simple structure's other weakness is that it is risky: Everything depends on one person. If anything happens to the owner-manager, the organization's information and decision-making center is lost.

Many organizations do not remain simple structures; that decision is often made by choice or because structural contingency factors dictate it. For example, as production or sales increase significantly, companies generally reach a point at which more employees are needed. As the number of employees rises, informal work rules of the simple structure give way to more formalized rules. Rules and regulations are implemented, departments are created, and levels of management are added to coordinate the activities of departmental people. At this point, a bureaucracy is formed. Two of the most popular bureaucratic design options grew out of the functional and product departmentalizations. These are appropriately called the functional and divisional structures, respectively.

THE FUNCTIONAL STRUCTURE

functional structure
An organization in which similar and related occupational specialties are grouped together.

We introduced functional departmentalization a few pages ago. The functional structure merely expands the functional orientation to make it the dominant form for the entire organization. As displayed in Exhibit 4-3, the company groups employees in similar and related occupational specialties together. The strength of the functional structure lies in the advantages that accrue from work specialization. Putting like specialties together results in economies of scale, minimizes duplication of personnel and equipment, and makes employees comfortable and satisfied because it gives them the opportunity to "talk the same language" as their peers. The most obvious weakness of the functional structure, however, is that the organization frequently loses sight of its best interests in the pursuit of functional goals. No one function is totally responsible for end results, so members within individual functions become insulated and have little understanding of what people in other functions are doing.

THE DIVISIONAL STRUCTURE

divisional structure
An organization made up of self-contained units.

The divisional structure is an organization design made up of self-contained units or divisions. Hershey Foods and PepsiCo are examples of companies that have implemented such a structure. Building on product departmentalization (see Exhibit 4-4), each division is generally autonomous, with a division manager responsible for performance and holding complete strategic and operational decision-making authority. In most divisional structures, central headquarters provides support services—such as financial and legal services—to the divisions. Of course, the headquarters also acts as an external overseer to coordinate and control the various divisions. Divisions are, therefore, autonomous within given parameters.

The chief advantage of the divisional structure is that it focuses on results. Division managers have full responsibility for a product or service. The divisional structure also frees the headquarters staff from being concerned with day-to-day operating details so that they can pay attention to long-term and strategic planning. The major disadvantage of the divisional structure is duplication of activities and resources. Each division, for instance, may have a marketing research department. In the absence of autonomous divisions, all of the organization's marketing research might be centralized and done for a fraction of the cost that divisionalization requires. Thus, the divisional form's duplication of functions increases the organization's costs and reduces efficiency.

THE MATRIX ORGANIZATION

The functional structure offers the advantages that accrue from specialization. The divisional structure has a greater focus on results but suffers from duplication of activities and resources. Does any structure combine the advantages of functional specialization with the focus and accountability that product departmentalization provides? The answer is yes, and it's called the matrix structure.[5]

Exhibit 4-8 illustrates the matrix structure of an aerospace firm. Notice that along the top of the figure are the familiar functions of engineering, accounting, human resources, manufacturing, and so forth. Along the vertical dimension, however, the various projects that the aerospace firm is currently working on have been added. Each program is directed by a supervisor who staffs his or her project with people from the functional departments. The addition of this vertical dimension to the traditional horizontal functional departments, in effect, weaves together elements of functional and product departmentalization—hence the term *matrix*.

The unique characteristic of the matrix is that employees in this structure have at least two bosses: their functional departmental supervisor and their product or project supervisors. Project supervisors have authority over the functional members who are part of that supervisor's project team. But authority is shared between the two supervisors. Typically, the project supervisor is given authority over project employees relative to

matrix
A structure that weaves together elements of functional and product departmentalization, creating a dual chain of command.

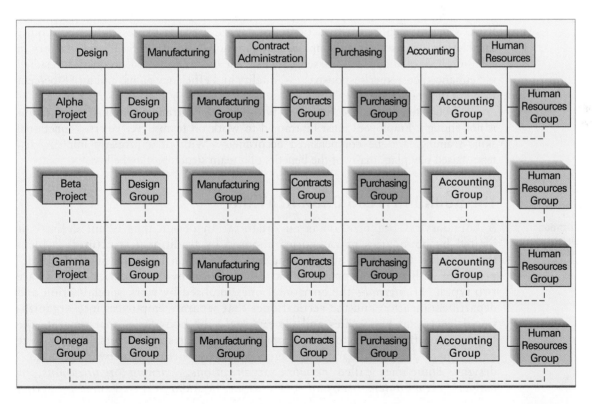

Exhibit 4-8

A matrix structure in an aerospace firm.

---

[5]See, for instance, J. Wolf and W. G. Egelhoff, "A Reexamination and Extension of International Strategy-Structure Theory," *IEEE Transaction on Engineering Management* 43, no. 1 (May 2001), 144–156.

the project's goals, but decisions such as promotions, salary recommendations, and annual reviews remain the functional supervisor's responsibility. To work effectively, project and functional supervisors must communicate regularly and coordinate the demands upon their common employees.

The primary strength of the matrix is that it can facilitate coordination of a multiple set of complex and interdependent projects while still retaining the economies that result from keeping functional specialists grouped together. The major disadvantages of the matrix lie in the confusion it creates and its propensity to foster power struggles. When you dispense with the chain-of-command principle, you significantly increase ambiguity. Confusion can exist over who reports to whom. This confusion and ambiguity, in turn, plant the seeds for power struggles.

TEAM-BASED STRUCTURES

team-based structure
An organization that consists entirely of workgroups, or teams.

In a team-based structure, the entire organization consists of workgroups or teams that perform the organization's work.[6] In such a structure, it goes without saying that team members have the authority to make decisions that affect them because there is no rigid chain of command in these work arrangements. How can team structures benefit the organization?

Let's look at what happened at the National Cooperative Bank in Washington, D.C.[7] Bank officials became aware of how their functional structure in the lending area was slowing decision making and constraining customer service; processing a loan often took as long as twenty weeks. To remedy the situation, they restructured the bank into teams representing specific industries, such as health care, distribution, and so on, based on the special regulatory issues in each industry. In doing so, the bank witnessed significant reductions in the time spent to process a loan; customer satisfaction increased, as did employee cooperation. And at AMS Hillend's factory in Edinburgh, Scotland, a team-based structure for its circuit board production resulted in "enhanced customer responsiveness, quality and efficiency gains, and an 88 percent increase in productivity."[8]

Although team structures have been positive, simply arranging employees into teams is not enough. Employees must be trained to work on teams, receive cross-functional skills training, and be compensated accordingly. Without a properly implemented team-based pay plan, many of the benefits of a team structure may be lost.[9]

THE BOUNDARYLESS ORGANIZATION

boundaryless organization
An organization that is not defined or limited by boundaries or categories imposed by traditional structures.

A boundaryless organization is an organization design that is not defined or limited by boundaries or categories imposed by traditional structures. It blurs the historical boundaries surrounding an organization by increasing its interdependence with its environment. What do we mean by "boundaries"? There are two types: (1) *internal*—the horizontal ones imposed by work specialization and departmentalization and the vertical ones that separate employees into organizational levels and hierarchies and (2) *external*—the boundaries that separate the organization from its customers, suppliers, and other stakeholders. To minimize or eliminate these boundaries, managers might use virtual or network structural designs. Sometimes called *network organizations*, *learning organizations*, or *barrier-free*, *modular*, or *virtual corporations*, boundaryless structures cut across

---

[6]M. Duffy, "Training for Success in a New Industrial World," *Industrial and Commercial Training* 26, no. 5 (February 2001), 48–54.

[7]R. L. Cross, A. Yan, and M. R. Louis, "Boundary Activities in 'Boundaryless' Organizations: A Case Study of a Transformation to a Team-Based Structure," *Human Relations* 53, no. 6 (June 2000), 841–868.

[8]D. Drickhamer, "Europe's Best Plants: Mission Critical," *Industry Week*, March 2002, 44–46.

[9]C. Garvey, "Steer Teams with the Right Pay," *HR Magazine*, May 2002, 70–78.

all aspects of the organization.[10] Rather than having functional specialties located in departments working on distinctive tasks, these internally boundaryless organizations group employees to accomplish some core competency.

But boundaryless organizations are not merely flatter organizations. They attempt to eliminate vertical, horizontal, and intraorganizational barriers. Supervisors must break down the traditional hierarchies that have often existed for many decades. Horizontal organizations require multidisciplinary work teams who have the authority to make the necessary decisions to do the work and be held accountable for measurable outcomes. What factors have contributed to the rise of boundaryless organization designs in today's organizations? Undoubtedly, many of the issues we covered in Chapter 2 have had an effect. Specifically, globalization of markets and competitors has played a major role. An organization's need to respond and adapt to the complex and dynamic environment is best served by boundaryless organizations. Changes in technology have also contributed to this movement. Advances in computer power, "intelligent" software, and telecommunications enable boundaryless e-commerce organizations to exist. Each of these supports the information network that makes the virtual workplace possible.

THE LEARNING ORGANIZATION

A learning organization is an organization that has developed a capacity to continuously adapt and change because all of its members take an active role in identifying and resolving work-related issues.[11] In learning organizations, employees are practicing knowledge management by continually acquiring and sharing new knowledge and are willing to apply that knowledge in making decisions or performing their work.

learning organization
An organization that has developed the capacity to adapt and change continuously.

What type of organizing elements would be necessary for learning to take place in an organization? In a learning organization, it's critical for members to share information and collaborate on work activities throughout the entire organization—across different functional specialties and even at different organizational levels. This can be done by minimizing or eliminating existing structural boundaries. In this type of boundaryless environment, employees are free to work together and collaborate in doing the organization's work the best way they can, and to learn from each other. Because of this need to collaborate, teams also tend to be an important feature of a learning organization's structural design. Employees work in teams on whatever activities need to be done, and these employee teams are empowered to make decisions about doing their work or resolving issues. With empowered employees and teams, there is little need for "supervisors" to direct and control. Instead, supervisors serve as facilitators, supporters, and advocates for employee teams.

Employees at Kimberly-Clark have found the learning-organization concept a positive way of work. Learning to work together and sharing information have helped transform how they do their jobs—and have led to successful improvements throughout the company.

---

[10]K. R. T. Larsen and C. R. McInerney, "Preparing to Work in the Virtual Organization," *Information and Management* 39, no. 6 (May 2002), 445–456; P. R. Sparrow, "New Employee Behaviors, Work Designs and Forms of Work Organization: What Is in Store for the Future of Work?" *Journal of Managerial Psychology* 15, no. 3, March 2000, 202–218; and P. Auditore, "Enabling Knowledge Management in Today's Knowledge Economy," *KM World,* January 2002, S8–S9.

[11]Initial work on the learning organization is credited to P. M. Senge, *The Fifth Discipline: The Art and Practice* (New York: Doubleday, 1990).

Organizing Your Employees

Once your departmental structure is in place, you need to organize the specific jobs of each of your employees. How do you do that? By identifying the tasks to be done, combining them into jobs, and then formalizing the process by creating job descriptions.

HOW DO YOU IDENTIFY THE TASKS TO BE DONE?

You begin the process by making a list of all the specific tasks with which your department has been charged. These are the tasks that, when effectively accomplished, result in your department successfully achieving its goals.[12] Exhibit 4-9 illustrates a partial list drawn up by a production supervisor in a large book publishing company.

It is unlikely that one person can do all the tasks that need to be accomplished. So, the tasks need to be combined into individual jobs. Work specialization typically drives the creation of jobs. When tasks are specialized and grouped by individuals, each person becomes more proficient at his or her job. So, the book production supervisor described previously will create specific jobs such as copyeditor, proofreader, photo editor, production coordinator, and designer.

In addition to grouping similar tasks, you need to be sure that workloads within your department are balanced. Employee morale and productivity will suffer if some employees' jobs are significantly more difficult or time consuming than others are. You should take into consideration the physical, mental, and time demands that the various tasks require to be accomplished, and use this information to help balance the workloads among department employees.

WHAT IS THE PURPOSE OF JOB DESCRIPTIONS?

A job description is a written statement of what a jobholder does, how the job is done, and why it is done. It typically portrays job duties, working conditions, and operating responsibilities. Exhibit 4-10 illustrates a job description for a production editor in a publishing company.

Why do you need to write job descriptions for each job under your jurisdiction? There are two reasons. First, it provides you with a formal document describing what each employee is supposed to be doing. It acts as a standard against which you can determine how well the employee is performing. This, in turn, can be used in the employee's performance appraisal, feedback, wage adjustment, and need-for-training decisions. Second, the job description helps employees learn their job duties and clarifies the results that you expect them to achieve.

Such information is crucial—especially when you empower your employees to perform certain duties that supervisors once performed.

job description
A written statement of job duties, working conditions, and operating responsibilities.

- Attend initial planning meeting with acquisition editor to launch a new book

- Contact with acquisition editors

- Contact with authors

- Contact with marketing personnel

- Contact with advertising group

- Contact with manufacturing buyers

- Develop production schedules for each book

- Design the internal layout of books and develop sample pages and design specifications

- Have figures and tables drawn; size and crop photos

- Lay out pages

- Design book covers

- Organize and direct weekly coordination meetings for each book

- Proofread and correct pages

Exhibit 4-9

Partial listing of tasks in a book production department.

---

[12]For a detailed explanation of this area, see D. D. DeCenzo and S. P. Robbins, *Human Resource Management*, 8th ed. (New York: John Wiley & Sons, 2005), Chapter 5.

Job Title: Production Editor

Department: College Book Editorial Production

Wage Category: Exempt

Reports to: Business Team Production Supervisor

Job Class: 7-12B

Job Statement:
    Performs and oversees editing work in the areas of book specifications, design, composition, printing, and binding. May carry a number of books at the same time. Works under general supervision. Exercises initiative and independent judgment in the performance of assigned tasks.

Job Duties:

1. Identifies activities to be completed, determines sequencing, and prepares a schedule for the six-month process.

2. Performs or contracts out copyediting of book manuscript.

3. Coordinates specification (size, color, paper, covers) and design (typefaces, art) with assigned designer. Coordinates preparation of pages with manufacturing buyers and compositor.

4. Distributes scheduling status reports to acquisition editors and others as needed.

5. Acts as liaison with authors on all production issues.

6. Checks all permissions for completeness and accuracy.

7. Responsible for maintaining in-stock date set at initial launch meeting.

8. Performs related duties as assigned by team supervisor.

Exhibit 4-10
A job description for a production editor in a publishing company.

Empowering Others through Delegation

Contemporary supervisors need to learn to empower others. Empowerment means increasing your employees' involvement in their work through greater participation in decisions that control their work and by expanding responsibility for work outcomes. Two ways to empower people are to delegate authority to them and to redesign their jobs. In this section, we address delegation. In Chapter 8, we show you how to empower people through job design.

empowerment
An increase in the decision-making discretion of workers.

WHAT IS DELEGATION?

There is no question that effective supervisors need to be able to delegate. Many supervisors find that this is hard for them. Why? They're typically afraid to give up control. In this section, we want to show that delegation can actually increase your effectiveness and that, when done properly, it still provides you control.

delegation
Allocation of duties, assignment of authority, assignment of responsibility, and creation of accountability.

Delegation is frequently depicted as a four-step process: (1) allocation of duties, (2) delegation of authority, (3) assignment of responsibility, and (4) creation of accountability. Let's briefly look at each of these:

1. **Allocation of duties.** Duties are the tasks and activities that a manager desires to have someone else do. Before you can delegate authority, you must allocate to an employee the duties over which the authority extends.

2. **Delegation of authority.** The essence of the delegation process is empowering the employee to act for you. It is passing to the employee the formal rights to act on your behalf.

3. **Assignment of responsibility.** When authority is delegated, you must assign responsibility. That is, when you give someone rights, you must also assign to that person a corresponding obligation to perform. Ask yourself: Did I give my employee enough authority to get the materials, the use of equipment, and the support from others necessary to get the job done?

4. **Creation of accountability.** To complete the delegation process, you must create accountability; that is, you must hold your employee answerable for properly carrying out his or her duties. So, although responsibility means an employee is obliged to carry out assigned duties, accountability means that he or she has to perform the assignment in a satisfactory manner. Employees are responsible for the completion of tasks assigned to them and are accountable to you for the satisfactory performance of that work.

ISN'T DELEGATION ABDICATION?

If you dump tasks on an employee without clarifying exactly what is to be done, the range of the employee's discretion, the expected level of performance, when the tasks are to be completed, and similar concerns, you are abdicating responsibility and inviting trouble. But don't fall into the trap of assuming that, to avoid the appearance of abdicating, you should minimize delegation. Unfortunately, this is the approach taken by many new and inexperienced supervisors. Lacking confidence in their employees, or fearful that they will be criticized for their employees' mistakes, they try to do everything themselves.

It may very well be true that you're capable of doing the tasks you delegate to your employees better, faster, or with fewer mistakes. The catch is that your time and energy are scarce resources. It's not possible for you to do everything yourself. So, you need to learn to delegate if you're going to be effective in your job (see the section titled "Delegating" at the end of this chapter). This suggests two important points. First, you should expect and accept some mistakes by your employees. It's part of delegation. Mistakes are often good learning experiences for your employees, as long as the costs of their mistakes are not excessive. Second, to ensure that the costs of mistakes don't exceed the value of the learning, you need to put adequate controls in place. Delegation without proper feedback controls that let you know when there are serious problems is abdication.

Comprehension Check 4-2

5. An organizational structure that consists primarily of workgroups is called a _____ structure.

    a. functional
    b. team-based
    c. matrix
    d. divisional

6. An organization that has developed the capacity to adapt to change continuously is called a _____organization.

    a. learning
    b. boundaryless
    c. functional
    d. work process engineering

7. A written statement of the duties, working conditions, and operating responsibilities of a job is called a

    a. work plan
    b. goal-setting plan
    c. job description
    d. benchmark

8. Allocating duties and assigning authority to others is called

    a. efficient management
    b. delegation
    c. responsibility
    d. leadership

Enhancing Understanding

SUMMARY

After reading this chapter, I can:

1. **Define** *organizing*. Organizing is arranging jobs and groups of jobs in a department so that activities can be accomplished as planned.

2. **Describe why work specialization should increase economic efficiency.** Work specialization increases economic efficiency by allocating the most difficult and complex tasks to the employees with the highest skill level and paying people less to do the less difficult and less skilled tasks.

3. **Explain how the span of control affects an organization's structure.** The narrower the span of control, the more supervisory levels are necessary to directly oversee activities. Wider spans create fewer managerial levels and flatter organizational structures.

4. **Contrast line and staff authority.** Line authority refers to the right to direct the work of employees. Staff authority, on the other hand, advises, services, and assists line authority in accomplishing its job. Only line authority allows individuals to make decisions independently and without consulting others.

5. **Explain why organizations are becoming increasingly decentralized.** Organizations are becoming increasingly decentralized to meet competitive challenges through knowledgeable and rapid decision making.

6. **Describe how flatter organizational structures can be beneficial to the organization.** Flatter organizational structures mean that job-related activities cut across all parts of the organization. Rather than having employees perform specialized jobs and work in departments with people who do similar tasks, the organization groups them with other employees who have different skills, forming a work team. Flatter organizational structures can be beneficial because they are flexible and more adaptable to conditions external to the organization.

7. **Explain the concept of a learning organization and how it influences organizational designs and supervisors.** A learning organization is an organization that has developed the capacity to continuously adapt and change because all members take an active role in making decisions or performing their work. It influences organizational designs because an organization's ability to learn is enhanced (or hindered) by its structural boundaries and the amount of collaborative work. Supervisors in a learning organization also play a different role. Rather than being the "boss," supervisors become facilitators, supporters, and advocates for their employees.

8. **Discuss the value of job descriptions.** Job descriptions (a) provide supervisors with a formal document describing what the employee is supposed to be doing, (b) help employees learn their job duties, and (c) clarify the results that management expects.

9. **Identify the four-step process of delegation.** Delegation consists of (1) allocation of duties, (2) delegation of authority, (3) assignment of responsibility, and (4) creation of accountability.

COMPREHENSION: Review and Discussion Questions

1. What are the limitations, if any, to work specialization?

2. How might wider spans of control lead to cost reductions for an organization?

3. What is functional authority? Why would an organization use it?

4. What happens when authority and responsibility are out of balance?

5. What are the advantages of (a) product, (b) geographic, (c) customer, and (d) process departmentalization?

6. Why would an organization use a matrix structure?

7. What are the purposes of a job description?

8. Is delegation synonymous with abdication? Discuss.

9. "A learning organization makes supervision obsolete." Do you agree or disagree with this statement? Defend your position.

KEY CONCEPT CROSSWORD

ACROSS

1. allocation of duties, assignment of authority, and accountability
4. a type of departmentalization in which activities are grouped based on how issues relate to a product
7. a type of structure that combines functional and product departmentalization
9. a type of authority in which one has control over individuals outside one's direct areas of responsibility
12. an organization not defined or limited by traditional structures
15. a type of departmentalization in which activities are grouped based on territory
18. a type of authority that supports line authority by advising, servicing, and assisting
19. supervisory obligation such as achieving a unit's goal
20. the grouping of work functions in an organization
22. a type of departmentalization in which activities are grouped based on the clients served
23. a type of departmentalization in which activities are grouped based on work flow
24. a type of organization that has developed the capacity to adapt and change continuously
25. a principle that states that an employee should report to one and only one supervisor

DOWN

2. a type of authority that allows a supervisor to direct the work of his or her employees
3. a type of structure that consists entirely of work groups
5. the continuous line of authority that extends from the highest levels to the lowest levels in an organization
6. a type of structure that is characterized as nonelaborate
8. a written statement of job duties
10. pushing down decision-making authority to those closest to the problem
11. process of breaking down jobs into a number of steps
13. the number of employees a supervisor can efficiently and effectively direct
14. decision-making responsibility in the hands of top management
16. a type of departmentalization in which activities are grouped based on the work performed
17. an increase in the decision-making discretion of workers
21. rights inherent in a supervisory position

ANSWERS TO COMPREHENSION CHECKS

Comprehension Check 4-1

1. b   2. a   3. c   4. c

Comprehension Check 4-2

5. b   6. a   7. c   8. b

Developing Your Supervisory Skills

GETTING TO KNOW YOURSELF

Before you can effectively supervise others, you must understand your present strengths and areas in need of development. To assist in this learning process, we encourage you to complete the following self-assessments from the Prentice Hall Self-Assessment Library 3.4.

1. How Power Oriented Am I? (II. C. 1.)

2. What's My Preferred Type of Power? (II. C. 2.)

3. What Type of Organization Structure Do I Prefer? (III. A. 1.)

4. What's the Right Organizational Culture for Me? (III. B. 1.)

After you complete the assessment, we suggest you retain the results and store them as part of your "portfolio of learning about yourself."

BUILDING A TEAM

➤ An Experiential Exercise: How Is Your School Organized?

Every college has a specific type of organizational structure. That is, if you are taking business courses, your classes are often "housed" in a department, school, or college of business. But have you ever asked why? Or is it something you just take for granted?

Analyze your school's overall structure in terms of formalization, centralization, and complexity. Furthermore, look at the departmentalization that exists.

Is your school's structure more functional or divisional? Does it exhibit learning-organization tendencies? Based on your assessments, what kind of structure would you predict your college to have? Does it have this structure now? Compare your findings with other classmates. Are there similarities in how each viewed the college? Differences? What do you believe has contributed to these findings?

➤ Internet: Web Activity

Go to http://www.pearsonhighered.com/robbins/. Find *Supervision Today!* 7th Ed. and click Companion Website.

DELEGATING

In learning to delegate, recognize that delegation is not the same as participation. In participative decision making, there's a sharing of authority. With delegation, employees make decisions on their own. That's why delegation is such a vital component of empowering workers! A number of actions are recommended that when followed can make you an effective delegator.

STEPS IN PRACTICING THE SKILL

STEP 1: Clarify the assignment. The place to begin is to determine what is to be delegated and to whom.

You need to identify the person best capable of doing the task, and then determine whether he or she has the time and motivation to do the job. Assuming you have a willing and able employee, it is your responsibility to provide clear information on what is being delegated, the results you expect, and any time or performance expectations you hold. Unless there is an overriding need to adhere to specific methods, you should delegate only the end results. That is, get agreement on what is to be done and the end results expected, but let the employee decide on the means. By focusing on goals and allowing the employee the freedom to use his or her own judgment as to how those goals are to be achieved, you increase trust between you and the employee, improve that employee's motivation, and enhance accountability for the results.

STEP 2: Specify the employee's range of discretion. Every act of delegation comes with constraints. You're delegating authority to act, but not unlimited authority. What you're delegating is authority to act on certain issues and, on those issues, within certain parameters. You need to specify what those parameters are so that employees know, in no uncertain terms, the range of their discretion. When this has been successfully communicated, both you and the employee will have the same idea of the limits to the latter's authority and how far he or she can go without checking further with you. How much authority do you give an employee? In other words, how tight do you draw the parameters? The best answer is that you should allocate enough authority to allow the individual to complete the task successfully.

STEP 3: Allow the employee to participate. One of the best sources for determining how much authority will be necessary to accomplish a task is the employee who will be held accountable for that task. If you allow employees to participate in determining what is delegated, how much authority is needed to get the job done, and the standards by which they'll be judged, you increase employee motivation, satisfaction, and accountability for performance. Be aware, however, that participation can present its own set of potential problems, as a result of employees' self-interest and biases in evaluating their own abilities. Some employees, for example, are personally motivated to expand their authority beyond what they need and beyond what they are capable of handling. Allowing such people too much participation in deciding which tasks they should take on and how much authority they must have to complete those tasks can undermine the effectiveness of the delegation process.

STEP 4: Inform others that delegation has occurred. Delegation should not take place in a vacuum. Not only do you and the employee need to know specifically what has been delegated and how much authority has been granted, but anyone else who may be affected by the delegation act also

needs to be informed. This includes people outside the organization as well as inside it. Essentially, you need to convey what has been delegated (the task and amount of authority) and to whom. If you fail to follow through on this step, the legitimacy of your employee's authority will probably be called into question. Failure to inform others makes conflicts likely and decreases the chances that your employee will be able to accomplish the delegated task efficiently.

STEP 5: Establish feedback controls. To delegate without instituting feedback controls is to invite problems. There is always the possibility that an employee will misuse the discretion that he or she has been delegated. The establishment of controls to monitor the employee's progress increases the likelihood that important problems will be identified early and that the task will be completed on time and to the desired specifications. Ideally, controls should be determined at the time of the initial assignment. Agree on a specific time for completion of the task, and then set progress dates when the employee will report back on how well he or she is doing and any major problems that have surfaced. This can be supplemented with periodic spot checks to ensure that authority guidelines are not being abused, organization policies are being followed, proper procedures are being used, and the like. But too much of a good thing can be dysfunctional. If the controls are too constraining, the employee will be deprived of the opportunity to build self-confidence and much of the motivational properties of delegation will be lost. A well-designed control system permits your employee to make small mistakes, but quickly alerts you when big mistakes are imminent.

STEP 6: When problems surface, insist on recommendations from the employee. Many supervisors fall into the trap of letting employees reverse the delegation process: The employee runs into a problem and then comes back to the supervisor for advice or a solution. Avoid being sucked into reverse delegation by insisting from the beginning that when employees want to discuss a problem with you, they come prepared with a recommendation. When you delegate downward, the employee's job includes making necessary decisions. Don't allow the employee to push decisions back upward to you.

➤ Communicating Effectively

1. Visit a McDonald's restaurant on a weekday around noon. On your first order, ask for a Big Mac or Quarter Pounder with Cheese. Record how long it takes to have your order filled. Leave, and return to the counter. On your second order, order the Big Mac or Quarter Pounder with (a) no lettuce, (b) extra pickles, and (c) no cheese. Record how long this special order takes. Compare the two times. Discuss the time differences in terms of efficiencies of work specialization. Also note whether the second order was completed correctly. What are the implications of this simple research for product specialization?

2. Discuss the pros and cons of a learning organization. Do you believe there are organizations that are better suited for a learning-organization environment? Discuss.

THINKING CRITICALLY

➤ Case 4-A: Using Plans

Jack Gibson is the building and grounds supervisor at a community college in a small city. His primary job responsibility is to ensure that the inside of the buildings and the grounds are clean and in good repair and are pleasant places for students, faculty, staff, and visitors. The range of his duties on a particular day can take him from supervising the repair of a water main to deciding which type of plants are best for the student lounge area. With the changes in the seasons he must pay attention to new plants, snow removal, adjusting the heat and air conditioning, and maintaining a constant level of humidity in the greenhouse used by the college biology department. His department includes seven full-time workers, many of whom have a specialty such as heating or plumbing, and he hires part-time employees as the need arises and the budget permits for grass cutting, snow removal, and special projects.

The needs are constantly changing with the seasons and special events. The college hosts many community events and a grand graduation ceremony, and last year the governor and the president of the United States visited during the campaign season. Jack is constantly monitoring different areas on the campus trying to balance the need for functionality and a desire for a beautiful space. He works very closely with the campus security department, the special events area, the construction manager, and the housekeeping staff.

RESPONDING TO THE CASE

1. Explain how work specialization is important to Jack as a building and grounds supervisor.

2. What type of organizational structure does this community college have? What are the strengths and weaknesses of this structure?

3. Discuss the factors that determine the size of Jack's span of control.

➤ Case 4-B: A Noble Supervisor

Sarah Travis is a supervisor at a Barnes and Noble university bookstore. She reports to the bookstore manager, and her primary job responsibility is to supervise three individuals who are responsible for ancillary items—clothing, gifts, and novelty items—that the bookstore sells. Sarah's job involves many activities, including ordering these items for the bookstore. Each semester her department must decide which traditional items should be stocked and which specialty or seasonal items might be needed. They must fill out a purchase order that identifies the number of items ordered and their costs; Sarah will receive the bill of sale that accompanies the invoice at delivery. When the goods arrive from various vendors, one of Sarah's employees logs them into the bookstore's inventory system. An employee then checks the goods to see that the order is correct. At that point, Sarah signs off on the invoice and forwards it to the bookkeeper, who handles all monies for the bookstore. One of Sarah's employees then unpacks the items and places them in a prearranged area of the stock room.

Unfortunately, simply placing goods into inventory won't create a sale. Sarah's department must set up displays on the bookstore floor, and then continually monitor the shelves and restock them whenever necessary.

During this time, Sarah must also keep track of what goods have sold. She needs to have this information entered in her inventory system so that she does not run out of items that are selling. To track inventories, Sarah receives cash register receipts twice daily during her shift. When a particular point is reached in remaining inventory, Sarah completes another purchase order and the process starts over again.

Sarah is also required to meet weekly with other supervisors to coordinate a variety of activities. For example, she and the person responsible for textbooks meet to discuss space utilization. At certain times, such as the beginning of a semester, more space is needed for textbook sales. After the first week of classes, the textbook space is reduced, enabling Sarah's employees to set up more ancillary item displays. Similar meetings take place with the individuals responsible for snack and personal hygiene products and office supplies and stationery.

RESPONDING TO THE CASE

1. What type of departmentalization is evident in the employee grouping of Sarah's department? Cite specific examples to support your point of view.

2. What are the strengths and weaknesses of this grouping?

3. If you were asked to group employees and activities in the bookstore in the most efficient manner from a customer (student) standpoint, what would that grouping be like? Explain your position.

Staffing and Recruiting

Key Concepts

After completing this chapter, you will be able to define these supervisory terms:

- affirmative action
- compensation administration
- employee benefits
- employee training
- employment planning
- human resource inventory
- human resource management
- layoff-survivor sickness
- orientation

- performance-simulation tests
- realistic job preview
- recruitment
- reliability
- selection process
- sexual harassment
- validity
- websumés

Chapter Outcomes

After reading this chapter, you will be able to:

1. Describe the human resource management process.
2. Discuss the influence of government regulations on human resource decisions.
3. Contrast recruitment and downsizing options.
4. Explain the importance of validity and reliability in selection.
5. Describe the selection devices that work best with various kinds of jobs.
6. Identify various training methods.
7. Describe the goals of compensation administration and factors that affect wage structures.
8. Explain what is meant by the terms *sexual harassment* and *layoff-survivor sickness*.

Responding to a Supervisory Dilemma

Your interview day has finally arrived. You are all dressed up to make that lasting first impression. You finally meet Mrs. Landers, as she shakes your hand firmly and invites you to get comfortable. Your interview has started! This is the moment you've waited for.

The first few moments appear mundane enough. The questions to this point, in fact, seem easy. Your confidence is growing. That little voice in your head keeps telling you that you are doing fine—just keep going. Suddenly, the questions get tougher. Mrs. Landers leans back and asks about why you want to leave your current job—the one you've been in for only eighteen months. As you begin to explain that you want to leave for personal reasons, she begins to probe more. Her smile is gone and her body language is different. All right, you think, be honest. So, you tell Mrs. Landers that you want to leave because you think your boss is unethical and you don't want your reputation tarnished by being associated with this person. This has led to a number of public disagreements with your boss, and you're tired of dealing with the situation any longer. Mrs. Landers looks at you and replies: "If you ask me, that's not a valid reason for wanting to leave. It appears to me that you should be more assertive about the situation. Are you sure you're confident enough and have what it takes to make it in this company?" How dare she talk to you that way! Who does she think she is? You respond with an angry tone in your voice. Guess what? You've just fallen victim to one of the tricks of the interviewing business—the stress interview.

Stress interviews are becoming more commonplace in today's business. Every job produces stress, and at some point every worker has a horrendous day. So, these types of interviews become predictors of how you may react at work under less than favorable conditions. How so? Interviewers want to observe how you'll react when you are put under pressure. Those who demonstrate the resolve and strength to handle the stress indicate a level of professionalism and confidence. Those are the characteristics being assessed. People who react to the pressure interview in a more positive manner indicate that they will likely be able to handle the day-to-day irritations that exist at work. Those who don't, well...

On the other hand, stress interviews are staged events. Interviewers deliberately lead applicants into a false sense of security—the comfortable interaction. Then, suddenly and drastically, they change. They go on the attack. And it's usually a personal affront that picks on a weakness they've uncovered about the applicant. It's possibly humiliating; at the very least it's demeaning. So, should stress interviews be used? Should interviewers be permitted to assess professionalism and confidence and how one reacts to the everyday nuisances of work by putting applicants in confrontational scenarios? Does getting angry in an interview when pressured indicate one's propensity toward violence should things not always go smoothly at work? Should supervisors advocate the use of an activity that could possibly get out of control?

The quality of a department and the entire organization is to a large degree determined by the quality of people it employs. Success for most supervisors depends on finding the right employees with the necessary skills to successfully perform the tasks required to attain the company's strategic goals. Staffing and human resource management decisions and methods are critical to ensuring that the organization hires and keeps the right personnel.

You may be thinking, Sure, personnel decisions are important. But aren't most of them made by people who specifically handle human resource issues? It's true that, in many organizations, a number of the activities grouped under the label human resource management (HRM) are done by specialists in human resources. In other cases, HRM activities may even be outsourced to companies. But not all supervisors may have HRM staff support. Small-business owners, for instance, are an obvious example of individuals who frequently must do their own hiring without the assistance of HRM specialists. Even supervisors in larger organizations are frequently involved in recruiting candidates, reviewing application forms, interviewing applicants, inducting new employees, making decisions about employee training, providing career advice to employees, and evaluating employees' performance. So, whether or not an organization provides HRM support activities, every supervisor is involved with human resource decisions in his or her unit.

Exhibit 5-1 introduces the key components of an organization's human resource management process. It represents eight activities or steps (Strategic human resource planning, Recruitment and downsizing, Selection, Orientation, Training and development, Performance appraisal, Compensation and benefits, Safety and health) that, if properly executed, will staff an organization with competent, high-performing employees who are capable of sustaining their performance level over the long term.

The first three steps represent employment planning, the adding of staff through recruitment, the reduction in staff through downsizing, and selection. When executed properly, these steps lead to the identification and selection of competent employees. These activities are important to assist organizations in achieving their goals. Accordingly, once an organization's plans have been established and the organization's structure has been designed, it's now time to "add" the people. That's one of the most critical roles for supervisors.

Once you have selected competent people, you need to help them adapt to the organization and to ensure that their job skills and knowledge are kept current. You do

human resource management
The process of finding, hiring, training, and keeping employees in the organization.

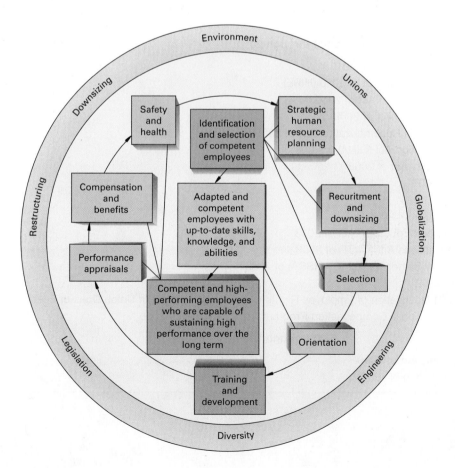

Exhibit 5-1

The human resource management process.

this through orientation, training, and development. The last steps in the HRM process are designed to identify performance goals, correct performance problems if necessary, and help employees sustain a high level of performance over their entire work life. The activities involved include performance appraisal, compensation and benefits, and safety and health.

Notice in Exhibit 5-1 that the entire employment process is influenced by the external environment. Many of the factors introduced in Chapter 2 (e.g., globalization, downsizing, and diversity) directly affect all management practices. But their effect is probably most severe in the management of human resources because whatever happens to an organization ultimately influences what happens to its employees. So, every supervisor must have a fundamental understanding of the current laws and regulations governing equal employment opportunity (see "Something to Think About: Is It Safe?").

The Legal Environment of HRM

Since the mid-1960s, the federal government has greatly expanded its influence over HRM decisions by enacting a wealth of laws and regulations (see Exhibit 5-2 for examples). As a result, today's supervisors must ensure that equal employment opportunities exist for job applicants and current employees. Decisions regarding who will be hired, for example, or which employees will be chosen for a training program must be made without regard to race, sex, religion, age, color, national origin, or disability. Exceptions can occur only when special circumstances exist. For instance, a community fire department can deny employment to a firefighter applicant who uses a wheelchair. But if that same individual is applying for a desk job, such as fire department dispatcher, the disability cannot be

---

Here is a comprehensive list of federal employment laws HR professionals and supervisors need to be familiar with. Work with a partner to select one law from each grouping. Go online to locate a brief description of the law for presentation to the class.

2000 through 2010

Patient Protection and Affordable Care Act of 2010
Hiring Incentives to Restore Employment Act of 2010 (HIRE)
Health Care Education and Reconciliation Act of 2010
American Recovery and Reinvestment Act of 2009
Children's Health Insurance Program Reauthorization Act of 2009 (CHIPRA)
Generic Information Nondiscrimination Act (GINA) of 2008
Mental Health and Addiction Equity Act of 2008
Lilly Ledbetter Fair Pay Act of 2007
Pension Protection Act (PPA) of 2006
Veterans Benefits Improvement Act of 2004
Workforce Reinvestment and Adult Education Act of 2003
Fair and Accurate Credit Transactions Act (FACT) of 2003
Contract Work Hours and Safety Standards Act (CWHSSA) of 2002
Sarbanes-Oxley Act (SOX) of 2002
Executive Order 13201 of 2001 Notification of Employee Rights Concerning Payment of Union Dues or Fees
Energy Employees Occupational Illness Compensation Program Act (EEOICPA) of 2000

1990 through 1999

Women's Health & Cancer Rights Act of 1998
Immigration and Nationality Act (INA) of 1996

Exhibit 5-2

Major U.S. federal laws and regulations related to HRM.

Mental Health Parity Act (MHPA) of 1996
Health Insurance Portability and Accountability Act (HIPAA) of 1996
Newborns' and Mothers' Health Protection Act of 1996
Uniformed Services Employment and Reemployment Rights Act (USERRA) of 1994
OSHA Hazard Communication Standard of 1994
Family and Medical Leave Act (FMLA) of 1993
Federal Employees' Compensation Act (FECA) of 1993
Civil Rights Act of 1991
Americans with Disabilities Act (ADA) of 1990

1980 through 1989

Drug-Free Workplace Act of 1988
Employee Polygraph Protection Act (EPPA) of 1988
Worker Adjustment and Retraining Notification Act (WARN) of 1988
Consolidated Omnibus Budget Reconciliation Act (COBRA) of 1986
Immigration Reform and Control Act of 1986 (IRCA)
Migrant and Seasonal Agricultural Worker Protection Act (MSPA) of 1983

1970 through 1979

Mandatory Retirement Act of 1978
Pregnancy Discrimination Act, Title VII of 1978
Uniform Guidelines on Employee Selection Procedures of 1978
Federal Mine Safety and Health Act (Mine Act) of 1977
Employee Retirement Income Security Act (ERISA) of 1974
Privacy Act of 1974
Vietnam-Era Veterans Readjustment Act (VEVRA) of 1974
Rehabilitation Act 1973, Section 503
Occupational Safety And Health Act (OSHA) of 1970

1960 through 1969

Black Lung Benefits Act (BLBA) authorized by Title IV, Federal Coal Mine Health and Safety Act of 1969
Fair Credit reporting Act (FCRA) of 1969
Consumer Credit Protection Act (CCPA) pf 1968
Jury Service and Selection Act of 1968
Age Discrimination in Employment Act (ADEA) of 1967
Executive Order 11246 of 1965 requiring Equal Employment Opportunity
McNamara-O'Hara Service Contract Act (SCA) of 1965
Title VII of the Civil Rights Act of 1964
Equal Pay Act (EPA) of 1963

1890 through 1959

Labor-Management Reporting and Disclosure Act (LMRDA) of 1959
National Labor Relations Act (NLRA) of 1947
Fair Labor Standards Act of (FLSA) of 1938
Walsh-Healey Act of 1936
Federal Insurance Contributions Act (FICA) of 1935
Copeland Act of 1934
Norris-LaGuardia Act of 1932
Davis Bacon Act of 1931
Longshore and Harbor Workers' Compensation Act (LHWCA) of 1927
Sherman Anti-Trust Act of 1890

Society for Human Resource Management (SHRM), "Federal Statues, Regulations and Guidance," http://www.shrm.org/LegalIssues/
FederalResources/FederalStatuesRegualtionsandGuidance/Pages/default.aspx (accessed May 14, 2011).

Exhibit 5-2 *Continued*

affirmative action
An active effort to recruit, select, train, and promote members of protected groups.

used as a reason to deny employment. The issues involved, however, are rarely that clear-cut. For example, employment laws protect most employees whose religious beliefs require a specific style of dress—robes, long shirts, long hair, and the like. However, if the individual's job involves operating machinery where the specific style of dress may be hazardous or unsafe in the work setting, a company could refuse to hire a person who would not adapt to a safer dress code.

Something to Think About (and promote class discussion)

IS IT SAFE?

Today, most supervisors know that their hiring practices must meet the requirements of employment laws. As a result, rarely will you find a supervisor who blatantly excludes certain groups of people. This doesn't mean, however, that discrimination cannot occur. Employment practices that appear harmless may, in fact, keep certain people from having an equal chance. To see how this can happen, read the following situations that may arise in the employment process. After reading each one, check whether you feel it is a safe or a risky practice for an organization to be using. Don't be concerned with whether you think the practice is legal or illegal. Just consider whether you believe it's okay to do, or whether it could create problems for the organization.

	Safe	Risky
1. "Wanted: Recent college graduate to teach first grade in the local public school."	☐	☐
2. A waiter in an exclusive restaurant is fired when his supervisor finds out he tested positive for HIV.	☐	☐
3. You want to take twelve weeks off without pay to care for your new child during the busiest part of your work year, and your supervisor denies the request.	☐	☐
4. A Broadway theater hires a woman for the job of restroom attendant and assigns her to the men's restroom.	☐	☐
5. An applicant who uses a wheelchair is denied a job as a computer programer. This seventy-five-person company is on the third floor and the building does not have elevators. Furthermore, door openings to offices are not wide enough for a wheelchair to pass safely—thus creating a safety hazard for the individual.	☐	☐
6. The company policy states: "Applicants applying for jobs in the organization must have, at a minimum, a high school diploma."	☐	☐
7. A pilot for Continental Airlines celebrates his sixty-fifth birthday. The following day, he is no longer permitted by his supervisor to fly the commercial flights he has been doing for the past twenty-eight years.	☐	☐
8. "Wanted: Sales rep to sell medical supplies to regional hospitals. The successful applicant must have five years of sales experience."	☐	☐

Trying to balance the "should" and "should-nots" of complying with these laws often falls under the realm of affirmative action. Many organizations have affirmative action programs to ensure that decisions and practices enhance the employment, upgrading, and retention of members from protected groups, such as minorities and females. That is, the supervisors in the organization not only refrain from discrimination but actively seek to enhance the status of members from protected groups.

Our conclusion is that supervisors are not completely free to choose whom they hire, promote, or fire. Although these regulations have significantly helped reduce employment discrimination and unfair employment practices in organizations, they have, at the same time, also reduced management's discretion over human resource decisions.

Employment Planning

Employment planning is the process by which supervisors ensure that they have the right number and kinds of people in the right places, and at the right times, who are capable of effectively and efficiently completing tasks that will help the organization achieve its overall objectives. Employment planning, then, translates the organization's and department's goals into a personnel plan that will allow those goals to be achieved. Employment planning can be condensed into two steps: (1) assessing current human resources and (2) assessing future human resource needs and developing a program to meet them.

employment planning
Assessing current human resources and future human resource needs; developing a program to meet future human resource needs.

HOW DOES A SUPERVISOR CONDUCT AN EMPLOYEE ASSESSMENT?

Supervisors begin by reviewing their current human resource status. This review is typically done by generating a human resource inventory. In an era of sophisticated computer systems, it is not too difficult a task for most supervisors to generate a human resource inventory report. The input for this report is derived from forms completed by employees. Such reports might list the name, education, training, prior employment, languages spoken, capabilities, and specialized skills of each employee in the organization. This inventory allows a supervisor to assess what talents and skills are currently available in the department and elsewhere in the organization.

human resource inventory
A database listing name, education, training, prior employer, languages spoken, and other information for each employee in the organization.

HOW ARE FUTURE EMPLOYEE NEEDS DETERMINED?

Future human resource needs are determined by the department's goals. Demand for human resources (its employees) is a result of demand for what the department produces. On the basis of its estimate of total work to be completed, a supervisor can attempt to establish the number and mix of human resources needed to reach that revenue.

After a supervisor has assessed both current capabilities and future needs, he or she is better able to estimate shortages—both in number and in kind—and to highlight areas in which the department is overstaffed. A program can then be developed that matches these estimates with forecasts of future labor supply. So, employment planning provides information not only to guide current staffing needs but also to project future employee needs and availability.

Recruitment and Selection

Once supervisors know their current staffing levels—whether they are understaffed or overstaffed—they can begin to do something about it. If one or more vacancies exist, they can use the information gathered through job analysis (see Chapter 4) to guide them in recruitment—the process of locating, identifying, and attracting capable applicants. On the other hand, if employment planning indicates a surplus, management will want to reduce the labor supply within the organization. This activity initiates downsizing or layoff activities.

recruitment
The process of locating, identifying, and attracting capable applicants.

WHERE DO SUPERVISORS LOOK TO RECRUIT CANDIDATES?

Candidates can be found by using several sources—including the World Wide Web. Exhibit 5-3 offers some guidance. The source that is used should reflect the local labor market, the type or level of position, and the size of the organization.

Are Certain Recruiting Sources Better Than Others? Do certain recruiting sources produce superior candidates? The answer is generally yes. The majority of studies have found

Source	Advantages	Disadvantages
Internal searches	Low cost; build employee morale; candidates are familiar with organization	Limited supply; may not increase proportion of protected-group employees
Advertisements	Wide distribution can be targeted to specific groups	Generate many unqualified candidates
Employee referrals	Knowledge about the organization provided by current employees; can generate strong candidates because a good referral reflects on the recommender	May not increase the diversity and mix of employees
Public employment agencies	Free or nominal cost	Candidates tend to be lower-skilled, although some skilled employees available
Private employment agencies	Wide contacts; careful screening; short-term guarantees often given	High cost
School placement	Large, centralized body of candidates	Limited to entry-level positions
Temporary help services	Fill temporary needs	Expensive
Employee leasing and independent contractors	Fill temporary needs, but usually for more specific, longer-term projects	Little commitment to organization other than current project

Exhibit 5-3

Traditional recruiting sources.

that employee referrals produce the best candidates.[1] The explanation for this finding is intuitively logical. First, applicants referred by current employees are prescreened by those employees. Because the recommenders know both the job and the person being recommended, they tend to refer applicants who are well qualified for the job. Second, because current employees often feel that their reputation in the organization is at stake with a referral, they tend to refer others only when they are reasonably confident that the referral won't make them look bad. But this finding should not be interpreted to mean that supervisors should always opt for the employee-referred candidate. Employee referrals may not increase the diversity and mix of employees.

A Special Case: Online Recruiting Newspaper advertisements and the like may be on their way to extinction as primary sources for identifying job candidates. The reason: Internet recruiting. Nearly four out of five companies currently use the Internet to recruit new employees—increasingly by adding a recruitment section to their website.[2] Because almost every organization—small as well as large—creates its own website, these become natural extensions for finding new employees. Organizations planning to do a lot of Internet recruiting often develop dedicated sites specifically designed for recruitment. They have the typical information you might find in an employment advertisement—qualifications sought, experience desired, benefits provided. But they

---

[1]"Employee Referral Programs: Highly Qualified New Hires Who Stick Around," *Canadian HR Reporter*, June 4, 2001, 21; and C. Lachnit, "Employee Referral Saves Time, Saves Money, Delivers Quality," *Workforce*, June 2001, 66–72.

[2]M. N. Martinez, "Get Job Seekers to Come to You," *HR Magazine*, August 2000, 42–52.

also allow the organization to showcase its products, services, corporate philosophy, and mission statement. This information increases the quality of applicants because those whose values don't mesh with the organization tend to self-select themselves out. The best designed of those websites include an online response form so that applicants don't need to send a separate résumé by mail, e-mail, or fax. Applicants only need to fill in a résumé page and click the "Submit" button. Many commercial Internet recruitment service companies—such as Monster.com—also provide these services.

Aggressive job candidates are also using the Internet. They set up their own web pages to "sell" their job candidacy—frequently called websumés. When they learn of a possible job opening, they encourage potential employers to "check me out at my website." There, applicants have standard résumé information, supporting documentation, and sometimes a video in which they introduce themselves to potential employers.

websumé
A web page used as a résumé.

Internet recruiting provides a low-cost means for most businesses to gain unprecedented access to potential employees worldwide. For example, a job posted online for San Francisco–based Joie de Vivre Hospitality cost $50. Had a supervisor used the more traditional local paper advertisement, the same ad would have cost $2,000.[3] It's also a way to increase diversity and find people with unique talents. Job-posting services create subgroup categories for employers looking, for example, to find bilingual workers, female attorneys, or African American engineers.

Finally, Internet recruiting won't be merely the choice of those looking to fill high-tech jobs. Computer availability and Internet access combined with increasing computer savvy have opened the door to the use of online recruiting for all kinds of nontechnical jobs—from those paying thousands of dollars a week to those paying minimum wage.

HOW DOES A SUPERVISOR HANDLE LAYOFFS?

In the past decade, most large U.S. corporations, as well as many government agencies and small businesses, have been forced to shrink the size of their workforce or restructure their skill composition. Downsizing has become a relevant means of meeting the demands of a dynamic environment.

What are a supervisor's downsizing options? Obviously, people can be "let go." But other choices may be more beneficial to the organization. Exhibit 5-4 summarizes a supervisor's major downsizing options. But keep in mind, regardless of the method chosen, employees may suffer. We discuss this phenomenon for employees—both victims and survivors—later in this chapter.

Option	Description
Firing	Permanent involuntary termination
Layoffs	Temporary involuntary termination; may last only a few days or extend to years
Attrition	Not filling openings created by voluntary resignations or normal retirements
Transfers	Moving employees either laterally or downward; usually does not reduce costs but can reduce intraorganizational supply–demand imbalances
Reduced workweeks	Having employees work fewer hours per week, share jobs, or perform their jobs on a part-time basis
Early retirements	Providing incentives to older and more-senior employees for retiring before their normal retirement date
Job sharing	Having employees, typically two part-timers, share one full-time position

Exhibit 5-4
Downsizing options.

[3]M. Zall, "Internet Recruiting," *Strategic Finance*, June 2000, 66; S. L. Thomas and K. Ray, "Recruiting and the Web: High-Tech Hiring," *Business Horizons*, May/June 2000, 43; and M. Whitford, "Hi-Tech HR, Hotel," *Hotel and Motel Management*, October 16, 2000, 49.

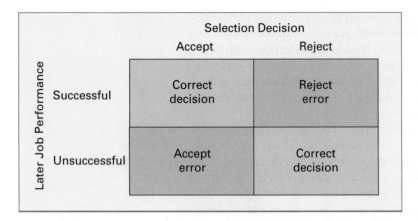

Exhibit 5-5
Selection decision outcomes.

selection process
The hiring process, designed to expand the organization's knowledge about an applicant's background, abilities, and motivation.

IS THERE A BASIC PREMISE TO SELECTING JOB CANDIDATES?

Once the recruiting effort has developed a pool of candidates, the next step in the employment process is to identify who is "best" qualified for the job. In essence, then, the selection process is a prediction exercise. It seeks to predict which applicants will be successful if hired. *Successful* in this case means performing well on the criteria the organization uses to evaluate its employees. In filling a network administrator position, for example, the selection process should be able to predict which applicants will be able to install, debug, and manage the organization's computer network properly. For a position as a sales representative, it should predict which applicants will be effective in generating high sales volumes. Consider, for a moment, that any selection decision can result in four possible outcomes. As shown in Exhibit 5-5, two of those outcomes would indicate correct decisions, but two would indicate errors.

A decision is correct (1) when the applicant was predicted to be successful (was accepted) and later proved to be successful on the job or (2) when the applicant was predicted to be unsuccessful (was rejected) and, if hired, would not have been able to do the job. In the former case, we have successfully accepted; in the latter case, we have successfully rejected. Problems occur, however, when we make errors by rejecting candidates who, if hired, would have performed successfully on the job (called reject errors) or by accepting those who subsequently perform poorly (accept errors). These problems are, unfortunately, far from insignificant.

A generation ago, reject errors meant only that the costs of selection would be increased because more candidates would have to be screened. Today, selection techniques that result in reject errors can open the organization to charges of employment discrimination, especially if applicants from protected groups are disproportionately rejected. Accept errors, on the other hand, have very obvious costs to supervisors and their organizations, including the cost of training the employee, the costs generated or profits forgone because of the employee's incompetence, and the cost of severance and the subsequent costs of further recruiting and selection screening. The major thrust of any selection activity is therefore to reduce the probability of making reject errors or accept errors while increasing the probability of making correct decisions. We do this by using selection activities that are both reliable and valid.

reliability
An indication of whether a test or device measures the same thing consistently.

What Is Reliability? Reliability addresses whether a selection device measures the same thing consistently. For example, if a test is reliable, any single individual's score should remain fairly stable over time, assuming that the characteristics it is measuring are also stable. The importance of reliability should be self-evident. No selection device can be effective if it is low in reliability. Using such a device would be the equivalent of weighing yourself every day on an erratic scale. If the scale is unreliable—randomly fluctuating, say, ten to fifteen pounds every time you step on it—the results will not mean much. To be effective predictors, selection devices must possess an acceptable level of consistency.

validity
A proven relationship between a selection device and some relevant criterion.

What Is Validity? Any selection device that a supervisor uses—such as application forms, tests, interviews, or physical examinations—must also demonstrate validity. That is, there must be a proven relationship between the selection device used and some relevant measure. For example, a few pages ago we introduced a firefighter applicant who uses a wheelchair. Because of the physical requirements of a firefighter's job, someone who uses a wheelchair would be unable to pass the physical endurance tests. In that case, denying employment could be considered valid. But requiring the same physical endurance tests for the dispatching job would not be job related. Thus, the law prohibits supervisors from using any selection device that cannot be shown to be directly related to successful job performance. And that constraint goes for "entrance" tests, too; supervisors must be able to demonstrate that, once on the job, individuals with high scores on this test outperform individuals with low test scores. Consequently, the burden is on supervisors and their organizations to verify that any selection device used to screen applicants is related to job performance.

HOW EFFECTIVE ARE TESTS AND INTERVIEWS AS SELECTION DEVICES?

Supervisors can use a number of selection devices to reduce accept and reject errors. The best-known devices include written tests, performance-simulation tests, and interviews. Let's briefly review these devices, giving particular attention to the validity of each in predicting job performance. After we review them, we discuss when each should be used.

How Do Written Tests Serve a Useful Purpose? Typical written tests include tests of intelligence, aptitude, ability, and interest. Such tests have long been used as selection devices, although their popularity has run in cycles. Written tests were widely used for twenty years after World War II. Beginning in the late 1960s, however, they fell into disfavor. Written tests were frequently characterized as discriminatory, and many organizations could not validate that their written tests were job related. But, since the late 1980s, written tests have made a comeback. Managers have become increasingly aware that poor hiring decisions are costly and that properly designed tests could reduce the likelihood of making such decisions. In addition, the cost of developing and validating a set of written tests for a specific job has come down markedly.

What Are Performance-Simulation Tests? What better way is there to find out whether an applicant for a technical writing position at Microsoft can write technical manuals than to have him or her do it? The logic of this question has led to the expanding interest in performance-simulation tests. Undoubtedly, the enthusiasm for these tests lies in the fact that they are based on job analysis data and therefore should more easily meet the requirement of job relatedness than do written tests. Performance-simulation tests are made up of actual job behaviors rather than substitutes. The best-known performance-simulation tests are work sampling (a miniature replica of the job) and assessment centers (simulating real problems a candidate may face on the job). The former is suited to routine jobs, the latter to selecting managerial personnel.

performance-simulation tests
Selection devices based on actual job behaviors, work sampling, and assessment centers.

What About Personality Profiles? Are there certain personality types that can be counted on to be more productive than others? And are there effective, reliable methods of selecting applicants who will perform well in the situations encountered on a particular job? Five factors of personality dimensions are identified by the Big Five model. They are the following:

Extroversion. Sociable, talkative, and assertive.
Agreeableness. Good-natured, cooperative, and trustworthy
Conscientiousness. Responsible, dependable, persistent, and achievement oriented.
Emotional stability. Calm, enthusiastic, and secure
Openness to experience. Imaginative, artistically sensitive, and intellectual.

Relationships have been shown to exist between these personality dimensions and on-the-job performance. One study of professionals, police, managers, salespeople, and skilled and semiskilled workers has shown conscientiousness to be a predictor of job performance for these occupational groups. The other factors figure differently depending on the occupational group and the situation.[4]

Is the Interview Effective? The interview, along with the application form, is an almost universal selection device. Few of us have ever gotten a job without one or more interviews. The irony of this fact is that the value of the interview as a selection device has been the subject of considerable debate.[5]

Interviews can be reliable and valid selection tools, but too often they are not. When interviews are structured and well organized, and when interviewers are held to common questioning, interviews are effective predictors.[6] But those conditions do not characterize many interviews. The typical interview—in which applicants are asked a varying set of essentially random questions in an informal setting—often provides little in the way of valuable information.

All kinds of potential biases can creep into interviews if they are not well structured and standardized. To illustrate, a review of the research leads us to the following conclusions:

- Prior knowledge about the applicant will bias the interviewer's evaluation.
- The interviewer tends to hold a stereotype of what represents a "good" applicant.
- The interviewer tends to favor applicants who share his or her own attitudes.
- The order in which applicants are interviewed will influence evaluations.
- The order in which information is elicited during the interview will influence evaluations.
- Negative information is given unduly high weight.
- The interviewer may make a decision concerning the applicant's suitability within the first four or five minutes of the interview.
- The interviewer may forget much of the interview's content within minutes after its conclusion.
- The interview is most valid in determining an applicant's intelligence, level of motivation, and interpersonal skills.
- Structured and well-organized interviews are more reliable than unstructured and unorganized ones.[7]

What can supervisors do to make interviews more valid and reliable? (See the "News Flash! The Realistic Job Preview" on page 127.) A number of suggestions have been made over the years. We list some in the section titled "Interviewing" at the end of this chapter.

---

[4]S. Robbins and D. Decenzo, *Fundamentals of Management: Essential Concepts and Applications* (Upper Saddle River, NJ: Pearson Prentice Hall, 2008), 224.
[5]R. A. Posthuma, F. P. Morgeson, and M. A. Campion, "Beyond Employment Interview Validity: A Comprehensive Narrative Review of Recent Research and Trends Over Time," *Personnel Psychology* 55, no. 1 (Spring 2002), 1–81.
[6]A. I. Huffcutt, J. M. Conway, P. L. Roth, and N. J. Stone, "Identification and Meta-Analysis Assessment of Psychological Constructs Measured in Employment Interviews," *Journal of Applied Psychology* 86, no. 5 (October 2001), 897–913; and A. I. Huffcutt, J. A. Weekley, W. H. Wiesner, T. G. Degroot, and C. Jones, "Comparison of Situational and Behavioral Description Interview Questions for Higher-Level Positions," *Personnel Psychology* 54, no. 3 (Autumn 2001), 619–644.
[7]See E. Hermelin and I. T. Robertson, "A Critique and Standardization of Meta-Analytic Coefficients in Personnel Selection," *Journal of Occupational and Organizational Psychology* 73, no. 4 (September 2001), 253–277; C. H. Middendorf and T. H. Macan, "Note-Taking in the Employment Interview: Effects on Recall and Judgments," *Journal of Applied Psychology* 87, no. 2 (April 2002), 293–303; D. Butcher, "The Interview Rights and Wrongs," *Management Today*, April 2002, 4; and P. L. Roth, C. H. Can Iddekinge, A. I. Huffcutt, C. E. Eidson, and P. Bobko, "Corrections for Range Restriction in Structured Interview Ethnic Group Differences: The Value May Be Larger than Researchers Thought," *Journal of Applied Psychology* 87 (April 2002), 369–376.

News Flash!

THE REALISTIC JOB PREVIEW

Supervisors who treat the recruiting and hiring of employees as if the applicants must be sold on the job and exposed only to an organization's positive characteristics set themselves up to have a workforce that is dissatisfied and prone to high turnover.

Every job applicant acquires, during the hiring process, a set of expectations about the company and about the job for which he or she is interviewing. When the information an applicant receives is excessively inflated, a number of things happen that have potentially negative effects on the company. First, mismatched applicants who would probably become dissatisfied with the job and quit soon would be less likely to withdraw from the search process. Second, the absence of accurate information builds unrealistic expectations. Consequently, the new employees are likely to become quickly dissatisfied—leading to premature resignations. Third, new hires are prone to become disillusioned and less committed to the organization when they face the "harsh" realities of the job. In many cases, these individuals feel that they were duped or misled during the hiring process and, therefore, may become problem employees.

To increase job satisfaction among employees and reduce turnover, supervisors should provide a realistic job preview (RJP). An RJP includes both positive and negative information about the job and the company. For example, in addition to the positive comments typically expressed in the interview, the candidate would be told of the downside of joining the company. He or she might be told that there are limited opportunities to talk to coworkers during work hours, that promotional advancement is slim, or that work hours fluctuate so erratically that employees may be required to work during typical off hours (nights and weekends). Applicants who have been given a more realistic job preview hold lower and more realistic job expectations for the jobs they'll be performing and are better able to cope with the job and its frustrating elements. The result is fewer unexpected resignations by new employees.

For supervisors, realistic job previews offer a major insight into the selection process—that retaining good people is as important as hiring them in the first place. Presenting only the positive aspects of a job to a job applicant may initially entice him or her to join the organization, but it may be an affiliation that both parties quickly regret.

Source: Based on S. L. Premack and J. P. Wanous, "A Meta-Analysis of Realistic Job Preview Experiments," *Journal of Applied Psychology* 70, no. 4 (November 1985), 706–720.

PREPARATION FOR THE INTERVIEW

Prepare for an interview with an applicant by reviewing job descriptions to find lists of tasks required by the job and lists of skills and experience required for the position. You may then use the lists as a guide during the interview. By using the lists, you can prepare and conduct multiple structured interviews while being certain you asked the same questions of all applicants.

Remember that all interview questions should be job related—don't ask if they're not! You may be able to determine the candidate's qualifications by stating the conditions/requirements of the job and then asking if the condition/requirement presents the candidate with a problem; this allows candidates to provide affirmative or negative responses without the necessity of providing details/specifics.

Remember to check federal, state, and local guidelines regarding employment regulations. You may wish to consult an attorney or the legal department of your organization before beginning the hiring process. Remember that you may inform the candidate that misleading statements or omissions of significant facts may be grounds for nonselection.

realistic job preview
A job interview that provides both positive and negative information about the job and the company.

INTERVIEW QUESTIONS YOU SHOULDN'T ASK

During an interview, supervisors should never ask questions that:

- Identify applicants between forty and sixty-four years of age
- Inquire about U.S. citizenship prior to hiring
- Identify applicant's ancestry, place of birth, or native language
- Directly or indirectly relate to race or color
- Identify religious preference, holidays, or customs
- Reveal sex or gender
- Relate to education or training not required for the job
- Identify membership in nonprofessional clubs or organizations that are not job related
- Reveal applicant's family or marital status
- Regard child-care, children's ages, or non-job-related areas
- Identify conditions of discharge from the military
- Identify security clearance level
- Relate to applicant's credit history
- Identify height and weight if these factors do not affect ability to perform job
- Regard home ownership or rental status
- Relate to applicant's arrest record
- Reveal names and addresses of relatives unless they are employed by the organization
- Inquire about pregnancy
- Regard disability-related issues until after a conditional job offer has been made

INTERVIEW QUESTIONS YOU SHOULD ASK

During an interview supervisors may ask questions:

- Related to the applicant's ability to speak English if it is required for the job
- Regarding academic, vocational, or professional education pertaining to Knowledge, Skills, and Abilities (KSAs) for the position
- Regarding membership in organizations if they are related to the job or KSAs for the position
- Related to travel, unusual hours, or overtime required by the job
- Stating the type of security clearance required for the position
- Regarding applicant's conviction for crimes
- Regarding applicant's physical ability to perform specific job functions
- Probing attendance at previous employers as long as you do not refer to illness or disability
- Identifying communication skills
- Demonstrating emotional maturity and behaviors
- Demonstrating decision-making ability
- Discussing applicant's experience in preparation for the position
- Identifying appropriate behaviors for specific work-related situations.[8]

---

[8]"Interview Skills for Supervisors: Finding the Best Match," www.nps.gov/training/tel/Guides/
Interview%20Skills_for_Supervisors_pg030405.pdf (accessed June 1, 2008); U.S. Equal Employment
Opportunity Commission, http://www.eeoc.gov (accessed June 1, 2008); and "Human Resources
Presents…Personnel Manager: Interview Subjects," www.doi.gov/hrm/pmanager/index.html (accessed
June 1, 2008).

Comprehension Check 5-1

1. Employer action to make an active effort to recruit, select, and promote protected group members is called

   a. equal employment opportunity
   b. effective supervision
   c. human resource management
   d. none of the above

2. Which one of the following is *not* a traditional recruiting source?

   a. Internal searches
   b. Cyberspace recruiting
   c. Employee referrals
   d. Advertisements

3. *Validity* means

   a. consistency of measurement
   b. equal employment opportunity for protected group members
   c. a proven relationship exists between a selection device and some relevant criterion
   d. all of the above

4. True or false? Interviewers tend to give more weight to negative information than to positive information from a job candidate?

Orientation, Training, and Development

If supervisors have done their recruiting and selecting properly, they should have hired competent individuals who can perform successfully. But successful performance requires more than possession of certain skills. New hires must be acclimated to the organization's culture and be trained to do the job in a manner consistent with the organization's objectives. To achieve these ends, supervisors embark on two processes—orientation and training.

HOW DO YOU INTRODUCE NEW HIRES TO THE ORGANIZATION?

Once a job candidate has been selected, he or she needs to be introduced to the job and organization. This introduction is called the new employee orientation or onboarding process. The major objectives of orientation are to reduce the initial anxiety all new employees feel as they begin a new job; to familiarize new employees with the job, the work unit, and the organization as a whole; and to facilitate the outsider–insider transition. Job orientation expands on the information the employee obtained during the recruitment and selection stages. The new employee's specific duties and responsibilities are clarified, as well as how his or her performance will be evaluated. This is also the time to rectify any unrealistic expectations new employees might hold about the job. Work-unit orientation familiarizes the employee with the goals of the work unit, makes clear how his or her job contributes to the unit's goals, and includes introduction to his or her coworkers. Organization orientation informs the new employee about the organization's objectives, history, philosophy, procedures, and rules. This information should include relevant personnel policies such as work hours, pay procedures, overtime requirements, and benefits. A tour of the organization's physical facilities is often part of the orientation.

Supervisors have an obligation to make the integration of the new employee into the organization as smooth and as free of anxiety as possible. Successful orientation,

orientation

An expansion on information a new employee obtained during the recruitment and selection stages; an attempt to familiarize new employees with the job, the work unit, and the organization as a whole.

How are most pilots trained? Through intensive flight simulation programs. Simulators let pilots actually experience a variety of situations—some of them life threatening—without having to suffer the ill consequences of poor decisions. As a result, the pilots are exposed to a wide variety of events, most of which they will never have to deal with on the job. But if they do, they have been prepared.

employee training
Changing the skills, knowledge, attitudes, or behavior of employees. Determination of training needs is made by supervisors.

whether formal or informal, results in an outsider–insider transition that makes the new member feel comfortable and fairly well adjusted, lowers the likelihood of poor work performance, and reduces the probability of a surprise resignation by the new employee only a week or two into the job.

WHAT IS EMPLOYEE TRAINING?

On the whole, planes don't cause airline accidents; people do. Most collisions, crashes, and other mishaps—nearly three-quarters of them—result from errors by the pilot or air traffic controller or from inadequate maintenance. These statistics illustrate the importance of training in the airline industry. These maintenance and human errors could be prevented or significantly reduced by better employee training.

Employee training is a learning experience in that it seeks a relatively permanent change in employees such that their ability to perform on the job improves. Thus, training involves changing skills, knowledge, attitudes, or behavior. This may mean changing what employees know; how they work; or their attitudes toward their jobs, coworkers, supervisors, and the organization. It has been estimated, for instance, that U.S. business firms alone spend billions of dollars a year on formal courses and training programs to develop workers' skills.[9] Supervisors, for the most part, are responsible for deciding when employees need training and what form that training should take. Determining training needs typically involves generating answers to several questions (see Exhibit 5-6). The leading questions in Exhibit 5-6 suggest the kinds of signals that can warn a supervisor that training may be necessary. The more obvious ones are related directly to productivity—that is, they may indicate that job performance is declining. These indications may include actual decreases in production numbers, lower quality, more accidents, and higher scrap or rejection rates. Any of these outcomes might suggest that worker skills need to be fine-tuned. Of course, we are assuming that the employee's performance decline is in no way related to lack of effort. Supervisors, too, must also recognize that training may be required because of a "future" element. Changes that are being imposed on employees as a result of job design or a technological breakthrough also require training.

How Are Employees Trained? Most training takes place on the job. The prevalence of on-the-job training can be attributed to the simplicity of such methods and their usually lower cost. However, on-the-job training can disrupt the workplace and result in an increase in errors while learning takes place. Also, some skill training is too complex to learn on the job. In such cases, it should take place outside the work setting.

What Are Some of the Typical Methods Used? Many different types of training methods are available. For the most part, however, we can classify them in two ways: on-the-job or off-the-job. We have summarized the most popular training methods in Exhibit 5-7.

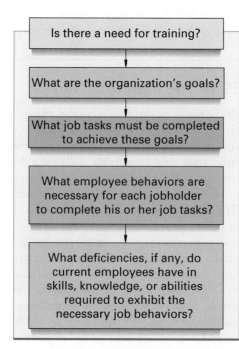

Exhibit 5-6
Determining training needs.

Is there a need for training?

What are the organization's goals?

What job tasks must be completed to achieve these goals?

What employee behaviors are necessary for each jobholder to complete his or her job tasks?

What deficiencies, if any, do current employees have in skills, knowledge, or abilities required to exhibit the necessary job behaviors?

---

[9]M. Dalahoussaye, "Show Me the Results," *Training*, March 2002, 28.

On-the-job training	Description
Apprenticeship	A time—typically two to five years—when an individual is under the guidance of a master worker to learn specific skills.
Job instruction training	A systematic approach to on-the-job training consisting of preparing the trainees by telling them about the job, presenting the instructions, having the trainees try the job to demonstrate their understanding, and placing trainees into the job under the lead of a resource person.
Off-the-job training	
Classroom lectures	Lectures designed to communicate specific interpersonal, technical, or problem-solving skills.
Multimedia	Using various media productions to demonstrate specialized skills and deliver specific information.
Simulation exercises	Training that occurs by actually performing the work. This may include case analysis, experiential exercises, roleplay, or group decision making.
Computer-based training	Simulating the work environment by programing a computer to imitate some of the realities of the job.
Vestibule training	Training on actual equipment used on the job, but conducted away from the actual work setting—a simulated workstation.
Programed instruction	Condensing training materials into highly organized, logical sequences. May include computer methods, interactive video disks, or virtual reality simulations.

Exhibit 5-7
Typical training methods.

How Can Supervisors Ensure That Training Is Working? It is easy to generate a new training program, but if the training effort is not evaluated, it becomes possible to rationalize any employee-training efforts.

Can we generalize how training programs are typically evaluated? The following is probably generalizable across organizations: Several supervisors, possibly representatives from HRM, and a group of workers who have recently completed a training program are asked for their opinions. If the comments are generally positive, the program may get a favorable evaluation and the organization will continue it until someone decides, for whatever reason, that it should be eliminated or replaced.

The reactions of participants or managers, although easy to acquire, are the least valid; their opinions are heavily influenced by factors that may have little to do with the training's effectiveness—such as difficulty, entertainment value, or personality characteristics of the instructor. However, trainees' reactions to the training may in fact provide feedback on how worthwhile the participants considered the training. Beyond general reactions, however, training must also be evaluated in terms of how much the participants learned, how well they are using their new skills on the job (did their behavior change?), and whether the training program achieved its desired results (reduced turnover, increased customer service, etc.)[10]

---

[10]See, for example, R. E. Catalano and D. L. Kirkpatrick, "Evaluating Training Programs—The State of the Art," *Training and Development Journal* 22, no. 5 (May 1968), 2–9.

Performance Appraisals

It is important for supervisors to get their employees to behave in ways that the organization considers desirable. How do managers ensure that employees are performing as they are supposed to? In organizations, the formal means of assessing the work of employees is through a systematic performance appraisal process. We look at this topic in depth in Chapter 12.

Compensation and Benefits

You open the newspaper and the following job advertisement grabs your attention. "Wanted: Hardworking individual who is willing to work sixty hours a week in a less-than-ideal environment. The job pays no money but gives you the opportunity to say 'I've done that.'" Sound intriguing to you? Probably not! In fact, although there are exceptions, most of us work for money. What our jobs pay and what benefits we get fall under the heading of compensation and benefits. Determining what these will be is by no means easy—and it's usually out of the hands of the immediate department supervisor. Although the supervisor will rarely set the wage rate, it's important to have an understanding of where the wage rate came from.

HOW ARE PAY LEVELS DETERMINED?

compensation administration
The process of determining a cost-effective pay structure that will attract and retain competent employees, provide an incentive for them to work hard, and ensure that pay levels will be perceived as fair.

How does an organization decide who gets paid $14.65 an hour and who receives $325,000 a year? The answer lies in compensation administration. The goals of compensation administration are to design a cost-effective pay structure that will attract and retain competent employees and to provide an incentive for these individuals to exert high energy levels at work. Compensation administration also attempts to ensure that whatever pay levels are determined will be perceived as fair by all employees. Fairness means that the established pay levels are adequate and consistent for the demands and requirements of the job. Therefore, the primary determination of pay is the kind of job an employee performs. Different jobs require different kinds and levels of skills, knowledge, and abilities—and these vary in their value to the organization. So, too, do the responsibility and authority held in certain positions. In short, the higher the skills, knowledge, and abilities—and the greater the authority and responsibility—the higher the pay.

Although skills, abilities, and the like directly affect pay levels, other factors may come into play. Pay levels may be influenced by the kind of business, the environment surrounding the job, geographic location, and employee performance levels and seniority. For example, private-sector jobs typically provide higher rates of pay than comparable positions in public and not-for-profit jobs. Employees who work under hazardous conditions (say, bridge builders operating two hundred feet in the air), work unusual hours (e.g., the overnight shift), or work in geographic areas where the cost of living is higher (e.g., New York City versus Tucson, Arizona) are typically more highly compensated. Likewise, employees who have been with an organization for a long time may have had a salary increase each year.

Irrespective of these factors, one other factor is most critical—the organization's compensation philosophy. Some organizations, for instance, don't pay employees any more than they have to. In the absence of a union contract that stipulates wage levels, those organizations have to pay only minimum wage for most of their jobs. On the other hand, some organizations are committed to paying their employees at or above area wage levels to emphasize that they want to attract and keep the best pool of talent.

WHY DO ORGANIZATIONS OFFER EMPLOYEE BENEFITS?

When an organization designs its overall compensation package, it has to look farther than just an hourly wage or annual salary. It has to take into account another element: employee benefits. Employee benefits are nonfinancial rewards that are designed to enrich employees' lives. They have grown in importance and variety over the past several decades. Once viewed as "fringes," today's benefit packages reflect great thought in an effort to provide something that each employee values.

employee benefits
Nonfinancial rewards designed to enrich employees' lives.

The benefits offered by an organization vary widely in scope. Most organizations are legally required to provide Social Security and workers' and unemployment compensation, but organizations also provide an array of benefits such as paid time off from work, life and disability insurance, retirement programs, and health insurance. The costs of some of these, such as retirement and health insurance benefits, are often paid by both the employer and the employee.

Current Issues in Human Resource Management

We conclude this chapter by looking at several human resource issues facing today's supervisors. These are dealing with workforce diversity, sexual harassment, and layoff-survivor sickness.

WORKFORCE DIVERSITY

We discussed the changing makeup of the workforce earlier in this book. Let's now consider how workforce diversity will affect such basic HRM concerns as recruitment, selection, and orientation.

Improving workforce diversity requires supervisors to widen their recruiting net. For example, the popular practice of relying on current employee referrals as a source of new job applicants tends to result in candidates who have similar characteristics to present employees. So, supervisors have to look for applicants in places where they haven't typically looked before. To increase diversity, supervisors are increasingly turning to nontraditional recruitment sources. These include women's job networks, over-fifty clubs, urban job banks, disabled people's training centers, ethnic newspapers, and gay-rights organizations. This type of outreach should enable the organization to broaden its pool of applicants.

Once a diverse set of applicants exists, efforts must be made to ensure that the selection process does not discriminate. Moreover, applicants need to be made comfortable with the organization's culture and be made aware of the supervisor's desire to accommodate their needs.

Finally, orientation is often difficult for women and minorities. Many organizations today, such as IBM and Hewlett-Packard, provide special workshops to raise diversity consciousness among current employees, as well as programs for new employees that focus on diversity issues. The thrust of these efforts is to increase individual understanding and appreciation of the differences each of us brings to the workplace.

WHAT IS SEXUAL HARASSMENT?

Sexual harassment is a serious issue in both public- and private-sector organizations. On average, more than twelve thousand complaints were filed from 2005 through 1010 with the Equal Employment Opportunity Commission (EEOC).[11] Not only have

---

[11]U.S. Equal Employment Opportunity Commission, "Sexual Harassment Charges EEOC & FEPAs Combined: FY 1997–FY 2010," EEOC, http://www.eeoc.gov/eeoc/statistics/enforcement/sexual_harassment.cfm (accessed May 15, 2011).

Is the action of this supervisor sexual harassment? It is if it makes the employee feel that such action is creating an offensive work environment.

sexual harassment

Anything of a sexual nature that is required for getting a job, has an employment consequence, or creates an offensive or hostile environment, including sexually suggestive remarks, unwanted touching, sexual advances, requests for sexual favors, and other verbal and physical conduct of a sexual nature.

settlements in these cases incurred a substantial cost to the companies in terms of litigation, but also it is estimated that sexual harassment is the single biggest financial risk facing companies today—and can result in a more than 30 percent decrease in a company's stock price. At Mitsubishi, for example, the company paid out more than $34 million to three hundred women for the rampant sexual harassment they were exposed to.[12] But it's more than just jury awards. Sexual harassment results in millions lost in absenteeism, low productivity, and turnover.[13] Furthermore, sexual harassment is not just a U.S. phenomenon. It's a global issue. For instance, sexual harassment charges have been filed against employers in such countries as Japan, Australia, the Netherlands, Belgium, New Zealand, Sweden, Ireland, and Mexico.[14] Although discussions of sexual harassment cases often focus on the large awards granted by a court, there are other concerns for supervisors. Sexual harassment creates an unpleasant work environment for organization members and undermines their ability to perform their job. But just what is sexual harassment?

Sexual harassment can be regarded as any unwanted activity of a sexual nature that affects an individual's employment. It can occur between members of the opposite sex or of the same sex—between employees of the organization or an employee and a nonemployee. Much of the problem associated with sexual harassment is determining what constitutes this illegal behavior. In 1993, the EEOC cited three situations in which sexual harassment can occur. These are instances in which verbal or physical conduct toward an individual

1. creates an intimidating, offensive, or hostile environment;
2. unreasonably interferes with an individual's work; or
3. adversely affects an employee's employment opportunities.

For many organizations and their supervisors, it's the offensive or hostile environment issue that is problematic.[15] Just what constitutes such an environment? For instance, does sexually explicit language in the office create a hostile environment? How about off-color jokes? Pictures of people totally undressed? The answer is: It could! It depends on the people in the department and the environment in which they work. What does this tell us? The point here is that we all must be attuned to what makes fellow employees uncomfortable—and if we don't know, then we should ask!

If sexual harassment carries with it potential costs to the organization, what can supervisors do for themselves and their organizations? The courts typically want to know two things—did the supervisor know about, or should the supervisor have known

---

[12]N. F. Foy, "Sexual Harassment Can Threaten Your Bottom Line," *Strategic Finance*, August 2000, 56–57; and "Federal Monitors Find Illinois Mitsubishi Unit Eradicating Harassment," *Wall Street Journal*, September 7, 2000, A-8.

[13]L. J. Munson, C. Hulin, and F. Drasgow, "Longitudinal Analysis of Dispositional Influences and Sexual Harassment: Effects on Job and Psychological Outcomes," *Personnel Psychology*, Spring 2000, 21.

[14]See, for instance, G. L. Maatman, Jr., "A Global View of Sexual Harassment," *HR Magazine*, July 2000, 151–158.

[15]R. L. Wiener and L. E. Hurt, "How Do People Evaluate Social Sexual Conduct at Work? A Psychological Model," *Journal of Applied Psychology* 85 (February 2000), 75.

about, the alleged behavior; and what was done to stop it? With the number and dollar amounts of the awards against organizations today, there is even a greater need for supervisors to educate their employees on sexual harassment matters. Furthermore, in June 1998, the Supreme Court ruled that sexual harassment may have occurred even if the employee did not experience any "negative" job repercussions.[16] The Supreme Court's decision in this case indicates that "harassment is defined by the ugly behavior of the supervisor, not by what happened to the worker subsequently."[17]

Finally, whenever involved in a sexual harassment matter, a supervisor must remember that the harasser may have rights, too. This means that no action should be taken against someone until a thorough investigation has been conducted. Furthermore, the results of the investigation should be reviewed by an independent and objective individual before any action against the alleged harasser is taken. Even then, the harasser should be given an opportunity to respond to the allegation and have a disciplinary hearing if desired. Additionally, an avenue for appeal should exist for the alleged harasser—an appeal heard by someone in a higher level of management who is not associated with the case.

HOW DO "SURVIVORS" RESPOND TO LAYOFFS?

As we discussed in Chapter 2, one of the significant organizational trends in the past decade has been organizational downsizing. Many organizations have done a fairly good job of helping layoff victims by offering a variety of job-help services, psychological counseling, support groups, severance pay, extended health insurance benefits, and detailed communications. Although some affected individuals react very negatively to being laid off (the worst cases involve returning to the separating organization and committing some form of violence), the assistance offered reveals that the organization does care about its former employees. Unfortunately, very little has been done for those who have been left behind and have the task of keeping the organization going or even of revitalizing it.

It may surprise you to learn that both victims and survivors experience feelings of frustration, anxiety, and loss.[18] But layoff victims get to start over with a clean slate and a clear conscience. Survivors don't. A new syndrome seems to be popping up in more and more departments across organizations: layoff-survivor sickness. It is a set of attitudes, perceptions, and behaviors of employees who remain after involuntary employee reductions. Symptoms include job insecurity, perceptions of unfairness, guilt, depression, stress from increased workloads, fear of change, loss of loyalty and commitment, reduced effort, and an unwillingness to do anything beyond the required minimum.

layoff-survivor sickness
A set of attitudes, perceptions, and behaviors of employees who survive involuntary staff reductions.

To address this survivor syndrome, supervisors may want to provide opportunities for employees to talk to counselors about their guilt, anger, and anxiety. Group discussions can also provide an opportunity for the "survivors" to vent their feelings. Some organizations have used downsizing efforts as the spark to implement increased employee-participation programs such as empowerment and self-managed work teams. In short, to keep morale and productivity high, every attempt should be made to ensure that individuals who are still working in the organization know that they are a valuable and much-needed resource.

---

[16]See, for instance, P. W. Dorfman, A. T. Cobb, and R. Cox, "Investigations of Sexual Harassment Allegations: Legal Means Fair—Or Does It?" *Human Resource Management* 39, no. 1 (Spring 2000), 33–39.

[17]W. L. Kosanovich, J. L. Rosenberg, and L. Swanson, "Preventing and Correcting Sexual Harassment: A Guide to the Ellerth/Faragher Affirmative Defense," *Employee Relations Law Journal* 28, no. 1 (Summer 2002), 79–99; and Milton Zall, "Workplace Harassment and Employer Liability," *Fleet Equipment*, January 2000, B1.

[18]P. P. Shah, "Network Destruction: The Structural Implications of Downsizing," *Academy of Management Journal* 43, no. 1 (February 2002), 101–112.

Here are eight practical tips supervisors can give to employees to help them overcome layoff survivor sickness:

1. Remain calm and overcome panic and anxiety by developing a personal and professional plan for what to do *in case* of a lay off.

2. Recognize that survivor guilt is normal and it won't help to deny or internalize the pain, so be prepared to grieve the loss of colleagues and a personal sense of stability.

3. Talk it out and remember that keeping grief and frustration bottled up is a recipe for trouble, and it's not a sign of weakness to vent personal feelings.

4. Be honest and efficient at work and keep in mind that layoff survivors usually end up with heavier workloads, so it may be best to eliminate distractions from the work environment and schedule meetings rather than discuss work issues spontaneously with colleagues who stop by.

5. Unhook self-esteem from the company by breaking organizational codependence and finding a sense of value and purpose in a profession rather than in the company.

6. Become empowered by developing transferrable skills and being proactive about professional development.

7. Manage stress by practicing stress-management techniques during after-hours, and keeping life in balance.

8. Maintain perspective by remembering that life is not the job, and if layoff survivor sickness is incapacitating or resulting in dramatic work overload with no respite in sight, quit the job.[19]

Comprehension Check 5-2

5. The process of determining a cost-effective pay structure is called
   a. compensation administration
   b. financial reward package
   c. human resource management
   d. human resource inventory

6. Nonfinancial rewards designed to enrich employees' lives are called
   a. compensation administration
   b. legally required perks
   c. perquisites
   d. employee benefits

7. Which of the following situations can lead toward sexual harassment?
   a. Something of a sexual nature creates an intimidating or offensive work environment.
   b. Something of a sexual nature interferes with an individual's work.
   c. Something of a sexual nature adversely affects an employee's employment opportunities.
   d. All of the above are matters that can lead to sexual harassment.

8. True or false? Those left in an organization after other workers have been laid off often experience similar feelings of frustration, anxiety, and loss.

---

[19] D. M. Noer, *Healing the Wounds: Overcoming the Trauma of Layoffs and Revitalizing Downsized Organizations* (San Francisco, CA: Jossey Bass, 2009); M. Malugani, "Coping with Layoff Survivor Sickness," *Monster*, May 9, 2011, http://career-advice.monster.com/in-the-office/workplace-issues/layoff-survivor-sickness/article.aspx (accessed May 15, 2011).

Enhancing Understanding

SUMMARY

After reading this chapter, I can:

1. **Describe the human resource management process.** The human resource management process seeks to staff the organization and to sustain high employee performance through strategic human resource planning, recruitment or downsizing, selection, orientation, training, performance appraisal, compensation and benefits, and safety and health and by dealing with contemporary issues in HRM.

2. **Discuss the influence of government regulations on human resource decisions.** Since the mid-1960s, the U.S. government has greatly expanded its influence over HRM decisions by enacting new laws and regulations. Because of the government's effort to provide equal employment opportunities, management must ensure that key HRM decisions—such as recruitment, selection, training, promotions, and terminations—are made without regard to race, sex, religion, age, color, national origin, or disability. Financial penalties can be imposed on organizations that fail to follow these laws and regulations.

3. **Contrast recruitment and downsizing options.** Recruitment seeks to develop a pool of potential job candidates. Typical sources include an internal search, advertisements, employee referrals, employment agencies, school placement centers, and temporary help services. Downsizing typically reduces the labor supply within an organization through options such as firing, layoffs, attrition, transfers, reduced workweeks, early retirements, and job sharing.

4. **Explain the importance of validity and reliability in selection.** All HRM decisions must be based on factors or criteria that are both reliable and valid. If a selection device is not reliable, it cannot be assumed to be a consistent measure. If a device is not valid, no proven relationship exists between it and relevant job criteria.

5. **Describe the selection devices that work best with various kinds of jobs.** Selection devices must match the job in question. Work sampling works best with low-level jobs. Assessment centers work best for managerial positions. The validity of the interview as a selection device increases at progressively higher levels of management.

6. **Identify various training methods.** Employee training can be on-the-job or off-the-job. Popular on-the-job methods include job rotation, understudying, and apprenticeships. The more popular off-the-job methods are classroom lectures, films, and simulation exercises.

7. **Describe the goals of compensation administration and factors that affect wage structures.** Compensation administration attempts to ensure that whatever pay levels are determined will be perceived as fair by all employees. Fairness means that the established levels of pay are adequate and consistent for the demands and requirements of the job. Therefore, the primary determination of pay is the kind of job an employee performs.

8. **Explain what is meant by** *sexual harassment* **and** *layoff-survivor sickness.* Sexual harassment is any unwanted activity of a sexual nature that affects an individual's employment—such as creating a hostile environment, interfering with work, or adversely affecting one's employment opportunities. Layoff-survivor sickness represents a set of attitudes, perceptions, and behaviors of employees who remain after involuntary employee reductions.

COMPREHENSION: Review and Discussion Questions

1. How does HRM affect all supervisors?

2. Contrast reject errors and accept errors. Which one is most likely to open a supervisor to charges of discrimination? Why?

3. What are the major problems of the interview as a selection device?

4. What is the relationship among selection, recruitment, and job analysis?

5. Compare and contrast orientation and employee training.

6. Should a supervisor have the right to choose employees without government interference in the hiring process? Explain your position.

7. What constitutes sexual harassment? Describe how supervisors and their companies can minimize the occurrences of sexual harassment in the workplace.

8. Why should supervisors be concerned with diversity in the workplace? What special HRM issues does diversity raise for them?

9. "Victims of downsizing are not those employees who were let go. Rather, the victims are the ones who have kept their jobs." Do you agree or disagree with this statement? Defend your position.

KEY CONCEPT CROSSWORD

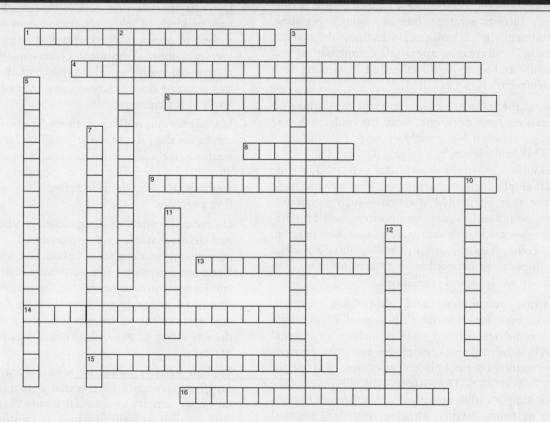

ACROSS

1. nonfinancial rewards designed to enrich employees' lives
4. determining a cost-effective pay structure
6. a selection device based on actual job behaviors
8. a web-based résumé
9. a database of employee skills, knowledge, and abilities
13. a formal introduction to the organization
14. assessing current employee resources and determining future employee needs
15. anything of a sexual nature that is required for getting or keeping a job, or one that creates an offensive work environment
16. making an effort to recruit, train, and promote minorities

DOWN

2. a means of changing the skills, attitudes, or behavior of employees
3. the process of finding, hiring, training, and keeping employees
5. an employment interview that reveals both positive and negative aspects about the job and the company
7. a means of determining who is the best candidate for a job opening
10. measuring consistently
11. showing a relationship between a selection device and some relevant criterion
12. the process of locating, identifying, and attracting capable applicants

ANSWERS TO COMPREHENSION CHECKS

Comprehension Check 5-1

1. d (affirmative action)   2. b   3. c   4. True

Comprehension Check 5-2

5. a   6. d   7. d   8. True

Developing Your Supervisory Skills

GETTING TO KNOW YOURSELF

Before you can effectively supervise others, you must understand your present strengths and areas in need of development. To assist in this learning process, we encourage you to complete the following self-assessment from the Prentice Hall Self-Assessment Library 3.4.

1. Am I Experiencing Work/Family Conflict? (III. B. 3.)

After you complete the assessment, we suggest you retain the results and store them as part of your "portfolio of learning about yourself."

BUILDING A TEAM

➤ An Experiential Exercise: Laying Off Workers

Every supervisor, at some point in his or her career, is likely to be faced with the difficult task of laying off employees. Assume that you are the supervisor in the accounting department of a 750-member organization. You have been notified by top management that you must permanently reduce your staff by two individuals. The following are some data about your five employees.

Janet McGraw: African American female, age thirty-six. Janet has been employed with your company for five years, all in the accounting department. Her evaluations over the past three years have been outstanding and above average. Janet has an MBA from a top-25 business school. She has been on short-term disability the past few weeks because of the birth of her second child and is expected to return to work in twenty weeks.

Bill Keeney: White male, age forty-nine. Bill has been with you for four months and has eleven years of experience in the company in payroll. He has an associate degree in business administration and bachelor's and master's degrees in accounting. He's also a CPA. Bill's evaluations over the past three years in the payroll department have been average, but he did save the company $150,000 on a suggestion he made regarding using electronic time sheets.

José Melendez: Hispanic male, age thirty-one. José has been with the company almost four years. His evaluations over the past three years in your department have been outstanding. He is committed to getting the job done and devoting whatever it takes. He has also shown initiative by taking job assignments that no one else wanted. And he has recovered a number of overdue and uncollected accounts that you had thought should be written off as a loss.

Lisa Parks: White female, age thirty-five. Lisa has been with your company seven years. Four years ago, Lisa was in an automobile accident while traveling on business to a customer's location. As a result of the accident, she was disabled and now uses a wheelchair. Rumors have it that she is about to receive several million dollars from the insurance company of the driver that hit her. Her performance the last two years has been above average. She has a bachelor's degree in accounting and specializes in computer information systems.

Charles Thomas: African American male, age forty-three. Charles just completed his joint master's degree in taxation and law, and recently passed the bar exam. He has been with your department the past four years. His evaluations have been good to above average. Five years ago, Charles won a lawsuit against your company for discriminating against him in a promotion to a supervisory position. Rumors have it that now, with his new degree, Charles is actively pursuing another job outside the company.

Given these five brief descriptions, make a recommendation on which two employees you will suggest to your boss be laid off. Discuss any other options that you feel can be used to meet the requirement of downsizing by two employees without resorting to layoffs. Discuss what you will do to (1) assist the two individuals who have been let go and (2) assist the remaining three employees. Then, in a group of three to five students, seek consensus on the question of who gets laid off. Be prepared to defend your actions.

➤ Internet: Web Activity

Go to http://www.pearsonhighered.com/robbins/. Find *Supervision Today!* 7th Ed. and click Companion Website.

INTERVIEWING

Every supervisor needs to develop his or her skills at interviewing. The following list highlights the key behaviors associated with this skill.

STEPS IN APPLYING THE SKILL

STEP 1: Review the job description and job specification. Reviewing pertinent information about the job provides valuable information about what you will assess the candidate on. Furthermore, relevant job requirements help eliminate interview bias.

STEP 2: Prepare a structured set of questions you want to ask all applicants for the job. By having a set of prepared questions, you ensure that the information you wish to elicit is attainable. Furthermore, by asking similar questions, you are able to better compare all candidates' answers against a common base.

STEP 3: Before meeting a candidate, review his or her application form and résumé. Doing so helps you to create a complete picture of the candidate in terms of what is represented on the résumé or application and what the job requires. You will also begin to identify areas to explore in the interview. That is, areas that are not clearly defined on the résumé or application but that are essential for the job will become a focal point in your discussion with the candidate.

STEP 4: Open the interview by putting the applicant at ease and by providing a brief preview of the topics to be discussed. Interviews are stressful for job candidates. By opening with small talk—such as about the weather—you give the candidate time to adjust to the interview setting. By providing a preview of topics to come, you are giving the candidate an "agenda." This helps the candidate begin framing what he or she will say in response to your questions.

STEP 5: Ask your questions and listen carefully to the applicant's answers. Select follow-up questions that naturally flow from the answers given. Focus on the responses as they relate to information you need to ensure that the candidate meets your job requirements. Any uncertainty you may still have requires a follow-up question to probe further for the information.

STEP 6: Close the interview by telling the applicant what is going to happen next. Applicants are anxious about the status of your hiring decision. Be upfront with the candidate regarding others who will be interviewed and the remaining steps in the hiring process. If you plan to make a decision in two weeks or so, let the candidate know what you intend to do. In addition, tell the applicant how you will let him or her know about your decision.

STEP 7: Write your evaluation of the applicant while the interview is still fresh in your mind. Don't wait until the end of your day, after interviewing several candidates, to write your analysis of a candidate. Memory can fail you! The sooner you complete your write-up after an interview, the better chance you have for accurately recording what occurred in the interview.

► Communicating Effectively

1. Visit your campus career center and make an appointment with a career counselor. During your meeting, ask the counselor for insight on how to succeed in interviews. Focus specifically on what kinds of things campus recruiters are looking for today, how you should prepare for the interview, and what kinds of questions you can expect to get in the interview. Once your appointment is completed, provide a three- to five-page summary of the interview, highlighting how the information can be useful for you in a future job search.

2. Go to the EEOC website at www.eeoc.gov. Research the process one must follow to file an EEOC charge. Also, review the sexual harassment data and summary statistics the EEOC collects. Identify the number of cases filed during the past three years in which data have been kept, how many of the cases were settled, and the amount of the monetary benefits awarded.

THINKING CRITICALLY

► Case 5-A: Net That Job

After you've planned effectively and grouped your employees accordingly, it's time to turn your attention to hiring the right people. The jobs that have been identified and their associated skills point to very specific types of employees. But these employees don't appear magically. Instead, you must embark on a process of finding, hiring, and retaining qualified people.

That process starts when you notify the "public" that openings exist. Typically, you attempt to get your information out so that a large number of potentially qualified applicants respond. Then, after several interactions with the most promising of these candidates, you hire the applicants who best demonstrate the skills, knowledge, and abilities to perform the job successfully.

Years ago, this entire process was dominated by paper and face-to-face interactions. Technology today is changing the process. For individuals like Henry Lu, the job search has gone to the Internet. Many jobs in organizations today are heavily influenced by technology. Accordingly, candidates must be able to demonstrate that they have the requisite skills and can offer something special to organizations. Explaining qualifications in a letter to an employer often doesn't have the same effect as showing potential employers what you can do. When Henry, a University of Pennsylvania senior, wanted to let employers know he understood technology, he opted for an electronic résumé. By developing a home page on the Net, Henry was able to refer potential employers to his web page, which he had designed. The electronic résumé, however, was only the beginning. Through the creation of links to other web pages, applicants like Henry can refer potential employers to a variety of websites that provide substantial data about him. For example, Henry

can provide the details about the college he attended and his major course of study. He can also show some of his completed works or graphically highlight other pertinent data about his "fit" with the organization.

Although the use of the Internet for job hunting is still growing, as more and more employers explore this technique, it's sure to continue to gain momentum. For now, though, it's safe to say that a competitive advantage can be gained for highly technical jobs by using the Internet as a means of displaying one's skills.

RESPONDING TO THE CASE

1. Describe the implications of job candidates placing résumés on the World Wide Web.

2. How can electronic résumés help you to identify that a job candidate possesses technical skills? How would you react if you found out that another person had developed the candidate's home page? Explain.

3. Describe a selection process in which you can verify that a candidate like Henry Lu does possess the technical skill required for a job using the Internet.

➤ Case 5-B: Staffing and Hiring

The temporary help industry plays an important role in the workplace by finding prequalified employees for employers who are undergoing seasonal or start-up operations or needing to fill positions open as a result of vacations or other employee work interruptions. Working for companies on a temporary basis can give job seekers a chance to test their desires and abilities at several situations before making a long-term commitment. Placement counselors in the temporary help industry generally need to have expertise in interviewing, understanding employer needs, finding temporary workers, explaining job functions, problem solving, and other communication-related skills.

Jameel Jackson worked for United Staffing during his college studies. The job started out as a standard part-time activity to help pay for expenses. Over time Jameel performed well in several assignments and was given the opportunity to learn more about the operations of a temporary help company. The experience was mutually beneficial. Jameel worked for different companies that did manufacturing, distribution, and service work; he performed work from assembly to loading and many types of office work. Jameel discovered that he was most interested in the office work using computer applications to record information, control functions, and analyze data. He found the office environment stimulating with its energy, variety of tasks, and creativity.

Jameel recently completed his undergraduate degree in management from a local college and has been offered

a position at United Staffing as a full-time staffing supervisor. His responsibilities will be to coordinate the part-time temporary work needs of several local companies. In addition he will work on two teams. One team responds to employer requests for a significant number of employees. The other team reviews the company's performance in meeting its customers' requests and analyzes the company's financial results.

RESPONDING TO THE CASE

1. Why is it important for Jameel to know about the laws and regulations that affect human resource practice?

2. Why is it important for Jameel to know how to determine staffing needs?

3. What are some recruiting methods that Jameel might use to ensure that he has the right employees to match the needs of employers?

4. Research the employment selection process of three businesses in your community. Ask questions like these: What type of and how much testing do they require? Is an application, résumé, or work sample required? Who conducts the interviews and how long are they? Who makes the final decision to hire a new employee? How long is the process?

Controlling

Key Concepts

After completing this chapter, you will be able to define these supervisory terms:

- basic corrective action
- cause-effect diagram
- concurrent control
- control by exception
- control chart
- control process
- corrective control
- flowchart
- immediate corrective action

- just-in-time (JIT) inventory system
- *kanban*
- preventive control
- quality control
- range of variation
- scatter diagram
- supply chain management
- value chain management

Chapter Outcomes

After reading this chapter, you will be able to:

1. Describe the control process.

2. Contrast two types of corrective action.

3. Compare preventive, concurrent, and corrective control.

4. Explain how a supervisor can reduce costs.

5. List the characteristics of an effective control system.

6. Explain potential negatives that controls can create.

7. Explain what is meant by the term *just-in-time inventory systems*.

8. Describe what is meant by the term *value chain management*.

9. Identify the ethical dilemmas in employee monitoring.

10. Explain what is meant by employee theft and its effect on the organization.

Responding to a Supervisory Dilemma

Technological advances have made the process of supervision in an organization much easier. But they have also provided supervisors a means of sophisticated employee monitoring. Although most of this monitoring is designed to enhance worker productivity, it could be, and has been, a source of concern over worker privacy. These advantages have also brought with them difficult questions regarding what supervisors have the right to know about employees and how far they can go in controlling employee behavior, both on and off the job.

Consider the following:

■ The mayor of Colorado Springs, Colorado, reads the e-mail messages that city council members send to each other from their homes. He defended his actions by saying he was making sure that e-mail was not being used to circumvent his state's "open-meeting" law that requires most council business to be conducted publicly.

■ The U.S. Internal Revenue Service's internal audit group monitors a computer log that shows employee access to taxpayers' accounts. This monitoring activity allows management to check and see what employees are doing on their computers.

■ American Express has an elaborate system for monitoring telephone calls. Daily reports are provided to supervisors that detail the frequency and length of calls made by employees, as well as how quickly incoming calls are answered.

■ Supervisors in several organizations require employees to wear badges at all times while on company premises. These badges contain a variety of data that allow employees to enter certain locations in the organization. Smart badges, too, can transmit where the employee is at all times!

Just how much control should a supervisor have over the private lives of employees? Where should a supervisor's rules and controls end? Does the supervisor have the right to dictate what you do on your own free time and in your own home? Could your supervisor, in essence, keep you from engaging in riding a motorcycle, skydiving, smoking, drinking alcohol, or eating junk food? Again, the answers may surprise you. What's more, supervisors' involvement in employees' off-work lives has been going on for decades. For instance, in the early 1900s, Ford Motor Company would send social workers to employees' homes to determine whether their off-the-job habits and finances were deserving of year-end bonuses. Other firms made sure employees regularly attended church services. Today, many organizations, in their quest to control safety and health insurance costs, are once again delving into their employees' private lives.

Although controlling employees' behaviors on and off the job may appear unjust or unfair, nothing in our legal system prevents employers from engaging in these practices. Rather, the law is based on the premise that if employees don't like the rules, they have the option of quitting. Supervisors, too, typically defend their actions in terms of ensuring quality, productivity, and proper employee behavior.

When does a supervisor's need for information about employee performance cross over the line and interfere with a worker's right to privacy? Is any action by a supervisor acceptable as long as employees are notified ahead of time that they will be monitored? And what about the distinction between monitoring work and nonwork behavior? When employees do work-related activities at home during evenings and weekends, does a supervisor's prerogative to monitor employees remain in force? What's your opinion?

Y ou've completed your planning. You know your own department's objectives. Your department is organized to maximize the possibility of completing your goals. You've hired quality employees, and you've jointly set specific job objectives with all the people that report to you. Standing plans are in place. So, too, are your department's budgets and important schedules. Your next concern should be this: How will I know if all my plans are being achieved? You won't, unless you've also developed controls!

As described in Chapter 1, controlling is the management function concerned with monitoring activities to ensure that they are being accomplished as planned and correcting any significant deviations. In this chapter, we show how effective supervisors perform the controlling function. Specifically, we detail the control process, discuss the timing of controls, identify the major areas where supervisors concentrate their control activity, and describe the characteristics of effective controls. We also discuss some of the potentially undesirable side effects of controls that supervisors need to be on guard against.

The Control Process

The control process consists of three separate and distinct steps: (1) measuring actual performance, (2) comparing results with standards, and (3) taking corrective action (see Exhibit 6-1). Before we discuss each of these steps, you should be aware that the control process assumes that standards of performance already exist. These standards are actually detailed in specific goals that you created in planning. So, planning must precede application of the control process.

If goal setting is used, the goals become the standards against which actual performance is compared. This is because goal setting integrates planning and control by providing supervisors with a set of objectives or standards to be attained. If goal setting is not practiced, then standards are the specific performance indicators for equipment use, resource use, quality, employee productivity, and the like. These standards can be applied to individuals, teams, departments, or the entire organization. Some examples of popular performance standards include percentage of plant capacity, number of units produced per work hour, average amount of scrap per unit produced, lost workdays resulting from injuries, absentee rates, return on investment, cost per unit sold, returns as a percentage of sales, and total dollar sales per sales territory.

control process
A three-step process that consists of (1) measuring actual performance, (2) comparing results with standards, and (3) taking corrective action.

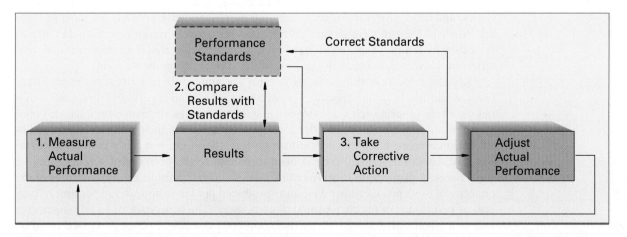

Exhibit 6-1
The control process.

HOW DO YOU MEASURE ACTUAL PERFORMANCE?

To determine actual performance, we must acquire information about it. The first step in control, then, is measuring. Let's consider both how we measure and what we measure.

Ways to Measure Four common sources of information used by supervisors to measure actual performance are personal observation, statistical reports, oral reports, and written reports.

Personal observation provides firsthand, intimate knowledge of the actual activity. As such, it is probably the most widely used means by which supervisors assess actual performance. In fact, it has even acquired its own label—MBWA, or management by walking around. It permits intensive coverage because minor as well as major performance activities can be observed. It also provides opportunities for the supervisor to "read between the lines." Personal observation can pick up verbal omissions, facial expressions, and tones of voice that may be missed by other methods.

The use of computers in organizations has led to supervisors increasingly relying on *statistical reports* for measuring actual performance. This measuring device, however, is not limited to computer outputs. It also includes graphs, bar charts, and numerical displays of any form that supervisors may use for assessing performance.

Information can also be acquired through *oral reports*, that is, through conferences, meetings, and one-to-one conversations. The advantages of oral reports are that they are fast; allow for feedback; and permit language expression and tone of voice, as well as words themselves, to convey meaning.

Finally, actual performance can be measured by *written reports*. The strength of written reports is that they offer greater comprehensiveness and conciseness than is typically found in oral reports. They are also easier to catalog and reference. Written reports are often combined with statistical reports. They may also be used to precede or follow up oral reports.

What to Measure What you measure is probably more critical to the control process than how you measure it. The selection of the wrong criteria can result in serious dysfunctional consequences (which we discuss later in this chapter). More important, what you measure determines, to a great extent, what employees will attempt to emphasize.

For instance, suppose you're a supervisor in the information systems department of a large hospital. You expect office staff to be at work at 8 a.m. Every morning, at precisely 8 a.m., you walk around the office to make sure everyone is in. What you typically find are purses and lunch bags on desks, open briefcases, coats over backs of chairs, and other physical evidence that your employees have arrived. But most of them are down in the cafeteria having coffee. Your employees make sure that they are at the office by 8 a.m. because you have communicated that this is an important control criterion. However, being in doesn't mean that they're actually working.

Keep in mind that some control criteria are applicable to most supervisory situations, while others are job specific. For instance, because all supervisors direct the activities of others, criteria such as employee satisfaction and absenteeism rates have universal application. Almost all supervisors also have budgets for their area of responsibility set in dollar costs. Keeping costs within budget, therefore, is a fairly common control measure. However, control criteria need to recognize the diversity of activities among supervisors. A production supervisor in a manufacturing plant might use measures of the quantity of units produced per day, units produced per labor hour, scrap per unit of output, or percentage of rejects returned by customers. The supervisor of an administrative unit in a government agency might use number of document pages processed per day, number of orders processed per hour, or average time required to process service calls. Sales supervisors often use measures such as percentage of market captured in a given territory, average dollar value per sale, or number of customer visits per salesperson. The key is that what you measure must be adjusted to fit the goals of your department.

HOW DO YOU COMPARE RESULTS WITH STANDARDS?

The comparing step determines the degree of variation between actual performance and the standard. Some variation in performance can be expected in all activities; it is therefore critical to determine the acceptable range of variation.

range of variation
Variation in performance that can be expected in all activities.

Determining Acceptable Ranges Deviations in excess of the acceptable range become significant and receive the supervisor's attention. In this comparison stage, you need to be concerned with the size and direction of the variation. An example should help make this clear.

Frank Singleton is the sales supervisor at Circle City Chevrolet/Buick in Indianapolis, Indiana. Frank prepares a report during the first week of each month that describes sales for the previous month, classified by model. Exhibit 6-2 displays both the standard (goal) and the actual sales figures for the month in review.

Should Frank be concerned with the July performance? If he focused on Chevrolet unit sales and Buick average dollar sales, the answer would be no. But there appear

Model	Goal	Actual	Over (under)
Chevrolet			
Aveo	2	3	1
Camaro	4	7	3
Corvette	2	1	−1
Cruze	3	2	−1
HHR	3	2	−1
Impala	3	4	1
Malibu	4	8	4
Volt	5	2	−3
Equinox	2	2	0
Suburban	1	2	1
Tahoe	1	2	1
Traverse	3	2	−1
Avalanche	2	0	−2
Colorado	2	1	−1
Express	2	2	0
Silverado	5	6	1
Total Units	44	46	2
Total Sales	$1,273,800.00	$1,285,475.00	
Average Sales	$28,950.00	$27,945.11	
Buick			
Enclave	8	6	−2
Lucerne	6	5	−1
Lacrosse	6	4	−2
Regal	10	8	−2
Total Units	30	23	−7
Total Sales	$937,500.00	$780,735.00	
Average Sales	$31,250.00	$33,945.00	

Exhibit 6-2

Circle City's sales performance for July.

to be some significant deviations. Average sales prices on Chevrolets were far below projection. A closer look at Exhibit 6-2 offers an explanation. The higher-priced SUVs weren't selling, whereas the lower-priced cars and pickups did better than expected. On the Buick side, Every model had disappointing sales.

Which performance deviations deserve Frank's attention? This depends on what Frank and his boss believe to be significant. How much tolerance should be allowed before corrective action is taken? The deviation on several models is very small and undoubtedly not worthy of special attention—for example, for some models the sales goal and actual sales were off by only one vehicle. The shortages for the Chevrolet Avalanche and Volt and the Buick Enclave, Lucerne, Lacrosse, and Regal may be more significant. That's a judgment Frank must make.

By the way, an error in understanding sales can be as troublesome as an overstatement. For instance, are the strong sales for the Chevrolet Camaro and Malibu a one-month abnormality, or are these models increasing in popularity? Frank has concluded that the Indianapolis economy is to blame. With some uncertainty about the economy, gas prices, and their job security, people appear to be moving to less expensive models. Reflecting national recessionary trends, sales of Buick cars are down across the board. This example illustrates that both overvariance and undervariance may require corrective action.

Some Special Measurement Tools Any discussion of control would be incomplete without a discussion of the basic statistical techniques used to control variability. In this section, we describe the more popular statistical process control techniques.

cause-effect diagram
A depiction of the causes of a problem that groups the causes according to common categories such as machinery, methods, personnel, finances, or management.

flowchart
Visual representation of the sequence of events for a particular process that clarifies how things are being done so that inefficiencies can be identified and the process can be improved.

scatter diagram
An illustration of the relationship between two variables that shows correlations and possible cause and effect.

Cause-Effect Diagrams Cause-effect diagrams (also sometimes called *fishbone diagrams*) are used to depict the causes of a certain problem and to group the causes according to common categories such as machinery, materials, methods, personnel, finances, or management.

As shown in Exhibit 6-3, these diagrams look somewhat like a fishbone, with the problem—the effect—defined as the head. On the "bones," growing out of the "spine," are the possible causes of production problems. They're listed in order of possible occurrence. Cause-effect diagrams provide guidance for analyzing the influence that alternative courses of action will have on a given problem.

Flowcharts Flowcharts are visual representations of the sequence of events for a particular process. They clarify exactly how things are being done so that inefficiencies can be identified and the process improved. Exhibit 6-4 provides an illustration.

Scatter Diagrams Scatter diagrams illustrate the relationship between two variables, such as height and weight or the hardness of a ball bearing and its diameter (see Exhibit 6-5).

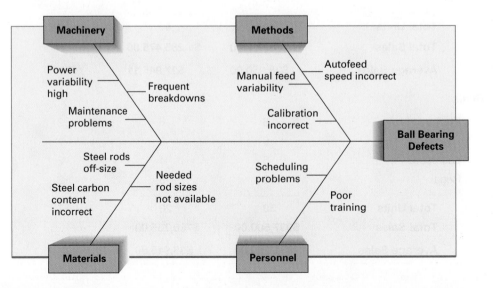

Exhibit 6-3

Example of a cause-effect (fishbone) diagram.

These diagrams visually depict correlations and possible cause and effect. So, for instance, a scatter diagram could reveal that the percentage of rejects increases as the size of production runs increases. This, in turn, might suggest the need to reduce production runs or reevaluate the process if quality is to be improved.

Control Charts Control charts are the most sophisticated of the statistical techniques we describe. They are used to reflect variation in a system. Control charts reflect measurements of sample products averaged with statistically determined upper and lower limits. For instance, Timkin, makers of ball bearings, samples its .215 ball bearings after they are produced to ensure that their measurements are within standards. As long as the process variables fall within the acceptable range, the system is said to be "in control" (see Exhibit 6-6). When a point falls outside the limits set, the variation is unacceptable. Improvements in quality should, over time, result in a narrowing of the range between the upper and lower limits through elimination of common causes.

WHEN SHOULD CORRECTIVE ACTION BE TAKEN?

The third and final step in the control process is the action that will correct the deviation. It will be an attempt either to adjust actual performance or to correct the standard, or both (see Exhibit 6-1).

There are two distinct types of corrective action. One is immediate and deals predominantly with symptoms. The other is basic and delves into the causes. Immediate corrective action is often described as "putting out fires." It adjusts something right now and gets things back on track. Basic corrective action gets to the source of the deviation and seeks to adjust the differences permanently. It asks how and why performance deviated. Unfortunately, many supervisors rationalize that they don't have the time to take basic corrective action and therefore must be content to perpetually "put out fires." Effective supervisors recognize that they must find the time to analyze deviations and, in situations where the benefits justify such action, permanently correct significant differences between standard and actual performance.

Referring back to our Frank Singleton example on page 148, he might take basic corrective action on the positive deviation for the Chevrolet Camaro and Malibu

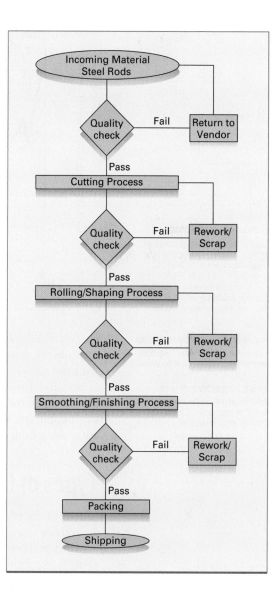

Exhibit 6-4

Example of a flowchart.

Source: *Reprinted with permission of the publisher. From* Putting Total Quality Management to Work, *copyright© 1993 by M. Sashkin and K.J'. Kiser, Berrett-Koehler Publishers, Inc., San Francisco, CA. All rights reserved. www.bkconnection.com*

control chart

A statistical technique used to measure variation in a system to produce an average standard with statistically determined upper and lower limits.

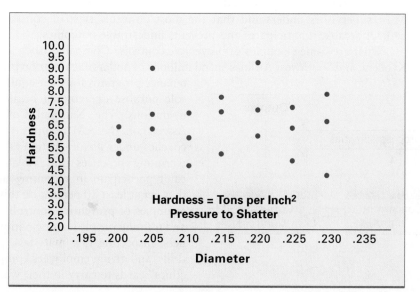

Exhibit 6-5

Example of a scatter diagram.

Source: *Reprinted with permission of the publisher. From* Putting Total Quality Management to Work, *copyright© 1993 by M. Sashkin and K.J. Kiser, Berrett-Koehler Publishers, Inc., San Francisco, CA. All rights reserved. www.bkconnection.com*

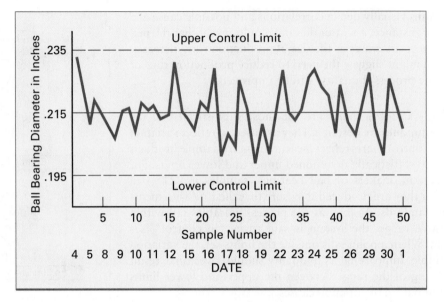

Exhibit 6-6

Example of a control chart.

Source: *Reprinted with permission of the publisher. From* Putting Total Quality Management to Work, *copyright© 1993 by M. Sashkin and K.J. Kiser, Berrett-Koehler Publishers, Inc., San Francisco, CA. All rights reserved. www.bkconnection.com*

immediate corrective action
Action that adjusts something right now and gets things back on track.

basic corrective action
Action that gets to the source of a deviation and seeks to adjust the differences permanently.

models. If sales have been greater than expected for the past several months, he might upgrade the standard for future months' sales of these models and increase his orders with the factory. The poor showing on all the Buick models might justify a number of actions—for instance, cutting back on orders of these cars, running a sales promotion to move the increased inventory, reworking the sales commission plan to reward salespeople for selling Buicks, and/or recommending an increase in his dealership's advertising budget.

Types of Controls

Where in the process should you apply controls? You can implement controls before an activity commences, while the activity is going on, or after the fact. The first type is called preventive control, the second is concurrent control, and the last is corrective control (see Exhibit 6-7). Some special types of statistical controls can also be used.

WHAT IS PREVENTIVE CONTROL?

There's an old saying: An ounce of prevention is worth a pound of cure. Its message is that the best way to handle a deviation from standard is to see that it doesn't occur. Most supervisors understand that the most desirable type of control is preventive control because it anticipates and prevents undesirable outcomes.

What are some examples of preventive controls? Companies such as McDonald's, Kyocera, and Southwest Airlines spend millions of dollars each year on preventive maintenance programs for their equipment with the sole purpose of avoiding breakdowns during operations. The National Collegiate Athletic Association (NCAA) requires that all college coaches under its jurisdiction take an exam on recruiting practices and violations. Coaches can't participate in recruiting athletes unless they get at least 80 percent on this exam. Other examples of preventive controls include hiring and training people in anticipation of new business, inspecting raw materials, practicing fire drills, and giving employees company "code of ethics" cards to carry in their wallets.

preventive control
A type of control that anticipates and prevents undesirable outcomes.

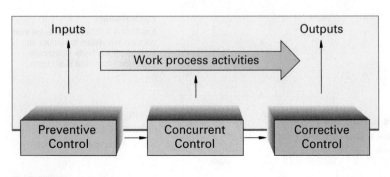

Exhibit 6-7
Three types of control.

WHEN ARE CONCURRENT CONTROLS USED?

As the name implies, concurrent control takes place while an activity is in progress. When control is enacted while the work is being done, you can correct problems before they get out of hand or become too costly.

Much of supervisors' day-to-day activities involve concurrent control. When they directly oversee the actions of employees, monitoring employees' work and correcting problems as they occur, concurrent control is taking place. Although there is obviously some delay between the action and a supervisor's corrective response, the delay is essentially minimal. You'll find other examples of concurrent control on factory machinery and computers. Temperature, pressure, and similar gauges that are checked regularly during a production process, and that automatically send a signal to an operator that there is a problem, are examples of concurrent controls. So, too, are programs on computers that give operators an immediate response when an error is made. If the operator inputs the wrong command, the program rejects it and may even provide the correct command.

concurrent control
A type of control that takes place while an activity is in progress.

WHAT IS CORRECTIVE CONTROL?

Corrective control provides feedback after an activity is finished to prevent any future deviations. Examples of corrective control include final inspection of finished goods, annual employee performance appraisals, financial audits, quarterly budget reports, and the like. The sales report that Frank Singleton at Circle City Chevrolet/Buick reviews each month, shown in Exhibit 6-2, is an example of a corrective control.

The obvious shortcoming of corrective control is that, by the time you have the information, it's often too late. The damage or mistakes have already occurred. For instance, where information controls are weak, you may learn for the first time in August that your employees have already spent 110 percent of the department's annual photocopying budget. Nothing can be done to correct the overexpenditure in August. But corrective control does alert you that there is a problem. Then, you can determine what went wrong and initiate basic corrective action.

corrective control
A type of control that provides feedback after an activity is finished to prevent future deviations.

The Focus of Control

What do supervisors control? Most of their control efforts are directed at four areas: costs, inventories, quality, and safety. It's important, too, to note that supervisors also control employee performance (see Exhibit 6-8). Because performance appraisals are a critical component of managing your employees, we devote more space to that discussion in Chapter 12.

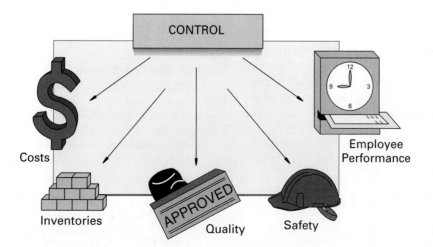

Exhibit 6-8
Focus of control.

News Flash!

ON THE ROCKS

Just after midnight on March 22, 2006, the *Queen of the North* ferry, part of the BC Ferries system, hit rocks off Gil Island, south of Prince Rupert. It was immediately clear that the ferry was in trouble, and within fifteen minutes, *all* the passengers and crew were off the ship and in the ferry's lifeboats. As local townspeople and the Coast Guard rescued the passengers from the lifeboats, the ferry sank, a little more than an hour after first striking the rocks. Initial media reports celebrated the fact that all ninety-nine passengers and crew had managed to get off the ferry safely. The crew was widely praised for conducting an orderly evacuation, something employees practice and train for at regular intervals.

On day two, passengers were reported missing. While international maritime regulations require that ferries record identifying information about all passengers (name, gender, and whether they are adults, children, or infants), the Canadian government doesn't require BC's ferry fleet to meet international standards. Passenger names aren't collected, and ferry staff don't even take a head count after loading. The number of passengers is only roughly determined by the number of tickets sold. Thus, the initial reports from BC Ferries that all passengers and crew survived were based on the simple belief that everyone had been evacuated. Demands for explanations of what had gone wrong arose.

The regional director of communications for Transport Canada (a governmental agency) reported the *Queen of the North* passed an annual safety inspection less than three weeks earlier, including a lifeboat drill that required passengers be evacuated in less than thirty minutes. "They did very well at it and they obviously did very well when it happened for real," he said.

The internal investigation BC Ferries conducted after the incident concluded that "human factors were the primary cause" of what happened. During the investigation, crew members responsible for navigating the ship that night claimed that they were unfamiliar with newly installed steering equipment. In addition, they had turned off a monitor displaying their course, because they could not turn on the night settings. The bridge crew used the equipment "in a way different than as instructed," the report noted, although this was not cited as a cause of running the boat aground. The report also concluded that the crew maintained a "casual watch-standing behavior," had "lost situational awareness," and "failed to appreciate the vessel's impending peril." A transcript of radio calls that evening noted that music was heard playing on the bridge.

Regarding the evacuation, though the crew was praised for acting quickly, several things made the evacuation more difficult than need be. There was no master key to the sleeping cabins; rather multiple keys had to be tried. A chalk X is supposed to be drawn on searched cabin doors, but no one had chalk. As well, only fifty-three of the fifty-five cabins were confirmed to have been searched.

Describe the type(s) of control that could be used to improve the BC Ferries service to prevent an accident such as this occurring again. Be specific. Assume that you are the president of BC Ferries. You have read the report of the investigation and noted some of the problems found. What would you do? Explain your reasoning. Would some types of controls be more important than others in this situation? Discuss.

Sources: Based on "Union Will Defend Fired Ferry Workers," *Kamloops Daily News,* May 7, 2007, A5; C. Montgomery and I. Austin, "Human Error Is Faulted for Ship Sinking," *Province* (Vancouver), March 27, 2007, A6; C. E. Harnett, "Human Error Sank B.C. Ferry," *Calgary Herald,* March 27, 2007, A5; C. E. Harnett, "Ferry Brass," *Times Colonist* (Victoria), June 6, 2006, A3; C. Montgomery, "Loose Manifest Rules Led to Miscount," *Province* (Vancouver), March 28, 2006, A4; E. Baron and E. O'Connor, "Why So Far Off Course?" *Province* (Vancouver), March 23, 2006, A3; and W. Boei, M. Bridge, and L. Pynn, "99 Escape After Ship Runs Aground, Slides into Depths," *Vancouver Sun,* March 23, 2006, A1.

Comprehension Check 6-1

1. Measuring performance, comparing against a standard, and taking corrective action are all part of the

    a. supervisory process
    b. control process
    c. value chain process
    d. none of the above

2. Variances in performance that can be expected in all activities are called the

    a. measurement process
    b. standard deviation
    c. range of variation
    d. benchmarking

3. A ____ is a visual representation of the sequence of events for a particular process.

    a. flowchart
    b. scatter diagram
    c. cause-effect diagram
    d. control chart

4. Which one of the following is *not* a type of control?

    a. Preventive control
    b. Concurrent control
    c. Immediate control
    d. Corrective control

WHAT COSTS SHOULD YOU CONTROL?

You are regularly under pressure to keep your costs in line. Let's look at the cost categories that you are likely to encounter and present a general program for cost reduction.

Major Cost Categories The following list describes the major cost categories that supervisors come in contact with and need to monitor.

1. **Direct labor costs.** Expenditures for labor that are directly applied in the creation or delivery of the product or service. Examples: machine operators in a factory or teachers in a school.

2. **Indirect labor costs.** Expenditures for labor that are not directly applied in the creation or delivery of the product or service. Examples: cost accountants, human resource recruiters, public relations specialists.

3. **Raw materials costs.** Expenditures for materials that go directly into the creation of a product or service. Examples: sheet steel at a Toyota plant or hamburger buns at a Wendy's restaurant.

4. **Supportive supplies costs.** Expenditures for necessary items that do not become part of the finished product or service. Examples: cleaning compounds at the Toyota plant or photocopying costs at Aetna Life.

5. **Utility costs.** Expenditures for electricity, gas, water, and similar utilities. Example: monthly electric bill for a regional office.

6. **Maintenance costs.** Material and labor expenditures incurred to repair and maintain equipment and facilities. Examples: repair parts for equipment or jet engine maintenance technicians at Continental Airlines.

7. **Waste costs.** Expenditures for products, parts, or services that cannot be reused. Examples: unsold french fries at Burger King or scrap metal at a Whirlpool Corporation plant.

Typically, you will have a budget for each major cost category. By monitoring expenditures in each category, you can keep costs within your total budget plans.

Cost Reduction Programs When costs are too high, you will more than likely be expected to implement a cost reduction program. Beginning in the late 1980s, U.S. corporations began a massive effort to reduce costs and improve their competitive position in relation to their global competitors. Much of this had a direct effect on supervisors. For instance, direct labor costs have been cut by automating jobs and redesigning work around teams that are more productive than individuals are. Indirect labor costs have been slashed by laying off tens of thousands of support personnel in research, finance, human resource, and clerical functions. Budgets for training, travel, telephone calls, photocopying, computer software, office supplies, and similar expenditures have undergone significant cuts.

The following list outlines a six-step program that can guide you in reducing costs in your department.[1]

1. **Improve methods.** Eliminate any unnecessary activities and introduce new work methods that can increase efficiency.
2. **Level the work flow.** Peaks and valleys in a work flow imply inefficiencies. By leveling the work flow, you can make do with fewer employees and cut down on overtime.
3. **Minimize waste.** Burning lights in unused areas, misuse of office supplies, idle employees, underused equipment, and wasteful use of raw materials add considerably to a supervisor's departmental costs.
4. **Install modern equipment.** Budget for new equipment to replace obsolete and worn-out machinery, computers, and the like.
5. **Invest in employee training.** People, like machines, can become obsolete if you allow their skills to become dated.
6. **Make cuts selectively.** Avoid across-the-board cuts. Some people and groups contribute significantly more than others. Make cuts where they will generate the greatest efficiencies.

WHY PAY ATTENTION TO INVENTORIES?

Supervisors are routinely responsible for ensuring that adequate inventories of materials and supplies are available for activities under their jurisdiction. For a shift supervisor at McDonald's, that would include paper products, buns, burger patties, french fries, condiments, cooking utensils, cleaning supplies, and even proper change for the cash register. For a nursing supervisor at a hospital, that might mean pharmaceuticals, gloves, hypodermic needles, and bed linens. The challenge in monitoring inventory cost is balancing the cost of maintaining inventories against the cost of running out of inventory. If excessive inventory is carried, money is needlessly tied up and unnecessary storage costs are incurred. Excessive inventory also adds to insurance premiums and taxes, and, of course, there are potential obsolescence costs. If Frank Singleton gets overstocked on Chevrolets and the new models begin to arrive, he might have to sell last year's models at below cost to get rid of them. If inventories drop too low, operations can be disrupted and sales lost. A stockout of paper can bring a publisher's printing presses to a halt. If the McDonald's supervisor fails to monitor his inventory

---

[1]Based on J. J. Semrodek, Jr., "Nine Steps to Cost Control," *Supervision Management*, April 1976, 29–32.

of frozen french fries, he might find himself with some very disgruntled customers. Frank Singleton may also find that many Chevrolet and Buick customers will expect his dealership to have the model and color they want available immediately, or they'll take their business to another dealer.

A popular inventory technique in today's organizations is called just-in-time (JIT) inventory systems. Large companies such as Boeing, Toyota, and General Electric have billions of dollars tied up in inventories. It is not unusual for even small firms to have a million dollars or more tied up in inventories. So, anything supervisors can do to significantly reduce the size of inventory will improve the organization's productivity. Just-in-time (JIT) inventory systems change the technology around which inventories are managed. With JIT, inventory items arrive when they are needed in the production process instead of being stored in stock. The ultimate goal of JIT is to have only enough inventory on hand to complete the day's work—thereby reducing a company's lead time, inventory, and associated costs.

In Japan, JIT systems are called kanban, a word that gets to the essence of the just-in-time concept.[2] *Kanban* is Japanese for "card" or "signal." Japanese suppliers ship parts in containers. Each container has a card, or *kanban*, slipped into a side pocket. When a production worker at the manufacturing plant opens a container, he or she takes out the card and sends it back to the supplier. Receipt of the card initiates the shipping of a second container of parts that, ideally, reaches the production worker just as the last part in the first container is being used up. This simple card system helped the Dana Corporation win the 2000 National Association of Manufacturers award for Workforce Excellence.[3] This system in part is helping the company save nearly $300,000 annually. It's also credited with decreasing inventory costs by 20 percent and reducing parts-dispatching errors by more than 50 percent at Waterville TG, the Quebec-based manufacturer of sealing systems for automotive assembly lines.[4]

The ultimate goal of a JIT inventory system is to eliminate raw material inventories by coordinating production and supply deliveries precisely. When the system works as designed, it results in a number of positive benefits for a manufacturer: reduced inventories, reduced setup time, better work flow, shorter manufacturing time, less space consumption, and even higher quality. Of course, suppliers that can be depended on to deliver quality materials on time must be found. Because there are no inventories, there is no slack in the system to compensate for defective materials or delays in shipments. Making this become a reality has focused supervisory attention on value chain management.

just-in-time (JIT) inventory system
A system in which inventory items arrive when they are needed in the production process instead of being stored in stock. See also kanban.

kanban
In Japanese, a "card" or "sign." Shipped in a container, a kanban is returned to the supplier when the container is opened, initiating the shipment of a second container that arrives just as the first container is emptied.

WHAT IS VALUE CHAIN MANAGEMENT?

Every organization needs customers if it's going to survive and prosper. Even not-for-profit organizations, such as churches and government agencies, must have customers who use its services or purchase its products. Customers want some type of value from the goods and services they purchase, or use, and these end users determine what has value.[5] Organizations must provide that value to attract and keep customers. Value is reflected in the performance characteristics, features, and attributes, or any other aspects of goods and services for which customers are willing to give up resources (usually money). For example, when you purchase Taylor Swift's new CD at Best Buy, a slice of pizza at a Sbarro's, or a haircut from your local hair salon, you're exchanging money

---

[2]See J. Cauhorn, "The Journey to World Class," *Industry Week*, April 6, 2001. Available online at www.industryweek.com.

[3]D. Bartholomew, "One Product, One Customer," *Industry Week*, September 12, 2002. Available online at www.industryweek.com.

[4]S. Chausse, S. Landry, F. Paisn, and S. Fortier, "Anatomy of a Kanban: A Case Study," *Production and Inventory Management Journal* 41, no. 4 (Fall 2000), 4–15.

[5]J. H. Sheridan, "Managing the Value Chain," *Industry Week*, September 6, 1999. Available online at www.industryweek.com.

in return for the value you desire from these products—providing music entertainment during your evening study time, alleviating your lunchtime hunger pangs, or looking professionally groomed for the job interview you have next week.

How is value provided to customers? Through the transformation of raw materials and other resources into some product or service that end users need or desire—in the form they want, when they want it. However, that seemingly simple act of turning a variety of resources into something that customers value and are willing to pay for involves a vast array of interrelated work activities performed by different participants. That is, this entire process involves the value chain. The value chain is the entire series of work activities that add value at each step beginning with the processing of raw materials and ending with a finished product in the hands of end users. The value chain can encompass anything from the supplier's suppliers to the customer's customers.[6]

The concept of value chain was popularized by Michael Porter in his book *Competitive Advantage: Creating and Sustaining Superior Performance.*[7] He wanted supervisors to understand the sequence of organizational activities that created value for customers. Although he focused primarily on what was happening within a single organization, he did emphasize that supervisors must understand how their organization's value chain fits into the industry's overall creation of value. In some cases, that's difficult to do. For example, organizations do a number of things that offer no value to the customer. Consider, for instance, the movie industry. A lot of film producers spend significant amounts of money on things that do little to make a movie better. Money well spent in this case is anything that is up on the screen where customers can see it. The money spent, however, for catering, limo services, and private jets for stars doesn't add value because those things don't end up on the screen. As such, they don't create value. A similar claim could be made about supervision. As one noted writer pointed out, "Supervisors are not value-added. A customer never buys a product because of the caliber of supervision. Supervision is, by definition, indirect. So if possible, less is better. One of the goals of reengineering [work process engineering] is to minimize the necessary amount of supervision."[8]

value chain management
The process of managing the entire sequence of integrated activities and information about product flows from start to finish—when the product is in the hands of the ultimate user.

supply chain management
An internally oriented process that focuses on the efficient flow of ncoming materials to the organization.

Value chain management is the process of managing the entire sequence of integrated activities and information about product flows along the entire value chain. In contrast to supply chain management, which is internally oriented and focuses on the efficient flow of incoming materials to the organization, value chain management is externally oriented and focuses on both incoming materials and outgoing products and services. Supply chain management is efficiency oriented (its goal is to reduce costs and make the organization more productive), whereas value chain management is effectiveness oriented and aims to create the highest value for customers.[9]

WHY THE FOCUS ON QUALITY?

With the possible exception of controlling costs, achieving high quality has become a primary focus of today's organizations. In years past, many American products were criticized for being shoddy in quality compared to their Japanese and German counterparts. On the other hand, companies such as Whirlpool Corporation, Motorola, and Ford have thrived in the past decade by focusing on quality products or services. With this new emphasis has come an increased demand on supervisors to engage in quality control.

Historically, *quality* referred to achieving some preestablished standard for an organization's product or service. Today, quality has taken on a larger meaning. We introduced continuous-improvement programs in Chapter 2, describing them as

[6]J. H. Sheridan, "Managing The Value Chain," Industry Week, September 6, 1999, 50–66. Available online at http://www.industryweek.com/articles/managing_the_value_chain_429.aspx.
[7]M. E. Porter, *Competitive Advantage: Creating and Sustaining Superior Performance* (New York: Simon & Schuster, 1998).
[8]R. Karkgaard, "ASAP Interview: Mike Hammer," *Forbes ASAP*, September 13, 1993, 70.
[9]See, for instance, K. P. O'Brien, "Value Chain Report: Supply Chain Success in the Aftermarket," *Industry Week*, July 15, 2002. Available online at www.industryweek.com.

comprehensive, customer-focused programs to continuously improve the quality of the organization's processes, products, and services. Whereas continuous-improvement programs emphasize actions to prevent mistakes, quality control emphasizes identifying mistakes that may have already occurred. Quality control continues to address monitoring quality—weight, strength, consistency, color, taste, reliability, finish, or any one of a myriad of quality characteristics—to ensure that it meets some preestablished standard.

quality control
Identification of mistakes that may have occurred; monitoring quality to ensure that (it) meets some preestablished standard.

Quality control is needed at multiple points in a process. It begins with the receipt of inputs. Are the raw materials satisfactory? Do new employees have the proper skills and abilities? It continues with work in process and all the steps up to the completion of the final product or service. Assessments at intermediate stages of the transformation process are typically part of quality control. Early detection of a defective part or process can save the cost of further work on the item.

A comprehensive quality-control program would encompass preventive, concurrent, and corrective controls. For example, controls would inspect incoming raw materials, monitor operations while they are in progress, and conduct final inspection and rejection of unsatisfactory outputs. This same comprehensive program could be applied to services. For instance, a claims supervisor for State Farm could hire and train her people to make sure they fully understand their jobs, monitor their daily work flow to ensure that it is done properly and on time, review completed claims for accuracy and thoroughness, and follow up with customers to determine their degree of satisfaction with the way their claims were handled.

WHAT ARE THE CHARACTERISTICS OF EFFECTIVE CONTROLS?

Effective control systems tend to have certain qualities in common. The importance of these characteristics varies with the situation, but the following checklist can guide supervisors in designing their unit's control system (see Exhibit 6-9).

Timeliness Controls should call attention to variations in time to prevent serious infringement on a unit's performance. The best information has little value if it is dated. Therefore, an effective control system must provide timely information.

Economy A control system must be economically reasonable to operate. Any system of control has to justify the benefits that it gives in relation to the costs it incurs. To minimize costs, you should try to impose the least amount of control that is necessary to produce the desired results. The widespread use of computers, to a large extent, is because of their ability to provide timely and accurate information in a highly efficient manner.

Flexibility Effective controls must be flexible enough to adjust to adverse change or to take advantage of new opportunities. In today's dynamic and rapidly changing world, you should design control systems that can adjust to the changing nature of your departmental objectives, work assignments, and job tasks.

Understandability Controls that cannot be understood by those who have to use them are of little value. It is sometimes necessary, therefore, to substitute less complex controls for sophisticated devices. A control system that is difficult to understand can cause unnecessary mistakes and frustrate employees; it will eventually be ignored.

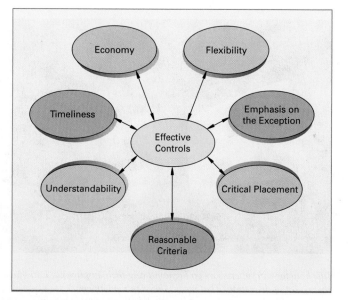

Exhibit 6-9
Characteristics of effective controls.

Reasonable Criteria Consistent with our discussion of goals in a previous chapter, control standards must be reasonable and attainable. If they are too high or unreasonable, they no longer motivate. Because most employees don't want to risk being labeled incompetent for telling their bosses that they ask too much, employees may resort to unethical or illegal shortcuts. Controls should, therefore, enforce standards that are reasonable; they should challenge and stretch people to reach higher performance levels without being demotivating or encouraging deception.

Critical Placement You can't control everything that goes on in your department. Even if you could, the benefits wouldn't justify the costs. As a result, you should place controls on those factors that are critical to your unit's performance goals. Controls should cover the critical activities, operations, and events within your unit. That is, you should focus on where variations from standard are most likely to occur or where a variation would do the greatest harm. For instance, if your labor costs are $20,000 a month and postage costs are $50 a month, a 5 percent overrun in the former is more critical than a 20 percent overrun in the latter. Hence, you should establish controls for labor and a critical dollar allocation, whereas postage expenses would not appear to be critical.

control by exception
A system that ensures that one is not overwhelmed by information on variations from standard.

Emphasis on the Exception Because you can't control all activities, you should place your control devices where they can call attention only to the exceptions. A control by exception system ensures that you are not overwhelmed by information on variations from standard. For instance, suppose that as an accounts receivable supervisor at a Sears store, you instruct your employees to inform you only when an account is fifteen days past due. The fact that 90 percent of your customers pay their bills on time or no more than two weeks late means you can devote your attention to the 10 percent of exceptions.

CAN CONTROLS CREATE PROBLEMS?

Yes, controls can create their own problems. The introduction of controls comes with potential negatives that need to be guarded against. These include employee resistance, misdirection of employee effort, and ethical dilemmas for supervisors concerning control devices. Let's take a brief look at each.

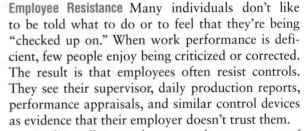

Employee Resistance Many individuals don't like to be told what to do or to feel that they're being "checked up on." When work performance is deficient, few people enjoy being criticized or corrected. The result is that employees often resist controls. They see their supervisor, daily production reports, performance appraisals, and similar control devices as evidence that their employer doesn't trust them.

Reality tells you that controls are a way of organizational life because you have a responsibility to ensure that activities are going as planned. So, what can you do to lessen this resistance?

First, wherever possible, encourage employee self-control. Once employees know their goals, give them the benefit of the doubt and leave them alone. Let them monitor and correct their own performance. Supplement this with regular communication so that they can let you know what problems they've encountered and how they've solved them. The assumption with self-control is that employees are responsible, trustworthy, and capable of personally

Just how far can supervisors go in monitoring their employees? Laws give them a lot of discretion. That means they can read an employee's e-mail or computer files, or even film employees while they are on company premises! The real question, however, is just how much of an employee's privacy can be invaded.

correcting any significant deviation from their goals. Only if this assumption proves incorrect do you need to introduce more formalized external control mechanisms.

When external controls are needed, there are some methods you can use to minimize employee resistance. Have employees participate in setting the standards. This lessens the likelihood that they'll view them as unrealistic or too demanding. Explain to employees how they will be evaluated. Surprisingly, the problem is often not the controls themselves that create resistance but the lack of understanding of how information will be gathered and how it will be used. Provide employees with regular feedback. Ambiguity causes stress and resistance, so let people know how they're doing. Finally, most people want the satisfaction that comes from doing their work better and want to avoid the pain and embarrassment that comes with discipline. As a result, supervisors should treat controls as devices for helping employees improve rather than for punishment.

Misdirection of Effort Did you ever notice that people who work in some government offices—for example, in departments that process motor vehicle licenses and building permits—sometimes appear not to care much about the problems of taxpayers? They become so fixated on ensuring that every rule is followed that they lose sight of the fact that their job is to serve the public, not hassle them!

This example illustrates another potential problem with controls: People may misdirect their efforts to look good on the control criteria. Because any control system has imperfections, problems occur when individuals or organizational units attempt to look good exclusively in terms of the control devices. In actuality, the result is dysfunctional in terms of the organization's goals. More often than not, this is caused by incomplete measures of performance. If the control system evaluates only the quantity of output, people will ignore quality. Similarly, if the system measures activities rather than results, people will spend their time attempting to look good on the activity measures.

What can you do to minimize this problem? Two things. First, make sure that control standards are reasonable. It is very important that this not be only your perception. Your employees must believe that the standards are fair and within their capability. Second, select and evaluate criteria that are directly related to achievement of employee job goals. If the licensing supervisor in the motor vehicle office evaluates her people on how well they follow rules, rather than on how effectively they serve the needs of clients, then her employees are not going to give much attention to satisfying clients. Finding the right criteria often means using a multiple set of standards. For instance, the goal of "serving clients" might require the licensing supervisor to evaluate her clerks on criteria such as "greets all clients with a smile and friendly greeting," "answers all client questions without seeking outside assistance," and "solves the client's problems in one visit." In addition, the supervisor might set up a client comment box in her licensing department where individual employees could be praised or criticized on their service, and then use this feedback as one measure of how well employees are doing their jobs.

Ethics and Control Devices Even as ethical issues can and do arise as supervisors design efficient and effective control systems, technological advances in computer hardware and software, for example, have made the process of controlling much easier. But these advantages have also brought with them difficult questions regarding what managers have the right to know about employees and how far they can go in controlling employee behavior both on and off the job. Special attention needs to be given to the topic of employee monitoring.

In Chapter 2, we briefly introduced how technology is changing our organizations. Many of these improvements enable organizations to become more productive; to help members work smarter, not harder; and to bring efficiencies into the organization that weren't possible just a decade ago. But technological advancements have also provided supervisors a means of sophisticated employee monitoring. Although most of this monitoring is designed to enhance worker productivity, it could be, and has been, a source of concern over worker privacy.

What can supervisors find out about their employees? You might be surprised by the answers! Supervisors can, among other things, read employees' e-mail (even confidential messages), tap their work telephone, determine their computer activities, and monitor employees anywhere on company property.

One area that has been a hot topic of debate over employee workplace privacy is e-mail communications. The use of e-mail is flourishing throughout global organizations, and employees are concerned about whether they can be fired or disciplined for things they have written and sent. Many companies can, and do, monitor these electronic transmissions.

Computer monitoring can be an excellent control mechanism. Computer monitoring systems can be used to collect, process, and provide performance feedback information about employees' work that can help supervisors with performance improvement suggestions and with employee development. They have also been used to help supervisors identify employee work practices that might be unethical or costly. For example, nursing supervisors in many hospitals and other health care organizations use computer monitoring to control costs of medical procedures and access to controlled medications. Likewise, many supervisors in business organizations use computer monitoring systems for controlling costs, employee work behavior, and a number of other areas of organizational activities. Telemarketing organizations often monitor telephone calls of their service operators. Other organizations monitor employees who deal with consumer complaints to ensure that the complaints are being handled appropriately. Unfortunately, computer monitoring has a questionable reputation because of instances of overuse and abuse.

Many individuals perceive computer monitoring as nothing more than a technologically sophisticated form of eavesdropping or a surveillance technique to catch employees slacking on the job. Critics also claim that these techniques lead to an increase in stress-related complaints from employees who feel pressured by being under constant surveillance. Supporters argue, however, that computer monitoring can be an effective employee-training device and a way to improve work performance levels.

How can supervisors benefit from the control information provided by computer monitoring systems and yet minimize the potential behavioral and legal drawbacks? Experts suggest that organizations do the following:

- Tell employees, both current and new, that they may be monitored.
- Have a written policy on monitoring that is posted where employees will see it; distribute it to each employee. Have all employees acknowledge in writing that they have received a copy of the policy and that they understand it.
- Monitor only those situations in which a legitimate business purpose is at stake, such as training or evaluating workers or controlling costs. When used in this manner, computer monitoring can be an effective—and ethical—supervisory control tool.

Contemporary Control Issues

Issues can arise as supervisors review control elements. Two of the more noteworthy control issues are employee theft and the Sarbanes-Oxley Act.

IS EMPLOYEE THEFT INCREASING?

Would you be surprised to find that up to 85 percent of all organizational theft and fraud is committed by employees, not outsiders?[10] And, it's a costly problem—estimated

---

[10]A. M. Bell and D. M. Smith, "Theft and Fraud May Be an Inside Job," *Workforce Online*, December 3, 2000, http://www.workforce.com.

Something to Think About (and promote class discussion)

OUT WITH E-MAIL

It's estimated that during 2008, each corporate user of e-mail sent or received over 150 messages per day. By 2011, that number is estimated to be well over 225. Another study found that one-third of e-mail users feel stressed by heavy e-mail volume. Once imagined to be a time-saver, has the inbox become a burden?

U.S. Cellular's chief operating officer Jay Ellison thought so and did something about it. He imposed a "no e-mail Friday" rule, a move that a growing number of companies are taking. Although most bans typically allow e-mailing clients and customers or responding to urgent matters, the intent is to slow down the routine internal e-mails that take up time and clog the organization's computer network. The limits also aim at encouraging more face-to-face and phone contact with coworkers and customers. Ellison also hoped that it would give his employees a small respite from the e-mail onslaught. What he got, however, was a rebellion. One employee confronted him saying that Ellison didn't understand how much work had to get done and how much easier it was when using e-mail.

What advantages and disadvantages are there to e-mail as a form of communication? In addition to your own personal experience with e-mail, you should do some research before answering this question. Why do you think the employees rebelled? What's your opinion about Ellison's actions? Was he right or wrong? Be sure to look at this from the perspective of both the organization and the employees. What other approaches might Ellison have taken to address this issue of out-of-control e-mail?

Sources: S. Shellenbarger, "A Day Without Email Is Like …,"*Wall Street Journal*, October 11, 2007, D1+; M. Kessler, "Fridays Go from Casual to E-Mail-Free," *USA Today*, October 5, 2007, 1A; D. Beizer, "Email Is Dead," *Fast Company*, July/August 2007, 46; O. Malik, "Why Email Is Bankrupt," *Business 2.0*, July 2007, 46; and D. Brady, "*!#?@ the E-Mail. Can We Talk?" *BusinessWeek*, December 4, 2006, 109.

to be around $4,500 per worker per year.[11] In a recent survey of U.S. companies, 20 percent said that workplace theft has become a moderate to very big problem.[12]

Employee theft is defined as any unauthorized taking of company property by employees for their personal use.[13] It can range from embezzlement to fraudulent filing of expense reports to removing equipment, parts, software, or office supplies from company premises. Although retail businesses have long faced serious potential losses from employee theft, loose financial controls at start-ups and small companies and the ready availability of information technology have made employee stealing an escalating problem in all kinds and sizes of organizations. It's a control issue that managers need to educate themselves about and be prepared to deal with.[14]

Why do employees steal? The answer depends on whom you ask.[15] Experts in various fields—industrial security, criminology, clinical psychology—have different perspectives.

[11]C. C. Verschoor, "New Evidence of Benefits from Effective Ethics Systems," *Strategic Finance* (May 2003), 20–21; and E. Krell, "Will Forensic Accounting Go Mainstream?" *Business Finance* (October 2002), 30–34.
[12]S. E. Needleman, "Businesses Say Theft by Their Workers Is Up," *Wall Street Journal*, December 11, 2008, B8.
[13]J. Greenberg, "The STEAL Motive: Managing the Social Determinants of Employee Theft," in R. Giacalone and J. Greenberg (eds.), *Antisocial Behavior in Organizations* (Newbury Park, CA: Sage, 1997), 85–108.
[14]B. E. Litzky, K. A. Eddleston, and D. L. Kidder, "The Good, the Bad, and the Misguided: How Managers Inadvertently Encourage Deviant Behaviors," *Academy of Management Perspective* (February 2006), 91–103; "Crime Spree," *BusinessWeek*, September 9, 2002, 8; B. P. Niehoff and R. J. Paul, "Causes of Employee Theft and Strategies That HR Managers Can Use for Prevention," *Human Resource Management* 39, no. 1 (Spring 2000), 51–64; and G. Winter, "Taking at the Office Reaches New Heights: Employee Larceny Is Bigger and Bolder," *New York Times*, July 12, 2000, C1+.
[15]This section is based on J. Greenberg, *Behavior in Organizations: Understanding and Managing the Human Side of Work*, 8th ed. (Upper Saddle River, NJ: Prentice Hall, 2003), 329–330.

The industrial security people propose that people steal because the opportunity presents itself through lax controls and favorable circumstances. Criminologists say that it's because people have financial-based pressures (e.g., personal financial problems) or vice-based pressures (e.g., gambling debts). And the clinical psychologists suggest that people steal because they can rationalize whatever they're doing as being correct and appropriate behavior ("everyone does it," "they had it coming," "this company makes enough money and they'll never miss anything this small," "I deserve this for all that I put up with," and so forth).[16] Although each approach provides compelling insights into employee theft and has been instrumental in attempts to deter it, unfortunately, employees continue to steal. What can managers do?

WHAT IS THE SARBANES-OXLEY ACT?

During the past several years, corporate scandals have received a lot of attention. The media have been filled with discussions of management practices at companies such as WorldCom, Enron, and ImClone. What executives at these companies did may be questionable, and some may have been illegal. For many, the aftermath of these corporate scandals has been a lack of trust for those who run organizations.[17] Although the law is not directed toward first-line supervisors, as a supervisor you should have some understanding about the implications of Sarbanes-Oxley. Let's briefly look at these.

Signed into law in July 2002 by President Bush, the Sarbanes-Oxley Act establishes procedures for public companies regarding how they handle and report their financial picture. The legislation also established penalties for noncompliance. For example, Sarbanes-Oxley requires the following[18]:

- Top management (the CEO and chief financial officer [CFO]) must personally certify the organization's financial reports.
- The organization must have in place procedures and guidelines for audit committees.
- CEOs and CFOs must reimburse the organization for bonuses and stock options when required by restatement of corporate profits.
- Personal loans or lines of credit for executives are now prohibited.

The penalty aspect of Sarbanes-Oxley for noncompliance is something that is getting executives' attention. Failure to comply with the requirements stipulated under Sarbanes-Oxley—such as falsely stating corporate financial position—can result in the executive being fined up to $1 million and imprisoned for up to ten years.[19] Moreover, if the executive's action is determined to be willful, both the fine and the jail time can be doubled.

Sarbanes-Oxley does not specifically identify general supervisory activities in the law, but it does require a number of items that generally fall under the topic of human resource management (see Chapter 5). For example, the act provides protection for employees who come forward (whistle-blowing) to report wrongdoing by executives. Supervisors must create an environment in which employees can come forward with allegations without fear of reprisal from the employer. Although this critical employee relations aspect is not limited solely to whistle-blowing, the act does require companies to have mechanisms in place for receiving complaints and undertaking an investigation. As a result, many companies are creating "organizational ombuds," professionals who

---

[16]A. H. Bell and D. M. Smith, "Why Some Employees Bite the Hand That Feeds Them," *Workforce Online*, December 3, 2000, http://www.workforce.com.
[17]"Coming Clean," *Money*, May 2002, 33.
[18]Based on J. A. Segal, "The Joy of Uncooking," *HR Magazine*, November 2002, 53.
[19]Ibid.

will offer confidential help for employees and "handle potentially unethical or illegal behavior" in the organization.[20]

Supervisors also have other responsibilities under the Sarbanes-Oxley Act. Someone in the organization must make sure that employees know about corporate ethics policies, and train employees and supervisory personnel on how to act ethically in organizations.

The bottom line is that corporate greed and unethical behavior must be stopped. Employees and other stakeholders demand it. Although regulations signed into law are attempting to legislate "proper" behavior, legislation alone cannot work. Instead, company officials must take the lead in establishing the moral fabric of the organization—and ensuring that it becomes part of the standard operating procedures of the enterprise.[21]

Comprehension Check 6-2

5. A system in which materials arrive when they are needed in the production process instead of being stored in stock is called

   a. work process engineering
   b. just-in-time inventory
   c. cause-effect diagram
   d. none of the above

6. The process of managing the entire sequence of integrated activities and information about product flows is called

   a. supply chain management
   b. *kaizen*
   c. value chain management
   d. process mapping

7. Which one of the following is *not* a characteristic of effective quality controls?

   a. Timeliness
   b. Reasonable criteria
   c. Placement on all activities
   d. Flexibility

8. True or false? Employee theft is a significant problem most organizations have to deal with.

---

[20]C. Hirschman, "Someone to Listen: Ombuds Can Offer Employees a Confidential, Discrete Way to Handle Problems—But Setup and Communication Are Crucial to Making This Role Work Properly," *HR Magazine*, January 2003, 46–52.
[21]B. McConnel, "Executives, HR Must Set Moral Compass, Says Ethics Group," *HR News*, August 19, 2003. Available online at www.shrm.org/hrnews.published/archives/CMS.003406.asp.

Enhancing Understanding

SUMMARY

After reading this chapter, I can:

1. **Describe the control process.** The control process consists of three separate and distinct steps: (1) measuring actual performance, (2) comparing results with standards, and (3) taking corrective action.

2. **Contrast two types of corrective action.** There are two types of corrective action: immediate and basic. Immediate corrective action deals predominantly with symptoms. Basic corrective action looks for the cause of the deviation and seeks to adjust the differences permanently.

3. **Compare preventive, concurrent, and corrective control.** Preventive control is implemented before an activity begins. It anticipates and prevents undesirable outcomes. Concurrent control takes place while an activity is in progress. Corrective control is implemented after an activity is finished and facilitates prevention of future deviations.

4. **Explain how a supervisor can reduce costs.** Supervisors can reduce costs by improving work methods, leveling the work flow, reducing waste, installing more modern equipment, investing in employee training, and making selective cuts that will generate the greatest efficiencies.

5. **List the characteristics of an effective control system.** An effective control system should be timely, be economical, be flexible, be understandable, have reasonable standards, be critically placed, and emphasize the exception.

6. **Explain potential negatives that controls can create.** Potential negatives include employee resistance, employees directing their efforts to the wrong activities, and ethical dilemmas created by advances in control technology.

7. **Explain what is meant by the term *just-in-time inventory systems*.** Just-in-time inventory systems change the technology around which inventories are managed. Inventory items arrive when they are needed in the production process instead of being stored in stock.

8. **Describe what is meant by the term *value chain management*.** Value chain management is the process of managing the entire sequence of integrated activities and information about product flows along the entire value chain.

9. **Identify the ethical dilemmas in employee monitoring.** The ethical dilemmas in employee monitoring revolve around the rights of employees versus the rights of employers. Employees are concerned with protecting their workplace privacy and intrusion into their personal lives. Employers, in contrast, are primarily concerned with enhancing productivity and ensuring that the workplace is safe.

10. **Explain what is meant by employee theft and describe its effect on the organization.** Employee theft is any unauthorized taking of property by employees for their personal use. Employee theft costs U.S. companies more than $29 billion annually.

COMPREHENSION: Review and Discussion Questions

1. Why may what we measure be more critical to the control process than how we measure it?

2. What constitutes an acceptable range of variation?

3. Which type of control is preferable—preventive, concurrent, or corrective? Why? What type do you think is most widely used in practice?

4. What is the challenge of monitoring inventory costs? Of implementing a just-in-time inventory system?

5. In terms of characteristics of an effective control system, where do you think most control systems fail? Why?

6. Why should a supervisor control by exception?

7. How can a supervisor lessen employee resistance to controls?

8. What can a supervisor do to minimize the problem of people trying to look good on control criteria?

KEY CONCEPT CROSSWORD

ACROSS

4. management of the efficient flow of incoming materials
7. a visual representation of the sequencing of events
8. expected difference in actual performance
10. an action that adjusts something right now and gets things back on track
11. a statistical technique used to measure variation to produce an average standard
12. measuring, comparing, and taking corrective action
13. a system that ensures that one is not overwhelmed by information on variations from standard
14. an illustration of the relationship between two variables
15. an inventory system in which items arrive as needed
16. identification of mistakes that may have occurred to ensure that preestablished standards are met
17. anticipating and preventing undesirable outcomes

DOWN

1. a diagram depicting the roots of a problem
2. an inventory system designed around a card system
3. management of the entire sequence of integrated activities
5. a type of control that provides feedback after an activity is finished to prevent future deviations
6. an action that gets to the source of a problem and adjusts it permanently
9. a type of control that takes place while an activity is in progress

ANSWERS TO COMPREHENSION CHECKS

Comprehension Check 6-1

1. a   2. c   3. a   4. c

Comprehension Check 6-2

5. b   6. c   7. c   8. True

Developing Your Supervisory Skills

GETTING TO KNOW YOURSELF

Before you can effectively supervise others, you must understand your present strengths and areas in need of development. To assist in this learning process, we encourage you to complete the following self-assessments from the Prentice Hall Self-Assessment Library 3.4.

1. How Confident Am I in My Abilities to Succeed? (I. C. 6.)

2. What's My Job's Motivating Potential? (I. C. 8.)

3. Do I Want an Enriched Job? (I. C. 9.)

After you complete the assessment, we suggest you retain the results, and store them as part of your "portfolio of learning about yourself."

BUILDING A TEAM

➤ An Experiential Exercise: Developing a Budget

You have recently been appointed advertising supervisor for a new monthly health magazine, *Today's Fitness*, being developed by the magazine division of the Rupert Murdoch organization. You were previously an advertising supervisor on one of the company's established magazines. You will report to the new magazine's publisher, Jennifer Clark.

Estimates of first-year subscription sales for *Today's Fitness* are 125,000. Magazine stand sales should add another $40,000 a month to this number. Your concern is with developing advertising revenue for the magazine. You and Jennifer have set a goal of selling advertising space totaling $6 million during *Today's Fitness*'s first

year. You think you can do this with a staff of about eight people. Because this is a completely new publication, there is no previous budget for your advertising group. You've been asked by Jennifer to submit a preliminary budget for your group.

Prepare a report no more than three pages long. (1) Describe in detail how you would go about this assignment. For example, where would you get budget categories? Whom would you contact? (2) Present your best effort at creating a budget for your department. (Your instructor will inform you whether this is to be turned in as a written assignment or discussed in class.)

➤ Internet: Web Activity

Go to http://www.pearsonhighered.com/robbins/. Find *Supervision Today!* 7th Ed. and click Companion Website.

ESTABLISHING BUDGETS

Budgets are an important component in running an effective department. If you've never been exposed to budgeting (other than your personal finances), developing a realistic budget can be difficult—especially the first few times. The following steps are designed to provide you with some guidance in developing an effective budget.

STEPS IN PRACTICING THE SKILL

STEP 1: Review the organization's overall strategy and goals. Understanding your organization's strategy and goals will help you focus on where the overall organization is going and your department's role in that plan.

STEP 2: Determine your department's goals and the means to attaining them. What activities will you do to reach your departmental goals and help the organization achieve its overall goals? What resources will you require to achieve these goals? Think in terms of things such as staffing requirements, workloads, and the materials and equipment you'll need. This is also your opportunity to formulate new programs and propose new responsibilities for your department.

STEP 3: Gather cost information. You'll need accurate cost estimates of the resources you identified in step 2. Old budgets may be of some help. But you'll also want to talk with your immediate boss, other supervisors, colleagues in similar positions, key employees, and other contacts you have developed inside and outside of your organization.

STEP 4: Share your goals and cost estimates with your boss. Your immediate boss will need to approve your budget, so his or her support is necessary. Discuss your goals, cost estimates, and other ideas with your immediate boss and key individuals in your organization before you include them in your budget. This will ensure that they align with upper management's vision of your department's role and will build consensus for your proposed submission.

STEP 5: Draw up your proposed budget. Once your goals and costs are in place, constructing the actual budget is fairly mechanical. Be sure to show the link between your budget items and your departmental goals. You need to justify your requests and be prepared to explain and sell your budget to your immediate boss and other people in management. If other supervisors are competing for some of the same resources that you want, your rationale will have to be especially strong.

STEP 6: Be prepared to negotiate. It's unlikely that your budget will be approved exactly as you submitted it. Be prepared to negotiate changes that management suggests and to revise your original budget. Recognize the politics in the budget process and negotiate from the perspective of building credits for future budgets. If certain projects aren't approved this time, use this point in the budget process to get some assurance that they will be reconsidered next time.

STEP 7: Monitor your budget. Once your budget is approved and implemented, you'll be judged on how well you manage it. Supervise by exception. Set variance targets that include both percentages and dollars. For instance, you could set a rule that says you'll investigate all monthly variances of 15 percent or larger where the actual dollar variance is $200 or more.

STEP 8: Keep your boss informed of your progress. Keep your immediate boss and other relevant parties advised on how you're doing in terms of meeting your budget. This is likely to help protect you if you exceed your budget for reasons beyond your control. Also, don't expect to be rewarded for underspending your budget. Underspending may indicate that you need less money than you expected, and this could adversely affect your next budgeting cycle.

➤ Communicating Effectively

1. "Controls have to be sophisticated to be effective." Present arguments for and against this statement. Conclude your paper with a persuasive argument why you agree or disagree with the statement.

2. Describe how you can use the concepts of control in your own personal life. Be specific in your examples and think in terms of the preventive, concurrent, and corrective controls that you use for different parts of your life.

3. Review the "Steps in Practicing the Skill" from the "Establishing Budgets" piece (earlier in this chapter) to develop your personal budget. Substitute yourself for the organization/department as you develop your goals and cost estimates related to completing an A.S. or B.S. degree at your school. Take on the role of the boss as you negotiate and monitor your own budget for the school year. Discuss what you learned as you reviewed your personal budget.

THINKING CRITICALLY

➤ Case 6-A: Walk the Talk

The hospitality industry has been hit hard by the economic turmoil. Not only are families not going on vacation, many companies are curtailing business travel. Hotel occupancy rates were down over previous years and forecasted to continue their decline in coming years. Hotel managers recognized that to attract guests and keep them returning, they had to offer exceptional customer service. That's why so many are taking control actions to ensure that employees are working efficiently and effectively to provide that service.

It's called the $10 test.[1] Managers at a Florida resort hotel felt that the instructional videos they used to train housekeepers on how to quickly and effectively clean guest rooms didn't seem to have a lasting impact. So they began doing surprise inspections evaluating room cleanliness based on the video information. A manager would choose a room that had just been cleaned, place 10 one-dollar bills on the bed, and then go through the room and look for areas not up to cleanliness standards. If, for instance, a hair was found on the bathroom counter or in the tub, the manager would pick up a dollar. Other cleaning "mistakes" also cost a dollar. After the inspection, any money left on the bed was given to the housekeeper as a bonus. At first, the housekeepers resented the "$10 tests" because there wasn't much left after the inspection. However, after doing the "tests" for a time, most of the housekeepers ended up with an extra $9 or $10 and actually started looking forward to the inspections. And managers got what they wanted…guest rooms cleaned to an impeccable standard, an important consideration since cleanliness is a critical component in customer satisfaction.

RESPONDING TO THE CASE

1. Refer to the steps of the control process (Exhibit 6-1). Where in the process do the steps taken by the Florida resort hotel fall?

2. As a supervisor, do you think the $10 test is a fair and appropriate method to measure the performance of the housekeeping staff? Why or why not?

3. Describe which type(s) of control(s) is/are illustrated in this case. How do you know?

[1] R. A. Clark, M. D. Hartline, and K. C. Jones, "The Effects of Leadership Style on Hotel Employees' Commitment to Service Quality," *Cornell Hospitality Quarterly* (May 2009), 209–231; C. Crowell, "Staff Management Is Key for Smaller Budgets," *Hotel & Motel Management*, February 2009, 4+; G. Withiam, "Scripts Can Ensure Quality but Must Be Used Carefully," *Hotel & Motel Management*, January 19, 2009, 20; B. De Lollis, "Most Hotels Likely to See Occupancy Rates Fall Next Year," *USA Today Online*, November 11, 2008; G. Kranz, "Hospitality's Sharpened Focus," *Workforce Management Online*, September 2008; A. Dombey, "How To: Excel in Service Delivery," *Caterer & Hotelkeeper*, June 12, 2008, 57; M. Nelson, "The Ten-Dollar Test Toward Customer Satisfaction," *Executive Housekeeping Today*, May 2008, 5+; and H. Dolezalek, "We Train to Please," *Training* (March/April 2008), 34–35.

➤ Case 6-B: Control Measures at Frito-Lay

All day long, each working day of the week, salespeople at Frito-Lay punch information into their handheld computers. At the end of each workday, these salespeople download the collected information to computers at local sales offices or in their homes. These downloaded data are then transmitted to corporate headquarters in Dallas, Texas, where within twenty-four hours they are made available to those who wish to review it. Information on one hundred Frito-Lay product lines in four hundred thousand stores is available on computer screens in easy-to-read, color-coded charts: Red means a sales drop; yellow, a slowdown; and green, an advance. This system allows problems to be identified and corrected quickly.

Frito-Lay's control system helped the company solve a recent problem in San Antonio and Houston. Sales were slumping in area supermarkets. One supervisor turned on his computer, called up data for south Texas, and quickly identified the cause. A regional competitor had introduced El Galindo, a white-corn tortilla chip. The chip was getting good word-of-mouth advertising and store managers were giving it more shelf space than Frito's traditional Tostitos tortilla chips. Using this information, the Frito-Lay supervisor sprang into action. He worked with a product development team to produce a white-corn version of Tostitos. Within three months a new product was on the shelves and the company won back lost market share. Interestingly, this control mechanism at Frito-Lay is relatively new. Before its installation, it would have required at least three months for supervisors to pinpoint the problem. But this new system gathers data daily from supermarkets, scans them for important clues about local trends, and warns executives about problems and opportunities in all Frito-Lay markets.

RESPONDING TO THE CASE

1. Describe the type of control that Frito-Lay is using. Why do you think they've chosen this type of control system?

2. Identify instances in the case where Frito-Lay is using preventive and corrective controls.

CHAPTER 7

Problem Analysis and Decision Making

Key Concepts

After completing this chapter, you will be able to define these supervisory terms:

- availability heuristic
- brainstorming
- decision-making process
- decision tree
- electronic meeting
- escalation of commitment
- expected value analysis
- groupthink
- ill-structured problems
- justice view of ethics

- marginal analysis
- nominal group technique
- nonprogrammed decision
- problem
- programmed decision
- representative heuristic
- rights view of ethics
- *ringisei*
- utilitarian view of ethics
- well-structured problems

Chapter Outcomes

After reading this chapter, you will be able to:

1. List the seven steps in the decision-making process.

2. Describe expected value analysis.

3. Explain the four types of decision styles.

4. Identify and explain the common decision-making errors.

5. Describe the two types of decision problems and the two types of decisions that are used to solve them.

6. Compare and contrast group decision making and individual decision making.

7. List and describe three techniques for improving group decision making.

8. Explain three different ethical viewpoints.

Responding to a Supervisory Dilemma

Consider the case of Advanced Cell Technology. It's embarking on a major activity—"to produce the world's first-ever cloned human embryo … a microscopic version of an already living person." Leaders of the organization have begun implementation of this goal by interviewing women to serve as egg donors. Combining these eggs with a human cell produces an embryo that permits scientists at Advanced Cell to capture stem cells. As the stem cells are captured, the embryo is destroyed. Stem cells are believed to be able to develop into human tissue that could help cure a variety of diseases, or even repair a severed spinal cord.

Advanced Cell Technology's goal, of course, is facing a major debate. People supporting both sides of the issue have voiced their opinions strongly. On one hand, if such research is proven effective, many diseases as we know them today—such as Parkinson's disease and muscular dystrophy—could be eliminated. That could be both a major scientific breakthrough in our world and a major financial coup for Advanced Cell. Moreover, similar research is being conducted in other parts of the globe, such as Europe, where it has received support. And in an attempt to ensure that the highest ethics prevail in all decisions made, the company has formed an ethical board of advisers consisting of scientists and professors of religion.

But critics of such research see this differently. They view stem cell research as the next step toward cloning humans—and at times, liken it to creating a "great society." Religious groups, too, have voiced this concern over Advanced Cell's decisions, claiming that it is working in an area that it shouldn't be. They also say that making decisions regarding such research raises significant ethical issues, particularly as to how far this research can go. The federal government has also entered into the discussion, and on March 9, 2009, President Barack Obama issued Executive Order (EO) 13505, entitled "Removing Barriers to Responsible Scientific Research Involving Human Stem Cells," effectively reversing the earlier presidential statement of President George W. Bush that set specific regulations on what kind of stem cell research is funded by the government. However, even some Advanced Cell ethics board members have resigned, complaining that Advanced Cell is more interested in "obtaining patents in the field and using the board as a rubber stamp."

Supervisors may not be fully involved in establishing lofty goals for organizations, but they may be responsible for implementing actions that make the goals achievable. Do you believe that company officials can make ethical decisions in this arena when so much is at stake? Should public opinion keep a company from doing something simply because it is unpopular—even though it is legal? If you were a supervisor at Advanced Cell and you were against this research for a number of personal reasons, would you voice your opinion and ask not to be part of this research? As a supervisor, what recourse might you have if you disagree with the decisions that are being handed down in the organization?

Sources: Based on A. Regalado, "Experiments in Controversy—Ethicists, Bodyguards Monitor Scientists' Effort to Create Copy of Human Embryo," *Wall Street Journal*, July 13, 2001, B1; and "Stem-Cell Research Is Forging Ahead in Europe," *Wall Street Journal*, July 13, 2001, B6; Federal Policy. In *Stem Cell Information* [World Wide Web site]. Bethesda, MD: National Institutes of Health, U.S. Department of Health and Human Services, 2010, http://stemcells.nih.gov/policy/defaultpage (accessed May 23, 2011).

Decisions, decisions, decisions! One of your employees has been coming to work late recently, and the quality of her work has fallen off. What do you do? You've got a vacancy in your department and your company's human resource representative has sent you six candidates. Which one do you choose? Several of your salespeople have told you that they're losing business to an innovative new product line introduced by one of your competitors. How do you respond?

As a supervisor, you are regularly confronted with problems that require decisions. For example, you help employees select goals, schedule workloads, and decide what information—and how much of it—to share with your boss.[1] How do you learn to make good decisions? Are you born with some intuitive talent? Probably not! Sure, some of you, because of your intelligence, knowledge, and experience, can unconsciously analyze problems; that can result, over time, in an impressive trail of decisions. There are, however, some conscious decision-making techniques that anyone can use to become a more effective decision maker. We review a number of these techniques in this chapter.

The Decision-Making Process

Let's begin by describing a rational and analytical way of looking at decisions. We call this approach the decision-making process. It's composed of seven steps (see also Exhibit 7-1):

1. Identify the problem.
2. Collect relevant information.
3. Develop alternatives.
4. Evaluate each alternative.
5. Select the best alternative.
6. Implement the decision.
7. Follow up and evaluate.

To help illustrate this process, we'll work through a problem faced by Carol Prince. Carol is head of operations at WCIV, a Fox affiliate in Charleston, South Carolina. She has just received the news that the syndicated program she runs in the 7:00–7:30 p.m. time slot, *COPS*, has been canceled by the syndicator. Let's look at how Carol handles this problem by working through the decision-making process.

HOW DO YOU IDENTIFY THE PROBLEM?

Step 1 in the decision-making process begins with identifying the existence of a problem or, more specifically, a discrepancy between an existing and a desired state of affairs. For Carol Prince it's suddenly having a half-hour gap in her early-evening program schedule, which she wants filled with profitable, high-rated shows.

In the real world, problems don't always come with neon signs identifying them as such. Many of the problems you will confront aren't as obvious as Carol's dilemma. One of the most difficult chores in this stage, then, is separating symptoms from problems. Is a 5 percent decline in sales a problem? Or are declining sales merely a symptom of another problem, such as product obsolescence or an inadequate advertising budget? To use a medical analogy, aspirin doesn't deal with the problem of stress on the job; it merely relieves the headache symptom. One last point: Solving the wrong problem perfectly is no better an outcome, and may be worse, than coming up with the wrong solution to the right problem! Correctly identifying the real problem is not an easy task and should not be taken lightly.

decision-making process
A seven-step process that provides a rational and analytical way of looking at decisions. The steps include identification of the problem, collection of relevant information, development of alternatives, evaluation of alternatives, selection of the best alternative, implementation of the decision, and follow-up and evaluation.

problem
A discrepancy between an existing and a desired state of affairs.

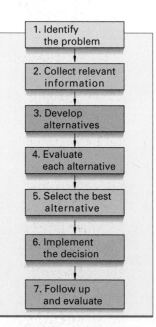

Exhibit 7-1
The decision-making process.

---

[1]See, for instance, K. Fracaro, "Pre-Planning: Key to Problem Solving," *Supervision*, November 2001, 9–12.

HOW DO YOU COLLECT RELEVANT INFORMATION?

Once the problem has been identified, you need to gather the facts and information relevant to the problem. Why has it occurred now? How is it affecting productivity in your department? What, if any, organizational policies are relevant for dealing with this problem? What time limitations exist for solving it? What costs are involved?

In Carol's case, she'll need to find answers to questions such as these: What was she paying the syndicator for *COPS*? For how much longer will the syndicator provide episodes? What are competitors currently showing in the 7:00–7:30 p.m. time slot? What are the ratings of these shows? What contractual obligations does she have that would constrain her options to shuffle other programs into this slot?

HOW DO YOU DEVELOP ALTERNATIVES?

Once you have collected the relevant information, it's now time to identify all possible alternatives. It is at this step in the decision process that you demonstrate your creativity (see the section titled "Becoming More Creative" at the end of this chapter) by considering which alternatives exist beyond the obvious or those that may have been used previously.

Keep in mind that this step requires only identifying alternatives. No alternative—no matter how unusual or unconventional—should be discarded at this point. If an alternative isn't viable, you'll find out at the next stage. Also, avoid the tendency to stop searching for alternatives after only a couple have been identified. If you see only two or three choices, you probably haven't thought hard enough. Generally speaking, the more alternatives you can generate, the better your final solution will be. Why? Because your final choice can be only as good as the best alternative you've generated.

What alternatives has Carol Prince been able to develop? Here's what she came up with:

1. Buy a syndicated tabloid news show for this time slot. *ET* is available.
2. Buy the syndicated program *Jeopardy*.
3. Buy comedy reruns in syndication. *Friends* is available.
4. Move *Bernie Mac* from the 7:30 p.m. slot and fill the gap with a local human-interest program—similar to *Atlanta Today*, a program that she had developed at her previous job at a station in Georgia.
5. Develop a new show around local college and professional sports teams.

HOW DO YOU EVALUATE EACH ALTERNATIVE?

Step 4, the next step in the decision-making process, is to evaluate all the strengths and weaknesses of each alternative. What will each cost? How long will each take to implement? What is the most favorable outcome you can expect from each? What is the most unfavorable outcome?

In this step, in particular, it is important to guard against biases. Undoubtedly, some alternatives will have looked more attractive when they were first identified. Others, at first glance, may have seemed unrealistic or exceedingly risky. As a result, you may tend to prematurely favor some outcomes over others and then bias your analysis accordingly. Try to put your initial biases on hold and evaluate each alternative as objectively as you can. Of course, no one is perfectly rational. However, you can improve the final outcome if you acknowledge your biases and overtly attempt to control them.

Exhibit 7-2 summarizes the highlights from Carol's evaluation of her five alternatives. Writing down key considerations—which in Carol's case are costs and audience market share—often makes it easier for decision makers to compare alternatives.

Alternative	Estimated Weekly Cost	Estimated Market Share*	Strengths	Weaknesses
1. Tabloid news show	$ 25,000	15–25	Competition does well with *Inside Edition* and *E! News* in this time slot.	High cost. Would leave little potential profit. Would split tabloid market further.
2. *Jeopardy*	$16,000	8–12	Known entity.	Low market potential.
3. Comedy reruns	$30,000	20–35	Could provide strong lead-in to 8:00 p.m. network programming. Might be perfect counterprogramming move against competitor's tabloid shows.	High cost. Would leave almost no profit.
4. Human-interest program	$12–15,000	8–12	Possible stopgap measure.	Low potential. Not a viable long-term solution.
5. New sports show	$6,000	6–20	Unique. Nothing like this in our market. Build goodwill in community. Low cost. Strong appeal among 18–39 male market.	Risky. Is there a market for a half hour of local sports coverage?

* Percentage of sets turned on that would be watching this show

Exhibit 7-2
Evaluating alternatives.

HOW DO YOU SELECT THE BEST ALTERNATIVE?

In Step 5, after analyzing the pros and cons for each alternative, it is time to select the best alternative. Of course, what's "best" will reflect any limitations or biases that you bring to the decision process. It depends on things such as the comprehensiveness and accuracy of the information gathered in Step 2, your ingenuity in developing alternatives in Step 3, the degree of risk that you're willing to take, and the quality of your analysis in Step 4.

Carol's analysis led her to choose development of a new program focusing on local college and professional sports teams (Alternative 5). Her logic went like this: "First of all, the syndicator advised me that they would offer *COPS* through the end of the season. That meant I had ten weeks more of the show. I wanted to make my decision permanent, so I eliminated the option of expanding the local news. The payoff of going with *Jeopardy* didn't seem high enough to justify the cost. I think the tabloid news market is saturated in this time slot, so I passed on buying *ET*. We're in business to make money and, although I felt confident we could get the highest ratings in this time period with *Friends*, the cost was too high. That left developing a sports show. I thought the sports show alternative offered me the highest potential market share for the lowest cost."

HOW DO YOU IMPLEMENT THE DECISION?

Even if you've made the proper choice, the decision may still fail if it is not implemented properly. This means that in Step 6 you need to convey the decision to those affected and get their commitment to it. You'll specifically want to assign responsibilities, allocate necessary resources, and clarify any deadlines.

In Carol's case, she called a meeting of her programming staff, explained the decision and how she arrived at it, and encouraged discussion on any problems people anticipated. She then created a three-member departmental task force to develop the concept, prepare a format, and suggest key personnel for the program. She appointed one of the team members as the project leader, and together they decided that the task force would make a formal presentation to Carol within three weeks.

HOW DO YOU FOLLOW UP AND EVALUATE?

In Step 7, the last phase in the decision-making process, you follow up and evaluate the outcomes of the decision. Did your choice accomplish the desired result? Did it correct the problem that you originally identified in Step 1? In Carol's decision, did she fill the time slot with a profitable, high-rated show? She hopes so, but she won't know the final answer until after the program has aired for a few months.

If the follow-up and evaluation indicate that the sought-after results weren't achieved, you'll want to review the decision process to see where you went wrong. You essentially have a brand-new problem, and you should go completely through the decision process again with a fresh perspective.

Decision Tools

A number of tools and techniques have been developed over the years to help supervisors improve their decision-making capabilities. In this section, we present several of the more popular ones. Let's begin, however, with a brief review of the conditions supervisors face when making decisions.

WHAT ARE THE CONDITIONS OF DECISION MAKING?

Supervisors may face three conditions as they make a decision: certainty, risk, and uncertainty. Let's briefly look at each of these.

Certainty Supervisors facing decisions in which certainty abounds are in the best possible situation. Certainty exists when the outcome and every alternative are known. For example, suppose a supervisor is deciding what transportation company to use to ship goods. The supervisor knows the exact weight of the item to be shipped and the cost incurred if it's shipped by UPS, FedEx, or DHL. The supervisor is also certain about the outcomes of each alternative—delivery will be made. As you might expect, most supervisory decisions aren't as clear-cut as this.

Risk A far more common situation supervisors face is one of risk, in which they must estimate the likelihood of certain outcomes. To assign probabilities to outcomes, supervisors can rely on personal experiences, secondary information, or historical data.

Uncertainty Supervisors who are not certain about the outcomes and can't even make a reasonable probability estimate are said to be making a decision under a condition of uncertainty. In this case, the choice of alternatives is influenced by the limited information available and by one's view of the problem. The optimistic supervisor will more than likely select an alternative that offers the highest possible payoff, whereas the pessimistic supervisor will often attempt to minimize the maximum loss. Although supervisors facing uncertainty will try to quantify the decision when possible, making a choice based on a "gut reaction" often results in the best outcome.

WHAT IS THE EXPECTED VALUE ANALYSIS?

The head of the skiing department at a Bass Pro Shops store in Houston is looking at several new brands of ski jackets. Given his space and budget limitations, he can purchase only one of these new brands to add to his selection. Which one should he choose?

Expected value analysis could help with this decision. It permits decision makers to place a monetary value on the various consequences likely to result from the selection of a particular course of action. The procedure is simple. You calculate the expected value of a particular alternative by weighting its possible outcomes by the probability (0 to 1.0, with 1.0 representing absolute certainty) of achieving the alternative, and then summing up the totals derived from the weighting process.

Let's say our Bass Pro Shops supervisor is looking at three lines of ski jackets: Nike, Adidas, and one that will carry the Bass label. He's constructed the payoff table in Exhibit 7-3 to summarize his analysis. Based on his past experience and personal judgment, he's calculated the potential yearly profit from each alternative and the probability of achieving that profit. The expected value of each alternative ranges from $6,500 to $8,800. Based on this analysis, the supervisor could anticipate the highest expected value by purchasing the Bass line of jackets.

Alternative	Possible Outcome	Probability	Expected Value
Nike	$12,000	0.1	$1,200
	8,000	0.7	5,600
	4,000	0.2	800
			$7,600
Adidas	$15,000	0.1	$1,500
	10,000	0.2	2,000
	6,000	0.4	2,400
	2,000	0.3	600
			$6,500
Bass label	$12,000	0.4	$4,800
	8,000	0.4	3,200
	4,000	0.2	800
			$8,800

Exhibit 7-3
Payoff table for ski jacket decision.

expected value analysis
A procedure that permits decision makers to place a monetary value on various consequences likely to result from the selection of a particular course of action.

HOW ARE DECISION TREES USEFUL?

Decision trees are a useful way to analyze hiring, marketing, investment, equipment purchase, pricing, and similar decisions that involve a progression of decisions. They're called decision trees because, when diagrammed, they look a lot like a tree with branches. Typical decision trees encompass expected value analysis by assigning probabilities to each possible outcome and calculating payoffs for each decision path.

Exhibit 7-4 illustrates a decision facing Mike Flynn, the midwestern region site-selection supervisor for the Barnes & Noble bookstore chain. Mike supervises a small group of specialists who analyze potential locations and make store site recommendations to the midwestern region's director. The lease on the company's store in Cleveland, Ohio, is expiring, and the landlord has decided not to renew it. Mike and his group have to make a relocation recommendation to the regional director.

decision tree
A diagram that analyzes hiring, marketing, investment, equipment purchases, pricing, and similar decisions that involve a progression of decisions. Decision trees assign probabilities to each possible outcome and calculate payoffs for each decision path.

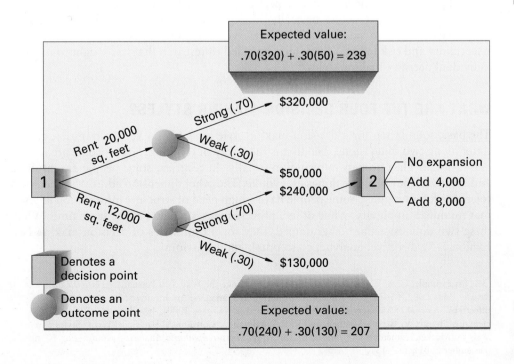

Exhibit 7-4
Decision tree and expected values for renting a large or small retail space.

Mike's group has identified an excellent site in a nearby shopping mall in North Olmsted. The mall owner has offered him two comparable locations: one with 12,000 square feet (the same as he has now) and the other a larger, 20,000-square-foot space. Mike has an initial decision to make about whether to recommend renting the larger or smaller location. If he chooses the larger space and the economy is strong, he estimates the store will make a $320,000 profit. However, if the economy is poor, the high operating costs of the larger store will mean that only $50,000 in profit will be made. With the smaller store, he estimates the profit at $240,000 with a good economy and $130,000 with a poor one.

As you can see from Exhibit 7-4, the expected value for the larger store is $239,000[(.70×320)+(.30×50)]. The expected value for the smaller store is $207,000[(.70×|240)+(.30×130)]. Given these results, Mike is planning to recommend renting the larger store space. But what if Mike wants to consider the implications of initially renting the smaller space, and then possibly expanding if the economy picks up? He can extend the decision tree to include this second decision point. He has calculated three options: no expansion, adding 4,000 square feet, and adding 8,000 square feet. Following the approach used for Decision Point 1, he could calculate the profit potential by extending the branches on the tree and calculating expected values for the various options.

WHAT IS MARGINAL ANALYSIS?

marginal analysis
A method that helps decision makers optimize returns or minimize costs by dealing with the additional cost in a particular decision, rather than the average cost.

The concept of marginal, or incremental, analysis helps decision makers optimize returns or minimize costs. Marginal analysis deals with the additional cost in a particular decision, rather than the average cost. For example, suppose the operations supervisor for a large commercial dry cleaner wonders whether she should take on a new customer. She should consider not the total revenue and the total cost that would result after the order was taken, but rather what additional revenue would be generated by this particular order and what additional costs. If the incremental revenues exceed the incremental costs, total profits would be increased by accepting the order.

Decision-Making Styles

Each of you brings your own unique personality and experiences to the decisions you make. For instance, if you're basically conservative and uncomfortable with uncertainty, you're likely to value decision alternatives differently from someone who enjoys uncertainty and risk taking. These facts have led to research that has sought to identify individual decision-making styles.[2]

WHAT ARE THE FOUR DECISION-MAKING STYLES?

The basic foundation for a decision-making style model is the recognition that people differ along two dimensions. The first is their way of thinking. Some people are logical and rational. They process information serially. In contrast, some people are intuitive and creative. They perceive things as a whole. The other dimension addresses a person's tolerance for ambiguity. Some people have a high need to structure information in ways that minimize ambiguity, while others process many thoughts at the same time. When these two dimensions are diagrammed, they form four styles of decision making (see Exhibit 7-5): directive, analytic, conceptual, and behavioral.

---

[2]See, for example, G. A. Williams and R. B. Miller, "Change the Way You Persuade," *Harvard Business Review*, May 2002, 65–73; J. A. Andersen, "Intuition in Managers: Are Intuitive Managers More Effective?" *Journal of Managerial Psychology* 15, no. 1–2 (January 2000), 46–63; and G. Walsh, T. Henning-Thurau, V. Wayne-Mitchell, and K. P. Wiedmann, "Consumers' Decision-Making Styles as a Basis for Market Segmentation," *Journal of Targeting, Measurement and Analysis for Marketing* 10, no. 2 (December 2001), 117–131.

Directive Style People using the directive style have low tolerance for ambiguity and seek rationality. They are efficient and logical. Their efficiency concerns may result in their making decisions with minimal information and after assessing few alternatives. Directive types make decisions quickly and focus on the short run.

Analytic Style Analytic types have a much greater tolerance for ambiguity than do directive managers. This leads to the desire for more information and consideration of more alternatives than is true for directives. Analytic supervisors would be best characterized as careful decision makers with the ability to adapt or cope with new situations.

Conceptual Style Individuals with a conceptual style tend to be very broad in their outlook and consider many alternatives. Their focus is long range, and they are very good at finding creative solutions to problems.

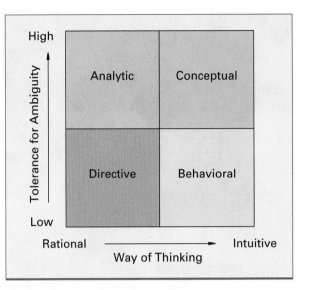

Exhibit 7-5
Decision-making style model.

Behavioral Style The behavioral style characterizes decision makers who work well with others. They're concerned with the achievement of their employees. They're receptive to suggestions from others and rely heavily on meetings for communicating. This type of decision maker tries to avoid conflict and seek acceptance.

WHAT'S THE POINT OF THESE FOUR DECISION-MAKING STYLES?

Although these four categories are distinct, most individuals have characteristics that fall into more than one. It's best to think in terms of an individual's dominant style and backup styles. Although some people rely almost exclusively on their dominant style, more flexible individuals can shift depending on the situation.

Business students, supervisors, and top executives tend to score highest in the analytic style. That's not surprising given the emphasis that formal education, particularly business education, gives to developing rational decision-making skills. For instance, courses in accounting, statistics, and finance all stress analytical thinking.

Focusing on decision styles can also be useful for helping you understand how two intelligent people, with access to the same information, can differ in the ways they approach decisions and in the final choices they make. It can also explain conflicts between you and your employees (or others you come in contact with). For example, if you are a directive supervisor, you expect work to be performed rapidly. You may get frustrated by the slowness and deliberate actions of a conceptual or analytic employee. On the other hand, if your style is analytic, you might criticize a decisive employee for incomplete work or acting too hastily. As an analytic, you may have great difficulty with your behavioral counterpart because of lack of understanding why feelings are used as the basis for decisions rather than rational logic.

Irrespective of your style, one must also be aware of some common decision-making errors. Let's look at the more common of these errors.

ARE COMMON ERRORS COMMITTED IN THE DECISION-MAKING PROCESS?

When supervisors have to make decisions, they must make choices. But doing so requires careful thought—and a lot of information. Complete information for any supervisor, however, would overload him or her. Consequently, supervisors often

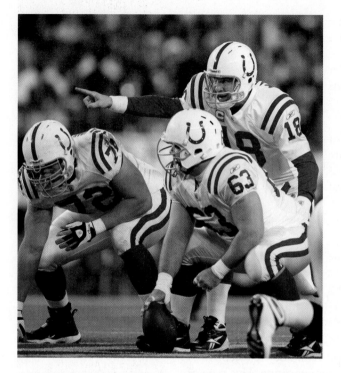

*Go to almost any youth foot-
ball game and you'll likely find
one thing in common. Someone
is playing football wearing
the jersey of Peyton Manning.
Why? Because many of these
players are trying to be just
like Peyton. After all, wearing
his jersey and playing like him
will help them one day fulfill a
dream and play in the NFL—
after a successful college career.
That dream is what we call
representative heuristic.*

availability heuristic
The tendency of people to base their
judgments on information that is readily available to them.

representative heuristic
The tendency of people to match the
likelihood of an occurrence with something they are familiar with.

escalation of commitment
An increased commitment to a
previous decision despite negative
information.

engage in behaviors that speed up the process. That is, to
avoid information overload, supervisors rely on judgmental shortcuts called *heuristics.*[3] Heuristics are commonly
found in two forms—availability and representative.
Both types create biases in a decision maker's judgment.
Another bias is the supervisor's tendency to escalate commitment to a failing course of action.

Availability Heuristic Availability heuristic is the tendency for
supervisors to base their judgments on readily available information. Events that evoke strong emotions, are vivid to the
imagination, or have recently occurred create a strong impression on them. As a result, supervisors are likely to overesti-
mate the frequency of the occurrence of unlikely events. For
instance, many people have a fear of flying. Although traveling in commercial aircraft is statistically safer than driving
a car, accidents in the former get much more attention. The
media coverage of an air disaster results in individuals' over-
stating the risk in flying and understating the risk of driving.
For supervisors, availability heuristic can also explain why,
when conducting performance appraisals (see Chapter 12),
they tend to give more weight to more recent behaviors of an
employee than behaviors of six or nine months ago.

Representative Heuristic Millions of recreational-league players dream of becoming professional football players someday. In reality, most of these youngsters have a better
chance of becoming medical doctors than they do of ever playing in the NFL. These
dreams are examples of what we call representative heuristic. Representative heuristic
causes individuals to match the likelihood of an occurrence with something that they are
familiar with. For example, our young football players may think about someone from
their local league who fifteen years ago went on to play in the NFL. Or they think, while
watching players on television, that they could perform as well.

In organizations, we can find several instances where representative heuristic
occurs. Decision makers may predict the future success of a new department process
by relating it to a previous process's success. Supervisors may also be affected by representative heuristic when they no longer hire college graduates from a particular college
program because the last three hired from that program were poor performers.

Escalation of Commitment A popular strategy in playing blackjack is to "guarantee" you
can't lose. When you lose a hand, double your next bet. This strategy, or decision rule,
may appear innocent enough, but if you start with a $5 bet and lose six hands in a row
(not uncommon for many of us), you will be wagering $320 on your seventh hand
merely to recoup your losses and win $5.

The blackjack strategy illustrates a phenomenon called escalation of commitment.
Specifically, it is defined as an increased commitment to a previous decision despite
negative information. That is, the escalation of commitment represents the tendency to
"stay the course," despite negative data that suggest one should do otherwise.

---

[3]See I. Yaniv, "Weighting and Trimming: Heuristics for Aggregating Judgments under Uncertainty,"
Organizational Behavior and Human Decision Processes 69, no. 3 (March 1997), 237–249; D. A. Duchon
and K. J. Donde-Dunegan, "Avoid Decision Making Disaster by Considering Psychological Biases," *Review
of Business,* Summer/Fall 1991, 13–18; C. G. Lundberg and B. M. Nagle, "Post-Decision Inference Editing
of Supportive and Counter Indicative Signals Among External Auditors in a Going Concern Judgment,"
European Journal of Operational Research 136, no. 2 (January 16, 2002), 264–281; and P. D. Windschitl
and M. E. Yong, "The Influence of Alternative Outcomes on Gut-Level Perceptions of Certainty," *Organizational Behavior and Human Decision Processes* 85, no. 1 (May 2001), 109–134.

Some of the best-recorded decisions involving escalation of commitment were made by presidents of the United States.[4] For example, Lyndon Johnson's administration increased the tonnage of bombs dropped on North Vietnam, despite continual information that bombing was not bringing the war any closer to conclusion. Richard Nixon refused to destroy his secret White House tapes. George H. W. Bush believed that, given his popularity after Operation Desert Storm and the fall of the Soviet Union, he had only to pay attention to foreign affairs to win the 1992 presidential election. History now tells us that staying the course proved detrimental to Johnson, Nixon, and Bush.

In organizations, supervisors may recognize evidence that their previous solution is not working. But rather than search for new alternatives, they further increase their commitment to the original solution. Why do they do this? In many cases, it's an effort to demonstrate that their initial decision was not wrong.

Comprehension Check 7-1

1. The first step in the decision-making process is
   a. collecting relevant information
   b. developing alternatives
   c. evaluating alternatives
   d. none of the above

2. A procedure that permits decision makers to place a monetary value on various consequences is called
   a. expected value analysis
   b. decision tree
   c. marginal analysis
   d. none of the above

3. People using a _____ style of decision making have a much greater tolerance for ambiguity than do those using other styles.
   a. directive
   b. analytic
   c. conceptual
   d. behavioral

4. Mental shortcuts in decision making, in which people base their judgments on information that they have easy access to, are called
   a. representative heuristics
   b. escalation of commitment
   c. availability heuristics
   d. none of the above

Problems Versus Decisions

The type of problem a supervisor faces in a decision-making situation often determines how the problem is treated. In this section, we present a categorization scheme for problems and for types of decisions. Then, we show how the type of decision a supervisor uses should reflect the characteristics of the problem (see also "News Flash! Global Decision Making").

---

[4]M. R. Beschloss, "Fateful Presidential Decisions," *Forbes FYI* 1 (1995), 171–172.

News Flash!

GLOBAL DECISION MAKING

Research shows that, to some extent, decision-making practices differ from country to country. The way decisions are made—whether by group, by team members, participatively, or autocratically by an individual supervisor—and the degree of risk a decision maker is willing to take are just two examples of decision variables that reflect a country's cultural environment. For example, in India, power distance and uncertainty avoidance (see Chapter 2) are high. There, only very senior-level people make decisions, and they are likely to make safe decisions. In contrast, in Sweden, power distance and uncertainty avoidance are low. Swedish supervisors are not afraid to make risky decisions. Senior managers in Sweden also push decisions down in the ranks. They encourage supervisors and employees to take part in decisions that affect them. In countries such as Egypt, where time pressures are low, supervisors make decisions at a slower and more deliberate pace than supervisors in the United States. And in Italy, where history and traditions are valued, supervisors tend to rely on tried and proven alternatives to resolve problems.

Decision making in Japan is much more group oriented than in the United States. The Japanese value conformity and cooperation. Before making decisions, Japanese supervisors collect a large amount of information, which is then used in consensus-forming group decisions called *ringisei*. Because employees in Japanese organizations have high job security, supervisory decisions take a long-term perspective rather than focusing on short-term profits, as is often the practice in the United States.

Supervisors in France and Germany also adapt their decision styles to their country's culture. In France, for instance, autocratic decision making is widely practiced, and supervisors tend to avoid risks. Supervisory styles in Germany reflect the German culture's concern for structure and order. Consequently, there are extensive rules and regulations in German organizations. Supervisors have well-defined responsibilities and accept that decisions must go through channels.

As supervisors deal with employees from diverse cultures, they need to recognize what is common and accepted behavior when asking them to make decisions. Some individuals may not be as comfortable being closely involved in decision making as others are, or they may not be willing to experiment with something radically different. Supervisors who accommodate the diversity in decision-making philosophies and practices can expect a high payoff: capturing the perspectives and strengths that a diverse workforce offers.

ringisei
In Japanese organizations, consensus-forming decision-making groups.

well-structured problems
Straightforward, familiar, easily defined problems.

ill-structured problems
New problems about which information is ambiguous or incomplete.

HOW DO PROBLEMS DIFFER?

Some problems are straightforward. The goal of the decision maker is clear, the problem familiar, and information about the problem easily defined and complete. Examples might include a supplier's being late with an important delivery, a customer's wanting to return a mail-order purchase, a news program's having to respond to an unexpected and fast-breaking news event, or a university's handling of a student who is applying for financial aid. Such situations are called well-structured problems.

Some situations faced by supervisors, however, are ill-structured problems. They are new or unusual. Information about such problems is ambiguous or incomplete. The decision on whether to restructure the department; to invest in and implement new, unproven technology; or to hire a consultant to redesign the work flow of the department is an example of ill-structured problems.

WHAT IS THE DIFFERENCE BETWEEN PROGRAMMED AND NONPROGRAMMED DECISIONS?

Just as problems can be divided into two categories, so too can decisions. As we will see, programmed, or routine, decision making is the most efficient way to handle well-structured problems. However, when problems are ill structured, supervisors must rely on nonprogrammed decision making to develop unique solutions.

Suppose a Goodyear Tire mechanic breaks an alloy wheel rim while installing new tires on a vehicle. What does the supervisor do? There is probably some standardized routine for handling this type of problem. For example, the supervisor replaces the rim at the company's expense. This is a programmed decision. Decisions are programmed to the extent that they are repetitive and routine and to the extent that a definite approach has been worked out for handling them. Because the problem is well structured, the supervisor does not have to go to the trouble and expense of working up an involved decision process.

programmed decision
A repetitive decision that can be handled by a routine approach.

Programmed decision making is relatively simple and tends to rely heavily on previous solutions. The "develop-the-alternatives" stage in the decision-making process is either nonexistent or given little attention. Why? Because once the structured problem is defined, its solution is usually self-evident or at least reduced to very few alternatives that are familiar and that have proved successful in the past. In many cases, programmed decision making becomes decision making by precedent. Supervisors simply do what they and others have done previously in the same situation. The broken wheel rim does not require the supervisor to identify and weight decision criteria or to develop a long list of possible solutions. Rather, the supervisor falls back on a systematic procedure, rule, or policy (see Chapter 3).

Nonprogrammed decisions, on the other hand, are decisions that are unique and nonrecurring. When a supervisor fronts an ill-structured problem, there is no cut-and-dried solution. A custom-made, nonprogrammed response is required.

nonprogrammed decision
A decision that must be custom-made to solve a unique and nonrecurring problem.

For example, setting strategy in the organization is a nonprogrammed decision. This decision is different from previous organizational decisions because the issue is new. The company faces a different set of environmental factors—like new laws or competition from countries that previously did not compete in the global marketplace. The conditions in which a decision is made often have changed. Accordingly, using the "tried and true" choices from the past may lead to problems in the future.

Group Decision Making

Decisions in organizations are increasingly being made by groups rather than by individuals. There seem to be at least two primary reasons for this. First is the desire to develop more and better alternatives. The adage "Two heads are better than one" translates into groups being able to generate a greater number, and potentially a more creative set, of decision alternatives. Second, organizations are relying less on the historical idea that departments and other organizational units should be separate and independent decision units. To get the best ideas and to improve their implementation, organizations are increasingly turning to teams that cut across traditional departmental lines for decision making. This requires group decision-making techniques.

WHAT ARE THE ADVANTAGES OF GROUP DECISIONS?

Individual and group decisions each have their own set of strengths. Neither is ideal for all situations. Let's begin, therefore, by reviewing the advantages that group decision making has over individual decision making (see Exhibit 7-6).

- **Provides more complete information.** A group brings a diversity of experience and perspective to the decision process that an individual, acting alone, cannot.
- **Generates more alternatives.** Because groups have a greater quantity and diversity of information, they can identify more alternatives than can an individual.
- **Increases acceptance of a solution.** Many decisions fail after the final choice has been made because people do not accept the solution. If the people who will be

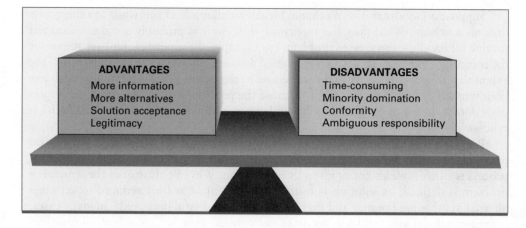

Exhibit 7-6
The advantages and disadvantages of group decision making.

affected by a certain solution and who will help implement it get to participate in the decision making itself, they will be more likely to accept the decision and to encourage others to accept it.

■ **Increases legitimacy.** The group decision-making process is consistent with democratic ideals and therefore may be perceived as more legitimate than decisions made by a single person.

ARE THERE DISADVANTAGES TO GROUP DECISION MAKING?

If groups are so good, how did the saying "A camel is a racehorse put together by a committee" become so popular? The answer, of course, is that group decisions are not without their drawbacks. The major disadvantages of group decision making are as follows:

■ **Time-consuming.** It takes time to assemble a group. Additionally, the interaction that takes place once the group is in place is frequently inefficient. The result is that groups almost always take more time to reach a solution than an individual making the decision alone.

■ **Minority domination.** Members of a group are never perfectly equal. They may differ in terms of rank in the organization, experience, knowledge about the problem, influence with other members, verbal skills, assertiveness, and the like. This creates the opportunity for one or more members to use their advantages to dominate others in the group and impose undue influence on the final decision.[5]

■ **Pressure to conform.** There are social pressures in groups. The desire of group members to be accepted and considered assets to the group can quash any overt disagreement and encourage conformity among viewpoints. The withholding by group members of different views to appear in agreement is called groupthink.

■ **Ambiguous responsibility.** Group members share responsibility, but who is actually responsible for the final outcome? In an individual decision, it is clear who is responsible, but in a group decision the responsibility of any single member is watered down.

groupthink
Withholding of differing views by group members to appear to be in agreement.

Groupthink Groupthink is a style of thinking often seen in cohesive groups. These groups attempt to reduce their conflict and reach agreement without thoroughly evaluating alternative actions. Eight symptoms often seen in groups experiencing groupthink are the following:

■ Feelings of invulnerability where danger is ignored and excessive risks are taken
■ Rationalizing anything contrary to group assumptions

---

[5]See C. K. W. De Drue and M. A. West, "Minority Dissent and Team Innovation: The Importance of Participation in Decision Making," *Journal of Applied Psychology* 86, no. 6 (December 2001), 1191–1201.

- Overriding belief in the morality of the group regardless of ethical outcomes
- Stereotyping opposition as weak and ineffectual
- Pressuring group members not to be disloyal to the group
- Self-censoring individual ideas not in harmony with the group viewpoint
- Illusion of unanimous agreement with silence viewed as assent
- Mindguards who shield the group from adverse outside information.[6]

IS THERE A GUIDE FOR WHEN TO USE GROUP DECISION MAKING?

When are groups better than individuals and vice versa? That depends on what you mean by *better*. Let's look at four criteria frequently associated with "better" decisions: accuracy, speed, creativity, and acceptance.

The evidence indicates that, on the average, groups make more accurate decisions than individuals do. This doesn't mean, of course, that all groups outperform every individual. Rather, group decisions have been found to be more effective than those that would have been reached by the average individual in the group. However, they seldom are as good as decisions by the best individual.

If *better* is defined in terms of decision speed, individuals are superior. Group decision processes are characterized by give-and-take, which consumes time.

Decision quality can also be assessed in terms of the degree to which a solution demonstrates creativity. If creativity is important, groups tend to do better than individuals. This requires, however, that the forces that foster groupthink—pressure to repress doubts about the group's shared views, the validity of favored arguments, excessive desire by the group to give an appearance of consensus, and the assumption that silence or abstention by members is a yes vote—be constrained.

As noted previously, because group decisions have input from more people, they are likely to result in solutions that have a higher degree of acceptance.

HOW CAN YOU IMPROVE GROUP DECISION MAKING?

When members of a group meet face to face and interact with one another, they create the potential for groupthink. They can censor themselves and pressure other group members into agreement. Three ways of making group decision making more creative have been suggested: brainstorming, the nominal group technique, and electronic meetings.

Brainstorming Brainstorming is a relatively simple technique for overcoming pressures for conformity that retard the development of creative alternatives.[7] It does this by using an idea-generating process that specifically encourages any and all alternatives while withholding any criticism of those alternatives. In a typical brainstorming session, a half-dozen to a dozen people sit around a table. The group leader states the problem in a clear manner that is understood by all participants. Members then "freewheel" as many alternatives as they can in a given time. No criticism is allowed, and all the alternatives are recorded for later discussion and analysis. Brainstorming, however, is merely a process for generating ideas. The next method, the nominal group technique, goes further by helping groups arrive at a preferred solution.[8]

brainstorming
A technique for overcoming pressures for conformity that retard the development of creative alternatives; an idea-generating process that specifically encourages alternatives while withholding criticism of those alternatives.

---

[6]I. L. Janis, *Victims of Groupthink: A Psychological Study of Foreign-Policy Decisions and Fiascoes* (Boston, MA: Houghton, Mifflin, 1972); and I. L. Janis and L. Mann, *Decision Making: A Psychological Analysis of Conflict, Choice, and Commitment* (New York: Free Press, 1977).

[7]J. Wagstaff, "Brainstorming Requires Drinks," *Far Eastern Economic Review*, May 2, 2002, 34.

[8]T. Kelley, "Six Ways to Kill a Brainstormer," *Across the Board*, March/April 2002, 12; and K. L. Dowling and R. D. St. Louis, "Asynchronous Implementation of the Nominal Group Technique: Is It Effective?" *Decision Support Systems* 29, no. 3 (October 2000), 229–248.

nominal group technique
A technique that restricts discussion during the decision-making process.

Nominal Group Technique The nominal group technique restricts discussion during the decision-making process, hence the term. Group members must be present, as in a traditional committee meeting, but they are required to operate independently. The chief advantage of this technique is that it permits the group to meet formally but does not restrict independent thinking, as so often happens in the traditional interacting group.

electronic meeting
A group decision-making technique in which participants are positioned in front of computer terminals as issues are presented. Participants type responses onto computer screens as their anonymous comments and aggregate votes are displayed on a projection screen in the room.

Electronic Meetings Electronic meetings are the most recent approach to group decision making; they blend the nominal group technique with sophisticated computer and videoconferencing technology. Once the technology for the meeting is in place, the concept is simple. Many individuals sit around a horseshoe-shaped table outfitted with computer terminals. Issues are presented to participants, and they type their responses onto their computer screens. Individual comments, as well as aggregate votes, are displayed on a projection screen in the room. Experts claim that electronic meetings and videoconferencing activities are much faster than traditional face-to-face meetings. Supervisors at Freeport-McMoRan Copper & Gold Inc. (formerly Phelps Dodge Mining), for instance, used the approach to cut its annual planning meeting from several days down to twelve hours. However, there are drawbacks. Those who can type quickly may outshine those who may be verbally eloquent but who are lousy typists; those with the best ideas don't get credit for them; and the process lacks the informational richness of face-to-face oral communication.

Something to Think About (and promote class discussion)

THE VALUE OF DIVERSITY IN DECISION MAKING

Have you decided what your major is going to be? How did you decide? Do you feel your decision is a good one? Is there anything you could have done differently to make sure that your decision was the best one?*

Making good decisions is tough! Supervisors continuously make decisions—for instance, developing new products, establishing weekly or monthly goals, implementing an advertising campaign, reassigning an employee to a different workgroup, resolving a customer's complaint, or purchasing new laptops for sales reps. One important suggestion for making better decisions is to tap into the diversity of the workgroup. Drawing upon diverse employees can prove valuable to a supervisor's decision making. Why? Diverse employees can provide fresh perspectives on issues. They can offer differing interpretations on how a problem is defined and may be more open to trying new ideas. Diverse employees can be more creative in generating alternatives and more flexible in resolving issues. And getting input from diverse sources increases the likelihood that creative and unique solutions will be generated.

Even though diversity in decision making can be valuable, there are drawbacks. The lack of a common perspective usually means that more time is spent discussing the issues. Communication may be a problem particularly if language barriers are present. In addition, seeking out diverse opinions can make the decision-making process more complex, confusing, and ambiguous. And with multiple perspectives on the decision, it may be difficult to reach a single agreement or to agree on specific actions. Although these drawbacks are valid concerns, the value of diversity in decision making outweighs the potential disadvantages.

Now, about that decision on a major. Did you ask others for their opinions? Did you seek out advice from professors, family members, friends, or coworkers? Getting diverse perspectives on an important decision like this could help you make the best decision! Supervisors also should consider the value to be gained from diversity in decision making.

*"Managing Diversity" box based on N. J. Adler (ed.), *International Dimensions of Organizational Behavior*, 4th ed. (Cincinnati: South-Western College Publishing, 2001); B. C. McDonald and D. Hutcheson, "Dealing with Diversity Is Key to Tapping Talent," *Atlanta Business Chronicle*, December 18, 1998, 45A+; and P. M. Elsass and L. M. Graves, "Demographic Diversity in Decision-Making Groups: The Experience of Women and People of Color," *Academy of Management Review* (October 1997), 946–973.

Ethics in Decision Making

In Chapter 2, we introduced the topic of ethics and described ways in which you can act ethically. Inherent in that discussion was the idea that when you face ethical choices, you face a problem. Ethical concerns then become a part of your decision making. For instance, one alternative may generate a considerably higher financial return than the others, but it might be ethically questionable because it compromises employee safety. Let's look at this important issue in greater detail.

WHAT ARE COMMON RATIONALIZATIONS?

Through the ages, people have developed some common rationalizations to justify questionable conduct.[9] These rationalizations provide some insights into why supervisors might make poor ethical choices.

- **"It's not really illegal or immoral."** Where is the line between being smart and being shady? Between an ingenious decision and an immoral one? Because this line is often ambiguous, people can rationalize that what they've done is not really wrong. If you put enough people in an ill-defined situation, some will conclude that whatever hasn't been labeled specifically as wrong must be okay. This is especially true if there are rich rewards for attaining certain goals and the organization's appraisal system doesn't look too carefully at how those goals are achieved. The practice of profiting on a stock tip through insider information often seems to fall into this category.

- **"It's in my (or the organization's) best interest."** The belief that unethical conduct is in a person's or an organization's best interest nearly always results from a narrow view of what those interests are. For instance, supervisors can come to believe that it's acceptable to bribe officials if the bribe results in the organization's getting a contract, or to falsify financial records if this improves their unit's performance record.

- **"No one will find out."** The third rationalization accepts the wrongdoing but assumes that it will never be uncovered. Philosophers ponder, If a tree falls in a forest and no one hears it, did it make a noise? Some supervisors answer the analogous question, "If an unethical act is committed and no one knows it, is it wrong?" in the negative. This rationalization is often stimulated by inadequate controls, strong pressures to perform, the appraisal of performance results while ignoring the means by which they're achieved, the allocation of big salary increases and promotions to those who achieve these results, and the absence of punishment for those who get caught in wrongdoing.

- **"Because it helps the organization, the organization will condone it and protect me."** This response represents loyalty gone berserk. Some supervisors come to believe that not only do the organization's interests override the laws and values of society but also that the organization expects its employees to exhibit unqualified loyalty. Even if the supervisor is caught, he or she believes that the organization will support and reward him or her for showing loyalty. Supervisors who use this rationalization to justify unethical practices place the organization's good name in jeopardy. This rationalization has motivated some supervisors for defense contractors to justify labor mischarges, cost duplications, product substitutions, and other contract abuses. Although supervisors should be expected to be loyal to the organization against competitors and detractors, that loyalty shouldn't put the organization above the law, common morality, or society itself.

---

[9]S. W. Gellerman, "Why Good Managers Make Bad Ethical Choices," *Harvard Business Review*, July–August 1986, 89.

WHAT ARE THE THREE VIEWS ON ETHICS?

In this section, we present three different ethical positions. They can help us see how individuals can make different decisions by using different ethical criteria (see Exhibit 7-7).

utilitarian view of ethics
A view in which decisions are made solely on the basis of their outcomes or consequences.

The Utilitarian View The first is the utilitarian view of ethics, in which decisions are made solely on the basis of their outcomes or consequences. The goal of utilitarianism is to provide the greatest good for the greatest number. This view tends to dominate business decision making. Why? Because it's consistent with goals such as efficiency, productivity, and high profits. By maximizing profits, for instance, a supervisor can argue that he or she is securing the greatest good for the greatest number.

rights view of ethics
A view that calls on individuals to make decisions consistent with fundamental liberties and privileges as set forth in documents such as the Bill of Rights.

The Rights View Another ethical perspective is the rights view of ethics, which calls on individuals to make decisions consistent with fundamental liberties and privileges as set forth in documents such as the Bill of Rights. The rights view of ethics is concerned with respecting and protecting the basic rights of individuals—for example, the right to privacy, free speech, and due process. This position would protect employees who report unethical or illegal practices by their organization to the press or government agencies, on the grounds of their right to free speech.

justice view of ethics
A view that requires individuals to impose and enforce rules fairly and impartially so that there is an equitable distribution of benefits and costs.

The Justice View The final perspective is the justice view of ethics, which requires individuals to impose and enforce rules fairly and impartially so that there is an equitable distribution of benefits and costs. Union members typically favor this view. It justifies paying people the same wage for a given job, regardless of performance differences, and it uses seniority as the criterion in making layoff decisions.

Each of these three perspectives has advantages and liabilities. The utilitarian view promotes efficiency and productivity, but it can result in ignoring the rights of some individuals, particularly those with minority representation in the organization. The rights perspective protects individuals from injury and is consistent with freedom and privacy, but it can create an overly legalistic work environment that hinders productivity and efficiency. The justice perspective protects the interests of the underrepresented and less powerful, but it can encourage a sense of entitlement that reduces risk taking, innovation, and productivity.

Even though each of these perspectives has its individual strengths and weaknesses, as we noted, individuals in business tend to focus on utilitarianism. But times are changing and so too must supervisors and other organizational members. New trends toward individual rights and social justice mean that supervisors need ethical standards based on nonutilitarian criteria. This is a solid challenge to today's supervisor because making decisions using criteria such as individual rights and social justice involves far more ambiguities than using utilitarian criteria such as effects on efficiency and profits.

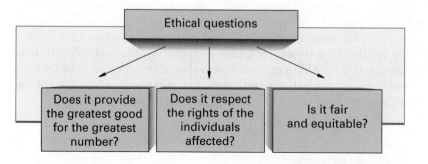

Exhibit 7-7
Three views on ethics.

IS THERE A GUIDE TO ACTING ETHICALLY?

We can provide no simple credo that will ensure that you won't err in your ethical judgments. What we can offer are some questions that you can and should ask yourself when making important decisions and decisions with obvious ethical implications.[10]

- How did this problem occur in the first place?
- Would you define the problem differently if you stood on the other side of the fence?
- To whom and to what do you give your loyalty as a person and as a member of your organization?
- What is your intention in making this decision?
- What is the potential for your intention to be misunderstood by others in the organization?
- How does your intention compare with the probable result?
- Whom could your decision injure?
- Can you discuss the problem with the affected parties before you make the decision?
- Are you confident that your position will be as valid over a long period of time as it seems now?
- Could you disclose your decision to your boss or your immediate family?
- How would you feel if your decision were described, in detail, on the front page of your local newspaper?

Comprehension Check 7-2

5. A repetitive decision can be best handled by
   a. a nonprogrammed decision
   b. a rule
   c. a programmed decision
   d. all of the above

6. Which one of the following is a disadvantage of group decision making?
   a. Conformity
   b. Legitimacy
   c. Solution acceptance
   d. More information

7. Withholding of deferring views by group members to appear to be in agreement is called
   a. minority domination
   b. groupthink
   c. brainstorming
   d. escalation of commitment

8. The view of ethics in which decisions are made solely on the basis of their outcomes or consequences is called the
   a. justice view of ethics
   b. rights view of ethics
   c. social obligation view of ethics
   d. utilitarian view of ethics

---

[10]Adapted from L. J. Hash, "Ethics without the Sermon," *Harvard Business Review*, November–December 1981, 81.

Enhancing Understanding

SUMMARY

After reading this chapter, I can:

1. **List the seven steps in the decision-making process.** The seven steps in the decision-making process are (1) identifying the problem, (2) collecting relevant information, (3) developing alternatives, (4) evaluating each alternative, (5) selecting the best alternative, (6) implementing the decision, and (7) following up and evaluating the decision.

2. **Describe expected value analysis.** Expected value analysis calculates the expected value of a particular alternative by weighting its possible outcomes by the probability of achieving the alternative, and then summing up the totals derived from the weighting process.

3. **Explain the four types of decision styles.** The four types of decision-making styles are directive, analytic, conceptual, and behavioral. The directive type is efficient and logical. The analytic type is careful, with the ability to adapt to or cope with new situations. The conceptual type considers many alternatives and is good at coming up with creative solutions. The behavioral type emphasizes suggestions from others and conflict avoidance.

4. **Identify and explain the common decision-making errors.** The common errors in decision making are called heuristics. Heuristics are shortcuts supervisors may take to speed up the decision-making process. Heuristics commonly exist in two forms—availability and representative. Both types can create biases in a supervisor's judgment. A third common error, called escalation of commitment, reflects an increased commitment to a previous decision despite negative information.

5. **Describe the two types of decision problems and the two types of decisions that are used to solve them.** Supervisors face well- and ill-structured problems. Well-structured problems are straightforward, familiar, easily defined, and solved using programmed decisions—repetitive decisions that can be handled by a routine approach, such as a policy, procedure, or rule. Ill-structured problems are new or unusual problems, involve ambiguous or incomplete information, and are solved using nonprogrammed decisions—decisions that must be custom-made to solve the unique and nonrecurring problem.

6. **Compare and contrast group decision making and individual decision making.** Group and individual decisions can be evaluated on the basis of accuracy, speed, creativity, and acceptance. The advantages of group decisions are that they have more complete information, generate more alternatives, and have an increased acceptance of a solution, which increases legitimacy (accuracy, creativity, and acceptance). Individual decision making, on the other hand, is typically faster (speed). Accordingly, when speed alone is the primary factor, individual decisions should be made. If speed alone is not the primary factor, group decisions are better.

7. **List and describe three techniques for improving group decision making.** Three techniques for improving group decision making are brainstorming, the nominal group technique, and electronic meetings. Brainstorming is a technique used for overcoming pressures to conform that retard development of creative alternatives. This idea-generating process specifically encourages alternatives while withholding criticism of those alternatives. The nominal group technique restricts discussion during the decision-making process. In electronic meetings, participants are positioned at computer terminals as issues are presented. Participants type anonymous responses into the computer, and aggregate votes are displayed on a projection system in the same room.

8. **Explain three different ethical viewpoints.** The three different viewpoints of ethical decisions are the utilitarian view, the rights view, and the justice view. The utilitarian view of ethics makes decisions based on the greatest good for the greatest number. The rights view of ethics makes decisions consistent with fundamental liberties and privileges. The justice view of ethics seeks fairness and impartiality.

COMPREHENSION: Review and Discussion Questions

1. Contrast symptoms with problems. Give three examples.

2. In which step of the decision-making process do you think creativity would be most helpful? In which step would quantitative analysis tools be most helpful?

3. Calculate your estimated grade point average this semester using expected value analysis.

4. How might certain decision styles fit better with specific jobs? Give examples.

5. How does escalation of commitment affect decision making? Give an example.

6. What rationalizations do people use to justify questionable conduct?

7. Which view of ethics do you believe dominates in business firms? Justify your response.

8. When should supervisors use groups for decision making? When should they make the decisions themselves?

9. Contrast the nominal group technique and electronic meetings.

KEY CONCEPT CROSSWORD

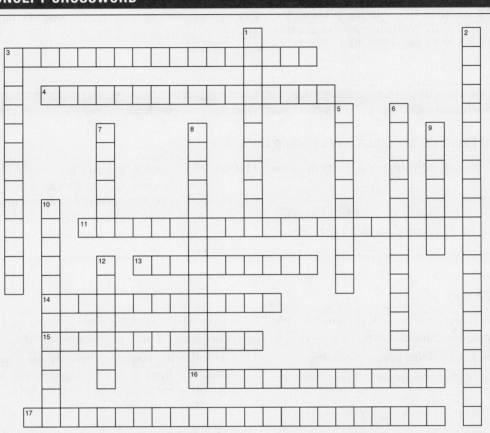

ACROSS

3. a group decision-making technique in which participants are positioned in front of computers
4. a method that helps decision makers optimize returns or minimize costs
11. an increasing support of a previous decision despite negative information
13. the withholding of differing views by group members in order to appear to be in agreement
14. new problems
15. a technique that restricts discussion during the decision-making process
16. a rational and analytical process of resolving problems
17. the tendency of people to match the likelihood of an occurrence with something they are familiar with

DOWN

1. a view of ethics in which decisions are made solely on the basis of their consequences
2. the tendency of people to base their judgments on information that is readily accessible
3. a procedure that permits one to place a monetary figure on likely consequences
5. a decision that is repetitive
6. a technique for overcoming pressures for conformity
7. a view of ethics that calls on individuals to make decisions consistent with fundamental liberties
8. straightforward, familiar, and easily defined problems
9. a discrepancy between an existing and a desired state
10. a diagram that shows a progression of decisions and their respective payoff calculations
12. a view of ethics that requires individuals to impose and enforce rules fairly

ANSWERS TO COMPREHENSION CHECKS

Comprehension Check 7-1

1. d (identifying the problem) 2. a 3. b 4. c

Comprehension Check 7-2

5. c 6. a 7. b 8. d

Developing Your Supervisory Skills

GETTING TO KNOW YOURSELF

Before you can effectively supervise others, you must understand your present strengths and areas in need of development. To assist in this learning process, we encourage you to complete the following self-assessments from the Prentice Hall Self-Assessment Library 3.4.

1. Am I a Procrastinator? (I. D. 1.)

After you complete the assessment, we suggest you retain the results and store them as part of your "portfolio of learning about yourself."

BUILDING A TEAM

➤ An Experiential Exercise: Individual versus Group Decisions

OBJECTIVE: To contrast individual and group decision making.

TIME: Fifteen minutes.

STEP 1: You have five minutes to read the following story and individually respond to each of the eleven statements as either true, false, or unknown.

THE STORY: A sales clerk had just turned off the lights in the store when a man appeared and demanded money. The owner opened a cash register. The contents of the cash register were scooped up, and the man sped away. A member of the police force was notified promptly.

Statements About the Story

1. A man appeared after the owner had turned off his store lights. True, false, or unknown?

2. The robber was a man. True, false, or unknown?

3. The man did not demand money. True, false, or unknown?

4. The man who opened the cash register was the owner. True, false, or unknown?

5. The store owner scooped up the contents of the cash register and ran away. True, false, or unknown?

6. Someone opened a cash register. True, false, or unknown?

7. After the man who demanded the money scooped up the contents of the cash register, he ran away. True, false, or unknown?

8. The cash register contained money, but the story does not state how much. True, false, or unknown?

9. The robber demanded money of the owner. True, false, or unknown?

10. The story concerns a series of events in which only three persons are referred to: the owner of the store,

a man who demanded money, and a member of the police force. True, false, or unknown?

11. The following events in the story are true: Someone demanded money; a cash register was opened; its contents were scooped up; a man dashed out of the store. True, false, or unknown?

STEP 2: After you have answered the eleven questions individually, form groups of four or five members each. The groups have ten minutes to discuss their answers and agree on the correct answers to each of the eleven statements.

STEP 3: Your instructor will give you the actual correct answers. How many correct answers did you get at the conclusion of step 1? How many did your group achieve at the conclusion of step 2? Did the group outperform the average individual? The best individual? Discuss the implications of these results.

➤ Internet: Web Activity

Go to http://www.pearsonhighered.com/robbins/. Find *Supervision Today!* 7th Ed. and click Companion Website.

BECOMING MORE CREATIVE

Creativity is the ability to combine ideas in a unique way to make unusual associations between them. Each of us has the ability to be creative, yet some use their creativity more than others. Although creative people are sometimes referred to as "artsy" and difficult to describe, there are certain steps you can take in becoming more creative.

STEPS IN PRACTICING THE SKILL

STEP 1: Think of yourself as creative. Although it's a simple suggestion, research shows that if you think that you can't be creative, you won't be. Just as the little engine in the children's fable says, "I think I can," if we believe in ourselves, we can become more creative.

STEP 2: Pay attention to your intuition. Everyone has a subconscious mind that works well. Sometimes answers come when we least expect them. For example, when you are about to go to sleep, your relaxed mind sometimes comes up with solutions to problems you face. You need to listen to this intuition. In fact, many creative people keep a notepad near their bed and write down those "great" ideas when they come to them. That way, the ideas are not forgotten.

STEP 3: Move away from your comfort zone. Every individual has a comfort zone in which certainty exists. But creativity and the known often don't mix. To be creative, we need to move away from the status quo and focus on something new.

STEP 4: Engage in activities that put you outside your comfort zone. Not only must we think differently, but we also need to do things differently. By engaging in activities that are different to us, we challenge ourselves. Learning to play a musical instrument or learning a foreign language, for example, opens the mind and allows it to be challenged.

STEP 5: Seek a change of scenery. As humans, we are creatures of habit. Creative people force themselves out of their habits by changing their scenery. Going into a quiet and serene area where you can be alone with your thoughts is a good way to enhance creativity.

STEP 6: Find several correct answers. Just as we set boundaries in rationality, we often seek solutions that are only good enough. Being creative means continuing to look for other solutions, even when you think you have solved the problem. A better, more creative solution just might be found.

STEP 7: Play your own devil's advocate. Challenging yourself to defend your solutions helps you develop confidence in your creative efforts. Second-guessing may also help you find more correct answers.

STEP 8: Believe in finding a workable solution. Like believing in yourself, you also need to believe in your ideas. If you don't think you can find a solution, you won't find one. Having a positive mental attitude, however, may become a self-fulfilling prophecy.

STEP 9: Brainstorm with others. Creativity is not an isolated activity. Bouncing ideas off others causes a synergistic effect.

STEP 10: Turn creative ideas into action. Coming up with ideas is only half of the process. Once the ideas are generated, they must be implemented. Great ideas that remain in someone's mind, or on papers that no one reads, do little to expand one's creative abilities.

Source: Adapted from J. Calano and J. Salzman, "Ten Ways to Fire Up Your Creativity," *Working Woman*, July 1989, 94–95.

➤ Communicating Effectively

1. "Supervisors often make decisions that are good enough, but may not be the best solution." Build a case that presents both sides of this argument. In your discussion, emphasize when "good enough" may be appropriate, and when the "best solution" may be critical. Provide specific examples in your paper.

2. Describe a situation in which a decision you made was influenced by availability or representative heuristics. In retrospect, provide an evaluation of how effective that decision was. Given your evaluation, are you more or less inclined to use judgmental shortcuts in your decision-making process? Explain.

THINKING CRITICALLY

➤ CASE 7-A: Developing a Decision-Making Style

Every supervisor brings a unique personality, varied experiences, and a variety of training to the decision-making process. Some supervisors are risk takers; some value certainty. Some supervisors are creative and intuitive; others are logical and rational. All supervisors are called on to make decisions and choices, which requires careful thought and information. Supervisors need to understand how to go about this process and the basic tendencies that may affect their process.

Toby Lyman has been hired as a supervisor in the new services department of a medium-sized call center. This department is responsible for assisting existing customers in using new services in a telecommunications call center. Other departments transfer calls to this department to alert customers to new services. The call center has high expectations for the results of this department. Toby's background is in sales and customer service at retail companies where she has also developed good problem-solving skills. A manager in a retail company where Toby worked is now a director and Toby's boss at the call center.

In the new services department Toby is one of four supervisors, each of whom has four to six associates to supervise. Two of the supervisors have ten years with the call center and five years as supervisors in the department. The other supervisor was recently transferred to this department from another department where she was

a supervisor. At the meeting in which Toby accepted the position, her new boss said, "Your sales background will help shake up our department and get people thinking in new ways." On the first day at the call center, one of the other supervisors welcomed Toby by saying, "Glad to have you; we'll take it easy on you until you understand how we do things here."

The new job is under way and there are decisions to make about people transfers, working hours, vacation coverage, customer handling, and website revisions, to name just a few. Toby is torn between a desire to fit in and another to recommend some actions that she suspects would work better in the call center. She knows that one path (fitting in) is conservative and has little risk. The alternative (recommending changes) might be the kind of action that makes her stand out.

RESPONDING TO THE CASE

1. In her new job, how might Toby make use of the knowledge she has about decision-making styles?

2. How would Toby benefit by examining the styles of her boss and those of the other supervisors?

3. In a popular television show *The Apprentice*, we see a particular style of decision making. Identify other public personalities by their decision-making styles.

➤ CASE 7-B: Improvement Ideas from a Car Sales Star

Jeff Scott, the general manager at Carr Chevrolet, had a problem he needed to solve. The new car sales force was not productive enough. Specifically, they were slow to greet, meet, and determine the new car buyer's needs and were not meeting the dealership's sales plan projections. Scott wanted to find a way to help them become more efficient.

To solve the problem, Scott called a meeting with the new and used car sales manager, he also included the parts and service manager in the hope there was a nugget of inspiration to be found. He and the other managers brainstormed a list of possible solutions. Afterward, they discussed the pros and cons of each of their ideas.

As Scott left the meeting, he passed a wall of plaques listing the names of past "Salesperson of the Month" and "Salesperson of the Year" awards. He noticed the name of Leroy Perez appeared on multiple plaques over the past

five years. Scott walked over to the cubicle where Perez was stationed and found him completing paper work for a sale he had just closed. Scott thanked Perez for his hard work and contributions to the performance of the store. Then he asked him how he managed to be such an effective sales person over the past several years—even during an economic downturn.

Scott learned more than he expected from that simple question. Perez explained that he had formed a team of individuals from the parts and service department, as well as the receptionists and cashiers. They listened to customers as they talked about old cars with problems, family members with car needs, safety concerns for teenage drivers, as well as upcoming birthdays and anniversaries. All of these team members were willing to share the information with Perez because he was willing to reward them with dinners and tickets to events if their information led to a sale. In addition he often bought lunch for them just because he genuinely liked them.

Scott asked Perez for other examples of salesmanship techniques and received many. He actually got more ideas for improving car sales in a fifteen-minute discussion than he and his fellow managers had thought of in their previous brainstorming session.

Scott thought Perez might be the key to turning around a slow sales period and offered Perez the opportunity to be sales trainer/sales manager—a position that offered the chance to learn a new skill while maintaining touch with the skills that made him so valuable to the organization. Perez worked with the sales force, passing on his ideas as well as uncovering many other sales techniques. Soon, the dealership was surpassing the sales plan projections, the sales force was setting monthly records, and Perez became much sought after as a sales consultant in the industry. Scott knew that the simple act of listening to a hidden in-house sales expert improved the attitudes and productivity of his sales force.

RESPONDING TO THE CASE

1. What was the difference in the way Scott and Perez viewed the problem in this case?

2. How did the initial problem definition affect the approach to, and solution of, the problem?

3. How does this case illustrate any advantages or disadvantages of group decision making?

4. List some ways Scott can apply what he learned from this situation to continue improving the quality and productivity of sales.

5. How might Scott continue to include the sales force in problem solving?

Motivating, Leading, Communicating, and Developing

If there is one thing common to employees wherever they work, it is the fact that they tend to give their effort to things that benefit them. Employees understand that they have to work—and work hard—but in doing so, they want something in return. They expect to work for supervisors who respect them, who keep them informed of things happening in the organization, and who can find a way to bring out their best.

CHAPTER 8

Motivating Followers

Key Concepts

After completing this chapter, you will be able to define these supervisory terms:

- competency-based compensation
- employee stock ownership plan (ESOP)
- equity theory
- expectancy theory
- hierarchy-of-needs theory
- hygiene factors
- job design
- job enrichment
- locus of control
- Machiavellianism

- motivation
- motivation-hygiene theory
- need
- need for achievement
- pay-for-performance programs
- risk propensity
- self-esteem
- self-monitoring
- Theory X–Theory Y

Chapter Outcomes

After reading this chapter, you will be able to:

1. Define *motivation*.

2. Identify and define five personality characteristics relevant to understanding the behavior of employees at work.

3. Explain the elements and the focus of the three early theories of motivation.

4. Identify the characteristics that stimulate the achievement drive in high achievers.

5. Identify the three relationships in expectancy theory that determine an individual's level of effort.

6. List actions a supervisor can take to maximize employee motivation.

7. Describe how supervisors can design individual jobs to maximize employee performance.

8. Explain the effect of workforce diversity on motivating employees.

Responding to a Supervisory Dilemma

Successful supervisors understand that what motivates them personally may have little or no effect on others. Just because you're motivated by being part of a cohesive work team, don't assume everyone is. Or just because you're motivated by your job doesn't mean that everyone is. Effective supervisors who get employees to put forth maximum effort know how and why those employees are motivated and tailor motivational practices to satisfy their needs and wants. Motivating and rewarding employees is one of the most important and challenging activities that supervisors do. To get employees to put forth maximum work effort, supervisors need to know how and why they're motivated.

Several CEOs were attending a meeting where the topic was, "What do employees want?"* Each CEO took turns describing the benefits they provided and how they gave out free M&Ms every Wednesday and offered their employees stock options and free parking spaces. However, the meeting's main speaker made the point that "employees don't want M&Ms; they want to love what they do." Half expecting his audience to laugh, the speaker was pleasantly surprised as the CEOs stood up one-by-one to agree. They all recognized that "the value in their companies comes from the employees who are motivated to be there."

These CEOs understand how important employee motivation is. Like them, all supervisors need to be able to motivate their employees. That requires understanding what motivation is. Let's begin by pointing out what motivation is not. Why? Because many people incorrectly view motivation as a personal trait; that is, they think some people are motivated and others aren't. Our knowledge of motivation tells us that we can't label people that way because individuals differ in motivational drive, and their overall motivation varies from situation to situation. For instance, you're probably more motivated in some classes than in others.

Motivating high levels of employee performance is an important organizational concern, and supervisors keep looking for answers. For instance, a recent Gallup poll found that a large majority of U.S. employees—some 73 percent—are not excited about their work. As the researchers stated, "These employees are essentially 'checked out.' They're sleepwalking through their workday, putting time, but not energy or passion, into their work."† It's no wonder then that supervisors want to understand and explain employee motivation.

In today's ongoing economic crisis, organizational downsizing is common and may include as many as half of the employees that work for the company. Many employees are going to be motivated to retain their jobs because they are scared, and as a result their performance and production may improve. The opposite may be true for other employees who think they will lose their job regardless of the work they do, so they feel it really doesn't matter. And still others might see the writing on the wall and leave the job before the downsizing occurs.

Whatever the situation, once cuts have been made in numbers of employees, supervisors are faced with the employees who remain. Supervisors need to invest energy in the people who remain after downsizing. Supervisors need to aid recovery, fuel productivity, boost morale, and minimize the damage to workplace trust. Showing value in the remaining employees is critical in motivating them. How could a supervisor motivate employees who just lost their long-time colleagues and friends? Faced with layoffs and organizational downsizing how would you treat the surviving employees? How could they be motivated? Do you think an organization can survive after losing employees through downsizing?

---

*P. Bronson, "What Should I Do with My Life Now?" *Fast Company*, April 2009, 35–37.
†J. Krueger and E. Killham, "At Work, Feeling Good Matters," *Gallup Management Journal*, December 8, 2005, http://gmj.gallup.com.

Tommy Sapp is a hard-driving, competitive person. He gives a maximum effort on everything he does—at his job, on his summer softball team, in detailing his classic 1963 Corvette. In contrast, his good friend Brad Wilson appears to have no discipline in his life. People who know him think he's lazy. Although Brad is smart and highly capable, he has trouble holding a job because of his inability to put forth much sustained effort. Tommy summed up his appraisal of Brad: "He can't stay with anything for more than a half hour or so. He gets bored and distracted easily."

Supervisors like having Tommy types working for them. Such people are essentially self-motivated. You don't have to do much to get them to produce a full day's effort. The Brad Wilsons of the world are another story. They're a supervisor's challenge. It's a challenge to develop creative ways to motivate them. Most employees, however, aren't like either Tommy or Brad. They're more like Samantha Carr. On some activities, Samantha is incredibly motivated. For example, she reads two or three romance novels a week, and she gets up at 5:30 every morning and religiously runs three or four miles before showering and going to work. But at her sales job at the local Bally's Fitness Center, she seems bored and unmotivated. Most people are like Samantha in that their levels of motivation vary across activities.

What can supervisors do to increase the motivation of people like Brad Wilson and Samantha Carr? In this chapter, we provide you with some insights and tools that can help answer this question, while exploring the exciting supervisory concept of motivation.

What Is Motivation?

First, let's describe what we mean by the term *motivation*. Motivation is the willingness to do something; it is conditioned by this action's ability to satisfy some need for the individual. A need, in our terminology, means a physiological or psychological deficiency that makes certain outcomes seem attractive.

An unsatisfied need creates tension, which sets off a drive to satisfy that need (see Exhibit 8-1). The greater the tension, the greater the drive or effort required to reduce that tension. When we see employees working hard at some activity, we can conclude that they're driven by a desire to satisfy one or more needs that they value.

motivation
The willingness to do something conditioned upon the action's ability to satisfy some need for the individual.

need
A physiological or psychological deficiency that makes certain outcomes seem attractive.

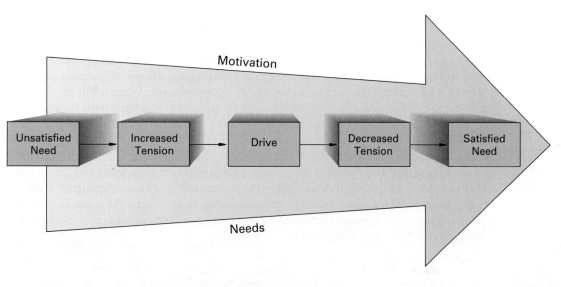

Exhibit 8-1
Needs and motivation.

Understanding Individual Differences

A common error that new supervisors often make is to assume that other people are like them. If they're ambitious, they think others will be ambitious just like them. If they place a high value on spending evenings and weekends with their family, they often assume that others feel the same way. These assumptions are frequently big mistakes! People are different. What's important to us is not necessarily important to others. Not everybody, for instance, is driven by the desire for money. Yet a lot of supervisors believe that a bonus or the opportunity for a pay increase should make every employee want to work harder. If you're going to be successful in motivating people, you have to begin by accepting and trying to understand individual differences.

To make our point, let's look at personality. Most of us know people who are loud and aggressive. We know others who are quiet and passive. A number of personality characteristics have been singled out as having relevance to understanding the behavior and motivation of employees at work. Five specific personality measures have proven most powerful in explaining individual behavior in organizations: locus of control, Machiavellianism, self-esteem, self-monitoring, and risk propensity. Let's look at these elements.

CAN PERSONALITY TYPES HELP PREDICT PRACTICAL WORK-RELATED BEHAVIORS?

locus of control
The source of control over an individual's behavior.

Who has control over an individual's behavior? Some people believe that they control their own fate. Others see themselves as pawns of fate, believing that what happens to them in their lives is a result of luck or chance. The locus of control in the first case is internal; these people believe that they control their destiny. In the second case it is external; these people believe that their lives are controlled by outside forces.[1] Studies tell us that employees who rate high in externality are less satisfied with their jobs, more alienated from the work setting, and less involved in their jobs than are those who rate high in internality. For instance, employees with an external locus of control may be less enthusiastic about their jobs because they believe that they have little personal influence on the outcome of their performance appraisals. If they get a poor appraisal, they're apt to blame it on their supervisor's prejudice, their coworkers, or other events outside their control.

Machiavellianism
Manipulative behavior based on the belief that the ends can justify the means.

The second characteristic is called Machiavellianism (Mach), named after Niccolo Machiavelli, who wrote in the sixteenth century on how to gain and manipulate power. An individual exhibiting strong Machiavellian tendencies is manipulative and believes that ends can justify means. Some might even see these people as ruthless. High Machs tend to be motivated on jobs that require bargaining (e.g., labor negotiator) or where there are substantial rewards for winning (as in commissioned sales). But they can get frustrated in jobs where specific rules must be followed or where rewards are based more on using the proper means than on the achievement of outcomes.

self-esteem
The degree to which an individual likes or dislikes himself or herself.

People differ in the degree to which they like or dislike themselves. This trait is called self-esteem. Studies confirm that people high in self-esteem (SE) believe that they possess more of the ability they need to succeed at work. But the most significant finding on self-esteem is that low-SEs are more susceptible to external influence than are high-SEs. Low-SEs depend on positive evaluations from others. As a result, they are more likely to seek approval from others and more prone to conform to the beliefs and behaviors of those they respect than are high-SEs.

[1]See, for example, J. Silvester, F. M. Anderson-Gough, N. R. Anderson, and A. R. Mohamed, "Locus of Control, Attributions and Impression Management in the Selection Interview, *Journal of Occupational and Organizational Psychology* 75, no. 1 (March 2002), 59–77; D. W. Organ and C. N. Greene, "Role Ambiguity, Locus of Control, and Work Satisfaction," *Journal of Applied Psychology* 59, no. 1 (February 1974), 101–102; and T. R. Mitchell, C. M. Smyser, and S. E. Weed, "Locus of Control: Supervision and Work Satisfaction," *Academy of Management Journal* 18, no. 1 (September 1975), 623–631.

Some individuals are very adaptable and can easily adjust their behavior to changing situations. Others are rigid and inflexible. The personality trait that captures this difference is called self-monitoring. Individuals high in self-monitoring show considerable adaptability in adjusting their behavior to external situational factors. They are highly sensitive to external cues and can behave differently in different situations. High self-monitors are capable of presenting striking contradictions between their public personas and their private selves. Low self-monitors can't disguise themselves this way. They tend to display their true feelings and beliefs in every situation. The evidence tells us that high self-monitors tend to pay closer attention to the behavior of others and are more capable of conforming than are low self-monitors. Additionally, because high self-monitors are flexible, they adjust better than low self-monitors to job situations that require individuals to play multiple roles in their workgroups.

People differ in their willingness to take chances. Individuals with a high risk propensity make more rapid decisions and use less information in making their choices than people with low risk propensity. Not surprisingly, high-risk seekers tend to prefer, and are more satisfied in, jobs such as stockbroker or putting out fires on oil platforms.

self-monitoring
The ability to adjust behavior to external situational factors. High self-monitors adapt easily and are capable of presenting striking contradictions between public personas and private selves; low self-monitors tend to display their true feelings and beliefs in almost every situation.

risk propensity
A willingness to take chances, characterized by rapid decision making with the use of less information.

DO YOU NEED TO DEVELOP YOUR EMOTIONAL INTELLIGENCE TO IMPROVE YOUR SUPERVISION SKILLS?

Becoming more attuned to your own emotions and those of others may increase your effectiveness on the job. Emotional intelligence consists of five dimensions that may help you cope with the daily demands and pressures of the workplace. The dimensions of emotional intelligence are the following:

- **Self-awareness.** An awareness of what/how you are feeling
- **Self-management.** The ability to manage your emotions and impulses
- **Self-motivation.** The ability to persist in the face of setbacks and failures
- **Empathy.** The ability to sense how others are feeling
- **Social skills.** The ability to handle the emotions of others

Multiple studies indicate that emotional intelligence characterizes high performers and they are better able to relate to others in individual as well as team environments. Many human resource managers indicate that emotional intelligence is essential for career success in the organization, especially in jobs requiring social interaction.[2]

HOW CAN AN UNDERSTANDING OF PERSONALITY HELP YOU BE A MORE EFFECTIVE SUPERVISOR?

The major value of understanding personality differences probably lies in selection. You are likely to have higher-performing and more satisfied employees if you match personality types with compatible jobs. In addition, there may be other benefits. By recognizing that people approach problem solving, decision making, and job interactions differently, you can better understand why, for instance, an employee is uncomfortable with making quick decisions or why an employee insists on gathering as much information as possible before addressing a problem. You can also anticipate that individuals with an external locus of control may be less satisfied with their jobs than internals, and also that they may be less willing to accept responsibility for their actions.

---

[2]S. Robbins and D. Decenzo, *Fundamentals of Management: Essential Concepts and Applications* (Upper Saddle River, NJ: Pearson Prentice Hall, 2008), 224–225.

The Early Theories of Motivation

Once we accept individual differences, we begin to understand why no single motivator applies to all employees. Because people are complex, any attempt to explain their motivations will also tend to be complex. We see this in the number of approaches that have been taken in developing theories of employee motivation. In the following pages, we review the most popular of these early theory approaches.

HOW DO YOU FOCUS ON NEEDS?

hierarchy-of-needs theory
A theory of Abraham Maslow that states that a satisfied need no longer creates tension and therefore doesn't motivate. Maslow believed that the key to motivation is to determine where an individual is along the needs hierarchy and to focus motivation efforts at the point where needs become essentially unfulfilled.

The most elementary approach to motivation was developed by Abraham Maslow.[3] He identified a set of basic needs that he argued were common to all individuals; he said individuals should be evaluated in terms of the degree to which these needs are fulfilled. According to Maslow's hierarchy-of-needs theory, a satisfied need no longer creates tension and therefore doesn't motivate. The key to motivation, then, at least according to Maslow, is to determine where an individual is along the needs hierarchy and to focus motivation efforts at the point where needs become essentially unfulfilled.

Maslow proposed that within every human being exists a hierarchy of five needs (see Exhibit 8-2):

1. **Physiological.** Includes hunger, thirst, shelter, sex, and other bodily needs
2. **Safety.** Includes security and protection from physical and emotional harm
3. **Social.** Includes affection, a sense of belonging, acceptance, and friendship
4. **Esteem.** Includes internal factors such as self-respect, autonomy, and achievement, and external factors such as status, recognition, and attention
5. **Self-actualization.** The drive to become what one is capable of becoming; includes growth, achieving one's potential, and self-fulfillment

As each of these needs becomes substantially satisfied, the next need becomes dominant. In terms of Exhibit 8-2, the individual moves up the hierarchy. From the perspective of motivation, the theory would say that although no need is ever completely fulfilled, a substantially satisfied need no longer motivates.

A number of studies to test the validity of Maslow's theory have been made over the years. Generally, these studies have not been able to support the theory. We can't say, for example, that everyone's need structure is organized along the dimensions

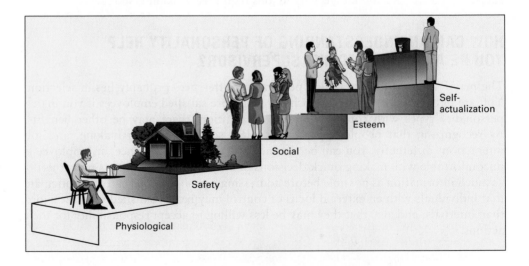

Exhibit 8-2

Maslow's hierarchy-of-needs theory.

Source: *By permission of the Instructional Communications Centre, McGill University, Montreal, Canada. Reprinted with permission.*

[3] A. Maslow, *Motivation and Personality* (New York: Harper & Row, 1954).

Maslow proposed. So, although this theory has been around for a long time and is certainly well known, it is probably not a very good guide for helping you motivate your employees.

DO SUPERVISORS FOCUS ON THE NATURE OF PEOPLE?

Some supervisors believe that their employees are hardworking, committed, and responsible. Others view their employees as essentially lazy, irresponsible, and lacking ambition. This observation led Douglas McGregor to propose his Theory X–Theory Y view of human nature and motivation.[4] McGregor argued that a supervisor's view of the nature of human beings is based on a certain grouping of assumptions, and that he or she tends to mold his or her behavior toward subordinates according to these assumptions.

Theory X–Theory Y
A theory of Douglas McGregor that a supervisor's view of human nature is based on a certain grouping of assumptions and that he or she tends to mold behavior toward subordinates according to those assumptions.

Under Theory X, the four assumptions held by supervisors are the following:

1. Employees inherently dislike work and, whenever possible, will attempt to avoid it.
2. Because employees dislike work, they must be coerced, controlled, or threatened with punishment to achieve desired goals.
3. Employees will shirk responsibilities and seek formal direction whenever possible.
4. Most workers place security above all other factors associated with work and will display little ambition.

In contrast to these negative views toward the nature of human beings, McGregor listed four other assumptions that he called Theory Y:

1. Employees can view work as being as natural as rest or play.
2. A person will exercise self-direction and self-control if he or she is committed to the objectives.
3. The average person can learn to accept, even seek, responsibility.
4. The ability to make good decisions is widely dispersed throughout the population and is not necessarily the sole province of supervisors.

What are the motivational implications of Theory X–Theory Y? McGregor argued that Theory Y assumptions were more valid than Theory X assumptions. As a result, he proposed ideas such as participation in decision making, responsible and challenging jobs, and good group relations as approaches that would maximize an employee's job motivation.

Unfortunately, there is no evidence to confirm that either set of assumptions is valid, or that acceptance of Theory Y assumptions and altering one's actions accordingly will lead to more motivated workers. As will become evident later in this chapter, either Theory X or Theory Y assumptions may be appropriate in a particular situation.

WHAT EFFECT DOES THE ORGANIZATION HAVE ON MOTIVATION?

"First, describe situations in which you felt exceptionally good about your job. Second, describe situations in which you felt exceptionally bad about your job." Beginning in the late 1950s, Frederick Herzberg asked these two questions of a number of workers. He then tabulated and categorized their responses. What he found was that the replies people gave when they felt good about their jobs were significantly different from the replies given when they felt bad. As shown in Exhibit 8-3, certain factors tend to be consistently related to job satisfaction (when they felt "good") and others to job dissatisfaction (when they felt "bad"). Intrinsic factors such as achievement, recognition, the work itself, responsibility, and advancement seemed to be related to job satisfaction. When those questioned felt good about their work, they tended to attribute these factors to themselves. On the other hand, when they were dissatisfied, they tended to cite external factors, such as company policy and administration, supervision, interpersonal relations, and working conditions.

[4]D. McGregor, *The Human Side of Enterprise* (New York: McGraw-Hill, 1960).

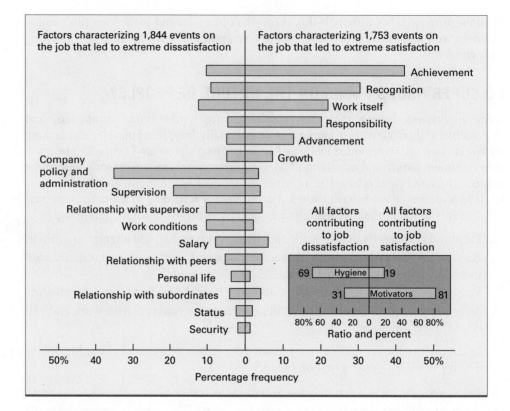

Exhibit 8-3

Comparison of satisfiers and dissatisfiers.

motivation-hygiene theory

A theory of Frederick Herzberg that the opposite of satisfaction is not "dissatisfaction" but "no satisfaction" and the opposite of dissatisfaction is not "satisfaction" but "no dissatisfaction."

Herzberg took these results and formulated his motivation-hygiene theory.[5] He said the responses suggest that the opposite of satisfaction is not dissatisfaction, as was traditionally believed. Removing dissatisfying characteristics from a job does not necessarily make the job satisfying. Herzberg proposed that his findings indicate the existence of a dual continuum: The opposite of "satisfaction" is "no satisfaction," and the opposite of "dissatisfaction" is "no dissatisfaction" (see Exhibit 8-4).

According to Herzberg, the factors leading to job satisfaction are separate and distinct from those that lead to job dissatisfaction. Therefore, supervisors who seek to eliminate factors that can create job dissatisfaction may bring about peace, but not necessarily motivation. They will be placating their employees rather than motivating them. As a result, such characteristics as company policy and administration, supervision, interpersonal relations, working conditions, and salary have been characterized by Herzberg as hygiene factors. When they're adequate, people will not be dissatisfied; however, neither will they be satisfied. If we want to motivate people in their jobs, Herzberg suggests emphasizing achievement, recognition, the work itself, responsibility, and growth. These are the characteristics that people find intrinsically rewarding.

hygiene factors

Herzberg's term for factors, such as working conditions and salary, that, when adequate, may eliminate job dissatisfaction but do not necessarily increase job satisfaction.

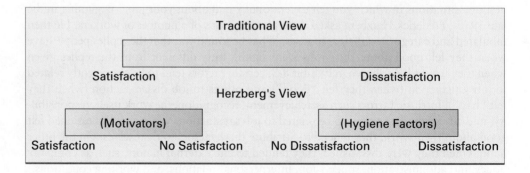

Exhibit 8-4

Contrasting views of satisfaction/dissatisfaction.

---

[5]F. Herzberg, B. Mauser, and B. Snyderman, *The Motivation to Work* (New York: John Wiley & Sons, 1959).

Comprehension Check 8-1

1. A physiological or psychological deficiency that makes certain outcomes seem attractive is called

   a. a need
   b. motivation
   c. increased tension
   d. drive

2. Manipulative behavior based on the belief that the ends justifies the means is called

   a. locus of control
   b. esteem
   c. Machiavellianism
   d. risk propensity

3. Which one of the following is *not* a need proposed in Maslow's hierarchy-of-needs theory?

   a. safety
   b. esteem
   c. locus of control
   d. physiological

4. Which motivation theory is attributed to Douglas McGregor?

   a. motivation-hygiene theory
   b. Theory X–Theory Y
   c. hierarchy-of-needs theory
   d. none of the above

Contemporary Theories of Motivation

Although the previous three theories are well known, they unfortunately have not held up well under close examination. However, all is not lost. Some contemporary theories have one thing in common: Each has a reasonable degree of valid supporting documentation. The following theories represent the current "state-of-the-art" explanations of employee motivation.

WHAT IS A FOCUS ON ACHIEVEMENT?

Some people have a compelling drive to succeed, but they are striving for personal achievement rather than the rewards of success. They have a desire to do something better or more efficiently than it has been done before. This drive is the need for achievement (nAch). People with a high need for achievement are intrinsically motivated.[6] As you'll see, when high achievers are placed into jobs that stimulate their achievement drive, they are self-motivated and require little of your time or energy.

need for achievement
A compelling drive to succeed; an intrinsic motivation to do something better or more efficiently than it has been done before.

High achievers differentiate themselves from others by their desire to do things better. They seek situations where they can attain personal responsibility for finding solutions to problems. They look for rapid and unambiguous feedback on their performance so that they can tell easily whether they are improving, and they set moderately challenging goals. High achievers are not gamblers; they dislike succeeding by chance. They prefer the challenge of working at a problem and accepting the personal responsibility for success or failure, rather than leaving the outcome to chance or the actions of others. They avoid what they perceive to be very easy or very difficult tasks.

---

[6]D. C. McClelland, *The Achieving Society* (New York: Van Nostrand Reinhold, 1961).

High achievers perform best when they perceive their probability of success as being 0.5; that is, when they estimate that they have a fifty–fifty chance of success. They dislike gambling with high odds because they get no achievement satisfaction from accidental success. Similarly, they dislike low odds (high probability of success) because then there is no challenge to their skills. They like to set goals that require stretching themselves a little. When there is an approximately equal chance of success or failure, there is the optimum opportunity to experience feelings of accomplishment and satisfaction from their efforts.

What proportion of the workforce is made up of high achievers? In developed countries, the answer appears to be between 10 and 20 percent. The percentage is considerably lower in developing countries. The reason is that the cultures of developed countries tend to socialize people more toward striving for personal achievement.

Based on an extensive amount of achievement research, we can draw three reasonably well-supported conclusions. First, individuals with a high nAch prefer job situations with personal responsibility, feedback, and an intermediate degree of risk. When these characteristics are prevalent, high achievers will be strongly motivated. The evidence consistently demonstrates, for instance, that high achievers are successful in entrepreneurial activities such as running their own businesses as well as in many sales positions.

Second, a high need to achieve does not necessarily lead to being a good supervisor or manager, especially in large organizations. High-nAch salespeople do not necessarily make good sales supervisors, and the good manager in a large organization does not typically have a high need to achieve. The reason seems to be that high achievers want to do things themselves rather than lead others toward accomplishments.

Last, employees can be successfully trained to stimulate their achievement need. If a job calls for a high achiever, you can select a person with a high nAch or develop your own candidate through achievement training. Achievement training focuses on teaching people to act, talk, and think like high achievers by having them write stories emphasizing achievement, play simulation games that stimulate feelings of achievement, meet with successful entrepreneurs, and learn how to develop specific and challenging goals.

HOW IMPORTANT IS EQUITY?

Suppose your company just hired someone new to work in your department, doing the same job you're doing. That person is essentially the same age as you, with almost identical educational qualifications and experience. The company is paying you $4,800 a month (which you consider very competitive). How would you feel if you found out that the company is paying the new person—whose credentials are not one bit better than yours—$5,600 a month? You'd probably be upset and angry. You'd probably think it wasn't fair. You're now likely to think you're underpaid. And you might direct your anger into actions such as reducing your work effort, taking longer coffee breaks, or taking extra days off by calling in "sick."

equity theory
The concept that employees perceive what they can get from a job situation (outcomes) in relation to what they put into it (inputs), and then compare their input–outcome ratio with the input–outcome ratio of others.

Your reactions illustrate the role that equity plays in motivation. People make comparisons of their job inputs and outcomes relative to others, and inequities have a strong bearing on the degree of effort that employees exert.[7] **Equity theory** states that employees perceive what they can get from a job situation (outcomes) in relation to what they put into it (inputs), and then compare their input–outcome ratio with the input–outcome ratio of others. If they perceive their ratio to be equal to the relevant others with whom they compare themselves, a state of equity is said to exist. They feel their situation is fair—that justice prevails. If the ratios are unequal, inequity exists; that is, the employees tend to view themselves as underrewarded or overrewarded. When inequities occur, employees attempt to correct them.

Equity theory recognizes that individuals are concerned not only with the absolute amount of rewards they receive for their efforts but also with the relationship of this

---

[7]J. S. Adams, "Inequity in Social Exchanges," in L. Berkowitz, ed., *Advances in Experimental Social Psychology*, Vol. 2 (New York: Academic Press, 1965), 267–300.

amount to what others receive (see Exhibit 8-5). Inputs such as effort, experience, education, and competence can be compared to outcomes such as salary levels, raises, recognition, and other factors. When people perceive an imbalance in their input–outcome ratio relative to others, tension is created. This tension provides the basis for motivation, as people strive for what they perceive as equity and fairness.

There is substantial evidence to confirm the equity thesis: Employee motivation is influenced significantly by relative rewards as well as absolute rewards. It helps to explain why, particularly when employees perceive themselves as underrewarded (we all seem to be pretty good at rationalizing being overrewarded), they may reduce their work effort, produce lower-quality work, sabotage the system, skip workdays, or even resign.

Individual outcomes	Compare with	Others' outcomes
Individual inputs		Others' inputs

Exhibit 8-5
Equity theory.

Do Employees Really Get What They Expect?

The final perspective we present is an integrative approach to motivation. It focuses on expectations. Specifically, expectancy theory argues that individuals analyze three relationships: effort–performance, performance–rewards, and rewards–personal goals. Their level of effort depends on the strengths of their expectations that these relationships can be achieved.[8] According to expectancy theory, an employee will be motivated to exert a high level of effort when he or she believes that effort will lead to a good performance appraisal; that a good appraisal will lead to organizational rewards such as a bonus, a salary increase, or a promotion; and that the rewards will satisfy the employee's personal goals. The theory is illustrated in Exhibit 8-6.

Expectancy theory has provided a powerful explanation of employee motivation. It helps explain why a lot of workers aren't motivated in their jobs and merely do the minimum necessary to get by. This can be made clearer if we look at the theory's three relationships in a little more detail. We present them as questions that employees need to answer affirmatively.

expectancy theory
A theory that individuals analyze effort–performance, performance–rewards, and rewards–personal goals relationships, and their level of effort depends on the strengths of their expectations that these relationships can be achieved.

- **First, if I give a maximum effort, will it be recognized in my performance evaluation?** For a lot of employees, the answer is no. Why? Their skill level may be deficient, which means that no matter how hard they try, they're not likely to be a high performer. The company's performance appraisal system may be poorly designed—assessing traits, for example, rather than behaviors—making it difficult or impossible for the employee to achieve a strong evaluation. Still another possibility is that employees, rightly or wrongly, perceive that their supervisors don't like them. As a result, they expect to get a poor appraisal regardless of their level of performance. These examples suggest that one possible source of low employee motivation is the belief of an employee that no matter how hard he or she works, the likelihood of getting a good performance appraisal is low.

- **Second, if I get a good performance appraisal, will it lead to organizational rewards?** Many employees see the performance–rewards relationship in their job

Exhibit 8-6
Expectancy theory.

[8]V. H. Vroom, *Work and Motivation* (New York: John Wiley & Sons, 1984).

as weak. The reason is that organizations reward a lot of things besides just performance. For example, when pay is allocated to employees based on factors such as seniority, being cooperative, or "kissing up" to the boss, employees are likely to see the performance–rewards relationship as being weak and demotivating.

- **Last, if I'm rewarded, do I find the rewards personally attractive?** The employee works hard in hope of getting a promotion, but gets a pay raise instead. Or the employee wants a more interesting and challenging job, but receives only a few words of praise. Unfortunately, many supervisors are limited in the rewards that they can distribute. This makes it difficult to tailor rewards to individual employees. Still other supervisors incorrectly assume that all employees want the same thing, thus overlooking the motivational effects of differentiating rewards. In either case, employee motivation is not fully maximized.

Something to Think About (and promote class discussion)

MOTIVATED TO DO WHAT?

Google gets over 777,000 applicants a year. And it's no wonder! With a massage every other week, on-site laundry, swimming pool and spa, free delicious all-you-can-eat gourmet meals, what more could an employee want? Sounds like an ideal job, doesn't it? However, at Google, many people are demonstrating by their decisions to leave the company that all those perks (and these are just a few) aren't enough to keep them there. As one analyst said, "Yes, Google's making gobs of money. Yes, it's full of smart people. Yes, it's a wonderful place to work. So why are so many people leaving?"

Google has been in the top ten list of "Best Companies to Work For" by *Fortune* magazine for three years running and was number one on the list for two of those three years. But make no mistake. Google's executives decided to offer all these fabulous perks for several reasons: to attract the best knowledge workers it can in an intensely competitive, cutthroat market; to help employees work long hours and not have to deal with time-consuming personal chores; to show employees they're valued; and to have employees remain Googlers (the name used for employees) for many years. But a number of Googlers have jumped ship and given up these fantastic benefits to go out on their own.

For instance, Sean Knapp and two colleagues, brothers Bismarck and Belsasar Lepe, came up with an idea on how to handle Web video. They left Google, or as one person put it, "expelled themselves from paradise to start their own company." When the threesome left the company, Google really wanted them and their project to stay. Google offered them a "blank check." But the trio realized they would do all the hard work and Google would own the product. So off they went, for the excitement of a start-up.

If this were an isolated occurrence, it would be easy to write off. But it's not. Other talented Google employees have done the same thing. In fact, there are so many of them who have left that they've formed an informal alumni club of ex-Googlers turned entrepreneurs.

If Google is such a motivational organization, what's it really like to work at Google? (Hint: Go to Google's website and click on "About Google." Find the section on Jobs at Google and go from there.) What's your assessment of the company's work environment? Even though Google is doing a lot for its employees, it obviously has not been enough to retain several of its talented employees. Reflecting on what you've learned from studying the various motivation theories, what does this situation tell you about employee motivation? What do you think is Google's biggest challenge in keeping employees motivated? If you were managing a team of Google employees, how would you keep them motivated? Will Google continue to hemorrhage talented workers? Should Google invest the time to correct the situation or accept it as a normal part of doing business in the IT world?

Sources: R. Levering and M. Moskowitz, "And the Winners Are...," *Fortune*, February 2, 2009, 67+; A. Lashinsky, "Where Does Google Go Next?" *CNNMoney.com*, May 12, 2008; K. Hafner, "Google Options Make Masseuse a Multimillionaire," *New York Times Online*, November 12, 2007; Q. Hardy, "Close to the Vest," *Forbes*, July 2, 2007, 40–42; K. J. Delaney, "Start-Ups Make Inroads with Google's Work Force," *Wall Street Journal Online*, June 28, 2007; and "Perk Place: The Benefits Offered by Google and Others May Be Grand, but They're All Business," *Knowledge @ Wharton*, http://knowledge.wharton.upenn.edu/article (accessed March 21, 2007).

HOW DO YOU CREATE AN ATMOSPHERE IN WHICH EMPLOYEES REALLY WANT TO WORK?

We've presented a number of approaches to motivation in this chapter. If you're a supervisor concerned with motivating your employees, how do you apply the various concepts introduced? Although there is no simple, all-encompassing set of guidelines, the essence of what we know about motivating employees is distilled in the following suggestions.

Recognize Individual Differences If we've learned one thing over the years, it's that employees are not the same. People have different needs. Whereas you may be driven by the need for recognition, I may be far more concerned with satisfying my desire for security. We know that a minority of employees have a high need for achievement. But if one or more of the people working for you are high achievers, make sure you design their jobs to provide them with the personal responsibility, feedback, and intermediate degree of risk that is most likely to provide them with motivation. Your job as a supervisor includes learning to recognize the dominant needs of each of your employees.

Match People to Jobs There is abundant evidence to support the idea that motivational benefits accrue from carefully matching people to jobs. Some people prefer routine work with repetitive tasks. Whereas many people enjoy being part of a team, others do their best work when they're isolated from other people and able to do their jobs independently. When jobs differ in terms of autonomy, the variety of tasks to be done, the range of skills they demand, and the like, you should try to match employees to jobs that best fit with their capabilities and personal preferences.

Set Challenging Goals We talked about the importance of goals in Chapter 3. In that discussion, we showed that challenging goals can be a source of motivation. When people accept and are committed to a set of specific and difficult goals, they will work hard to achieve them. Although we haven't directly addressed goals as motivators in this chapter, our earlier review of the evidence clearly indicates the power of goals in influencing employee behavior. Based on that earlier evidence, we suggest that you sit down with each of your employees and jointly set tangible, verifiable, and measurable goals for a specific time period. Then, create a mechanism by which these employees will receive ongoing feedback as to their progress toward achieving these goals. If done properly, this goal-setting process should act to motivate employees.

Encourage Participation Allowing employees to participate in decisions that affect them has been shown to increase their motivation. Participation is empowering. It allows people to take ownership of decisions. Examples of decisions in which employees might participate include setting work goals, choosing their own benefits packages, and selecting preferred work schedules and assignments. Participation, of course, should be at the option of the employee. No one should feel compelled to participate in decision making. While participation is associated with increasing employee commitment and motivation, consistent with our earlier discussion of individual differences, some people may prefer to waive their rights to participate in decisions that affect them. Those preferences should be heeded.

Individualize Rewards Because employees have different needs, what acts as a reinforcer for one may not work for another. You should use your knowledge of individual differences to individualize the rewards over which you have control. Some of the more obvious rewards that supervisors allocate include pay, job assignments, work hours, and the opportunity to participate in goal setting and decision making.

Link Rewards to Performance In both reinforcement theory and expectancy theory, motivation is maximized when supervisors make rewards contingent on performance. Rewarding factors other than performance only acts to reinforce and encourage those other factors. Key rewards such as pay increases and promotions should be allocated for the attainment of the employee's specific goals. To maximize the impact of the reward contingencies, supervisors should look for ways to increase the visibility of rewards. Publicizing performance bonuses and allocating annual salary increases in a lump sum rather than spreading them out over the entire year are examples of actions that will make rewards more visible and potentially more motivating.

Check for Equity Rewards or outcomes should be perceived by employees as equaling the inputs they give. At a simplistic level, this should mean that experience, abilities, effort, and other obvious inputs should explain differences in pay, responsibility, and other obvious outcomes. The problem, however, is complicated by the fact that there are dozens of inputs and outcomes, and that employee groups place different degrees of importance on them. This suggests that one person's equity is another's inequity, so an ideal reward system should probably weight inputs differently to arrive at the proper rewards for each job.

Don't Ignore Money! Our last suggestion may seem incredibly obvious. But it's easy to get so caught up in setting goals or providing opportunities for participation that you forget that money is a major reason most people work. The allocation of performance-based wage increases, piecework bonuses, and other pay incentives is important in determining employee motivation. Maybe the best case for not overlooking money as a motivator is a review of eighty studies evaluating motivational methods and their impacts on employee productivity.[9] Goal setting alone produced, on average, a 16 percent increase in productivity; efforts to redesign jobs to make them more interesting and challenging yielded 8 to 16 percent increases; and employee participation in decision making produced a median increase of less than 1 percent. In contrast, monetary incentives led to an average increase of 30 percent.

Designing Motivating Jobs

One of the most important factors that influence an employee's motivational level is the structure of the work itself. Is there a lot of variety or is the job repetitive? Is the work closely supervised? Does the job allow the employee discretion? The answers to questions such as these will have a major impact on the motivational properties inherent in the job and, hence, the level of productivity an employee can expect to achieve.

job design
Combining tasks to form complete jobs.

We use the term job design to refer to the way that tasks are combined to form complete jobs. Some jobs are routine because the tasks are standardized and repetitive; others are nonroutine. Some require a large number of varied and diverse skills; others are narrow in scope. Some jobs constrain the employee by requiring him or her to follow very precise procedures; others allow employees substantial freedom in how they do their work. The point is that jobs differ in the way tasks are combined, and these different combinations create a variety of job designs.

What are the key characteristics that define a job? There are five, and together they constitute the core dimensions of any job[10]:

1. **Skill variety.** The degree to which the job requires a variety of different activities so that the worker can use a number of different skills and talents

---

[9]E. A. Locke, "The Relative Effectiveness of Four Methods of Motivating Employee Performance," in K. D. Duncan, M. M. Gruneberg, and D. Wallis, eds., *Changes in Working Life* (London: John Wiley & Sons, 1980), 363–383.
[10]J. R. Hackman and G. R. Oldham, "Motivation through the Design of Work: Test of a Theory," *Organizational Behavior and Human Performance*, August 1976, 250–279.

2. **Task identity.** The degree to which the job requires completion of a whole and identifiable piece of work

3. **Task significance.** The degree to which the job has a substantial impact on the lives or work of other people

4. **Autonomy.** The degree to which the job provides substantial freedom, independence, and discretion to the individual in scheduling the work and in determining the procedures to be used in carrying it out

5. **Feedback.** The degree to which carrying out the work activities required by the job results in the individual obtaining direct and clear information about the effectiveness of his or her performance

Exhibit 8-7 offers examples of job activities that rate high and low for each characteristic. When these five characteristics are all present in a job, the job becomes enriched and potentially motivating. Notice that we said *potentially* motivating. Whether that potential is actualized largely depends on the strength of the employee's growth need. Individuals with a high growth need are more likely to be motivated in enriched jobs than their counterparts with a low growth need.

Job enrichment increases the degree to which a worker controls the planning, execution, and evaluation of his or her work. An enriched job organizes tasks so as to allow the worker to do a complete activity, increases the employee's freedom and independence, increases responsibility, and provides feedback so that an individual can assess and correct his or her own performance (see the section titled "Designing Jobs" at the end of this chapter).

job enrichment
The degree to which a worker controls the planning, execution, and evaluation of his or her work.

Flow in the Workplace The design of a job provides the organization an opportunity to match workers' skills with the conditions of the task and the workplace. When workers are able to find intrinsic motivation to complete a task, indeed when they become engaged in the task, to the apparent exclusion of outside influences, they can be said

Skill Variety	
High variety	The owner-operator of a garage who does electrical repair, rebuilds engines, does body work, and interacts with customers
Low variety	A body shop worker who sprays paint eight hours a day
Task Identity	
High identity	A cabinet maker who designs a piece of furniture, selects the wood, builds the object, and finishes it to perfection
Low identity	A worker in a furniture factory who operates a lathe solely to make table legs
Task Significance	
High significance	A nurse who cares for the sick in a hospital intensive-care unit
Low significance	A janitor who sweeps hospital floors
Autonomy	
High autonomy	A telephone installer who schedules his or her own work for the day, makes visits without supervision, and decides on the most effective techniques for a particular installation
Low autonomy	A telephone operator who must handle calls as they come according to a routine, highly specified procedure
Feedback	
High feedback	An electronics factory worker who assembles a radio and then tests it to determine whether it operates properly
Low feedback	An electronics factory worker who assembles a radio and then routes it to a quality control inspector who tests it for proper operation and makes needed adjustments

Exhibit 8-7

Examples of high and low levels of job characteristics.

to be in the flow of the task, job, or even their career. Flow is basically a high level of intrinsic motivation occurring when individuals becomes so absorbed in what they are doing they lose all awareness of things external to the task.

Flow is most common during work activities, often occurring when

- One's skills are appropriately matched by challenges.
- Concentration is so intense that there is no excess attention to focus on irrelevant problems or everyday worries.
- The concept of the self disappears and one loses a sense of time.
- An activity is so rewarding that people undertake the activity for its own sake.

Supervisors seeking to improve workplace conditions and provide motivational opportunities for workers should realize that when employee skills surpass their job challenges, they easily become bored. Conversely, job challenges greater than the skills of the employee may cause anxiety over inability to complete the task successfully. When challenges are appropriate for the skill set possessed by the employee, the employee is more likely to engage fully with the task and optimize the experience. In a modern highly competitive workplace it is important to identify work environments that possess the potential to increase employee engagement.[11]

Motivation Challenges for Today's Supervisors

Today's supervisors have challenges in motivating their employees that their counterparts of thirty or forty years ago didn't have. This includes motivating a diverse workforce, paying for performance, motivating minimum-wage employees, motivating professional and technical employees, and introducing employee stock ownership plans.

WHAT IS THE KEY TO MOTIVATING A DIVERSE WORKFORCE?

To maximize motivation among today's diversified workforce, supervisors need to think in terms of flexibility.[12] For instance, studies tell us that men place considerably more importance on having autonomy in their jobs than do women. In contrast, the opportunity to learn, convenient work hours, and good interpersonal relations appear more important to women than to men. Supervisors need to recognize that what motivates a single mother with two dependent children who is working full-time to support her family may be very different from what motivates a young, single, part-time worker or the older employee who is working to supplement his or her pension income. Employees have different personal needs and goals that they're hoping to satisfy through their job. The offer of various types of rewards to meet their diverse needs can be highly motivating for employees.

Motivating a diverse workforce also means that supervisors must be flexible by being aware of cultural differences. The theories of motivation we have been studying were developed largely by U.S. psychologists and were validated by studying American

---

[11]M. Csíkszentmihályi, *Flow: The Psychology of Optimal Experience* (New York: Harper & Row, 1990); J. Chamberlin and Monitor staff, "Reaching Flow to Optimize Work and Play," *APA Online* 29, no. 7 (July 1998), www.apa.org/monitor/jul98/joy.html (accessed June 10, 2008); M. Csíkszentmihályi, *Good Business: Leadership, Flow, and the Making of Meaning* (New York: Penguin Books, 2003); Hindu Business Line Internet Edition, "Discern Opportunities Around When Others Don't," March 8, 2004, www.thehindubusinessline.com/mentor/2004/03/08/stories/2004030800251100.htm (accessed June 10, 2008); and A. Marsh, "The Art of Work," *FastCompany.com*, December 19, 2007, www.fastcompany.com/magazine/97/art-of-work.html (accessed June 10, 2008).

[12]See S. Bates, "Getting Engaged," *HR Magazine*, February 2004, 44–51; and G. M. Combs, "Meeting the Leadership Challenge of a Diverse and Pluralistic Workplace: Implications of Self-Efficacy for Diversity Training," *Journal of Leadership Studies* 8, no. 4 (Spring 2002), 1–17.

workers. Therefore, these theories need to be modified for different cultures.[13] For instance, the self-interest concept is consistent with capitalism and the extremely high value placed on individualism in countries such as the United States. Because almost all the motivation theories presented in this chapter are based on the self-interest motive, they should be applicable to employees in such countries as Great Britain and Australia, where capitalism and individualism are highly valued. In more collectivist nations—such as Venezuela, Singapore, Japan, and Mexico—the link to the organization is the individual's loyalty to the organization or society, rather than his or her self-interest. Employees in collectivist cultures should be more receptive to team-based job design, group goals, and group-performance evaluations. Reliance on the fear of being fired in such cultures is likely to be less effective, even if the laws in those countries allow managers to fire employees.

Lincoln Electric's pay-for-performance culture, rewards employees for their contributions to the success and profitability of the Company.

The need-for-achievement concept provides another example of a motivation theory with a U.S. bias. The view that a high need for achievement acts as an internal motivator presupposes the existence of two cultural characteristics: a willingness to accept a moderate degree of risk and a concern with performance. These characteristics would exclude countries with high uncertainty-avoidance scores and high quality-of-life ratings. The remaining countries are exclusively Anglo-American countries such as New Zealand, South Africa, Ireland, the United States, and Canada.

However, results of several recent studies among employees in countries other than the United States indicate that some aspects of motivation theory are transferable.[14] For instance, motivational techniques presented earlier in this chapter were shown to be effective in changing performance-related behaviors of Russian textile mill workers. However, we should not assume that motivation concepts are universally applicable. Supervisors must change their motivational techniques to fit the culture. The technique used by a large department store in Xian, China—recognizing and embarrassing the worst sales clerks by giving them awards—may be a means of supervising in China, but doing something that humiliates employees isn't likely to work in North America or Western Europe.

SHOULD EMPLOYEES BE PAID FOR PERFORMANCE OR TIME ON THE JOB?

What's in it for me? That's a question every person consciously or unconsciously asks before engaging in any form of behavior. Our knowledge of motivation tells us that people do what they do to satisfy some need. Before they do anything, therefore, they look for a payoff or reward. Although many different rewards may be offered by organizations, most of us are concerned with earning an amount of money that allows us to satisfy our needs and wants. Because pay is an important variable in motivation as one type of reward, we need to look at how we can use pay to motivate high levels of employee performance. This concern explains the intent and logic behind pay-for-performance programs.

[13]G. Hofstede, "Motivation, Leadership, and Organizations: Do American Theories Apply Abroad?" *Organizational Dynamics* 9, no. 1 (Summer 1980), 55.

[14]D. H. B. Walsh, F. Luthens, and S. M. Sommer, "Organizational Behavior Modification Goes to Russia: Replicating an Experimental Analysis across Cultures and Tasks," *Journal of Organizational Behavior Management* 13, no. 2 (Fall 1993), 15–35; and J. R. Baum, J. D. Olian, M. Erez, and E. R. Schnell, "Nationality and Work Role Interactions: A Cultural Contrast of Israel and U.S. Entrepreneurs' versus Managers' Needs," *Journal of Business Venturing* 8, no. 6 (November 1993), 499–512.

pay-for-performance programs
Compensation plans that pay employees on the basis of some performance measure.

Pay-for-performance programs are compensation plans that pay employees on the basis of some performance measure. Piece-rate plans, gain sharing, wage incentive plans, profit sharing, and lump-sum bonuses are examples of pay-for-performance programs. What differentiates these forms of pay from the more traditional compensation plans is that instead of paying an employee for time on the job, pay is adjusted to reflect some performance measures. These performance measures might include such things as individual productivity, team or workgroup productivity, departmental productivity, or the overall organization's profits for a given period.

Performance-based compensation is probably most compatible with expectancy theory. That is, employees should perceive a strong relationship between their performance and the rewards they receive if motivation is to be maximized. If rewards are allocated solely on nonperformance factors—such as seniority, job title, or across-the-board cost-of-living raises—then employees are likely to reduce their efforts.

Pay-for-performance programs are gaining in popularity in organizations. A study found that almost 80 percent of firms surveyed were practicing some form of pay-for-performance for salaried employees.[15] The growing popularity can be explained in terms of both motivation and cost control.[16] From a motivation perspective, making some or all of a worker's pay conditional on performance measures focuses his or her attention and effort on that measure, and then reinforces the continuation of that effort with rewards. However, if the employee's, team's, or organization's performance declines, so too does the reward. Thus, there is an incentive to keep efforts and motivation strong.

competency-based compensation
Payments and rewards to employees on the basis of skills, knowledge, and behaviors.

A recent extension of the pay-for-performance concept is called competency-based compensation.[17] A competency-based compensation program pays and rewards employees on the basis of the skills, knowledge, or behaviors employees possess. These competencies may include such behaviors and skills as leadership, problem solving, decision making, or strategic planning. Pay levels are established on the basis of the degree to which these competencies exist. Pay increases in a competency-based system are awarded for growth in personal competencies as well as for the contributions one makes to the overall organization. Accordingly, an employee's rewards are tied directly to how capable he or she is of contributing to the achievement of the organization's goals and objectives.

HOW CAN SUPERVISORS MOTIVATE MINIMUM-WAGE EMPLOYEES?

Imagine for a moment that your first supervisory job after graduating from college involves overseeing a group made up of minimum-wage employees. Offering more pay to these employees for high levels of performance is out of the question. Your company just can't afford it. What are your motivational options at this point?[18] One of the toughest motivational challenges facing many supervisors today is how to achieve high performance levels among minimum-wage workers.

One trap many supervisors fall into is thinking that employees are motivated only by money. Although money is important as a motivator, it's not the only "reward" that people seek and that supervisors can use. In motivating minimum-wage employees, supervisors should look at other types of rewards that help motivate employees. What are some other types of rewards that supervisors can use? Many companies use employee recognition programs such as employee of the month, quarterly employee-performance

[15]J. Wiscombe, "Can Pay for Performance Really Work?" *Workforce*, August 2001, 28.

[16]"Exclusive PFP Survey: Latest Data—What's Hot and What's Not in PFP," *Pay for Performance Report*, May 2002, 1.

[17]See D. A. DeCenzo and S. P. Robbins, *Human Resource Management*, 8th ed. (New York: John Wiley & Sons, 2005), 286.

[18]P. Falcone, "Motivating Staff Without Money," *HR Magazine*, August 2002, 105–108.

award ceremonies, or other celebrations of employee accomplishment. For instance, at many fast-food restaurants such as McDonald's and Wendy's, you'll often see plaques hanging in prominent places that feature the "Crew Member of the Month." These types of programs serve the purpose of highlighting employees whose work performance has been of the type and level the organization wants to encourage. Many supervisors also recognize the power of praise. When praise is used, you need to be sure that these "pats on the back" are sincere and done for the right reasons; otherwise, employees can see such actions as manipulative.

But we know from the motivation theories presented earlier that rewards are only part of the motivation equation. We can look to job design and expectancy theories for additional insights. In service industries such as travel and hospitality, retail sales, child care, and maintenance, where pay for frontline employees generally doesn't get much above the minimum-wage level, successful companies are empowering these front-line employees with more authority to address customers' problems. If we use the key characteristics that define a job to examine this change, we can see that this type of job redesign provides enhanced motivating potential because employees now experience increased skill variety, task identity, task significance, autonomy, and feedback.

WHAT'S DIFFERENT IN MOTIVATING PROFESSIONAL AND TECHNICAL EMPLOYEES?

Professional and technical employees are typically different from nonprofessionals. They have a strong and long-term commitment to their field of expertise. Their loyalty, however, is more often to their profession than to their employer. To keep current in their field, they need to regularly update their knowledge. And their commitment to their profession or technical field means they rarely define their workweek in terms of a nine-to-five schedule, five days a week.[19]

So, what motivates these types of employees? Money and promotions into supervisory positions typically are low on their priority list. Why? They tend to be well paid, and they enjoy what they do. In contrast, job challenge tends to be ranked high. They like to tackle problems and find solutions. Their chief reward in their job is the work itself. Professional and technical employees generally also value support. They want others to think that what they are working on is important.[20]

This implies that supervisors should provide professional and technical employees with new assignments and challenging projects. Give them autonomy to follow their interests and allow them to structure their work in ways they find productive. Reward them with educational opportunities—training, workshops, attending conferences—that enable them to keep current in their field and to network with their peers. Also reward them with recognition. And supervisors should ask questions and engage in other actions that demonstrate to their professional and technical employees that they're sincerely interested in what they're doing.

An increasing number of companies are creating alternative career paths for these employees—especially those in highly technical fields such as IT. These allow employees to earn more money and status, without assuming managerial responsibilities. At Merck, IBM, and AT&T, the best scientists, engineers, and researchers gain titles such as Fellow and Senior Scientist. Their pay and prestige are comparable to those of managers, but without the corresponding authority.

---

[19]See, for instance, P. J. Sauer, "Open-Door Management," *Inc.*, June 2003, 44.
[20]"One's CEO's Perspective on Power of Recognition," *Workforce Management*, March 2, 2004. Available online at www.workforce.com; and R. Fournier, "Teamwork Is the Key to Remote Development—Inspiring Trust and Maintaining Motivation Are Critical for a Distributive Development Team," *InfoWorld*, March 5, 2001, 48.

WHAT CAN A SUPERVISOR DO TO IMPROVE EMPLOYEES' WORK–LIFE BALANCE?

The typical employee in the 1960s or 1970s showed up at the workplace Monday through Friday and did his or her job in eight- or nine-hour chunks of time. The workplace and hours were clearly specified. That's not the case anymore for a large segment of the workforce. Employees are increasingly complaining that the line between work and nonwork time has blurred, creating personal conflicts and stress.[21] Several factors have contributed to this blurring between work and personal life. One is that in a world of global business, work never ends. At any time and on any day, for instance, thousands of Caterpillar employees are working somewhere in the company's facilities. The need to consult with colleagues or customers eight or ten time zones away means that many employees of global companies are "on call" twenty-four hours a day. Another factor is that communication technology allows employees to do their work at home, in their cars, or on the beach in Tahiti. Although this capability allows those in technical and professional jobs to do their work anywhere and at anytime, it means there's no escaping from work. Another factor is that as organizations have had to lay off employees during the economic downturn, "surviving" employees have had to work longer hours. It's not unusual for employees to work more than forty-five hours a week, and some work more than fifty. Finally, fewer families today have a single wage earner. Today's married employee is typically part of a dual-career couple, which makes it increasingly difficult for married employees to find time to fulfill commitments to home, spouse, children, parents, and friends.[22]

More and more, employees recognize that work is squeezing out their personal lives, and they're not happy about it. Today's progressive workplaces must accommodate the varied needs of a diverse workforce. In response, many organizations are offering *family-friendly benefits*, benefits that provide a wide range of scheduling options that allow employees more flexibility at work, accommodating their need for work–life balance. They've introduced programs such as on-site child care, summer day camps, flextime, job sharing, time off for school functions, telecommuting, and part-time employment. Younger people, particularly, put a higher priority on family and a lower priority on jobs and are looking for organizations that give them more work flexibility.[23]

Flextime (short for "flexible work time") is a scheduling option that allows employees, within specific parameters, to decide when to go to work. Employees have to work a specific number of hours a week, but they are free to vary the hours of work within certain limits. Flextime has become a popular scheduling option, especially among professional employees and Gen-Xers.[24] For instance, a recent study of firms' practices to enhance the work–life balance found that about 60 percent offered employees some form of flextime.[25]

The potential benefits of flextime are numerous for both the employee and the employer. They include improved employee motivation and morale, reduced absenteeism as a result of enabling employees to better balance work and family responsibilities, increased wages as a result of productivity gains, and the ability of the organization to recruit higher-quality and more diverse employees.[26]

---

[21]See, for instance, P. Cappelli, J. Constantine, and C. Chadwick, "It Pays to Value Family: Work and Family Trade-Offs Reconsidered," *Industrial Relations* 39, no. 2 (April 2000), 175–198; R. C. Barnett and D. T. Hall, "How to Use Reduced Hours to Win the War for Talent," *Organizational Dynamics* 29 (March 2001), 42; and M. A. Verespej, "Balancing Act," *Industry Week*, May 15, 2000, 81–85.

[22]M. Conlin, "The New Debate over Working Moms," *BusinessWeek*, November 18, 2000, 102–103.

[23]M. Elias, "The Family-First Generation," *USA Today*, December 13, 2004, 5D.

[24]J. Wiscombe, "Flex Appeal—Not Just for Moms," *Workforce*, March 2002, 18.

[25]S. Roberts, "Companies Slow to Employ Alternative Work Options; Use of Arrangements Such as Flextime Is Up Slightly, If at All," *Business Insurance*, April 8, 2002, T3.

[26]S. F. Gale, "Formalized Flextime: The Perk That Brings Productivity," *Workforce*, February 2001, 38; and B. S. Gariety and S. Shaffer, "Wage Differentials Associated with Flextime," *Monthly Labor Review* 124, no. 3 (March 2001), 68–75.

News Flash!

THE GROWING URGENCY FOR WORK–LIFE BALANCE

Tough economic times place pressure on employees worried over their job security, and they tend to seek out employers offering a better work–life balance. Work–life balance ranks second only to compensation in terms of importance to employees, according to research conducted by the Corporate Executive Board among more than 50,000 global workers. Employees who feel they have a better work–life balance tend to work 21 percent harder than those that don't.

Ensuring an adequate work–life balance for employees is largely being neglected by employers as more and more pressure is put onto employees. In 2006, 53 percent of employees felt they had a good work–life balance; that number fell to 30 percent in the first quarter of 2009. Incredibly, many organizations shirk the opportunity to deliver on the work–life balance promise, and others mistakenly provide costly services, such as an on-site gym or healthcare services when, in fact, fewer than 20 percent of employees actually value these types of benefits.

With the nuclear family feeling increasing pressure to provide quality family time, many organizations recognize the most appreciated service they provide their employees is the "gift of time." More than 60 percent of the employees polled in the CEB study identified flexible schedules as the most important work–life practice their employer could provide.

The fact that nearly 60 percent of HR executives polled felt satisfied with the work–life services of their organization, while just 16 percent of employees felt the same, illustrates a fundamental disconnect when it comes to work–life benefits. The companies who most effectively address and close that gap stand the best chance of achieving the high levels of employee attraction and retention they seek.

Source: The Staff of the Corporate Executive Board, "The Increasing Call for Work-Life Balance," Bloomberg Business Week, *Bloomberg.com*, March, 2009, http://www.businessweek.com/managing/content/mar2009/ca20090327_734197.htm?chan=careers_special+report+--+work-life+balance_special+report+--+work-life+balance (accessed May 23, 2011).

Job sharing is a special type of part-time work. It allows two or more individuals to split a traditional forty-hour-a-week job. One person might perform the job from 8 a.m. to noon while another performs the same job from 1 p.m. to 5 p.m., or both could work full, but alternate, days. Job sharing, growing in popularity, allows organizations to draw on the talents of more than one individual for a given job. It provides the opportunity to acquire skilled workers—for instance, single parents with young children and retirees—who might not be available on a full-time basis.

HOW CAN EMPLOYEE STOCK OWNERSHIP PLANS AFFECT MOTIVATION?

Many companies are using employee stock ownership plans for improving and motivating employee performance. An employee stock ownership plan (ESOP) is a compensation program in which employees become part owners of the organization by receiving stock as a performance incentive. Also, many ESOPs allow employees to purchase additional stocks at attractive, below-market prices. Under an ESOP, employees often are motivated to give more effort because it makes them owners who will share in any gains and losses. The fruits of their labors are no longer just going into the pockets of some unknown owners—the employees *are* the owners! Do ESOPs positively affect productivity and employee satisfaction? The answer appears to be yes.

employee stock ownership plan (ESOP)
A compensation program that allows employees to become part owners of an organization by receiving stock as a performance incentive.

Comprehension Check **8-2**

5. A person who has a compelling drive to succeed, to do something better than others, has a high _____ .

   a. esteem need
   b. need for achievement
   c. need for people
   d. equity need

6. Which one of the following is *not* a direct linkage in expectancy theory?

   a. Effort–performance
   b. Rewards–personal goals
   c. Effort–personal goals
   d. Performance–rewards

7. Which one of the following is *not* a component of the core dimensions of a job?

   a. Skill variety
   b. Feedback
   c. Autonomy
   d. Role identity

8. A compensation plan that pays employees on the basis of the work they did is called

   a. competency-based compensation
   b. pay-for-performance
   c. compensation administration
   d. none of the above

Enhancing Understanding

SUMMARY

After reading this chapter, I can:

1. **Define** *motivation.* Motivation is the willingness to do something and is conditioned by this action's ability to satisfy some need for the individual.

2. **Identify and define five personality characteristics relevant to understanding the behavior of employees at work.** Five personality characteristics are (1) locus of control—the degree to which people believe they are masters of their own fate, (2) Machiavellianism—the degree to which an individual is manipulative and believes that ends can justify means, (3) self-esteem—an individual's degree of liking or disliking himself or herself, (4) self-monitoring—an individual's ability to adjust his or her behavior to external, situational factors, and (5) risk propensity—the degree of an individual's willingness to take chances.

3. **Explain the elements and the focus of the three early theories of motivation.** Maslow focused on the self. Maslow's hierarchy of needs proposes that there are five needs—physiological, safety, social, esteem, and self-actualization—and as each need is sequentially satisfied, the next need becomes dominant. McGregor focused on management's perception of the self. Theory X–Theory Y proposes two views of human nature, and then argues that employees are essentially hardworking, committed, and responsible. Therefore, to maximize motivation, employees should be allowed to participate in decision making and should be given responsible and challenging jobs, and supervisors should strive to achieve good group relations among employees. Herzberg focused on the organization's effect on the self. According to motivation-hygiene theory, if you want to motivate employees, you have to emphasize achievement, recognition, the work itself, responsibility, and growth. These are the characteristics that people find intrinsically rewarding.

4. **Identify the characteristics that stimulate the achievement drive in high achievers.** High achievers prefer jobs that give them personal responsibility for finding solutions to problems, where they can receive rapid and unambiguous feedback on their performance, and where they can set moderately challenging goals.

5. **Identify the three relationships in expectancy theory that determine an individual's level of effort.** The three relationships in expectancy theory that determine an individual's level of effort are effort–performance, performance–rewards, and rewards–personal goals. The effort–performance linkage implies that an employee who puts forth the effort has a greater likelihood that he or she will successfully perform the job. The performance–rewards linkage implies that if the performance is successful, the employee will receive a reward. Finally, the rewards–personal goals linkage implies that the rewards received are something the employee wants and finds value in—it helps fulfill an individual need.

6. **List actions a supervisor can take to maximize employee motivation.** To maximize employee motivation, supervisors should recognize individual differences, match people to jobs, set challenging goals, encourage participation, individualize rewards, link rewards to performance, check for equity, and not ignore money.

7. **Describe how supervisors can design individual jobs to maximize employee performance.** Supervisors can design individual jobs to maximize employee performance by offering skill variety, task identity, task significance, and autonomy and by providing feedback. These five elements have been identified as key characteristics that define a job.

8. **Explain the effect of workforce diversity on motivating employees.** Maximizing motivation in contemporary organizations requires that supervisors be flexible in their practices. They must recognize that employees have different personal needs and goals that they are attempting to satisfy through work. Supervisors must also recognize that cultural differences may play a role. Various types of rewards must be developed to meet and motivate people with these diverse needs.

COMPREHENSION: Review and Discussion Questions

1. How does an unsatisfied need create motivation?

2. Contrast behavioral predictions about people with an internal versus an external locus of control.

3. Compare the assumptions of Theory X with those of Theory Y. Do you believe that there are types of jobs that require one focus or another? Explain.

4. What is the importance of the dual continuum in the motivation-hygiene theory?

5. What does a supervisor need to do to motivate a high achiever?

6. What role would money play in (a) the hierarchy-of-needs theory, (b) motivation-hygiene theory, (c) equity theory, (d) expectancy theory, and (e) the case of employees with a high nAch?

7. Describe expectancy theory. What are the critical linkages?

8. What motivational challenges does a diversified workforce create for supervisors?

9. Identify and explain the five core dimensions in a job.

10. How can a supervisor enrich a job?

KEY CONCEPT CROSSWORD

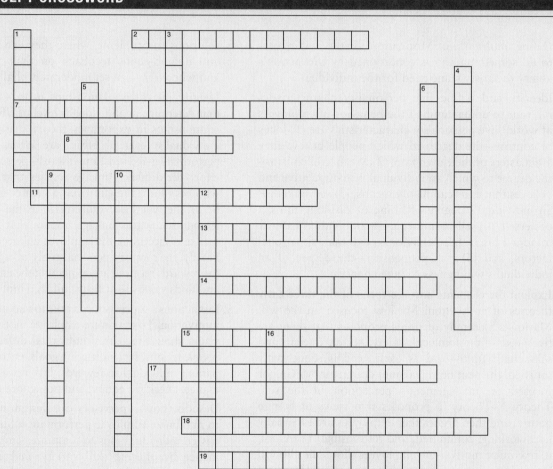

ACROSS

2. McGregor's motivation theory
7. a compensation plan that allows employees to become part owners in the organization
8. the degree to which an individual likes or dislikes himself or herself
11. Herzberg's motivation theory
13. a motivation theory that looks at the effort–performance–reward linkages
14. a willingness to take chances
15. Herzberg's terms for such things as working conditions and salary
17. compensation plans that compensate employees based on tasks completed
18. a compelling drive to succeed
19. the ability to adjust behavior to external situational factors

DOWN

1. combining tasks to form complete jobs
3. a motivation theory that states that employees' inputs equal outcomes
4. a compensation program in which payments and rewards are based on skills, knowledge, and abilities
5. the degree to which a worker controls the planning, execution, and evaluation of his or her work
6. the willingness to do something to satisfy a need
9. a source of the power over an individual's behavior
10. manipulative behavior based on the belief that the ends justify the means
12. Maslow's motivation theory
16. a deficiency that makes certain outcomes attractive

ANSWERS TO COMPREHENSION CHECKS

Comprehension Check 8-1

1. a   2. c   3. c   4. b

Comprehension Check 8-2

5. b   6. c   7. d   8. b

Developing Your Supervisory Skills

GETTING TO KNOW YOURSELF

Before you can effectively supervise others, you must understand your present strengths and areas in need of development. To assist in this learning process, we encourage you to complete the following self-assessments from the Prentice Hall Self-Assessment Library 3.4.

1. What Do I Value? (I. B. 1.)
2. What Rewards Do I Value Most? (I. C. 3.)

3. What's My View on the Nature of People? (I. C. 4.)
4. What Motivates Me? (I. C. 1.)
5. What's My Attitude toward Achievement? (I. C. 7.)

After you complete the assessment, we suggest you retain the results and store them as part of your "portfolio of learning about yourself."

BUILDING A TEAM

➤ An Experiential Exercise: Motivating Others

This exercise is designed to help increase your awareness of how and why you motivate others and to help focus on the needs of those you are attempting to motivate.

STEP 1: Break into groups of five to seven people. Each group member is to individually respond to the following:

SITUATION 1: You are the supervisor of eleven employees. Your goal is to motivate all eleven employees to their highest effort level.

Task 1: On a separate piece of paper, list the factors you would use to motivate your employees. Avoid general statements such as "give them a raise." Rather, be as specific as possible.

Task 2: Rank (from highest to lowest) all the factors listed in Task 1.

SITUATION 2: Consider now that you are one of the eleven employees who has been given insight as to what motivates you.

Task 3: As an employee, list the factors that would most effectively motivate you. Again, be as specific as possible.

Task 4: Rank (from highest to lowest) all the factors listed in Task 3.

STEP 2: Each member should share his or her prioritized lists (the lists from Tasks 2 and 4) with the other members of the group.

STEP 3: After each member has presented his or her lists, the group should respond to the following questions:

1. Are each individual's lists (Task 2 and Task 4) similar or dissimilar? What do the differences or similarities suggest to you?
2. What have you learned about how and why you motivate others, and how can you apply these data?

➤ Internet: Web Activity

Go to http://www.pearsonhighered.com/robbins/. Find *Supervision Today!* 7th Ed. and click Companion Website.

DESIGNING JOBS

As a supervisor, what can you do regarding job design to maximize your employees' performance? Based on the research, we suggest that you improve the five core job dimensions.

STEPS IN PRACTICING THE SKILL

STEP 1: **Combine tasks.** Put existing fractionalized tasks back together to form a new, larger module of work. This increases skill variety and task identity.

STEP 2: Create natural work units. Design tasks that form an identifiable and meaningful whole. This increases employee ownership of the work and encourages your employees to view their work as meaningful and important rather than as irrelevant and boring.

STEP 3: Establish client relationships. The client is the user of the product or service that your employees work on. Wherever possible, you should establish direct relationships between your workers and their clients. This increases skill variety, autonomy, and feedback for the employees.

STEP 4: Expand jobs vertically. Vertical expansion means giving employees responsibilities and controls that were formerly reserved for you, the supervisor. It partially closes the gap between the "doing" and "controlling" aspects of the job, and it increases employee autonomy.

STEP 5: Open feedback channels. By increasing feedback, employees not only learn how well they are performing their jobs but also whether their performances are improving, deteriorating, or remaining at a constant level. Ideally, employees should receive performance feedback directly as they do their jobs rather than on an occasional basis.

Source: J. R. Hackman and G. R. Oldham, "Motivation through the Design of Work: Test of a Theory," *Organizational Behavior and Human Performance*, August 1976, 250–279.

➤ Communicating Effectively

1. Develop a two- to three-page paper that answers the following questions: What motivates me? What rewards can an employer provide that will make me give the extra effort at work?

2. Go to http://www.chartcourse.com/articlehappy.htm. Review the article "Happy Employees Make Productive Employees." Summarize the key points of the article and relate the focus to motivating minimum-wage employees.

THINKING CRITICALLY

➤ Case 8-A: Unequal Pay for Equal Work

The new world economic order has changed the work environment for employees over the past decade. Companies have restructured jobs and processes, resulting in thousands of workers being laid off. For the luckier ones who remain employed, pay levels have either held constant for several years (no raises given), or worse, pay has been cut. What effect has this had on employee motivation?

One researcher explored that question. The study reviewed the practices of three plants of a large Midwest manufacturing organization. Not unlike many manufacturing companies, this organization was struggling to survive. In an effort to do so, the company decided, among other things, to implement pay cuts for all its employees.

No one expected workers to be happy about making less money. However, it was the supervisors' perception that a pay cut would cause less harm than eliminating several jobs altogether. In fact, by reducing pay levels, layoffs could be prevented. What happened next was clearly not the reaction anyone expected.

Employees did change their behaviors and attitudes toward the company. Sure, they were disgruntled, but they did more than complain. Employees began stealing from the company. Anything and everything that they could take was looted. In fact, in two of the three plants, theft skyrocketed to unprecedented levels.

RESPONDING TO THE CASE

1. Describe the behaviors (stealing) by these employees in terms of (a) their needs, (b) the organization's effect on them, (c) equating their inputs and outcomes, and (d) what employees expect from their employer.

2. What do you believe supervisors could have done differently to avert this "potential" problem?

➤ Case 8-B: Doldrums in the Dental Office

Caroline was happy to achieve her Associate Degree in Dental Hygiene with an emphasis in children's prophylaxis. At the very least, she had a job that made her family happy and got them off her back about a career. Her mom and dad constantly pointed out that even during hard times children would still need to have their teeth cleaned and parents would work to ensure the health of their children so her job was recession proof. Additionally, her family felt that a job in the medical profession gave her more status and others would see her as someone important.

After working with the placement service of the university, Caroline found a job at a large family dental practice in the valley. She wanted to appear as professional as possible so she joined all of the local, state, and national dental hygienist organizations she could find, even though she had no real intention of participating or assuming a leadership role in any of the organizations.

After a two-week orientation period at the dental practice, Caroline was assigned to her own room and began to receive new clients. Her work focused on children and she worked hard to build their confidence in her and overcome their fear of going to the dentist. Caroline thought it was strange that she and the other hygienists did most of the work on the patients, with the dentists doing a cursory once over at the end of the cleaning session, yet the dentists were paid much more of the per-patient fees.

One weekend working out at the local gym she had joined for exercise and networking opportunities, Caroline ran into Julia, one of her former classmates. After exchanging some idle chit chat, Julia asked her how she liked her new job. Caroline explained to her that the job was boring and terribly repetitive. She explained that she received little satisfaction from the job other than seeing the smiles of the children she worked on and she realized now that it was a job, just like any other.

One evening Caroline was waiting in line to place her order at a local carry-out diner. In front of her was Chrystal, the accounts manager for the dental practice. Chrystal invited Caroline to sit with her in the dining room after they paid the cashier. As they ate their dinner, Chrystal remarked to Caroline that she had some feedback she would like to share with her. Caroline remarked that she hoped it was not a problem with the insurance billing she had completed for a family earlier in the week.

Chrystal assured her it had nothing to do with the insurance. She went on to tell Caroline that she had overheard several of the dentists in the practice referring to her as automatic and emotionless when dealing with the children who were her patients. They were concerned that Caroline had no passion for her job and could make a critical mistake due to her blasé attitude.

Caroline became defensive and angry, telling Chrystal she loved the children and would never do anything to hurt them. She went on to tell her that if she were paid a little more she might be more inclined to be more passionate about the job. But, as it was, well...

RESPONDING TO THE CASE

1. What can Caroline do to become more motivated about her work and overcome the reputation of being passionless about her job?

2. What motivational opportunities could Caroline expect from her bosses at the dentist office?

3. Explain Caroline's behavior using the equity theory.

4. How would Herzberg explain Caroline's lack of passion for her job?

Leading Followers

Key Concepts

After completing this chapter, you will be able to define these supervisory terms:

- autocratic leader
- charismatic leader
- consultative-participative leadership
- credibility
- democratic-participative leadership
- free-rein leader
- leadership
- leadership traits
- participative leadership

- people-centered leader
- readiness
- situational leadership
- task-centered leader
- transactional leader
- transformational leader
- trust
- visionary leadership

Chapter Outcomes

After reading this chapter, you will be able to:

1. Define *leadership* and describe the difference between a leader and a supervisor.
2. Identify the traits that may help you become a successful leader.
3. Define *charisma* and its key components.
4. Describe the skills of a visionary leader.
5. Differentiate between task-centered and people-centered leadership behaviors.
6. Identify and describe three types of participative leadership styles.
7. Explain situational leadership.
8. Describe situations in which leadership is irrelevant.

Responding to a Supervisory Dilemma

Are there gender differences in leadership styles? Are men more effective leaders, or does that honor belong to women? Even asking those questions is certain to evoke reactions on both sides of the debate.

The evidence indicates that the two sexes are more alike than different in the ways they lead. Much of this similarity is based on the fact that leaders, regardless of gender, perform similar activities in influencing others. That's their job, and the two sexes do it equally well. The same holds true in other professions. For instance, although the stereotypical nurse is a woman, men are equally effective and successful in this career.

Although the sexes are more alike than different, they are not exactly the same. The most common difference lies in leadership styles. Women tend to use a more democratic style. They encourage the participation of their followers and are willing to share their positional power with others. In addition, women tend to influence others best through their ability to be charmingly influential. Men, on the other hand, tend to use a task-centered leadership style. This includes directing the activities of others and relying on their positional power to control the organization's activities. But surprisingly, even this difference is blurred. All things considered, when a woman is a leader in a traditionally male-dominated job (e.g., that of a police officer), she tends to lead in a manner that is more task centered.

Further compounding this issue are the changing roles of leaders in today's organizations. With an increased emphasis on teams, employee involvement, and interpersonal skills, democratic leadership styles are more in demand. Leaders need to be more sensitive to their followers' needs and more open in their communications; they need to build more trusting relationships. And many of these factors are behaviors that women have typically grown up developing.

So what do you think? Is there a difference between the sexes in terms of leadership styles? Do men or women make better leaders? Would you prefer to work for a man or a woman?

Sources: Vignette based on M. L. Van Engen, R. Van Der Leeden, and T. M. Willemsen, "Gender, Context and Leadership Styles: A Field Study," *Journal of Occupational and Organizational Psychology* 74, no. 5 (December 2001), 581–599; R. F. Martell and A. L. DeSmet, "A Diagnostic-Ratio Approach to Measuring Beliefs about the Leadership Abilities of Male and Female Managers," *Journal of Applied Psychology* 86, no. 6 (December 2001), 1223–1232; "Are Women Better Leaders?" *U.S. News and World Report*, January 29, 2001, 10; R. Sharpe, "As Leaders, Women Rule," *Business Week*, November 20, 2000, 75–84; J. K. Winter, J. C. Neal, and K. K. Waner, "How Male, Female, and Mixed-Gender Groups Regard Interaction and Leadership Differences in the Business Communication Course," *Business Communication Quarterly* 64, no. 3 (September 2001), 43; N. Z. Stelter, "Gender Differences in Leadership: Current Social Issues and Future Organizational Implications," *Journal of Leadership Studies* 8, no. 4 (Spring 2002), 88–100; and W. H. Decker and D. M. Rotondo, "Relationships Among Gender, Types of Humor, and Perceived Leader Effectiveness," *Journal of Managerial Issues* 13, no. 4 (Winter 2001), 450–466.

The activities ongoing in an organization tell us something about leadership. On one hand, it's the leaders in organizations and departments who make things happen, and make the difference between success and failure. On the other hand, the way they do this may differ widely. The potential for success and the different ways it is achieved are addressed in this very important chapter on leadership.

Understanding Leadership

Leadership is the ability you demonstrate when you influence others to act in a particular way. Through direction, encouragement, sensitivity, consideration, and support, you inspire your followers to accept challenges and achieve goals that may be viewed as difficult to achieve. As a leader, you're also someone who sees and can get the best out of others—helping them develop a sense of personal and professional accomplishment. Being a leader means building a commitment to goal attainment among those being led, as well as a strong desire for them to continue following.

You may think of leaders as individuals who are in charge of others. These would include you, as an authority over your employees; your boss; and anyone else who holds a position of power over you—such as your professor in this class. Obviously, through a variety of actions, you and the others have the ability to influence. Yet leadership frequently goes beyond formal positions. In fact, sometimes this person of power isn't around, yet leadership may still exist.

Let's begin by clarifying the distinction between those who supervise others and those we call leaders. The words *leader* and *supervisor* are frequently used to mean the same thing, but they do not.

Those who supervise others are appointed by the organization. They have legitimate power that allows them to reward and punish their employees. Their ability to influence employees is based on the formal authority inherent in their positions. In contrast, leaders may either be appointed or emerge from within a group. Leaders can influence others to perform beyond the actions dictated by formal authority.

Should all those who supervise others be leaders? Conversely, should all leaders formally direct the activities of others? Because no one yet has been able to demonstrate through research or logical argument that leadership ability is a hindrance to those who supervise, we can state that anyone who supervises employees should ideally be a leader. However, not all leaders necessarily have the capabilities in other supervisory functions, and thus not all should have formal authority. Therefore, when we refer to a leader in this chapter, we are talking about anyone who can influence others.

leadership
The ability an individual demonstrates to influence others to act in a particular way through direction, encouragement, sensitivity, consideration, and support.

leadership traits
Qualities such as intelligence, charm, decisiveness, enthusiasm, strength, bravery, integrity, and self-confidence.

Are Leaders Born or Made?

Ask the average person on the street what comes to mind when he or she thinks of leadership. You're likely to get a list of qualities such as intelligence, charm, decisiveness, enthusiasm, strength, bravery, integrity, and self-confidence. In fact, these are probably some of the same characteristics you would have listed if you had been asked that question. The responses that we get, in essence, represent leadership traits. The search for traits or characteristics that separate leaders from nonleaders, though done in a more sophisticated manner than an on-the-street survey, dominated early research efforts in the study of leadership.

Is it possible to isolate one or more traits in individuals who are generally acknowledged to be able to influence others—such as Nikki Haley, Ken Chenault, Irene Rosenfeld, Mark Zuckerberg, Indra Nooyi, and Steve Jobs—that nonleaders do not possess? You may agree that these individuals meet the fundamental definition of a leader, but they have completely different characteristics. If the concept of leadership traits is to prove valid, there must be identifiable characteristics that all leaders are born with.

What is it about Rupert Murdoch that makes him a visionary leader? Research tells us it's his ability to explain the vision, express the vision, and extend the vision. In doing so, he helps his employees look at problems in new ways and inspires them to put in extra effort.

WHAT ARE THE TRAITS OF SUCCESSFUL LEADERS?

Research efforts at isolating specific leadership traits resulted in a number of dead ends. Attempts failed to identify a set of traits that would always differentiate leaders from

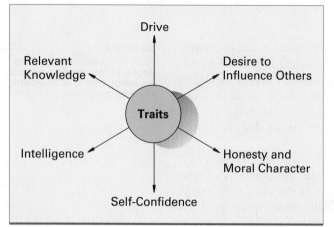

Exhibit 9-1
Six traits of effective leaders.

followers and effective leaders from ineffective leaders. Perhaps it was a bit optimistic to believe that a set of consistent and unique personality traits could apply across the board to all effective leaders—in such widely diverse organizations as Dell Computer, the Indianapolis Colts, the archdiocese of Washington, Walmart, and Toyota.

Attempts to identify traits consistently associated with those who are successful in influencing others have been more promising. For example, six traits on which leaders are seen to differ from nonleaders are drive, the desire to influence others, honesty and moral character, self-confidence, intelligence, and relevant knowledge (see Exhibit 9-1).[1]

A person's *drive* reflects his or her desire to exert a high level of effort to complete a task. This type of individual often has a strong need to achieve and excel in what he or she does. Ambitious, this leader demonstrates high energy levels in his or her endless persistence in all activities. Furthermore, a person who has this drive frequently shows a willingness to take initiative.

Leaders have a clear *desire to influence others*. Often this desire to lead is viewed as a willingness to accept responsibility for a variety of tasks. A leader also builds trusting relationships with those he or she influences, by being truthful and by showing a high consistency between spoken words and actions. In other words, others are more apt to be influenced by someone whom they view as exhibiting *honesty and moral character*.

A person who leads also shows *self-confidence* to convince others of the correctness of goals and decisions. It has been shown that employees prefer to be influenced by individuals who are free of self-doubt. In other words, they are influenced more by a supervisor who has a strong belief as opposed to one who frequently waffles on decisions made.

Influencing others requires a level of *intelligence*, too. To influence others successfully, one needs to be able to gather, synthesize, and interpret a lot of information. He or she must also be able to create a vision (a plan), communicate it in such a way that others understand it, solve problems, and make good decisions. Many of these intelligence requirements come from education and experience.

Finally, an effective leader has a high degree of *relevant knowledge* about the department and the unit's employees. This in-depth knowledge helps the supervisor make well-informed decisions, as well as understand the implications those decisions have on others in the department.

WHAT IS THIS THING CALLED CHARISMA?

charismatic leader
An individual with a compelling vision or sense of purpose, an ability to communicate that vision in clear terms that followers can understand, a demonstrated consistency and focus in pursuit of the vision, and an understanding of his or her own strengths.

What do people like Jay Leno, Payton Manning, Suze Orman, and Oprah Winfrey have in common? They all have something in their personality construct called *charisma*. Each of these individuals are what we call a charismatic leader—that is, an enthusiastic, self-confident leader whose personality and actions influence people to behave in certain ways. Charisma is a magnetism that inspires followers to go the "extra mile" to reach goals that are perceived as difficult or unpopular. Being charismatic, however, is not attributed to a single factor. Instead, it too evolves from one's possession of several characteristics.[2]

[1]S. A. Kirkpatrick and E. A. Locke, "Leadership: Do Traits Matter?" *Academy of Management Executive* 5, no. 2 (May 1991), 48–60.
[2]J. A. Conger and R. N. Kanungo, Charismatic Leadership in Organizations (Thousand Oaks, CA: Sage, 1998). See also, A. M. O'Roark, The Quest for Executive Effectiveness: Turning Inside-Out Charismatic-Participatory Leadership (Nevada City, CA: Symposium, 2000); C. G. Emrich, H. H. Brower, J. M. Feldman, and H. Garland, "Images in Words: Presidential Rhetoric, Charisma, and Greatness," Administrative Science Quarterly 46, no. 3 (September 2001), 527–561; and J. J. Sosik, "The Role of Personal Meaning in Charismatic Leadership," Journal of Leadership Studies 7, no. 2 (Spring 2000), 60–75.

Several authors have attempted to identify personal characteristics of the charismatic leader.[3] The most comprehensive analysis identified five such characteristics: they have a vision, the ability to articulate that vision, willingness to take risks to achieve that vision, sensitivity to both environmental constraints and follower needs, and behaviors that are out of the ordinary.[4]

There's an increasing body of evidence that shows impressive correlations between charismatic leadership and high performance and satisfaction among followers.[5] If charisma is desirable, can people learn to be charismatic leaders? Or are charismatic leaders born with their qualities? Although a small number of experts still think that charisma can't be learned, most believe that individuals can be trained to exhibit charismatic behaviors.[6] For example, researchers have succeeded in teaching undergraduate students to "be" charismatic. How? They were taught to articulate a far-reaching goal, communicate high performance expectations, exhibit confidence in the ability of subordinates to meet those expectations, and empathize with the needs of their subordinates; they learned to project a powerful, confident, and dynamic presence; and they practiced using a captivating and engaging voice tone. The researchers also trained the student leaders to use charismatic nonverbal behaviors including leaning toward the follower when communicating, maintaining direct eye contact, and having a relaxed posture and animated facial expressions. In groups with these "trained" charismatic leaders, members had higher task performance, higher task adjustment, and better adjustment to the leader and to the group than did group members who worked in groups led by noncharismatic leaders.

In Chapter 8, we introduced the personality dimension called self-monitoring. As you'll recall, we described high self-monitors as individuals who can easily adjust their behavior to different situations. They can read verbal and nonverbal social cues and

---

[3]J. M. Crant and T. S. Bateman, "Charismatic Leadership Viewed from Above: The Impact of Proactive Personality," *Journal of Organizational Behavior* 21, no. 1 (February 2000), 63–75; G. Yukl and J. M. Howell, "Organizational and Contextual Influences on the Emergence and Effectiveness of Charismatic Leadership," *Leadership Quarterly* 10, no. 2 (Summer 1999), 257–283; and J. A. Conger and R. N. Kanungo, "Behavioral Dimensions of Charismatic Leadership," in J. A. Conger, R. N. Kanungo and Associates (eds.), *Charismatic Leadership* (San Francisco, CA: Jossey-Bass, 1988), 78–97.

[4]J. A. Conger and R. N. Kanungo, *Charismatic Leadership in Organizations* (Thousand Oaks, CA: Sage, 1998).

[5]K. S. Groves, "Linking Leader Skills, Follower Attitudes, and Contextual Variables via an Integrated Model of Charismatic Leadership," *Journal of Management* 31, no. 2 (April 2005), 255–277; J. J. Sosik, "The Role of Personal Values in the Charismatic Leadership of Corporate Managers: A Model and Preliminary Field Study," *Leadership Quarterly* 16, no. 2 (April 2005), 221–244; A. H. B. deHoogh, D. N. den Hartog, P. L. Koopman, H. Thierry, P. T. van den Berg, J. G. van der Weide, and C. P. M. Wilderom, "Leader Motives, Charismatic Leadership, and Subordinates' Work Attitudes in the Profit and Voluntary Sector," *Leadership Quarterly* 16 (February 2005), 17–38; J. M. Howell and B. Shamir, "The Role of Followers in the Charismatic Leadership Process: Relationships and Their Consequences," *Academy of Management Review* 30, no. 1 (January 2005), 96–112; J. Paul, D. L. Costley, J. P. Howell, P. W. Dorfman, and D. Trafimow, "The Effects of Charismatic Leadership on Followers' Self-Concept Accessibility," *Journal of Applied Social Psychology* 31, no. 9 (September 2001), 1821–1844; J. A. Conger, R. N. Kanungo, and S. T. Menon, "Charismatic Leadership and Follower Effects," *Journal of Organizational Behavior* 21, no. 7 (2000), 747–767; R. W. Rowden, "The Relationship Between Charismatic Leadership Behaviors and Organizational Commitment," *Leadership & Organization Development Journal* 21, no. 1 (January 2000), 30–35; G. P. Shea and C. M. Howell, "Charismatic Leadership and Task Feedback: A Laboratory Study of Their Effects on Self-Efficacy," *Leadership Quarterly* 10 (Fall 1999), 375–396; S. A. Kirkpatrick and E. A. Locke, "Direct and Indirect Effects of Three Core Charismatic Leadership Components on Performance and Attitudes," *Journal of Applied Psychology* 81, no. 1 (February 1996), 36–51; D. A. Waldman, B. M. Bass, and F. J. Yammarino, "Adding to Contingent-Reward Behavior: The Augmenting Effect of Charismatic Leadership," *Group & Organization Studies* 15, no. 4 (December 1990), 381–394; and R. J. House, J. Woycke, and E. M. Fodor, "Charismatic and Noncharismatic Leaders: Differences in Behavior and Effectiveness," in Conger and Kanungo, *Charismatic Leadership*, 103–104.

[6]R. Birchfield, "Creating Charismatic Leaders," *Management* (June 2000), 30–31; S. Caudron, "Growing Charisma," *IndustryWeek*, May 4, 1998, 54–55; and J. A. Conger and R. N. Kanungo, "Training Charismatic Leadership: A Risky and Critical Task," in J. A. Conger and R. N. Kanungo (eds.), *Charismatic Leadership* (San Francisco, CA: Jossey-Bass, 1988), 309–323.

alter their behavior accordingly. This ability to be a "good actor" has been found to be associated with charismatic leadership. Because high self-monitors can accurately read a situation, understand the feelings of employees, and then exhibit behaviors that match employees' expectations, they tend to emerge as effective and charismatic supervisors.

One last thing we should say about charismatic leadership is that it may not always be necessary to achieve high levels of employee performance. It may be most appropriate when the follower's task has an ideological purpose or when the environment involves a high degree of stress and uncertainty.[7] This may explain why, when charismatic leaders surface, it's more likely to be in politics, religion, or wartime; or when a business firm is starting up or facing a survival crisis. For example, Martin Luther King Jr. used his charisma to bring about social equality through nonviolent means; and Steve Jobs achieved unwavering loyalty and commitment from Apple's technical staff in the early 1980s by articulating a vision of personal computers that would dramatically change the way people lived.

What can be said about the charismatic leader's effect on his or her followers? There is increasing support for the idea that there is a strong link between charismatic leadership and high performance and satisfaction among followers—that is, people working for charismatic leaders are motivated to exert extra work effort and, because they like their leader, express greater satisfaction.[8] Although one study found that charismatic CEOs had no impact on subsequent organizational performance, charisma is still believed to be a desirable leadership quality.[9]

Although traits of successful leaders have been identified over the years, these traits alone are not adequate for entirely explaining leadership effectiveness. If they were, then leaders could be identified from childhood. Although you may have been the natural line leader in kindergarten—exhibiting your influencing abilities at an early age—leading requires more. The problem with focusing solely on traits is that it ignores the skills leaders must have, as well as the behaviors they must demonstrate in a number of situations. Fortunately, these latter two—skills and behaviors—can both be learned! Therefore, it is more correct to say that leaders are made.

WHAT IS VISIONARY LEADERSHIP?

The term *vision* appeared a few paragraphs ago in our discussion of charismatic leadership. But visionary leadership goes beyond charisma. In this section, we review recent revelations about the importance of visionary leadership.

visionary leadership
The ability to create and articulate a realistic, credible, attractive vision of the future that grows out of, and improves upon, the present.

Visionary leadership is the ability to create and articulate a realistic, credible, attractive vision of the future for an organization or organizational unit, a vision that grows out of and improves upon the present.[10] This vision, if properly selected and implemented, is so energizing that it "in effect jump-starts the future by calling forth the skills, talents, and resources to make it happen."[11]

---

[7]J. G. Hunt, K. B. Boal, and G. E. Dodge, "The Effects of Visionary and Crisis-Responsive Charisma on Followers: An Experimental Examination," *Leadership Quarterly* (Fall 1999), 423–448; R. J. House and R. N. Aditya, "The Social Scientific Study of Leadership: Quo Vadis?" *Journal of Management* 23, no. 3 (1997), 316–323; and House, "A 1976 Theory of Charismatic Leadership."
[8]Conger and Kanungo, "Behavioral Dimensions," 79.
[9]B. R. Agle, N J. Nagarajan, J. A. Sonnenfeld, and D. Srinivasan, "Does CEO Charisma Matter? An Empirical Analysis of the Relationships Among Organizational Performance, Environmental Uncertainty, and Top Management Team Perceptions of CEO Charisma," *Academy of Management Journal* 49 (February 2006), 161–174.
[10]This definition is based on M. Sashkin, "The Visionary Leader," in *Charismatic Leadership: The Elusive Factor in Organizational Effectiveness*, ed. J. A. Conger, R. N. Kanungo, et al. (San Francisco, CA: Jossey-Bass, 1988), 124–125; B. Nanus, *Visionary Leadership* (New York: Free Press, 1992), 8; N. H. Snyder and M. Graves, "Leadership and Vision," *Business Horizons* 37, no. 1 (January–February 1994), 1; J. R. Lucas, "Anatomy of a Vision Statement," *Management Review* 87, no. 2 (February 1998), 22–26; and S. Marino, "Where There Is No Visionary, Companies Falter," *Industry Week*, March 15, 1999, 20.
[11]Nanus, *Visionary Leadership*, 8.

The key properties of a vision seem to be inspirational possibilities that are value centered, attainable, and well articulated. Visions should be able to create possibilities that are inspirational and unique and offer a new order that can produce organizational distinction. A vision is likely to fail if it doesn't offer a view of the future that is clearly and demonstrably better for the organization and its members. Desirable visions fit the times and circumstances and reflect the uniqueness of the organization. People in the organization must also believe that the vision is attainable. It should be perceived as challenging, yet doable. Visions that have clear articulation and powerful imagery are more easily grasped and accepted.

What are some examples of visions? Sir Richard Branson is the visionary founder and president of Virgin Group, one of the world's most recognized and respected brands in aviation, hospitality and leisure, telecommunications, financial services, health and wellness, and clean energy. Virgin Group operates more than 200 companies worldwide, employing approximately 50,000 people in over thirty countries. Mary Kay Ash's vision of women as entrepreneurs selling products that improved their self-image gave impetus to her cosmetics company. Michael Dell created a vision of a business that allows Dell Computer to sell and deliver a finished PC directly to a customer in fewer than eight days.

What skills do visionary leaders exhibit? Once the vision is identified, these leaders appear to have three qualities that are related to effectiveness in their visionary roles.[12] First is the *ability to explain the vision* to others. The leader needs to make the vision clear in terms of required actions and aims through clear oral and written communication. Former president Ronald Reagan—the so-called great communicator—used his years of acting experience to help him articulate a simple vision for his presidency: a return to happier and more prosperous times through less government, lower taxes, and a strong military.

Second is the *ability to express the vision* not just verbally but through the leader's behavior. This requires behaving in ways that continually convey and reinforce the vision. Herb Kelleher, when he was at the helm of Southwest Airlines, lived and breathed his commitment to customer service. He was famous within the company for jumping in when needed to help check in passengers, load baggage, fill in for flight attendants, or do anything else to make the customer's experience more pleasant. The third skill is the *ability to extend the vision* to different leadership contexts. This is the ability to sequence activities so that the vision can be applied in a variety of situations.

Comprehension Check 9-1

1. The ability to influence others to act in a particular way is called

   a. supervision
   b. leadership
   c. motivation
   d. all of the above

2. Which one of the following is *not* regarded as a leadership trait?

   a. Drive
   b. Self-confidence
   c. Honesty
   d. Vision

   (Continued)

[12]J. R. Baum, E. A. Locke, and S. A. Kirkpatrick, "A Longitudinal Study of the Relation of Vision and Vision Communication to Venture Growth in Entrepreneurial Firms," *Journal of Applied Psychology* 83, no. 1 (February 1998), 43–54.

(Continued)

3. An individual with a compelling sense of purpose that is communicated so that followers can understand is often regarded as a
    a. charismatic leader
    b. transactional leader
    c. autocratic leader
    d. participative leader

4. The ability to create and articulate a realistic and credible view of the future of the organization is called
    a. participative leadership
    b. visionary leadership
    c. charismatic leadership
    d. none of the above

How Do You Become a Leader?

Whether or not you currently hold a formal position of authority over others, you may be in a position to influence others. Becoming a leader, however, requires certain skills (as well as many of the traits described earlier): technical, conceptual, networking, and human relations skills. You're probably thinking you've heard these before. If you are, congratulations. You're paying close attention. Some of these are the competencies that effective supervisors need—as we discussed in Chapter 1. Because of their importance to leadership, let's look at them again—this time with an eye on leadership!

WHY DOES A LEADER NEED TECHNICAL SKILLS?

It's a rare occurrence when you can influence others even though you have absolutely no idea of what they are doing. Although people may respect you as a person, when it comes to influencing them, they would like to believe that you have the experience to make recommendations. This experience generally comes from your technical skills.

Technical skills are the tools, procedures, and techniques that are unique to your specialized situation. You need to master your job in your attempt to be viewed as a source of help—the expert. Others generally won't come to you unless they need assistance. It's often the exceptions that they can't—or are ill equipped to—handle. That's when they'll look to you for guidance. By having the technical skills, you're able to assist. But imagine if you didn't. You'd constantly have to ask someone else for the information. When you got it, you might be unable to adequately explain it to the employee who requested it. At some point, employees may simply go around you and talk directly to the source of the technical information. When that happens, you've lost some of your influence!

The need for knowledge of technical skills related to your job cannot be overstated. Those "in the know" do influence others. If you want followers to have confidence in your advice and the direction you give, they've got to perceive you as a technically competent supervisor.

HOW DO CONCEPTUAL SKILLS AFFECT YOUR LEADERSHIP?

Conceptual skills are your mental ability to coordinate a variety of interests and activities. It means having the ability to think in the abstract, analyze lots of information, and make connections between the data. Earlier, we described an effective leader as someone who could create a vision. To do this, you must be able to think critically and conceptualize things regarding how they could be.

Thinking conceptually is not as easy as you may believe. For some, it may be impossible! That's because to think conceptually, you must look at the infamous "big picture." Too many times, we get caught up in the daily grind, focusing our attention on the minute details. This is not to say that focusing on the details isn't important; without it, little may be accomplished. But setting long-term directions requires you to think about the future, to deal with the uncertainty and the risks of the unknown. To be a good leader, then, you must be able to make some sense out of this chaos and envision what can be.

HOW DO NETWORKING SKILLS MAKE YOU A BETTER LEADER?

Networking skills are your ability to socialize and interact with outsiders—those not associated with your unit. As a leader, it's understood that you cannot do everything by yourself. Obviously, if you did, you'd not be a leader, but rather a superworker! Therefore, you need to know where to go to get the things your followers need. This may mean "fighting" for more resources or establishing relationships outside your area that will provide some benefit to your followers. Networking, if you're making the connection, means having good political skills—a point that shouldn't be overlooked.

Your employees will often look to you to provide them with what they need to do an excellent job. If they can depend on you for providing the tools (or running the interference) they need, you'll once again inspire a level of confidence in your employees. They will also more likely respond better if they know you're willing to fight for them. Instead of finding a hundred reasons why they can't do something, they can come to you for help in finding the one way that will work. You somehow muster the necessary resources and defend what "your people" are doing. In challenging employees to go beyond what they think they are capable of achieving, however, you know that mistakes will be made. When they are, you view them as a learning experience—and something from which to grow.

WHAT ROLE DO HUMAN RELATIONS SKILLS PLAY IN EFFECTIVE LEADERSHIP?

Human relations skills focus on your ability to work with, understand, and motivate those around you. As you've been reading this book, these skills have been highlighted. Good human relations skills require you to communicate effectively—especially your vision—with your employees and those outside of your unit. It also means listening to what they have to say. A good leader is not a know-it-all, but rather someone who freely accepts and encourages involvement from his or her followers.

Human relations skills are the "people skills" frequently mentioned in today's discussion of effective supervision. It's coaching, facilitating, and supporting others around you. It's understanding yourself and being confident in your abilities. It's your honesty in dealing with others and the values you live by. It's your confidence in knowing that by helping others succeed—and letting them get the credit—you're doing the right thing for them, the organization, and yourself.

A coach helps people grow, improve, and perform better. However, a supervisor acting as coach to employees has to deal with the dynamics of the organization as well as the relationship with the employee. Their relationship is more than a coaching one because the supervisor is in a position to know the requirements of the job, the performance of the employee, and the expectations of the organization. In his classic book *A Passion for Excellence*, Tom Peters writes about leaders using coaching as a methodology for leading. He states, "Coaching is face-to-face leadership that pulls together people with diverse backgrounds, talents, experiences and interests, encourages them to step up to responsibility and continued achievement, and treats them as full-scale partners and contributors. Coaching is not about memorizing techniques or devising the perfect game plan. It is about really paying attention to people—really believing them, really caring about them, really involving them."[13]

If an employee's low performance is related to a skill deficiency, training methods may be used to correct the behavior. If substandard performance is not the result of a

Something to Think About (and promote class discussion)

GROWING LEADERS

How important are excellent leaders to organizations? If you were to ask 3M CEO George Buckley, he'd say extremely important. But he'd also say that excellent leaders don't just pop up out of nowhere. A company has to cultivate leaders who have the skills and abilities to help it survive and thrive. And like a successful baseball team with strong performance statistics that has a player development plan in place, 3M has its own farm system. Except that its farm system is designed to develop company leaders.

3M's leadership development program is so effective that in 2009 *Chief Executive* magazine and Hay Consulting Group named the company the best at developing future leaders. What is 3M's leadership program all about? About eight years ago, the company's former CEO (Jim McNerney, who is now Boeing's CEO) and his top team spent eighteen months developing a new leadership model for the company. After numerous brainstorming sessions and much heated debate, the group finally agreed on six "leadership attributes" that they believed were essential for the company to become skilled at executing strategy and being accountable. Those six attributes included the ability to "chart the course; energize and inspire others; demonstrate ethics, integrity, and compliance; deliver results; raise the bar; and innovate resourcefully." And now under Buckley's guidance, the company is continuing and reinforcing its pursuit of leadership excellence with these six attributes.

When asked about his views on leadership, Buckley said that he believes there is a difference between leaders and supervisors. "A leader is as much about inspiration as anything else. A supervisor is more about process." He believes that the key to developing leaders is to focus on those things that can be developed—like strategic thinking. Buckley also believes that leaders should not be promoted up and through the organization too quickly. They need time to experience failures and what it takes to rebuild.

Finally, when asked about his own leadership style, Buckley responded, "The absolutely best way for me to be successful is to have people working for me who are better. Having that kind of emotional self-confidence is vital to leaders. You build respect in those people because you admire what they do. Having built respect, you build trust. However hokey it sounds, it works." And it must be working as the company was named the number one most admired company in the medical and other precision equipment division of *Fortune's* most admired ranking for 2009.

Knowing that you want to advance through the ranks in your organization and become a leader in your own right, what do you think about Buckley's statement that leaders and supervisors differ? Do you agree? Why or why not? Chapter 9 references a number of leadership topics. Out of those topics, which leadership models/theories/issues do you see in this case? List and describe. In regard to 3M, take each of the six leadership attributes that the company feels is important. Explain what you think each one involves. Then discuss how those attributes might be developed and measured. What did you learn about leadership from this discussion?

Sources: J. Kerr and R. Albright, "Finding and Cultivating Finishers," *Leadership Excellence* (July 2009), 20; D. Jones, "3M CEO Emphasizes Importance of Leaders," *USA Today*, May 18, 2009, 4B; G. Colvin, "World's Most Admired Companies 2009," *Fortune*, March 16, 2009, 75+; and M. C. Mankins and R. Steele, "Turning Great Strategy into Great Performance," *Harvard Business Review* (July/August 2005), 64–72.

---

[13]T. Peters and N. Austin, *A Passion for Excellence: The Leadership Difference* (New York: Random House, 1985), 325–326.

skill deficiency, then coaching may be the appropriate response. The dynamic process of coaching requires the supervisor to monitor the employee's performance while reacting to changes in organizational needs and all the while adjusting their approach to the employee. Peters goes on to state, "Coaching is the process of enabling others to act, of building on their strengths. It's counting on people to use their own special skill and competence, and then giving them enough room and enough time to do it. Coaching at its heart involves caring enough about people to take the time to build a personal relationship with them."[14] The coaching process is heavily leveraged by the trust that has been developed between the supervisor and the employee. In all coaching situations, supervisors play active roles in the success and improvement of the employee(s) supervised.

There's one aspect that's almost a guarantee with respect to leadership—that is, if you fail as a leader, it most likely won't be because you lack technical skills. Rather, it's more likely that your followers, as well as others, have lost respect for you because of your lack of human relations skills. If that ever happens, your ability to influence others will be seriously impaired.

One of the interesting aspects of leadership is that traits and skills are difficult for followers to detect. As a result, followers define your leadership by the behaviors they see in you. As the adage goes, actions speak louder than words. It's what you do that matters. Therefore, you need to understand leadership behaviors.

Leadership Behaviors and Styles

The inability to explain leadership solely from traits and skills has led researchers to look at the behaviors and styles that specific leaders have exhibited. Researchers wonder whether there is something unique in the behavior of effective leaders and the style in which they practice their craft. For example, do leaders tend to be more participative than autocratic?

A number of studies have looked at behavioral styles. The most comprehensive and most replicated of the behavioral theories resulted from research that began at Ohio State University in the late 1940s.[15] This study (as well as others) sought to identify independent dimensions of leader behavior. Beginning with more than a thousand dimensions, researchers eventually narrowed the list down to two categories that accounted for most of the leadership behavior described by employees. These are best identified as task-centered and employee-centered behaviors (see Exhibit 9-2).[16]

WHAT IS TASK-CENTERED BEHAVIOR?

A task-centered leader has a strong tendency to emphasize the technical or task aspects of the job. This individual's major concern is ensuring that employees know precisely what is expected of them and providing any guidance necessary for goals to be met. Employees, as viewed by this leader, are a means to an end. That is, to achieve goals, employees have to do their jobs. As long as they do what is expected, this leader is happy. Calling a production-oriented person a leader may be somewhat of a misnomer.

task-centered leader
An individual with a strong tendency to emphasize the technical or task aspects of a job.

---

[14]Ibid, p. 328.
[15]R. M. Stodgill and A. E. Coons, eds., *Leader Behavior: Its Description and Measurement, Research Monograph No. 88* (Columbus, OH: Ohio State University, Bureau of Business Research, 1951).
[16]Stodgill and Coons, *Leader Behavior*; and R. Kahn and D. Katz, "Leadership Practices in Relation to Productivity and Morale," in *Group Dynamics: Research and Theory*, 2nd ed., ed. D. Cartwright and A. Zander (Elmsford, NY: Row, Paterson, 1960), 41.

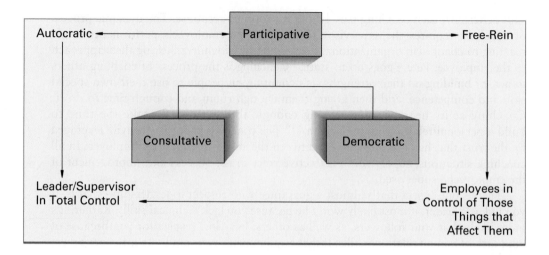

Exhibit 9-2
Supervisory leadership behaviors.

This individual may not lead in the classic sense, but simply ensures compliance with stated rules, regulations, and production goals. In motivational terms, a production-oriented leader frequently exhibits a Theory X orientation (see Chapter 8) or an autocratic/authoritarian leadership style.

An autocratic leader can best be described as a taskmaster. This individual leaves no doubt as to who's in charge and who has the authority and power in the group. He or she makes all the decisions affecting the group and tells others what to do. This telling frequently happens in the form of orders—mandates that are expected to be followed. Failure to obey these orders usually results in some negative reinforcement at the hands of the authoritarian leader. Obviously, autocratic leadership is inappropriate in today's organization. Right? Well, maybe not. There are leaders in all types of organizations—business, government, and the military—for whom the autocratic style works best.

WHAT ARE PEOPLE-CENTERED BEHAVIORS?

A people-centered leader emphasizes interpersonal relations with those he or she leads. This leader takes a personal interest in the needs of his or her employees. A people-centered leader is concerned for employees' welfare. Interactions between this leader and his or her employees are characterized as trusting, friendly, and supportive. Furthermore, this leader is very sensitive to the concerns and feelings of employees. Likewise, from a motivational point of view, a people-centered leader exhibits more Theory Y orientations (see Chapter 8). As a result, this individual often exhibits a participative (or democratic) leadership style.

In a participative leadership style, the leader actively seeks input from followers for many of the activities in the organization. Thus, establishing plans, solving problems, and making decisions are not done solely by the supervisor. Instead, the entire workgroup participates. The only question that really remains is who has the final say. That is, participative leadership can be viewed from two perspectives. First is one where the leader seeks input and hears the concerns and issues of the followers, but makes the final decision. In this capacity, the leader is using the input as an information-seeking exercise. We call this consultative-participative leadership. On the other hand, a participative leader may allow the followers to have a say in what's decided. Here, decisions are made truly by the group. This is referred to as democratic-participative leadership.

autocratic leader
A taskmaster who leaves no doubt as to who's in charge, and who has the authority and power in the group.

people-centered leader
An individual who emphasizes interpersonal relations with those he or she leads.

participative leadership
The leadership style of an individual who actively seeks input from followers for many of the activities in the organization.

consultative-participative leadership
The leadership style of an individual who seeks input and hears the concerns and issues of followers, but makes the final decision using input as an information-seeking exercise.

democratic-participative leadership
A leadership behavior whereby the leader offers followers a say in what is decided; decisions are made by the group.

Beyond participative leadership, there is one other behavioral leadership style. This is often referred to as free-reining. A free-rein (or *laissez-faire*) leader gives employees total autonomy to make the decisions that will affect them. After the leader establishes overall objectives and general guidelines, the employees are free to establish their own plans for achieving their goals. This is not meant to imply that there's a lack of leadership. Rather, it implies that the leader is removed from the day-to-day activities of the employees—but is always available to deal with the exceptions.

free-rein leader
An individual who gives employees total autonomy to make decisions that will affect them.

WHAT BEHAVIOR SHOULD YOU EXHIBIT?

In today's organizations, many employees appear to prefer to work for a supervisor with a people-centered leadership style. However, just because this style appears "friendlier" to employees, we cannot make a sweeping generalization that a people-centered leadership style will make you a more effective supervisor. There has actually been very little success in identifying consistent relationships between patterns of leadership behavior and successful organizational performance. Results vary. In some cases, people-centered styles generate both high productivity and high follower satisfaction. However, in others, followers are happy, but productivity suffers. What sometimes is overlooked in trying to pinpoint one style over the other are the situational factors that influence effective leadership. Our advice is that a supervisor should be prepared to use any style the situation calls for.

Effective Leadership

It became increasingly clear to those studying leadership that predicting leadership success involved something more complex than isolating a few traits or preferable behaviors. The failure to find answers led to a new focus on situational influences. The relationship between leadership style and effectiveness suggested that under Condition A, Style X would be appropriate, whereas Style Y would be more suitable for Condition B, and Style Z for Condition C. But what were the Conditions A, B, C, and so forth? It was one thing to say that leadership effectiveness depended on the situation and another to be able to isolate those situational conditions. The key to many of these situational theories was their inclusion of followers.

Paul Hersey and Kenneth Blanchard proposed a leadership model called situational leadership. They emphasize that leadership styles must adjust to specific situations.[17] Given that without employees there is no leader, situational leadership shows how you should adjust your leadership style to reflect employees' needs.

situational leadership
Adjustment of a leadership style to specific situations to reflect employee needs.

Situational leadership focuses attention on the readiness of employees. Readiness in this context reflects how able and willing an employee is to do a job. Hersey and Blanchard identified four stages of follower readiness:

readiness
The ability and willingness of an employee to complete a task.

- R1: An employee is both unable and unwilling to do a job.
- R2: An employee is unable to do the job but is willing to perform the necessary tasks.
- R3: An employee is able to do the job but is unwilling to do so.
- R4: An employee is both able and willing to do the job.

A point should be made here concerning willingness. As defined, for example, in R1, an employee is unwilling to do something. This is not the same unwillingness that you would associate with being insubordinate. Rather, it's unwillingness because that individual is not confident or competent to do a job.

---

[17]P. Hersey and K. Blanchard, *Management of Organization Behavior: Utilizing Human Resources*, 5th ed. (Upper Saddle River, NJ: Prentice Hall, 1988).

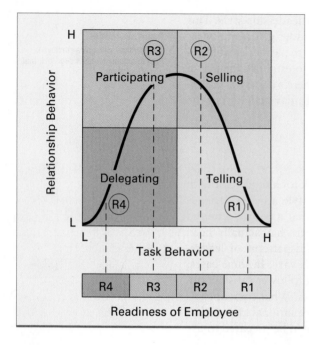

Exhibit 9-3
Situational leadership.

A second component of the model focuses on leader behavior. Leaders must behave in a given way contingent on where an employee is in terms of readiness. Leader behavior in this model reflects the leader–employee communications taking place. Task behavior is viewed as one-way communication—from the leader to the employee. Relationship behavior reflects two-way communication—between the leader and the employee. Given that high and low degrees of these two behaviors can exist, Hersey and Blanchard identified four specific leadership styles based on the maturity of the follower (see Exhibit 9-3).

The Telling leadership style is appropriate with a new employee (R1) uncertain about the job responsibilities and the tasks required. Communication between you and the employee, at this point, needs to be one-way. You need to tell her what to do and give her specific directions on how to do it. The employee will not remain at this stage for long and, after being provided with ample directions and getting more familiar with the job, she'll move to stage R2.

The Selling leadership style works well with an employee at the R2 stage of work development. The employee is more involved in her job, but still lacks some ability and is not fully trained. The R2 employee asks questions about things not fully understood and may question why certain things have to be done as you have asked. There may be a need to sell your ideas to get this employee to accept what you feel is necessary. High degrees of both one-way and two-way communication are happening simultaneously.

The Participating leadership style comes into play after the employee has become expert on her job (R3). Knowing her duties better than anybody, she's beginning to put her special mark on things. You no longer need to tell her what to do, but you still need to be involved in what she's doing. She's not to the point yet where you feel comfortable leaving her totally alone, and you recognize this employee still has some developing to do. This leadership style is supportive and not overly task-centered.

The Delegating leadership style emerges when the employee has fully developed. She has your trust and can carry out her duties with little, if any, direction (R4). She basically needs to be left alone, and you simply assign the tasks and let her do her job. After appraising her performance you know she can and will get the job done. If she needs help, you're always available to deal with the exceptions.

An important aspect of situational leadership is that an employee can be in all four quadrants at the same time. To lead properly, you must be able to exhibit the correct leadership style given what each employee needs. You also need to demonstrate a leadership style that's consistent with your employees' abilities (see "News Flash! National Culture Could Affect Your Leadership Style").

Contemporary Leadership Roles

credibility
Honesty, competence, and the ability to inspire.

trust
The belief in the integrity, character, and ability of a leader.

Let's turn our attention to important issues that every effective supervisor must consider. Specifically, how do you build credibility and trust with your employees, and how can you become a more empowering supervisor?

DO CREDIBILITY AND TRUST REALLY MATTER?

The central component of credibility is honesty. Surveys show that honesty is consistently singled out as the number one characteristic of admired supervisors. "Honesty is absolutely essential to leadership. If people are going to follow someone willingly, whether it

News Flash!

NATIONAL CULTURE COULD AFFECT YOUR LEADERSHIP STYLE

One general conclusion that surfaces from learning about leadership is that you shouldn't use any single leadership style in every case. Instead, you should adjust your style to the situation. Although not mentioned specifically in any of the theories we've presented, national culture is clearly an important situational variable in determining which leadership style will be most effective for you.

National culture affects leadership by way of your employees. You cannot choose your leadership styles at will. Rather, you are constrained by the cultural conditions your employees come to expect. For example, an autocratic leadership style is more compatible with cultures where power is unequal, such as those found in Arab, Far Eastern, and Latin American countries. This cultural "power" ranking should be a good indicator of employees' willingness to accept participative leadership. Participation is likely to be most

effective in cultures where power is more equally distributed—such as those in Norway, Finland, Denmark, and Sweden.

It's important to remember that most leadership theories were developed by North American researchers using North American subjects. The United States, Canada, and the Scandinavian countries all rate below average on "power" criteria. This realization may help explain why our theories tend to favor more participative and empowering styles of leadership. Accordingly, you need to consider national culture as yet another contingency variable in determining your most effective leadership style.

Sources: G. Hofstede, "Motivation, Leadership, and Organization: Do American Theories Apply Abroad?" *Organizational Dynamics* 9, no. 1 (Summer 1980), 57; and A. Ede, "Leadership and Decision Making: Management Styles and Culture," *Journal of Managerial Psychology*, July 1992, 28–31.

be into battle or into the boardroom, they first want to assure themselves that the person is worthy of their trust."[18] In addition to being honest, credible supervisors are competent and inspiring. They need to appear capable and they can be effectively communicating confidence and enthusiasm to their employees. Employees judge their supervisors' credibility in terms of their honesty, competence, and ability to inspire. Ultimately, a supervisor's credibility separates supervisors with followers from supervisors with subordinates and is built on the quality of relationships that exist between the supervisors and their employees.

Trust, closely connected with the concept of credibility, is defined as the belief in the integrity, character, and ability of a leader. When employees trust their supervisor, they're willing to be vulnerable to their supervisor's actions because they're confident that their rights and interests won't be abused.[19] Research has identified five dimensions that make up the concept of trust:[20]

■ Integrity: honesty and truthfulness
■ Competence: technical and interpersonal knowledge and skills
■ Consistency: reliability, predictability, and good judgment in handling situations
■ Loyalty: willingness to protect a person, physically and emotionally
■ Openness: willingness to share ideas and information freely

Of these five dimensions, integrity seems to be the most critical when someone assesses another's trustworthiness.[21] Additionally, both integrity and competence are leadership traits consistently associated with successful supervisors.

---

[18]J. M. Kouzes and B. Z. Posner, *Credibility: How Leaders Gain and Lose It, and Why People Demand It* (San Francisco, CA: Jossey-Bass, 1993), 14.

[19]J. D. Lewis and A. Weigert, "Trust as a Social Reality," *Social Forces*, June 1985, 970.

[20]P. L. Schindler and C. C. Thomas, "The Structure of Interpersonal Trust in the Workplace," *Psychological Reports*, October 1993, 563–573.

[21]H. H. Tan and C. S. F. Tan, "Toward the Differentiation of Trust in Supervisor and Trust in Organization," *Genetic, Social, and General Psychology Monographs* 126, no. 2 (May 2000), 241–260.

WHY ARE CREDIBILITY AND TRUST IMPORTANT?

The top rating of honesty as an identifying characteristic of admired supervisors indicates the importance of credibility and trust to leadership effectiveness.[22] This has probably always been true. However, recent changes in the workplace have reignited interest and concern about supervisors building trust.

The trend toward empowering employees and creating self-managed work teams has reduced or removed many of the traditional control mechanisms used to monitor employees. As employees become increasingly free to schedule their own work, evaluate their own performance, and in some cases, even make their own team hiring decisions, trust becomes critical. Employees have to trust supervisors to treat them fairly, and supervisors have to trust employees to fulfill their responsibilities conscientiously.

Supervisors must increasingly lead others who are not in their direct line of authority—members of project teams, individuals who work for suppliers, customers, and people who represent other organizations through such arrangements as corporate partnerships. These situations don't allow supervisors to fall back on their formal positions to exact compliance. Many of the relationships, in fact, are dynamic. The ability to develop trust quickly may be crucial to the success of such relationships (see the section titled "Building Trust" at the end of this chapter).

Now, more than ever, supervisory leadership effectiveness depends on the ability to gain the trust of followers.[23] Downsizing, corporate financial misrepresentations, and the increased use of temporary employees have undermined employees' trust in their leaders and shaken the confidence of investors, suppliers, and customers. A survey found that only 39 percent of U.S. employees and 51 percent of Canadian employees trusted their executive leaders.[24] Today's supervisors have the challenge of rebuilding and restoring trust with their employees.

WHAT IF YOU PLAY FAVORITES?

You would think that one way to undermine employees' trust in you would be for you to be seen as someone who plays favorites. In many cases you'd be right. But many supervisors, it appears, play favorites. That is, they do not treat all their employees in the same manner. You're likely to have favorite employees who make up your "in-group." You'll have a special relationship with this small group. You'll trust them, give them a lot of your attention, and often give them special privileges. Not surprisingly, they'll perceive themselves as having preferred status. Be aware that this creation of a favored in-group can undermine your credibility, especially among employees outside this in-group.

Be cautious of this tendency to create favorites in your department. You're human, so you'll naturally find some employees you feel closer to and with whom you'll want to be more open. What you need to think through is whether you want this favoritism to show. When this favored-employee status is granted to someone based on nonperformance criteria—for example, because you share similar interests or common personality traits—it is likely to lessen your leadership effectiveness. However, it may have a place when you favor employees who are high performers. In such cases, you are rewarding a behavior that you want to reinforce. Be careful when you follow this practice. Unless performance measures are objective and widely visible, you may be seen as arbitrary and unfair.

---

[22]J. M. Kouzes and B. Z. Posner, *Credibility: How Leaders Gain and Lose It, and Why People Demand It* (San Francisco, CA: Jossey-Bass, 1993), 14.

[23]R. Zemke, "The Confidence Crisis," *Training* (June 2004), 22–30; J.A. Byrne, "Restoring Trust in Corporate America," *Business Week*, June 24, 2002, 30–35; S. Armour, "Employees' New Motto: Trust No One," *USA Today*, February 5, 2002, 1B; J. Scott, "Once Bitten, Twice Shy: A World of Eroding Trust," *New York Times*, April 21, 2002, WK5; J. Brockner, P. A. Siegel, J. P. Daly, T. Tyler, and C. Martin, "When Trust Matters: The Moderating Effect of Outcome Favorability," *Administrative Science Quarterly* 42 (September 1997), 558.

[24]"Weathering the Storm: A Study of Employee Attitudes and Opinions," *WorkUSA 2002 Study*, Watson Wyatt, http://www.watsonwyatt.com/research/printable.asp?id=w-557, accessed August 1, 2011.

HOW CAN YOU LEAD THROUGH EMPOWERMENT?

Several times in different sections of this text, we've stated that supervisors increasingly lead by empowering their employees. Millions of individual employees and teams of employees are making key operating decisions that directly affect their work. They are developing budgets, scheduling workloads, controlling inventories, solving quality problems, evaluating their own performance, and so on—activities that until very recently were viewed exclusively as part of the supervisor's job.

The increased use of empowerment is being driven by two forces. First is the need for quick decisions by people who are most knowledgeable about the issues. That requires, at times, moving decisions to employee levels. If organizations are to compete successfully in a dynamic global village, they have to be able to make decisions and implement changes quickly. Second is the reality that the downsizing and restructuring of organizations left many supervisors with considerably larger spans of control than they had earlier. To cope with the demands of an increased workload, supervisors have to empower their people. As a result, they are sharing power and responsibility with their employees. This means their role is to show trust on, provide vision to, remove performance-blocking barriers from the path of, offer encouragement to, motivate, and coach employees.

Does this wholesale support of shared leadership appear strange, given the attention paid earlier to contingency theories of leadership? If it doesn't, it should. Why? Because empowerment proponents are essentially advocating a noncontingent approach to leadership. That means they claim that empowerment will work anywhere. So, directive, task-oriented, autocratic leadership is out.

The problem with this kind of thinking is that the current empowerment movement ignores the extent to which leadership can be shared and the conditions facilitating successful shared leadership. Because of factors such as downsizing—which results in the need for higher-level employee skills, continuous employee training, implementation of continuous-improvement programs, and introduction of self-managed teams—the need for shared leadership is increasing. But that is not true in all situations. Blanket acceptance of empowerment or any universal approach to leadership is inconsistent with the best and most current evidence we have on leadership.

Leadership Issues Today

We finish this chapter by looking at two current debates surrounding leadership: the movement from transactional to transformational leadership and team leadership. The section ends with a discussion on leadership relevance.

WHAT ARE TRANSACTIONAL AND TRANSFORMATIONAL LEADERS?

It is important to differentiate between transactional leaders and transformational leaders.[25] As you'll see, because transformational leaders are also charismatic, there is some overlap between this topic and the preceding discussion on charismatic traits.

Most leadership models address transactional leaders. These leaders guide or motivate their employees in the direction of established goals by clarifying role and task requirements. Another type of leader inspires followers to transcend their own self-interests for the good of the organization. This leader is capable of having a profound and extraordinary effect on his or her followers. These are called transformational leaders. They pay attention to the concerns and developmental needs of employees;

transactional leader
A leader who guides or motivates employees in the direction of established goals by clarifying role and task requirements.

transformational leader
A leader who inspires followers to transcend self-interests for the good of the organization and who is capable of having a profound and extraordinary effect on followers.

---

[25]B. M. Bass, "From Transactional to Transformational Leadership: Learning to Share the Vision," *Organizational Dynamics* 18, no. 3 (Winter 1990), 19–31.

they change employees' awareness of issues by helping them look at old problems in new ways; and they excite, arouse, and inspire followers to put out extra effort to achieve group goals.

Transactional and transformational supervision should not be viewed as opposing approaches to getting things done. Transformational supervision is built on top of transactional supervision. Transformational supervision produces levels of employee effort and performance that go beyond what would occur with a transactional approach alone. Moreover, transformational supervision is more than charisma. "The purely charismatic [leader] may want employees to adopt the charismatic's world view and go no further. The transformational supervisor will attempt to instill in employees the ability to question not only established views but eventually those established by the leader."[26]

The evidence supporting the superiority of transformational supervision over the transactional variety is overwhelmingly impressive. In summary, it indicates that transformational supervision leads to lower turnover rates, higher productivity, and higher employee satisfaction.

WHAT IS TEAM LEADERSHIP?

Leadership is increasingly taking place within a team context. As teams grow in popularity, the role of the leader in guiding team members takes on heightened importance. And the role of team leader is different from the traditional leadership role performed by first-line supervisors. J. D. Bryant, a supervisor at Texas Instruments' Forest Lane plant in Dallas, found that out.[27] One day he was happily overseeing a staff of fifteen circuit-board assemblers. The next day he was informed that the company was moving to teams and that he was to become a "facilitator." "I'm supposed to teach the teams everything I know and then let them make their own decisions," he said. Confused about his new role, he admitted, "There was no clear plan on what I was supposed to do." In this section, we consider the challenge of being a team leader, review the new roles that team leaders take on, and offer some tips on how to increase the likelihood that you can perform effectively in this position.

Many leaders are not equipped to handle the change to teams. As one prominent consultant noted, "Even the most capable managers have trouble making the transition because all the command-and-control-type things they were encouraged to do before are no longer appropriate. There's no reason to have any skill or sense of this." This same consultant estimated that "probably 15 percent of managers are natural team leaders; another 15 percent could never lead a team because it runs counter to their personality. [They're unable to sublimate their dominating style for the good of the team.] Then there's that huge group in the middle: Team leadership doesn't come naturally to them, but they can learn it."[28]

The challenge for most supervisors, then, is to learn how to become an effective team leader. They have to learn skills such as the patience to share information, to trust others, and to give up authority, and understanding when to intervene. Effective leaders have mastered the difficult balancing act of knowing when to leave their teams alone and when to intercede. New team leaders may try to retain too much control at a time when team members need more autonomy, or they may abandon their teams at times when the teams need support and help.[29]

---

[26]B. J. Avolio and B. M. Bass, "Transformational Leadership: Charisma and Beyond," working paper, School of Management, State University of New York, Binghamton (1995), 14.

[27]S. Caminiti, "What Team Leaders Need to Know," *Fortune*, February 20, 1995, 93–100.

[28]Caminiti, "What Team Leaders Need to Know," 93–100.

[29]W. H. Decker and D. M. Rotondo, "Relationships Among Gender, Types of Humor, and Perceived Leader Effectiveness," *Journal of Managerial Issues* 13, no. 4 (Winter 2001), 450–466; and S. Simsarian, "Leadership and Trust Facilitating Cross-Functional Team Success," *Journal of Management Development* 21, no. 3 (March–April 2002), 201–215.

WHAT IS E-LEADERSHIP?

Leading employees physically separated from the organization is a challenge for supervisors in the twenty-first century. Generally, leadership is viewed as an interaction between personnel who are physically present in the organization and able to receive face-to-face communication. Changes in communication technology have changed the reality of modern supervisors, and they are often called upon to manage workers geographically dispersed around the country or even the globe. Virtual teams and telecommuting employees are linked to the office via computers and Internet connections, receiving all official communication by e-mail.

Because e-leadership is a relatively new phenomenon in the business world, there is a paucity of information regarding motivation techniques for dispersed employees. However, it is important for leaders to consider their behavior in situations defined by Internet interactions. Communications lacking the support of nonverbal behavior can easily be misunderstood and terse messages in an all caps format may be misinterpreted as aggressive regardless of the use of emoticons in an attempt to soften the message.

Effective e-leadership requires supervisors to be judicious in their choice of words while monitoring their messages for anything that may appear to have subliminal meaning to the reader. E-leaders must consider what they want their readers to perceive and keep in mind that the development of trust in long-distance leadership situations may be difficult to achieve. The writing ability of the e-leader will be a necessary component of effective interpersonal leadership skills as more supervisors find themselves managing widely geographically dispersed employees.[30]

IS LEADERSHIP ALWAYS RELEVANT?

We conclude this section by offering this opinion: The belief that a particular leadership style will always be effective regardless of the situation may not be true. Leadership may not always be important. Data from numerous studies demonstrate that, in many situations, any behaviors a leader exhibits are irrelevant. Certain individual, job, and organizational variables can act as substitutes for leadership or neutralize the leader's ability to influence followers.[31] These things make it impossible for leader behavior to make any difference in follower outcomes. They negate the leader's influence.

Substitutes, on the other hand, make a leader's influence not only impossible but also unnecessary. They act as a replacement for the leader's influence. For instance, characteristics of employees such as experience, training, professional orientation, or indifference toward organizational matters can substitute for, or neutralize, the effect of leadership. Experience and training, for instance, can replace the need for a leader to organize jobs and reduce task ambiguity. Jobs that are inherently unambiguous and routine (e.g., working on an assembly line) or that are intrinsically satisfying (e.g., a research scientist) may place fewer demands on the leadership variable. Organizational characteristics such as explicit formalized goals, rigid rules and procedures, and cohesive workgroups can also substitute for leadership.

---

[30]S. Robbins and T. Judge, *Organizational Behavior*, 13th ed. (Upper Saddle River, NJ: Pearson Prentice Hall, 2009), 431–432.

[31]See, for example, S. Kerr and J. M. Jermier, "Substitutes for Leadership: Their Meaning and Measurement," *Organization Behavior and Human Performance* 22, no. 3 (December 1978), 375–403; J. P. Howell and P. W. Dorfman, "Substitutes for Leadership: Test of a Construct," *Academy of Management Journal* 24, no. 4 (December 1981), 714–728; J. P. Howell, P. W. Dorfman, and S. Kerr, "Leadership and Substitutes for Leadership," *Journal of Applied Behavioral Science* 22, no. 1 (1986), 29–46; J. P. Howell, D. E. Bowen, P. W. Dorfman, S. Kerr, and P. M. Podsakoff, "Substitutes for Leadership: Effective Alternatives to Ineffective Leadership," *Organizational Dynamics*, 19, no. 1 (Summer 1990), 21–38; P. M. Podsakoff, S. B. MacKenzie, and W. H. Bommer, "Meta-Analysis of the Relationships between Kerr and Jermier's Substitutes for Leadership and Employee Attitudes, Role Perceptions, and Performance," *Journal of Applied Psychology* 81 (August 1996), 380–399; and J. M. Jermier and S. Kerr, "Substitutes for Leadership: Their Meaning and Measurement—Contextual Recollections and Current Observations," *Leadership Quarterly* 8, no. 2 (1997), 95–101.

This realization that leaders don't always have an effect on those they are suppose to lead should not be that alarming. After all, factors such as attitudes, personality, ability, and group norms have been documented as having an effect on employee performance and satisfaction. Yet supporters of the leadership concept have tended to place an undue burden on leadership for explaining and predicting behavior. It is too simplistic to state that employees are guided to goal accomplishment solely by the actions of a leader. It's important, therefore, to recognize that leadership is another variable in organizational effectiveness. In some situations, it may contribute a lot to employee productivity, absence, turnover, citizenship, and satisfaction. But in other situations, it may contribute little toward those ends.

Comprehension Check 9-2

5. A taskmaster is often referred to as a(n) _____ leader.
   a. task-centered
   b. autocratic
   c. people-centered
   d. participative

6. A person who gives employees total autonomy to make decisions that will affect them is called a _____ leader.
   a. participative
   b. democratic
   c. free-reign
   d. people-centered

7. An employee who is able to do the job, but unwilling to be told by a leader what to do, would be classified at which readiness level in the situational leadership model?
   a. R-4
   b. R-3
   c. R-2
   d. R-1

8. Which one of the following is *not* a dimension of trust?
   a. Consistency
   b. Loyalty
   c. Openness
   d. Risk taking

Enhancing Understanding

SUMMARY

After reading this chapter, I can:

1. **Define *leadership* and describe the difference between a leader and a supervisor.** Leadership is the ability to influence others. The main difference between a leader and a supervisor is that a supervisor is appointed. A supervisor has legitimate power that allows him or her to reward and punish. A supervisor's ability to influence is founded on the formal authority inherent in his or her position. In contrast, a leader may either be appointed or emerge from within a group. A leader can influence others to perform beyond the actions dictated by formal authority.

2. **Identify the traits that may help you become a successful leader.** Six traits have been found on which leaders differ from nonleaders: drive, the desire to influence others, honesty and moral character, self-confidence, intelligence, and relevant knowledge. Yet possession of these traits is no guarantee of leadership because they ignore situational factors.

3. **Define *charisma* and its key components.** Charisma is a magnetism that inspires employees to reach goals that are perceived as difficult or unpopular. Charismatic leaders are self-confident, possess a vision of a better future, have a strong belief in that vision, engage in unconventional behaviors, have a high degree of self-monitoring, and are perceived as agents of radical change.

4. **Describe the skills of a visionary leader.** Several skills are associated with visionary leaders. Although possessing these skills is not a guarantee that someone will be a visionary leader, those who are visionary leaders frequently exhibit them: (1) the ability to explain, both verbally and in writing, the vision to others in a way that is clear in terms of required actions; (2) the ability to express the vision through one's behavior so that it reinforces to organizational members the importance of the vision; and (3) the ability to extend the vision to different leadership contexts, gaining commitment and understanding from organizational members regardless of their department affiliation or location.

5. **Differentiate between task-centered and people-centered leadership behaviors.** Task-centered leadership behaviors focus on the technical or task aspects of a job. People-centered leadership behaviors focus on interpersonal relations with employees.

6. **Identify and describe three types of participative leadership styles.** The three types of participative leadership styles are consultative (seeking input from employees), democratic (giving employees a role in making decisions), and free-rein (giving employees total autonomy to make the decisions that affect them).

7. **Explain situational leadership.** Situational leadership involves adjusting one's leadership style to the readiness level of the employee for a given set of tasks. Given an employee's ability and willingness to do a specific job, a situational leader will use one of four leadership styles—telling, selling, participating, or delegating.

8. **Describe situations in which leadership is irrelevant.** Leadership may be irrelevant in situations where certain individual, job, or organizational variables substitute for a leader. These situations may involve experience, professional orientation, routine jobs, or formalized rules and procedures.

COMPREHENSION: Review and Discussion Questions

1. "All supervisors should be leaders, but not all leaders should be supervisors." Do you agree or disagree? Support your position.

2. How is intelligence related to leadership?

3. What is charismatic leadership? Why might high self-monitors be more effective leaders? Discuss.

4. How are technical, conceptual, networking, and human relations skills linked to effective leadership?

5. What's the difference between a task-centered and a people-centered supervisor? Which do you believe employees would rather work for? Why? Which would you prefer to work for? Explain.

6. Compare and contrast consultative, democratic, and free-rein styles of participative leadership.

7. How can supervisors be both flexible and consistent in their leadership styles? Aren't these contradictory? Explain.

8. How could a professor apply situational leadership with students in a classroom setting?

9. What role do credibility and trust play in leadership?

10. "Given the emphasis on caring for employees, women may be more effective supervisors." Do you agree or disagree? Support your position.

KEY CONCEPT CROSSWORD

ACROSS

1. a leader who seeks input from followers but makes the final decision
6. a leader who guides or motivates employees in the direction of established goals
7. the belief in the integrity and character of a leader
8. the ability to influence others to act in a particular way
9. a leadership style of an individual who actively seeks input from followers
10. the adjustment of leadership type based on employee needs
14. the ability and willingness of an employee to complete a task
15. an individual with a compelling vision or sense of purpose
16. a leader who offers followers a say in what is decided and the group makes the decision
17. a leader who inspires followers to transcend their self-interests for the good of the organization

DOWN

2. qualities such as intelligence, charm, decisiveness, and enthusiasm
3. a leader who emphasizes interpersonal relations with those he or she leads
4. honesty, competency, and the ability to inspire
5. the ability to create and articulate a realistic, credible, attractive picture of the future
11. a leader with a strong tendency to emphasize the technical aspects of a job
12. a leader who is characterized as a taskmaster
13. a leader who gives employees total autonomy to make decisions that will affect them

ANSWERS TO COMPREHENSION CHECKS

Comprehension Check 9-1

1. b 2. d 3. a 4. b

Comprehension Check 9-2

5. b 6. c 7. b 8. d

Developing Your Supervisory Skills

GETTING TO KNOW YOURSELF

Before you can effectively supervise others, you must understand your present strengths and areas in need of development. To assist in this learning process, we encourage you to complete the following self-assessments from the Prentice Hall Self-Assessment Library 3.4.

1. What's My Leadership Style? (II. B. 1.)
2. Do Others See Me as Trusting? (II. B. 4.)

3. How Willing Am I to Delegate? (III. A. 2.)
4. How Charismatic Am I? (II. B. 2)
5. Do I Trust Others? (II. B. 3.)

After you complete the assessment, we suggest you retain the results and store them as part of your "portfolio of learning about yourself."

BUILDING A TEAM

➤ An Experiential Exercise: Leadership Characteristics

Objective: To compare characteristics intuitively related to leadership with leadership characteristics found in leadership theory.

Procedure: Identify three people (friends, relatives, previous boss, public figures, etc.) whom you consider to be outstanding leaders. For each individual, list why you feel he or she is a good leader. Compare your lists of the three individuals. Which traits, if any, are common to all three?

Your instructor will lead the class in a discussion of leadership characteristics based on your lists. Students will call out what they identified, and your instructor

will write down the traits. When all students have shared their lists, class discussion will focus on the following questions:

1. Which characteristics consistently appeared on students' lists?
2. Were these characteristics more trait oriented or behavior oriented?
3. In which situations were these characteristics useful?
4. What, if anything, does this exercise suggest about leadership attributes?

➤ Internet: Web Activity

Go to http://www.pearsonhighered.com/robbins/. Find *Supervision Today!* 7th Ed. and click Companion Website.

MENTORING OTHERS

➤ Building Trust

Given the importance trust plays in the leadership equation, today's leaders should actively seek to build trust with their followers. Here are some suggestions for achieving that goal.

STEPS IN PRACTICING THE SKILL

STEP 1: **Practice openness.** Mistrust comes as much from what people don't know as from what they do know. Openness leads to confidence and trust. So, keep

people informed, make clear the criteria on how decisions are made, explain the rationale for your decisions, be candid about problems, and fully disclose relevant information.

STEP 2: **Be fair.** Before making decisions or taking actions, consider how others will perceive them in terms of objectivity and fairness. Give credit where credit is due, be objective and impartial in performance appraisals, and pay attention to equity perceptions in reward distributions.

STEP 3: Speak your feelings. Leaders who convey only hard facts come across as cold and distant. When you share your feelings, others will see you as real and human. They will know who you are and their respect for you will increase.

STEP 4: Tell the truth. If honesty is critical to credibility, you must be perceived as someone who tells the truth. Followers are more tolerant of learning something they "don't want to hear" than of finding out that their leader lied to them.

STEP 5: Be consistent. People want predictability. Mistrust comes from not knowing what to expect. Take the time to think about your values and beliefs. Then, let them consistently guide your decisions. When you know your central purpose, your actions will follow accordingly, and you will project a consistency that earns trust.

STEP 6: Fulfill your promises. Trust requires that people believe that you are dependable. So, you need to keep your word. Promises made must be promises kept.

STEP 7: Maintain confidences. You trust those whom you believe to be discreet and whom you can rely on. If people make themselves vulnerable by telling you something in confidence, they need to feel assured that you won't discuss it with others or betray that confidence. If people perceive you as someone who leaks personal confidences or someone who can't be depended on, you won't be perceived as trustworthy.

STEP 8: Demonstrate confidence. Develop the admiration and respect of others by demonstrating technical and professional ability. Pay particular attention to developing and displaying your communication, negotiating, and other interpersonal skills.

_____

Sources: Based on F. Bartolome, "Nobody Trusts the Boss Completely—Now What?" *Harvard Business Review* 67 (March–April 1989), 135–142; J. K. Butler, Jr., "Toward Understanding and Measuring Conditions of Trust: Evolution of a Condition of Trust Inventory," *Journal of Management* 17 (September 1991), 643–663; and J. Finegan, "Ready, Aim, Focus," *Inc.,* March 1997, 53.

➤ Communicating Effectively

1. Think about a person in your life (a parent, a supervisor, a teacher, etc.) who influenced you to the extent that you enthusiastically gave 110 percent. Describe the characteristics of this individual. Pick one of the contemporary leadership theories in this chapter and relate your list to the model, explaining how your "leader" demonstrated the attributes of your selected theory.

THINKING CRITICALLY

➤ Case 9-A: Making a Mark as a Leader

Robert Mark is twenty-two years old and will be receiving his BS degree in mathematics from Concordia University in Montreal at the end of this semester. He spent the past two summers working for Montreal Insurance Services (MIS), filling in on a number of different jobs while employees took their vacations. He's received and accepted an offer to join MIS as a supervisor in the policy renewal department on a permanent basis upon graduation.

Montreal Insurance Services is a large insurance company. In the headquarters office alone, where Robert will work, there are 11,000 employees. The company believes strongly in the personal development of its employees. This translates into a philosophy, flowing down from senior officials, of trust and respect for all MIS employees.

The job Robert will be assuming requires him to work with and supervise the activities of eighteen policy renewal representatives. The unit's job responsibility is to ensure that renewal notices are sent on current policies, to tabulate any changes in premiums from a standardized table, and to advise the sales division if a policy is to be canceled as a result of nonresponse to renewal notices.

Robert's department is composed of individuals ranging in age from nineteen to sixty-two years. The median age is thirty-eight. The salary range for policy renewal representatives is $2,480 to $3,000 per month (in U.S. dollars). Robert will be replacing a longtime MIS employee, Peter Finch. Peter is retiring after thirty-seven years with MIS, the last eleven spent as the policy renewal supervisor. Because Robert spent a few weeks in Peter's department last summer, he's familiar with Peter's leadership style and knows most of the departmental employees. He anticipates no problems from any of his soon-to-be employees, except, possibly, for Uri Garavich. Uri is well into his forties, has been a policy renewal representative for more than sixteen years, and as one of the senior members of the department, carries a lot of weight with other employees. It may be important to note that Uri didn't apply for the supervisor's job Robert got. He simply didn't want the formal responsibility of being a supervisor—even though it would have meant about a 15 percent pay raise! He felt the job duties might interfere with his primary outside interest—coaching his son's ice hockey team. Nonetheless, Robert has concluded that his job could prove very difficult without Uri's support.

Robert is determined to get his leadership of the department off on the right foot. As a result, he's been doing a lot of thinking about the qualities of an effective supervisor.

➤ Case 9-B: Order Up!

As chief executive chef of a large, national, themed restaurant chain, hoping to go international in the next five years, Koptra Galwal worked hard to inspire the restaurant's employees. He planned to expand the number of restaurants, improve profitability, and enhance all aspects of customer service. His active leadership style matches his big plans, but many have commented on his ability to lead from both directions. That is, he inspires people from the top down and the bottom up.

Galwal's top-down style was evident in his approach to assessment of organizational decisions. His bottom-up approach showed as he recruited from the nation-wide chain of restaurants to find employees willing to participate in and report on benchmarking customer service, menu items, and competitive advantages. He knew in his heart that employees working in the company's restaurants were the ones who innovated on a daily basis, as he once had while working as a chef in the back of the house.

Galwal is confident working simultaneously in multiple directions, but not all of his supervisory management team was. It took awhile for everyone to adjust to information flowing in from far-flung locations and from the bottom up as well as the top down, but eventually the culture took hold in the organization. His supervisors were also encouraged to develop and implement new ideas to add to the corporate body of knowledge. He sets the direction but he believes in the process he has developed and so he lets his people run with their ideas.

Galwal is also a stickler for detail. He reviewed company-wide training procedures for front of the house employees and found wide variation in the normative behaviors of multiple locations of the restaurant chain. He sought input and then designed the menu as well as the script for hosts and hostesses in his restaurants in an attempt to provide a feeling of familiarity for customers regardless of where in the country they dined. He established back-of-the-house procedures for cooks and food prep and sanitation employees based on his considerable personal experience in the food service industry.

RESPONDING TO THE CASE

1. What critical factors will affect Robert's success as a leader? Do you believe these factors would be the same if success were defined as group satisfaction rather than group productivity?

2. Do you think that Robert can choose a leadership style? If so, describe the style you think would be most effective for him. If not, why?

3. What suggestions might you make to Robert to help him win the support of Uri Garavich? What factors may be important in determining the leadership style to use with Uri?

RESPONDING TO THE CASE

1. How would you describe Koptra Galwal's leadership style? Why?

2. Do you think these leadership styles were beneficial for this organization? Why or why not?

3. Imagine you are a supervisor working for Koptra Galwal, how would his style influence your behavior as a leader? Is he transformative or transactional?

Communicating Effectively

Key Concepts

After completing this chapter, you will be able to define these supervisory terms:

- active listening
- assertiveness training
- body language
- channel
- communication
- decoding
- encoding
- feedback loop

- formal communication
- grapevine
- informal communication
- message
- nonverbal communication
- richness of information
- roles
- verbal intonation

Chapter Outcomes

After reading this chapter, you will be able to:

1. Define *communication* and the communication process.
2. Contrast formal and informal communication.
3. Explain how electronic communication affects the supervisor's job.
4. List barriers to effective communication.
5. Describe techniques for overcoming communication barriers.
6. List the requirements for active listening.
7. Explain the behaviors necessary for providing effective feedback.

Responding to a Supervisory Dilemma

Communication takes place every day in every organization, in all areas, and by all organizational members. Most of that communication tends to be work related, but as the following story shows, sometimes that communication doesn't lead to positive outcomes.

Sixty percent of respondents in a recent employee survey said that gossip was their biggest pet peeve about their jobs. Most gossip centers around the workplace and the personal lives of coworkers. How often have you gossiped at work—either as a sender or as a receiver? Although you may think workplace gossip is harmless, it can have some pretty serious consequences. First, spreading rumors can damage morale and increase anxiety. Second, it can hamper productivity and impact performance. And it can lead to something you might not even have considered, as it did for four former employees of the town of Hooksett, New Hampshire. Fired by the city council for gossiping about their boss, they learned the hard way that gossip can cost you your job.*

The longtime employees were fired because one of the women had used derogatory terms to describe the town administrator and because all of them had discussed a rumor that he was having an affair with a female subordinate. All four of the women acknowledged feeling resentment toward the woman, who worked in a specially created position and was paid more than two of the gossiping employees, despite having less experience and seniority.

Despite an appeal of their dismissal by the four employees, the Hooksett council didn't budge and stated, "These employees do not represent the best interests of the town of Hooksett and the false rumors, gossip and derogatory statements have contributed to a negative working environment and malcontent among their fellow employees." Despite national media attention and a petition signed by 419 residents asking for the women to be reinstated, the city council didn't waver on its decision. An attorney for the four women said that his clients were "legitimately questioning the conduct of their supervisor, and whether the female subordinate was getting preferential treatment. It almost cheapens it to call it gossip. It might have been idle, not particularly thoughtful, talk. But there was no harm intended."

Although the four women represented nearly fifty years of combined service to the city and all had positive performance reviews, the town council believed that the women's actions were "insubordinate" and "dishonest." All four received a settlement for being fired, which cost the town a total of $330,000. The settlement agreement also stipulated, however, that two of the women can never apply for a job with the town again.

What do you think? Gossip is interpersonal communication, but it presents an ethical dilemma relating to the distortion of information and is something that supervisors have to deal with. Is it okay for employees to openly gossip about others in the organization? Do you agree with the action of the city council? If the women in this story had taken their concerns to management regarding the alleged affair, how do you think it would have changed the outcome? Viewed in a different context, does the story shift from one of malicious gossip to one of concern over a potential sexual harassment situation? What guidelines would you suggest for supervisors who want guidance in deciding when it is appropriate to control workplace gossip?

*J. McGregor, "Mining the Office Chatter," *BusinessWeek*, May 19, 2008, 54; E. Zimmerman, "Gossip Is Information by Another Name," *New York Times Online*, February 3, 2008; A. Fisher, "Harmless Office Chitchat or Poisonous Gossip?" *CNNMoney.com*, November 12, 2007; S. Armour, "Did You Hear the Story About Office Gossip?" *USA Today*, September 10, 2007, 1B+; "Women Lose Jobs over Office Scuttlebutt," *AARP Bulletin*, July–August 2007, 11; G. Cuyler, "Hooksett 4 to Seek Judge's Aid in Getting Jobs Back," *New Hampshire Union Leader*, June 25, 2007; and P. B. Erickson, "Drawing the Line Between Gossip, Watercooler Chat," *NewsOK.com*, June 15, 2007.

The following episodes occurred in one eight-hour day at a large Marriott hotel in Phoenix, Arizona.

Episode 1: The supervisor of convention sales, Ronnie Barnes, was reviewing last quarter's sales report in preparation for a performance review with each of her three employees. Concerned particularly about Patti Williams's performance, Ronnie called Patti into her office. "Patti, I just saw your last quarter's sales numbers. I thought we had agreed on a goal of six major conventions [1,000 or more room nights] for the quarter. Now I'm looking at the data and it says you booked only four. What happened?" "I don't understand the problem," Patti responded. "Six was our goal—my target. It was something we were trying to reach. I didn't understand that to mean that it was a do-or-die proposition." Patti was noticeably upset, and Ronnie was trying to control her frustration. "Patti, six was our goal all right. But it wasn't some 'pie-in-the-sky' number. It was the minimum number of bookings we were counting on you to make. You're responsible for getting us the big conventions. Robin and Carlos handle the smaller ones. You know we rely on the big conventions to keep our occupancy rates up. I told Liz [the hotel's general manager and Ronnie's immediate boss] we'd book at least six big conventions in the second quarter. Now I've got to explain why we missed our goal!"

Episode 2: A memo had gone out a number of months previously from the hotel's director of human resources to all managers and supervisors. The topic of the memo was a change in the hotel's leave-without-pay policy. A complaint from the buyer in the food and beverage department had just been received by the director of human resources. The employee's complaint was that his request for a two-week leave without pay to handle personal and financial problems related to the death of his mother had been denied by his supervisor. He felt his request was reasonable and should have been approved. Interestingly, the memo in question specifically stated that leaves of up to three weeks because of a death in the family were to be uniformly approved. When the human resource director called the food and beverage supervisor to follow up on the employee complaint, she was told by the supervisor, "I never knew there was a change of policy on leaves without pay."

Episode 3: The following conversation took place between two bellhops. "Did you hear the latest? The general manager's daughter is marrying some guy from New Jersey who's serving a five-year sentence for some offense he committed in his franchise. Heard it involved millions of dollars." "You're kidding!" responded the other. "No, I'm not kidding! I heard it this morning from Larry in maintenance. Can you imagine how the family must feel?"

This rumor had some basis in fact but was far from accurate. The truth was that the previous week, the general manager had announced the engagement of her daughter to a football player with the New York Jets—an offensive lineman who just happened to have the "franchise player" label put on him—and had just signed a new five-year multimillion-dollar contract.

These three episodes demonstrate three facts about communication. First, words mean different things to different people. In the first instance, to Ronnie Barnes a goal meant a minimum level of attainment, while to Patti Williams it meant a maximum target that one tried to reach. Second, the initiation of a message is no assurance that it is received or understood as intended. Third, communications often become distorted as they are transmitted from person to person. As the marriage rumor illustrates, "facts" in messages can lose much of their accuracy as they are transmitted and translated.

These episodes illustrate potential communication problems for supervisors. The importance of effective communication for supervisors can't be overemphasized—for one specific reason. Everything a supervisor does involves communicating. Not some things, but everything! You can't make a decision without information, and that information has to be communicated. Once a decision is made, communication must again take place. Otherwise, no one will know you've made a decision. The best idea, the most creative suggestion, or the finest plan cannot take form without communication. Supervisors work with their employees, peers, immediate managers, people in other departments, customers, and others to get their own department's objectives accomplished; the interactions with these various individuals all require communication of some type. The successful supervisor, therefore, needs effective communication skills. We are not suggesting, of course, that good communication skills alone make a successful supervisor. We can say, however, that ineffective communication skills can lead to a continuous stream of problems for the supervisor.

What Is Communication?

communication
The transference and understanding of meaning.

Communication involves the transfer of meaning. If no information or ideas have been conveyed, communication has not taken place. The speaker who is not heard or the writer who is not read does not communicate. However, for communication to be successful, the meaning must not only be imparted but also understood. A memo addressed to us in Japanese (a language of which we're totally ignorant) cannot be considered a communication until we have it translated. Therefore, communication is the transference and understanding of meaning.

A final point before we move on. Good communication is often erroneously defined by the communicator as "agreement" instead of "clarity of understanding." If someone disagrees with us, many of us assume the person just didn't fully understand our position. In other words, many of us define good communication as having someone accept our views. But a person can understand very clearly what you mean and not agree with what you say. In fact, when a supervisor concludes that a lack of communication must exist because a conflict between two of her employees has continued for a prolonged time, a closer examination often reveals that there is plenty of effective communication going on. Each fully understands the other's position. The problem is one of equating effective communication with agreement.

The Communication Process

Communication can be thought of as a process or flow. Communication problems occur when there are deviations or blockages in that flow. Before communication can take place, a purpose, expressed as a message to be conveyed, is needed. It passes between a source (the sender) and a receiver. The message is encoded (converted to symbolic form) and is passed by way of some medium (channel) to the receiver, who retranslates (decodes) the message initiated by the sender. The result is transference of meaning from one person to another.[1]

Exhibit 10-1 depicts the *communication process*. This model is made up of seven parts: (1) the sender, (2) encoding, (3) the message, (4) the channel, (5) decoding, (6) the receiver, and (7) feedback.

The sender initiates a message by encoding a thought. Three primary conditions affect the encoded message: skill, knowledge, and the social-cultural system.

encoding
The conversion of a message into symbolic form.

The message we want to communicate to you depends on our writing skills; if the authors of textbooks do not have the requisite writing skills, their messages will not reach students in the form desired. One's total communicative success includes speaking, reading, listening, and reasoning skills as well. We are restricted in our communicative activity by the extent of our knowledge of the particular topic. We cannot communicate what we don't know, and should our knowledge be too extensive, it's possible that our receiver will not understand our message. Clearly, the amount of knowledge the sender holds about his or her subject will affect the message he or she seeks to transfer. And, finally, just as knowledge influences our behavior, so does our

---

[1]D. K. Berlo, *The Process of Communication* (New York: Holt, Rinehart & Winston, 1960), 30–32.

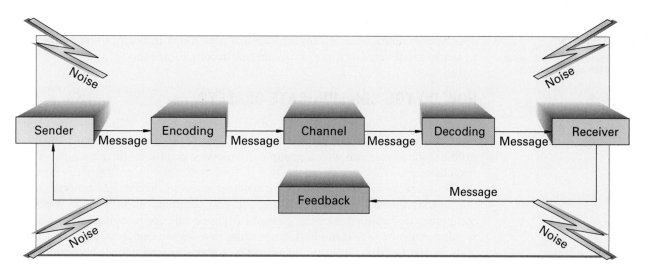

Exhibit 10-1
The communication process.

position in the social-cultural system in which we exist. Your beliefs and values, all part of your culture, act to influence you as a communicative source.

The **message** is the actual physical product from the sender's encoding. "When we speak, the speech is the message. When we write, the writing is the message. When we paint, the picture is the message. When we gesture, the movements of our arms, the expressions on our face are the message."[2] Our message is affected by the code or group of symbols we use to transfer meaning, the content of the message itself, and the decisions that we make in selecting and arranging both codes and content.

The **channel** is the medium through which the message travels. It is selected by the sender, who must determine which channel is formal and which one is informal. Formal channels are established by the organization and transmit messages that pertain to the job-related activities of members. They traditionally follow the authority network within the organization. Other forms of messages, such as personal or social, follow the informal channels in the organization.

The receiver is the object to whom the message is directed. But before the message can be received, the symbols in it must be translated into a form that can be understood by the receiver. This is the **decoding** of the message. Just as the encoder was limited by his or her skills, attitudes, knowledge, and social-cultural system, the receiver is equally restricted. Accordingly, the sender must be skillful in writing or speaking, the receiver must be skillful in reading or listening, and both must be able to reason. One's knowledge, attitudes, and cultural background influence one's ability to receive, just as they do the ability to send.

The final link in the communication process is a **feedback loop**. Feedback is the check on how successful we have been in transferring our messages as originally intended. It determines whether understanding has been achieved.

message
Information that is sent.

channel
The medium by which a message travels.

decoding
A receiver's translation of a sender's message.

feedback loop
Information received by the sender from a receiver regarding a message that was sent.

Methods of Communication

Supervisors participate in two types of communication. One is **formal communication**. It addresses task-related issues and tends to follow the organization's authority chain. When supervisors give directions to an employee, provide advice to a work team in their department, are offered suggestions by employees, interact with other supervisors on a project, or respond to a request made by their boss, they are engaged in formal communication. Supervisors engage in formal communication through speech, written documents,

formal communication
Communication that addresses task-related issues and tends to follow the organization's authority chain.

---

[2]Berlo, *Process of Communication*, 30–32.

informal communication
Communication that moves in any direction, skips authority levels, and is as likely to satisfy social needs as it is to facilitate task accomplishments.

electronic media, and nonverbal behavior. The other type is informal communication. This type of communication moves in any direction, skips authority levels, and is as likely to satisfy social needs as it is to facilitate task accomplishments.

HOW DO YOU COMMUNICATE ORALLY?

As a supervisor, you'll rely heavily on oral communication. Examples are when you meet one-on-one with an employee, give a speech to your department, engage in a problem-solving session with a group of employees, or talk on the phone to a disgruntled customer.

What are the advantages to this form of communication? You can transmit information quickly through the spoken word, and oral communication includes a nonverbal component that can enhance the message. A phone call, for instance, conveys not only words but also tone and mood. Conversation in a one-on-one meeting further includes gestures and facial expressions. Additionally, today's supervisors are becoming increasingly aware that oral communication not only is an effective means for quickly conveying information but has positive symbolic value as well. In contrast to a memo or electronic message, the spoken word is more personal. It conveys more intimacy and caring. As a result, some of the best supervisors rely extensively on oral communication even when the use of written or electronic channels would seem to be as effective. They have found, through experience, that reliance on oral communication tends to build trust with employees and creates a climate of openness and support (see "Something to Think About").

WHY DO YOU USE WRITTEN COMMUNICATION?

When your message is intended to be official, if it has long-term implications, or if it is highly complex, you'll want to convey it in written form. Introducing a new departmental procedure, for instance, should be conveyed in writing so that there is a permanent record to which all employees can refer. Providing a written summary to employees following performance reviews is a good idea because it helps reduce

Something to Think About (and to promote class discussion)

DO WOMEN AND MEN COMMUNICATE DIFFERENTLY?

We know that leadership styles of men and women differ. So, can we conclude that men and women communicate differently, too? The answer is yes! The differences in communication styles between men and women may lead to some interesting insights. When men talk, they do so to emphasize status and independence, whereas women talk to create connections and intimacy. For instance, men frequently complain that women talk on and on about their problems. Women, however, criticize men for not listening. What's happening is that when a man hears a woman talking about a problem, he frequently asserts his desire for independence and control by providing solutions. Many women, in contrast, view conversing about a problem as a means to promote closeness. The woman presents the problem to gain support and connection—not to get the male's advice.

Because effective communication between the sexes is important to all supervisors for meeting departmental goals, how can you manage the differences in communication style? To keep gender differences from becoming persistent barriers to effective communication requires acceptance, understanding, and a commitment to communicate adaptively across gender lines. Both men and women need to acknowledge that there are differences in communication styles, that one style isn't better than the other, and that it takes real effort to talk with each other successfully.

What do you think? Do men and women really communicate differently? What examples have you witnessed that would support your position?

misunderstandings and creates a formal record of what was discussed. Departmental reports that contain lots of detailed numbers and facts are best conveyed in writing because of their complexity.

The fact that written communications provide better documentation than the spoken word is both a plus and a minus. On the plus side, written documents provide a reliable "paper trail" for decisions or actions that are later called into question. They also reduce ambiguity for recipients. On the negative side, obsessive concern with documenting everything "in writing" leads to risk avoidance, decision paralysis, and creation of a highly politicized work environment. At the extreme, task accomplishment becomes subordinated to writing documents that "cover your rear" and make sure that no one person is held responsible for any questionable decision.

IS ELECTRONIC COMMUNICATION MORE EFFICIENT?

Computers, microchips, and digitalization are dramatically increasing a supervisor's communication options. Today, you can rely on a number of sophisticated electronic media to carry your communications.[3] These include e-mail, text messaging, voice mail, electronic paging, cellular telephones, videoconferencing, modem-based transmissions, Internet and intranet communications, and other forms of network-related communication. Whatever electronic media is selected, limit liability risks and improve the overall effectiveness of the organization's e-communications by requiring employees to use appropriate, businesslike language in e-mail and other electronic documents. Be sure to avoid the shouting of ALL CAPS!

Supervisors are increasingly using many of these technological advances. E-mail and voice mail allow people to transmit messages twenty-four hours a day. When you're away from your office, others can leave messages for you to review on your return. For important and complex communications, a permanent record of e-mail messages can be obtained by merely printing out a hard copy. Cellular phones are dramatically changing the role of the telephone as a communication device. In the past, telephone numbers were attached to physical locations. Now, with cellular technology, the phone number attaches to mobile phones. You can be in constant contact with your employees, other supervisors, and key members in the organization regardless of where they are physically located. Network-related communication also allows you to monitor the work of employees whose jobs are done on computers in remote locations, to participate in electronic meetings, and to communicate with suppliers and customers on inter- and intraorganizational networks.

What Issues Are Created by IM and Text Messaging?

A technology designed initially for conducting one-on-one personal chats has permeated the workplace. Many employees are choosing text-based instant messaging (IM) over phone calls and e-mail. IM is essentially the text version of a phone call. Immediate, streamlined, and real-time, it often serves as a backstop for e-mail problems.

Okay…how well do you know the Net lingo?[4] If you received an e-mail or text message with GFTD (gone for the day) written in it, would you know what that meant? What about NSFW, FYEO (for your eyes only), BTW (by the way), or BIL

---

[3]"Technology Can Enhance Employee Communications, Help Attract and Retain Workers," *Employee Benefit Plan Review*, June 2000, 24–28.

[4]S. Raposo, "Quick! Tell Us What KUTGW Means," *Wall Street Journal*, August 5, 2009, D1+; and C. Tuna, "Corporate Blogs and Tweets Must Keep SEC in Mind," *Wall Street Journal*, April 27, 2009, B4.

(boss is listening)? When an employee received an e-mail at work from a friend with an attached slideshow entitled "Awkward Family Photos," she clicked through it and saw some pretty unusual—yes, awkward—photos. Looking back at the e-mail, that's when she also saw the abbreviation "NSFW" written at the bottom. Not knowing what that was, she looked the abbreviation up on netlingo.com and verified it on internetslang.com (websites that translate Internet and texting abbreviations). Come to find out, she should have paid more attention to the abbreviation since NSFW stands for "not safe for work."

"As text-messaging shorthand becomes increasingly widespread in e-mails, text messages, and Tweets," people need to be aware of what it means. At many workplaces, a working knowledge of Net lingo is becoming necessary. As employees use social media sites like Twitter and Facebook and even text messaging to communicate with colleagues and customers, the shorthand abbreviations are often necessary to stay within message length limits. However, as the NSFW example showed, not knowing or even misunderstanding the lingo can lead to surprises, inappropriate responses, or miscommunications.

IM benefits businesses that work in teams or on projects because it enhances collaboration. Be aware, along with time and cost savings, there are risks and downsides to its use. Here are ten instant messaging do's and don'ts.[5]

1. DO adopt a user policy containing at least general guidelines for instant messaging between employees, customers, or business partners.

2. DON'T use instant messaging to communicate confidential or sensitive information. Leave the IM for quick information about project status, meeting times, or a person's whereabouts.

3. DO organize your contact lists to separate business contacts from family and friends to eliminate the possibility that a social contact could be included in a business chat with employees, customers, or business partners.

4. DON'T allow excessive personal messaging at work; instead urge that personal chats be done during breaks or the lunch hour, or that the chats generate new customers or revenue to the business.

5. DO be aware that instant messages can be saved and the record is not always wiped when users are done. Parties to conversations can copy and paste the chat onto a Notepad or Word document and some IM services allow users to archive entire messages. Be careful what is written, just as you would in an e-mail!

6. DON'T compromise the company's liability or individual reputation making statements that could damage personal, or company, integrity or credibility. Again, be careful what is written.

7. DO be aware of virus infections and related security risks. Since most IM services allow file transfer with messages, learn about the organization's quality of firewall protection and decide whether or not to restrict transferring files through IM.

8. DON'T share personal data or information through instant messaging because the chat text is relayed to a Web server en route to your contact and IM providers or hackers can see it. Send critical info through an encrypted e-mail only.

9. DO keep instant messages simple by limiting the inquiry, avoiding unnecessary blather, getting to the point, and knowing when to say goodbye.

10. DON'T confuse contacts with a misleading user name or status; update status throughout the day so contacts know whether users are available for messages or offline.

---

[5]M. Enbysk, "10 Tips for Using Instant Messaging for Business," 2011, Microsoft Corporation, Microsoft Business, http://www.microsoft.com/business/en-us/resources/ArticleReader/website/default.aspx?Print=1& ArticleId=tipsforusinginstantmessagingforbusiness&fbid=W5j9HZ3WlNn (accessed May 24, 2011).

HOW DOES NONVERBAL COMMUNICATION AFFECT YOUR COMMUNICATION?

Some of the most meaningful communication is not spoken, written, or transmitted on a computer. This is nonverbal communication. A loud siren or a red light at an intersection tells you something without words. When you are conducting a training session, you don't need words to tell you that employees are bored when their eyes get glassy—or they simply fall asleep. Similarly, generally you can tell in an instant by your boss's body language and verbal intonations whether he's angry, upbeat, anxious, or distracted.

Body language refers to gestures, facial configurations, and other movements of the body. Narrowed eyes, a clenched jaw, or a beet-red face, for example, says something different from a smile. Hand motions, facial expressions, and other gestures can communicate emotions or temperaments such as aggression, fear, shyness, arrogance, joy, and anger.[6]

Verbal intonation refers to the emphasis one gives to words or phrases. To illustrate how intonations can change the meaning of a message, consider the supervisor who asks a colleague a question. The colleague replies, "What do you mean by that?" The supervisor's reaction will vary, depending on the tone of the colleague's response. A soft, smooth tone creates a different meaning from one that is abrasive and puts a strong emphasis on the last word. Most of us would view the first intonation as coming from someone who sincerely seeks clarification, whereas the second suggests that the person is aggressive or defensive.

The fact that every oral communication also has a nonverbal message cannot be overemphasized. Why? Because the nonverbal component is likely to carry the greatest impact. Most of us know that animals respond to how we say something rather than what we say. Apparently, people aren't much different.

nonverbal communication
Communication that is not spoken, written, or transmitted on a computer.

body language
Gestures, facial configurations, and other movements of the body that communicate emotions or temperaments such as aggression, fear, shyness, arrogance, joy, and anger.

verbal intonation
The emphasis an individual gives to words or phrases through speech.

WHAT IS THE GRAPEVINE?

The grapevine is active in almost all organizations. In fact, studies typically find that the grapevine is the means of communication by which most operative employees first hear about important changes introduced by organizational leaders. It rates ahead of supervisors, official memoranda, and other formal sources.

Is the information that flows along the grapevine accurate? Sometimes yes, and sometimes no. Accuracy aside, it's important to consider the conditions that foster an active grapevine. It is frequently assumed that rumors start because they make titillating gossip. Such is rarely the case. Rumors have at least four purposes: to structure and reduce anxiety; to make sense of limited or fragmented information; to serve as a vehicle to organize group members, and possibly outsiders, into coalitions; and to signal a sender's status ("I'm an insider and you're not") or power ("I have the power to make you an insider"). Studies have found that rumors emerge in response to situations that are important to us or where there is ambiguity, or under conditions that arouse anxiety. Work situations frequently contain these three elements, which explains why rumors flourish in organizations. The secrecy and competition that typically prevail in large organizations—around such issues as appointment of new bosses, relocation of offices, realignment of work assignments, and layoffs—create conditions that encourage and sustain rumors on the grapevine. A rumor will persist either until the wants and expectations creating the uncertainty underlying the rumor are fulfilled or until the anxiety is reduced.

What can we conclude from this discussion? Certainly the grapevine is an important part of any group's or organization's communication system and well

grapevine
The means of communication by which most operative employees first hear about important changes introduced by organizational leaders; the rumor mill.

---

[6]M. Fulfer, "Nonverbal Communication: How to Read What's Plain as the Nose…or Eyelid…or Chin…on Their Faces," *Journal of Occupational Excellence* 20, no. 2 (Spring 2001), 19–38.

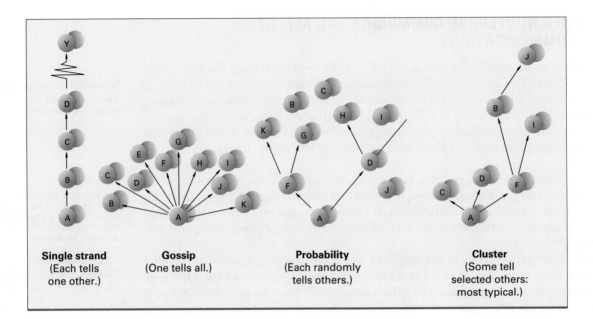

Single strand
(Each tells
one other.)

Gossip
(One tells all.)

Probability
(Each randomly
tells others.)

Cluster
(Some tell
selected others:
most typical.)

Exhibit 10-2

Grapevine patterns.

Source: John W. Newstrom and Keith Davis, Organizational Behavior: Human Behavior at Work, *9th ed. (New York: McGraw-Hill, 1993), 445. Reprinted with permission of the McGraw-Hill Companies.*

worth understanding. Moreover, it's never going to be eliminated, so supervisors should use it in beneficial ways. Given that only a small set of employees typically passes information to more than one other person, you can analyze grapevine information and predict its flow (see Exhibit 10-2). Certain messages are likely to follow predictable patterns. You might even consider using the grapevine informally to transmit information to specific individuals by planting messages with key people who are active on the grapevine and are likely to find a given message worthy of passing on.

You should not lose sight of the grapevine's value for identifying issues that employees consider important and that create anxiety among them. It acts as both a filter and a feedback mechanism, picking up issues that employees consider relevant and planting messages that employees want passed on to those "running" the organization. For instance, the grapevine can tap employee concerns. If the grapevine is hopping with a rumor of a mass layoff, and if you know the rumor is totally false, the message still has meaning. It reflects the fears and concerns of employees and, hence, should not be ignored.

Electronic communication is affecting everything and the grapevine is no exception. Corporate blogs are reshaping the grapevine. Weblogs, or blogs, are used internally to disseminate information to employees or externally to aid in marketing and public relations; corporate blogs are being used to reach corporate goals. Blogs display information in reverse chronological order, allowing participants to ask questions, make comments, and receive comments from a variety of sources in a logical evolving fashion, similar to an ongoing conversation around the watercooler. Because the blog is available to a wide audience, many organizations institute a code of ethics that is applied to all postings. Internal blogs allow individuals in multiple locations and time zones to participate in discussions of concern to employees and management so that the blog becomes an electronic grapevine![7]

[7]"Corporate Blog," *Wikipedia*, June 18, 2008, en.wikipedia.org/wiki/Corporate_blog; "Is Blogging Really Good for My Company? Or Just a Buzz Word?" *Intra Focus*, January 18, 2007, intrafocus.wordpress. com/2007/01/18/is-blogging-really-good-for-my-company-or-just-a-buzz-word/; "GM Blogger's Code of Ethics," *GM FastLane Blog*, June 18, 2008, fastlane.gmblogs.com/about.html; and J. Sessum, "Why CEOs Should Blog," *Global PR Blog Week* 2.0, September 19, 2005, www.globalprblogweek.com/2005/09/19/ sessum-why-ceos-should-blog/ (all accessed June 19, 2008).

Barriers to Effective Communication

As noted earlier, the goal of perfect communication is to transmit a thought or idea from a sender to a receiver so that it is perceived by the receiver exactly the same as it was envisioned by the sender. That goal is almost never achieved because of distortions and other barriers. In this section, we describe some of the more serious barriers that hinder effective communication (see Exhibit 10-3). In the following section, we offer some suggestions for how to overcome these barriers.

HOW DOES LANGUAGE AFFECT COMMUNICATION?

Words mean different things to different people. Age, education, and cultural background are three of the most obvious variables that influence the language people use and the definitions they give to words. In an organization, employees usually come from diverse backgrounds. Furthermore, horizontal differentiation creates specialists who develop their own jargon or technical language. In large organizations, members are often widely dispersed geographically, and those in each locale use terms and phrases that are unique to their area. Vertical differentiation can also cause language problems. For instance, differences in the meaning of words such as *incentives* and *quotas* occur at different levels of managerial personnel. Senior managers, for example, often speak about the need for incentives and quotas. Yet these terms have been found to imply manipulation and create resentment among supervisors.

The point is that although we may speak the same language (e.g., English), our use of that language is far from uniform. A knowledge of how each of us modifies the language would minimize communication difficulties. The problem is that you don't know how your various employees, peers, superiors, customers, and others with whom you interact have modified the language. Senders tend to assume that the words and terms they use mean the same to the receiver as they do to them. This, of course, is often incorrect, and thus creates communication difficulties.

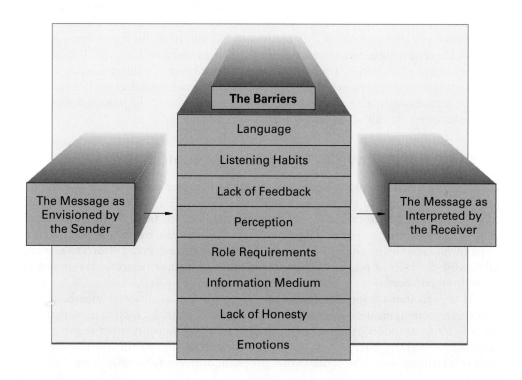

Exhibit 10-3

Barriers to effective communication.

Exhibit 10-4
What do you see—an old woman or a young lady?

WHAT DID YOU SAY?

Most of us hear, but we don't listen! Hearing is merely picking up sound vibrations. Listening is making sense out of what we hear. That is, listening requires paying attention, interpreting, and remembering what is being said.

Many of us are pretty poor listeners. At this point, it suffices to say that if you don't have good listening skills, you're not going to get the full message as the sender meant to convey it. For example, many of us share common flaws regarding listening. We get distracted and end up hearing only parts of a message. Instead of listening for meaning, we listen to determine whether we agree or disagree with what's being said. We begin thinking about our response to what's being said rather than listening for the complete message. Each of these flaws in our listening habits contributes to messages being received differently from what the sender intended. We'll come back to active listening shortly.

DID YOU GET MY MESSAGE?

Effective communication means the transference and understanding of meaning. But how do you know whether someone has received your message and comprehended it in the way that you meant? The answer is: Use feedback. When you request that each member of your staff submit a specific report, receipt of the report is feedback. Likewise, when your instructor tests you on the material in this book, you're getting feedback on your understanding of the material.

When you fail to use feedback, you never know whether the message has been received as intended. Thus, lack of feedback creates the potential for inaccuracies and distortions.

DO YOU SEE WHAT I SEE?

Your attitudes, interests, past experiences, and expectations determine how you organize and interpret your surroundings. This explains how you can look at the same thing as someone else and perceive it differently (see Exhibit 10-4). In the communication process, the receiver selectively sees and hears messages based on his or her background and personal characteristics. The receiver also projects his or her interests and expectations into communications when interpreting them. Because senders and receivers of communications each bring their own set of perceptual biases, the messages they seek to transfer often are subject to distortions.

WHAT DO ROLES HAVE TO DO WITH COMMUNICATION?

roles
Behavior patterns that correspond to the positions individuals occupy in an organization.

People in organizations play roles. They engage in behavior patterns that go with the positions they occupy in the organization. Supervisory jobs, for instance, come with role identities. Supervisors know that they are supposed to be loyal to, and defend, their boss and the organization. Union leaders' roles typically require loyalty to union goals such as improving employee security. Marketing roles demand efforts to increase sales, while the roles of people working in the credit department emphasize minimizing losses from bad debts.

As organizations impose different role requirements on different members, they also create communication barriers. Each role comes with its own jargon that sets the role off from others. Additionally, fulfilling role requirements often requires individuals to selectively interpret events. They hear and see the world consistently with their role requirements. The result is that people in different roles often have difficulty

Comprehension Check **10-1**

1. Effective communication does not include

    a. transference of meaning
    b. agreement
    c. a sender and a receiver
    d. feedback

2. The conversion of a message into symbolic form is commonly referred to as

    a. the message
    b. feedback
    c. encoding
    d. a symbol

3. The emphasis one gives to words or phrases is called

    a. verbal intonation
    b. body language
    c. the grapevine
    d. feedback

4. Which one of the following is *not* regarded as a barrier to effective communication?

    a. Agreement
    b. Language
    c. Perception
    d. Emotions

communicating with each other. Marketing people say they want to "increase sales." So, too, do the people in the credit department, except the marketing people want to sell everything to anybody, while those in the credit department want to sell only to those who are creditworthy. Labor and company representatives sometimes have difficulty negotiating because their roles encompass very different language and interests. A lot of internal communication breakdowns in organizations are merely individuals enacting behaviors consistent with the roles they are playing.

IS THERE A PREFERRED INFORMATION MEDIUM?

The amount of information transmitted in a face-to-face conversation is considerably greater than that received from a flyer posted on an organization's bulletin board. The former offers multiple information cues (words, posture, facial expressions, gestures, intonations), immediate feedback, and the personal touch of "being there" that the flyer doesn't. This reminds us that media differ in the **richness of information** they transmit. Exhibit 10-5 illustrates a hierarchy of information richness. The higher a medium rates in richness, the more information it is capable of transmitting. Generally speaking, the more ambiguous and complicated the message, the more the sender should rely on a rich communication medium.

High-performing supervisors tend to be media sensitive, and their selection of a communication channel targets the use of a rich medium to overcome ambiguity in their message. Using face-to-face meetings, as well as opportunities that arise from

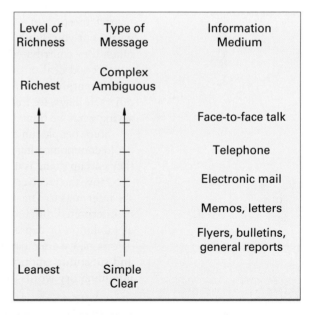

Exhibit 10-5

Hierarchy of information richness.

richness of information

A measure of the amount of information that is transmitted based on multiple information cues (words, posture, facial expressions, gestures, intonations), immediate feedback, and the personal touch.

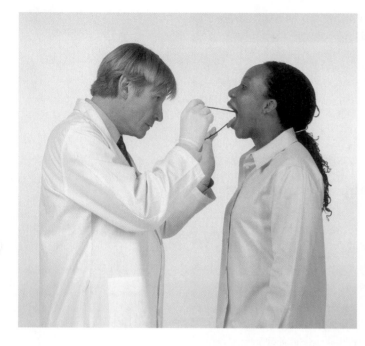

Doctors and nurses need to adjust their language constantly. Using medical terminology is required when communicating with other health care professionals but is usually not appropriate when talking to a patient unless accompanied by an explanation in "lay terms."

the simple supervisory act of walking around the department instead of sitting in the office, supervisors are engaging in rich communication with employees. Richness comes from the ability of the channel to handle multiple cues at the same time while providing rapid feedback in a personal manner. Face-to-face meetings, video conferences, and phone conversations provide supervisors the opportunity to maximize the information they transmit, and the medium is especially appropriate for messages needing great clarity.

For example, as a supervisor, if you want to share with your employees a major new product line that your company will be introducing—and that will affect everyone in your department—your communication is more likely to be effective in a face-to-face departmental meeting than through use of a memo. Why? Because this message is likely to initiate apprehension among employees and require clarification. Bulletins, memos, prerecorded speeches, and e-mail lack the richness of personal communication, but they are effective in transmitting routine messages with a minimum of ambiguity. Modest changes in tomorrow's departmental production schedule can be effectively communicated in a memo or with an e-mail. Unfortunately, people in organizations don't always match the medium to the message and, thereby, create communication problems.[8]

HOW DOES HONESTY AFFECT COMMUNICATION?

Suppose a colleague asked you what you thought of the ideas he suggested in the recent project meeting in which you both participated. You thought his suggestions were weak, but you didn't tell him that. Rather, you complimented his ideas and said how much they contributed to the final results.

A good deal of what passes as "poor communication" is nothing other than individuals purposely avoiding honesty and openness. To avoid confrontations and hurting others' feelings, we frequently engage in practices such as conveying ambiguous messages, saying what we think others want to hear, or cutting off communication altogether.

Some people run from confrontation. They want everyone to like them. As such, they avoid communicating any messages they think might be displeasing to the receiver. What they end up doing is increasing tension and further hindering effective communication.

How the receiver feels at the time of receipt of a message will influence how he or she interprets it. The same message received when you're angry or distraught is likely to be interpreted differently when you're in a neutral disposition. Extreme emotions such as jubilation or depression are most likely to hinder effective communication. In such instances, we are most prone to disregard our rational and objective thinking processes and substitute emotional judgments. These are also the times we're most likely to use inflammatory words or language that we later regret.

HOW CAN YOU IMPROVE YOUR COMMUNICATION EFFECTIVENESS?

A few of the barriers we've described are part of organizational life and will never be fully eliminated. Perceptual and role differences, for example, should be recognized as barriers but are not easily corrected. However, most barriers to effective communication can be overcome. The following provides some guidance.

---

[8]S. Robbins and T. Judge, *Organizational Behavior*, 13th ed. (Upper Saddle River, NJ: Pearson Prentice Hall, 2009), 367–368.

Think First Think before you speak! That cliché can be expanded to include all forms of communication. Before you speak or write, ask yourself: What message am I trying to convey? Then ask: How can I organize and present my message so that it will achieve the desired outcome? Most of us follow the "Think first" dictum when writing a message. The formal and deliberate process of writing encourages thinking through what we want to say and how best to say it. The concept of working on a draft implies that the written document will be edited and revised. Few of us give anywhere near the same attention to our verbal communications. That's a mistake. Before you speak, make sure you know what you want to say. Then, present your message in a logical and organized fashion so that it is clear and can be understood by your receiver.

Constrain Emotions It would be naïve to assume that you always communicate in a fully rational manner. Yet you know that emotions can severely cloud and distort the transference of meaning. If you are emotionally upset over an issue, you're more likely to misconstrue incoming messages and fail to express your outgoing messages clearly and accurately. What can you do? The simplest answer is to discontinue further communication until you have regained composure.

Learn to Listen We stated earlier that most of us are poor listeners. That doesn't mean, though, that we can't improve our listening skills. Some specific behaviors have been found to be related to effective listening. We present those skills in the section titled "Active Listening" at the end of this chapter.

Tailor Language to the Receiver Because language can be a barrier, you should choose words and structure your messages in ways that will be clear and understandable to the receiver. You need to simplify your language and consider the audience to whom the message is directed so that the language is tailored to the receivers. Remember, effective communication is achieved when a message is both received and understood (see "News Flash! Communication Differences in the Global Village" later in this chapter). Understanding is improved by simplifying the language used in relation to the audience intended. For example, a nursing supervisor should always try to communicate to the staff in clear and easily understood terms. At the same time, the language used in messages to a patient should be purposely different from that used with the medical staff. Jargon can facilitate understanding when used with those who know what it means, but it can cause innumerable problems when used outside that group.

Match Words and Actions Actions speak louder than words. Therefore, it is important to watch your actions to make sure they align with and reinforce the words that go along with them. We noted earlier that nonverbal messages carry a great deal of weight. Given this fact, the effective supervisor watches his or her nonverbal cues to ensure that they too convey the message desired. Remember also that as a supervisor, your employees will look at your behavior as a model. If your verbal comments are backed up by your actions, you will gain credibility and build trust. If, on the other hand, you say one thing and do another, your employees will ignore what you say and model themselves on what you do. At the extreme, people stop listening because they no longer believe that your words have credibility. Incidentally, this problem often plagues politicians.

Use Feedback Many communication problems can be directly attributed to misunderstandings and inaccuracies. These are less likely to occur if you use feedback. This feedback can be verbal or nonverbal. If you ask someone, "Did you understand what I said?" the response represents feedback. But feedback should include more than yes and no answers. You can ask a set of questions about a message to determine whether the message was received as intended. Better yet, you can ask the receiver to restate the message in his or her own words. If you then hear what was intended, understanding and accuracy should be enhanced.

Feedback also includes subtler things than asking direct questions or summarizing messages. General comments can give you a sense of the receiver's reaction to a message. Of course, performance appraisals, salary reviews, and promotions also represent forms of feedback. Feedback does not have to be conveyed in words. The sales supervisor who sends out a staff directive describing a new monthly sales report that all sales personnel will need to complete receives feedback if some of the salespeople fail to turn in the new report. This feedback suggests that he or she needs to clarify further the initial directive. Similarly, when you give a speech to a group of people, watch their eyes and look for other nonverbal clues to tell you whether they are getting your message. This may explain why television performers on comedy shows prefer to tape their programs in front of a live audience. Immediate laughter and applause—or their absence—convey to the performer whether the message is getting across as intended.

Participate in Assertiveness Training Many people have no trouble asserting themselves. Being open and honest comes naturally to them. Some, in fact, are too assertive. They cross the line and become aggressive and abrasive. Other individuals suffer from a constant fear of upsetting others and fall back on avoidance or ambiguous communication when they need to be open and assertive. Such people would benefit from participation in assertiveness training. An effective supervisor needn't always be assertive, but should be capable of being so when it's needed.

Assertiveness training is designed to make people more open and self-expressive. They confront issues in a straightforward manner. They say what they mean, without being rude or thoughtless. Individuals who take assertiveness training learn verbal and nonverbal behaviors that enhance their ability to communicate openly and unambiguously. These behaviors include direct and unambiguous language; the use of "I" statements and cooperative "we" statements; a strong, steady, audible voice; good eye contact; facial expressions matched to the message; an appropriately serious tone; and a comfortable but firm posture.

assertiveness training
A technique designed to make people more open and self-expressive, saying what they mean without being rude or thoughtless.

Help Immigrant Workers Assimilate Into the Culture Immigrant workers have a responsibility to learn English and adapt to the cultural norms in the American workplace, but this can take time and employers can gain a lot by helping their workers bridge the cultural divide. Many employers, however, have the "sink or swim" attitude and expect immigrant workers to figure things out for themselves. This does not work in many cases, and it is not a wise business decision. Employers benefit by investing in helping immigrant workers adapt to the workplace. When help is given by the employer, it results in increased productivity, higher performance, improved safety, greater trust, and more loyalty among workers. All of these things impact the bottom line in terms of higher business profits in the long term. HR professionals offer these tips for employers who want to enhance and retain their immigrant workforce.

Learn as much as you can about the culture of the people you are dealing with.

Recognize the broad ethnic diversity that exists within groups such as Hispanics or Asians.

Respect individual differences, abilities, and personalities by getting to know a person's culture as you get to know them as individuals.

Provide orientation programs for new hires to address cultural differences and language barriers.

Encourage coworkers to serve as mentors or coaches to help new workers adapt to the culture and vocabulary of the workplace.

When working with immigrants, refrain from using jargon or slang that might not translate.

When training immigrant employees, make sure they understand your training material and why it is useful to them.

Never assume your communications with someone with limited English-speaking abilities have been understood, and remember to ask for feedback or for demonstration when you are training them.

Be patient when working with immigrants; this will help to prevent feelings of inadequacy and embarrassment when a person cannot express himself or herself clearly or fully.

Recruit bilingual managers and supervisors to serve as the communication link between cultures and/or engage coworkers to serve as translators while people are learning English.

If you have a number of people in need of learning English, consider partnering with a school to offer on-site English as a Second Language (ESL) classes. This helps to create a safe environment for learning, and helping people learn English is a way to build trust and loyalty.

Help workers take care of their basic survival needs by helping them find transportation, establish credit, and file income tax returns.

Provide sensitivity training to native workers in the company to make them aware of, and sensitive toward, cultural differences.

Promote immigrants when appropriate; this gives people more opportunities and demonstrates to other immigrants that they can advance if they prove themselves.

Keep current on immigration regulations by reading the INS *Handbook for Employers* and make sure proper employment forms are completed and maintained.[9]

A Special Communication Skill: Active Listening

Effective listening is active rather than passive. In passive listening, you're like a tape recorder. You absorb the information given. If the speaker provides a clear message and makes his or her delivery interesting enough to keep your attention, you'll probably get most of what the speaker is trying to communicate. But active listening requires you to "get inside" the speaker's mind so that you can understand the communication from his or her point of view. As you'll see, active listening is hard work.[10] You have to concentrate, and you have to want to fully understand what a speaker is saying (see the section titled "Active Listening" at the end of this chapter). Students who use active listening techniques for an entire lecture are as tired as their instructor when the lecture is over because they've put as much energy into listening as the instructor puts into speaking.

> **active listening**
> A technique that requires an individual to "get inside" a speaker's mind to understand the communication from the speaker's point of view.

There are four requirements for active listening. You need to listen with (1) intensity, (2) empathy, (3) acceptance, and (4) a willingness to take responsibility for completeness. Because listening presents the opportunity for the mind to wander, the active listener concentrates intensely on what the speaker is saying and tunes out thousands of miscellaneous thoughts (work deadlines, money, personal problems) that create distractions. What do active listeners do with their idle brain time? They summarize and integrate what has been said! They put each new bit of information into the context of what has preceded it.

Empathy requires you to put yourself in the speaker's shoes. Try to understand what the speaker wants to communicate rather than what you want to understand. Notice that empathy demands both knowledge of the speaker and flexibility on your part. Suspend your own thoughts and feelings and adjust what you see and feel to your speaker's world. In that way, you increase the likelihood that you will interpret the message being spoken in the way the speaker intended.

An active listener demonstrates acceptance. You listen objectively without judging content. This is no easy task. It is natural to be distracted by the content of what a speaker says, especially when you disagree with it. When you hear something you disagree with, you have a tendency to begin formulating mental arguments to counter what is being said. Of course, in doing so, you often miss the rest of the message. The challenge is to absorb what is being said and to withhold judgment on content until the speaker is finished.

---

[9]Charlotte-Mecklenburg Workforce Development Board, "Cultural and Language Barriers in the Workplace," February 2002, http://www.charlotteworks.org/clbpositionpaper.pdf (accessed May 24, 2011).

[10]R. B. Cousins, "Active Listening Is More Than Just Hearing," *Supervision* 61, no. 9 (September 2000), 14.

News Flash!

COMMUNICATION DIFFERENCES IN THE GLOBAL VILLAGE

It's important to recognize that communication isn't conducted in the same way around the world. For example, compare countries that place a high value on individualism (e.g., the United States) with countries where the emphasis is on collectivism (e.g., Japan). Owing to the emphasis on the individual in countries such as the United States, communication patterns are individual oriented and rather clearly spelled out. For example, U.S. supervisors rely heavily on memoranda, announcements, position papers, and other formal forms of communication to stake out their positions in the organization. They frequently also keep information secret in an attempt to promote their own advancement and as a way of inducing their employees to accept decisions and plans. For their own protection, lower-level employees also engage in this practice.

In collectivist countries such as Japan, there is more interaction for its own sake and a more informal manner of interpersonal contact. The Japanese supervisor, in contrast to U.S. supervisors, engages in extensive verbal consultation over an issue first and draws up a formal document later, only to outline the agreement that was made. Face-to-face communication is encouraged. Additionally, open communication is an inherent part of the Japanese work setting. Work spaces are open and crowded with individuals at different levels in the work hierarchy. In contrast, U.S. organizations emphasize authority, hierarchy, and formal lines of communication.

Sources: Based on M. K. Kozan, "Subcultures and Conflict Management Styles," *Management International Review* 42, no. 1 (January 2002), 89–106; and A. Mehrabian, "Communication without Words," *Psychology Today,* September 1968, 53–55.

The final ingredient of active listening is taking responsibility for completeness. That is, as an active listener, you do whatever is necessary to get the full intended meaning from the speaker's communication.[11]

The Importance of Feedback Skills

Ask a supervisor about the feedback he or she gives to employees, and you're likely to get a qualified answer. If the feedback is positive, it's likely to be given promptly and enthusiastically. Feedback for improvement commonly referred to as negative feedback is often treated very differently.[12] Like most of us, supervisors don't particularly enjoy communicating bad news. They fear offending or having to deal with the receiver's defensiveness. The result is that feedback for improvement may be avoided, delayed, or distorted. The purposes of this section are to show you the importance of providing both positive feedback and feedback for improvement and to identify specific techniques to help make your feedback more effective.

WHAT'S THE DIFFERENCE BETWEEN POSITIVE FEEDBACK AND FEEDBACK FOR IMPROVEMENT?

We said that supervisors treat positive feedback and feedback for improvement differently. So, too, do receivers. You need to understand this fact and adjust your feedback style accordingly. Positive feedback is more readily and accurately perceived than is

---

[11]See, for instance, K. Fracaro, "Two Ears and One Mouth," *Supervision,* February 2001, 3–5.

[12]See, for example, K. Leung, S. Su, and M. W. Morris, "When Is Criticism Not Constructive? The Roles of Fairness Perceptions and Dispositional Attributions in Employee Acceptance of Critical Supervisory Feedback," *Human Relations* 54, no. 1 (September 2001), 1155; and C. A. Walker, "Saving Your Rookie Managers from Themselves," *Harvard Business Review* 80, no. 4 (April 2002), 97–103.

feedback for improvement. Furthermore, although positive feedback is almost always accepted, you can expect feedback for improvement to meet resistance. Why? The logical answer appears to be that people want to hear good news and block out the rest. Positive feedback fits what most people wish to hear and already believe about themselves. Does this mean, then, that you should avoid giving feedback for improvement? No! What it means is that you need to be aware of potential resistance and learn to use feedback for improvement in situations in which it's most likely to be accepted. That is, feedback for improvement should be used when it's supported by hard data—numbers, specific examples, and the like.

> • Focus on specific behaviors
> • Keep feedback impersonal
> • Keep feedback goal oriented
> • Make feedback well timed
> • Ensure understanding
> • Direct feedback for improvement toward behavior that the receiver can control

Exhibit 10-6
Suggestions for effective feedback.

HOW DO YOU GIVE EFFECTIVE FEEDBACK?

We have six specific suggestions to help you become more effective in providing feedback. We discuss them here and summarize them in Exhibit 10-6.

Focus on Specific Behaviors Feedback should be specific rather than general. Avoid such statements as, "You have a bad attitude" or "I'm really impressed with the good job you did." They're vague and, although they provide information, they don't tell the receiver enough to correct the "bad attitude" or to know on what basis you concluded that a "good job" has been done so that the person knows what behaviors to repeat.

Keep Feedback Impersonal Feedback, particularly for improvement, should be descriptive rather than judgmental or evaluative. No matter how upset you are, keep the feedback focused on job-related behaviors and never criticize someone personally because of an inappropriate action. Telling people they're incompetent, lazy, or the like is almost always counterproductive. It provokes such an emotional reaction that the performance deviation itself is apt to be overlooked. When you're criticizing, remember that you're censuring job-related behavior, not the person. You might be tempted to tell someone he or she is rude and insensitive (which might just be true); however, that's hardly impersonal. It's better to say something more specific, such as, "You've interrupted me three times with questions that weren't urgent when you knew I was talking long-distance to a customer in Brazil."

Keep Feedback Goal Oriented Feedback should not be given primarily to "dump" or "unload" on another person. If you have to provide feedback for improvement, make sure it's directed toward the receiver's goals. Ask yourself whom the feedback is supposed to help. If the answer is essentially you—"I've got something I just want to get off my chest"—bite your tongue and hold the comment. Such feedback undermines your credibility and lessens the meaning and influence of future feedback sessions.

Make Feedback Well Timed Feedback is most meaningful to a receiver when there is a very short interval between his or her behavior and the receipt of feedback about that behavior. For example, a new employee who makes a mistake is more likely to respond to suggestions for improving right after the mistake or at the end of the workday—rather than during a performance review session six months later. If you have to spend time re-creating a situation and refreshing someone's memory of it, the feedback you're providing is likely to be ineffective. Moreover, if you're particularly concerned with changing behavior, delays in providing timely feedback on the undesirable actions lessen the likelihood that the feedback will be effective in bringing about the desired change. Of course, making feedback prompt merely for promptness's sake can backfire if you have insufficient information or if you're otherwise emotionally upset. In such instances, "well timed" could mean "somewhat delayed."

Ensure Understanding Is your feedback concise and complete enough that the receiver clearly and fully understands your communication? Remember that every successful communication requires both transference and understanding of meaning. If feedback is to be effective, you need to ensure that the receiver understands it. Consistent with our discussion of listening techniques, you should have the receiver rephrase the content of your feedback to find out whether it fully captured the meaning you intended.

Direct Feedback for Improvement Feedback for improvement should be directed toward behavior the receiver can do something about. There's little value in reminding a person of some shortcoming over which he or she has no control. For instance, to criticize an employee who's late for work because she forgot to set her alarm clock is valid. To criticize her for being late for work when the subway she takes to work every day had a power failure, stranding her for ninety minutes, is pointless. There's nothing she could have done to correct what happened—short of finding a different means of traveling to work, which may be unrealistic.

In addition, when feedback for improvement is given concerning something that the receiver can control, it might be a good idea to indicate specifically what can be done to improve the situation. This takes some of the sting out of the criticism and offers guidance to employees who understand the problem—but don't know how to resolve it.

Comprehension Check 10-2

5. Active listening is best described as

   a. agreeing with what the sender communicates
   b. asking lots of questions
   c. concentrating on what's being communicated
   d. providing a lot of feedback

6. The most crucial linkage in communications is

   a. agreement
   b. constraining emotions
   c. feedback
   d. tailoring language to the receiver

7. Which one of the following is *not* a recommendation on giving effective feedback?

   a. Keep feedback personal
   b. Focus on specific behavior
   c. Keep feedback goal oriented
   d. Make feedback well timed

8. A technique to make people more open and self-expressive is called

   a. feedback training
   b. assertiveness training
   c. grapevine training
   d. communications training

Enhancing Understanding

SUMMARY

After reading this chapter, I can:

1. **Define *communication* and the communication process.** Communication is the transference and understanding of meaning. Effective communication, however, does not imply agreement. The communication process begins with a communication sender (a source) who has a message to convey. The message is converted to symbolic form (encoding) and passed by way of a channel to the receiver, who decodes the message. To ensure accuracy, the receiver should provide the sender with feedback as a check on whether understanding has been achieved.

2. **Contrast formal and informal communication.** Formal communication addresses task-related issues and tends to follow the organization's authority chain. Informal communication moves in any direction, skips authority levels, and is as likely to satisfy social needs as it is to facilitate task accomplishments.

3. **Explain how electronic communication affects the supervisor's job.** Electronic communication allows supervisors to transmit messages twenty-four hours a day and stay in constant contact with department members, other supervisors, and key members of the organization regardless of where they are physically located. Networks also allow supervisors to participate in electronic meetings and interact with key people outside the organization.

4. **List barriers to effective communication.** Barriers to effective communication include language differences, poor listening habits, lack of feedback, differences in perception, role requirements, poor choice of information medium, lack of honesty, and emotions.

5. **Describe techniques for overcoming communication barriers.** Techniques for overcoming communication barriers include thinking through what you want to say before communicating, constraining emotions, learning to listen, tailoring language to the receiver, matching words and actions, using feedback, and participating in assertiveness training.

6. **List the requirements for active listening.** The requirements for active listening are (1) intensity, (2) empathy, (3) acceptance, and (4) a willingness to take responsibility for completeness.

7. **Explain the behaviors necessary for providing effective feedback.** Behaviors that are necessary for providing effective feedback include focusing on specific behaviors; keeping feedback impersonal, goal oriented, and well timed; ensuring understanding; and directing feedback for improvement toward behavior that the recipient can control.

COMPREHENSION: Review and Discussion Questions

1. "Everything a supervisor does involves communicating." Build an argument to support this statement.

2. Why isn't agreement necessarily a part of good communication?

3. When is a written communication preferable to an oral one? When is it not preferred?

4. Which type of communication method do you prefer to use at work when sending a message to someone else? Why? Do you have the same preference when messages are being sent to you? Explain.

5. "Do as I say, not as I do." Analyze this phrase in terms of supervisors being effective communicators, and in terms of its effect on credibility and trust among the supervisor's employees.

6. How can nonverbal messages be powerful communicators? How can supervisors use nonverbal messages to their advantage?

7. What use, if any, can the grapevine serve? Provide a specific example.

8. Do you believe that supervisors can control the grapevine? Explain your position.

9. Contrast passive and active listening.

10. Why are feedback skills so important to a supervisor's success?

KEY CONCEPT CROSSWORD

ACROSS

2. the emphasis an individual gives to words or phrases in a speech
6. communication that is not spoken, written, or transmitted on a computer
7. the rumor mill in an organization
10. a receiver's translation of a sender's message
12. communication that addresses task-related issues
13. transference of meaning
16. training that focuses on making people more open and self-expressive

DOWN

1. communication that moves in any direction and skips authority levels
3. a measure of the amount of information that is transmitted
4. a technique that requires an individual to concentrate on what is being said
5. information received by the sender from a receiver regarding a message that had been sent
8. gestures and other personal movements that communicate emotions or temperaments
9. the conversion of a message into symbolic form
11. the medium by which a message travels
14. information that is being sent
15. behavior patterns that correspond to the positions people occupy in an organization

ANSWERS TO COMPREHENSION CHECKS

Comprehension Check 10-1

1. b   2. c   3. a   4. a

Comprehension Check 10-2

5. c   6. c   7. a   8. b

Developing Your Supervisory Skills

GETTING TO KNOW YOURSELF

Before you can effectively supervise others, you must understand your present strengths and areas in need of development. To assist in this learning process, we encourage you to complete the following self-assessments from the Prentice Hall Self-Assessment Library 3.4.

1. How Good Are My Listening Skills? (II. A. 2.)

2. What's My Face-to-Face Communications Style? (II. A. 1.)

After you complete the assessment, we suggest you retain the results and store them as part of your "portfolio of learning about yourself."

BUILDING A TEAM

➤ An Experiential Exercise: Practicing Listening Skills

This is a role-play to practice listening skills. Break into groups of three. One person will be the observer. He or she will evaluate the two other role players and provide feedback on their listening skills using the eight points listed in the section titled "Active Listening," which follows.

The second person will take the role of Chris Humphries. Chris is a regional sales supervisor with Hershey Chocolate who is spending the month recruiting on college campuses. Chris joined Hershey three years ago, directly out of college, and went through the company's marketing management training program.

The third person in the group will take the role of Lee Pleasant. Lee is a college senior, graduating at the end of the semester.

Note to the role players: The role descriptions in this exercise establish each character. Follow the guidelines. Don't make up or change the facts you're given, but, within the guidelines, try to involve yourself in the character.

Situation

Preliminary interview (in a college placement center) for a marketing management trainee position with Hershey Chocolate. A brief job description and Lee's résumé follow.

Abbreviated Job Description

Title: Marketing Management Trainee—Chocolate Division
Reports To: Regional Sales Supervisor
Duties and Responsibilities: Completes formal training program at headquarters in Hershey, Pennsylvania. After training:

- Calls on retail stores
- Introduces new products to store personnel
- Distributes sales promotion materials
- Stocks and arranges shelves in stores
- Takes sales orders
- Follows up on complaints or problems
- Completes all necessary sales reports

Abbreviated Résumé

Name: Lee Pleasant
Education: B.S. in Business; GPA 3.6 (out of 4.0). Major: Marketing. Minor: Economics.
Work Experience: Worked fifteen hours a week during semesters and full-time during summer vacations at Barnes & Noble bookstore.
Honors: Dean's list (ranked in top 5 percent of business class).
Other: Intercollegiate tennis team (two-year letter winner); vice president, College Marketing Club.

Stop!

The observer should read both Chris's and Lee's roles. The people playing Chris and Lee, however, should read only their own roles. After all have read their appropriate roles, begin the exercise. You have up to fifteen minutes. When completed, the observer should provide feedback to both of the role players.

Chris Humphries's Role

You will be interviewing approximately 150 students over the next six weeks to fill four trainee positions. You're looking for candidates who are bright, articulate, and ambitious, and have management potential. The Hershey training program is eighteen months long. Trainees will be sales representatives calling on retail stores and will spend the first six weeks taking formal classes at Hershey's head office. The compensation to start is $37,500 a year plus a car. You are to improvise other information as needed. Examples of questions you might ask are the following: Where do you expect to be in five years? What's important to you in a job? What courses did you like best in college? Which did you like least? What makes you think you would do well in this job?

Lee Pleasant's Role

Review your résumé. You are a very good student whose previous work experience has been limited to selling in retail stores part-time while going to school and full-time during the summers. This is your first interview with Hershey, but you're very interested in their training program. Fill in any voids in information as you see fit.

➤ Internet: Web Activity

Go to http://www.pearsonhighered.com/robbins/. Find *Supervision Today!* 7th Ed. and click Companion Website.

ACTIVE LISTENING

Active listening requires you to concentrate on what is being said. It's more than just hearing the words. It involves a concerted effort to understand and interpret the speaker's message.

STEPS IN PRACTICING THE SKILL

STEP 1: Make eye contact. How do you feel when somebody doesn't look at you when you're speaking? If you're like most people, you're likely to interpret this behavior as aloofness or disinterest. Making eye contact with the speaker focuses your attention, reduces the likelihood that you will become distracted, and encourages the speaker.

STEP 2: Exhibit affirmative nods and appropriate facial expressions. The effective listener shows interest in what is being said through nonverbal signals. Affirmative nods and appropriate facial expressions, when added to good eye contact, convey to the speaker that you're listening.

STEP 3: Avoid distracting actions or gestures that suggest boredom. The other side of showing interest is avoiding actions that suggest that your mind is some-where else. When listening, don't look at your watch, shuffle papers, play with your pencil, or engage in similar distractions. They make the speaker feel that you're bored or disinterested or indicate that you aren't fully attentive.

STEP 4: Ask questions. The critical listener analyzes what he or she hears and asks questions. This behavior provides clarification, ensures understanding, and assures the speaker that you're listening.

STEP 5: Paraphrase using your own words. The effective listener uses phrases such as, "What I hear you saying is…" or "Do you mean…?" Paraphrasing is an excellent control device to check on whether you're listening carefully and to verify that what you heard is accurate.

STEP 6: Avoid interrupting the speaker. Let the speaker complete his or her thought before you try to respond. Don't try to second-guess where the speaker's thoughts are going. When the speaker is finished, you'll know it.

STEP 7: Don't overtalk. Most of us would rather speak our own ideas than listen to what someone else says. Talking might be more fun and silence might be uncomfortable, but you can't talk and listen at the same time. The good listener recognizes this fact and doesn't overtalk.

STEP 8: Make smooth transitions between the roles of speaker and listener. The effective listener makes transitions smoothly from speaker to listener and back to speaker. From a listening perspective this means concentrating on what a speaker has to say and practicing not thinking about what you're going to say as soon as you get your chance.

➤ Communicating Effectively

1. Develop a two- to three-page report describing what you can do to improve the likelihood that your verbal communications will be received and understood as you intended them to be.

2. List the common communication shortcuts you use in text messaging or e-mails. Identify fifteen acronyms and describe what they mean. How and when would these acronyms be used appropriately? What barriers might these acronyms create for a user? A receiver? Someone unfamiliar with texting?

THINKING CRITICALLY

➤ Case 10-A: Communication Problems at Ozark Corporation

March is the busiest time of the year at Ozark Corporation. Thus, when the production line in Section A has trouble for the second time in a week, Sam Case decides he'd better get it straightened out immediately. As the lead supervisor, Sam is directly in charge of Sections A and B.

Sam calls in Paul Banks, the new supervisor in Section A. Their conversation is as follows:

SAM: Paul, we seem to be having some problems in your section. The line has been down twice in the last three days. This is our busiest time of the year. We can't afford to have recurring problems of this type. I want you to stop that quality-control project I have you working on, find out what the problem is out on the line, and get rid of it.

PAUL: Okay, I'll get out there, find out what's causing the problem, and get rid of it.

SAM: Fine.

A quick check of the line reveals that there was a problem with the automatic control unit. Paul checks and finds that it would take four hours to replace the unit. "If you put in a new one," the maintenance man tells him, "you won't have a problem with it for at least sixteen months. It's up to you. I'll do whatever you tell me." Paul tells the man to replace the automatic control unit.

By late afternoon the new unit is installed and the line is operating at full speed. However, the next morning, after Sam receives the previous day's production figures, he calls Paul in. "What happened in your section? I thought you were going to fix the problem."

"I did," Paul tells him. "The automatic control unit was giving us trouble, so I replaced it."

Sam's voice indicates that he is not happy with this decision. "You pulled the unit in the middle of a workday? Why didn't you wait until the shift was over and have the unit pulled then? You could have done preventive maintenance to get through the rest of the day. You gave up two hours of production time to replace a unit that could have waited for maintenance."

Paul is shocked. He thought he had done the right thing. "Look, Sam," he says, "you told me to get rid of the problem and I did. You didn't say anything about preventive maintenance or not stopping the line."

Sam realizes that the discussion is beginning to get out of hand. "Look, let's stand back and quietly discuss this matter." With that, the two men start discussing the matter from the beginning.

RESPONDING TO THE CASE

1. Analyze the communication between the lead supervisor, Sam Case, and the new supervisor in Section A, Paul Banks. What did Sam do wrong?

2. How could the problem have been prevented? In your answer discuss the requirement for active listening.

3. Discuss the barriers to effective communication. What should Sam and Paul learn from this experience that will make them better communicators and more effective supervisors?

➤ Case 10-B: A Pinch of this and a Dash of that

How do you combine two packaged-food companies, both with very well-known household brand names, and make it work? That's the challenge managers at General Mills faced when it acquired Pillsbury. The company's chief learning officer, Kevin Wilde, said, "Let's get the best out of both of our marketing organizations. And let's not stop there." So they decided to identify, share, and integrate the best practices from both companies. And employee teams played a major role in how the company proceeded.

An intensive training program called "Brand Champions" was created and launched. The program was designed not just for marketing specialists, but for all employees from different functional areas who worked on particular brands. These cross-functional teams attended the in-house training together as a unified group. According to one of the program developers, Beth Gunderson, specific benefits of including these teams soon became evident. "A person from human resources, for instance, would ask a provocative question precisely because she wasn't a marketer. And you'd see the look on the marketers' faces: Whoa, I never thought of that." It helped employees understand and appreciate different perspectives.

Another benefit of including people from different functions was improved communication throughout the company. People were no longer griping about what other functional areas were doing. Employees began to understand how the other functional areas worked and how each area's contribution was important to the overall success of the company.

The training program has been so successful that now General Mills' production plants have asked for a mini-version of the course. "They want to understand the language marketers speak and why things are done as they are." Oh...and one other example of how successful the program has been. Betty Crocker is well known for packaged cake mixes, but less so for cookie mixes. Inspired by input from the group, the cookie-mix team decided to go after scratch bakers. (These are people who bake from scratch rather than from a boxed mix. As one person said, they were "taking on grandma.") The cookie mixes were reformulated and now the brand owns 90 percent of the dry cookie mix category.

RESPONDING TO THE CASE

1. What barriers were there to communication between the employees of General Mills and Pillsbury?

2. Although not a "different language" per se, how might the language of the functional areas within the organization have interfered with communication?

3. How did the employee roles from the combined organizations impact the communication process?

4. As a supervisor, what suggestions would you offer to improve the communication between groups?

Sources: Based on L. Gratton and T. J. Erickson, "8 Ways to Build Collaborative Teams," *Harvard Business Review*, November 2007, 100–109; and J. Gordon, "Building Brand Champions," *Training* January/February 2007, 14–17.

11

Developing Groups

Key Concepts

After completing this chapter, you will be able to define these supervisory terms:

- cohesiveness
- emergent leader
- formal group
- group

- informal group
- social loafing
- team

Chapter Outcomes

After reading this chapter, you will be able to:

1. Contrast a group and a team.
2. Define *norms*.
3. Explain the relationship between cohesiveness and group productivity.
4. Describe who is likely to become an emergent leader in an informal group.
5. Explain what a supervisor can do when group norms are hindering department performance.
6. Identify three categories of teams.
7. List the characteristics of real teams.
8. List actions a supervisor can take to improve team performance.
9. Describe the role of teams in continuous-improvement programs.

Responding to a Supervisory Dilemma

You're a production supervisor at a company that makes circuit breakers and other electrical parts. One of your newest employees is Chris Petersen, who has a bachelor's degree in engineering and a master's in business. You hired Chris out of college for a position in supply chain management.

You've recently been chosen to supervise a cross-functional team to look at ways to reduce inventory costs. This team would essentially be a permanent task force. You've decided to have team members come from supplier relations, cost accounting, transportation, and production systems. You've also decided to include Chris on the team. Although an employee of only four months, Chris has impressed you with energy, smarts, and industriousness. You think this would be an excellent opportunity for Chris to increase visibility in the company and expand understanding of the company's inventory system.

When you called Chris into your office to give the good news, you were quite surprised by the response. "I'm not a team player," Chris said, "I didn't join clubs in high school. I was on the track team and I did well, but track is an individual sport. We were a team only in the sense that we rode together in the same bus to away meets. In college, I avoided the whole Greek-life thing. Some people may call me a loner. I don't think that's true. I can work well with others, but I hate meetings and committees. To me, they waste so much time. And anything you're working on with a group, you've got all these different personalities that you have to adjust for. I'm an independent operator. Give me a job and I'll get it done. I work harder than anyone I know—and I give my employer 150 percent. But I don't want my performance to be dependent on the other people in my group. They may not work as hard as I will. Someone is sure to shirk some of their responsibilities. I just don't want to be a team player."

You are somewhat perplexed by Chris's comments. You had discussed the possibility of working in teams with Chris during the job interview, and you did not get this reaction. You believe Chris would be an asset to your team.

What do you do? Should you make joining the inventory cost reduction team optional for Chris? Is it unethical for you to require someone like Chris to be part of a team? Conversely, is it unethical for you to excuse people like Chris from working on a team just because they don't like teams—especially when it's in the best interest of the organization to have such talent on a particular team? Will you change how you address teamwork in your interviewing?

T he behavior of individuals in groups is not the same as the total of all the individuals' behavior. Individuals act differently in groups than they do when they are alone. Therefore, if we want to understand organizational behavior more fully, we need to study groups.

group
Two or more interacting and interdependent individuals who come together to achieve particular objectives.

formal group
A workgroup established by the organization and given designated work assignments and established tasks.

What Is a Group?

A group is defined as two or more interacting and interdependent individuals who come together to achieve particular objectives. Groups can be either formal or informal. Formal groups are workgroups established by the organization that have designated work assignments and established tasks. In formal groups, the behaviors in which one should engage are stipulated by and directed toward organizational goals. Examples of formal groups include committees, group meetings, task forces, and work teams.

Formal groups can be either permanent or temporary. Some committees, for instance, are permanent in that they meet on a planned and regular basis. At Cedars-Sinai Hospital in New York, all nursing supervisors in the surgical unit meet every Monday morning. There is also a committee made up of supervisors and employees who study ways to continually improve patient services. After they've finished their work and presented their recommendations to the hospital's administrators, the committee is dissolved. This is an illustration of a temporary formal group.

In contrast, informal groups are of a social nature. These groups are natural formations that appear in the work environment in response to the need for social contact. Informal groups tend to form around friendships and common interests. For instance, people who carpool together, individuals who share an interest in golf or eat lunch with each other, or employees who band together to support a peer who has had a tragedy at home are all examples of informal groups.

Are formal workgroups the same thing as teams? Not necessarily. Many formal workgroups are merely individuals who sporadically interact but who have no collective commitment that requires joint efforts. That is, the group's total performance is merely the summation of the individual group members' performance.

What differentiates a team is that members are committed to a common purpose, have a set of specific performance goals, and hold themselves mutually accountable for the team's results. Teams, in other words, are greater than the sum of their parts. Later in this chapter, we elaborate on the characteristics that differentiate successful teams from ordinary workgroups.

informal group
A social group that forms naturally in the work environment in response to the need for social contact.

team
A workgroup whose members are committed to a common purpose, have a set of specific performance goals, and hold themselves mutually accountable for the team's results.

Why Do People Join Groups?

There is no single reason why individuals join groups. Because most people belong to a number of groups, it's obvious that different groups provide different benefits to their members. Most people join a group out of needs for security, status, self-esteem, affiliation, power, or goal achievement (see Exhibit 11-1).

Security reflects strength in numbers. By joining a group, individuals can reduce the insecurity of "standing alone." The group helps the individual to feel stronger, have fewer self-doubts, and be more resistant to threats. Status indicates prestige that comes from belonging to a particular group. Inclusion in a group that others view as important

REASON	PERCEIVED BENEFIT
Security	Gaining strength in numbers; reducing the insecurity of standing alone
Status	Achieving some level of prestige from belonging to a particular group
Self-esteem	Enhancing one's feeling of self-worth—especially membership in a highly valued group
Affiliation	Satisfying one's social needs through social interaction
Power	Achieving something through a group action not possible individually; protecting group members from unreasonable demands of others
Goal achievement	Providing an opportunity to accomplish a particular task when it takes more than one person's talents, knowledge, or power to complete the job

Exhibit 11-1
Reasons people join groups.

provides recognition and status for its members. Self-esteem conveys people's feelings of self-worth. That is, in addition to conveying status to those outside the group, membership can also raise feelings of self-esteem—being accepted into a highly valued group.

Affiliation with groups can fulfill one's social needs. People enjoy the regular interaction that comes with group membership. For many people, on-the-job interactions are their primary means of fulfilling their need for affiliation. For almost all people, workgroups contribute significantly to fulfilling their need for friendships and social relations. One of the appealing aspects of groups is that they represent power. What often cannot be achieved individually becomes possible through group action. Of course, this power might not be sought only to make demands on others. It might be desired merely as a countermeasure. To protect themselves from unreasonable demands by supervisors, individuals may align with others. Informal groups additionally provide opportunities for individuals to exercise power over others. For individuals who desire to influence others, groups can offer power without a formal position of authority in the organization. As a group leader, you might be able to make requests of group members and obtain compliance without any of the responsibilities that traditionally go with formal managerial positions. For people with a high power need, groups can be a vehicle for fulfillment. Finally, people may join a group for goal achievement. There are times when it takes more than one person to accomplish a particular task; there is a need to pool talents, knowledge, or power to get a job completed. In such instances, management will rely on a formal group.

Understanding Informal Workgroups

Supervisors must learn to live with the fact that, like the grapevine (discussed in Chapter 10), informal workgroups emerge naturally in organizations. You should expect that your employees will be members of many informal workgroups. The reason you should be interested in the workings of informal groups is simple. These groups can shape the behavior of employees and affect productivity in your department.

To fully appreciate and to begin our understanding of informal workgroups, we need to look at three factors: norms, cohesiveness, and emergent leadership.

WHAT ARE NORMS AND HOW DO THEY AFFECT WORK BEHAVIOR?

Did you ever notice that golfers don't speak while their partners are putting on the green, or that employees generally don't criticize their bosses in public? This is because of *norms*. All groups have established norms, or acceptable standards that are shared by the group's members. Norms dictate things such as output levels, absenteeism rates, promptness or tardiness, and the amount of socializing allowed on the job.

Norms, for example, dictate the dress code among customer service representatives at one cellular phone company. Most workers who have little face-to-face customer contact come to work dressed very casually. However, on occasion, a newly hired employee will come to work the first few days dressed in a suit. Those who do are often teased and pressured until their dress conforms to the group's standard.

Although each group has its own unique set of norms, common classes of norms appear in most organizations. These focus on effort and performance, dress, and loyalty. Probably the most widespread norms are related to levels of effort and performance. Workgroups typically provide their members with very explicit cues on how hard to work, what level of output to have, when to look busy, when it's acceptable to goof off, and the like. These norms are extremely powerful in affecting an individual employee's performance. They are so powerful that performance predictions that are based solely on an employee's ability and level of personal motivation often prove to be wrong.

Some organizations have formal dress codes—explicit statements regarding how employees are to dress while at work. However, even in their absence, norms frequently

News Flash!

SOLOMON ASCH AND GROUP CONFORMITY

Does one's desire to be accepted as part of a group leave him or her susceptible to conforming to the group's norms? Will the group place strong enough pressure to change a member's attitude and behavior? In the research by Solomon Asch, the answer appears to be yes.

Asch's study involved groups of seven or eight people who sat in a classroom and were asked to compare two cards held by an investigator. One card had one line; the other had three lines of varying length. As shown in Exhibit 11-2, one of the lines on the three-line card was identical to the line on the one-line card. Also, as shown in Exhibit 11-2, the difference in line length was quite obvious; under ordinary conditions, subjects made fewer than 1 percent errors. The object was to announce aloud which of the three lines matched the single line. But what happens if all the other members in the group begin to give incorrect answers? Will the pressure to conform cause the unsuspecting subject (USS) to alter his or her answers to align with those of the others? That was what Asch wanted to know. He arranged the group so that only the USS was unaware that the experiment was fixed. The seating was prearranged so that the USS was the last to announce his or her decision.

The experiment began with two sets of matching exercises. All the subjects gave the right answers. On the third set, however, the first subject gave an obviously wrong answer—for example, saying C in Exhibit 11-2. The next subject gave the same wrong answer, and so did the others, until it got to the unsuspecting subject. He or she knew that B was the same as X, but everyone else had said C. The decision confronting the USS was this: Do you publicly state a perception that differs from the announced position of the others? Or do you give an answer that you strongly believe is incorrect to have your response agree with the other group members? Asch's subjects conformed in about 35 percent of many experiments and many trials. That is, the subjects gave answers that they knew were wrong but that were consistent with the replies of other group members.

For supervisors, the Asch study provides considerable insight into workgroup behaviors. The tendency, as Asch showed, is for individual members to go along with the "pack." To diminish the negative aspects of conformity, supervisors should create a climate of openness in which employees are free to discuss problems without fear of retaliation.

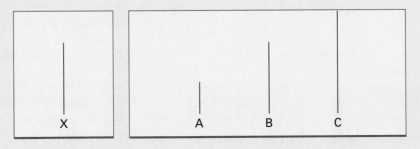

Exhibit 11-2

Examples of cards used in the Asch study.

Source: S. E. Asch, "Effects of Group Pressure upon the Modification and Distortion of Judgements," in H. Guetzkow (ed.), *Groups, Leadership and Men* (Pittsburgh, PA: Carnegie Press, 1951), 177–190.

develop to dictate the kind of clothing that should be worn to work. College seniors, interviewing for their first postgraduate job, pick up this norm quickly. Every spring, on college campuses throughout the country, the students who are interviewing for jobs can usually be spotted; they are the ones walking around in the dark gray or blue suits. They are enacting the dress norms that they have learned are expected in professional positions. Of course, what connotes acceptable dress in one organization may be very different from the norms in another.

Few supervisors appreciate employees who ridicule the organization. Similarly, professional employees and those in the supervisory ranks recognize that most employers view people who actively look for another job unfavorably. People who are unhappy know that they should keep their job searches secret. These examples demonstrate that loyalty norms are widespread in organizations. This concern for demonstrating loyalty, by the way, often explains why ambitious candidates to positions of greater authority in an organization willingly take work home at night, come in on weekends, and accept transfers to cities where they would otherwise not prefer to live.

Because individuals desire acceptance by the groups to which they belong, they are susceptible to conformity pressures (see "News Flash! Solomon Asch and Group Conformity"). The impact that group pressures for conformity can have on an individual member's judgment and attitudes was demonstrated in the now-classic studies by Solomon Asch. Asch's results suggest that there are group norms that press us toward conformity.[1] We desire to be one of the group and avoid being visibly different. We can generalize this finding further to say that when an individual's opinion of objective data differs significantly from that of others in the group, he or she feels extensive pressure to align his or her opinion to conform with those of the others.

ARE COHESIVE GROUPS MORE EFFECTIVE?

cohesiveness
The degree to which group members are attracted to each other and are motivated to stay in the group.

Informal groups differ in their cohesiveness. Cohesiveness is the degree to which members are attracted to each other and are motivated to stay in the group. For instance, some workgroups are more cohesive because the members have spent a great deal of time together; the group's size is small and facilitates high interaction; the group has experienced external threats, which have brought members closer together; or the group has developed a history of previous success. Cohesiveness is important because it's been found to be related to the group's productivity.

Studies consistently show that the relationship of cohesiveness and productivity depends on the performance-related norms established by the group. The more cohesive the group, the more its members will follow its goals. If performance-related norms are high (e.g., high output, quality work, cooperation with individuals outside the group), a cohesive group will be more productive than a less cohesive group will be. But if cohesiveness is high and performance norms are low, productivity will be low. If cohesiveness is low and performance norms are high, productivity will increase, but less than in the high cohesiveness–high norms situation. And where cohesiveness and performance-related norms are both low, productivity will tend to fall into the low to moderate range. These conclusions are summarized in Exhibit 11-3.

emergent leader
A leader who emerges within a workgroup without having formal authority in the organization.

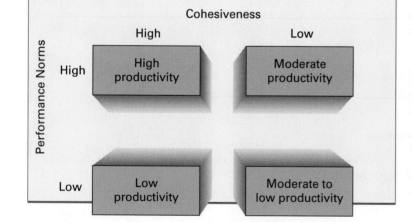

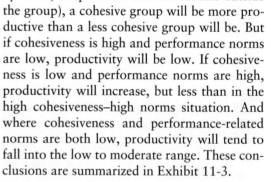

Exhibit 11-3

Relationship among group cohesiveness, performance norms, and productivity.

WHAT IS AN EMERGENT LEADER?

As noted in Chapter 9, leaders aren't always supervisors or managers. Leaders frequently emerge within workgroups, yet they have no formal authority in the organization. Despite their lack of formal authority, these emergent leaders are a force that supervisors must be prepared to reckon with.

[1]S. E. Asch, "Effects of Group Pressure upon the Modification and Distortion of Judgements," in H. Guetzkow (ed.), *Groups, Leadership and Men* (Pittsburgh, PA: Carnegie Press, 1951), pp. 177–190.

How do you spot an emergent leader? They are the ones that others like to be with. People naturally gravitate to them. When they speak, others are more likely to listen. They often become the spokespersons for their groups. They also tend to be central links in the informal communication chain—important information tends to reach them early, and they pass on information to others. In many cases, they have become informal leaders largely because of their contacts in the organization and their ability to use those contacts to access important information.

Identify the emergent leaders within workgroups and build ties with them. Recognize that they have influence over their group members. By respecting their leadership positions and gaining their cooperation, you can turn potential enemies into allies. The effective supervisor also uses the grapevine as a means to identify the needs that the formal system isn't fulfilling. In doing so, supervisors are able to identify fairly accurately which individuals and groups are gaining and losing influence.

Who is likely to become an emergent leader? Look for people with charismatic traits and those with important but scarce knowledge about the organization or technical aspects of the group's work. Charismatic qualities such as self-confidence and the ability to articulate goals clearly tend to attract followers. Similarly, the group often projects leadership status onto individuals who possess knowledge that group members believe they need to function well.

Also keep in mind that emergent leaders change over time. As issues, problems, and people change within a department and the organization, new leaders will arise. Ongoing monitoring of the grapevine will typically signal those changes to you. It is important to keep track because different leaders seek to impose different agendas on their groups.

HOW CAN INFORMAL GROUPS BE HELPFUL?

A final point that helps us understand informal groups better is that they arise to fill gaps that exist in the formal system.

Every organization—no matter how well it's structured—has voids. Despite well-designed formal communication paths, departmental designations, and job descriptions, there will always be gaps. Informal groups fill these holes. For instance, in jobs where employees experience high levels of stress (e.g., air traffic controllers), informal groups often develop as a means for stressed employees to share their frustrations and let off steam. That's because such jobs come with pressure created by time constraints, have drastic consequences if mistakes are made, or involve dealing with extremely demanding customers. In jobs where everyone essentially does similar tasks, informal groups can fulfill the need for status. Those included in the informal group can gain recognition and prestige that their work alone doesn't provide. And in departments or organizational units where formal communication with employees is limited, informal groups typically arise to fill the information void.

ARE THERE WAYS TO INFLUENCE THE INFORMAL WORKGROUP?

Informal workgroups can have positive benefits to an organization and to a supervisor. They fill gaps in the formal organization, provide a useful channel of communication, and fill other unmet needs of employees. Of course, they can also be dysfunctional—especially when their performance-related norms are low. Some facets of these informal groups are beyond a supervisor's control. But there are also some actions that supervisors can take to manage these groups and turn them into an asset for the department and the organization. Let's look at some of these.

Group Norms   As a supervisor, pay attention to the norms of the informal groups that include members of your department. Who belongs to what groups? What do these groups value? How do they enforce their norms?

If these norms are hindering your department's performance, you can consider doing a few things. You can request transfers for one or more of the group's members. Physical separation can undermine the group's influence by reducing cohesiveness. Also consider rewarding departmental members who act against the dysfunctional norms. For example, give preferred work assignments, paid time off, or praise to employees who don't restrict their work output to satisfy the group's modest performance norms.

Department Goals Ambiguity works in favor of informal groups whose goals are at odds with the formal goals of the department. When supervisors fail to make their department goals clear or allow employees to lose sight of those goals, employee behaviors that hinder those goals don't tend to be too visible. In contrast, when supervisors consistently reiterate formal departmental goals and make clear which behaviors are consistent with achieving those goals, dysfunctional behaviors become more readily evident (and employees are discouraged from engaging in those dysfunctional behaviors).

So, if you find informal groups in your department encouraging low-performance-related norms by doing such things as emphasizing quantity over quality, failing to cooperate with other departments, taking the customer for granted, ignoring safety regulations, or showing disrespect for minority employees, make the department's formal goals clear. Show how dysfunctional behaviors undermine those goals, and drive home these points by consistently articulating what the department is trying to accomplish.

Comprehension Check 11-1

1. Two or more interacting and interdependent individuals who come together to achieve a particular objective are called a
   a. team
   b. group
   c. task force
   d. all of the above

2. Acceptable standards that are shared by team members are called
   a. behaviors
   b. organization culture
   c. norms
   d. work rules

3. Which one of the following is *not* a reason people join groups?
   a. Self-esteem
   b. Security
   c. Money
   d. Power

4. An emergent leader is one who
   a. develops group norms for the group to follow
   b. establishes group goals to be achieved
   c. develops group cohesiveness
   d. leads without having formal authority in the organization

The Increasing Use of Teams

Teams are increasingly becoming the prime vehicle around which work is being designed. Why? Because teams typically outperform individuals when the tasks being done require multiple skills, judgment, and experience. As organizations restructure themselves to compete more effectively and efficiently, they are turning to teams as a way to use employee talents better. We are finding that teams are more flexible and responsive to changing events than departments or other forms of permanent groupings. They can be quickly assembled, deployed, refocused, and disbanded.

Teams fall into three categories depending on their objectives. Some organizations use teams to provide advice. For instance, they create temporary task forces to recommend ways to cut costs, improve quality, or select a site for a new plant. Some organizations use teams to manage. They introduce management teams at various levels in the organization to run things. However, supervisors are most likely to be involved with teams that are created to make or do things. They include production teams, design teams, and office teams that handle administrative work.

Companies such as General Electric, AT&T, Hewlett-Packard, Motorola, Chrysler Group LLC., and 3M are making work teams the centerpiece around which they create work units. For instance, at a GE factory in Puerto Rico, every one of the plant's workers is a member of a team. Even the not-for-profit sector is getting on the team bandwagon. The San Diego Zoo, for example, has created permanent teams to share responsibility for running native habitat zones.

In organizations that are reorganizing work around work teams, supervisors must learn how to coordinate team activity effectively. In many cases, management's emphasis has been on creating self-managed teams. As we'll see, this is redefining the supervisor's managerial role.

TURNING GROUPS INTO TEAMS

As we noted at the opening of this chapter, groups and teams are not necessarily the same thing. Exhibit 11-4 illustrates how a workgroup evolves into a real team. The primary force that moves a workgroup toward being a real high-performing team is its emphasis on performance.

A *working group* is merely a group of individuals who interact primarily to share information and to make decisions to help each other perform within a given area of responsibility. There is no need or opportunity to engage in collective work that requires joint effort, so performance is merely the summation of each group member's individual contribution.

A *pseudo team* is the product of negative synergy. The sum of the whole is less than the potential of the individual parts because of factors such as poor communication, antagonistic conflicts, and avoidance of responsibilities. This is not a team because it doesn't focus on collective performance and members have no interest in shaping a common purpose.

A *potential team* is going in the right direction. It recognizes the need for higher performance and is really trying hard to achieve it, but its purpose and goals need greater clarity or the team may need better coordination. The result is that it has not yet established a sense of collective accountability.

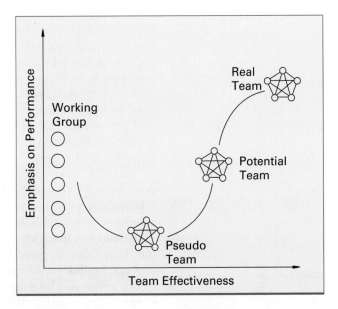

Exhibit 11-4

Comparing groups and teams.

A *real team* is the ultimate goal. This is a unit with a set of common characteristics that lead to consistently high performance.

THE FIVE-STAGE MODEL OF GROUP DEVELOPMENT

Groups tend to pass through developmental stages as they mature, and several different models of group development exist. One popular model of group development was formulated by Tuckman and Jensen in 1977.

Their model proposes five distinct stages of group development, and the suggestion is that groups must experience the first four stages to achieve their maximum development. The five stages are Forming, Storming, Norming, Performing, and Adjourning. Progression through the stages may be accomplished without an awareness of them, but supervisors with knowledge of the stages can facilitate their group, thereby speeding progress to the performing stage.

Stage 1: Forming In the Forming stage, individuals know little about the other members of the group, and even though they display independent behavior, they are on their best behavior because they want to be accepted by others and avoid conflict. In this stage, individuals are motivated but unclear or uncertain about what they are supposed to do in the group. Individuals focus on the duties of group members and what needs to be done while simultaneously gathering information and forming impressions of each other and the task of the group. During this stage, many mature, experienced group members model appropriate group behavior. This developmental stage is important because members get to know one another and make new friends.

This stage is very supervisor directed, and group members depend on the leader for goals, guidance, and direction. Supervisors can use this opportunity to see how individuals work and respond to pressure. At the same time they must spend time explaining the purpose, objectives, and external relationships. Group members learn about the opportunity and challenges, agree on goals, and begin to tackle the tasks. Sharing group development information with the group members is helpful during this stage, and even though this is a comfortable stage for the group members, there is not much task accomplishment.

Stage 2: Storming In the Storming stage, supervisors may become more accessible to group members but still need to direct and guide decision making while modeling professional behavior. Supervisors must focus the group on its goals to keep members from becoming distracted by relationship and emotional issues. With the leadership of the supervisor, the group can address issues surrounding the problems they are supposed to solve, determine how to function independently and together, and define the leadership model they are willing to accept. During this stage, the supervisor has the opportunity to coach the group members and sell them on the importance of the task.

Growth occurs during the Storming stage, in which different ideas compete for consideration. This can be a destructive stage for the group and can lower motivation if allowed to get out of control. Sometimes storming is quickly resolved, but occasionally groups never leave this stage. Decisions don't come easily for any group, and individuals remain nice to each other for only so long as issues are addressed. Generally, groups are clear in their purpose, but uncertainties related to the work of the group or to roles and responsibilities within the group persist, and compromises may be required to enable progress. This stage will be contentious, unpleasant, and even painful to group members averse to conflict, and some people's patience may break early. Many minor confrontations will arise that are quickly dealt with or glossed over, and some team members may continue to focus on minutiae to evade real issues. Many group members may feel relieved to be getting into the real issues, whereas others will prefer to remain in the comfort and security of stage 1.

During this stage, the tolerance of each team member and their differences needs to be emphasized because without tolerance and patience the team will fail. Group members will open up and confront the ideas and perspectives of others as they vie for position in an attempt to establish themselves in relation to other team members and the leader. In-groups and factions often form, and power struggles may arise as members challenge the leader. Many group members feel as if they are winning or losing battles and often look to structure and rules to end the conflict. As members work through this stage, the conflict may appear to be suppressed, but it is often there under the surface. Group member maturity is a factor in determining whether the group will move out of this stage. It is not unusual to see immature members of the group act out to demonstrate their knowledge and convince others their ideas are correct.

Stage 3: Norming The Norming stage begins after the group members have worked through their arguments and learned to understand each other better. Eventually, they begin to appreciate each other's skills and experience. They listen to each other, appreciate and support each other, and are prepared to change preconceived views. They feel they are part of a cohesive, effective group where commitment and unity are strong, with roles and responsibilities clear and accepted. The scope of the group's tasks or responsibilities is clear and agreed on. Big decisions are made by group agreement and consensus but smaller decisions may be delegated to individuals or small teams within the group.

At this point, the group may become more gregarious, engaging in social activities as they discuss and develop their processes and working style. Group members modify their behavior and develop work habits that make group work seem easier. This stage is marked by agreement on rules, values, professional behavior, shared methods, working tools, and even taboos. Trust begins to develop and individual motivation increases as the group gets more acquainted with the project.

During this time, respect for the leader increases and leadership begins to be shared by the group. Group members begin to take responsibility for making decisions and for their professional behavior. Supervisors become more participative than they are in the earlier stages, often doing more facilitating and empowering the group to make decisions. Supervisors should be aware that because group members have worked hard to attain this stage they may resist internal and external pressure to change because they fear the group might break up or revert to a storm. Supervisors must bear in mind that groups in this phase may lose their creativity if the norming behaviors are so strong that they begin to stifle healthy dissent and exhibit groupthink.

Stage 4: Performing The Performing stage is marked by the apparent flexibility of the group as it works toward the accomplishment of its tasks. At this point, the group appears strategically aware and knows why it is doing what it is doing. This shared vision, coupled with the motivation and knowledge of the group, results in autonomous behavior and the ability to work through the decision-making process without supervision. Extremely task oriented, the group works to achieve goals and makes most task-related decisions by judging against criteria agreed on with the leader.

Group members are interdependent, but dissent is expected, and when disagreements occur, they are resolved in a positive manner with changes to processes and structure made by the group. The group is in a high-performance mode and functions as a unit to get the job done smoothly and effectively without inappropriate conflict or the need for external supervision. Working to achieve their goal, the group also attends to relationship, style, and process issues along the way. There is a high level of group identity, loyalty, and morale with everyone trusting each other enough to allow independent activity. This high comfort level results in all of the group's energy being directed toward the task(s).

At this point, supervisors delegate and oversee tasks, but the group makes most of the necessary decisions. The group requires delegated tasks and projects but does not need to be instructed or assisted. However, the group may ask the leader for assistance with personal and interpersonal development. Supervisors must be aware that even high-performing groups will revert to earlier stages, going through the stages many times as a reaction to changing circumstances. For example, changes in supervision may cause the group to revert to storming as the new supervisor challenges existing norms and dynamics of the group.

Stage 5: Adjourning The Adjourning stage addresses the group from a perspective beyond the purpose of the first four stages and is relevant to the people in the group and their well-being. In this stage, group members recognize the task is completed and begin to disengage from other group members. If the task has been completed successfully, and the group has fulfilled its purpose, group members can move on to new things, feeling good about what the group has achieved. Group members need to recognize what they have done and consciously prepare to move on. Supervisors should encourage group members to be proud of their achievements and of having the opportunity to be part of such a productive group. However, supervisors should recognize there may be a sense of loss felt by group members, and they should be sensitive to the potential for group members to feel vulnerable, particularly if members of the group have been closely bonded and feel a sense of insecurity or threat from adjournment of the group.

The five-stage model assumes that groups progress through the stages and become more effective as they persist to completion of a task, but groups do not always move cleanly from one stage to the next. Groups may be in several stages simultaneously and may regress and move ahead unpredictably. Supervisors should consider that the process is dynamic rather than static and that even though progression through the stages appears linear, groups can move back and forth between stages as group membership changes. Experienced supervisors are aware of this and always strive to lead groups back to the performance stage. Supervisors should also be aware that groups may become comfortable with a particular stage and resist moving to a new stage.[2]

A MODEL OF DEVELOPMENT FOR DEADLINE-DRIVEN AD HOC GROUPS

Ad hoc groups facing tight deadlines appear to have a two-phase development cycle all their own. This cycle is referred to as the *punctuated-equilibrium model*. The first phase includes the initial meeting of the group and determines the direction of the group. In this initial period, many norms of behavior as well as assumptions regarding the process of the group are established. Even though these norms may not be in the best interest of the group, they usually continue to guide the group during the project. During this period, the group is locked into an unchanging process that resists change even if new information is discovered. The group continues to operate this way until it reaches the midpoint of the time allotted for the existence of the group (for student groups this could be halfway through the semester).

At the halfway point in the existence of the group, a crisis of personality conflict, dissatisfaction with the progress or direction of the project, or some other internal or external force results in a wake-up call of awareness that something needs to be accomplished, and soon! This crisis is the beginning of the second phase of the cycle. During the second phase, the group becomes highly effective, functioning as a team instead of a group of disconnected individuals. This heightened effort continues until the last meeting of the group when there is usually a last-minute burst of frenzied effort to complete the task.

---

[2]S. Robbins and T. Judge, *Organizational Behavior*, 13th ed. (Upper Saddle River, NJ: Pearson Prentice Hall, 2009), 286–287; B. Tuckman, "Developmental Sequences in Small Groups," *Psychological Bulletin* 63, no. 6 (June 1965), 384–399; and B. Tuckman and M. Jensen, "Stages of Small-Group Development Revisited," *Group and Organizational Studies* 2, no. 4 (December 1977), 419–427.

Supervisors must realize this model is limited to deadline-driven ad hoc groups, and they should pay attention to the task and behavior tone set during the startup phase of the project. Because groups reach the crisis point halfway through the duration of the project, supervisors must plan for it, monitor for signs of it, and outline steps for a positive transition out of the crisis. Because group members are often frustrated by an apparent lack of progress, supervisors should periodically appraise the group of its progress toward the goal.[3]

HOW DO YOU BUILD EFFECTIVE TEAMS?

Studies of effective teams have found that they contain a small number of people with complementary skills who are equally committed to a common purpose, common goals, and a common working approach for which they hold themselves mutually accountable.[4]

Small Size The best teams tend to be small. Teams with more than about ten members can have difficulty getting much done. They have trouble interacting constructively and agreeing. Large numbers of people usually cannot develop the common purpose, goals, approach, and mutual accountability of a real team. They tend merely to go through the motions. So, in designing effective teams, keep them to ten or fewer people. If the natural working unit is larger, and you want a team effort, break the group into subteams. Federal Express, for instance, has divided the one-thousand clerical workers at its headquarters into teams of five to ten members each.

Complementary Skills To perform effectively, a team requires three types of skills. First, it needs people with *technical expertise*. Second, it needs people with *problem-solving and decision-making skills* to identify problems, generate alternatives, evaluate those alternatives, and make competent choices. Finally, teams need people with good *interpersonal skills* (listening, feedback, conflict resolution). No team can achieve its performance potential without developing all three types of skills. The right mix is crucial. Too much of one at the expense of others results in lower team performance.

Incidentally, teams don't need to have all the complementary skills at the beginning. In teams in which members value personal growth and development, one or more members often take responsibility for learning the skills in which the group is deficient, as long as the skill potential exists. Additionally, personal compatibility among members is not crucial to the team's success if the technical, decision-making, and interpersonal skills are in place.

Common Purpose Does the team have a meaningful purpose to which all members aspire? This purpose is a vision. It's broader than any specific goals. High-performing teams have a common and meaningful purpose that provides direction, momentum, and commitment for members.

The development team at Apple Computer that designed the Macintosh, for example, was almost religiously committed to creating a user-friendly machine that would revolutionize the way people used computers. Production teams at Ford are united by the common purpose of building an American automobile that can successfully compete in terms of quality and price with the best Japanese cars.

Members of successful teams put a tremendous amount of time and effort into discussing, shaping, and agreeing on a purpose that belongs to them collectively and individually. This common purpose, when accepted by the team, becomes the equivalent of what navigation is to a ship captain—it provides direction and guidance under any and all conditions.

---

[3]Robbins and Judge, *Organizational Behavior*, 287–288; C. Gersick, "Time and Transition in Work Teams: Toward a New Model of Group Development," *Academy of Management Journal* 31, no. 1 (March 1998), 9–41; and A. Seers and S. Woodruff, "Temporal Pacing in Task Forces: Group Development or Deadline Pressure?" *Journal of Management* 23, no. 2 (March–April 1997), 169–187, findarticles.com/p/articles/mi_m4256/is_n2_v23/ai_19498953 (accessed June 21, 2008).
[4]P. Strozniak, "Teams at Work," *Industry Week*, September 18, 2000, 47–50.

Specific Goals Successful teams translate their common purpose into specific, measurable, and realistic performance goals. Just as goals lead individuals to higher performance (see Chapter 3), they also energize teams. Specific goals facilitate clear communication and help teams maintain their focus on getting results. Examples of specific team goals might be responding to all customers within twenty-four hours, cutting production-cycle time by 30 percent over the next six months, or maintaining equipment at a level of zero downtime every month.

Common Approach Goals are the ends a team strives to attain. Defining and agreeing on a common approach ensures that the team is unified on the means for achieving those ends.

Team members must contribute equally in sharing the workload and agree on who is to do what. Additionally, the team needs to determine how schedules will be set, what skills need to be developed, how conflicts will be resolved, and how decisions will be made and modified. The implementation of work teams at Olin Chemicals' McIntosh, Alabama, plant included having teams complete questionnaires on how they would organize themselves and share specific responsibilities. Integrating individual skills to further the team's performance is the essence of shaping a common approach.

Mutual Accountability The final characteristic of high-performing teams is accountability at both the individual and group levels. Successful teams make members individually and jointly accountable for the team's purpose, goals, and approach. Members understand what they are individually responsible for and what they are jointly responsible for.

Studies have shown that when teams focus only on group-level performance targets, and ignore individual contributions and responsibilities, team members often engage in social loafing.[5] They reduce their efforts because their individual contributions can't be identified. In effect, they become "free riders" and coast on the group's effort. The result is that the team's overall performance suffers. This reaffirms the importance of measuring individual contributions to the team as well as the team's overall performance. Successful teams have members who collectively feel responsible for their team's performance.

social loafing
Becoming a free rider in a group because individual contributions to the group effort cannot be identified. As a result, the overall team's performance suffers.

Team Challenges for Supervisors

Teams have long been popular in Japan. When American managers began to broadly introduce them into the United States in the late 1980s, critics warned that they were destined to fail: Japan is a collectivist society. American culture is based on the values of individualism. American workers won't sublimate their needs for individual responsibility and recognition to be anonymous parts of a team. Although the introduction of work teams in some organizations has met with resistance and disappointment, the overall picture has been encouraging. When teams are properly used in organizations and when the organization's internal climate is consistent with a team approach, the results have been largely positive.

In this section, we discuss obstacles to creating effective teams and offer some suggestions to supervisors for overcoming those obstacles.

WHAT OBSTACLES EXIST IN CREATING EFFECTIVE TEAMS?

The following critical obstacles can prevent your teams from becoming high performers.

---

[5]R. Albanese and D. D. Van Fleet, "Rational Behavior in Groups: The Free Riding Tendency," *Academy of Management Review* 10, no. 2 (April 1985), 244–255.

Something to Think About (and to promote class discussion)

FAST TIMES!

Imagine working for an organization that employs more than 2,700 individuals with each one having the identical focus.* Imagine, too, that company supervisors in this organization want you to work hard *and* be the best at what you do. If you're employed by Ferrari S.p.A., such realities aren't hard to imagine.

When most people hear the name *Ferrari*, they think of expensive, super-fast sports cars. That reputation for speed is why Ferraris continue to be well known and respected in racing groups around the world. The Italian company was founded by Enzo Ferrari in 1928, and even in its early days, racing was an important part of the Ferrari legend. Today, Luca Cordero, president and managing director of the company, believes that his employees truly make a difference in producing one of the world's greatest sports cars. He recognizes that to be the best, he needs employees who understand how to work together and how to achieve common goals. At Ferrari, employee teams combine their efforts to produce an outstanding automobile, with quality befitting its iconic reputation. You won't find traditional assembly lines in the Ferrari factory, nor will you find production quotas. With prices for a Ferrari starting at $140,000, auto assembly time isn't measured in seconds. Rather, team tasks often last more than ninety minutes for each portion of a car. Then the team proudly passes its finished work to the next team so its work can begin. Average time to manufacture one car: three days. The company produces around 6,000 Ferraris in any one year, although the company hopes to boost that number to 10,000 cars in the future. To achieve that goal, the company is expanding current capacity, although its singular focus on quality and teamwork won't change.

Employees at Ferrari truly enjoy being part of a team. They say that working toward a common goal is one of the most satisfying elements in their jobs. They also appreciate what the company does for them. They enjoy a state-of-the-art fitness center, annual physicals at the company's on-site clinic, an employee cafeteria, and home-based training for employees to learn English. They feel as if Cordero and his team treat them as associates, not just as cogs in the Ferrari wheel. As one employee stated, "For many of us working for Ferrari is like working in the Vatican." Recently, the company won an award for Best Place to Work in Europe. The prize resulted from the company's "Formula-1-inspired workplace initiative called Formula Uomo," which took the principles of Ferrari's success in Formula 1 racing and applied them to the workplace. The main thrust was recognizing its people as the "fulcrum of the company's work system."

Is the team concept at Ferrari working? By all accounts, yes. The company has achieved over $2.3 billion in sales. And more importantly, the car still retains its appeal as one of the best and most desired in the world. Although profits have been nominal during the global economic downturn, there are always going to be customers who want to own the car with the rearing-horse logo.

Like company executives at Ferrari, many supervisors today believe the use of teams allows their organizations to increase sales or manufacture better products faster and at lower costs. Although the effort to create teams isn't always successful, well-planned teams can reinvigorate productivity and better position an organization to deal with a rapidly changing environment.

---

* " Ferrari London Store Opening Stops Traffic," *License Magazine Online*, June 2009; S. Oster, "Open a Bank Account and Test Drive a Ferrari," *Wall Street Journal*, June 1, 2007, B3; "Kudos: Ferrari Named 'Best Place to Work' in Europe," http://www.edmonds.com (May 4, 2007); and M. Moskowitz and R. Levering, "100 Best Companies to Work For," "10 Great Companies to Work for in Europe," "Ferrari: Good Food, Good People, Lots of Fun—Sound Like a European Holiday? No, It's a Great Job," *Fortune*, January 7, 2003.

A Weak Sense of Direction Teams perform poorly when members are not sure of their purpose, goals, and approach. Add weak leadership and you have a recipe for failure. Nothing undermines enthusiasm for the team concept as quickly as the frustration of being an involuntary member of a team that has no focus.

Infighting When team members are spending time bickering and undermining their colleagues, energy is being misdirected. Effective teams are not necessarily composed of people who all like each other; however, members must respect each other and be willing to put aside petty differences to facilitate goal achievement.

Shirking of Responsibilities Members may exhibit a lack of commitment to the team, deviously maneuver to have others do part of their job, or be quick to blame colleagues or management for any personal or team failures. The result is a pseudo team—a team in name only and one that consistently underperforms even what the members could accomplish independently.

Lack of Trust When there is trust, team members believe in each other's integrity, character, and ability. When this is lacking, members cannot depend on each other. Teams that lack trust tend to be short lived.

Critical Skill Gaps When skill gaps occur and the team doesn't fill those gaps, the team flounders. Members have trouble communicating with each other, destructive conflicts aren't resolved, decisions are never made, or technical problems overwhelm the team.

Lack of External Support Teams exist within the larger organization. They rely on that larger organization for a variety of resources—money, people, equipment—and if those resources aren't there, it's difficult for teams to reach their potential. For example, teams must live with the organization's employee selection process, formal rules and regulations, budgeting procedures, and compensation system. If these are inconsistent with the team's needs and goals, the team suffers.

HOW CAN TEAM OBSTACLES BE OVERCOME?

Supervisors can do a number of things to overcome the obstacles mentioned and help teams to reach their full potential. These are listed in Exhibit 11-5.

Create a Clear Purpose and Goals High-performance teams have both a clear understanding of their goals and a belief that the goals embody a worthwhile or important result. Moreover, the importance of these goals encourages individuals to sublimate personal concerns to these team goals. In effective teams, members are committed to the team's goals, know what they are expected to accomplish, and understand how they will work together to achieve these goals.

As a supervisor, your job is to ensure that teams under your leadership have a clear purpose and goals. Whether you participate in setting them or delegate this task to the team itself, it's your responsibility to make sure that this is accomplished.

Encourage Small Wins The building of real teams takes time. Team members have to learn to think and work as a team. New teams can't be expected to hit home runs, right at the beginning, every time they come to bat. So, encourage the team to begin by trying to hit singles.

Help the team identify and set attainable goals. The eventual goal of cutting overall costs by 30 percent, for instance, can be dissected into five or ten smaller and more easily attainable goals. As the smaller goals are attained, the team's success is reinforced. Cohesiveness is increased and morale improves. Confidence builds. Success breeds success, but it's a lot easier for young teams to reach their goals if they start with small wins.

Build Mutual Trust Trust is fragile. It takes a long time to build and can be easily destroyed. As discussed in Chapter 9, there are things a supervisor can do to create a climate of mutual trust.[6]

---

[6]K. T. Dirks, "The Effects of Interpersonal Trust on Work Group Performance," *Journal of Applied Psychology* 54, no. 3 (June 1999), 445–455.

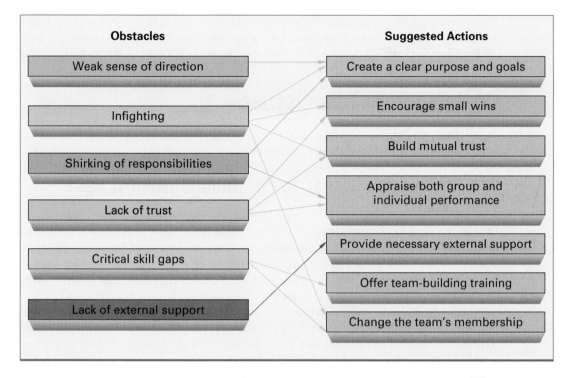

Obstacles	Suggested Actions
Weak sense of direction	Create a clear purpose and goals
Infighting	Encourage small wins
Shirking of responsibilities	Build mutual trust
Lack of trust	Appraise both group and individual performance
Critical skill gaps	Provide necessary external support
Lack of external support	Offer team-building training
	Change the team's membership

Exhibit 11-5
Creating effective teams.

Keep team members informed by explaining upper-management decisions and policies and by providing accurate feedback. Create a climate of openness where employees are free to discuss problems without fear of retaliation. Be candid about your own problems and limitations. Make sure you're available and approachable when employees need support. Be respectful and listen to team members' ideas. Develop a reputation for being fair, objective, and impartial in your treatment of team members. Show consistency in your actions, and avoid erratic and unpredictable behavior. Coach team members as needed (see the section titled "Developing Your Coaching Skills" later in this chapter). Finally, be dependable and honest. Make sure you follow through on all explicit and implied promises.

Appraise Both Group and Individual Performance Team members should all share in the glory when their team succeeds, and they should share in the blame when it fails. So, a large measure of each member's performance appraisal should be based on the overall team's performance. But members need to know that they can't ride on the backs of others. Therefore, each member's individual contribution should be identified and made part of his or her overall performance appraisal.

Provide Necessary External Support You're the link between teams and upper management. As such, it's your responsibility to make sure teams have the necessary organizational resources to accomplish their goals. That means you should be prepared to make the case to your boss and other key decision makers in the organization for tools, equipment, training, personnel, physical space, or other resources that teams may require.

Offer Team-Building Training Teams, especially in their early stages of formation, need training to build their skills. Typically, these include problem-solving, communication, negotiation, conflict resolution, and group-processing skills. If you can't personally provide this kind of skill training for your team members, look to specialists in your organization who can, or secure funds to bring in outside facilitators who specialize in this kind of training.

Change the Team's Membership When teams get bogged down in their own inertia or internal fighting, allow them to rotate members. You might want to manage this change by considering how certain personalities mesh and re-forming teams in ways that better complement skills. If lack of leadership is the problem, use your knowledge of the people involved to create teams in which there is high probability that a leader will emerge.

Contemporary Team Issues

As we close this chapter, we address two issues related to supervising teams: continuous-improvement programs and diversity in teams.

WHY ARE TEAMS CENTRAL TO CONTINUOUS-IMPROVEMENT PROGRAMS?

One of the central characteristics of continuous-improvement programs is the use of teams. Why teams? The essence of continuous improvement is process improvement, and employee participation is the linchpin of process improvement. In other words, continuous improvement requires management to encourage employees to share ideas and to act on what the employees suggest.

Teams provide the natural vehicle for employees to share ideas and implement improvements. For example, at BASF, the world's largest chemical company, a process called *Verbund* permits all of the company's 385 facilities and more than 100,000 employees worldwide to be connected to each other—forming teams to address specific issues. For example, one project team tested thirteen different production factors using thirty-two experiments. As a result of their work, more than $700,000 was cut from annual production costs, and nearly $1 million for a one-time capital improvement expenditure was eliminated.[7]

HOW DOES WORKFORCE DIVERSITY AFFECT TEAMS?

Managing diversity on teams is a balancing act. Diversity typically provides fresh perspectives on issues, but it makes it more difficult to unify the team and reach agreements.

The strongest case for diversity on work teams is when these teams are engaged in problem-solving and decision-making tasks. Heterogeneous teams bring multiple perspectives to the discussion, thus increasing the likelihood that the team will identify creative or unique solutions. Additionally, the lack of a common perspective usually means that diverse teams spend more time discussing issues, which decreases the chances that a weak alternative will be chosen. However, keep in mind that the positive contribution that diversity makes to decision-making teams undoubtedly declines over time. Diverse groups have more difficulty working together and solving problems, but this dissipates with time.[8] Expect the value-added component of diverse teams to increase as members become more familiar with each other and the team becomes more cohesive.

Studies tell us that members of cohesive teams have greater satisfaction, lower absenteeism, and lower attrition from the group.[9] Yet cohesiveness is likely to be lower on diverse teams. So, here is a potential negative of diversity: It may be detrimental to group cohesiveness.[10] However, we suggest that if the norms of the team support diversity, a team can maximize the value of heterogeneity while also achieving the benefits of high cohesiveness.[11] This makes a strong case for team members to participate in diversity training.

---

[7]See BASF's website (www.basf.com); and D. Drickhamer, "BASF Breaks Through with Statistics," *Industry Week*, June 2002, 81–82.

[8]"Diversity Enhances Decision-Making," *Industry Week*, April 2, 2001, 9.

[9]See S. G. Barsade, A. J. Ward, J. D. F. Turner, and J. A. Sonnenfeld, "To Your Heart's Content: A Model of Effective Diversity in Top Management Teams," *Administrative Science Quarterly* 45 (December 2000), 802.

[10]L. H. Pelled, K. M. Eisenhardt, and K. R. Xin, "Exploring the Black Box: An Analysis of Work Group Diversity, Conflict, and Performance," *Administrative Science Quarterly* 46, no. 2 (March 1999), 128.

[11]H. E. Joy, D. Joyendu, and M. Bhadury, "Maximizing Workforce Diversity in Project Teams: A Network Flow Approach," *Omega* 28, no. 2 (April 2000), 143–155.

Comprehension Check 11-2

5. A potential team is one that

    a. represents a group of individuals who interact primarily to share information and make decisions
    b. is heavily influenced by negative synergy
    c. is moving in the right direction but is not quite there yet
    d. has a set of common characteristics that lead to consistently high performance

6. Becoming a "free rider" in a group is frequently called

    a. social loafing
    b. social norming
    c. social work teams
    d. none of the above

7. Which one of the following is *not* an obstacle to effective teams?

    a. Lack of trust
    b. Lack of infighting
    c. Lack of external support
    d. Weak sense of direction

8. Why are teams central to continuous-improvement programs?

    a. They allow for specific goals to be set.
    b. They provide a natural vehicle for employees to share ideas and implement improvements.
    c. They allow for greater efficiencies and better use of resources.
    d. They promote workforce diversity.

Enhancing Understanding

SUMMARY

After reading this chapter, I can:

1. **Contrast a group and a team.** A group is merely two or more people who come together to achieve a particular objective. A team is a formal workgroup composed of individuals who are committed to a common purpose, who have a set of performance goals, and who hold themselves mutually accountable for the team's results. In contrast to formal workgroups, teams achieve positive synergy by producing a whole that is greater than the sum of its parts through joint effort.

2. **Define *norms*.** Norms are acceptable standards of behavior within a group that are shared by the group's members.

3. **Explain the relationship between cohesiveness and group productivity.** Whether cohesiveness affects productivity depends on the group's performance-related norms. If performance-related norms are high, a more cohesive group will be more productive than a less cohesive group will. If cohesiveness is high and performance norms are low, productivity will be low. If cohesiveness is low and performance norms are high, productivity increases modestly. If cohesiveness and performance-related norms are both low, productivity will tend to be low to moderate.

4. **Describe who is likely to become an emergent leader in an informal group.** Emergent leaders tend to be people with charismatic traits and those with important but scarce knowledge about the organization or technical aspects of the group's work.

5. **Explain what a supervisor can do when group norms are hindering department performance.** When norms are hindering department performance, the supervisor can transfer one or more group members, physically separate members, or reward members who act against dysfunctional norms.

6. **Identify three categories of teams.** Teams can be categorized in three ways: teams that provide advice, teams that manage things, and teams that make or do things.

7. **List the characteristics of real teams.** Real teams are characterized by a small number of people with complementary skills who are equally committed to a common purpose, common goals, and a common working approach for which they hold themselves mutually accountable.

8. **List actions a supervisor can take to improve team performance.** Supervisors can improve team performance by creating a clear purpose and goals, encouraging small wins, building mutual trust, appraising both group and individual performance, providing necessary external support, offering team-building training, and changing the team's membership.

9. **Describe the role of teams in continuous-improvement programs.** Continuous-improvement programs provide a natural vehicle for employees to share ideas and to implement improvements as part of the process. Teams are particularly effective for resolving complex problems.

COMPREHENSION: Review and Discussion Questions

1. How do norms affect the behavior of employees?
2. Give examples of low performance-related norms.
3. Do cohesive groups always outperform less cohesive groups? Explain.
4. Why can't formal systems be designed to completely eliminate the need for informal groups?
5. Explain the increasing popularity of teams.
6. Compare a pseudo team with a real team.
7. What skills do all teams need to perform effectively?
8. Contrast a team's purpose and its goals.
9. How do you build trust in a team?
10. What is the supervisor's role in gaining external support for teams?

KEY CONCEPT CROSSWORD

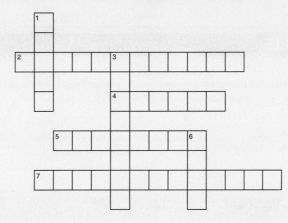

ACROSS

2. the degree to which group members are attracted to each other and are motivated to stay in a group
4. a type of work group established by the organization and given specific work assignments
5. a leader who arises within a work group without having formal authority in the organization
7. becoming a free rider in a group

DOWN

1. two or more individuals interacting interdependently to achieve a particular objective
3. a type of work group that forms naturally in the work environment in response to the need for social contact
6. a work group whose members are committed to a common purpose

ANSWERS TO COMPREHENSION CHECKS

Comprehension Check 11-1

1. b 2. c 3. c 4. d

Comprehension Check 11-2

5. c 6. a 7. b 8. b

Developing Your Supervisory Skills

GETTING TO KNOW YOURSELF

Before you can effectively supervise others, you must understand your present strengths and areas in need of development. To assist in this learning process, we encourage you to complete the following self-assessment from the Prentice Hall Self-Assessment Library 3.4.

1. How Good Am I at Building and Leading a Team? (II. B. 6.)

After you complete the assessment, we suggest you retain the results and store them as part of your "portfolio of learning about yourself."

BUILDING A TEAM

➤ An Experiential Exercise: Building Effective Work Teams

Objective: This exercise is designed to allow class members to (a) experience working together as a team on a specific task and (b) analyze this experience.

Time: Teams will have forty-five minutes to engage in Steps 2 and 3, which follow. Another thirty minutes will be used in class to critique and evaluate the exercise.

Procedure

1. Class members are assigned to teams of about six people.

2. Each team may be required to

   a. determine a team name
   b. compose a team song

3. Each team is to try to find the following items on its scavenger hunt:

   a. a picture of a team
   b. a newspaper article about a group or team
   c. a piece of apparel with the college name or logo
   d. a drinking straw
   e. a ball of cotton
   f. a piece of stationery from a college department
   g. a pad of sticky notes
   h. a flash drive
   i. a beverage cup from a fast-food restaurant
   j. a pet leash
   k. a book by Ernest Hemingway
   l. an ad brochure for a Ford product
   m. a test tube
   n. a pack of gum
   o. a college catalog

4. After forty-five minutes, all teams are to be back in the classroom. (A penalty, determined by the instructor,

will be imposed on late teams.) The team with the most items on the list will be declared the winner. The class and instructor will determine whether the items meet the requirements of the exercise.

5. Debriefing will begin by having each team engage in self-evaluation. Specifically, it should answer the following questions:

   a. What was the team's strategy?
   b. What roles did individual members perform?
   c. How effective was the team?
   d. What could the team have done to be more effective?

6. Full class discussion will focus on issues such as the following:

   a. What differentiated the more effective teams from the less effective teams?
   b. What did you learn from this experience that is relevant to the design of effective teams?

Source: Adapted from M. R. Manning and P. J. Schmidt, "Building Effective Work Teams: A Quick Exercise Based on a Scavenger Hunt," *Journal of Management Education* 19, no. 3 (August 1995), 392–398.

➤ Internet: Web Activity

Go to http://www.pearsonhighered.com/robbins/. Find *Supervision Today!* 7th Ed. and click Companion Website.

DEVELOPING YOUR COACHING SKILLS

Effective supervisors are increasingly being described as coaches rather than bosses. Just like coaches they are expected to provide instruction, guidance, advice, and encouragement to help team members improve their job performance.

STEPS IN PRACTICING THE SKILL

STEP 1: Analyze ways to improve the team's performance and capabilities. A coach looks for opportunities for team members to expand their capabilities and improve performance. How? By using the following behaviors: Observe your team members' behavior on a day-to-day basis. Ask questions of them: Why do you do a task this way? Can it be improved? What other approaches might be used? Show genuine interest in team members as individuals, not merely as employees. Respect them individually. Listen to the employee.

STEP 2: Create a supportive climate. It's the coach's responsibility to reduce barriers to development and to facilitate a climate that encourages personal performance improvement. How? By using the following behaviors: Create a climate that contributes to a free and open exchange of ideas. Offer help and assistance. Give guidance and advice when asked.

Encourage your team. Be positive and upbeat. Don't use threats. Ask, What did we learn from this that can help us in the future? Reduce obstacles. Express to team members that you value their contribution to the team's goals. Take personal responsibility for the outcome, but don't rob team members of their full responsibility. Validate the team members' efforts when they succeed. Point to what was missing when they fail. Never blame team members for poor results.

STEP 3: Influence team members to change their behavior. The ultimate test of coaching effectiveness is whether an employee's performance improves. The concern is with ongoing growth and development. How can you do this? By using the following behaviors: Recognize and reward small improvements and treat coaching as a way of helping employees continually work toward improvement. Use a collaborative style by allowing team members to participate in identifying and choosing among improvement ideas. Break difficult tasks down into simpler ones. Model the qualities that you expect from your team. If you want openness, dedication, commitment, and responsibility from your team members, you must demonstrate these qualities yourself.

➤ Communicating Effectively

1. Describe why work teams are more acceptable in Japan than in the United States or Canada. Explain how Japanese firms in the United States can still use teams even though the cultural dimensions are different.

2. In two to three pages, explain whether you would prefer to work alone or as part of a team. What does your response indicate in terms of organizational cultures in which you might work? Explain.

THINKING CRITICALLY

➤ Case 11-A: Distribution at Hewlett-Packard

Even well-managed organizations don't always work as efficiently and effectively as management would like. At Hewlett-Packard (HP), billions of dollars of products—from computers and diagnostic devices to toner cartridges—are shipped each year. Customer orders come in 24 hours a day, 365 days a year. Nearly sixteen thousand different products are requested daily and must be shipped from six different warehouses—often located thirty or more miles apart. It often takes weeks to get the products into the customer's hand. This is a serious problem with customers who have contracts with HP stating that deliveries are to be made in four hours or less. That means that from the time a customer calls the HP customer service line, they should have their replacement part and be

back in operation within four hours—irrespective of where the customer is located!

One characteristic that distinguishes an outstanding organization is its ability to know when problems need to be addressed, and then proceed to do something about it. The job of correcting this problem fell on the shoulders of HP's distribution supervisor, Loretta Wilson.

Loretta quickly assembled a team of experts—both from within and external to the organization. These included logistics, systems, and operations experts. They quickly assessed the situation and established their goals. In essence, the team wanted to "find smarter and simpler ways to handle parts fewer times at several points in the distribution channel." They concluded that a new, high-tech facility was needed—one in which the distribution process could maximize efficiencies. The team designed a 405,000-square-foot facility and specified the precise equipment and layout of the operation. For example, the new distribution facility has over a mile of conveyor belts that run constantly. New sorting machines can sort more than forty-five pieces a minute, enabling the company to process more than sixty thousand products each day. Inventory is now stocked after it's received in the warehouse in minutes—rather than the nearly eight days it previously took. Packing and crating is done with the assistance of robotics. Workstations for employees were redesigned to reduce their involvement in handling products. And a special shipping dock is equipped such that shipments can be held and their weight determined right up to the moment that Federal Express backs up to the dock. The cargo is then immediately placed into the trucks and the drivers are sent to the airport. As the FedEx drivers head to the airport, they use their cell phones to call in the cargo's weight and drive to a waiting aircraft—and the cargo is off to the customer.

Was Loretta's team successful? Yes. The new distribution facility is getting its orders filled within the four-hour limit as contractually required. Additionally, by consolidating the previous six independent facilities into one operation, productivity has risen by more than 33 percent.

RESPONDING TO THE CASE

1. Why do you think a team was needed for the design of a complex project like the distribution center for HP? How would you classify this team?

2. Do you believe that the advantages accrued from specialization (see Chapter 4, "Organizing") are lost or diminished when individuals from different specialties are put together on a team? Discuss.

3. Do you think Loretta Wilson's team achieved its objective? Explain.

Source: Based on T. Feare, "Speeding HP Orders 'Out the Door in Four,' " *Modern Materials Management,* May 1999, 40–43.

➤ Case 11-B: Welcome to Barnes City Hospital

Paula Meers has been the supervisor of nursing for the night shift at Barnes City Hospital for nearly four years. Paula supervises twenty-four nurses who work from 11:00 p.m. until 7:30 a.m. Seven of the nurses have been very close to one another, both inside and outside the hospital. Each of these seven nurses has been with the hospital for more than twenty years, and they have gained the respect and confidence of the medical staff and the administration. One of these nurses, Bonnie Lin, is an excellent nurse, a very friendly and outgoing person, and well respected by this group of seven nurses.

When new nurses are brought on to the shift, they are assigned a mentor for the first three months. In addition, the seven nurses also engage in a welcoming routine of some jokes and a few nonharmful tricks. Many of the new nurses recognize this as a harmless rite of passage for new members of the nursing night shift. But Paula, as supervisor, has become concerned that the jokes and tricks may be causing some problems. Three newly hired nurses have left Barnes City Hospital after only two weeks on the job.

Paula arranges a meeting with Bonnie to express concerns over the jokes and tricks. Bonnie states that the jokes and tricks are harmless fun that is necessary to break the tension and constant pressure of caring for the patients. In addition, she says, "Any nurse who can't take the jokes should not be working the night shift at Barnes City Hospital."

Three weeks later, three more newly hired nurses resign after telling Paula that they did not like the "jokes and tricks treatment." These nurses tell Paula that they believe nursing is a serious profession and that they cannot work under the present conditions. The nurses leave the meeting stating that they intend to communicate their concerns to the hospital administrator.

RESPONDING TO THE CASE

1. What type of a group do the seven nurses on the night shift represent? Does this type of group improve the performance of the night shift?

2. Discuss the topic of group norms as related to this case. How might revising the group norms improve this situation?

3. As the supervisor, should Paula work on improving the norms of the informal group, or should she work on transforming it into a cohesive formal group?

Appraisal, Safety, Negotiation, Change, and Labor Relations

If there is one thing common to most supervisors' jobs, it's the fact that things will never remain calm—at least not for a long period of time. Supervisors know that they must evaluate their employees as well as deal with problems that may arise. So, too, must supervisors work to ensure that the work environment is safe and healthy, and they must be prepared to deal with the dynamic change that takes place in organizations. All of these areas are subjects of Part 4.

Performance Appraisal

Key Concepts

After completing this chapter, you will be able to define these supervisory terms:

- adjective rating scale
- appraisal process
- behaviorally anchored rating scale (BARS)
- central tendency error
- checklist
- critical incidents
- employee counseling
- extrinsic feedback
- group-order ranking

- halo error
- individual ranking
- intrinsic feedback
- leniency error
- performance appraisal
- performance feedback
- recency error
- similarity error
- written essay
- 360-degree appraisal

Chapter Outcomes

After reading this chapter, you will be able to:

1. Describe the three purposes of the performance appraisal.
2. Differentiate formal and informal performance appraisals.
3. Describe key legal concerns in performance appraisals.
4. Identify the three most popular sets of criteria that supervisors appraise.
5. Contrast absolute and relative standards.
6. List human errors that can distort performance appraisal ratings.
7. Describe what is meant by the term *360-degree appraisal.*
8. Describe the purpose of employee counseling.

Responding to a Supervisory Dilemma

"On any given day in most organizations in North America, you'll find a supervisor informing an employee that it's time for their regular performance review. And usually, the news is neither delivered or received with joy. Second only to firing an employee, supervisors rate performance appraisals as the task they dislike the most. Jim Heskett, writing in the *Harvard Business Review*, says employee performance reviews rank with root canals on the list of least favorite things to do both for employees and managers. Heskett argues that the debate over the utility of performance reviews centers around a 'forced ranking' system, made popular by GE, which not only purports to identify the top performers, but also the underperformers who can subsequently be 'advised' to leave the organization."*

Performance appraisal may be defined as a structured formal interaction between an employee and a supervisor that usually takes the form of a periodic interview (annual or semiannual), in which the work performance of the employee is examined and discussed, with a view to identifying weaknesses and strengths as well as opportunities for improvement and skills development. The goal of the review process is to recognize achievement, to evaluate job progress, and then to design training for the further development of skills and strengths. A performance appraisal may stimulate an employee's interest and improve his or her job performance. The real potential of appraisal is as a tool for motivation and development.

Fortunate or not, supervisors are likely be the ones doing the review/appraisal. Most supervisors recognize the importance of effective performance management systems in an organization. They know that employee performance is essential to a company's success or failure and that a unified system for performance evaluations should be in place for organizations to give feedback to their employees. The larger the company, the more likely there is a standardized appraisal form and formal procedures to follow. The procedures are critical to ensure equal opportunities are given, and most supervisors would agree that performance appraisals must meet equal employment opportunity (EEO) requirements. That is, they must be administered in such a way that they result in a fair and equitable treatment of all employees in today's diverse workforce.

The performance appraisal should contain standards that are measurable, understandable, verifiable, equitable, and achievable. The performance appraisal should tell employees what they have to do and tell them how well they have to do it. Performance standards should be set and reviewed with each employee so they know what is expected of them. Used effectively, appraisals can be beneficial working documents available for discussion, and not merely paperwork filed in a drawer to be seen only when ratings are required. Additionally, the standards must describe work assignments and responsibilities that are significantly influenced by an employee's work effort and within the employee's control.

Embedded in the document should be statements of quality intended to address how well the employee is expected to perform the work and/or the accuracy or effectiveness of the final product. The standards for quantity must address how much work the employee is expected to produce. While the indicators for timeliness should be in place to address how quickly, when, or by what date the employee is expected to produce the work. Supervisors should remember that a performance appraisal is a review and discussion of an employee's performance of assigned duties and responsibilities.

---

*Ray Williams, "Why CEOs need to scrap employee performance reviews," Wired for Success, May 17, 2011, *Psychology Today*, http://www.psychologytoday.com/blog/wired-success/201105/ why-ceos-need-scrap-employee-performance-reviews (accessed May 25, 2011).

The appraisal must be based on results obtained by the employee in his/her job, not on the employee's personality characteristics.

Supervisors should plan to provide ongoing feedback to their employees. Designing effective feedback into a performance management program will improve individual performance and make the organization more effective. With effective feedback processes, employees can see their progress and that may motivate them to reach their performance goals. Feedback works best when it relates to a specific goal, and employees should receive information about how they are doing in as timely a fashion as possible. Feedback should be given in a manner that will best help improve performance. In some cases an employee's peers, who work with them on a day-to-day basis, are going to know their job performance and may assist in providing feedback.

No legislative regulations, such as EEO laws, exist to enforce ethical standards in performance appraisal. Thus, the evaluation process may be, and frequently is, lacking in ethical practice. Because of this, there are many who believe that organizations should do away with performance appraisals and evaluations. Because there are gray areas when it comes to evaluations, they may meet legal requirements but verge on questionable practices.

There are many reputable sources—researchers, management commentators, and psychometricians—who have expressed doubts about the validity and reliability of the performance appraisal process. Some have even suggested that the process is so inherently flawed that it may be impossible to perfect it.[†] Indeed, some drawbacks of the appraisal process are such that even though supervisors acknowledge the "intentions of the appraisal is a means to provide constructive feedback and write good development plans and goals,...people with less-than superior ratings are preoccupied with the numerical rating rather than the message. Except for those receiving top ratings, the good conversation they had hoped for rarely happens. Employees tune out and politely complete the interview. Others become defensive and resentful."[‡]

So what is the answer? Why do supervisors use performance appraisals? Do you feel employee appraisals are a valuable tool in assisting supervisors in understanding how their employees are performing? Do they accomplish their intended goals? What are their real effects? Do supervisors really need performance appraisals? Are there other ways to accomplish these goals? Do you believe an organization can have an effective performance appraisal process without sincerity and honesty dominating the system? How would you handle employee evaluations as the supervisor?

[†]M. G. Derven, "The Paradox of Performance Appraisals," *Personnel Journal* 69 (February, 1990), 107–111.

[‡]T. Coens and M. Jenkins, *Abolishing Performance Appraisals: Why They Backfire and What to Do Instead* (San Francisco, CA: Berrett-Koehler Publishers, 2000), http://www.bkconnection.com/static/Abolishing_Performance_Appraisals_EXCERPT.pdf (accessed May 25, 2011).

Additional Sources: See T. Juncaj, "Do Appraisals Work?" *Quality Progress* 35, no. 11 (November 2002), 45–50; M. Brown and J. Benson, "Rated to Exhaustion? Reaction to Performance Appraisal Process," *Industrial Relations Journal* 34, no. 1 (March 2003), 67–81; and B. Erdogan, M. L. Kraimer, and R. C. Liden, "Procedural Justice as a Two-Dimensional Construct: An Examination in the Performance Appraisal Context," *Journal of Applied Behavioral Science* (June 2001), 205–223.

"I know it's wrong," remarked Ron Connors. "I know I should do more in terms of performance appraisals with my employees, but I don't. As long as my boss doesn't get on my case, I sort of ignore them. The reason is that when I do appraisals and give people feedback, we almost never agree. Everybody thinks they're doing an above-average job. How can everybody be above-average? If I believed their self-appraisals, I'd have only three kinds of people working for me—stars, all-stars, and superstars!"

Ron Connors's comments suggest why a lot of supervisors find appraising employee performance one of their most difficult tasks. In this chapter, we review the performance appraisal and provide you and the Ron Connorses of this world with some techniques that can make the appraisal and performance review a less traumatic experience.

The Purpose of Employee Performance Appraisals

Thirty-five years ago, the typical supervisor would sit down annually with his or her employees individually and critique their job performance. The purpose was to review how well they worked toward achieving their work goals. Employees who failed to achieve their goals found that performance appraisals resulted in little more than their supervisor documenting a list of their shortcomings. Of course, because the performance appraisal is a key determinant in pay adjustments and promotion decisions, anything to do with appraising job performance struck fear into the hearts of employees. Not surprisingly, in this climate supervisors often wanted to avoid the whole appraisal process.

Today, effective supervisors treat the performance appraisal as an evaluation and development tool, as well as a formal legal document. It reviews past performance—emphasizing positive accomplishments as well as deficiencies. In addition, supervisors are using the performance appraisal to help employees improve future performance. If deficiencies are found, the supervisor can help employees draft a detailed plan to correct the situation. By emphasizing the future as well as the past, employees are less likely to respond defensively to performance feedback, and the appraisal process is more likely to motivate employees to correct their performance deficiencies. Finally, remember from Chapter 5 the issue of employee discrimination. Taking action against an employee for poor performance can create a problem if the problem is not well documented. The performance evaluation serves a vital purpose in providing the documentation necessary for any personnel action that is taken.[1]

performance appraisal
A review of past performance that emphasizes positive accomplishments as well as deficiencies; a means for helping employees improve future performance.

WHEN SHOULD APPRAISALS OCCUR?

The performance appraisal is both a formal and an informal activity. Formal performance reviews should be conducted once a year at a minimum. Twice a year may even be better. Just as students don't like to have their entire course grade hanging on the results of one final exam, neither do employees relish having their careers depend on an annual review. Two formal reviews a year means that less "performance" will be appraised at each one, and lessens the tension employees often associate with the formal review.

Proactive supervisors may even establish the practice of having periodic informal reviews instead of waiting for the annual or biannual review. Informal performance appraisal is the day-to-day assessment a supervisor makes of an employee's performance and the ongoing feedback the supervisor gives the employee about that performance. The effective supervisor continually provides informal information to employees—commenting on the positive aspects of their work and pointing out problems when they surface. So, whereas formal reviews may occur only once or twice a year, informal reviews should be taking place all the time. Moreover, when the informal feedback

---

[1]Material in this chapter is derived from D. A. DeCenzo and S. P. Robbins, *Fundamentals of Human Resource Management*, 8th ed. (Hoboken, NJ: John Wiley & Sons, 2005), Chapter 10.

has been open and honest, the formal reviews will probably be less threatening to the employee and won't present any great surprises. When reviews indicate deficiencies or goals have not been achieved, supervisors may use a coaching process to analyze why and to aid the employee in developing an internal locus of personal accountability. A supervisor may find that employees with an external locus will blame a poor performance evaluation on their boss's prejudice, their coworkers, or other events outside their control, whereas employees with an internal locus of control will explain the same evaluation in terms of their own actions.

WHAT IS YOUR ROLE IN PERFORMANCE APPRAISALS?

How much latitude do supervisors have in the appraisal process? The larger your organization, the more likely it is that there will be standardized appraisal forms and formal procedures for you to follow. Even small companies tend to standardize some appraisal procedures to ensure that equal employment opportunity requirements are met.

Will You Be the Sole Appraiser? Most employee performance appraisals are conducted by supervisors. However, a supervisor isn't always the sole source of pertinent information about employees' performance. In recent years, some organizations have added self-evaluations and peer evaluations to supplement those made by supervisors. Employees themselves often have valuable insights to provide. So, too, do their peers.

Self-evaluations get high marks from employees themselves. They tend to lessen employees' defensiveness about the appraisal process, and they make excellent vehicles for stimulating the job performance discussion. Self-evaluations tend to suffer from inflated assessments, so they should be used to enhance your evaluation rather than to replace it. The use of self-evaluations, however, is fully consistent with viewing performance appraisal as a developmental tool rather than for purely evaluative purposes.

There are some elements of an employee's job that peers are better at judging than you are as a supervisor. In some jobs, for instance, you don't regularly observe an employee's work because your span of control is quite large or because of physical separation. When work is built largely around teams, team members are often better at evaluating each other because they have a more comprehensive view of each member's job performance. In such instances, supplementing your appraisals with peer evaluations can increase the accuracy of the appraisal process.

appraisal process
The elements of a performance appraisal as defined by the organization; may involve self-evaluation and peer evaluation in addition to a supervisor's input.

What Forms or Documentation Does the Organization Provide? It is the unusual organization that doesn't require its supervisors to use a standardized form to guide them in doing performance appraisals. In some cases, top management or the human resource department provides an abbreviated form and allows considerable freedom in identifying and assessing job performance factors. At the other extreme, organizations provide detailed forms and instructions that all supervisors must follow (see Exhibit 12-1).

Our point is that you rarely have complete discretion in evaluating your employees. Begin by reviewing any standard forms that your organization uses for appraisals. Familiarize yourself with the information you'll be expected to provide and make sure all of the people reporting to you—especially new employees—understand how and on what criteria they will be evaluated.

How Do You Set Performance Expectations? As a supervisor, you should be involved in determining performance standards for your employees. This ties back to the discussion of goal setting in Chapter 3. Ideally, you and each employee should jointly review the employee's job, identify the processes and results needed, and then determine performance standards that will define how well the results are accomplished. Remember, before an employee's performance can be appraised, some standard must exist against which the appraisal can be made. You must ensure that performance expectations have been defined for every employee and that employees fully understand these expectations.

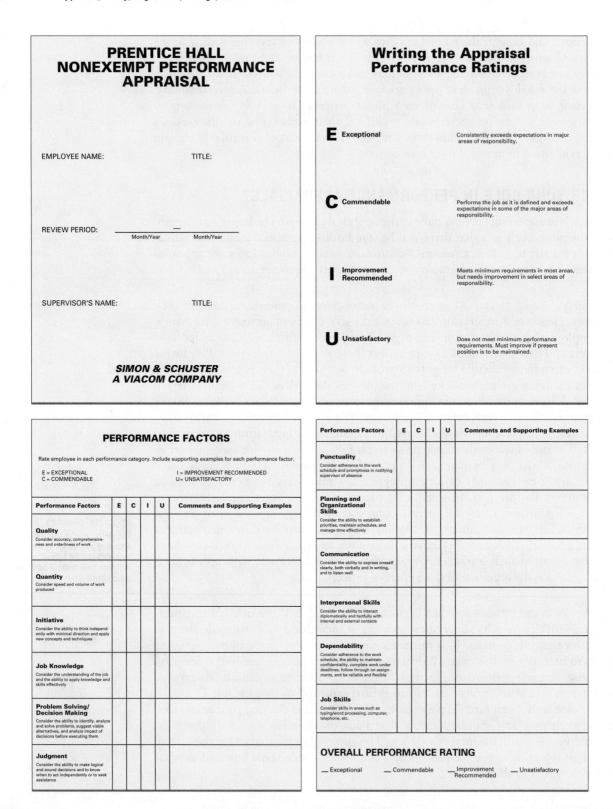

PRENTICE HALL NONEXEMPT PERFORMANCE APPRAISAL

EMPLOYEE NAME: TITLE:

REVIEW PERIOD: _____ — _____
                  Month/Year   Month/Year

SUPERVISOR'S NAME: TITLE:

**SIMON & SCHUSTER
A VIACOM COMPANY**

Writing the Appraisal Performance Ratings

E Exceptional — Consistently exceeds expectations in major areas of responsibility.

C Commendable — Performs the job as it is defined and exceeds expectations in some of the major areas of responsibility.

I Improvement Recommended — Meets minimum requirements in most areas, but needs improvement in select areas of responsibility.

U Unsatisfactory — Does not meet minimum performance requirements. Must improve if present position is to be maintained.

PERFORMANCE FACTORS

Rate employee in each performance category. Include supporting examples for each performance factor.

E = EXCEPTIONAL   I = IMPROVEMENT RECOMMENDED
C = COMMENDABLE   U = UNSATISFACTORY

Performance Factors	E	C	I	U	Comments and Supporting Examples
Quality Consider accuracy, comprehensiveness and orderliness of work					
Quantity Consider speed and volume of work produced					
Initiative Consider the ability to think independently with minimal direction and apply new concepts and techniques					
Job Knowledge Consider the understanding of the job and the ability to apply knowledge and skills effectively					
Problem Solving/ Decision Making Consider the ability to identify, analyze and solve problems, suggest viable alternatives, and analyze impact of decisions before executing them					
Judgment Consider the ability to make logical and sound decisions and to know when to act independently or to seek assistance					

Performance Factors	E	C	I	U	Comments and Supporting Examples
Punctuality Consider adherence to the work schedule and promptness in notifying supervisor of absence					
Planning and Organizational Skills Consider the ability to establish priorities, maintain schedules, and manage time effectively					
Communication Consider the ability to express oneself clearly, both verbally and in writing, and to listen well					
Interpersonal Skills Consider the ability to interact diplomatically and tactfully with internal and external contacts					
Dependability Consider adherence to the work schedule, the ability to maintain confidentiality, complete work under deadlines, follow through on assignments, and be reliable and flexible					
Job Skills Consider skills in areas such as typing/word processing, computer, telephone, etc.					

OVERALL PERFORMANCE RATING

___ Exceptional   ___ Commendable   ___ Improvement Recommended   ___ Unsatisfactory

Exhibit 12-1

Examples of employee appraisal forms.

performance feedback

Information that lets an employee know how well he or she is performing a job; may be intrinsic (provided by the work itself) or extrinsic (provided by a supervisor or some other source).

What Is Performance Feedback? Employees can receive performance feedback in one of two forms. It can be provided intrinsically by the work itself, or it can be given extrinsically by a supervisor or some other external source (see the section titled "Conducting a Performance Evaluation" at the end of this chapter).

In some jobs, employees regularly get feedback on how well they're doing because the feedback is built into the job. For example, a claims specialist who processes health

PERFORMANCE SUMMARY

I. **Performance vs. Goals for Past Year:**

Describe how the employee met stated goals for past year and met additional goals if applicable.

II. **Goals for Upcoming Year:**

List quantifiable goals with timetables for completion.

PERFORMANCE SUMMARY

III. **Strengths**

Identify employee unique strengths in relation to performance factors previously listed.

IV. **Areas for Improvement**

Identify areas in which employee can focus to achieve improved performance.

PERFORMANCE SUMMARY

V. **Personal Growth and Development**

Describe activities to be undertaken that will maximize the employee's career development. These may include educational programs, counseling, on-the-job training, etc.

_____   _____
Supervisor's Signature   Date

EMPLOYEE'S COMMENTS
Your comments are beneficial to the performance appraisal process. Additional comments may be attached on a separate page if desired.

THE EVALUATION AND COMMENTS WERE DISCUSSED WITH THE EMPLOYEE

Employee's signature and date

Supervisor's signature and date   Title

Exhibit 12-1 (continued)

care claims gets self-generated feedback. Her computer terminal often tracks the forms she has processed, the time she has spent on any one of them, and their accuracy (assuming that incomplete forms aren't forwarded). Similarly, a freight clerk in a shipping department at a trucking company keeps an ongoing tally of the number of boxes he packs and the weight of each. At the end of the day, he totals the numbers and compares them to his daily goals. These calculations provide him with self-generated or intrinsic feedback on how he did that day.

intrinsic feedback
Self-generated feedback.
See also performance feedback.

extrinsic feedback
Feedback provided to an employee by an outside source. *See also* performance feedback.

Extrinsic feedback is provided to an employee by an outside source. If the claims specialist routes the completed claims form to her supervisor, who checks it for thoroughness and makes any necessary adjustments, her performance feedback is extrinsic. If the freight clerk's shipping totals are calculated each day by his supervisor and posted on the department's bulletin board, his performance feedback is also extrinsic.

You should provide your employees with ongoing extrinsic feedback, even if their jobs are rich in the intrinsic variety. This can be accomplished through informal performance reviews—ongoing comments that let an employee know how he or she is doing—and through formal performance reviews on a semiannual or annual basis.

WHAT ARE THE LEGAL ISSUES IN PERFORMANCE APPRAISALS?

A great many lawsuits have arisen because supervisors said or did something that their employees believed adversely affected them. One supervisor told an employee that he had downgraded the employee's evaluation because he had taken off work for religious holidays. An employee argued that her supervisor's appraisals were arbitrary and based on subjective judgments. Another employee was awarded damages because his supervisor failed to follow the company's performance appraisal policies and procedures.

Maybe the two most important legal facts you need to keep in mind concerning performance appraisals are the following: (1) Performance appraisal policies and procedures, as set forth in organizational handbooks, are being increasingly construed by the courts as binding unilateral contracts; and (2) you must do everything possible to avoid the appearance of prejudice and discrimination.

Does your company have a published handbook that describes its performance appraisal procedures? If so, make sure you fully understand its contents. The courts, in most states, consider it a binding contract. The organization can be held accountable if those procedures are not followed or are followed improperly. If the handbook states, for instance, that appraisals must be performed annually or that managers will counsel employees to correct deficiencies, then you are obligated to fulfill these commitments. On the other hand, the courts have generally supported giving supervisors a wide range of discretion, as long as fairness and equity are not compromised, when their organizations have no published performance appraisal policies.

The second point is a reminder that equal employment opportunity laws require that all human resource practices be bias-free—including employee performance appraisals. The appraisal criteria, methods, and documentation must be designed to ensure that they are job related. They must not create a different effect on women or minorities. Appraisal judgments must be neutral regarding an employee's race, color, religion, age, gender, or national origin. An increasing number of organizations are providing supervisory training in the mechanics of performance appraisal specifically to minimize the likelihood that discrimination might occur in the process.

ARE THERE APPROPRIATE CRITERIA FOR APPRAISING PERFORMANCE?

The criteria that you choose to appraise employee performance will have a major influence on what employees do. In a public employment agency that served workers seeking employment and employers seeking workers, employment interviewers were appraised by the number of interviews they conducted. Consistent with the thesis that the evaluating criteria influence behavior, employees emphasized the number of interviews conducted rather than the placement of clients in jobs.[2]

The preceding example demonstrates the importance of criteria in performance appraisal. What should you appraise? The three most popular sets of criteria are individual task outcomes, behaviors, and traits.

---

[2]P. M. Blau, *The Dynamics of Bureaucracy*, rev. ed. (Chicago, IL: University of Chicago Press, 1963).

What Are Individual Task Outcomes? If ends count, rather than means, you should evaluate an employee's task outcomes. Using task outcomes, a carpet cleaner might be judged on the number of square yards he or she was able to clean per day. A salesperson could be assessed on overall sales volume in his or her territory, dollar increase in sales, and number of new accounts established.

Which Behaviors Matter? Evaluating employees on behavior requires the opportunity to observe employees or devising a system for reporting on specific behavior criteria. Using the previous examples, behaviors of a carpet cleaner that could be used for performance appraisal purposes might include promptness in reporting to work sites or thoroughness in cleaning equipment at the end of the workday. Pertinent salesperson behaviors could be the average number of contact calls made per day or sick days used per year.

In many cases, it is difficult to identify specific outcomes that are directly attributable to an employee's actions. This is particularly true of personnel in staff positions and individuals whose work assignments are intrinsically part of a group effort. In the latter case, the group's performance may be readily evaluated, but the contribution of each group member may be difficult or impossible to identify clearly. In such instances, it is not unusual to appraise the employee's behavior.

Is Evaluating Traits Useful? When you rate people on the degree to which they are dependable, confident, aggressive, loyal, cooperative, and the like, you are judging traits. Experts seem to agree that traits are inferior to both task outcomes and behaviors as appraisal criteria. The reason is that traits refer to potential predictors of performance, not performance itself. So, the link between traits and job performance is often weak. Additionally, traits typically have a strong subjective component. What, for instance, does *aggressive* mean? Is it pushy, dominating, or assertive? Your evaluation of someone on this trait is largely determined by what the term means to you. Despite the drawbacks of traits as a criterion, they are still widely used in organizations for appraising employee performance.

HOW DO YOU GATHER PERFORMANCE DATA?

Once performance standards have been set, expectations communicated, and appraisal criteria defined, you need to gather performance data. This is an activity every supervisor can and should do.

The best approach is to gather performance data on a continual basis. Don't wait until a week or so before you are due to formally evaluate an employee to begin gathering your information. You should keep an ongoing file for each of your employees in which you record actual incidents (behaviors and/or outcomes) that affect his or her job success or failure. Such documentation reduces the potential for errors caused by overreliance on your recall of events and provides supportive evidence to back up your eventual ratings. Remember, too, that frequency of observation will improve the quality of the data you gather. The more opportunities you have to observe your employees' performance firsthand, the more accurate your performance appraisals are likely to be.

Performance Appraisal Methods

Once you have your data, you can begin your actual performance appraisals. If available, use the forms provided by the organization; otherwise, develop your own rating forms. The object is to replace the "global impression" each of us creates about someone else's overall performance with a systematic procedure for assessing performance. This systematic procedure increases the accuracy and consistency of results.

There are three different approaches for doing appraisals. Employees can be appraised against (1) absolute standards, (2) relative standards, or (3) objectives. No one approach is always best; each has its strengths and weaknesses. However, keep in mind that your choice may be dictated, or at least limited, by the human resource policies and procedures in your organization.

WHAT ARE THE ABSOLUTE-STANDARDS MEASUREMENTS?

The absolute-standards measurement means that employees are not compared against any other person. Included in this group are the following methods: written essays, critical incidents, checklists, adjective rating scales, and behaviorally anchored rating scales.

written essay

A written narrative describing an employee's strengths, weaknesses, past performance, potential, and suggestions for improvement.

Written Essays Probably the simplest method of appraisal is to write a narrative describing an employee's strengths, weaknesses, past performance, potential, and suggestions for improvement. The written essay requires no complex forms or extensive training to complete. A drawback is that the results tend to reflect the ability of the writer. A good or bad appraisal may be determined as much by your writing style as by the employee's actual level of performance.

critical incidents

Incidents that focus attention on employee behaviors that are key in making the difference between executing a job effectively and executing it ineffectively.

Critical Incidents Critical incidents focus attention on employee behaviors that are key in making the difference between executing a job effectively and executing it ineffectively. That is, you write down anecdotes that describe what the employee did that was especially effective or ineffective. The key here is that only specific behaviors, not vaguely defined personality traits, are cited. A list of critical incidents provides a rich set of examples from which the employee can be shown those behaviors that are desirable and those that call for improvement.

checklist

A list of behavioral descriptions that are checked off when they apply to an employee.

Checklists With a checklist, you use a list of behavioral descriptions and check off behaviors that apply to the employee. As Exhibit 12-2 illustrates, you merely go down the list and check off yes or no to each question. Checklists are quick and relatively easy to administer. However, they have drawbacks. One drawback is their cost. Organizations with a number of job categories must develop checklist items for each category. Second, simply checking yes or no provides few data for employees—especially if you expect them to improve their work.

	Yes	No
1. Are the supervisor's orders usually followed?	____	____
2. Does the individual approach customers promptly?	____	____
3. Does the individual suggest additional merchandise to customers?	____	____
4. Does the individual keep busy when not servicing a customer?	____	____
5. Does the individual lose his or her temper in public?	____	____
6. Does the individual volunteer to help other employees?	____	____

Exhibit 12-2

Sample items from a checklist appraisal form.

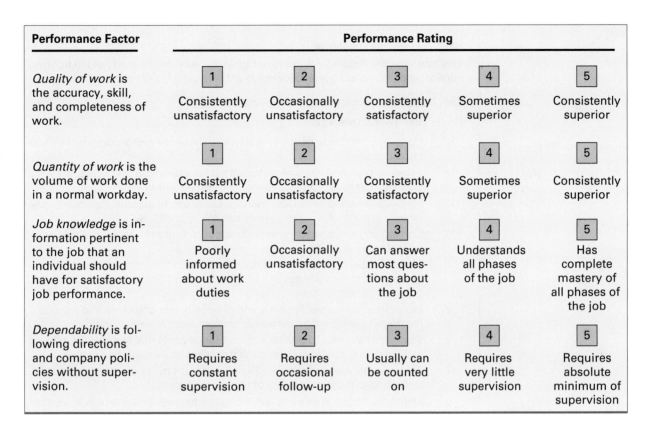

Performance Factor	Performance Rating				
Quality of work is the accuracy, skill, and completeness of work.	**1** Consistently unsatisfactory	**2** Occasionally unsatisfactory	**3** Consistently satisfactory	**4** Sometimes superior	**5** Consistently superior
Quantity of work is the volume of work done in a normal workday.	**1** Consistently unsatisfactory	**2** Occasionally unsatisfactory	**3** Consistently satisfactory	**4** Sometimes superior	**5** Consistently superior
Job knowledge is information pertinent to the job that an individual should have for satisfactory job performance.	**1** Poorly informed about work duties	**2** Occasionally unsatisfactory	**3** Can answer most questions about the job	**4** Understands all phases of the job	**5** Has complete mastery of all phases of the job
Dependability is following directions and company policies without supervision.	**1** Requires constant supervision	**2** Requires occasional follow-up	**3** Usually can be counted on	**4** Requires very little supervision	**5** Requires absolute minimum of supervision

Exhibit 12-3

Example of adjective rating scale items.

adjective rating scale

A method of appraisal that uses a scale or continuum that best describes the employee using factors such as quantity and quality of work, job knowledge, cooperation, loyalty, dependability, attendance, honesty, integrity, attitudes, and initiative.

Adjective Rating Scales One of the oldest and most popular methods of appraisal is the adjective rating scale. An example of some adjective rating scale items is shown in Exhibit 12-3.

Adjective rating scales can be used to assess factors such as quantity and quality of work, job knowledge, cooperation, loyalty, dependability, attendance, honesty, integrity, attitudes, and initiative. This method is most valid when subjective traits such as loyalty or integrity are avoided, unless they can be defined in specific behavioral terms.

With the adjective rating scale, you go down the list of factors and note the point along the scale or continuum that best describes the employee. There are typically five to ten points on the continuum. In the design of the rating scale, the challenge is to ensure that both the factors evaluated and the scale points are clearly understood by the supervisor doing the rating.

Why are adjective rating scales so popular? Though they don't provide the depth of information that essays or critical incidents do, they do have a number of advantages. They are less time consuming to develop and administer; they provide for quantitative aggregation and comparison; and in contrast to the checklist, there is greater standardization of items so that comparison with other employees in diverse job categories is possible. Furthermore, having this quantifiable assessment helps support or defend supervisory personnel decisions when challenged.

Behaviorally Anchored Rating Scales Behaviorally anchored rating scales (BARS) combine major elements from the critical incident and adjective rating scale approaches. You rate your employees based on items along a continuum, but the points are examples of actual behavior on the given job rather than general descriptions or traits.

Behaviorally anchored rating scales specify definite, observable, and measurable job behaviors. Examples of job-related behaviors and performance dimensions are found by obtaining specific illustrations of effective and ineffective behavior for each performance dimension. These behavioral examples are then translated into a set of performance dimensions, each dimension having varying levels of performance. The results of this process are behavioral descriptions, such as *anticipates, plans, executes, solves*

behaviorally anchored rating scale (BARS)

A scale that helps a supervisor rate an employee based on items along a continuum; points are examples of actual behavior on a given job rather than general descriptions or traits.

BARS for Frontline Supervisor

This performance dimension scale is designed to measure the ability of the frontline supervisor to focus and guide followers to achieve work objectives.

This frontline supervisor can be expected to:

Rank	Behavioral Description
14	Consistently provide needed feedback to maximize performance of individuals and teams
13	Establish high performance expectations for individuals and teams while creating high levels of commitment and buy-in for results
12	Take action to find resources, training, tools, etc. to support staff needs while remaining accessible to and approachable by staff
11	Consistently emphasize the importance of high quality work while holding subordinates accountable for marginal quality work
10	Coach followers and work with them to create developmental opportunities to expand their knowledge and skill level by providing positive feedback and guidance for career development
9	Monitor employee performance and provide timely, objective, and specific feedback to supplement the annual performance review
8	Work with followers to generate performance goals that are specific, measurable, and time-bound and establish a process to monitor their progress
7	Find opportunities to leverage strengths of team members and manage limitations to facilitate delivery of strong team results
6	Identify appropriate rewards and recognize follower excellence in ways that motivate others
5	Be unwilling or unable to provide followers with regular feedback on work performance
4	Be unable to define and describe expectations of work success
3	Be unapproachable to staff who have questions
2	Be inconsistent in emphasizing the importance of high quality work
1	View the organizational performance appraisal/rating system as an obstacle to completing the work

---

Exhibit 12-4
Sample BARS for frontline supervisor.

immediate problems, carries out orders, and *handles emergency situations.* Exhibit 12-4 provides an example of a BARS for an employee relations specialist.

Studies conducted using the BARS method indicate that they tend to reduce rating errors. But this tool's biggest plus may stem from the dimensions a BARS generates rather than from any particular superiority of behavior anchors over trait anchors. The process of developing the behavioral scales is valuable in and of itself for clarifying to both the employee and the supervisor which behaviors mean good performance and which mean bad.

However, the BARS method is not without its drawbacks. It, too, suffers from the distortions inherent in most rating methods. A BARS is also costly to develop and maintain.

HOW DO YOU USE RELATIVE STANDARDS?

In the second category of performance appraisals—relative standards—employees are compared against other employees in evaluating their performance. We discuss two relative methods: group-order ranking and individual ranking.

group-order ranking
Placing employees into classifications, such as "top one-fifth" or "second one-fifth." This method prevents a supervisor from inflating or equalizing employee evaluations.

Group-Order Ranking Group-order ranking requires you to place your employees into particular classifications, such as "top one-fifth" or "second one-fifth." If you have twenty employees, and you're using the group-order ranking method, only four of your employees can be in the top fifth, and, of course, four also must be relegated to the bottom fifth (see Exhibit 12-5).

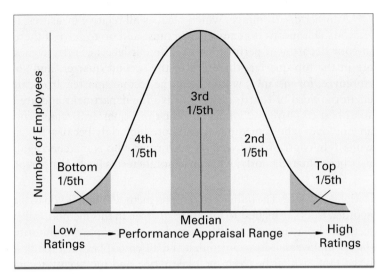

Exhibit 12-5
Group-order ranking distribution.

Comprehension Check 12-1

1. Which one of the following is *not* a component of an effective performance appraisal system?

   a. Feedback
   b. Development
   c. Salary increase
   d. Documentation

2. Self-generated feedback about one's performance is best referred to as

   a. extrinsic feedback
   b. supervisory feedback
   c. intrinsic feedback
   d. self-performance feedback

3. The type of appraisal method that involves a narrative of an employee's strengths, weaknesses, past performance, potential, and suggestions for improvement is the

   a. critical incident
   b. written essay
   c. checklist
   d. behaviorally anchored rating scale

4. Which one of the following is *not* an absolute-standards measurement?

   a. Group-order ranking
   b. Critical incident
   c. Checklist
   d. Adjective rating scale

The advantage of group ordering is that it prevents you from inflating employee evaluations so that everyone looks good or equalizing the evaluations so that everyone is rated near the average—outcomes that are not unusual with the graphic rating scale. The predominant disadvantages surface when the number of employees being compared is small. At the extreme, if you are looking at only four employees, all of whom may actually be excellent, you are forced to rank them into top quarter, second quarter, third quarter, and bottom quarter. Of course, as the sample size increases, the validity of relative scores as an accurate measure increases.

Another disadvantage, which plagues all relative measures, is the zero-sum consideration. This means that any change must add up to zero. If there are twelve employees in your department performing at different levels of effectiveness, by definition, three are in the top quarter, three are in the second quarter, and so forth. The sixth-best employee, for instance, would be in the second quarter. Ironically, if two of the workers in the third or fourth quarters leave the department and are not replaced, then the sixth-best employee now falls into the third quarter. Because comparisons are relative, an employee who is mediocre may score high only because he or she is the "best of the worst." In contrast, an excellent performer who is matched against tough competition may be evaluated poorly, when in absolute terms his or her performance is outstanding.

individual ranking
A method that requires supervisors to list all employees in order from the highest to lowest performer.

Individual Ranking The individual ranking method requires you to list all of your employees, in order, from the highest to lowest performer. In this method, only one can be "best." This method also assumes that differences between people are uniform. That is, in appraising thirty employees, it is assumed that the difference between the first and second employee is the same as that between the twenty-first and the twenty-second. This method allows for no ties, which can be an advantage because it doesn't allow you to avoid confronting differences in performance levels. But its major drawback is that in situations where differences are small or nonexistent, this method magnifies and overemphasizes differences.

OBJECTIVES

The final method for appraising performance is by using objectives. This is essentially an application of goal setting, introduced in Chapter 3.

Once you and your employee have established a set of tangible, verifiable, and measurable goals that encompass the key results he or she is expected to achieve, you have the standard in place against which the employee's performance can be assessed. At the end of the goal-setting period—which might be monthly, quarterly, semiannually, or annually—you and your employee can sit down and appraise how well he or she performed. If the goals were carefully chosen to capture the essential performance dimensions in the employee's job and written so that they can be readily measured, they should provide you with a fairly accurate appraisal of the employee's overall job performance.

You've just read about the types of appraisal methods. How are they demonstrated in your class? How does your professor's evaluation of you meet the three purposes of evaluations? (See "Something to Think About.")

Potential Problems in Performance Appraisals

Although you and your employer may seek to make the performance appraisal process free from personal biases, prejudices, and idiosyncrasies, a number of potential problems can creep into the process. To the degree that the following factors are prevalent, an employee's performance appraisal is likely to be distorted.

WHAT IS LENIENCY ERROR?

leniency error
Positive or negative leniency that overstates or understates performance, giving an individual a higher or lower appraisal than deserved.

Every appraiser has his or her own value system that acts as a standard against which appraisals are made. Relative to the true or actual performance an individual exhibits, some appraisers mark high and others low. The former is referred to as positive leniency error, and the latter as negative leniency error. When appraisers are positively lenient in their evaluations, an employee's performance becomes overstated—that is, rated higher than it actually should be. Similarly, a negative leniency error understates performance, giving the individual a lower appraisal than deserved.

If all employees in an organization were appraised by the same person, there would be no problem. Although there would be an error factor, it would be applied equally to everyone. The difficulty arises when we have different raters with different leniency errors making judgments. For example, assume that Jean and Steven are performing the same job for different supervisors, but they have absolutely identical job performance. If Jean's supervisor tends to err toward positive leniency, while Steven's supervisor errs toward negative leniency, we might be confronted with two dramatically different performance appraisals.

HOW DO HALO ERRORS AFFECT APPRAISALS?

The halo error is a tendency to rate an individual high or low on all factors as a result of the impression of a high or low rating on some specific factor. For example, if an employee tends to be dependable, you might become biased toward that individual to the extent that you rate him or her high on many desirable traits.

halo error
A tendency to rate an individual high or low on all factors as a result of the impression of a high or low rating on some specific factor.

People who design teaching appraisal forms for college students to fill out to evaluate the effectiveness of their instructors each semester must confront the halo error. Students tend to rate a faculty member as outstanding on all criteria when they are particularly appreciative of a few things he or she does in the classroom. Similarly, a few bad habits—such as showing up late for lectures, being slow in returning papers, or assigning an extremely demanding reading assignment—might result in students evaluating the instructor as "lousy" across the board.

WHAT IS SIMILARITY ERROR?

When appraisers rate other people by giving special consideration to qualities that they perceive in themselves, they are making a similarity error. The supervisor who perceives himself as aggressive may evaluate others by looking for aggressiveness. Those who demonstrate this characteristic tend to benefit, while others are penalized.

similarity error
Rating others in a way that gives special consideration to qualities that appraisers perceive in themselves.

Again, this error would tend to wash out if the same evaluator appraised all the people in the organization. However, multiple-rater reliability obviously suffers when various evaluators use their own similarity criteria.

WHAT IS RECENCY ERROR?

It's easier for most of us to remember vividly what happened yesterday than what happened six months ago. This creates the potential for recency error to surface in performance appraisals.

Something to Think About (and promote class discussion)

EVALUATING STUDENTS

Nearly everything you've been reading so far in this chapter can be directly applied to your classroom. Every day you come to class, every quiz or test you take, and any assignments you turn in are evaluated in some form. You're being appraised—even if you hadn't thought about it that way.

Let's look at how you are evaluated. More than likely, your instructor has laid out his or her grading policy in the course syllabus. Is it based on absolute standards, relative standards, objectives—or a combination of all of these? For example, on an exam based on 100 points, your grade on that exam is being rated against an absolute standard (100 points). If your instructor curves the exam, some relative standards are appearing. Maybe the final grade in the course is determined by how well you met certain goals (objectives). Of course, the list could go on. Consider how you are evaluated. Do you believe it meets the three purposes of evaluations—feedback, development, and documentation? If you had the opportunity to redesign the evaluation component of your class, what would you recommend? Of course, you realize that "no evaluation" is not acceptable!

recency error
An error that occurs when appraisers recall and give greater importance to employee job behaviors that have occurred near the end of the performance-measuring period.

Recency error results when evaluators recall, and then give greater importance to, employee job behaviors that have occurred near the end of the performance-measuring period. If you have to complete an appraisal form on each of your employees every June 1, accomplishments and mistakes that took place in May might tend to be remembered, while behaviors exhibited during the previous November tend to be forgotten. Given the reality that we all have good and bad days—even good and bad months—and that they don't occur at the same time for all employees, a semiannual or annual review may be significantly biased by employee behaviors that occurred just prior to the review.

HOW DOES CENTRAL TENDENCY ERROR AFFECT APPRAISALS?

It's possible that, regardless of whom the appraiser evaluates and what characteristics are used, the pattern of evaluation remains the same. It is also possible that a supervisor's ability to appraise objectively and accurately has been impeded by a failure to use the extremes of the appraising scale. This reluctance to assign extreme ratings, in either direction, is the central tendency error.

central tendency error
Appraisers' tendency to avoid the "excellent" category as well as the "unacceptable" category and assign all ratings around the "average" or midpoint range.

Raters who are prone to the central tendency error avoid the "excellent" category as well as the "unacceptable" category and assign all ratings around the "average" or midpoint range. For example, if you rate all employees as 3 on a scale of 1 to 5, then no differentiation among them exists. Suppressing differences makes employees' work performances appear considerably more homogeneous than they really are.

ARE YOU INCLINED TO USE INFLATIONARY PRESSURES?

A clerical employee at a large insurance company was disappointed by the small salary increase she received following her recent performance review. After all, her supervisor had given her an 86 overall rating. She knew that the company's appraisal system defined "outstanding performance" as 90 and above, "good" as 80 to 89, "average" as 70 to 79, and "unacceptable" performance as anything below 70. This employee was really bewildered when she heard from some friends at work that her pay increase was below the company average. You can imagine her surprise when, after meeting with the assistant director of human resources, she learned that the "average" rating of clerical personnel in the company was 92!

This example illustrates a potential problem in appraisals—inflationary pressures. Here, you as a supervisor minimize differences among your employees and push all evaluations into the upper range of the rating scale. Inflationary pressures have always existed but have become more of a problem over the past three decades. As equality values have grown in importance, as well as fear of retribution from disgruntled employees who fail to achieve excellent appraisals, evaluators have tended to be less rigorous and to reduce the negative repercussions from the appraisal process by generally inflating or upgrading evaluations.

HOW CAN YOU OVERCOME THE HURDLES?

Just because there are potential hurdles to effective appraisals doesn't mean that you should give up on the process. There are some things you can do to help overcome these hurdles.

Continually Document Employee Performance Keep a file for each of your employees and continually put notes into these files describing specific incidents of accomplishments and behaviors. Include dates and details. When the time comes for you to conduct formal employee appraisals, you'll have a comprehensive history of each employee's performance record during the appraisal period. This will minimize the recency error, increase the accuracy of your ratings, and provide specific documentation to support your assessments.

Use Behaviorally Based Measures As we've noted previously, behaviorally based measures are superior to those developed around traits. Many traits often considered related to good performance may in fact have little or no performance relationship. Traits such as loyalty, initiative, courage, and reliability are intuitively appealing as desirable characteristics in employees. But the relevant question is, Are employees who are evaluated as high on these traits better performers than those who rate low? We can't answer that question. We know that some employees rate high on these characteristics and are poor performers. We can find others who are excellent performers but don't score well on traits such as these. Our conclusion is that traits such as loyalty and initiative may be prized by organizations, but there is no evidence to support that certain traits will be adequate substitutes for performance in a large cross-section of jobs. Additionally, as we noted previously, traits suffer from weak agreement among multiple raters. What you consider loyalty, I may not.

Behaviorally based measures can deal with both of these objections. Because they deal with specific examples of performance—both good and bad—you avoid the problem of using inappropriate substitutes. Moreover, because you're evaluating specific behaviors, you increase the likelihood that two or more evaluators will see the same thing. You might consider a given employee friendly, while I rate her as standoffish. But when asked to rate her in terms of specific behaviors, we might both agree that she frequently says "Good morning" to customers, rarely gives advice or assistance to coworkers, and almost always avoids idle chatter with coworkers.

Combine Absolute and Relative Standards A major drawback to absolute standards is that they tend to be biased by inflationary pressures—evaluators lean toward packing their subjects into the high part of the rankings. On the other hand, relative standards suffer when there is little actual variability among the subjects.

The obvious solution is to consider using appraisal methods that combine absolute and relative standards. For example, you might want to use the adjective rating scale and the individual ranking method. It's much more meaningful to compare two employees' performance records when you know that Supervisor A gave Bob Carter an overall rating of 86, which ranked fourth in a department of seventeen; while Supervisor B also gave Tina Blackstone an 86 rating, but ranked her twelfth in a department of fourteen. It's possible that Supervisor B has higher-performing employees than Supervisor A. Supervisor B's ratings may also suffer from inflationary pressures. By providing both absolute and relative assessments, it is easier to more accurately compare employees across departments.

Use Multiple Raters As the number of evaluators increases, the probability of attaining more accurate information increases. If rater error tends to follow a normal curve, an increase in the number of appraisers will tend to find the majority congregating about the middle. You see this approach being used in athletic competitions in such sports as diving, gymnastics, and figure skating. A set of evaluators judges a performance, the highest and lowest scores are dropped, and the final performance appraisal is made up from the cumulative scores of those remaining. The logic of multiple raters applies to organizations as well.

If an employee has had ten supervisors, nine having rated her excellent and one poor, the one poor appraisal takes on less importance. Multiple raters, therefore, increase the reliability of results by tending to lessen the importance of rater personal biases such as leniency, similarity, and central tendency errors.

A special case of multiple raters involves a trend in today's organizations referred to as the 360-degree appraisal. The 360-degree appraisal seeks performance feedback from such sources as oneself, bosses, peers, team members, customers, and suppliers and has become very popular in contemporary organizations.[3]

360-degree appraisal
Performance feedback provided by supervisors, employees, peers, and possibly others.

[3]T. J. Maurer, D. R. D. Mitchell, and F. G. Barbeite, "Predictors of Attitudes Toward a 360-Degree Feedback System and Involvement in Post-Feedback Management Development Activity," *Journal of Occupational and Organizational Psychology* 75 (March 2002), 87–107.

As a supervisor appraising this individual's classroom performance, if you give him a positive rating based on his ability to entertain rather than his ability to teach, you may be allowing the halo effect to bias your appraisal.

In today's dynamic organizations, traditional performance evaluations systems may be archaic. Downsizing has resulted in supervisors having greater work responsibility and more employees reporting directly to them. Accordingly, in some instances, it is almost impossible for supervisors to have extensive job knowledge of each of their employees. Furthermore, the growth of project teams and employee involvement in today's companies places the responsibility of evaluation where people are better able to make an accurate assessment.[4] The 360-degree appraisal process also has some positive benefits for development concerns. Many supervisors simply do not know how their employees truly view them and the work they have done.

Research studies into the effectiveness of 360-degree performance appraisals are reporting positive results. These stem from having more accurate feedback, empowering employees, reducing the subjective factors in the evaluation process, and developing leadership in an organization.[5] Moreover, to enhance honesty and efficiency in feedback, some companies have put their 360-degree appraisal on the Internet.

Rate Selectively As an employee's direct supervisor, you are not always in a position to comprehensively appraise all the key aspects of that employee's performance. You should rate only in areas in which you have significant job knowledge and have been able to observe firsthand the employee's job performance. If you appraise only the dimensions that you are in a good position to rate, you make the performance appraisal a more valid process.

If there are important parts of an employee's job in which you aren't able to make accurate judgments, you should supplement your appraisal with self-appraisals, peer evaluations, or even customer appraisals, if that's more appropriate. A number of sales supervisors use customer input as part of their evaluation of sales representatives. Supervisors who have to be away from their work areas frequently, which limits their opportunities to observe their employees' job behavior, use peer reviews to improve the validity of the appraisal process.

Participate in Appraisal Training Good appraisers aren't necessarily born. If your appraisal skills are deficient, you should participate in performance appraisal training because there is evidence that training can make you a more accurate rater.

Common errors such as leniency and halo have been minimized or eliminated in workshops where supervisors practice observing and rating behaviors. These workshops typically run from one to three days, but allocating many hours to training may not always be necessary. One case has been cited in which both halo and leniency errors were decreased immediately after exposing evaluators to explanatory training sessions lasting only five minutes.[6] However, the effects of training appear to diminish over time, which suggests the need for regular refresher sessions.

[4]C. Hymowitz, "In the Lead: Do 360 Job Reviews by Colleagues Promote Honesty or Insults?" *Wall Street Journal*, December 12, 2000, B-1.

[5]J. S. Miller, P. W. Hom, and L. R. Gomez-Mejia, "The High Cost of Low Wages: Does Maquiladora Compensation Reduce Turnover?" *Journal of International Business Studies* 32, no. 3 (Third Quarter 2001), 585–595.

[6]C. P. Neck, G. L. Stewart, and C. C. Manz, "Thought Self-Leadership as a Framework for Enhancing the Performance of Performance Appraisers," *Journal of Applied Behavior Science* 31, no.3 (September 1995), 278–302.

Conduct Performance Appraisals of Teams Performance appraisal concepts have been developed almost exclusively with the individual employee as the focus point. This reflects the historic belief that individuals are the core building block around which organizations are built. Recently, as we've noted a number of times in this book, more and more organizations are restructuring themselves around teams (see "News Flash! Performance Appraisals in Contemporary Organizations").

In team-based departments, job performance is a function of each individual's contribution to the team and his or her ability to be a good team player. Both of these performance dimensions are often better assessed by the team's members than by the team's supervisor. We suggest, therefore, that you include peer evaluations from team members in the performance appraisals of those whose jobs are inherently designed around teamwork. This enhances the autonomy of the team, reinforces the importance of cooperation, and increases the validity of the appraisal process. Additionally, consider the benefits of downplaying individual contributions by substituting group performance measures. When teams have clear responsibilities for achieving specific objectives, it makes more sense to appraise the team's overall performance than to focus on its individual members.

RESPONDING TO PERFORMANCE PROBLEMS

Whenever one of your employees exhibits work behaviors that are inconsistent with the work environment (e.g., fighting, stealing, or unexcused absences) or is unable to perform his or her job satisfactorily, you must intervene. But before any intervention can begin, it is imperative for you to identify the problem. If you realize that the performance problem is ability related, your emphasis becomes one of encouraging training and development efforts. However, when the performance problem is desire related, whether the unwillingness to correct the problem is voluntary or involuntary, employee counseling is the next logical approach.[7]

employee counseling
An emphasis on encouraging training and development efforts in a situation in which an employee's unwillingness or inability to perform his or her job satisfactorily is either voluntary or involuntary.

News Flash!

PERFORMANCE APPRAISALS IN CONTEMPORARY ORGANIZATIONS

The foundation of the performance appraisal process is the concept that performance standards are clearly identified. This fundamental fact implies that for workers to perform effectively, they must know and understand what is expected of them. This concept, however, applies only where clear job descriptions and specifications exist, and where variations to the job are minimal. In other words, conventional performance appraisals were designed to fit the needs of the traditional organization. But what happens to these when the organization is far from traditional? Let's look at some possibilities.

First, setting goals for an employee could become a thing of the past. Your workers may go from project to project, with the demands and requirements of their work rapidly changing. No formalized performance appraisal system may be able to capture the complexities of the jobs being done. Second, employees will likely have several bosses, not just you. Just who, then, will have the responsibility for the performance appraisal? It is more likely to be the team members themselves—setting their own goals and evaluating each other's performance. One can even speculate that this will take the format of an ongoing informal process, rather than some formal "ritual" held every twelve months.

All in all, while we surmise a drastic change in the performance appraisal process, you should not infer that you will become less concerned with evaluating employee performance. On the contrary, individual performance will still matter most. The major difference is that employee performance information is likely to be collected from a number of sources—from anyone who's familiar with the employee's work.

---

[7]M. Scott, "7 Pitfalls for Managers When Handling Poor Performers and How to Overcome Them," *Manage*, February 2000, 12–13.

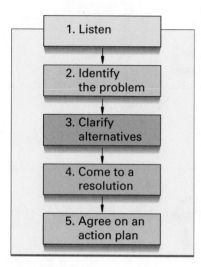

Exhibit 12-6
The counseling process.

WHAT DO YOU NEED TO KNOW ABOUT COUNSELING EMPLOYEES?

Although employee counseling processes differ, some fundamental steps should be followed when counseling an employee (see Exhibit 12-6).

Listen to What the Employee Has to Say You can't effectively counsel others unless you listen to what they have to say. Your actions should be tailored to the needs, demands, and personality of your employee. These factors can't be accurately assessed without active listening.

When you sit down with your employee, demonstrate your willingness and desire to be helpful. Then, listen to what he or she has to say. Also listen to what is not being said. How is the employee framing the problem? Who does the employee think is to blame? Are his or her emotions driving out rational thinking? Don't make judgments too quickly. Try to grasp the employee's perception of the situation without agreeing or disagreeing with that perception. At this point, it's not so important to determine whether the employee is right or wrong as it is to try to fully understand the problem from his or her point of view.

Identify the Problem After you've listened to your employee's initial assessment of the situation, begin the search to identify the problem and its causes. What does the employee think is the problem? Who or what is the cause? How is this problem affecting the employee? What, if any, responsibility is your employee taking for the problem? You must remember, though, you're attacking some behavior, not the employee!

Clarify Alternatives Problems come with options. In most cases, a number of alternatives can correct the problem. These need to be explored and clarified. This is a point at which a participative approach can be particularly valuable because you may see and know things that escape the employee's perception. As a result, merging your insights and the employee's can result in a greater number of quality options.

Once alternatives are identified, they need to be evaluated. What are the strengths and weaknesses of each? Again, two heads are better than one. Your goal should be to have the employee weigh the pluses and minuses of each course of action.

Come to a Resolution What's the best option for the employee? Remember, the best option for one employee is not necessarily the best option for another. The solution should reflect the unique characteristics of the employee. Ideally, both you and the employee will agree on the solution. You want to be sure the employee buys into the final choice, whether that final choice was made by you, by the employee, or jointly. A terrific solution that's not accepted by the employee is unlikely to result in any meaningful change.

Agree on an Action Plan Finally, the employee needs to develop a concrete plan of action for implementing the solution. What, specifically, is the employee going to do? When will he or she do it? What resources, if any, will be needed?

It's usually a good idea to end a counseling session with the employee summarizing what has taken place and the specific actions he or she plans on taking. Establish a follow-up point at some specific date in the future for reassessing the employee's progress. If a formal meeting isn't needed, request a short memo from the employee updating you on his or her progress. This can be effective as a reminder to the employee that progress is expected and as a control device for you to assess the employee's progress.

IS YOUR ACTION ETHICAL?

What business do you have delving into an employee's personal life? That's a valid question and requires us to look at the ethics of counseling. Employees bring a multitude of problems and frustrations from their personal lives to their jobs. They have difficulty finding quality day care for infants. A teenage child is expelled from high school. They have fights with their spouses. A family member suffers a nervous breakdown. They get behind in their bills and they're harassed by creditors. A close friend is seriously hurt in an automobile accident. A parent is diagnosed with Alzheimer's disease.

It may seem wise to keep your nose out of your employees' personal lives, but that is often unreasonable. Why? Because there is no clear demarcation that separates personal and work lives. Consider the following scenario involving one of your employees, Denise. Denise's son was arrested last night for possession of drugs. She spent most of the night with police and lawyers. Today, at work, she is tired and psychologically distant. She has trouble concentrating. Her mind is not on her job. It's naïve to believe that employees can somehow leave their personal problems at the door when they come to work each morning.

Do employees have a right to privacy? Absolutely! However, when personal problems interfere with work performance, you should not consider it beyond your jurisdiction to inquire about the problem, offer yourself as an open ear, and genuinely seek to help with the problem. If your offer is rejected, don't push. If the employee understands how his or her personal problem is affecting work performance, and you make clear what the consequences will be if the work performance doesn't improve, you've reached the ethical limit of your involvement. If the employee is protective of his or her personal life, your rights as a supervisor don't extend to helping solve his or her personal problems. However, you do have the right and the obligation to make sure employees understand that if personal problems interfere with their work, they need to solve those personal problems—and you're there to help, if asked.

Comprehension Check 12-2

5. The type of performance appraisal error that overstates or understates performance based on the rater's value system is called
   a. similarity error
   b. recency error
   c. halo error
   d. leniency error

6. Central tendency is
   a. rating others in a way that gives special consideration to qualities that appraisers perceive in themselves
   b. a tendency to rate an individual high or low based on the impression of some specific factor
   c. assigning all ratings as average
   d. none of the above

7. Which one of the following is *not* a recommendation for overcoming performance appraisal hurdles?
   a. Use single raters
   b. Use behaviorally based measures
   c. Rate selectively
   d. Train appraisers

8. An emphasis on encouraging training and development efforts in a situation in which an employee's unwillingness or inability to perform his or her job satisfactorily is either voluntary or involuntary is descriptive of
   a. performance feedback
   b. employee counseling
   c. 360-degree appraisal
   d. discipline

Enhancing Understanding

SUMMARY

After reading this chapter, I can:

1. **Describe the three purposes of the performance appraisal.** The performance appraisal is both an evaluation and development tool and a legal document. It reviews past performance to identify accomplishments and deficiencies; it offers a detailed plan to improve future performance through training and development; and it also becomes a legal document that can be used to support and justify personnel actions.

2. **Differentiate formal and informal performance appraisals.** Formal performance appraisals are regular, planned meetings where the supervisor and employee discuss and review the latter's work performance. Informal performance appraisal is the day-to-day assessment a supervisor makes of an employee's performance and the ongoing feedback the supervisor gives the employee about that performance.

3. **Describe key legal concerns in performance appraisals.** To minimize legal problems, supervisors should make sure that they carefully follow all performance appraisal policies and procedures set forth in the organization's employee handbook (if it exists) and make every effort to avoid prejudice and discrimination.

4. **Identify the three most popular sets of criteria that supervisors appraise.** The three most popular sets of criteria used by supervisors in appraisals are individual task outcomes, behaviors, and traits. The first two are almost always preferred to the third.

5. **Contrast absolute and relative standards.** Absolute standards compare the employee's performance against specific tasks, behaviors, or traits rather than against other employees. In contrast, relative standards compare employee performance against that of other employees.

6. **List human errors that can distort performance appraisal ratings.** Common human errors that can distort appraisals include leniency error, halo error, similarity error, recency error, central tendency error, and inflationary pressures.

7. **Describe what is meant by the term *360-degree appraisal*.** In 360-degree performance appraisals, evaluations are made by the employee being appraised, supervisors, other employees, team members, customers, suppliers, and the like. In doing so, a complete picture of performance can be assessed.

8. **Describe the purpose of employee counseling.** The purpose of employee counseling is to address performance problems when the deficiencies are desire related.

COMPREHENSION: Review and Discussion Questions

1. Why, in your opinion, do many supervisors dislike or even avoid giving employees performance feedback?

2. Contrast the advantages of supervisor-conducted appraisals, self-evaluations, and peer evaluations.

3. What is the relationship between goal setting and performance appraisal?

4. Contrast intrinsic and extrinsic feedback.

5. If appraising behaviors are superior to appraising traits, why do you think so many organizations evaluate their employees on criteria such as effort, loyalty, and dependability?

6. Compare written essay appraisals with BARS appraisals.

7. Would human errors in the appraisal process be eliminated in small organizations where one person does all the appraisals? Explain.

8. What can a supervisor do to minimize distortions in the appraisal process?

9. What is a 360-degree appraisal? What are the advantages and disadvantages of using this method of appraising?

10. Do you believe employee counseling is preferable to disciplining employees? Support your position.

KEY CONCEPT CROSSWORDS

ACROSS

5. elements of performance evaluation as defined by the organization
7. a type of performance evaluation whereby information is obtained from supervisors, employees, peers, and maybe others
11. ranking employees into such classifications as top fifth, second fifth, etc.
15. key behaviors that make a difference in an employee's job effectiveness
16. an emphasis on encouraging training and development when an employee's performance problem is desire related
17. a ranking method of listing employees from highest to lowest
18. an evaluation scale that combines major elements of critical incidents and adjective rating scales
19. a type of feedback that is provided by an outside source

DOWN

1. a type of performance evaluation error in which the most current behaviors influence the evaluation
2. a type of performance evaluation error whereby someone's rating is related to how appraisers perceive themselves
3. a type of performance evaluation error whereby one is evaluated high or low based on some specific factor
4. a review of past performance that emphasizes accomplishments and deficiencies
6. information that lets an employee know how well he or she performed
8. an evaluation method involving behavioral descriptions that are either present or not
9. an appraisal method that uses a scale or continuum that describes the degree to which an employee performed his or her work
10. a type of performance evaluation error in which all ratings end up average
12. a type of performance evaluation error that overstates or understates one's performance
13. a type of feedback that is self-generated
14. a type of employee evaluation involving a narrative description of an employee's performance

ANSWERS TO COMPREHENSION CHECKS

Comprehension Check 12-1

1. c   2. c   3. b   4. a

Comprehension Check 12-2

5. d   6. c   7. a   8. b

Developing Your Supervisory Skills

GETTING TO KNOW YOURSELF

Before you can effectively supervise others, you must understand your present strengths and areas in need of development. To assist in this learning process, we encourage you to complete the following self-assessments from the Prentice Hall Self-Assessment Library 3.4.

1. How Good Am I at Giving Performance Feedback? (III. A. 3.)
2. What Are My Course Performance Goals? (I. C. 5.)

After you complete the assessment, we suggest you retain the results and store them as part of your "portfolio of learning about yourself."

BUILDING A TEAM

➤ An Experiential Exercise: The 360-Degree Appraisal

As a student in a supervision class, you and your class team have been asked to conduct a fifteen-minute presentation for ten to fifteen supervisors at the next supervisors' meeting because supervisors have not adapted as well as desired by management to a change in the appraisal system.

Develop a fifteen-minute presentation about the purposes of the performance management systems, who benefits, the basic six steps, the difference between relative and absolute standards, possible distortions, and the 360-degree appraisal system.

➤ Internet: Web Activity

Go to http://www.pearsonhighered.com/robbins/. Find *Supervision Today!* 7th Ed. and click Companion Website.

CONDUCTING A PERFORMANCE EVALUATION

How does one properly conduct the performance appraisal process? We offer the following steps that can assist in this endeavor.

STEP 1: Prepare for, and schedule, the appraisal in advance. Before meeting with employees, some preliminary activities should be performed. You should at a minimum review employee job descriptions, period goals that may have been set, and performance data you may have on employees. Furthermore, you should schedule the appraisal well in advance to give employees the opportunity to prepare their own data for the meeting.

STEP 2: Create a supportive environment to put employees at ease. Performance appraisals conjure

up several emotions. As such, every effort should be made to make employees comfortable during the meeting so that they are receptive to constructive feedback.

STEP 3: Describe the purpose of the appraisal to employees. Make sure employees know precisely what the appraisal is to be used for. Will it have implications for pay increases or other personnel decisions? If so, make sure employees understand exactly how the appraisal process works, and its consequences.

STEP 4: Involve the employee in the appraisal discussion, including a self-evaluation. Performance appraisals should not be a one-way communication event. Although as supervisor, you may believe that you have to talk more in the meeting, that needn't be the case. Instead, employees should have ample opportunity to discuss their performance, raise questions about the facts you raise, and add their own data/perceptions about their work. One means of ensuring that two-way communication occurs is to have employees conduct a self-evaluation. You should actively listen to their assessment. This involvement helps create an environment of participation.[8]

STEP 5: Focus discussion on work behaviors, not on the employee. One way of creating emotional difficulties is to attack the employee. Keep your discussion on the behaviors you've observed. For instance, telling an employee that his report stinks doesn't do a thing. That's not focusing on behaviors. Instead, indicating that you believe that not enough time was devoted to proofreading the report describes the behavior you may be having a problem with.

STEP 6: Support your evaluation with specific examples. Specific performance behaviors help clarify to employees the issues you raise. Rather than saying something wasn't good (subjective evaluation), be as specific as possible in your explanations. So, for the employee who failed to proof the work, describing that the report had five grammatical mistakes in the first two pages alone would be a specific example.

STEP 7: Give both positive feedback and feedback for improvement. Performance appraisals needn't be all negative. Although there is a perception that this process focuses on the negative, it should also be used to compliment and recognize good work. Positive feedback, as well as feedback for improvement, helps employees to gain a better understanding of their performance. For example, although the report was not up to the quality you expected, the employee did do the work and completed the report in a timely fashion. That's behavior that deserves some positive reinforcement.

STEP 8: Ensure that employees understand what was discussed in the appraisal. At the end of the appraisal, especially when some improvement is warranted, you should ask employees to summarize what was discussed in the meeting. This will help ensure that you have gotten your information through to the employee.

STEP 9: Generate a development plan. Most of the performance appraisal revolves around feedback and documentation. But another component is needed. When development efforts are encouraged, a plan should be developed to describe what is to be done, by when, and what support you as the supervisor will provide to aid in the improvement/enhancement effort.

Source: See also P. Peters, "7 Tips for Delivering Performance Feedback," *Supervision* 61, no. 5 (May 2000), 12–14.

[8]See W. R. Boswell and J. W. Boudreau, "Employee Satisfaction with Performance Appraisals and Appraisers: The Role of Perceived Appraisal Use," *Human Resource Development Quarterly* 11, no.3 (Fall 2000), 283–299.

➤ Communicating Effectively

1. Develop a two- to three-page paper describing the relationship that exists between the job analysis and the performance evaluation. Cite specific examples where appropriate.

2. Conduct an Internet search for articles providing data on the pros and cons of using a 360-degree performance appraisal in an organization. Summarize the articles and end the paper with your beliefs on whether 360-degree evaluations should be used in all organizations.

THINKING CRITICALLY

➤ Case 12-A: Using 360-Degree Performance Appraisals

Margaret Jenkins is an administrative assistant in the engineering department. She is responsible to Adam Clark, one of the engineering directors. Margaret is a ten-year veteran in the engineering department but has only reported to Adam for six months. She has a reputation as a good performer and steady contributor to the department with an excellent attendance record. All of the other administrative assistants and engineering personnel like Margaret because she is a social person who takes an interest in everyone.

In a typical day, Margaret arrives at work on time, and then goes to the cafeteria for coffee and conversation with her many friends and coworkers. This usually lasts about half an hour. Margaret does receive personal phone calls during the day and makes phone calls on personal matters quite often. She is also the first person to be involved with gatherings for birthdays and retirement activities. The engineering section is involved in several large and complex new projects that will demand close attention to communication and follow-up activities.

Adam is interested in finding ways to improve Margaret's job scope and her job performance. He believes that Margaret's long service and experience in the department could be of greater value to their work. Being a new director, he is very aware of the stature that Margaret holds in the department, and he wants to take a very positive approach to Margaret's performance. Adam has enrolled Margaret in the company's new plan where she will be provided with several feedback and assessment instruments from her department and company coworkers. As a result of this feedback, Margaret is given a plan to correct some of her oversocializing behaviors. She is also to return to her normal activities and seek clarification with Adam and other employees on ways she can improve her value to the company.

RESPONDING TO THE CASE

1. How would this new type of performance appraisal plan help Margaret, and how would it help Adam?

2. What else needs to go on in an organization for this type of performance appraisal to work?

3. What type of potential problems might one be on the lookout for when using this type of appraisal instrument?

➤ Case 12-B: Performance Appraisal at the Athletic Shoe Shop

At the Athletic Shoe Shop, formal performance appraisals are conducted annually. Each supervisor is expected to conduct a performance review for every employee during October—in time to recommend end-of-the-year employee bonuses. As a supervisor, it is essential that Bill Martin take this responsibility seriously.

After Bill and his area manager discuss the review for each employee in his store, Bill is expected to sit down with each employee individually to go over their performance review. He is expected to have these appraisal feedback meetings during November. This face-to-face meeting gives each employee feedback about performance and also addresses areas of performance that could be improved.

The company uses a standard form to evaluate employees. The form was developed by a group of employees representing all levels of workers in the company. It includes the following elements: job knowledge and skills, quality of work, productivity or quantity of work, following company policies and procedures, planning and organizing work, prioritizing work assignments, communication in speaking and writing, attitude toward job, teamwork and working with coworkers, cooperation and loyalty, adaptability to change, dependability and punctuality, and initiative and resourcefulness.

It is now time for Bill Martin to evaluate his employees. He really doesn't like this aspect of his job because it is so hard to be objective. He distinctly remembers last year's meeting with his boss, Leslie Hines. Bill can still hear her saying, "It is remarkable that all of your employees rate so high in all areas. How can this be?" Bill knew that he had difficulty responding to her not-so-subtle way of telling him he was not adequately evaluating his personnel. He didn't want a repeat performance of that incident this year.

RESPONDING TO THE CASE

1. Why do you think Bill Martin is so concerned about his meeting with his area manager? Should he change the rating methods he uses to evaluate his employees? Why or why not?

2. What are some of the benefits Bill Martin's employees get from their performance reviews? What are some drawbacks?

3. What could Bill do to improve the performance evaluation process in his store?

4. What are the legal issues Martin and other supervisors need to consider in conducting performance appraisals? Develop a list of guidelines Bill could follow to avoid legal problems.

Workplace Health and Safety

Key Concepts

After completing this chapter, you will be able to define these supervisory terms:

- carpal tunnel syndrome
- employee assistance program (EAP)
- imminent danger
- incidence rate
- *karoshi*
- musculoskeletal disorders (MSDs)
- National Institute for Occupational Safety and Health (NIOSH)

- Occupational Safety and Health Act
- repetitive stress injuries
- sick buildings
- stress
- stressors
- wellness program

Chapter Outcomes

After reading this chapter, you will be able to:

1. Discuss the supervisory effects of the Occupational Safety and Health Act.

2. List the enforcement priorities of the Occupational Safety and Health Administration (OSHA).

3. Explain what punitive actions OSHA can impose on an organization.

4. Describe what supervisors must do to comply with OSHA record-keeping requirements.

5. Describe the leading causes of safety and health accidents.

6. Explain what supervisors can do to prevent workplace violence.

7. Define *stress*.

8. Explain how a supervisor can create a healthy work site.

9. Describe the purposes of employee assistance and wellness programs.

Responding to a Supervisory Dilemma

A trend occurring in organizations today continues to raise important questions for a number of people. Indeed, workplace wellness programs encourage people to take steps to prevent the onset or worsening of a health condition or sickness and to adopt lifestyles that are healthier. Some organizations have comprehensive workplace wellness programs while others achieve savings or increase productivity with relatively easy activities designed to promote healthier lifestyles.

Workplace wellness programs are an effective tool in slowing the growth of health care costs by providing health options that may reduce a worker's chances of suffering from illness. Less illness means lower health plan utilization, and that can lower health benefit costs for organizations while consequently increasing earnings. Research shows that medically high-risk workers are medically high-cost workers as they use additional health care and generate higher claims.

The fact that smoking can create health problems has been well documented. Accordingly, health insurance premiums, as well as other premiums such as life insurance, are significantly higher for those who light up. And in most cases, employers have passed these increased premium costs on to the worker. Companies have become more stringent in developing policies on smoking, and many have banned smoking on company premises altogether. Clearly, the smoker today is disadvantaged, but how far can that go? Can supervisors refuse to hire people simply because they smoke? Depending on the organization, the requirement of the job, and the state in which one lives, they might have that right! Even so, some employers may take this one step further. Companies may, in fact, be able to terminate an employee for smoking off the job—on the employee's own time. Do you agree with an organization's right to terminate an employee for smoking off the job?

The Wellness Council of America (WELCOA) was established as a national not-for-profit organization in the mid-1980s. WELCOA believes healthcare costs are an issue of significant concern and that a healthy workforce is essential to America's continued growth and prosperity. Their belief is that much of the illness in the United States is directly preventable and the workplace is an ideal setting to address health and well-being. Their vision is that workplace wellness programs can transform corporate culture and change lives.[*]

In an attempt to change its corporate culture, Rothman Gordon, a law firm, paid about $3,750 for health club privileges for its thirty-one lawyers and more than thirty support personnel. The facility is open to members twenty-four hours a day, seven days a week so they can work out before, after, or even during office hours. The managing shareholder Bill Lestitian believes that it is a smart and effective way to boost employee wellness and morale. Other on-site wellness programs include yoga and smoking cessation. Lestitian feels that in the long run it could help reduce the firm's medical costs.[†] Is this a better way to control the wellness of employees? What about an employee who does not lead a healthy lifestyle? He or she may not participate in the wellness program regardless of its cost.

The Bryan/College Station Chamber of Commerce states that when it comes to workplace wellness at least 50 percent of an organization's health care costs are driven by the lifestyle-related behaviors of employees, such as smoking, poor diet, and lack of exercise. However, in the past ten years, the annual return on investment for worksite

---

[*]Wellness Council of America, "Creating Well Workplaces," http://www.welcoa.org/wellworkplace/ (accessed May 16, 2011).

[†]J. Gannon, "Companies Offer Wellness Programs to Cut Insurance Costs" *Pittsburgh Post-Gazette*, May 11, 2008, http://www.post-gazette.com/pg/08132/880660-28.stm#ixzz1MTakApni (accessed May 16, 2011).

wellness programs has been as much as $6 saved for every $1 spent and the average reduction in health plan costs, sick leave, disability costs, and workers' compensation is more than 25 percent for well-designed worksite wellness programs. Their thought is that workplace wellness initiatives improve company productivity by attracting superior quality staff, thereby reducing the rate of absenteeism and time lost, which in turn results in enhanced on-the-job time utilization and decision making that leads to improved worker morale, which in turn lowers turnover.[‡]

The Centers for Disease Control and Prevention encourage businesses to invest in a workplace wellness program and help the United States achieve two of its major Healthy People 2010 workplace objectives: to have 75 percent of all employers, regardless of size, provide a wide-reaching staff workplace wellness program; and to have 75 percent of all company staff to participate in employer-sponsored workplace wellness program activities.[§]

So, do you believe companies have the right to dictate what employees do outside of work? If an organization can take action against employees for smoking, and justify it on the grounds that it creates a health problem, what about other things we do? Should employees be disciplined for eating too much fatty food? Should they be fired for having a glass of wine with dinner, or drinking a beer at a sporting event? Smoking a cigar? If these are the policies you must abide by as a supervisor in the organization, would you be willing to discipline or even terminate an employee you saw violating rules outside of the workplace? What do you think? How far should we go in regulating "wellness" in our organizations?

[‡]Bryan/College Station Chamber of Commerce, Bryan, TX, http://www.bcschamber.org/LiveWork/Health-Wellness (accessed May 16, 2011).
[§]Centers for Disease Control and Prevention, "About Healthy People 2010," http://www.cdc.gov/nchs/healthy_people/hp2010.htm (accessed May 16, 2011).

Supervisors have a legal responsibility, if not a moral one, to ensure that the workplace is free from unnecessary hazards and that conditions surrounding the workplace are not hazardous to their employees' physical or mental health. Of course, accidents can and do occur. In 2009, according to preliminary data from the Bureau of Labor Statistics, 4,340 workers were killed on the job—an average of twelve workers every day—and an estimated 50,000 died from occupational diseases. More than 4.1 million work-related injuries and illnesses were reported, but this number understates the problem. The true toll of job injuries is two to three times greater—about 8 million to 12 million job injuries and illnesses each year. The cost of job injuries and illnesses is enormous—estimated at $159 billion to $318 billion a year for direct and indirect costs of disabling injuries.[1] Heartless as it sounds, supervisors must be concerned about their employees' health and safety if for no other reason than that accidents cost money.

From the turn of the last century through the late 1960s, remarkable progress was made in reducing the rate and severity of job-related accidents and illnesses. Yet the most significant piece of legislation in the area of employee health and safety was not enacted until 1970. This law is called the Occupational Safety and Health Act.[2]

Occupational Safety and Health Act
A law that enforces, through standards and regulations, healthful working conditions and preservation of human resources.

---

[1]AFL-CIO Safety and Health Department, "Death on the Job: The Toll of Neglect," 20th ed., April 2011, http://www.aflcio.org/issues/safety/memorial/upload/dotj_2011.pdf (accessed May 16, 2011). See also U.S. Department of Labor, Bureau of Labor Statistics, "Injuries, Illnesses, and Fatalities," 2011, http://www.bls.gov/iif/ (accessed May 16, 2011).
[2]The material in this chapter is adapted from D. A. DeCenzo and S. P. Robbins, *Fundamentals of Human Resource Management*, 8th ed. (Hoboken, NJ: John Wiley & Sons, 2005), Chapter 13.

The Occupational Safety and Health Act

The passage of the Occupational Safety and Health Act (OSH Act) dramatically changed the role that supervisors must play in ensuring that physical working conditions meet adequate standards.

OSH Act legislation established comprehensive and specific health standards, authorized inspections to ensure that standards are met, empowered the Occupational Safety and Health Administration (OSHA) to police organizations' compliance, and required employers to keep records of illnesses and injuries and to calculate accident ratios. The act applies to almost every U.S. business engaged in interstate commerce. Organizations not meeting the interstate commerce criteria of the OSH Act are generally covered by state occupational safety and health laws.

The safety and health standards the OSH Act established are quite complex. Standards exist for such diverse conditions as noise levels, air impurities, physical protection equipment, the height of toilet partitions, and the correct size of ladders. Furthermore, OSHA researches repetitive stress (or motion) injuries, problems associated with the eyestrain that accompanies video display terminal use, problems of needlesticks in health care activities, and developing training and education programs for businesses.

The initial OSH Act standards took up 350 pages in the *Federal Register*, and some of the annual revisions and interpretations are equally extensive. Nevertheless, supervisors are responsible for knowing these standards and ensuring that those that apply to them are followed (see Exhibit 13-1).

WHAT ARE THE OSHA ENFORCEMENT PRIORITIES?

imminent danger
A condition under which an accident is about to occur.

Enforcement procedures of OSHA standards vary depending on the nature of the event and the organization. Typically, OSHA enforces the standards based on a five-item priority listing. These are, in descending priority, as follows: imminent danger; serious accidents that have occurred within the past eight hours; a current employee complaint; inspections of target industries with a high injury ratio; and random inspections.

Imminent danger refers to a condition in which an accident is about to occur. Although this is given top priority and acts as a preventive measure, imminent danger situations are hard to define. In fact, in some cases, the definition of imminent danger appears to be an accident in progress, and interpretation leaves much to the imagination. For example, suppose you were withdrawing cash at an ATM. As you remove your cash, you are grabbed by an individual who places a gun in your face and angrily demands your cash. Are you in imminent danger? Of course, most of us would say, absolutely! But according to one interpretation of imminent danger, you may not be in "imminent" danger. That state would not exist until the assailant pulled the trigger of the weapon, and the bullet was rifling through the barrel. Tragically, by that time it is too late to worry about imminent danger. One's safety has already been threatened.

This has given rise to priority-two accidents—those that have led to serious injuries or death. Under the law, a supervisor must report these serious accidents to the OSHA field office within eight hours of occurrence. This permits the investigators to review the scene and try to determine the cause of the accident.

Priority three, employee complaints, is a major concern for any supervisor. If an employee sees a violation of OSHA standards, that employee has the right to call OSHA and request an investigation. The worker may even refuse to work on the item in question until OSHA has investigated the complaint. This is especially true when there is a union. For instance, in some union contracts, workers may

Exhibit 13-1

OSHA poster.

Note: *Original poster is available as PDF file at www.osha.gov/Publications/poster.html.*

legally refuse to work if they believe they are in significant danger. Accordingly, they may stay off the job with pay until OSHA arrives and either finds the complaint invalid or cites the company and mandates compliance.

Next in the priority of enforcement is the inspection of targeted industries. With several million workplaces in the United States, inspecting each would require several hundred thousand full-time inspectors. OSHA, however, has limited resources, and its budget has been significantly cut in the past decade. So, to have the largest effect, OSHA began to partner with state health and safety agencies, who together direct their attention to industries with the highest injury rates—industries such as chemical processing, roofing and sheet metal, meat processing, lumber and wood products, mobile homes and campers, and stevedoring.

A new rule established in 1990 also requires supervisors whose employees handle hazardous waste (e.g., chemicals and medical waste) to follow strict operating procedures; such supervisors are required to monitor employee exposure, develop and communicate safety plans, and provide necessary protective equipment.

The final OSHA priority is the random inspection. Originally, OSHA inspectors were authorized to enter any work area premise, without notice, to ensure that the workplace is in compliance. In 1978, however, the Supreme Court ruled in *Marshall v. Barlow's Inc.*[3] that a supervisor and his or her organization are not required to let OSHA inspectors enter the premises unless the inspectors have a search warrant. This decision, although not destroying OSHA's ability to conduct inspections, forces inspectors to justify their choice of inspection sites more rigorously. But don't let the warrant requirement mislead you into a false sense of security. If needed, an OSHA inspector will obtain the necessary legal document. For example, when inspectors attempted to evaluate conditions at the Hollywood, Florida, Hotel Diplomat construction site, the general contractor would not let them in. A few days later, however, the OSHA inspectors returned with warrant in hand.[4]

Attorneys who deal with OSHA suggest that supervisors cooperate rather than viewing this event as confrontational. This cooperation focuses on permitting the inspection, but only after reaching consensus on the inspection process. That's not to say, however, that you can keep inspectors from finding violations. If they are found, inspectors can take the necessary action. Finally, it is recommended that any information regarding the company's safety program be discussed with the OSHA inspector, emphasizing how the program is communicated to employees and how it is enforced.

Should supervisors feel that the fine levied is unjust, or too harsh, the law permits the supervisor and the organization to file an appeal. This appeal is reviewed by the Occupational Safety and Health Review Commission, an independently operating safety and health board. Although this commission's decisions are generally final, employers may still appeal commission decisions through the federal courts.

HOW DOES A SUPERVISOR KEEP OSHA RECORDS?

To fulfill part of the requirements established under the Occupational Safety and Health Act, supervisors in industries where a high percentage of accidents and injuries occur must maintain safety and health records. It's important to note, however, that organizations that are exempt from record-keeping requirements—such as universities and retail establishments—still must comply with the law itself; their only exception is the reduction of time spent on maintaining safety records. The basis of record keeping for the OSH Act is the completion of OSHA Form 300 (see Exhibit 13-2). Employers are required to keep these safety records for five years. In complying with OSHA record-keeping requirements, one issue arises for supervisors—just what is a reportable accident or illness? According to the act, any work-related illness (no matter how

[3]*Marshall v. Barlow's Inc.*, 436 U.S. 307 (1978).
[4]"OSHA Inspection Delay Is Legal," *ENR*, May 3, 1999, 21.

Exhibit 13-2

OSHA's Forms 300 and 300A.

Source: www.osha.gov/recordkeeping/
new-osha300form1-1-04.pdf.

incidence rate

A measure of the number of injuries, illnesses, or lost workdays as it relates to a common base rate of 100 full-time employees.

insignificant it may appear) must be reported on Form 300. Injuries, on the other hand, are reported only when they require medical treatment (besides first aid), involve loss of consciousness or restriction of work or motion, or require transfer to another job.

To help supervisors decide whether an incident should be recorded, OSHA offers a schematic diagram for organizations to follow (see Exhibit 13-3). By using this decision tree, supervisors can decide whether an event should be recorded. If so, the supervisor must record it under one of three areas: fatality, lost workdays, or neither fatality nor lost workdays. Part of this information is then used to determine an organization's incidence rate. An incidence rate reflects the "number of injuries, illnesses, or (lost) workdays related to a common exposure base rate of 100 full-time workers." This rate

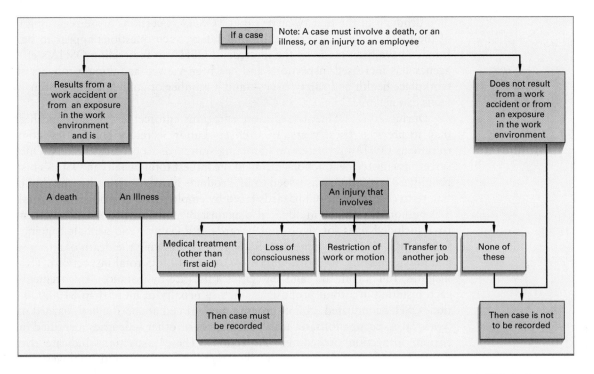

Exhibit 13-3

Determining the recordability of cases under the OSH Act.

is then used by OSHA for determining industries and organizations that are more susceptible to injury. Let's look at the incidence rate formula and use it in an example.

To determine the incidence rate, the formula $(N/EH) \times 200{,}000$ is used, where

- N is the number of injuries and/or illnesses or lost workdays.
- EH is the total hours worked by all employees during the year.
- $200{,}000$ is the base hour rate equivalent (100 workers × 40 hours per week × 50 weeks per year).

In using the formula and calculating an organization's incidence rate, assume we have an organization with 1,800 employees that experienced 195 reported accidents over the past year. We would calculate the incidence rate as follows: $(195/3{,}600{,}000) \times 200{,}000$.[5] The incidence rate, then, is 10.8. What does that 10.8 represent? That depends on a number of factors. If the organization is in the meatpacking industry, where the industry average incidence rate is 32.1, then they are doing well. If, however, it is in the oil and gas extraction industry, where the industry incidence rate is 4.1, then a 10.8 indicates a major concern.

WHAT ARE THE OSHA PUNITIVE ACTIONS?

An OSHA inspector has the right to levy a fine against an organization for noncompliance. Although levying the fine is more complicated than described here, if supervisors and their organizations do not bring a "red-flagged" item into compliance, they can be assessed a severe penalty. As originally passed in 1970, the maximum penalty was $10,000 per occurrence per day. However, with the Omnibus Budget Reconciliation Act of 1990, that $10,000 penalty can increase to $70,000 if the violation is severe, willful, and repetitive. But fines are not for safety violations alone. A company that fails to keep its OSH Act records properly can also be subjected to stiff penalties, or under certain circumstances, company executives can be held criminally liable.

---

[5]The number 3,600,000 is determined as follows: 1,800 employees, working 40-hour weeks, for 50 weeks a year [1,800 × 40 × 50].

Although in the first twenty years of OSHA, questions arose regarding the value of the OSH Act to workers' health and safety, such questions appear to be abating. Inroads have been made by the director of OSHA in redirecting OSHA's efforts. The agency has increased inspections and has been viewed as taking a tougher stance on workplace health and safety issues—and a number of companies have seen what that focus can mean.

During 2009, OSHA issued more egregious enforcement actions and higher fines than in previous fiscal years. This reflects Labor Secretary Hilda Solis' commitment to refocus OSHA's priorities on enforcing standards to protect workers. One of these egregious enforcement actions included the largest total penalty in OSHA's history. The penalty, $81,340,000, was issued to BP Products North America Inc. for the company's failure to correct potential hazards faced by employees. The prior largest total penalty, $21 million, was issued in 2005, also against BP. Other egregious enforcement actions have included fines for significant hazards at a cement and asphalt bagging plant in Scotia, New York, and more than $1.6 million following the death of a teen worker at a grain storage site. In 2010, OSHA conducted 40,993 total inspections. This number includes 164 significant and egregious (instance-by-instance) enforcement actions, each resulting in a total proposed monetary penalty of more than $100,000. In addition, OSHA conducted 24,759 programmed (aimed at specific high-hazard industries, workplaces, occupations, or health substances or other industries identified in OSHA's current inspection procedures) inspections. These inspections indicate that OSHA devoted more resources to proactively target the industries and employers that experienced the greatest number of workplace injuries and illnesses. OSHA also conducted 16,234 unprogrammed (based on complaints, accidents, referrals, reports of imminent danger, reports of fatality/catastrophe, or follow-up) inspections.[6]

DOES OSHA WORK?

Has the OSH Act worked? The answer is a qualified yes. In fact, the act has had a direct and significant effect on almost every organization and every supervisor in the United States. In some of the largest organizations, an additional administrator has been created who is solely responsible for safety. The impact of the OSH Act standards has made organizations more aware of health and safety.

National Institute for Occupational Safety and Health (NIOSH)
The government agency that researches and sets OSHA standards.

What can supervisors expect from OSHA over the next decade? Although its efforts will continue to concentrate on safety and health violations in organizations, OSHA is addressing problems associated with contemporary organizations, concentrating its efforts through the National Institute for Occupational Safety and Health (NIOSH) for research and setting standards in such areas as blood-borne pathogens and chemical process safety (see "News Flash! OSHA and Needlesticks"). It is even focusing its attention on preventing Lyme disease in workers who work in areas where exposure to ticks carrying the disease is high. Similarly, OSHA continues to explore motor vehicle safety, as well as focusing on fitting the work environment to the individual.

Setting standards for blood-borne pathogens is designed to protect individuals such as medical personnel from becoming infected with such diseases as AIDS and hepatitis. In doing so, OSHA has established guidelines regarding protective equipment (e.g., latex gloves and eye shields), and in cases where a vaccine is available, it ensures that exposed workers have access to it. Chemical processing standards reflect specific guidelines that must be adhered to when employees work with chemicals or other

---

[6]US Department of Labor, Occupational Safety and Health Administration, http://www.osha.gov/dep/2009_enforcement_summary.html (accessed May 18, 2011) and US Department of Labor, Occupational Safety and Health Administration, http://www.osha.gov/dep/2010_enforcement_summary.html (accessed May 18, 2011).

hazardous toxic substances. This requires supervisors to perform hazard analyses and take any corrective action required.

These concerns over chemical hazards led to a number of states passing *right-to-know laws*. These laws helped identify hazardous chemicals in the workplace and required supervisors to inform employees of the chemicals they might be exposed to, the health risk associated with that exposure, and other policies guiding their use. Although these state laws made progress in providing information regarding workplace toxins, there were variations among the states—and some states didn't have these laws at all. Consequently, to provide some uniformity in protection, OSHA developed the Hazard Communication Standard in 1983. This policy "requires supervisors to communicate chemical hazards to their employees by labeling containers, and by distributing data information (called Material Safety Data Sheets) provided by the manufacturer" to employees. In addition, employees exposed to various hazardous chemicals must be trained in their safe handling. As enacted in 1983, this standard applied only to manufacturing industries. But by mid-1989, meeting the requirements of the Hazard Communication Standard became the responsibility of all industries.[7]

The third area, motor vehicle safety, reflects OSHA's interest in addressing the problems associated with workers who drive extensively as part of their job duties. This interest exists, in part, because nearly half of all worker deaths in any given year are attributed to motor vehicle accidents. Accordingly, emphasis is placed on substance-abuse testing of drivers, safety equipment, and driver's education.

Fourth, OSHA has been continuing its efforts in studying the proper design of the work environment such that it is conducive to productive work, called *ergonomics*. OSHA has established a website (www.osha.gov/SLTC/ergonomics/index.html) that helps organizations understand how ergonomics operates and how it can help. We come back to ergonomics later in this chapter.

Finally, OSHA is interested in employee training and has basic requirements for employees based on the job in question. General training categories may pertain to multiple jobs. However, most requirements pertain to general safety and health provisions, medical services and first aid, gases, vapors, fumes, dusts and mists, fire protection, fall protection, general protection requirements, ladders, electrical equipment, as well as hand and power tools. Some occupations require additional training. For example, construction positions demand training on demolition, scaffolding, and excavations. In general, OSHA requirements demand employers to establish and supervise programs for the education and training of employers. Employees are expected to be able to recognize, avoid, and prevent unsafe conditions. Supervisors should be trained in all areas demanded of the employee before instructing them. Employees require training in regulations applicable to their work environments to control or eliminate potential hazards or exposure to possible illness or injury. OSHA's training guidelines follow a model that consists of the following steps:

1. Determine if training is needed.
2. Identify training needs.
3. Identify goals and objectives.
4. Develop learning activities.
5. Conduct the training.
6. Assess and evaluate training program effectiveness.
7. Improve the program based on the assessment.[8]

---

[7]See U.S. Department of Labor, Occupational Safety and Health Administration, *Hazard Communication Guidelines for Compliance* (Washington, DC: Government Printing Office, 2000).

[8]U.S. Department of Labor, Occupational Safety and Health Administration, "Training Requirements in OSHA Standards and Training Guidelines," 1998, http://www.osha.gov/Publications/osha2254.pdf (accessed May 18, 2011).

News Flash!

OSHA AND NEEDLESTICKS

As mandated by the Needlestick Safety and Prevention Act, OSHA has revised its blood-borne pathogens standard to clarify the need for employers to select safer needle devices as they become available and to involve employees in identifying and choosing the devices. The updated standard also requires supervisors to maintain a log of injuries from contaminated sharps. "These changes in the OSHA blood-borne pathogens standard reaffirm our commitment to protecting health care providers who care for us all," said Labor Secretary Alexis M. Herman. "Newer, safer medical devices can reduce the risk of needlesticks and the chance of contracting deadly blood-borne diseases such as AIDS and hepatitis C. Employers need to consult their workers and use the safer devices when possible." According to the Needlestick Act, in March 2000 the Centers for Disease Control and Prevention estimated that selecting safer medical devices could prevent 62 to 88 percent of sharps injuries in hospital settings.

"Our revised blood-borne pathogen standard sets forth clearly the importance of re-evaluating needle systems to identify safer devices every year. The new requirement to record all needlesticks will help employers determine the effectiveness of the devices they use and track how many needlesticks

are occurring within their workplaces," said OSHA administrator Charles N. Jeffress.

The revised OSHA blood-borne pathogen standard specifically mandates consideration of safer needle devices as part of the reevaluation of appropriate engineering controls during the annual review of the employer's exposure control plan. It calls for employers to solicit front-line employee input in choosing safer devices. New provisions require employers to establish a log to track needlesticks rather than only recording cuts or sticks that actually lead to illness, and to maintain the privacy of employees who have suffered these injuries.

Passed unanimously by Congress and signed by President Clinton on November 6, 2000, the Needlestick Safety and Prevention Act mandated specific revisions of OSHA's blood-borne pathogens standard within six months. The legislation exempted OSHA from certain standard rule-making requirements so that the changes could be adopted quickly. The revised blood-borne pathogens standard became effective April 18, 2001.

Source: National News Release USDL: 01-26, www.osha.gov/media/oshnews/jan01/national-20010118a.html, January 18, 2001.

Comprehension Check 13-1

1. A condition in which an accident is about to happen is called

   a. an OSHA violation
   b. imminent danger
   c. serious injury or death
   d. none of the above

2. A "standard" metric used to compare injuries, illness, or lost workdays in organizations is the

   a. incidence rate
   b. work-related injury log
   c. recordability metric
   d. OSHA Form 100

3. The maximum fine imposed by OSHA on an organization should the violation be severe, willful, and repetitive is

   a. $10,000
   b. $25,000
   c. $55,000
   d. $70,000

4. Laws that help to identify hazardous chemicals in the workplace and require organizations to inform employees of potential exposures are called
   a. right-to-work laws
   b. right-to-know laws
   c. right-to-life laws
   d. rights and ethics laws

Job Safety Programs

If businesses are concerned with efficiency and profits, you may ask, why would they spend money to create conditions that exceed those required by law? The answer is the profit motive itself. The cost of accidents can be, and for many organizations is, a substantial additional cost of doing business. The direct cost of an accident to an employer shows itself in the organization's workers' compensation premium. This cost is largely determined by the insured's accident history. Indirect costs, which generally far exceed direct costs, also must be paid by the employer. These include wages paid for time lost as a result of injury, damage to equipment and materials, personnel to investigate and report on accidents, and lost production as a result of work stoppages and personnel changeover. The impact of these indirect costs can be seen in statistics that describe the costs of accidents for American industry as a whole.

As we mentioned at the beginning of this chapter, accidents cost employers additional billions of dollars in wages and lost production. The significance of this latter figure is emphasized when we note that this cost is approximately ten times greater than losses caused by strikes, an issue that historically has received much more attention.

WHAT CAUSES WORK-RELATED ACCIDENTS?

The cause of an accident can be generally classified as either human or environmental. Human causes are directly attributable to human error brought about by carelessness, intoxication, daydreaming, inability to do the job, or other human deficiency. Environmental causes, in contrast, are attributable to the workplace and include the tools, equipment, physical plant, and general work environment. Both of these sources are important, but in terms of numbers, the human factor is responsible for the vast majority of accidents. No matter how much effort is made to create an accident-free work environment, a low accident rate record can be achieved only by concentrating on the human element.

One of the main objectives of safety engineers is to scrutinize the work environment to locate sources of potential accidents. In addition to looking for such obvious factors as loose steps or carpets, oil on walkways, or a sharp protrusion on a piece of equipment at eye level, safety engineers seek those that are less obvious. Standards established by OSHA provide an excellent guide in the search for potential hazards.

HOW CAN ACCIDENTS BE PREVENTED?

What traditional measures can supervisors look to for preventing accidents? The answer lies in education, skills training, engineering, protective devices, and regulation enforcement. We have summarized these in Exhibit 13-4.

HOW DO SUPERVISORS ENSURE JOB SAFETY?

One way supervisors can be assured that rules and regulations are being enforced is to develop some type of feedback system. This can be provided by inspecting the

Education	Create safety awareness by posting highly visible signs that proclaim safety slogans, placing articles on accident prevention in organization newsletters, or exhibiting a sign proclaiming the number of days the plant has operated without a lost-day accident.
Skills Training	Incorporate accident prevention measures into the learning process.
Engineering	Prevent accidents through both the design of the equipment and the design of the jobs themselves. This may also include eliminating factors that promote operator fatigue, boredom, and daydreaming.
Protection	Provide protective equipment where necessary. This may include safety shoes, gloves, hard hats, safety glasses, and noise mufflers. Protection also includes performing preventive maintenance on machinery.
Regulation Enforcement	The best safety rules and regulations will be ineffective in reducing accidents if they are not enforced. Additionally, if such rules are not enforced, the employer may be liable for any injuries that occur.

Exhibit 13-4
Accident prevention mechanisms.

work surroundings. Supervisors can rely on oral or written reports for information on enforcement. Another approach is to get firsthand information by periodically walking through the work areas to make observations.

Although safety is everyone's responsibility, it should be part of the organization's culture. Top management must show its commitment to safety by providing resources to purchase safety devices and maintaining equipment. Furthermore, safety should become part of every employee's performance goals. As we mentioned in Chapter 12 on performance evaluations, if something isn't included, there's a tendency to diminish its importance. Holding employees accountable for safety issues by evaluating their performance sends the message that the company is serious about safety.

Another means of promoting safety is to empower the employees so that they can take action. In organizations, such employee groups are called safety committees. Although prevalent chiefly in unionized settings, these committees serve a vital role in helping the company and its employees implement and maintain a good safety program.

A Special Case of Safety: Workplace Violence

Inasmuch as there is growing concern for the job safety of our workers, a much greater emphasis today is being placed on the increasing violence that has erupted on the job. No organization is immune from it, and the problem appears to be getting worse.[9] On June 25, 2008, in Henderson, Kentucky, an employee at a plastics plant returned hours after arguing with his supervisor over his not wearing safety goggles and for using his cell phone while working on the assembly line. He shot and killed the supervisor, four other coworkers, and himself. In April 2007, the same month in which the Virginia Tech shootings occurred, a gunman at his former workplace in Troy, Michigan, and one at NASA in Houston shot and killed a person. On January 30, 2006, a former employee who was once removed from a Santa Barbara, California, postal facility because of "strange behavior" came back and shot five workers to death, critically wounded another, and killed herself. On January 26, 2005, an autoworker at a Jeep plant in Toledo, Ohio, who had met the day before with plant managers about a problem with

---

[9]D. Costello, "Stressed Out: Can Workplace Stress Get Worse? Incidents of 'Desk Rage' Disrupt America's Offices—Long Hours, Cramped Quarters Produce Some Short Fuses; Flinging Phones at the Wall," *Wall Street Journal*, January 16, 2001, B-1.

his work, came in and killed a supervisor and wounded two other employees before killing himself.[10]

Is workplace violence really an issue for managers? Yes. The latest data available (2007) showed an increase in workplace homicides (610). However, despite this increase, workplace homicides have declined 44 percent from the high of 1,080 reported in 1994.[11] But workplace violence doesn't just include homicides. The U.S. National Institute of Occupational Safety and Health says that each year, some 2 million American workers are victims of some form of workplace violence such as verbal abuse, yelling at coworkers, purposeful damage of machines or furniture, or assaulting coworkers. In an average week, one employee is killed and at least twenty-five are seriously injured in violent assaults by current or former coworkers. And according to a Department of Labor survey, 58 percent of firms reported that managers received verbal threats from workers.[12] Anger, rage, and violence in the workplace are intimidating to coworkers and adversely affect their productivity. The annual cost to U.S. businesses is estimated to be between $20 billion and $35 billion.[13] The issue for supervisors, then, is how to prevent violence from occurring on the job, and to reduce their organization's liability should an unfortunate event occur.

Because the circumstances of each incident are different, a specific plan of action for companies to follow is difficult to detail. However, several suggestions can be made. First, the organization must develop a plan to deal with the issue. This may mean reviewing all corporate policies to ensure that they are not adversely affecting employees. In fact, in many cases where violent individuals caused mayhem in an office setting, and didn't commit suicide, one common factor arose: These employees were not treated with respect or dignity. They were laid off without any warning, or they perceived that they were being treated too harshly in the discipline process. Sound human resource management practices can help ensure that respect and dignity exist for employees, even in the most difficult issues such as terminations.

Supervisors must also be trained to identify troubled employees before the problem results in violence.[14] *Employee assistance programs (EAPs)* can be designed specifically to help these individuals. As we address shortly in our discussion of EAPs, rarely does an individual go from being happy to committing some act of violence overnight! Furthermore, if supervisors are better able to spot the types of demonstrated behaviors that may lead to violence, those who cannot be helped through the EAP can be removed from the organization before others are harmed. Organizations and their supervisors should also implement stronger security mechanisms. For example, many women who are killed at work following a domestic dispute die at the hands of someone who didn't belong on company premises. These individuals, as well as violence paraphernalia—guns, knives, and so on—must be kept from entering the facilities altogether.

Sadly, no matter how careful the organization is, and how much it attempts to prevent workplace violence, some will occur. In those cases, supervisors must be prepared to deal with the situation and, together with their company leaders, offer whatever assistance they can to deal with the aftermath.

[10]R. Lenz, "Gunman Kills Five, Himself at Plant," *The Associated Press, Springfield, Missouri, News-Leader*, June 26, 2008, 6A; S. Oppermann, "Violence in the Workplace: Is Your Agency Prepared?" *FedSmith*, May 30, 2007, http://www.fedsmith.com; CBS News, "Former Postal Worker Kills 5, Herself," *CBS News*, January 31, 2006, http://www.cbsnews.com/stories; CBS News, "Autoworker's Grudge Turns Deadly," January 27, 2005, http://www.cbsnews.com/stories; D. Sharp, "Gunman Just Hated a Lot of People," *USA Today*, July 10, 2003, 3A; and M. Prince, "Violence in the Workplace on the Rise; Training, Zero Tolerance Can Prevent Aggression," *Business Insurance*, May 12, 2003, 1.

[11]"Workplace Homicides in 2007," *U.S. Bureau of Labor Statistics Division of Information Services*, August 26, 2008, http://data.blg.gov.

[12]J. McCafferty, "Verbal Chills," *CFO*, June 2005, 17; S. Armour, "Managers Not Prepared for Workplace Violence," *USA Today*, July 15, 2004, 1B+; and "Workplace Violence," OSHA Fact Sheet, U.S. Department of Labor, Occupational Safety and Health Administration, 2002.

[13]"Ten Tips on Recognizing and Minimizing Violence," *Workforce Online*, December 3, 2000, http://www.workforce.com.

[14]P. Falcone, "Dealing with Employees in Crisis: Use This Blueprint for Proactive Management Intervention," *HR Magazine*, May 2003, 117–122. For another insight into this matter, see E. Roche, "Do Something—He's About to Snap," *Harvard Business Review*, July 2003, 23–30.

Maintaining a Healthy Work Environment

sick building
An unhealthy work environment.

Unhealthy work environments are a concern for every supervisor. If workers cannot function properly at their jobs because of constant headaches, watering eyes, breathing difficulties, or fear of exposure to materials that may cause long-term health problems, productivity will decrease. Consequently, creating a healthy work environment not only is the proper thing to do but also benefits the organization. Often referred to as sick buildings, office environments that contain harmful airborne chemicals, asbestos, or indoor pollution (possibly caused by smoking) have forced employers to take drastic steps. For many, it has meant the removal of asbestos from their buildings. Because extended exposure to asbestos has been linked to lung cancer, companies are required by various federal agencies such as the Environmental Protection Agency (EPA) to remove it altogether, or at least seal it so that it cannot escape into the air. But asbestos is not the only culprit! Germs, fungi, mold, and a variety of synthetic pollutants cause problems, too.

Although specific problems and their elimination go beyond the scope of this text, here are some suggestions for keeping the workplace healthy[15]:

- **Make sure workers get enough fresh air.** The cost of providing it is peanuts compared with the expense of cleaning up a problem. One simple tactic: unsealing vents closed in overzealous efforts to conserve energy.

- **Avoid suspect building materials and furnishings.** A general rule is that if it stinks, it may be unhealthy. For instance, substitute tacks for smelly carpet glue or natural wood for chemically treated plywood.

- **Test new buildings for toxins before occupancy.** Failure to do so may lead to health problems. Most consultants say that letting a new building sit temporarily vacant allows the worst fumes to dissipate.

- **Provide a smoke-free environment.** If you don't want to ban smoking entirely, establish an area for smokers that has its own ventilation system.

- **Keep air ducts clean and dry.** Water in air ducts is a fertile breeding ground for fungi. Servicing the air ducts periodically can help eliminate the fungi before they cause harm.

- **Pay attention to workers' complaints.** Have a designated employee record dates and particulars. Because employees are often closest to the problems, they are a valuable source of information.

Whereas these suggestions are important to follow, one in particular is noteworthy for us to explore a bit further: the smoke-free environment.

HOW DO YOU CREATE A SMOKE-FREE ENVIRONMENT?

Should smoking be prohibited in a public place of business? Even, say, in a bar, where forbidding smoking could put the establishment out of business? The dangers and health problems associated with smoking have been well documented—and this is translating into increased health insurance costs. Furthermore, smokers have been found to be absent more than nonsmokers, to lose productivity as a result of smoke breaks, to damage property with cigarette burns, to require more routine maintenance (ash/butt cleanup), and to create problems for other employees through secondhand smoke. Recognized as a means to control these maladies associated with smoking, in conjunction with society's emphasis on wellness, smoke-free policies have appeared. In fact, most U.S. organizations have banned smoking altogether, or significantly restrict smoking to designated areas.

---

[15]See M. Conlin and J. Carey, "Is Your Office Killing You?" *BusinessWeek,* June 5, 2000, 114–128; R. Schneider, "Sick Buildings Threaten Health of Those Who Inhabit Them," *Indianapolis Star,* September 23, 2000, A-1; and F. Rice, "Do You Work in a Sick Building?" *Fortune,* July 2, 1990, 88.

Although many nonsmokers would agree that a total ban on smoking in the workplace is the most desirable, it may not be the most practical. For employees who smoke, quitting immediately may be impossible. The nicotine addiction may prohibit a "cold turkey" approach for the most ardent smoker. Accordingly, a total ban on smoking should be viewed as a phased-in approach. For example, this gradual process may begin with the involvement of representative employees to determine what the organization's smoke-free goals and timetables should be. This means deciding whether the organization will ban smoking altogether over a period of time, or whether special areas will be designated as smoking rooms. If the latter is chosen, these rooms must be properly ventilated to keep the smoke fumes from permeating other parts of the facility.

Consequently, the organization needs to look at incentives for getting people not to smoke. As mentioned previously, health care premiums—as well as the costs of life insurance policies—for smokers are significantly higher than those for nonsmokers. Employers may decide to pay only the nonsmoking premium, and pass the additional premium costs on to the smokers. Companies also need to offer various options for individuals to seek help. Through various assistance programs—such as smoking-cessation classes—the organization can show that it is making a deliberate commitment to eliminate the problems associated with smoking in the workplace.

Something to Think About (and promote class discussion)

SAVE LIVES, SAVE MONEY: MAKE YOUR BUSINESS SMOKE-FREE

Think of a lit cigarette as a miniature toxic waste dump. Its secondhand smoke contains more than fifty cancer-causing chemicals, and the toxins in secondhand smoke can cause heart disease and lung cancer in nonsmokers. In fact, breathing secondhand smoke for even a short time could have immediate effects on blood and blood vessels, potentially increasing the risk of a heart attack.

The American Productivity Audit, a national survey of over 29,000 workers, found that tobacco use was a leading cause of workers' lost production time, even greater than alcohol abuse or family emergencies. One large company found that their employees who smoked had more hospital admissions (124 vs. 76 admissions per 1,000 workers) and a higher average insured payment for health care ($1,145 vs. $762) than their nonsmoking employees in an eleven-month period. However, quitting smoking, or even just cutting back, improves a worker's productivity.

Going smoke-free lowers the risk of fires and accidental injuries, which can reduce insurance costs. Many smoke-free businesses have negotiated for lower fire and property insurance premiums, with some businesses winning reductions of 25–30 percent.

Going smoke-free also reduces cleaning and maintenance costs. The Building Owners and Managers Association, a national trade group, reports that indoor smoking increases cleaning costs and states "secondhand smoke does not belong in buildings." Unigard Insurance, in Seattle, WA, saved $500 a month after going smoke-free when its maintenance contractor reduced its monthly fee because the staff no longer had to clean ashtrays, dust desks, and clean carpets or furniture as often.

Going smoke-free reduces potential legal liability. Nonsmokers harmed by secondhand smoke at work have won lawsuits and disability claims against their employers under a variety of legal remedies. Everyone benefits when the air is cleared of secondhand smoke, including smokers, some of whom will quit or at least cut back. In a smoke-free environment workers become healthier, and healthier workers miss less work, are more productive, and have lower health care costs.

Sources: Centers for Disease Control and Prevention, "*Save Lives, Save Money: Make Your Business Smoke-Free*," Atlanta, Georgia: U.S. Department of Health and Human Services, Centers for Disease Control and Prevention, National Center for Chronic Disease Prevention and Health Promotion, Office on Smoking and Health, June 2006, http://www.cdc.gov/tobacco/basic_information/secondhand_smoke/guides/business/pdfs/save_lives_save_money. pdf (accessed May 18, 2011).

Repetitive stress injuries and related musculoskeletal disorders caused by improper workstation design have been reduced by adherence to OSHA-issued ergonomic standards.

WHAT ARE REPETITIVE STRESS INJURIES?

Whenever workers are subjected to a continuous motion such as keyboarding, without proper workstation design (seat and keyboard height adjustments), they run the risk of developing repetitive stress injuries. This phenomenon is referred to as musculoskeletal disorders (MSDs). These disorders, which account for nearly 40 percent of annual workplace illnesses, result in headaches, swollen feet, back pain, or nerve damage and cost U.S. companies several billion dollars annually. The most frequent form of this disorder, found in the wrist, is called carpal tunnel syndrome and affects thousands of workers. Given the magnitude of problems associated with MSDs, OSHA issued its final ergonomics standards in late 2000 to combat this workplace problem—standards that will hopefully save nearly $10 billion in reduced work-related injuries.[16]

One chief means of reducing the potential effects of repetitive stress injuries for an organization is through the use of *ergonomics*. Ergonomics involves fitting the work environment to the individual. Reality tells us that every employee is different—different shape, size, height, and so on. Expecting each worker to adjust to "standard" office furnishings is just not practical. Instead, by recognizing and acting on these differences, ergonomics looks at customizing the work environment so that it not only is conducive to productive work but also keeps the employee healthy.

When we speak of ergonomics, we are primarily addressing two main areas: the office environment and office furniture. Organizations are reviewing their office settings, their work environment, and their space utilization in an effort to provide more productive atmospheres. This means that new furniture designed to reduce back strain and fatigue is being purchased. Properly designed and fitted office equipment can also help reduce repetitive stress injuries. Furthermore, companies are using colors such as mauves and grays, which are more pleasing to the eye, and experimenting with lighting brightness as a means of lessening employee exposure to harmful eyestrain associated with today's video display terminals.

repetitive stress injuries
Injuries sustained by continuous and repetitive movements of a body part.

musculoskeletal disorders (MSDs)
Continuous-motion disorders caused by repetitive stress injuries.

carpal tunnel syndrome
A repetitive stress injury of the wrist.

Stress

stress
Something an individual feels when faced with opportunities, constraints, or demands perceived to be both uncertain and important. Stress can show itself in both positive and negative ways.

Stress is a dynamic condition in which an individual is confronted with an opportunity, constraint, or demand related to what he or she desires, and for which the outcome is perceived to be both uncertain and important. Stress is a complex issue, so let us look at it more closely. Stress can manifest itself in both positive and negative ways. Stress is said to be positive when the situation offers an opportunity for one to gain something; for example, the "psyching up" that an athlete goes through can be stressful, but this can lead to maximum performance. But when constraints or demands are placed on us, stress can become negative. Let us explore these two features—constraints and demands.

Constraints are barriers that keep us from doing what we desire. Purchasing a hybrid sport utility vehicle (SUV) may be your desire, but if you cannot afford the

[16]See Occupational Safety and Health Administration, *OSHA's Ergonomics Enforcement Plan* (Washington, DC: Government Printing Office, March 6, 2003); and www.osha.gov/SLTC/ergonomics/enforcement_plan.html

$38,000 price, you are constrained from purchasing it. Accordingly, constraints inhibit you in ways that take control of a situation out of your hands. If you cannot afford the hybrid SUV, you cannot get it. Demands, on the other hand, may cause you to give up something you desire. If you wish to go to a movie with friends on Tuesday night but have a major exam on Wednesday, the exam may take precedence. Thus, demands preoccupy your time and force you to shift priorities.

Constraints and demands can lead to potential stress. When they are coupled with uncertainty about the outcome and importance of the outcome, potential stress becomes actual stress. Regardless of the situation, if you remove the uncertainty or the importance, you remove stress. For instance, you may have been constrained from purchasing the hybrid SUV because of your budget, but if you just won one in GM's OnStar giveaway, the uncertainty element is significantly reduced. Furthermore, if you are auditing a class for no grade, the importance of the major exam is essentially nil. However, when constraints or demands have an effect on an important event and the outcome is unknown, pressure is added—resulting in stress.

Whereas we are not attempting to minimize stress in people's lives, it is important to recognize that both good and bad personal factors may cause stress. Of course, when you consider the changes, such as restructuring, that are occurring in U.S. companies, it is little wonder that stress is so rampant in today's companies. Just how rampant? Stress-related problems cost U.S. companies hundreds of billions of dollars annually! And stress on the job knows no boundaries. In Japan, worker stress has been identified in nearly three-fourths of workers. In fact, in Japan there is a concept called *karoshi*, which means "death from overworking"—employees who die after working more than three thousand hours the previous year.

karoshi
A Japanese term for sudden death caused by overwork.

ARE THERE COMMON CAUSES OF STRESS?

Stress can be caused by a number of factors called stressors. Factors that create stress can be grouped into two major categories—organizational and personal (see Exhibit 13-5). Both directly affect employees, and ultimately their jobs.

Many factors within the organization can cause stress. Pressures to avoid errors or complete tasks in a limited time period, a demanding supervisor, and unpleasant coworkers are a few examples.

stressors
Conditions that cause stress in an individual.

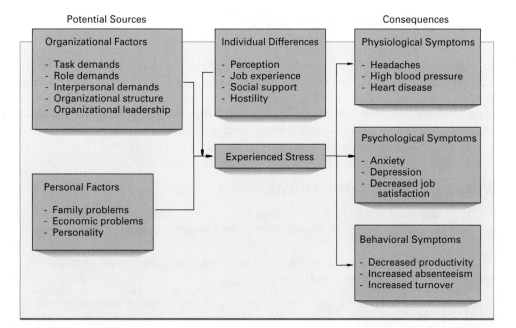

Exhibit 13-5
Potential sources of stress.

WHAT ARE THE SYMPTOMS OF STRESS?

What signs indicate that an employee's stress level might be too high? Stress reveals itself in three general ways: physiological, psychological, and behavioral symptoms.

Most of the early interest in stress focused heavily on health-related or *physiological concerns*. High stress levels result in changes in metabolism, increased heart and breathing rates, increased blood pressure, headaches, and increased risk of heart attacks. Because detecting many of these requires the skills of trained medical personnel, their immediate and direct relevance to the supervisor is negligible.

Of greater importance to supervisors are psychological and behavioral symptoms of stress—symptoms that can be witnessed in the person. The *psychological symptoms* can be seen as increased tension and anxiety, boredom, and procrastination—which can all lead to productivity decreases. So too can *behavioral symptoms*—changes in eating habits, increased smoking or substance consumption, rapid speech, or sleep disorders.

HOW CAN STRESS BE REDUCED?

Reducing stress presents a dilemma for supervisors. Some stress in organizations is absolutely necessary. Without it, people have no energy. Accordingly, whenever one considers stress reduction, what is at issue is reducing its dysfunctional aspects.

One of the first means of reducing stress is to make sure that employees are properly matched to their jobs—and that they understand the extent of their "authority." Furthermore, letting employees know precisely what is expected of them can reduce ambiguity. Redesigning jobs can also help ease work overload–related stressors. Employees should have some input in those things that affect them. Their involvement and participation have been found to lessen stress.

Supervisors must recognize that no matter what they do to eliminate organizational stressors, some employees will still be "stressed out." Supervisors simply have little or no control over the employee's personal factors. Supervisors also face an ethical issue when personal factors cause stress—just how far can one intrude on an employee's personal life? To help deal with this issue, many companies have started employee assistance and wellness programs. These employer-offered programs are designed to assist employees in areas where they may be having difficulties, such as financial planning, legal matters, health, fitness, and handling stress.[17]

Helping the Whole Employee

No matter what kind of organization or industry one works in, one thing is certain: At times, employees will have personal problems. Whether that problem is job stress, legal, marital, financial, or health-related, one commonality exists: If an employee experiences a personal problem, sooner or later it will manifest itself at the workplace in terms of lowered productivity, increased absenteeism, or turnover (behavioral symptoms of stress). To help employees deal with these personal problems, more and more companies are implementing employee assistance programs (EAPs).

employee assistance program (EAP)
A program designed to act as a first stop for individuals seeking help with the goal of getting productive employees back on the job as swiftly as possible.

WHERE DID EAPS COME FROM?

EAPs, as they exist today in about half of U.S. organizations, are extensions of programs that had their birth in U.S. companies in the 1940s.[18] Companies such as DuPont,

---

[17]See Institute for Management Excellence, "Reducing Stress in the Workplace," October 2002. www. itstime.com/oct2002.htm (accessed June 22, 2008).

[18]F. Hansen, "Employee Assistance Programs (EAPs) Grow and Expand Their Reach," *Compensation and Benefits Review*, March/April 2000, 13; "EAPs with the Most," *Managing Benefits Plans*, March 2003, 8; and K. Tyler, "Helping Employees Cope with Grief," *HR Magazine*, September 2003, 55–58.

Standard Oil, and Kodak recognized that a number of their employees were experiencing problems with alcohol. To help these employees, formalized programs were implemented on the company's site to educate these workers on the dangers of alcohol and to help them overcome their addiction. The premise behind these programs, which still holds today, is getting a productive employee back on the job as swiftly as possible. Let's examine this for a moment.

Suppose you have a worker, Robert, who has been with you for a number of years. Robert has been a solid performer for several years, but lately something has happened. You notice his performance declining. The quality of his work is diminishing, he has been late three times in the past five weeks, and rumor has it that Robert is having marital problems. You could, and would have every right to, discipline Robert according to the organization's discipline process. But it is doubtful that discipline alone would help. Consequently, after a period of time, you may end up firing him. You've now lost a once good performer and must fill the position with another—a process that may take eighteen months to finally achieve the productivity level Robert had. However, instead of firing him, you decide to refer this individual to the organization's EAP. This confidential program works with Robert to determine the cause(s) of the problems and seeks to help him overcome them. Although Robert meets more frequently at first with the EAP counselor, you notice that after a short period of time Robert is back on the job, and his performance is improving. After four months, he is performing at the level prior to the problem getting out of hand. In this scenario, you now have your fully productive employee back in four months, as opposed to possibly eighteen months had you fired and replaced Robert.

WHY PROVIDE WELLNESS PROGRAMS?

When we mention wellness programs in any organization, we are talking about any type of program that is designed to keep employees healthy. These programs are varied and may focus on such things as smoking cessation, weight control, stress management, physical fitness, nutrition education, blood pressure control, violence protection, and work team problem intervention. Wellness programs are designed to help cut employer health costs and to lower absenteeism and turnover by preventing health-related problems.[19]

It is interesting to note that, similar to EAPs, wellness programs don't work unless employees view them as having some value. Unfortunately for wellness, the numbers across the United States are not as promising. Less than one-fourth of all employees use them. To help combat this low turnout, a number of key criteria must exist. First of all, there must be top supervisory support—without supervisors' support in terms of resources and in personally using the programs, the wrong message may be sent to employees. Second, there appears to be a need to have the programs serve the family as well as the employees themselves. This not only provides an atmosphere where families can get healthy together, but it also reduces possible medical costs for the dependents. And finally comes the issue of employee input. If programs are designed without considering employees' needs, even the best ones may fail. Supervisors need to invite participation by asking employees what they'd use if available. Although many supervisors know that exercise is beneficial, few initially addressed how to get employees involved. But after finding out that employees would like such things as on-site exercise facilities or aerobics, they were able to begin appropriate program development.

wellness program
Any type of program that is designed to keep employees healthy, focusing on such things as smoking cessation, weight control, stress management, physical fitness, nutrition education, blood pressure control, and so on.

[19]C. Petersen, "Value of Complementary Care Rises, But Poses Challenges," *Managed Healthcare*, November 2000, 47–48.

Comprehension Check **13-2**

5. Which one of the following is *not* an accident prevention mechanism?

   a. Skills training
   b. Protection
   c. Valid selection criteria
   d. Regulation enforcement

6. Workplace homicide is the number _____ cause of work-related deaths in the United States.

   a. four
   b. three
   c. two
   d. one

7. An unhealthy work environment is best described as a(n)

   a. OSHA violation
   b. sick building
   c. imminent danger
   d. none of the above

8. Injuries sustained by continuous movements of a body part are called

   a. musculoskeletal problems
   b. carpal tunnel syndrome
   c. eye–hand coordination disease
   d. none of the above

9. What two factors must be present for stress to exist?

   a. Importance and uncertainty
   b. Importance and certainty
   c. Unimportance and certainty
   d. Unimportance and uncertainty

Enhancing Understanding

SUMMARY

After reading this chapter, I can:

1. **Discuss the supervisory effects of the Occupational Safety and Health Act.** The Occupational Safety and Health Act (OSH Act) outlines comprehensive and specific safety and health standards for organizations. These standards are usually translated into organizational policies, which are enforced by supervisors.

2. **List the enforcement priorities of the Occupational Safety and Health Administration (OSHA).** OSHA has an established five-step priority enforcement process consisting of imminent danger, serious accidents, employee complaints, inspection of targeted industries, and random inspections.

3. **Explain what punitive actions OSHA can impose on an organization.** OSHA can fine an organization up to a maximum penalty of $70,000 if the violation is severe, willful, and repetitive. For violations not meeting those criteria, the maximum fine is $10,000. OSHA may, at its discretion, seek criminal or civil charges against an organization's management if they willfully violate health and safety regulations.

4. **Describe what supervisors must do to comply with OSHA record-keeping requirements.** Supervisors in selected industries must complete OSHA Form 300 to record accidents, injuries, and illnesses that are job related. This information is then used to calculate the organization's incidence rate.

5. **Describe the leading causes of safety and health accidents.** The leading causes of accidents are

human and environmental factors. Human factors include carelessness, intoxication, daydreaming, inability to do the job, and other human deficiencies. Environmental factors include tools, equipment, the physical plant, and the general work environment.

6. **Explain what supervisors can do to prevent workplace violence.** A supervisor can help prevent workplace violence by ensuring that organizational policies are not adversely affecting employees, by developing a plan to deal with the issue, and by being trained in identifying troubled employees.

7. **Define *stress*.** Stress is a dynamic condition in which an individual is confronted with an opportunity, constraint, or demand for which the outcome is perceived as important and uncertain.

8. **Explain how a supervisor can create a healthy work site.** A supervisor can assist in creating a healthy work site by removing harmful substances such as asbestos, germs, mold, fungi, and cigarette smoke, thus limiting employee exposure.

9. **Describe the purposes of employee assistance and wellness programs.** Employee assistance and wellness programs are designed to offer employees a variety of services that will help them become mentally and physically healthy, which in turn helps contain the organization's health care costs.

COMPREHENSION: Review and Discussion Questions

1. What are the objectives of the Occupational Safety and Health Act?

2. Describe the priority of OSHA investigations.

3. Identify three methods of preventing accidents. How can supervisors assist in ensuring that accidents are prevented?

4. How are incidence rates calculated? Give an example.

5. What is stress? How can it be positive?

6. Differentiate among physiological, psychological, and behavioral stress symptoms. Which are the greatest concerns for supervisors?

7. "Supervisors should be concerned with helping their employees cope with both job-related stress and off-the-job stress." Do you agree or disagree? Discuss.

8. Some medical experts believe that regular daily exercise results in better health, improved conditioning, and greater tolerance of stressful situations. What would you think about being employed by a company that required you to work out daily on company time? Do you think this would help or hurt the company's recruiting ability? Explain your position.

KEY CONCEPT CROSSWORD

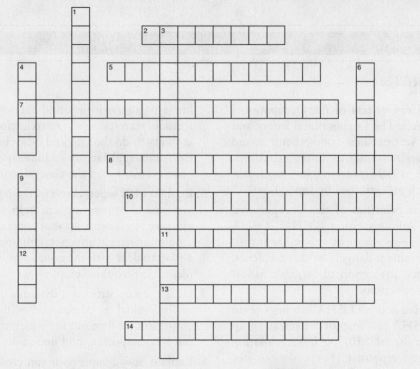

ACROSS

2. a type of program designed to keep employees healthy
5. a repetitive stress injury of the wrist
7. part one of the law that enforces healthy working conditions and the preservation of human resources
8. injuries sustained by continuous movements of a body part
10. a continuous motion disorder caused by repetitive stress injuries
11. a condition under which an accident is about to happen
12. conditions that cause stress in an individual
13. part two of the law that enforces healthy working conditions and preservation of human resources
14. a measure of the number of illnesses, injuries, and lost days as it relates to a common base of one hundred full-time employees

DOWN

1. a term referring to an unhealthy work environment
3. a program designed to act as a first stop for individuals in an organization seeking help with a personal problem
4. the government agency that researches and sets OSHA standards
6. something an individual feels when faced with an opportunity or constraint that is perceived to be both uncertain and important
9. a Japanese term for sudden death caused by overwork

ANSWERS TO COMPREHENSION CHECKS

Comprehension Check 13-1

1. b   2. a   3. d   4. b

Comprehension Check 13-2

5. c   6. c   7. b   8. d (repetitive stress injuries)   9. a

Developing Your Supervisory Skills

GETTING TO KNOW YOURSELF

Before you can effectively supervise others, you must understand your present strengths and areas in need of development. To assist in this learning process, we encourage you to complete the following self-assessment from the Prentice Hall Self-Assessment Library 3.4.

1. Am I Burned Out? (III. C. 3.)
2. How Stressful Is My Life? (III. C. 2.)

After you complete the assessment, we suggest you retain the results and store them as part of your "portfolio of learning about yourself."

BUILDING A TEAM

➤ An Experiential Exercise: Health and Safety

Your team may wish to role-play this case for the class, and then discuss what the supervisor should do and how the supervisor should respond.

The Situation

Dana Robbins has been a machinist for Minneo Tool and Die, a manufacturer of engine parts for large motors, for sixteen years. Lately, more of Dana's parts have been rejected for errors; Dana seems preoccupied with outside matters—leaving early, asking to take days beyond sick days allowed, and so on. Dana has missed work three days in two weeks, and Chris Lynch, Dana's supervisor, wonders if that was alcohol on Dana's breath after lunch yesterday. Chris hasn't said anything yet. She doesn't want to invade Dana's privacy. Chris thinks Dana may just be going through a tough time because Dana has been cooperative, positive, highly productive, and rarely sick or absent in the past. Besides, it has been difficult in the last month because a major shipment has required overtime, and all machinists have been asked to work eighty to ninety-five hours a week until the shipment is complete.

At lunch Chris overhears an argument between Dana and a coworker, Terry, each blaming the other for a part being rejected by quality assurance. Dana threatens Terry to "stay out of the way" and "the next time we'll settle it outside," poking Terry in the chest with a finger. Dana then slams a $250 gauge down on the floor, shouts profanities, and adds, "I don't care if the part falls off or if this place burns to the ground anymore; I've about had all I can take of you and this place! You know my spouse left me for my best friend last week, left me with a two-year-old to raise by myself, and my other kid got expelled for possession. It just doesn't much matter to me what you think; so I'd leave me alone if I were you!"

Chris is unsure how to proceed.

GROUP QUESTIONS

1. What should Chris do?
2. What advice would you give Chris?
3. How should Chris respond to the immediate situation?
4. What advice can you give Chris regarding workplace violence to help her handle future situations more effectively?

➤ Internet: Web Activity

Go to http://www.pearsonhighered.com/robbins/. Find *Supervision Today!* 7th Ed. and click Companion Website.

DEVELOPING SAFETY SKILLS

Several steps can be recommended for developing an organization's safety and health program. Whether or not such programs are chiefly the responsibility of one individual, every supervisor must work to ensure that the work environment is safe for all employees.

STEPS IN PRACTICING THE SKILL

STEP 1: Involve supervisors and employees in the development of a safety and health plan. If neither group can see the usefulness and the benefit of such a plan, even the best plan will fail.

STEP 2: Hold someone accountable for implementing the plan. Plans do not work by themselves. They need someone to champion the cause. This person must be given the resources to put the plan in place, but also must be held accountable for what it's intended to accomplish.

STEP 3: Determine the safety and health requirements for your work site. Just as each individual is different, so too is each workplace. Understanding the specific needs of the facility will help you determine what safety and health requirements will be necessary.

STEP 4: Assess what workplace hazards exist in the facility. Identify the potential health and safety problems that may exist on the job. By understanding what exists, you can develop preventive measures.

STEP 5: Correct hazards that exist. If certain hazards were identified in the assessment, fix or eliminate them. This may mean decreasing the effect of the hazard or controlling it through other means (e.g., protective clothing).

STEP 6: Train employees in safety and health techniques. Make safety and health training mandatory for all employees. Employees should be instructed how to do their jobs in the safest manner and understand that any protective equipment provided must be used.

STEP 7: Develop the mind-set in employees that the organization is to be kept hazard-free. Often employees are the first to witness problems. Establish a means for them to report their findings, including having emergency procedures in place, if necessary. Ensuring that preventive maintenance of equipment follows a recommended schedule can also prevent breakdowns from becoming a hazard.

STEP 8: Continually update and refine the safety and health program. Once the program has been implemented, it must continually be evaluated, and necessary changes must be made. Documenting the progress of the program is necessary for use in this analysis.

➤ Communicating Effectively

1. Visit OSHA's website (www.osha.gov). Go to a page that discusses a news release on something OSHA is doing. Provide a two- to three-page summary of the news release, focusing on what OSHA is intending to do, its effect on workers, and its effect on supervisors.

2. Use the Internet to locate descriptions of company employee assistance programs (EAPs). Determine the areas of assistance and wellness these companies typically offer their employees. In a two- to three-page paper explain why an organization would/should offer these benefits to employees. From an employee perspective explain why you would/would not participate in a company-sponsored EAP.

THINKING CRITICALLY

➤ Case 13-A: Get Healthy or Get Out

CEO Oliver Warren decided that today was the day he was going to take a stand and make a change in not only his health but also the health of his entire company. He just received the report from his Human Resources department and he was upset by what he read. Health care costs were skyrocketing and the health care industry did not seem interested in fixing a problem that was helping to fill their pockets with money. The active participation of the employees in the available health care program had increased to the point where the company's health care rates had tripled in the last four years. This led to an increase in the employee's premium contributions to the health care insurance, and they were as unhappy as he was.

In his no-nonsense style, Warren decided to tell his employees "like it is" and let them know the true cost of health care—but he was also going to tell them what he and everyone else in the company was going to do about it. Over 30 percent of the company's net profits were funding the health care program. The health-risk assessment conducted earlier in the year showed that over half of the employees were overweight and a majority of them were smokers. His response to this information was to mandate a company-wide no-smoking policy and a wellness program focused on smoking cessation and weight loss.

The company's HR department and legal advisors were concerned that he might overstep his authority by mandating draconian approaches, but after zealous research he found that his state was one of twenty-one where it was not illegal to hire and fire people based on their smoking habits. He also hired a third party to manage the proposed wellness system, thereby removing his supervisors from a system where they might inadvertently discriminate against health-challenged employees.

Five years later, the company encourages yearly intensive health-risk assessments and charges higher insurance premiums to those who decline to participate. Everyone has a health coach to work with them on an individual wellness program; those who do not follow the programs are also charged higher premiums. Many employees do not like the "new" reality of their healthy work place, but Warren has not budged and remains steadfast in his commitment to reign in health care costs and promote healthy lifestyles for his employees.

RESPONDING TO THE CASE

1. What do you think about Warren's approach to controlling employee health care costs? Do you agree with it? Why or why not?

2. What benefits or drawbacks are there to this type of wellness program for employees and the company?

3. Research company wellness programs. What types of things are companies doing to encourage employee wellness? Are there any things you found that you would recommend Warren implement? Describe.

_____

Sources: L. Alderman, "Getting Healthy, with a Little Help from the Boss," *New York Times Online,* May 23, 2009; P. B. Kavilanz, "Unhealthy Habits Cost You More at Work," *CNNMoney.com,* March 24, 2009; M. Freudenheim, "Seeking Savings, Employers Help Smokers Quit," *New York Times Online,* October 26, 2007; and M. Conlin, "Get Healthy or Else," *BusinessWeek,* February 26, 2007, 58–69.

➤ Case 13-B: Safety First at the Samson Company

The Samson Company is in the middle of a contest to boost production. Joe Miller's and Al Scott's departments have been running nip and tuck, with Joe's team currently in the lead. However, last week Joe had some machine downtime, and it looked as though his department might finish behind schedule and be pushed out of first place. There was some good-natured heckling about it between departments, and the machine operators in Joe's department decided they were not going to give up without a struggle. That fact is obvious when Joe arrives at the plant on Monday morning. He is about fifteen minutes early, but most of his people are already at their machines waiting for the starting bell.

That's the way it goes all week. Joe's people work at peak performance, and by Thursday it looks as if they have a good chance of being on top again.

Then, Thursday afternoon, one of the machines jams. The operator, Tim Hanley, one of Joe's best workers, tries to save time by fixing it himself. He reaches in to free the jammed part and one of his fingers is severely gashed. Another worker gets the first-aid kit and fixes a temporary bandage. Then, Joe rushes Tim to the infirmary.

"How is he?" the others ask when Joe returns.

"The nurse did what he could and sent Tim to the hospital," Joe answers.

"Tim really meant it when he said we'd lose over his dead body," one of the workers says admiringly. Several others make similar comments, and Joe realizes that Tim is regarded as a hero by his coworkers.

What Tim did was stupid, Joe thinks, as well as a violation of a basic safety rule. What troubles Joe most, however, is the admiration shown by other members of the group for Tim's actions.

Joe is at a loss as to what he can do to handle the situation. Tim is a top-flight worker, but he did violate a safety procedure when he reached into the jammed machine with the power still on. Also, he is not authorized to make repairs. The normal punishment for such a safety violation is a three-day suspension, but this will put Joe's department further behind and definitely out of the running in the contest. Joe also knows that Tim was only thinking of his department when he tried to repair the machine. Suspending him will be considered by the others as a penalty for loyalty to the company and to his fellow workers. Joe decides to wait for Tim's return before making a decision. He leaves work that day without filing the report of the accident as required by both company policy and OSHA standards.

The following afternoon, Tim returns with a bandage around his hand. All the workers gather around to welcome him back. After much good-natured kidding and sincere welcomes, Joe decides to join the group. After welcoming Tim back, he tells him that what he did was wrong. Joe explains his appreciation for Tim's efforts to save time, and he tells Tim that he will waive the three-day suspension this time because of the circumstances, but that if a similar incident occurs in the future, the suspension will be doubled. Joe turns to the assembled group and makes this statement: "The next time, I will have no choice but to suspend the person according to the rules. I trust that Tim's experience is warning enough. Now get back to work, all of you." Joe returns to his office and begins to fill out the accident report. In the space provided for an explanation of the causes of the accident Joe writes, "Operator's machine malfunctioned, causing a minor injury to the worker's right index finger."

RESPONDING TO THE CASE

1. Do you think Joe would have handled the situation differently if Tim had been a less valued worker? Why?

2. What is the probable outcome of not filing the accident report on time and with complete honesty?

3. If you had been the supervisor in the case, what would you have done to deal with Tim and your workgroup?

4. What does this case suggest about a supervisor's responsibilities for safety and his or her efforts to achieve higher production levels?

Conflict, Politics, Discipline, and Negotiation

Key Concepts

After completing this chapter, you will be able to define these supervisory terms:

- accommodation
- avoidance
- collaboration
- compromise
- conflict
- conflict management
- culture
- devil's advocate
- discipline
- dismissal
- distributive bargaining
- employment-at-will

- forcing
- "hot stove" rule
- integrative bargaining
- negotiation
- politicking
- progressive discipline
- status
- suspension
- verbal warning
- written warning
- wrongful discharge

Chapter Outcomes

After reading this chapter, you will be able to:

1. Define *conflict*.
2. Identify the three general sources of conflict.
3. List the five basic techniques for resolving conflict.
4. Describe how a supervisor could stimulate conflict.
5. Define *politicking*.
6. Explain the existence of politics in organizations.
7. Define *discipline* and the four most common types of discipline problems.
8. List the typical steps in progressive discipline.
9. Contrast distributive and integrative bargaining.

Responding to a Supervisory Dilemma

Hostage and *supervisor*. These are not two words that you would usually expect to hear spoken in the same breath. However, during the first few months of 2009, workers at manufacturing facilities of 3M Company, Sony Corporation, and Caterpillar Inc. in France have taken supervisors hostage. Why? To negotiate better severance packages and benefits for laid-off employees.

French workers have long been known for their aggressive and radical responses to what they feel is wrong or oppressive treatment. Says one French executive, "Protest is inscribed in the genes of French culture. In the past, peasants protested against their lords. Today the difference is that the lords are chief executives." Protesting French workers have been known to burn piles of tires in city streets or tie up traffic with caravans of farm tractors. In one instance, striking truckers blockaded roads and highways to highlight their campaign for retirement at age fifty-five. The labor blockade worked, as the French government relented when food supplies started to run out. And the tactic of taking the boss hostage has been used previously, as well. For instance, in 1997, workers at the state-run mortgage bank Crédit Foncier de France took their boss hostage for five days to try and prevent the bank's closing even though it had been losing money. Although kidnapping your boss isn't legal, a French sociologist who surveyed 3,000 companies in 2004 found that eighteen of them had experienced an "executive detention" in the prior three years.

The actions being taken by workers, which have been peaceful and more of a symbolic protest, are in response to a continuing economic downturn. Although France isn't in any worse shape than the other big industrialized economies, the country's "strong tradition of egalitarianism triggers strong reactions when people think they are being mistreated or when better-off people appear to flaunt their wealth at a time of general hardship." At Caterpillar's French facility near Grenoble, unhappy workers first went on strike for a day. The next day, they detained the plant director and four other supervisors for about twenty-four hours. The supervisors were released only after the company agreed to resume talks with unions and a government mediator on "how to improve compensation for workers being laid off." The incident at Caterpillar followed others at Sony and 3M, where supervisors also were held captive by workers angry over being laid off. Although all the hostage-taking incidents were resolved peacefully, some analysts wonder if more violent actions may be in store especially if workers feel they have nothing to lose.

What's your reaction to these events? Do you think your reaction is influenced by the culture, values, and traditions of the country in which you find yourself? Explain. Review Hofstede's findings (Chapter 2) and use it to explain these workers' actions. How important is it for supervisors to be aware of external environmental forces. Discuss this in light of these events.

What might the French supervisors have done differently in this situation, especially prior to the point where workers felt they had to make their point by taking them hostage? Explain.

Do you think something like this could happen in the United States? Why or why not?

Sources: J. Marquez, "French Hostage Situations Have Some Wondering If U.S. Is Next," *Workforce Management Online*, April 3, 2009; D. Gauthier-Villars and L. Abboud, "In France, Boss Can Become a Hostage," *Wall Street Journal*, April 3, 2009, B1+; L. Abboud and M. Colchester, "French Bosses Besieged as Worker Anger Rises," *Wall Street Journal*, April 1, 2009, B1+; D. Gauthier-Villars, "French Business Leaders Vow to Give Up 'Abusive' Benefits," *Wall Street Journal*, October 8, 2008, A14; and F. Coleman, "Take A Hostage, Save Your Job," *U.S. News & World Report*, February 3, 1997, 43.

ealing with conflicts and political issues is a part of every supervisor's job. Those who learn how to handle these matters are likely to reap significant benefits.

In this chapter, we define conflict, explore what brings it about, and examine the various ways you can handle it. Then, we discuss organizational politics—why understanding politics is important for all supervisors and how you can make politics work for you. We then look at one of the more difficult issues facing a supervisor, disciplining employees, and the conflict it causes. Finally, we conclude with some suggestions on how to be more successful at negotiation.

What Is Conflict?

Conflict is a process in which one party consciously interferes in the goal-achievement efforts of another party. This interference can be between a supervisor and a member of his or her department or between two operatives within a department. It also might exist between a supervisor and his or her boss, or it might involve interdepartmental parties, such as two supervisors in separate departments.

conflict
A process in which one party consciously interferes in the goal-achievement efforts of another party.

IS ALL CONFLICT BAD?

Most of us have grown up with the idea that all conflicts are bad. We were told not to argue with our parents or teachers, to get along with our brothers and sisters, and that countries spend billions of dollars on military outlays to preserve peace. But conflicts aren't all bad, especially in organizations.[1]

Conflict is a natural phenomenon of organizational life.[2] It can't be completely eliminated. Why? Because (1) organizational members have different goals; (2) there are scarce resources, such as budget allocations, that various people want and are willing to fight over; and (3) people in organizations don't all see things alike, as a result of their diverse backgrounds, education, experiences, and interests. However, the existence of conflict in organizations has a positive side. It stimulates creativity, innovation, and change—and only through change can an organization adapt and survive (see Exhibit 14-1). A positive level of conflict in an organization supports disagreements, open questioning of others, and challenging the status quo. If organizations were completely devoid of conflict, they would become apathetic, stagnant, and unresponsive to change.

You should look at conflict as having an upside as well as a downside. You should encourage enough conflict to keep your department viable, self-critical, and creative. Of course, too much conflict is bad and should be reduced. Your goal should be to have enough conflict in your department to keep the unit responsive and innovative, but not so much as to hinder departmental performance.

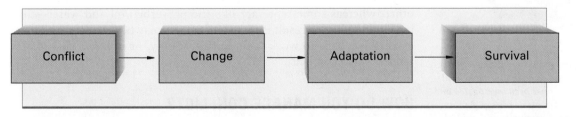

Exhibit 14-1
The positive role of conflict.

---

[1]See S. P. Robbins, *Managing Organizational Conflict: A Non-Traditional Approach* (Upper Saddle River, NJ: Prentice Hall, 1974).

[2]See, for example, C. Noble, "Resolving Co-Worker Disputes through 'Coaching Conflict Management,'" *Canadian HR Reporter*, September 24, 2001, 18–20.

WHERE DO CONFLICTS COME FROM?

Conflicts don't pop out of thin air. They have causes. These causes can be separated into three general categories: communication differences, structural differentiation, and personal differences. Let's briefly look at each of these.

Communication Differences Communication differences encompass conflicts arising from misunderstandings and different meanings attached to words. One of the major myths that most of us carry around with us is that poor communication is the reason for all conflicts—"If we could just communicate with each other, we could eliminate our differences." Such a conclusion is not unreasonable, given the amount of time each of us spends communicating. Poor communication is certainly not the source of all conflicts, though there is considerable evidence to suggest that problems in the communication process act to retard collaboration and stimulate misunderstanding.

Structural Differentiation As we explained in Chapter 4, organizations are horizontally and vertically differentiated. Company officials divide up tasks, group common tasks into departments, and establish rules and regulations to facilitate standardized practices among departments.

This structural differentiation often causes conflicts. Individuals may disagree over goals, decision alternatives, performance criteria, and resource allocations. These conflicts, however, are not caused by poor communication or personal hostility. Rather, they are rooted in the structure of the organization itself. The "goodies" that supervisors want—budgets, promotions, pay increases, additions to staff, office space, influence over decisions—are scarce resources that must be divided up. The creation of horizontal units (departments) and vertical levels (the organizational hierarchy) brings about efficiencies through specialization and coordination, but at the same time produces the potential for structural conflicts.

Personal Differences The third source of conflict is personal differences. These include value systems and personality characteristics that account for individual idiosyncrasies and differences.

Imagine the following situations. Your values emphasize developing close family ties; your boss' focus on acquiring material possessions. An employee in your department thinks salary increases should be based on seniority; you think the criterion should be job performance. These value differences stimulate conflicts. Similarly, the chemistry between some people makes it hard for them to work together. Factors such as background, education, experience, and training mold each individual into a unique personality. Some personality types are attracted to each other, whereas some types are like the proverbial oil and water—they just don't mix. The result is that some people may be perceived by others as abrasive, hard to work with, untrustworthy, or strange. This creates interpersonal conflicts.

What should a disciplinary process be? It should be reasonable and fair, and it should deal with the issues at hand. Decisions shouldn't be made until the appropriate behavior has been investigated and the alleged wrongdoer has his or her say. As this symbol of justice typifies, an employee should be considered "innocent until proven guilty."

Conflict management
A method of identifying and resolving conflicts in a reasonable, equitable, competent manner.

HOW DO YOU MANAGE CONFLICT?

As a supervisor, you want to have the optimal level of conflict in your department. That means you need to manage it. You want to resolve conflict when it's too high and disrupting your department's performance. You want to stimulate conflict when it's too low. So, conflict management is the application of resolution and stimulation techniques to achieve the optimal level of departmental conflict.

WHAT RESOLUTION TECHNIQUES CAN YOU USE?

What options do you have available to eliminate or reduce conflicts? There are five basic approaches or techniques for resolving conflict: avoidance, accommodation, forcing, compromise, and collaboration. As shown in Exhibit 14-2, they differ in terms of the emphasis they place on concern for others versus concern for oneself. Each technique has particular strengths and weaknesses, and no one technique is ideal for every situation. You should consider each technique as a tool in your conflict management portfolio. Although you may be better at using some tools than others, the skilled supervisor knows what each tool can do and when it is likely to be most effective.

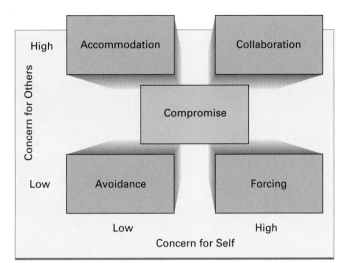

Exhibit 14-2
Basic techniques for resolving conflicts.

Avoidance Sometimes *avoidance* is the best solution for you—just withdrawing from the conflict or ignoring it. When would that be? When the conflict you face is trivial, when emotions are running high and time can help cool things down, or when the potential disruption from a more assertive action outweighs the benefits of resolution, avoidance can work best. The thing to be concerned about with this approach is that some supervisors believe that all conflicts can be ignored. These conflict avoiders are often very poor supervisors. They frustrate their employees and usually lose their respect. There are times when the best action is no action, but that shouldn't be the way you respond to every conflict.

avoidance
Intentionally keeping away from places, people, thoughts, feelings, or conversations related to a conflict situation.

Accommodation The goal of *accommodation* is to maintain harmonious relationships by placing another's needs and concerns above your own. You might, for example, yield to another person's position on an issue or try to defuse a conflict by focusing on points of agreement. This approach is most viable when the issue under dispute isn't that important to you or when you want to build up credits for later issues.

accommodation
A method of maintaining harmonious relationships by placing others' needs and concerns above one's own.

Forcing With *forcing*, you attempt to satisfy your own needs at the expense of the other party. In organizations, this is most often illustrated by supervisors using their formal authority to resolve a dispute. The use of intimidation, majority-rule voting, or stubbornly refusing to give in on your position are other examples of force. Force works well (1) when you need a quick resolution, (2) on important issues for which unpopular actions must be taken, and (3) when commitment by others to your solution is not critical.

forcing
Attempting to satisfy one's own needs at the expense of the other party.

Compromise A *compromise* approach requires each party to give up something of value. This is typically the approach taken by management personnel and labor unions in negotiating a new labor contract. Supervisors also often use compromise to deal with interpersonal conflicts. For instance, a supervisor in a small printing company wanted one of his employees to come in over a weekend to finish an important project. The employee didn't want to spend his whole weekend at work. After considerable discussion, they arrived at a compromise solution: The employee would come in on Saturday only, the supervisor would also come in and help out, and the employee would get eight hours of overtime pay plus the following Friday off.

When should you look to compromise as an option? You do so when the party with whom you have the conflict has power about equal to yours, when it is desirable to achieve a temporary solution to a complex issue, or when time pressures demand an expedient solution.

compromise
An approach to conflict that requires each party to give up something of value.

collaboration

An approach to conflict in which all parties seek to satisfy their interests.

Collaboration The ultimate win–win solution is collaboration. All parties to the conflict seek to satisfy their interests. This technique is typically characterized by open and honest discussion among the parties, intensive listening to understand differences and identify areas of mutual agreement, and careful deliberation over a full range of alternatives to find a solution that is advantageous to all.

When is collaboration the best conflict approach for you? Collaboration is best used when time pressures are minimal, when all parties in the conflict seriously want a solution, and when the issue is too important to be compromised.

WHICH CONFLICTS DO YOU HANDLE?

Not every conflict justifies your attention. Some might not be worth the effort; others might be unmanageable. Although avoidance might appear to be a "cop-out," it can sometimes be the most appropriate response. You can improve your overall supervisory effectiveness, and your conflict management skills in particular, by avoiding trivial conflicts. Choose your battles judiciously, saving your efforts for the ones that count.

Regardless of our desires, some conflicts may be unmanageable. When antagonisms are deeply rooted, when one or both parties wish to prolong a conflict, or when emotions run so high that constructive interaction is impossible, your efforts to manage the conflict are unlikely to meet with much success. Don't be lured into the naïve belief that a good supervisor can resolve every conflict effectively. Some aren't worth the effort. Some are outside your realm of influence. Still others may be functional and, as such, are best left alone. Those you choose to handle, you need to know how to handle in the best way possible.

HOW DO YOU CHOOSE THE APPROPRIATE RESOLUTION TECHNIQUE?

Given that you're familiar with your options, how should you proceed if you find you have a conflict that needs resolving? We summarize your options in Exhibit 14-3 and we describe them in this section. Start by considering your preferred conflict-handling style. Each of us has a basic approach to handling conflict with which we feel most comfortable. Do you try to postpone dealing with conflicts, hoping they'll go away

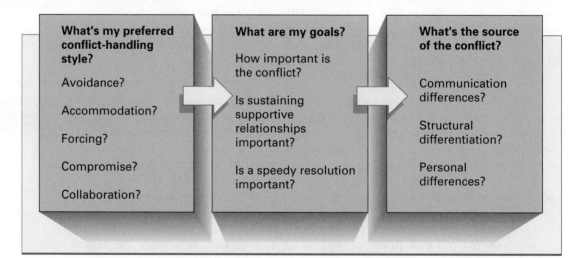

Exhibit 14-3

Choosing the appropriate resolution technique: a guideline.

(avoidance)? Do you prefer soothing the other party's feelings so that the disagreement doesn't damage your relationship (accommodation)? Are you stubborn and determined to get your way (forcing)? Do you look for middle-ground solutions (compromise)? Or maybe you prefer to sit down and discuss differences to find a solution that will make everybody happy (collaboration).

Everyone has a basic resolution approach that reflects his or her personality. You should understand what yours is. Most people aren't held prisoner to their basic approach. They're flexible and can use different approaches if they need to. Unfortunately, some people are extremely rigid and incapable of adjusting their styles. These people are at a severe disadvantage because they can't use all of the resolution options. You should know your basic resolution style and try to show flexibility in using others. However, keep in mind that when push comes to shove, most of us fall back on our basic approach because it's the one we know best and feel most comfortable with.

The next thing you should look at is your goals. The best solution is closely intertwined with your definition of *best*. Three goals seemed to dominate our discussion of resolution approaches: the importance of the conflict, concern over maintaining long-term interpersonal relations, and the speed with which you need to resolve the conflict. All other things held constant, if the issue is critical to your unit's success, collaboration is preferred. If sustaining supportive relationships is important, the best approaches, in order of preference, are accommodation, collaboration, compromise, and avoidance. If it's crucial to resolve the conflict as quickly as possible, force, accommodation, and compromise—in that order—are preferred.

Finally, you need to consider the source of the conflict. What works best depends, to a large degree, on the cause of the conflict. Communication-based conflicts revolve around misinformation and misunderstandings. Such conflicts lend themselves to collaboration. In contrast, conflicts based on personal differences arise out of disparities between the parties' values and personalities. Such conflicts are most susceptible to avoidance because these differences are often deeply entrenched. When you have to resolve conflicts rooted in personal differences, you'll frequently rely on force—not so much because it placates everyone involved, but because it works! The third category, structural conflicts, offers opportunities to use most of the conflict approaches.

This process of blending your personal style, your goals, and the source of the conflict should result in identifying the approach or set of approaches most likely to be effective for you in any specific conflict.

HOW DO YOU STIMULATE CONFLICT?

What about the other side of conflict management—situations that require supervisors to stimulate conflict? The notion of stimulating conflict is often difficult to accept. For almost all of us, the term *conflict* has a negative connotation, and the idea of purposely creating conflict seems to be counter to good supervisory practices. Few of us personally enjoy being in conflictive situations. Yet there are situations where an increase in conflict is constructive. Exhibit 14-4 provides a set of questions that can help you determine whether a situation might justify conflict stimulation. An affirmative answer to one or more of these questions suggests that an increase in conflict might help your unit's performance.

1. Are you surrounded by "yes people"?

2. Are subordinates afraid to admit ignorance and uncertainties to you?

3. Do you and department members concentrate so hard on reaching a compromise that you lose sight of key values, long-term objectives, or the organization's welfare?

4. Do you believe that it is in your best interest to maintain the impression of peace and cooperation in your unit, regardless of the price?

5. Is there an excessive concern in your department not to hurt the feelings of others?

6. Do people in your department believe that popularity is more important for obtaining rewards than competence and high performance?

7. Is your department unduly enamored with obtaining consensus for all decisions?

8. Do employees show unusually high resistance to change?

9. Is there a lack of new ideas?

10. Is there an unusually low level of employee turnover?

Exhibit 14-4

An affirmative answer to any of these questions suggests the need for conflict stimulation.

We know a lot more about resolving conflict than stimulating it. However, the following are some suggestions you might want to consider if you find your department needs an increased level of conflict.

Use Communication As far back as Franklin Roosevelt's administration, and probably before, the White House has consistently used communication to stimulate conflict. Senior officials float trial balloons by "planting" possible decisions with the media through the infamous "reliable source" route. For example, the name of a prominent judge is leaked as a possible Supreme Court appointment. If the candidate survives the public scrutiny, his or her appointment is announced by the president. However, if the candidate is found lacking by the media and public, the president's press secretary or other high-level official will make a formal statement such as, "At no time was this individual under consideration."

You can use rumors and ambiguous messages to stimulate conflict in your department. Information that some employees might be transferred, that serious budget cuts are coming, or that a layoff is possible can reduce apathy, stimulate new ideas, and force reevaluation—all positive outcomes as a result of increased conflict.

Bring in Outsiders A widely used method for shaking up a stagnant department is to bring in—either by hiring from outside or by internal transfer—individuals whose backgrounds, values, attitudes, or personalities differ from those of present members. One of the major benefits of the diversity movement (encouraging the hiring and promotion of people who are different) is that it can stimulate conflict and improve an organization's performance.

Restructure the Department We know that structural variables are a source of conflict. It is therefore only logical to look to structure as a conflict stimulation device. Centralizing decisions, realigning workgroups, and increasing formalization are examples of structural devices that disrupt the status quo and act to increase conflict levels.

devil's advocate
A person who purposely presents arguments that run counter to those proposed by the majority or against current practices.

Appoint a Devil's Advocate A devil's advocate is a person who purposely presents arguments that run counter to those proposed by the majority or against current practices. He or she plays the role of the critic, even to the point of arguing against positions with which he or she actually agrees.

A devil's advocate acts as a check against groupthink and practices that have no better justification than "that's the way we've always done it around here." When thoughtfully listened to, the advocate can improve the quality of group decision making. On the other hand, others in the group often view advocates as time wasters; appointment of an advocate is almost certain to delay any decision process.

HOW CAUTIOUSLY SHOULD YOU PROCEED IN STIMULATING CONFLICT?

Even though there are situations where departmental performance can be enhanced through conflict stimulation, it may not be in your best career interests to use stimulation techniques.

If your organizational culture or your immediate superior views any kind of conflict in your department as a negative reflection on your supervisory performance, think twice before stimulating conflict or even allowing low levels of conflict to exist. When company officials believe that all conflicts are bad, it's not uncommon for you to be evaluated on how peaceful and harmonious conditions are in your department. Although a conflict-free climate tends to create stagnant and apathetic organizations, and eventually lower performance, it is important for your survival to adopt a conflict management style that's compatible with your organization. In some cases, that might mean using only resolution techniques.

Comprehension Check 14-1

1. *True or false?* All conflict is bad.

2. The conflict management technique involving withdrawing from or ignoring the conflict is referred to as
   a. accommodation
   b. avoidance
   c. compromise
   d. forcing

3. When you need a quick resolution to an important issue and when commitment to your solution is not critical, the _____ style of conflict resolution works best.
   a. compromise
   b. avoidance
   c. forcing
   d. accommodation

4. Conflict can occur for all of the following reasons except
   a. communication differences
   b. personal differences
   c. structural differences
   d. strategic differences

Understanding Organizational Politics

Don't use conflict stimulation techniques, even if they would improve your department's performance, if your organization's senior management views all conflicts as bad. This summary of the previous paragraph acknowledges the political nature of organizations. You're not always rewarded for doing the right things. In the real world of organizations, the good guys don't always win. Demonstrating openness, trust, objectivity, support, and similar humane qualities in relationships with others doesn't always lead to improved supervisory performance. There will be times when, to get things done or to protect your interests against the maneuvering of others, you'll have to engage in politicking. Effective supervisors understand the political nature of organizations and adjust their actions accordingly.

WHAT IS POLITICS?

Politics relates to who gets what, when, and how. Politicking consists of the actions you can take to influence, or attempt to influence, the distribution of advantages and disadvantages within your organization. Some examples of political behavior include withholding key information from decision makers, whistle-blowing, spreading rumors, leaking confidential information about organizational activities to the media, exchanging favors with others in the organization for mutual benefit, and lobbying for or against a particular individual or decision alternative.[3]

One of the most interesting insights about politics is that what constitutes a political action is almost entirely a judgment call. Like beauty, politics is in the eye of the beholder. A behavior that one person labels "organizational politics" is very

politicking
The actions one can take to influence, or attempt to influence, the distribution of advantages and disadvantages within an organization.

---

[3]See, for example, D. A. DeCenzo and B. Silhanek, *Human Relations: Personal and Professional Development* (Upper Saddle River, NJ: Prentice Hall, 2002), 177–179.

POLITICAL LABEL		EFFECTIVE SUPERVISION LABEL
1. Blaming others	or	Fixing responsibility
2. Kissing up	or	Developing working relationships
3. Apple polishing	or	Demonstrating loyalty
4. Passing the buck	or	Delegating authority
5. Covering your rear	or	Documenting decisions
6. Creating conflict	or	Encouraging change and innovation
7. Forming coalitions	or	Facilitating teamwork
8. Whistle-blowing	or	Improving efficiency
9. Nitpicking	or	Meticulous attention to detail
10. Scheming	or	Planning ahead

Exhibit 14-5

Is it politics or effective supervision?

likely to be characterized as an instance of "effective supervision" by another. Effective supervision is not necessarily political, though in some cases it might be. Rather, a person's reference point determines what he or she classifies as organizational politics. Take a look at the labels in Exhibit 14-5 that are used to describe the same activities.

WHY DOES POLITICS EXIST IN ORGANIZATIONS?

Can you conceive of an organization that is free of politics? It's possible, but most unlikely. Organizations are made up of individuals and groups with different values, goals, and interests. This sets up the potential for conflict over resources. Departmental budgets, space allocations, project responsibilities, and salary adjustments are just a few examples of the resources about which organizational members will disagree.

Resources in organizations are limited. This often turns potential conflict into real conflict. If resources were abundant, all the various interests within the organization could satisfy their goals. Because resources are limited, not everyone's interests can be provided for. Further, whether true or not, gains by one individual or group are often perceived as being at the expense of others within the organization. These forces create competition among members for the organization's limited resources.

Maybe the most important factor leading to politics within organizations is the realization that most of the "facts" that are used to allocate limited resources are open to interpretation. What, for instance, is "good" performance? What's a "good" job? What's an "adequate" improvement? The coach of any National Football League team knows that a quarterback like Peyton Manning, with a consistent rating in the range of 90 to 105, is a high performer and one with a 43 rating is a poor performer. You don't need to be a football genius to know you should play the top quarterback and keep the lower-rated one on the bench. But what if you have to choose between two quarterbacks who have ratings of 87 and 84? Then, other factors—less objective ones—come into play: attitude, potential, ability to perform in the clutch, and so on.

Most supervisory decisions in organizations more closely resemble choosing between two fairly equally rated quarterbacks than deciding between a superstar and a bench warmer. It is in this large and ambiguous middle ground of organizational life—where the facts don't speak for themselves—that politics takes place.

Finally, because most decisions have to be made in a climate of ambiguity (where facts are rarely fully objective, and thus are open to interpretation), people within the organization will use whatever influence they can to taint the facts to support their goals and interests. That, of course, creates motivation for the activities we call politicking.

CAN YOU PLAY POLITICS AND STILL BE ETHICAL?

Not all political actions are necessarily unethical. To help guide you in differentiating ethical from unethical politicking, there are some questions you should consider. Exhibit 14-6 illustrates a decision tree to guide ethical actions. The first question you need to answer addresses self-interest versus organizational goals. Ethical actions are consistent with the organization's goals. Spreading untrue rumors about the safety of a new product introduced by your company, to make that product's design group look bad, is unethical. However, there may be nothing unethical if you, as a department head, exchange favors with your division's purchasing supervisor to get a critical contract processed quickly.

The second question concerns the rights of other parties. If you went down to the mail room during your lunch hour and read through the mail directed to the purchasing supervisor (described in the previous paragraph) with the intent of "getting something on him" so that he'd expedite your contract, you'd be acting unethically. You would have violated the purchasing supervisor's right to privacy.

The final question relates to whether the political activity conforms to standards of equity and justice. If you inflate the performance evaluation of a favored employee and deflate the evaluation of a disfavored employee, and then use these evaluations to justify giving the former a big raise and nothing to the latter, you have treated the disfavored employee unfairly and acted unethically.

HOW DO YOU KNOW WHEN YOU SHOULD PLAY POLITICS?

Before you consider your political options in any situation, you need to evaluate that situation. The key situational factors are your organization's culture, the power of others, and your own power.

Your Organization's Culture The place to begin is with assessing your organization's culture to determine which behaviors are desirable and which aren't.

Every organization has a system of shared meaning called its culture. This culture is a set of unwritten norms that members of the organization accept and understand and that guide their actions. For example, some organizations' cultures encourage risk taking, accept conflicts and disagreements, allow employees a great deal of autonomy, and reward members according to performance criteria. Other organizations' cultures differ by 180 degrees: They punish risk taking, seek harmony and cooperation at any price, minimize opportunities for employees to show initiative, and allocate rewards to

culture

A set of unwritten norms that members of the organization accept and understand, and that guide their actions.

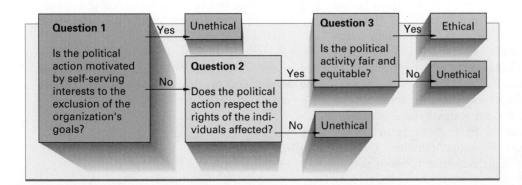

Exhibit 14-6

Is a political action ethical?

people according to such criteria as seniority, effort, or loyalty. The point is that every organization's culture is somewhat different, and if a political strategy is to succeed, it must be compatible with the culture (see "News Flash! Status in Organizations").

The Power of Others   Either people are powerful or they're not, right? Wrong! Power is differential. On some issues, a person may be very powerful. Yet that same person may be relatively powerless on other issues. What you need to do, therefore, is determine which individuals or groups will be powerful in a given situation.

Some people have influence as a result of their formal position in the organization. That is probably the best place to begin your power assessment. What decision or issue do you want to influence? Who has formal authority to affect that issue? The answer to that is only the beginning. After determining who has formal authority, consider others—individuals, coalitions, departments—who may have a vested interest in the decision's outcome. Who might gain or lose as a result of one choice being selected over another? This helps identify the power players—those motivated to engage in politicking. It also pinpoints your likely adversaries.

status
A social rank or the importance one has in a group.

News Flash!

STATUS IN ORGANIZATIONS

Traditionally in organizations, individuals who are politically shrewd often have the trimmings that go along with it. These things are grouped under the heading of status. Status is a social rank or the importance one has in a group. Status is not something a person gives himself or herself. Although an individual may have worked hard to achieve something, having status requires at least two people. That is, someone else must view that individual as having a higher ranking (in some capacity) than he or she does. A supervisor's status may come from a number of sources. Generally, these sources are grouped in two ways—formal and informal. Much of the discussion on power and politics, as well as authority, focuses on the formal aspects of status. For instance, the title *supervisor* carries a certain level of prestige with it. It implies that you have the ability to direct others and affect their work lives.

On the other hand, status may be informally conferred on a supervisor by characteristics such as education, age, skill, or experience. Anything a supervisor has can have status value if others evaluate it as such. Of course, just because status is informal does not mean that it is less important to a supervisor or that there is less agreement on whether one has it.

It is especially important in organizations to believe that the formal status system is fitting. That is, there should be fairness between perceived ranking and the status "symbols" given. If it is lacking, problems can arise between people

in organizations.[*] Consider a situation where the supervisor of the quality-control department has an office that is smaller, is located in a more isolated part of the organization, and is not as well furnished as that of a new employee just joining the unit. If one views importance in terms of the office and its furnishings, one might come to the conclusion that the new employee is more highly regarded than the supervisor is. That's probably not the case! Yet inconsistencies in status ranking have sent the wrong message.

Status may also affect employees' willingness to work hard. For instance, imagine the potential for conflict if employees earn more than their supervisor—and that's not as unrealistic as one might think! That's because the supervisor may be paid a fixed salary and be ineligible for overtime pay. The employees, on the other hand, are paid on an hourly basis and, after working more than forty hours in a week, earn time-and-a-half. If an employee works a lot of overtime, he or she could conceivably be making more money than the supervisor does. That can easily be controlled if the supervisor simply stops overtime outright. However, in doing so, the supervisor may be losing sight of the goals of the department. In such a case, status gets in the way of goal attainment!

---

[*]W. F. Whyte, "The Social Structure of the Restaurant," *American Journal of Sociology* 54 (January 1954), 302–308.

Now you need to specifically assess the power of each player or group of players. In addition to each one's formal authority, evaluate the resources each controls and his or her location in the organization. The control of scarce and important resources is a source of power in organizations. Control and access to key information, expert knowledge, and possession of special skills are examples of resources that may be scarce and important to the organization; hence, they become potential means of influencing organizational decisions. In addition, being in the right place in the organization can be a source of power. This explains, for example, the frequent power of administrative assistants. They are often in the direct flow of key information and control the access of others to their bosses.

Assess your boss's influence in any power analysis. What is his or her position on the issue under concern—for, against, or neutral? If it's for or against, how intense is your boss's stand? What is your boss's power status in the organization? Strong or weak? Answers to these questions can help you assess whether the support or opposition of your boss will be relevant.

Your Own Power After looking at others' power, assess your own power base. What's your personal power? What power does your supervisory position in the organization provide? Where do you stand relative to others who hold power?

Your power can come from several sources. If you've got a charismatic personality, for instance, you can exert power because others will want to know your position on issues, your arguments will often be perceived as persuasive, and your position is likely to carry considerable weight in others' decisions. Another frequent source of power for supervisors is access to important information that others in the organization need.

The Disciplinary Process

The phrase *conflict in an organization* conjures up some of the more emotional elements in any organization. But at no other time is conflict more evident that when a supervisor has to discipline an employee.

The purpose of this section is to help you understand why you may have to discipline an employee, how to do it properly, and how to minimize any potential and undue conflict that may arise. That's because any form of discipline can create fear or anger in employees. The supervisor who makes the discipline process less painful for the employee, behaves with compassion, and treats the employee with dignity is likely to find that more severe forms of disciplinary action become unnecessary. In cases where termination does occur, the employee is better able to handle it.

What specifically do we mean when we use the term discipline in the workplace? It refers to actions taken by a supervisor to enforce the organization's standards and regulations. It generally follows a typical sequence of four steps: verbal warning, written warning, suspension, and dismissal (see Exhibit 14-7).

The mildest form of discipline is the documented verbal warning. A verbal warning is a temporary record of a reprimand that a supervisor keeps. This verbal warning typically states the purpose, date, and outcome of the feedback session. If the verbal warning is effective, no further disciplinary action is needed. However, an employee who fails to improve his or her performance encounters more severe action—the written warning. The written warning is the first formal stage of the disciplinary procedure. This is because the written warning becomes part of an employee's official personnel file. In all other ways, however, the written warning is similar to the verbal warning. That is, the employee is advised in private of the violation, its effects, and potential consequences of future violations. Also, if no further disciplinary problems arise after a period of time, the warning is removed from the employee's file.

discipline
Actions taken by supervisors to enforce an organization's standards and regulations.

verbal warning
A reprimand, a temporary record of which is kept by the supervisor.

written warning
The first formal stage of the disciplinary procedure; the warning becomes part of an employee's official personnel file.

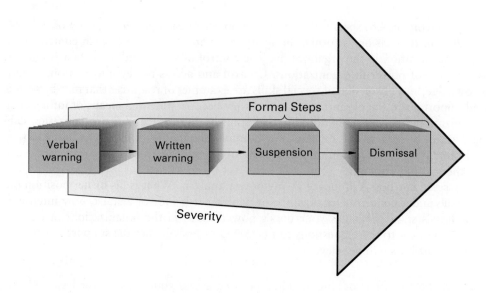

Exhibit 14-7
The discipline process.

suspension
Time off without pay; this step is usually taken only if neither verbal nor written warnings have achieved desired results.

dismissal
Termination of employment.

A suspension, or time off without pay, may be the next disciplinary step, usually taken only if the prior two steps have not achieved the desired results—although exceptions do exist where suspension may be given without any prior verbal or written warning if the infraction is of a serious nature. Why would you suspend an employee? One reason is that a short layoff, without pay, is potentially a rude awakening. It may convince the employee that you are serious and help him or her to fully understand and accept responsibility for following the organization's rules.

Your ultimate disciplinary punishment is terminating employment. Dismissal is often used for the most serious offenses, and it may be the only feasible alternative if your employee's behavior seriously interferes with a department's or the organization's operation.

Although many organizations may follow the process described here, recognize that it may be bypassed if an employee's behavior is extremely severe. For example, stealing or attacking another employee with intent to inflict serious harm may result in immediate suspension or dismissal. Regardless of any action taken, however, discipline should be fair and consistent. That is, the punishment an employee receives should be appropriate for what he or she did, and others doing the same thing should be disciplined in a like manner.

WHAT TYPES OF DISCIPLINE PROBLEMS MIGHT YOU FACE?

With very little difficulty, we could list several dozen or more infractions that supervisors might believe require disciplinary action. Basically, if the problem is associated with an employee's lack of desire to do the job, not with his or her abilities, it becomes a discipline problem. For simplicity's sake, we have classified the more frequent violations into four categories: attendance, on-the-job behaviors, dishonesty, and outside activities.

Attendance The most frequent disciplinary problems facing supervisors undoubtedly involve attendance. Attendance problems appear to be even more widespread than those related to productivity (carelessness in doing work, neglect of duty, and not following established procedures).

On-the-Job Behaviors The second category of discipline problems covers on-the-job behaviors. This blanket label includes insubordination, horseplay, fighting, gambling, failure to use safety devices, carelessness, and two of the most widely discussed problems in organizations today—alcohol and drug abuse.

Dishonesty Although it is not one of the more widespread employee problems confronting supervisors, dishonesty has traditionally resulted in the most severe disciplinary actions. It's a matter of trust. As a supervisor, you need to be able to trust your employees to do certain things or to handle information properly. Lying, cheating, or other aspects of dishonesty simply destroy an employee's credibility—and your trust in him or her.

Outside Activities This final problem category covers activities that employees engage in outside of work, but that either affect their on-the-job performance or generally reflect negatively on the organization's image. Included here are unauthorized strike activity, outside criminal activities, and working for a competing organization.

IS DISCIPLINE ALWAYS THE SOLUTION?

Just because you have a problem with an employee, don't assume that discipline is the automatic answer. Before you consider disciplining an employee, be sure that the employee has both the ability and the influence to correct his or her behavior.

If an employee doesn't have the ability—that is, he or she can't perform—disciplinary action is not the answer. Some employee coaching is! Employee coaching is a process designed to help employees overcome performance-related problems. Rather than viewing the performance problem from a punitive standpoint (discipline), employee coaching attempts to uncover why employees have lost their desire or ability to work productively. More importantly, it's designed to find ways to fix the problem. The premise behind employee coaching is fairly simple: It's beneficial to both the organization and the employee. Just as it's costly to have an employee quit shortly after being hired, it's costly to fire someone. But make no mistake about it, employee coaching is not intended to lessen the effect of an employee's poor performance, nor is it intended to reduce his or her responsibility to change inappropriate work behavior. If the employee can't or won't accept coaching help, then disciplinary actions must be taken.

Similarly, if there are external factors that block goal attainment and are beyond the employee's control—such as inadequate equipment, disruptive colleagues, or excessive noise—discipline doesn't make much sense either. If an employee can perform but won't, disciplinary action is called for. However, ability problems should be responded to with solutions such as skill training, job redesign, or a job transfer. Serious personal problems that interfere with work performance are typically best met with professional counseling, a medical referral, or employee assistance programs. Of course, if there are external obstacles in the employee's way, you should act to remove them. The point is that if the cause of an employee's problem is outside his or her control, discipline is not the answer.

BASIC TENETS OF DISCIPLINE

Based on decades of experience, supervisors have learned what works best when administering discipline. In the following sections, we review some of the lessons learned. We present the basic groundwork that needs to be laid prior to any punitive action, the importance of making discipline progressive, and how the "hot stove" rule can guide your actions (see the section titled "Disciplining an Employee" at the end of this chapter).

HOW DO YOU LAY THE GROUNDWORK FOR DISCIPLINE?

Any disciplinary action you take should be perceived as fair and reasonable. This increases the likelihood that the employee will change his or her behavior to align with the organization's standards. Such action also prevents unnecessary legal entanglements.

The foundation of a fair and reasonable disciplinary climate is created by ensuring that employees are given adequate advance notice of disciplining rules and that a proper investigation precedes any action.

Advance Notice "The best surprise is no surprise." This phrase, used a number of years ago by a national hotel chain to describe its rooms and service, is a valid guide for supervisors when considering discipline. Employees have a right to know what is expected of them and the probable consequences should they fail to meet those expectations. They should also understand just how serious different types of offenses are. This information can be communicated in employee handbooks, company newsletters, posted rules, or labor contracts. It is always preferable to have these expectations in writing. This provides protection for you, the organization, and your employees.

Paper trail
Documentary written evidence of an employee's activities that tells what has transpired over a given period of time.

Paper Trail A paper trail is extremely important when disciplinary action is taken. Employees and supervisors may be asked to explain what happened in detail. A supervisor can be protected if careful documentation is done. If an employee tries to refute the claim leading to discipline, a supervisor can use the paper trail to prove that appropriate steps were taken in the disciplinary process.

A paper trail begins with providing the supervisor with written job descriptions that establish expectations for each specific job. Employees should be aware of and sign their job description. Also, the organization should have written employee policies that establish expectations for all employees along with written acknowledgements of receipt. Poor performance, behavior, attitude, and so on should never be allowed to continue without comment because failing to do so implies acceptance. Supervisors should keep a log of observations and conversations and, after a number of conversations, a note should be written to the employee's personnel file. Employee training and/or coaching where appropriate along with training completion certificates and file memos to document what transpired are all part of the paper trail. If the complaint involves attendance issues, all written notes/e-mails regarding absences should be retained. Verbal warnings should be documented when given and a file memo drafted to document what transpired. Written warnings should include copies to the personnel file and employee. An attempt should be made to have the employee sign the file copy of the warning or the supervisor should write "refused to sign." Supervisors should also create a separate file memo to document any conversation occurring when the warning was given. Always remember to have employees sign written acknowledgements of policies received and similar other things. Accurate annual performance appraisals should never include inappropriate "satisfactory" ratings when the performance is not acceptable. Finally, the employee's file should include evidence of all communication of employee expectations, as well as evidence of employee's ability, or inability, to meet those expectations, and finally, evidence of any coaching, counseling, or discipline given the employee.[4]

Proper Investigation Fair treatment of employees demands that a proper investigation precede any decision. Just as in the U.S. legal system, employees should be treated as innocent until proven guilty. Also important is that no judgment occur before all the relevant facts have been gathered.

As the employee's supervisor, you will typically be responsible for conducting the investigation. However, if the problem includes an interpersonal conflict between you and the employee, a neutral third party should be chosen to conduct the investigation.

---

[4]D. Lindeman, "Creating a Paper Trail Supports Discipline and Discharge Decisions," *Human Resouces IQ*, August 2008, http://www.humanresourcesiq.com/employment-law/columns/creating-a-paper-trail-supports-discipline-and-dis/ (accessed May 26, 2011).

The investigation should focus not only on the event that might lead to discipline but also on any related matters. This is important because these related concerns may reveal extenuating factors that will need to be considered. Of course, the employee must be notified of the offense with which he or she is being charged so that a defense can be prepared. Remember, you have an obligation to listen objectively to the employee's interpretation and explanation of the offense. A fair and objective investigation includes identifying and interviewing any witnesses and documenting all evidence that is uncovered.

Failure to conduct a full and impartial investigation can carry high costs. A good employee may be unjustly punished, the trust of other employees may be severely jeopardized, and you may place your organization under risk for financial damages should the employee file a lawsuit.

HOW DO YOU MAKE DISCIPLINE PROGRESSIVE?

Punishment should be applied in steps. That is, penalties should get progressively stronger if, or when, an offense is repeated. As we mentioned previously (see Exhibit 14-7), progressive disciplinary action begins with a verbal warning, and then proceeds through written reprimands, suspension, and finally, in the most serious cases, dismissal.

The logic underlying progressive discipline is twofold. First, stronger penalties for repeated offenses discourage repetition. Second, progressive discipline is consistent with court and arbitration rulings that mitigating factors (e.g., length of service, past performance record, or ambiguous organizational policies) be considered when taking disciplinary action.[5]

The "hot stove" rule is a frequently suggested set of principles that can guide you in effectively disciplining an employee. The name comes from the similarities between touching a hot stove and receiving discipline (see Exhibit 14-8).

Both are painful, but the analogy goes further. When you touch a hot stove, you get an immediate response. The burn you receive is instantaneous, leaving no doubt in your mind about the cause and the effect. You have ample warning. You know what happens if you touch a red-hot stove. Further, the result is consistent. Every time you touch a hot stove, you get the same response—you get burned. Finally, the result is impartial. Regardless of who you are, if you touch a hot stove, you will be burned. The analogy with discipline should be apparent, but let's briefly expand on each of these four points because they are central tenets in developing your disciplining skills.

Immediacy The impact of a disciplinary action is reduced as the time between the infraction and the penalty's implementation lengthens. The more quickly the discipline follows the offense, the more likely that the employee will associate the discipline with the offense rather than with you as the imposer of the discipline. Therefore, it is best to begin the disciplinary process as soon as possible after you notice a violation. Of course, the immediacy requirement should not

progressive discipline
Action that begins with a verbal warning, and then proceeds through written reprimands, suspension, and finally, in the most serious cases, dismissal.

"hot stove" rule
A set of principles for effectively disciplining an employee that demonstrates the analogy between touching a hot stove and receiving discipline.

Exhibit 14-8
The "hot stove" rule.

---

[5] S. Bahls and J. E. Bahls, "Fire Proof," *Entrepreneur*, July 2002, 70.

result in undue haste. Fair and objective treatment should not be compromised for expediency.

Advance Warning As noted earlier, you have an obligation to give advance warning before initiating formal disciplinary action. This means that the employee must be aware of the organization's rules and accept its standards of behavior. Disciplinary action is more likely to be interpreted as fair by employees when they have received clear warning that a given violation will lead to discipline and when they know what that discipline will be.

Consistency Fair treatment of employees demands that disciplinary action be consistent. If you enforce rule violations in an inconsistent manner, the rules will lose their impact. Morale will decline and employees will question your competence. Productivity will suffer as a result of employee insecurity and anxiety. Your employees want to know the limits of permissible behavior, and they look to your actions for guidance. If Cindy is reprimanded today for something that she also did last week, when nothing was said, these limits become blurry. Similarly, if Sam and John are both goofing around at their desks and only Sam is reprimanded, Sam is likely to question the fairness of the action. The point, then, is that discipline should be consistent. This need not result in treating everyone exactly alike because that ignores mitigating circumstances. It does put the responsibility on you to clearly justify disciplinary actions that may appear inconsistent to employees.

Impartiality The last guideline that flows from the "hot stove" rule is to keep the discipline impartial. Penalties should be connected with a given violation, not with the personality of the violator. That is, discipline should be directed at what the employee has done, not at the employee personally. As a supervisor, you should make it clear that you are avoiding personal judgments about the employee's character. You are penalizing the rule violation, not the individual. All employees committing the violation can expect to be penalized. Further, once the penalty has been imposed, you must make every effort to forget the incident. You should attempt to treat the employee in the same manner that you did prior to the infraction.

WHAT FACTORS SHOULD YOU CONSIDER IN DISCIPLINE?

Defining what is "reasonable in relation to the offense" is one of the most challenging aspects of the discipline process. Why? Because infractions vary greatly in terms of severity. Suspending an employee is considerably more stringent than issuing a verbal warning. Similarly, firing someone—the organizational equivalent of the death penalty—is dramatically more punitive than a two-week suspension without pay. If you fail to recognize relevant extenuating factors and make the proper adjustments in the severity of penalties, you risk having your action perceived as unfair. The factors summarized in Exhibit 14-9 should be taken into consideration when applying discipline.

WHAT ABOUT THE LAW?

Making a mistake in disciplining an employee can have very serious repercussions for an organization. As a result, most

- Seriousness of the problem
- Duration of the problem
- Frequency and nature of the problem
- Employee's work history
- Extenuating circumstances
- Degree of warning
- History of the organization's discipline practices
- Implications for other employees
- Upper-management support

Exhibit 14-9
Relevant factors determining the severity of penalties.

large organizations have specific procedures that supervisors are required to follow. Supervisors typically are trained in how to handle the discipline process.

Beginning in the late 1800s, the major legal doctrine that defined an employer's right to discipline or discharge an employee was the concept of employment-at-will. The employment-at-will doctrine permitted employers to discipline or discharge employees at their discretion. The premise behind this doctrine is to equalize the playing field. If employees can resign at any time they want, shouldn't an employer have the same right to terminate the relationship?

Under the employment-at-will doctrine, an employer can dismiss an employee "for good cause, for no cause, or even for a cause morally wrong, without being guilty of a legal wrong."[6] Of course, even so, you can't fire on the basis of race, religion, sex, national origin, age, or disability. Although this doctrine has existed for more than a hundred years, the courts, labor unions, and legislation have attempted to lessen its use. In these instances, jobs are being likened to private property. That is, individuals have a right to these jobs unless the organization has specified otherwise. Employees today are challenging the legality of their discharge more frequently. Employees fired without cause may seek the assistance of the courts to address their wrongful discharge. Most states permit employees to sue their employers if they believe their termination was unjust. At issue in these suits is whether, through some action on the part of the employer, exceptions to the employment-at-will doctrine exist. Today, should you fire an employee, you and your employer may end up in court defending yourselves against claims of wrongful discharge or improperly terminating the employee.

As the courts have moved to protect an employee's right to his or her job, most organizations have responded by tightening up their hiring and discipline practices. They are carefully reviewing their hiring processes to remove any implied employment contracts. In the past, employment handbooks, interviewers, and supervisors often gave implied guarantees or promises about continued employment. The courts have interpreted such written and verbal statements as implied contracts that protect employees against termination. So, as a supervisor, you should be careful not to make any statement to an employee such as "we never lay people off here" or "you'll have a place with this company as long as you do your job."

The courts have also become increasingly concerned with ensuring that when an employee is terminated, the employee's rights have not been abused and discipline has been fairly imposed. Proper documentation of all disciplinary action is the best protection against employees who claim, "I never knew there was any problem," or "I was treated unfairly." In addition, you will want to obey due process when taking any disciplinary action. This includes (1) a presumption of innocence until reasonable proof of an employee's role in an offense is substantiated; (2) the right of the employee to be heard, and in some cases to be represented by another person; and (3) discipline that is reasonable in relation to the offense involved.

Negotiation

We know that lawyers and auto salespeople spend a significant amount of time on their jobs negotiating. So, too, do supervisors. They have to negotiate salaries for incoming employees, cut deals with their bosses, work out differences with their peers, and resolve conflicts with employees. For our purposes, we define negotiation as a process in which two or more parties who have different preferences must make a joint decision and come to an agreement. To achieve this goal, both parties typically use a bargaining strategy.

employment-at-will
A legal doctrine that defines an employer's rights to discipline or discharge an employee.

wrongful discharge
Improper or unjust termination of an employee.

negotiation
A process in which two or more parties who have different preferences and priorities must make a joint decision and come to an agreement.

---

[6]*Payne v. Western and Atlantic Railroad Co.*, 812 Tenn. 507 (1884). See also C. Hirschman, "Off Duty, Out of Work," *HR Magazine*, February 2003, 51–52.

HOW DO BARGAINING STRATEGIES DIFFER?

There are two general approaches to negotiation—distributive bargaining and integrative bargaining.[7] Let's see what's involved in each of these approaches.

Suppose you see a used car advertised for sale in the newspaper. It appears to be just what you've been looking for. You go out to see the car. It's great and you want it. The owner tells you the asking price. You don't want to pay that much. The two of you then negotiate over the price. The negotiating process you are engaging in is called distributive bargaining. Its most identifying feature is that it operates under zero-sum conditions. That is, any gain you make is at the expense of the other person, and vice versa. Referring to the used car example, every dollar you can get the seller to cut from the car's price is a dollar you save. Conversely, every dollar more he or she can get from you comes at your expense. Thus, the essence of distributive bargaining is negotiating over who gets what share of a fixed pie.

Probably the most widely cited example of distributive bargaining is in labor–management negotiations over wages and benefits (see Chapter 16). Typically, labor's representatives come to the bargaining table determined to get as much as they can from management. Because every cent more that labor negotiates increases management's costs, each party bargains aggressively and often treats the other as an opponent who must be defeated. In distributive bargaining, each party has a target point that defines what it would like to achieve. Each also has a resistance point that marks the lowest outcome that's acceptable (see Exhibit 14-10). The area between their resistance points is the settlement range. As long as there is some overlap in their aspiration ranges, there exists a settlement area where each one's aspirations can be met.

When you are engaged in distributive bargaining, your tactics should focus on trying to get your opponent to agree to your specific target point or to get as close to it as possible. Examples of such tactics are persuading your opponent of the impossibility of getting to his or her target point and the advisability of accepting a settlement near yours; arguing that your target is fair, while your opponent's isn't; and attempting to get your opponent to feel emotionally generous toward you and thus accept an outcome close to your target point.

Suppose a sales representative for a women's sportswear manufacturer has just closed a $35,000 order from a small clothing retailer. The sales rep calls in the order to her firm's credit department. She is told that the firm can't approve credit to this customer because of a past slow-pay record. The next day, the sales rep and the firm's credit supervisor meet to discuss the problem. The sales rep doesn't want to lose the business. Neither does the credit supervisor, but he also doesn't want to get stuck with an uncollectible debt. The two openly review their options. After considerable

distributive bargaining
A negotiating process that operates under zero-sum conditions; any gain made is at the expense of the other person, and vice versa.

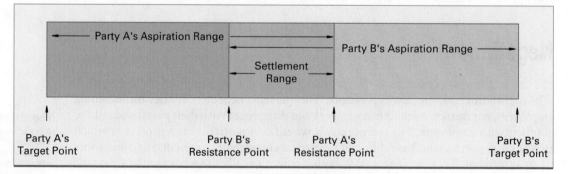

Exhibit 14-10

Staking out the bargaining zone, or settlement range.

[7]R. E. Walton and R. B. McKersie, *Behavioral Theory of Labor Relations: An Analysis of a Social Interaction System* (New York: McGraw-Hill, 1965).

discussion, they agree on a solution that meets both their needs. The credit supervisor will approve the sale, but the clothing store's owner must provide a bank guarantee that assures payment if the bill isn't paid within sixty days.

The sales credit negotiation is an example of integrative bargaining. In contrast to distributive bargaining, integrative problem solving operates under the assumption that there is at least one settlement that can create a win–win solution. In general, integrative bargaining is preferable to distributive bargaining. Why? Because the former builds long-term relationships and facilitates working together in the future. It bonds negotiators and allows each to leave the bargaining table feeling that he or she has achieved a victory. Distributive bargaining, on the other hand, leaves one party a potential loser. It tends to build animosities and deepen divisions between people who have to work together on an ongoing basis.

Why, then, don't we see more integrative bargaining in organizations? The answer lies in the conditions necessary for this type of negotiation to succeed. These conditions include openness with information and frankness between parties; a sensitivity by each party to the other's needs; the ability to trust one another; and a willingness by both parties to maintain flexibility.[8] Because many organizational cultures and intraorganizational relationships are not characterized by openness, trust, and flexibility, it isn't surprising that negotiations often take on a win-at-any-cost dynamic. With that in mind, let's look at some suggestions for negotiating successfully.

integrative bargaining
A negotiating process that operates under the assumption that there is at least one settlement that can create a win–win solution.

HOW DO YOU DEVELOP EFFECTIVE NEGOTIATION SKILLS?

The essence of effective negotiation can be summarized in the following six recommendations.[9]

Consider the Other Party's Situation Acquire as much information as you can about your opponent's interests and goals. What constituencies must he or she appease? What is his or her strategy? This information will help you understand your opponent's behavior, predict responses to your offers, and frame solutions in terms of the opponent's interests. Additionally, when you can anticipate your opponent's position, you are better equipped to counter his or her arguments with the facts and figures that support your position.

Have a Concrete Strategy Treat negotiation like a chess match. Expert chess players have a strategy. They know ahead of time how they will respond to any given situation. How strong is your situation and how important is the issue? Are you willing to split differences to achieve an early solution? If the issue is very important to you, is your position strong enough to let you play hardball and show little or no willingness to compromise? These are questions you should address before you begin bargaining.

Begin with a Positive Overture Studies on negotiation show that concessions tend to be reciprocated and lead to agreements. Thus, you should begin bargaining with a positive overture—perhaps a small concession—and then reciprocate your opponent's concessions.

---

[8]K. W. Thomas, "Conflict and Negotiation Processes in Organizations," in M. D. Dunnette and L. M. Hough (ed.), *Handbook of Industrial and Organizational Psychology*, 2nd ed., vol. 3, (Palo Alto, CA: Consulting Psychologists Press, 1992), pp. 651–717.
[9]Based on R. Fisher and W. Ury, *Getting to Yes: Negotiating Agreement without Giving In* (Boston, MA: Houghton Mifflin, 1981); J. A. Wall, Jr., and M. W. Blum, "Negotiations," *Journal of Management,* 17, no. 2 (June 1991), 295–296; and M. H. Bazerman and M. A. Neale, *Negotiating Rationally* (New York: Free Press, 1992).

Address Problems, Not Personalities Concentrate on the negotiation issues, not on the personal characteristics of your opponent. When negotiations get tough, avoid the tendency to attack your opponent. It's your opponent's ideas or position that you disagree with, not him or her personally. Separate the people from the problem, and don't personalize differences.

Something to Think About (and promote class discussion)

HAND ME A TOWEL

Like many revolts, it began with something simple.[*] At Microsoft, it was the vanishing towels. For employees who biked to work through the often-drizzly weather in Seattle, the provided towels had become an entitlement. However, one day when employees came to work, the towels were gone—pulled without notice from the locker rooms in the company's underground garage. The company's human resources manager thought removing the towels, which had been done as a cost-saving measure, "wouldn't even be a blip." But it was. Irate employees waged war on company message boards and blogs. One post fumed, "It is a dark and dreary day at One Microsoft Way. Do yourself a favor and stay away." The intensity of the comments shocked senior executives. The towel fiasco, in conjunction with a languishing stock price and a little bit of "Google envy," suggested a serious morale problem and a need to bring in a new face to HR. Lisa Brummel, a successful Microsoft product development manager with no HR experience, was tapped to become the new HR chief. Her mandate: Improve the mood around here. And Lisa, who had always been a strong people leader, stepped up to do just that.

In addition to reinstating the towels (a no-brainer), Lisa looked for other ways that the company could reshape HR at Microsoft. And in doing so, she brought a unique and insightful understanding of human behavior. One thing she did was to introduce innovative office designs that allowed employees to reconfigure their workspaces for the task they were working on. The customized workspaces included options such as sliding doors, movable walls, and features that made the space seem more like an urban loft than an office. When beginning a workspace redesign, "employees are first divided into four worker types: providers (the godfathers of work groups), travelers (the types who work anywhere but work), concentrators (head-down, always-at-work types), and orchestrators (the company's natural diplomats)." Based on their "type," employees then pick the kind of workspace that works best for them. By allowing their creative, quirky, and talented people freedom to design their workspaces, the company was able to give them some control over their chaotic and often hectic environment.

With Lisa at the helm of HR, the company has made progress in its people policies. Yet, sometimes a decision coming out of One Microsoft Way (company headquarters) still makes you scratch your head and wonder why. The most recent was when twenty-five recently laid-off employees were asked to return an overpayment of severance pay. The amount, a small sum, came to about $5,000 per employee. But by asking for this money back, this billion-dollar organization didn't send a very good message, especially when trying to improve morale and keep employees excited and engaged with their work. Once again, Lisa stepped up. She made the calls to the employees involved and said that the company hadn't handled the situation in a "thoughtful manner" and the money was theirs to keep. Like any successful manager, Lisa recognizes the importance of people skills.

What do you think? Should Microsoft have stayed firm in its resolve to cut costs, even at the risk of upsetting the corporate culture? Did the employees have any bargaining power in this situation? Was the original towel resolution an example of distributive or integrative bargaining? How would you classify Lisa's solution—distributive or integrative bargaining? Why, what makes it one or the other? Did this conflict result in a creative outcome? Why or why not?

---

[*]M. Conlin, "Making the Case for Unequal Pay and Perks," *BusinessWeek Online*, March 12, 2009; "Good Job, Microsoft," *The Bing Blog*, http://stanleybing.blogs.fortune.cnn.com (February 24, 2009); M. Conlin and J. Greene, "How to Make a Microserf Smile," *BusinessWeek*, September 10, 2007, 56–59; M. Conlin, "Online Extra: Microsoft's Meet-My-Mood Offices," *BusinessWeek Online*, September 10, 2007; and M. Conlin and J. Greene, "Online Extra: Reshaping Microsoft's HR Agenda," *BusinessWeek Online*, September 10, 2007.

Pay Little Attention to Initial Offers Treat an initial offer as merely a point of departure. Everyone has to have an initial position. These initial offers tend to be extreme and idealistic. Treat them as such.

Emphasize Win–Win Solutions Bargainers often assume that their gain must come at the expense of the other party. As noted with integrative bargaining, that needn't be the case. There are often win–win solutions. If you assume a zero-sum game, you may miss opportunities for trade-offs that could benefit both sides. So, if conditions are supportive, look for an integrative solution. Frame options in terms of your opponent's interests and look for solutions that can allow your opponent, as well as you, to declare a victory.

Comprehension Check 14-2

5. Actions taken to influence the distribution of advantages and disadvantages in the organization are called

   a. power
   b. influence
   c. politicking
   d. all of the above

6. A set of unwritten norms that organizational members accept and understand is called

   a. a code of ethics
   b. a culture
   c. influence
   d. supervision

7. One's social rank in an organization reflects one's

   a. position
   b. influence
   c. authority
   d. status

8. The first formal step in the disciplinary process is the

   a. suspension
   b. written warning
   c. verbal warning
   d. none of the above

9. Which one of the following is *not* a characteristic of the "hot stove" rule?

   a. Advance warning
   b. Flexibility
   c. Impartiality
   d. Immediacy

Enhancing Understanding

SUMMARY

After reading this chapter, I can:

1. **Define** *conflict*. Conflict is a process in which one party consciously interferes with the goal-achievement efforts of another party.

2. **Identify the three general sources of conflict.** Conflicts generally come from one of three sources: communication differences, structural differentiation, or personal differences.

3. **List the five basic techniques for resolving conflict.** The five basic techniques for resolving conflict are avoidance, accommodation, forcing, compromise, and collaboration.

4. **Describe how a supervisor could stimulate conflict.** A supervisor could stimulate conflict by communicating ambiguous messages or planting rumors, bringing in outsiders with different backgrounds or personalities, restructuring the department, or appointing a devil's advocate.

5. **Define** *politicking*. Politicking consists of the actions you can take to influence, or attempt to influence, the distribution of advantages and disadvantages within your department.

6. **Explain the existence of politics in organizations.** Politics exist in organizations because individuals have different values, goals, and interests; organizational resources are limited; the criteria for allocating the limited resources are ambiguous; and individuals seek influence so that they can shape the criteria to support their goals and interests.

7. **Define** *discipline* **and the four most common types of discipline problems.** Discipline refers to actions taken to enforce the organization's rules and standards. The four most common types of discipline problems facing a supervisor are (1) attendance issues such as absenteeism, tardiness, and abuse of sick leave; (2) on-the-job behaviors such as insubordination and substance abuse; (3) dishonesty; and (4) outside activities that affect on-the-job performance or reflect poorly on the organization.

8. **List the typical steps in progressive discipline.** The typical steps in a progressive disciplinary process are (1) a verbal warning that is documented, (2) a written reprimand, (3) suspension, and (4) dismissal.

9. **Contrast distributive and integrative bargaining.** Distributive bargaining creates a win–lose situation because the object of negotiation is treated as fixed in amount. Integrative bargaining treats available resources as variable, and hence creates the potential for win–win solutions.

COMPREHENSION: Review and Discussion Questions

1. How can conflict benefit an organization?

2. What is conflict management?

3. When should you avoid conflict? When should you seek compromise?

4. What is a devil's advocate? How does a devil's advocate produce conflict in a department?

5. Can an organization be free of politics? Explain.

6. How do you assess another person's power in an organization?

7. "A good supervisor will never have to use discipline." Do you agree or disagree with this statement? Discuss.

8. Why is it important to document any disciplinary action you take against an employee?

9. Why is discipline not always the best solution?

10. Assume you found an apartment that you wanted to rent and the ad said: "$550/month negotiable." What could you do to improve the likelihood that you would negotiate the lowest possible price?

KEY CONCEPT CROSSWORD

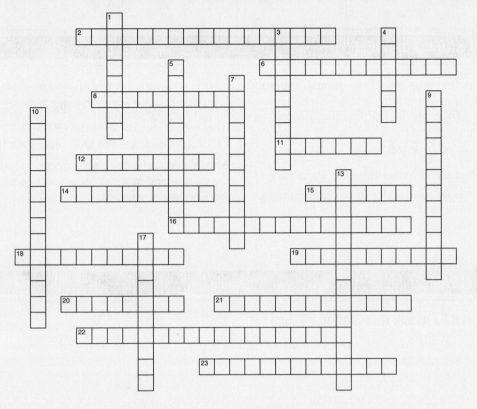

ACROSS

2. improper or unjust termination of an employee
6. an approach to conflict in which all parties seek to satisfy their interests
8. an approach to conflict that requires each party to give up something of value
11. a set of unwritten norms that members of the organization accept and understand, and that guide their actions
12. termination of employment
14. time off without pay
15. an approach to conflict in which one attempts to satisfy one's own needs at the expense of the other party
16. a legal doctrine that defines an employer's rights to discipline or discharge an employee
18. the actions one can take to influence the distribution of advantages
19. a bargaining process that operates under the assumption that there is at least one settlement that can create a win–win situation
20. a process in which one part consciously interferes in the efforts of another party
21. a method of maintaining harmonious relationships by placing others' needs above one's own
22. an application of techniques designed to achieve the optimum level of departmental conflict
23. an oral reprimand

DOWN

1. an analogy for a set of principles for effectively disciplining an employee
3. an approach to conflict whereby one withdraws from a conflict
4. a social rank of the importance one has in a group
5. a type of discipline that begins with a verbal warning and may end in dismissal
7. a process in which two or more parties who have different preferences come together to reach an agreement
9. a bargaining process that operates under the zero-sum premise
10. a person who purposely presents arguments that run counter to those proposed by the majority
13. the first formal stage of the disciplinary process
17. actions taken by a supervisor to enforce an organization's standards

ANSWERS TO COMPREHENSION CHECKS

Comprehension Check 14-1

1. False   2. b   3. c   4. d

Comprehension Check 14-2

5. c   6. b   7. d   8. b   9. b

Developing Your Supervisory Skills

GETTING TO KNOW YOURSELF

Before you can effectively supervise others, you must understand your present strengths and areas in need of development. To assist in this learning process, we encourage you to complete the following self-assessments from the Prentice Hall Self-Assessment Library 3.4.

1. What's My Preferred Conflict-Handling Style? (II. C. 5.)
2. What's My Negotiating Style? (II. C. 6.)

3. How Creative Am I? (I. A. 5.)
4. How Good Am I at Playing Politics? (II. C. 3.)
5. How Well Do I Manage Impressions? (II. C. 4.)
6. How Good Am I at Disciplining Others? (II. B. 5.)

After you complete the assessment, we suggest you retain the results and store them as part of your "portfolio of learning about yourself."

BUILDING A TEAM

➤ An Experiential Exercise: Negotiating a Raise

Break into pairs for this role-play exercise. One person will play the role of Terry, the department supervisor. The other person will play Dale, Terry's boss.

The Situation

Terry and Dale work for Nike in Portland, Oregon. They are both former college runners who have worked for Nike for more than six years. Terry supervises a research laboratory. Dale is the manager of research and development. Dale has been Terry's boss for two years.

One of Terry's employees, Barbara, has greatly impressed Terry. Barbara was hired eleven months ago. She is twenty-six years old and holds a master's degree in mechanical engineering. Her entry-level salary was $42,500 a year. Terry told her that, in accordance with corporate policy, she would receive an initial performance evaluation at six months and a comprehensive review after one year. Based on her performance record, Barbara was told she could expect a salary adjustment at the time of the one-year evaluation.

Terry's evaluation of Barbara after six months was very positive. Terry commented on the long hours Barbara was putting in, her cooperative spirit, the fact that others in the lab enjoyed working with her, and that she was making an immediate positive impact on the project she had been assigned. Now that Barbara's first anniversary is coming up, Terry has again reviewed Barbara's performance. Terry thinks Barbara may be the best new person the R&D group has ever hired. After only a year, Terry has rated Barbara as the number-three-ranked performer in a department of eleven. Salaries in the department vary greatly. Terry, for instance, has a basic salary of $67,000, plus eligibility for a bonus that might add another $8,000 to $11,000 a year. The salary range of the eleven department members is $36,400 to $61,350. The lowest salary is a recent hire with a bachelor's degree in physics. The two people that Terry has rated above Barbara earn base salaries of $49,700 and $53,350. They're both thirty-one years old and have been at Nike for three and four years, respectively. The median salary in Terry's department is $52,660.

Terry's Role

You want to give Barbara a big raise. Although she's been with your unit only eleven months, she has proven to be an excellent addition to the department. You don't want to lose her. More important, she knows in general what other people in the department are earning and she thinks she's underpaid. The company typically gives one-year raises of 5 percent, although 10 percent is not unusual and 20 to 30 percent increases have been approved on occasion. You'd like to get Barbara as large an increase as Dale will approve.

Dale's Role

All your supervisors typically try to squeeze you for as much money as they can for their people. You understand this because you did the same thing when you were a supervisor. However, your boss wants to keep a lid on costs. He wants you to keep raises for recent hires generally in the 5 to 8 percent range. In fact, he's sent a memo to all managers and supervisors saying this. However, your boss is also very concerned with equity and paying people what they're worth. You feel assured that he will support any salary recommendation you make, as long as it can be justified. Your goal, consistent with cost reduction, is to keep salary increases as low as possible.

Terry has a meeting scheduled with Dale to discuss Barbara's performance review and salary adjustment. Take up to fifteen minutes to conduct your negotiation. When your negotiation is complete, the class will compare the various negotiation strategies used and compare outcomes.

Six Steps to Resolve Conflict

Conflict often results from unmet needs, disruptive behaviors of others, and circumstances arising as the result of the behavior of others. The most effective conflict resolution strategies depend on communication of the problem to the parties involved. A simple strategy to resolve conflict follows six steps.

1. **Identify problem ownership.** You may own the problem because you are the one bothered or someone else may own the problem because your behavior is offensive to them.
2. **Research and reflect.** Gather information related to the problem as you check your facts and test your assumptions and perceptions by self-reflecting on the problem.
3. **Select an alternative to follow.** When a conflict results from a behavior or an unacceptable situation, you can choose one of three alternatives. You can (1) change your attitude, (2) change your environment, or (3) confront the person regarding their behavior.
4. **Rehearse.** Get somone to role-play the situation with you and rehearse multiple scenarios so that you can experience your own emotional reaction to the issue before you interact with the involved parties.
5. **Meet to resolve the issue.** You have two goals in this step. First, you want to make the other person aware of your problem by engaging in a conversation regarding the issues, but you must control your anger and remember to send I-messages. Second, you must engage in conflict resolution by offering and agreeing to options acceptable to you and the other party.
6. **Follow through and follow up.** After implementing the resolution, you must continuously monitor the situation to ensure that the agreement is being honored, and you must look for unforseen problems that may have been created.

Source: C. Goodwin and D. Griffith, *The Conflict Survival Kit: Tools for Resolving Conflict at Work* (Upper Saddle River, NJ: Pearson Prentice Hall, 2007), 133–144.

➤ Internet: Web Activity

Go to http://www.pearsonhighered.com/robbins/. Find *Supervision Today!* 7th Ed. and click Companion Website.

DISCIPLINING AN EMPLOYEE

Disciplining an employee is not an easy task. It is often painful for both parties involved. The following dozen principles, however, should guide you when you have to discipline an employee.

STEPS IN PRACTICING THE SKILL

STEP 1: Before you accuse anyone, do your homework. What happened? If you didn't personally see the infraction, investigate and verify any accusations made by others. Was it completely the employee's fault? If not, who or what else was involved? Did the employee know and understand the rule or regulation that was broken? Document the facts: date, time, place, individuals involved, mitigating circumstances, and the like.

STEP 2: Was ample warning provided? Before you take formal action, be sure you've provided the employee with reasonable previous warnings and that those warnings have been documented. Ask yourself: If challenged, will my action be defensible? Did I provide ample warning to the employee before taking formal action? It's very likely that applying stiffer punitive actions later on will be judged as unjust by the employee, an arbitrator, and the courts if it is determined that these punitive actions could not be readily anticipated by the employee.

STEP 3: Act in a timely fashion. When you become aware of an infraction and it has been supported by your investigation, do something and do it quickly. Delay weakens the linkage between actions and consequences, sends the wrong message to others, undermines your credibility with your subordinates, creates doubt that any action will be taken, and invites repetition of the problem.

STEP 4: Conduct the discipline session in private. Praise employees in public but keep punishment private. Your objective is not to humiliate the violator. Public reprimands embarrass an employee

and are unlikely to produce the change in behavior you desire.

STEP 5: Adopt a calm and serious tone. Many interpersonal situations are facilitated by a loose, informal, and relaxed manner on the part of a supervisor. The idea in such situations is to put the employee at ease. Administering discipline is not one of those situations. Avoid anger or other emotional responses, but convey your comments in a calm and serious tone. Do not try to lessen the tension by cracking jokes or making small talk. Such actions are only likely to confuse the employee because they send out conflicting signals.

STEP 6: Be specific about the problem. When you sit down with the employee, indicate that you have documentation and be specific about the problem. Define the violation in exact terms instead of just citing company regulations or the union contract. It's not the breaking of the rules per se that you want to convey concern over. It's the effect that the rule violation has on the work unit's performance. Explain why the behavior can't be continued by showing how it specifically affects the employee's job performance, the unit's effectiveness, and the employee's coworkers.

STEP 7: Keep it impersonal. Criticism should be focused on the employee's behavior rather than on the individual personally. For instance, if an employee has been late for work several times, point out how this behavior has increased the workload of others or has lowered departmental morale. Don't criticize the person for being thoughtless or irresponsible.

STEP 8: Get the employee's side of the story. Regardless of what your investigation has revealed, and even if you have the proverbial "smoking gun" to support your accusations, due process demands that you give the employee the opportunity to explain his or her position. From the employee's perspective, what happened? Why did it happen? What was his or her perception of the rules, regulations, and circumstances? If there are significant discrepancies between your version of the violation and the employee's, you may need to do more investigating. Of course, you'll want to document your employee's response for the record.

STEP 9: Keep control of the discussion. In most interpersonal exchanges with employees, you want to encourage open dialogue. You want to give up control and create a climate of communication between equals. This won't work in administering discipline. Why? Violators are prone to use any allowed egalitarianism to put you on the defensive. In other words, if you don't take control, they will. Discipline, by definition, is an authority-based act. You are enforcing the organization's standards and regulations. So take control. Ask the employee for his or her side of the story. Get the facts. But don't let the employee interrupt you or divert you from your objective.

STEP 10: Agree on how mistakes can be prevented next time. Discipline should include guidance and direction for correcting the problem. Let the employee state what he or she plans to do in the future to ensure that the violation isn't repeated. For serious violations, have the employee draft a step-by-step plan to change the problem behavior. Then, set a timetable, with follow-up meetings in which progress can be evaluated.

STEP 11: Select progressive disciplinary action and consider mitigating circumstances. Choose a punishment that is appropriate to the crime. The punishment you select should be viewed as fair and consistent. Once you've arrived at your decision, tell the employee what the action will be, your reasons for taking it, and when it will be carried out.

STEP 12: Fully document the disciplinary session. To complete your disciplinary action, make sure that your ongoing documentation (what occurred, the results of your investigation, your initial warnings, the employee's explanation and responses, the discipline decision, and the consequences of further misconduct) is complete and accurate. This full documentation should be made part of the employee's permanent file. In addition, it's a good idea to give the employee a formal letter that highlights what was resolved during your discussion, specifics about the punishment, future expectations, and what actions you are prepared to take if the behavior isn't corrected or the violation is repeated.

➤ Communicating Effectively

1. Do some research on male versus female conflict-handling styles. Provide a two- to three-page summary of what you've found. Here are two guiding questions: Do women and men handle conflict differently? If so, what are the implications of your findings for supervisors?

2. Develop a paper arguing the pros and cons of the employment-at-will doctrine from the supervisor's perspective. After presenting both sides of the issue, select the side you support and describe why.

THINKING CRITICALLY

➤ Case 14-A: Social Networking Gone Wrong

A young doctor at a local community hospital was upset by content posted by other doctors, nurses, and interns on a popular social networking site. These doctors and nurses discussed their work, including specific cases they had. Their postings included derogatory comments and slurs about the economically disadvantaged, mentally disturbed, and homosexual clients they treated on a regular basis. They also commented that the upper class citizenry and politicians of the city deigned to use the services of the hospital, preferring instead to go to a large privately owned hospital outside of town. Photos of these doctors and nurses on their pages showed them in hospital uniforms with the logo and name of the hospital clearly visible.

The young doctor who was upset by the material viewable on the website reported it to his supervising physician. The supervisor worked with hospital administration to pursue the complaints. The hospital made sure to work with the city's legal department in order to respect the First Amendment rights of the doctors and nurses involved. A hospital review board met behind closed doors to examine the complaint and the behavior of the doctors and nurses in order to recommend discipline in the matter.

Ultimately, the review board recommended written censure of the doctors and nurses involved along with their loss of hospital privileges for six months, during which time they were to work in the local poverty health center. They were also to participate in extensive sensitivity training programs. The hospital administration accepted the recommendations and presented them to the doctors and nurses.

The doctors and nurses accepted their discipline with the stipulation that after completing the six-month they were to return to full hospital status. The expectation of hospital administration was that the doctors and nurses would be committed to moving ahead and working to get the incident behind them, while the hospital would work to improve relationships with the community.

RESPONDING TO THE CASE

1. Was it appropriate for hospital administration to discipline the doctors and nurses for behavior that occurred outside the hospital environment? Why or why not?

2. If you were the supervisor who received the information regarding the social networking site postings, what would your reaction have been?

3. Was this case an example of effective discipline? Why or why not?

➤ Case 14-B: Dealing with Conflict at Eco Landscape

Janet Ramirez is the supervisor of a ten-person design section at Eco Landscape, an employee-owned company that plans, designs, and builds exteriors of large commercial development projects. Although the company has projects all around the Unites States, their work is heavily concentrated in the Minnesota area, where the exterior building season is limited to six months in the spring and summer. The schedule forces the company to rely very heavily on the winter months to complete all the design work for its projects. Janet is very aware that the quality and output of her department during January through March will have serious impacts on the company's financial performance for the year.

During December, Janet notices that one of her designers, Alex, is drafting plans for a lot his family owns near a local vacation lake. Alex is an employee who Janet values for his competence in design and his initiative on projects. For the moment Janet decides not to do anything about this incident, thinking that it may just be an unusual occurrence. Two weeks later Janet is reviewing some design plans for a major project with another two of her designers. In the meeting Janet is made aware that this project is running seriously behind schedule and has a number of problems that must be addressed. Janet asks the two designers what is holding up the project and what is being done to get the project completed on schedule. Ted, an experienced and senior designer, says, "Well, we need some input from Alex that we have asked for several times, but he seems busy with other things." Becky, the other designer, chimes in with, "And we are not going to stay late and work on this project when some other members of the department are leaving early to work on personal projects."

At this point Janet realizes there is a potentially serious problem with Alex and sets up a meeting with him. At the meeting Alex denies working on personal projects and cannot remember or understand the items that the other designers claim are late. Alex thinks about the situation and says to Janet, "You know, those two designers are constantly late on projects and always blaming someone else for their poor planning and sloppy work. Remember last year when the Bank project was delayed? That was their project, and I worked overtime for three weeks to fix their design and to complete their paperwork." A week later Janet stops for coffee with a group of designers in the cafeteria, and one of the designers says, "Well, morale and productivity are as low as I have ever seen it.

I guess the arguments will cost us all our year-end bonus payments, not to mention the fun of working at Eco."

RESPONDING TO THE CASE

1. Where did this conflict originate?

2. What type of conflict resolution is called for in this case?

3. What would you suggest is a good first step for the supervisor to do in this case?

Change Management

Key Concepts

After completing this chapter, you will be able to define these supervisory terms:

- attitudes
- change
- change agent
- change process
- creativity
- innovation
- organization development (OD)

Chapter Outcomes

After reading this chapter, you will be able to:

1. Describe the traditional and contemporary views of change.
2. Explain why employees resist change.
3. Identify ways that supervisors can reduce resistance to change.
4. List the steps a supervisor can use in changing negative employee attitudes.
5. Differentiate between creativity and innovation.
6. Explain how supervisors can stimulate innovation.

Responding to a Supervisory Dilemma

"There is nothing so practical as a good theory."

"If you want truly to understand something, try to change it."

These two quotes by Kurt Lewin provide unique insights into who he was and how he approached studying supervision.* Lewin, who's often called the father of modern social psychology (a discipline that uses scientific methods to "understand and explain how the thought, feeling, and behavior of individuals are influenced by the actual, imagined, or implied presence of other human beings"), made his name in supervision circles through his studies of group dynamics. His approach was based on the belief that "group behavior is an intricate set of symbolic interactions and forces that not only affect group structure but also modify individual behavior."

One of his research studies that looked at modifying family food habits during World War II provided new and important insights into introducing change. He found that "changes were more easily induced through group decision making than through lectures and individual appeals." So what did this mean? His findings suggested that changes would be more readily accepted when people felt they had an opportunity to be involved and participate in the change rather than when they were simply asked or told to change. That's an important lesson for any supervisor, even today, to learn and apply.

Another of Lewin's major contributions was the idea of force field analysis, a framework for looking at the factors (forces) that influenced a situation. Those forces could either be *driving* movement toward a goal or *blocking* movement toward a goal. When you view this idea in terms of managing change, you can see how this process also could contribute to understanding the dynamics of what makes change work and how supervisors can overcome resistance to change, that is, increase the driving forces, decrease the blocking forces, or both.

When supervisors, in cooperation with company officials, make sweeping changes in departments to produce positive change, that effort is frequently called *organization development (OD)*. Because OD interventions often rely on the participation of organization members, they can foster an atmosphere of openness, trust, and respect among coworkers. Interventions can also empower employees and encourage them to take risks. The hope is that these characteristics (openness, trust, respect, empowerment, and risk taking) will lead to better organizational performance.

Based on what Lewin suggested, active participation can cause employees to speak their minds. But that carries some risk. For example, imagine an employee questioning a supervisor's reason for change in the workplace. This employee fully believes the supervisor's reasoning is detrimental to the work unit. But voicing such a concern could lead to retaliation from the supervisor. Although the supervisor might appear to be receptive to the feedback at first, he or she may strike back later. In either case—participation or not—employees could be hurt.

Do you think supervisors should be involved in change initiatives such as OD interventions? Should they involve their employees? When they do—even with the assistance of someone outside the department—do you think coworkers can be too participative as they drive or block movement toward an OD intervention goal? What do you think you as a supervisor can do to ensure that employees who participate in the change process will be protected?

---

* "From the Past to the Present" box based on D. A. Wren and A. G. Bedeian, *The Evolution of Management Thought,* 6th ed. (New York: John Wiley & Sons, Inc., 2009); "Biography and Quotes of Kurt Lewin," *About.com,* http://psychology.about.com (July 15, 2009); and K. T. Lewin, "The Dynamics of Group Action," *Educational Leadership* 1, no. 4 (January 1944), 195–200.

Change is an alteration of an organization's environment, structure, technology, or people. If it weren't for change, the supervisor's job would be relatively easy. Planning would be without problems because tomorrow would be no different from today. Given that the environment would be free from uncertainty, there would be no need to adapt. Decision making would be dramatically simplified because the outcome of each alternative could be predicted with almost certain accuracy. It would, indeed, simplify the supervisor's job if, for example, no new products were introduced, government regulations were never modified, technology never changed, or employees' needs didn't shift.

However, change is an organizational reality. Handling change is an integral part of every supervisor's job. The forces that are "out there" simply demand it (see "News Flash! EA Sports").

Change in a dynamic environment is typically filled with uncertainty. Just as these whitewater rafters have to deal with "rapid" changes, so too must supervisors as they react to unexpected events.

change
An alteration of an organization's environment, structure, technology, or people.

The Forces for Change

In Chapter 2, we pointed out that both external and internal forces constrain supervisors. These same forces also bring about the need for change. Let's briefly look at the factors that can create the need for change (see Exhibit 15-1).

WHAT ARE THE EXTERNAL FORCES CREATING A NEED FOR CHANGE?

The external forces that create the need for change come from various sources. In recent years, the marketplace has affected companies such as Domino's Pizza by introducing new competition. For instance, Domino's must contend with a host of competitors such as Pizza Hut and Pizza Boli's, which have moved into the home-delivery market. Government laws and regulations are a frequent impetus for change. In 1990, the passage of the Americans with Disabilities Act required thousands of businesses to widen doorways, reconfigure restrooms, add ramps, and take other actions to improve accessibility. In the mid-1990s, the Internet became a multifaceted vehicle for getting information and selling products.

Technology also creates the need for change. Recent developments in sophisticated equipment have created significant economies of scale for many organizations. At Charles Schwab and TD Ameritrade (discount brokerage firms), for example, new technology has provided the ability to process thousands of mutual fund trades a day. The assembly line in many industries is undergoing dramatic changes as employers replace human labor with technologically advanced mechanical robots, and the fluctuation in labor markets is forcing managers to initiate changes.

Economic changes, of course, affect almost all of us. The dramatic increases in crude oil and gasoline prices in 2011 caused many U.S. companies that depended on fuel products to transport their goods to look for alternative delivery techniques to help them reduce the costs of delivery services.

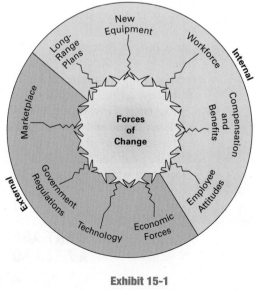

Exhibit 15-1
Forces of change.

News Flash!

EA SPORTS

Walk into any well-furnished college dorm and you'll likely find all the basic necessities—a bed, dresser, desk, and computer. You'll also more than likely find some sort of video game device. It's no wonder that the video game industry is a serious business. It's everywhere. But in an industry in which customers are looking for the "next best game," and in which competition abounds, one company, Electronic Arts (EA), has prospered. EA is now the number one video game publisher in the United States, offering its products under three primary brand names—EA Sports, EA Games, and EA Sports Big. Currently offering such game titles as Skate 3, Need for Speed World, Madden NFL 2011, Tiger Woods PGA Tour 11, and NBA Jam, EA has created more than fifty best-sellers. In fiscal 2010, EA had twenty-seven titles that sold more than 1 million copies, and five titles that each sold more than 4 million copies, including FIFA 10, Madden NFL 10, Need for Speed SHIFT, The SIMS 3, and Battlefield: Bad Company 2. Their net revenue for the fiscal year ended March 31, 2010, was $3.654 billion.

EA is not resting on its previous accomplishments. Quite the contrary. Company management is paranoid about keeping its market leadership. They continue to risk time and money to develop new, creative, market-leading games. For instance, it takes EA from twelve to thirty-six months to produce a top-selling game, with costs upward of $10 million to develop. John Riccitello, president and chief operating officer at EA, says that "the forgotten aspect of creativity is discipline." Creativity at EA is an absolute must, as employees relentlessly pursue games people want to play. To reach that goal, EA assembles the best development team it can, solves every and any technical problem it encounters, completes new games on schedule, and markets them appropriately. How does EA do all of this?

It starts and ends with discipline. Game designers try to identify the creative center of a game—what they call the "creative X"—so that they can understand what the game is all about. Then, they address the discipline of understanding the customers by using focus groups to pinpoint their likes and dislikes. This information is placed on the company's intranet library so that everyone in the company will have the latest information—the discipline of sharing. The company is also committed to the discipline of developing the next generation of creative leaders. The emerging leaders program gives selected employees the opportunity to work in departments outside their own to gain an appreciation of how other parts of the company function.

EA also engages in the discipline of studying the competition. Employees are encouraged to know the features of competitors' products. The final discipline is project management. As Riccitello states, "If you're working on a game and you miss your deadlines, you won't be working here long."

The pressure of creating constant winners might appear to be an incredible strain on employees. Yet, that doesn't appear to be the case at EA. Sometimes programmers spend days working on something that takes three seconds in the actual game. That's because the programmers, like everyone at EA, have a passion for what they do. They love the creative challenge video games present, and they are inspired to accept the next creative challenge. It's this kind of passion, devotion, discipline, and innovation that serves EA so well.

Source: Based on information from the Electronic Arts website (www.ea.com), 2011; C. Salter, "Playing to Win," *Fast Company*, December 2002, 80–91; G. L. Cooper and E. K. Brown, "Video Game Industry Update," *Bank of America Equity Research Brief*, June 7, 2002; and M. Athitakis, "Steve Rechschaffner, Game Wizard," *Business 2.0*, May 2002, 82; Electronic Arts Inc., "EA Reports Fourth Quarter and Fiscal Year 2010 Results," May 11, 2010, http://files.shareholder.com/downloads/ERTS/1269808588x0x373418/f2f6fb54-936c-4283-bfb9-e5bd333a36d0/ERTS_Q410_Earnings_Release_5_11_10_final_with_financial_tables_-_REVISED.pdf (accessed May 26, 2011).

WHAT ARE THE INTERNAL FORCES CREATING A NEED FOR CHANGE?

In addition to the external forces noted previously, internal forces can also stimulate the need for change. These internal forces tend to originate primarily from the internal operations of the organization or from the impact of external changes.

When company officials redefine or modify the organization's strategy, they often introduce a host of changes. For example, when Herman Miller, Inc., developed a new strategy of competing more aggressively in the office furniture market, organizational members had to change how they performed their jobs: Marketing efforts shifted dramatically, and manufacturing processes were revamped.[1] The introduction of new equipment represents another internal force for change. Employees may have their jobs redesigned, need to undergo training to operate the new equipment, or be required to establish new interaction patterns within their formal group.

An organization's workforce is rarely static. Its composition changes in terms of age, education, gender, nationality, and so forth. In a stable organization where supervisors have been in their positions for years, there might be a need to restructure jobs to retain more ambitious employees, affording them more scheduling flexibility and possibly some upward mobility. The compensation and benefits systems might also need to be reworked to reflect the needs of a diverse workforce—and market forces where certain skills are in short supply. Employee attitudes such as increased job dissatisfaction may lead to increased absenteeism, more voluntary resignations, and even strikes. Such events will, in turn, often lead to changes in company policies and practices.

HOW CAN SUPERVISORS SERVE AS CHANGE AGENTS?

Changes within an organization need a catalyst. People who act as catalysts and assume the responsibility for overseeing the change process are called change agents. They do so in a process called organization development (OD).

> **change agent**
> A person who acts as a catalyst and assumes the responsibility for overseeing the change process.

Any supervisor can be a change agent. The change agent can also be a nonsupervisor—for example, an internal staff specialist or outside consultant whose expertise is in change implementation. For major system-wide changes, company officials often hire outside consultants to provide advice and assistance. Because they are from the outside, they often can offer an objective perspective usually lacking in insiders. However, outside consultants may be at a disadvantage because they have an inadequate understanding of the organization's history, culture, operating procedures, and personnel. Outside consultants are also prone to initiate more drastic changes than insiders are—which can be either a benefit or a disadvantage—because they do not have to live with the repercussions after the change is implemented. In contrast, supervisors who act as change agents may be more thoughtful (and possibly more cautious) because they must live with the consequences of their actions.

> **organization development (OD)**
> The process of making systematic change in an organization.

Two Views of the Change Process

There are two very different ways to view the change process. The traditional way is to view the organization as a large ship crossing a calm sea. The ship's captain and crew know exactly where they're going because they've made the trip many times before. Change surfaces as the occasional storm, a brief distraction in an otherwise calm and predictable trip. The contemporary view sees the organization as a small raft navigating a raging river with uninterrupted whitewater rapids. Aboard the raft are half a dozen people who've never worked together before, who are totally unfamiliar with the river, who are unsure of their eventual destination, and, as if things weren't bad enough, who are traveling in the pitch dark of night. In the contemporary view, change is a natural state, and directing change is a continual process. These two ways of viewing change present very different approaches to understanding and responding to change. Let's take a closer look at each one.

> **change process**
> A model that allows for successful change by requiring unfreezing of the status quo (equilibrium state), changing to a new state, and refreezing the new change to make it permanent. Unfreezing the equilibrium state is achieved by (1) increasing driving forces, (2) decreasing restraining forces, or (3) combining these two approaches.

---

[1] D. Rocks, "Reinventing Herman Miller," *BusinessWeek E.Biz*, April 3, 2000, EB89–EB96.

Exhibit 15-2

The three-step traditional view of the change process.

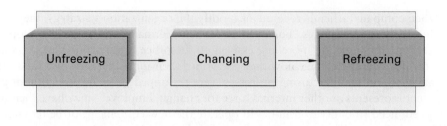

WHAT IS THE TRADITIONAL VIEW OF CHANGE?

The traditional view of change at one time dominated the thinking of most individuals familiar with organizations. It is best illustrated in a three-step description of the change process[2] (see Exhibit 15-2).

According to this model, successful change requires unfreezing the status quo, changing to a new state, and refreezing the new state to make it permanent. The status quo can be considered an equilibrium state. To move from this equilibrium, unfreezing is necessary. It can be achieved in one of three ways:

1. The driving forces, which direct behavior away from the status quo, can be increased.
2. The restraining forces, which hinder movement from the existing equilibrium, can be decreased.
3. The two approaches can be combined.

Once unfreezing has been accomplished, the change itself can be implemented. However, mere introduction of change does not ensure that it will take hold. The new situation, therefore, needs to be refrozen so that it can be sustained over time. Unless this last step is attended to, there is a strong chance that the change will be short lived and employees will revert to the previous equilibrium state. The objective of refreezing, then, is to stabilize the new situation by balancing the driving and restraining forces.

Note how this three-step process treats change as a break in the organization's equilibrium state. The status quo has been disturbed, and change is necessary to establish a new equilibrium state. This view might have been appropriate to the relatively calm environment that most organizations faced in the 1950s, 1960s, and early 1970s. But the traditional view of change is increasingly obsolete as a way to describe the kind of seas that current managers have to navigate.

WHAT IS THE CONTEMPORARY VIEW OF CHANGE?

The contemporary view of change takes into consideration the idea that environments are both uncertain and dynamic. To get a feeling for what directing change might be like when you have to continually maneuver in uninterrupted rapids, consider going on a ski trip and facing the following: Ski slopes that are open vary in length and difficulty. Unfortunately, when you start a "run," you don't know what the ski course will be. It might be a simple course or one that is very challenging. Furthermore, you've planned your ski vacation assuming that the slopes will be open. After all, it's January—and that is prime ski time at the resort. But the course does not always open. If that is not bad enough, on some days, the slopes are closed for no apparent reason at all. Oh yes, there is one more thing: Lift ticket prices can change dramatically on the hour. And there is no apparent pattern to the price fluctuations. To succeed under these conditions, you would have to be incredibly flexible and be able to respond quickly to every changing condition. Those who are too slow or too structured will have difficulty—and clearly no fun!

---

[2]K. Lewin, *Field Theory in Social Science* (New York: Harper & Row, 1951).

A growing number of supervisors are coming to accept that their job is much like what one might face on such a ski vacation. The stability and predictability of the traditional view of change may not exist. Disruptions in the status quo are not occasional and temporary, followed by a return to calm waters. Many of today's supervisors never get out of the rapids. They face constant change, bordering on chaos. These supervisors are being forced to play a game they've never played before, which is governed by rules that are created as the game progresses.

WILL YOU FACE A WORLD OF CONSTANT AND CHAOTIC CHANGE?

Not every supervisor faces a world of constant and chaotic change. However, the set of supervisors who don't is dwindling rapidly. Few supervisors today can treat change as an occasional disturbance in an otherwise peaceful world. Doing so can put you at great risk. Too much is changing too fast for anyone to be complacent. As business writer Tom Peters aptly noted, the old saying "If it ain't broke, don't fix it" no longer applies. In its place, he suggested, "If it ain't broke, you just haven't looked hard enough. Fix it anyway."[3]

WHY DO PEOPLE RESIST CHANGE?

One of the best-documented findings in the study of people at work is that individuals resist change. As one person once put it, "Most people hate any change that doesn't jingle in their pockets."

Resistance to change surfaces in many forms. It can be overt, implicit, immediate, or deferred. It is easiest for supervisors to deal with resistance when it is overt and immediate. For instance, a change is proposed and employees quickly respond by voicing complaints, engaging in a work slowdown, threatening to go on strike, or the like. The greater challenge is managing resistance that is implicit or deferred. Implicit resistance efforts are more subtle (loss of loyalty to the organization, loss of motivation to work, increased errors or mistakes, increased absenteeism resulting from "sickness"), and hence more difficult to recognize. Similarly, deferred actions cloud the link between the source of the resistance and the reaction to it. A change may produce what appears to be only a minimal reaction at the time it is initiated, but then resistance surfaces weeks, months, or even years later. A single change that in and of itself might have little impact can become the straw that breaks the camel's back. Reactions to change can build up and then explode in some response that seems totally out of proportion to the change action it follows. The resistance, of course, has merely been deferred and stockpiled. What surfaces is a response to an accumulation of previous changes.

So, why do people resist change? There are a number of reasons. We've listed them in Exhibit 15-3 and describe them in the following section.

Habit As human beings, we're creatures of habit. Life is complex enough; we don't need to consider the full range of options for the hundreds of decisions we have to make every day. To cope with this complexity, we all rely on habits or

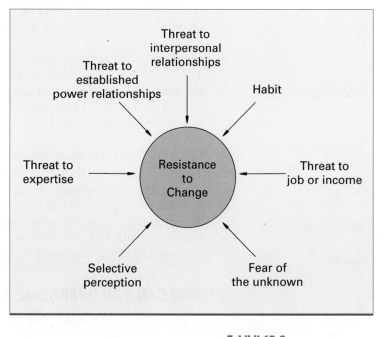

[3]T. Peters, *Thriving on Chaos* (New York: Knopf, 1987).

Exhibit 15-3
Why people resist change.

programmed responses. When we are confronted with change, this tendency to respond in our accustomed ways becomes a source of resistance. So, when your department is moved to a new office building across town, it means your employees are likely to have to change many habits: waking up ten minutes earlier, taking a new set of streets to work, finding a new parking place, adjusting to the new office layout, developing a new lunchtime routine, and so on.

Threat to Job and Income Employees often fear any change that may reduce their job security or income. New labor-saving equipment, for instance, may be interpreted as the forerunner of layoffs. People are also often threatened by changes in job tasks or established work routines if they fear that they won't be able to perform them successfully. This is particularly threatening where pay is closely tied to productivity.

Fear of the Unknown Changes substitute ambiguity and uncertainty for the known, and human beings don't like ambiguity. If the introduction of a desktop publishing system by a small book publisher means that editorial people will have to learn to do their entire jobs on computers, some of these people may fear that they will be unable to learn the intricacies of the system. They may, therefore, develop a negative attitude toward working with desktop publishing or behave dysfunctionally—complaining, purposely working slowly, undermining department morale—if required to use the system.

Selective Perception Individuals shape the world through their perceptions. Once they have created this world, it resists change. So, individuals are guilty of selectively processing what they see and hear to keep their perceptions intact. They often hear what they want to hear. They ignore information that challenges the world they've created. The book editors faced with the introduction of desktop publishing may ignore the arguments that their supervisors make in explaining why the new equipment has been purchased or the potential benefits that the change will provide them.

Threat to Expertise Changes in organizational policies and practices may threaten the expertise of specialized groups and departments. The introduction of personal computers, which give supervisors access to information directly from a company's mainframe, is an example of a change that was strongly resisted by many information systems departments in the early 1980s. Why? Because decentralized end-user computing was a threat to the specialized skills held by those in the centralized information systems departments.

Threat to Established Power Relationships Any redistribution of decision-making authority can threaten long-established power relationships within an organization. Efforts by company officials to empower operating employees or to introduce self-directed work teams have frequently been met with resistance from supervisors who are threatened by a redistribution of power.

Threat to Interpersonal Relationships Work is more than a means to earn a living. The interpersonal relationships that are part of a person's job often play an important role in satisfying the individual's social needs. We look forward to going to work to interact with coworkers and make friends. Change can be a threat to those relationships. Reorganizations, transfers, and restructuring of work layouts change the people that employees work with, report to, and regularly interact with. Because such changes are often seen as threats, they tend to be resisted.

HOW CAN YOU OVERCOME RESISTANCE TO CHANGE?

The resistance to change we've previously described can be overcome. We offer five specific techniques. Resistance is most likely to be eliminated when you implement all five techniques.

Build Trust If employees trust and have confidence in you, they're less likely to be threatened by changes you propose. The implementation of self-directed work teams at Ocean Spray's Vero Beach, Florida, processing plant initially met with considerable resistance because employees didn't trust supervisors. For years, supervisors hadn't trusted their employees to make decisions; then, all of a sudden, these same supervisors were telling workers to make their own decisions. It took more than a year for employees to accept responsibility for solving their own problems. Trust takes a long time to develop. It's also very fragile; it can be destroyed easily. The ideas we offer in Chapter 9 should help you to build trust with your employees.

Open Channels of Communication Resistance can be reduced through communicating with employees to help them see the logic of a change. When employees receive the full facts and get misunderstandings cleared up, resistance often fades. This explains why, for example, company officials at Stathakis, a Michigan-based janitorial, maintenance, and painting company, allow any of the company's employees to review the company's profit and loss statements and get questions answered about the firm's financial performance.

Opening communication channels, however, will be effective only when there is a climate of trust and when the organization is truly concerned with the welfare of its employees. Improved communication is particularly effective in reducing threats created by ambiguity. For instance, when the grapevine is active with rumors of cutbacks and layoffs, honest and open communication of the true facts can be a calming force. Even if the news is bad, a clear message often wins points and opens people to accepting change. When communication is ambiguous and people are threatened, they often contrive scenarios that are considerably worse than the actual "bad news."

Involve Your Employees Organizations as varied as American Express, Boeing, Delmarva Power, the U.S. Internal Revenue Service, and SEI Investments are asking employees to help plan major change programs. Why? It's difficult for individuals to resist a change decision in which they participated. So, solicit employee inputs early in the change process. When affected employees have been involved in a change from its beginning, they will usually actively support the change. No one wants to oppose something that he or she helped develop.

Provide Incentives Make sure that people see how supporting a change is in their best interests. What's the source of their resistance? What do you control that might overcome that resistance? Are they afraid they won't be able to do a new task? Provide them with new-skills training or maybe a short paid leave of absence so that they'll have time to rethink their fears, calm down, and come to the realization that their concerns are unfounded.

Similarly, layoffs can become opportunities for those who remain. Jobs can be redesigned to provide new challenges and responsibilities. A pay increase, a new title, flexible work hours, or increased job autonomy are additional examples of incentives that can help reduce resistance. JLG Industries, Inc. offers a skill-based pay plan because it wants employees to broaden their skills and become more flexible. To encourage this, it offers pay premiums to employees who develop new skill competencies.

Deal with Employee Feelings "I hate my job." "My boss is insensitive to women." "I think the medical products we're producing make a real difference in people's lives." These employee statements are examples of attitudes. That is, they're evaluative statements or judgments concerning objects, people, or events. They reflect how people feel about something. What can you do, as a supervisor, to change negative employee attitudes? First, identify the attitude you want to change. Then, determine what sustains that attitude. Next, unfreeze the attitude and offer an alternative attitude. Finally, reinforce and support the new attitude.

attitudes
Evaluative statements or judgments concerning objects, people, or events.

Something To Think About (and promote class discussion)

ROBOT DOC

Imagine lying as a patient in a hospital bed and being visited by a 5-foot robot.* You might attribute such a "vision" to too many drugs or too little sleep. But in Methodist Hospital in Houston, that 5-foot robot isn't a vision. It's real. The robot, which looks like "an oversize carpet cleaner with a computer monitor stuck on top," visits patients, being guided remotely by a patient's doctor from a command center on another floor. With this type of technology, especially in a critical care unit, a medical team can do its rounds and "read" vital signs and "see" how patients are doing without disturbing or distressing them.

Robots roaming hospital hallways aren't the only technological advancements transforming how medical centers and health care systems work. Radio-frequency ID tags keep track of doctors, nurses, and pieces of equipment in real time, leading to faster emergency response times. "Smart beds automatically transfer patients' breathing and heart rates to their charts," quickly alerting nurses to potential or developing problems. And one of the biggest technological changes is in medical records information keeping. Rather than having massive numbers of paper-based files, health care organizations are moving toward completely digital medical records. But the rate of change has been slow. Currently, only 1.5 percent of private hospitals have a comprehensive electronic medical records system in all clinical units. Only 7.6 percent have a basic system in at least one unit. Yet, it's a major change with significant promise. "Putting patient records into digital form...can provide a wealth of information about which treatments work and which don't, and speed diagnosis and medical care."

The investment that hospitals and other health care organizations are making in technology has basically two goals: (1) to improve medical care and reduce error rates and (2) to minimize patient stress, which encourages healing. "Ironically, one of the most anticipated developments is that technology will allow hospitals to keep people out of them." The vice president of the innovation and technology group at Kaiser Permanente's Sidney R. Garfield Health Care Innovation Center says, "By 2015, the home will be the hub of health care." And such changes are already taking place. In many rural areas of the United States where specialized medical care is scarce, telemedicine is in place to cover the gaps. For instance, thirty-one hospitals in remote locations in Michigan use robots, similar to the one described earlier, for diagnosis and follow-up. Robots are even found in operating rooms—the "assembly line" of a health care system—just as they are in other organization's assembly lines, *and* for the same reasons: quality control and cost control.

In an industry where you'd expect up-to-date technology, the changes in the way health care organizations do their work haven't been occurring as rapidly as you might think. However, technological changes will continue to transform the industry and the organizations and the people who make it work.

What do you think? Will employees and the general population embrace this type of technological change or feel threatened by it? Why or why not? Will supervisors be expected to evaluate and appraise their employees on their ability to communicate via the robot doc? As a supervisor, how would you approach the introduction of this new technology to your employees?

---

*M. Andrews, "The Hospital of the Future," *U.S. News & World Report*, August 2009, 68–74; C. Salter, "The Doctor of the Future," *Fast Company*, May 2009, 64–70; L. Landro, "An Affordable Fix for Modernizing Medical Records," *Wall Street Journal*, April 30, 2009, A11; and J. Ioffe, "Tech Rx for Health Care," *Fortune*, March 16, 2009.

Comprehension Check 15-1

1. The alteration of an organization's environment, structure, technology, or people is called
   a. change
   b. strategic planning
   c. conflict management
   d. none of the above

2. Which one of the following is *not* an internal force for change?

   a. New environment
   b. Workforce
   c. Employee attitudes
   d. Marketplace

3. The person who acts as a catalyst for change and assumes the responsibility for that change is called a

   a. manager
   b. change agent
   c. top-level manager
   d. consultant

4. Which one of the following items is *not* associated with the traditional view of change?

   a. Refreezing
   b. Changing
   c. Chaos
   d. Freezing

5. People resist change for all of the following reasons *except*

   a. threat to job and income
   b. habit
   c. fear of the unknown
   d. threat to building trust

Stimulating Innovation

"Innovate or die!" These harsh words are increasingly becoming the rallying cry of today's supervisors. In the dynamic world of global competition, organizations must create new products and services and adopt state-of-the-art technology if they are to compete successfully.[4] The standard of innovation to which many organizations strive is that achieved by such companies as DuPont, Sharp, Eastman Chemical, and 3M.[5] Supervisors at 3M, for example, have developed a reputation for being able to stimulate innovation over a long period of time. One of its stated objectives is that 25 percent of each division's profits are to come from products less than five years old. Toward that end, 3M typically launches more than two hundred new products each year. During one recent five-year period, 3M generated better than 30 percent of its $13 billion in revenues from products introduced during the previous five years.

What's the secret to 3M's success? What, if anything, can other supervisors do to make their organizations more innovative? In the following pages, we try to answer those questions as we discuss the factors behind innovation.

HOW ARE CREATIVITY AND INNOVATION RELATED?

In general usage, creativity means the ability to combine ideas in a unique way or to make unusual associations between ideas. For example, at Mattel, company officials have introduced Project Platypus. This special division brings people from all disciplines—such as engineering, marketing, design, and sales—to get employees to "think

creativity
The ability to combine ideas in a unique way or to make unusual associations between ideas.

---

[4]J. Benditt, "Lessons from Innovation," *Technology Review*, July–August 2002, 9.

[5]K. H. Hammonds, "How to Design the Perfect Product Start with Craig Vogel and Jonathan Cagan: Integrate Style and Technology with a Dash of Fantasy. Apply Everything from Toasters to Cars," *Fast Company*, July 2002, 122–127.

outside the box" to "understand the sociology and psychology behind children's play patterns." To help make this happen, team members embark on such activities as imagination exercises, group crying, and stuffed-bunny throwing.[6] The first Project Platypus product, Ello, hit the market in 2002 after two years in development.

innovation
The process of turning a creative idea into a useful product, service, or method of operation.

Innovation is the process of taking a creative idea and turning it into a useful product, service, or method of operation.[7] The innovative organization is characterized by the ability to channel its creative juices into useful outcomes. When managers talk about changing an organization to make it more creative, they usually mean that they want to stimulate innovation. The 3M company is aptly described as innovative because it has taken novel ideas and turned them into profitable products such as cellophane tape, Scotch Guard protective coatings, Post-It notepads, and diapers with elastic waistbands. Also innovative is the highly successful microchip manufacturer Intel. It leads all chip manufacturers and the success of its Intel Core Processors helped give the company an 81.0 percent share of global microprocessor revenue in 2010. With full-year revenue of $43.6 billion reported in 2010, Intel's commitment to staying ahead of the competition by introducing a stream of new and more powerful products is supported by planned annual capital spending for 2011 of $10.2 billion. Its research and development budget increased from slightly more than $5 billion in 2005 to a budget of $6.6 billion in 2010.[8]

Often operating as organizational change agents, corporate human resource managers specializing in training recognize change as one of the biggest challenges faced by supervisors. Constant change in organizations struggling to remain profitable often interrupts the normal responsibility of employees. At such times, a supervisor must be masterful in communicating the need for change.

WHAT IS INVOLVED IN INNOVATION?

Some people believe that creativity is inborn; others believe that with training, anyone can be creative. In this latter view, creativity can be viewed as a fourfold process consisting of perception, incubation, inspiration, and innovation.[9]

Perception involves how you see things. Being creative means seeing things from a unique perspective. That is, an employee may see solutions to a problem that others cannot or will not see at all. Going from perception to reality, however, doesn't occur instantaneously. Instead, ideas go through a process of *incubation*. Sometimes, employees need to "sit" on their ideas. This doesn't mean sitting and doing nothing. Rather, during this incubation period, employees should collect massive data that they store, retrieve, study, reshape, and finally mold into something new. This period can sometimes take years.

[6]L. Bannon, "Think Tank in Toyland," *Wall Street Journal,* June 6, 2002, B1, B3.

[7]"Learning from Leading Innovators," *The Futurist,* May 2002, 62.

[8]See, for example, L. P. Livinstone, L. E. Palicyh, and G. R. Carini, "Promotion Creativity Through the Logic of Contradiction," *Journal of Organizational Behavior* 23, no. 3 (May 2002), 321–327; IC Insights, Inc., "Samsung Poised to Overtake Intel as Largest Semiconductor Maker," August 25, 2010, http://www.icinsights.com/news/bulletins/Samsung-Poised-To-Overtake-Intel-As-Largest-Semiconductor-Maker/ (accessed May 26, 2011); E. Savitz, "Update: Intel Opens Wallet, Semi Equipment Shares Rally," *Forbes,* April 20, 2011, http://blogs.forbes.com/ericsavitz/2011/04/20/update-intel-opens-wallet-semi-equipment-shares-rally/?partner=contextstory (accessed May 26, 2011); P. Darling, "Intel Reports Record Year and Record Fourth Quarter," *Intel Newsroom,* January 13, 2011, http://newsroom.intel.com/community/intel_newsroom/blog/2011/01/13/intel-reports-record-year-and-record-fourth-quarter (accessed May 26, 2011); N. Eddy, "Intel, AMD Hold Lead on Microprocessor Market Share: Report," *e-Week.com, Midmarket News,* March 2011, http://www.eweek.com/c/a/Midmarket/Intel-AMD-Hold-Lead-on-Microprocessor-Market-Share-Report-654921/ (accessed May 26, 2011).

[9]C. Vogel and J. Cagan, *Creating Breakthrough Products: Innovation from Product Planning to Program Approval* (Upper Saddle River, NJ: Prentice Hall, 2002).

Think for a moment about a time you struggled for an answer on a test. Although you tried hard to jog your memory, nothing worked. Then, suddenly, like a flash of light, the answer popped into your head. You found it! *Inspiration* in the creative process is similar. Inspiration is the moment when all your prior efforts come together successfully.

Although inspiration leads to euphoria, the creative work is not complete. It requires an innovative effort. *Innovation* involves taking that inspiration and turning it into a useful product, service, or way of doing things. Thomas Edison is often credited with saying that "creativity is 1 percent inspiration and 99 percent perspiration." That 99 percent, or the innovation, involves testing, evaluating, and retesting what the inspiration found. It is usually at this stage that an individual involves others more in what he or she had been working on. That involvement is critical because even the greatest invention may be delayed, or lost, if an individual cannot effectively deal with others in communicating and achieving what the creative idea is supposed to do!

HOW CAN A SUPERVISOR FOSTER INNOVATION?

Three sets of variables have been found to stimulate innovation. They pertain to the organization's structure, culture, and human resource practices.

Structural Variables On the basis of extensive research, we can make three statements regarding the effect of structural variables on innovation. First, less formalized structures positively influence innovation. Because they are lower in work specialization, have fewer rules, and are more decentralized than bureaucracies, they facilitate the flexibility, adaptation, and cross-fertilization that make the adoption of innovations easier. Second, easy availability of plentiful resources provides a key building block for innovation. An abundance of resources allows supervisors to afford to purchase innovations, bear the cost of instituting innovations, and absorb failures. Finally, frequent interunit communication helps break down possible barriers to innovation by facilitating interaction across departmental lines.

Cultural Variables Innovative organizations tend to have similar cultures.[10] They encourage experimentation. They reward both successes and failures. They celebrate mistakes. For example, at Sony, employees are encouraged and rewarded for experimenting with new products in the marketplace. Unlike other organizations, Sony takes many products to market knowing that not all of them will be market successes. Their culture, therefore, promotes this risk-taking behavior. An innovative culture is likely to have the following seven characteristics:

- **Acceptance of ambiguity.** Too much emphasis on objectivity and specificity constrains creativity.
- **Tolerance of the impractical.** Individuals who offer impractical, even foolish, answers to "what if" questions are not stifled. What seems impractical at first might lead to innovative solutions.
- **Low external controls.** Rules, regulations, policies, and similar controls are kept to a minimum.
- **Tolerance of risk.** Employees are encouraged to experiment without fear of consequences should they fail. Mistakes are treated as learning opportunities.
- **Tolerance of conflict.** Diversity of opinions is encouraged. Harmony and agreement between individuals or units are not assumed to be evidence of high performance.
- **Focus on ends rather than on means.** Goals are made clear, and individuals are encouraged to consider alternative routes to their attainment. Focusing on ends suggests that there might be several right answers to any given problem.
- **Open systems focus.** The organization closely monitors the environment and responds rapidly to changes as they occur.

---

[10]Ibid., p. 63.

Human Resource Variables Within the human resource category, we find that innovative organizations actively promote the training and development of their members so that their knowledge remains current, offer their employees high job security to reduce the fear of getting fired for making mistakes, and encourage individuals to become champions of change. Once a new idea is developed, champions of change actively and enthusiastically promote the idea, build support, overcome resistance, and ensure that the innovation is implemented.

Research finds that champions have common personality characteristics: extremely high self-confidence, persistence, energy, and a tendency to take risks. Champions also display characteristics associated with dynamic leadership. They inspire and energize others with their vision of the potential of an innovation and through their strong personal conviction in their mission. They are also good at gaining the commitment of others to support their mission. In addition, champions have jobs that provide considerable decision-making discretion. This autonomy helps them introduce and implement innovations.

Comprehension Check 15-2

6. The ability to combine ideas in a unique way is called

    a. creativity
    b. innovation
    c. work process engineering
    d. all of the above

7. Taking a new idea and turning it into a useful product, service, or method of operation is called

    a. creativity
    b. innovation
    c. work process engineering
    d. all of the above

8. Keeping rules, regulations, and policies to a minimum is what type of cultural variable?

    a. Tolerance of conflict
    b. Tolerance of the impractical
    c. Low external controls
    d. Tolerance of risks

9. Encouraging employees to experiment without fear of consequences should they fail is what type of cultural variable?

    a. Tolerance of risk
    b. Tolerance of conflict
    c. Focus on ends rather than on means
    d. Open system focus

Enhancing Understanding

SUMMARY

After reading this chapter, I can:

1. **Describe the traditional and contemporary views of change.** The traditional view of change treats change as a break in the organization's equilibrium state. Change is initiated and then stabilized at a new equilibrium. The contemporary view of change is that it is constant. Disequilibrium is the natural state.

2. **Explain why employees resist change.** Employees resist change because of habit, fear of the unknown, or selective perception, or if they perceive the change as a threat to their job, income, expertise, established power relationships, or interpersonal relationships.

3. **Identify ways that supervisors can reduce resistance to change.** Supervisors can reduce resistance by building trust, opening channels of communication, involving employees in change decisions, providing incentives to employees for accepting change, and helping employees change their attitudes.

4. **List the steps a supervisor can use in changing negative employee attitudes.** The five steps in changing attitudes are (1) identifying the attitude you want to change, (2) determining what sustains the attitude, (3) unfreezing the attitude, (4) offering an alternative attitude, and (5) refreezing the new attitude.

5. **Differentiate between creativity and innovation.** Creativity is the ability to combine ideas in a unique way or to make unusual associations between ideas. Innovation is the process of taking creative ideas and turning them into a useful product, service, or method of operation.

6. **Explain how supervisors can stimulate innovation.** Supervisors can stimulate innovation through structures that are flexible, provide easy access to resources, and have fluid communication; a culture that is relaxed, supports new ideas, and encourages monitoring of the environment; and creative people who are well trained, current in their fields, and secure in their jobs.

COMPREHENSION: Review and Discussion Questions

1. Give several examples of environmental forces that might affect supervisors and require changes in a department.

2. Describe the traditional model of the change process. How does it differ from the contemporary view of change?

3. What signals or cues might tell you that an employee is resistant to a change you're planning to implement?

4. How does an employee's perception relate to his or her resistance to change?

5. How can building trust lessen change resistance?

6. Why should supervisors be concerned with an employee's work-related attitudes?

7. What happens if an attitude change is not refrozen?

8. How do creativity and innovation differ? Give an example of each.

9. How does an innovative culture make an organization more effective? Do you think such an innovative culture could make an organization less effective? Why or why not?

10. Do you think changes can occur in an organization without a champion to foster new and innovative ways of doing things? Explain.

KEY CONCEPT CROSSWORD

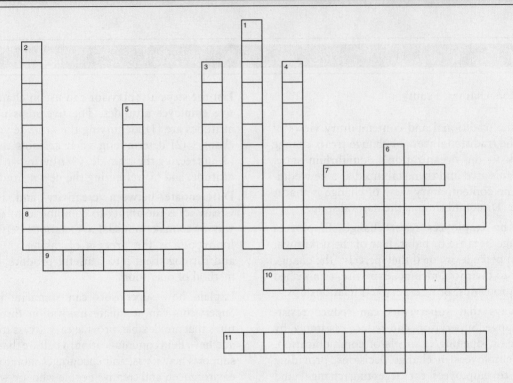

ACROSS

7. an alteration of the organization
8. the process of making systematic change in an organization
9. forces that direct behavior away from the status quo
10. a person who acts as a catalyst for change in an organization
11. a model that allows for successful change through unfreezing, changing, and refreezing

DOWN

1. forces that hinder movement from the existing equilibrium
2. the process of turning a creative idea into a useful product
3. how one sees things
4. evaluative statements concerning objects, people, or events
5. the ability to combine ideas in a unique way to make an unusual association
6. the moment when all one's prior efforts successfully come together

ANSWERS TO COMPREHENSION CHECKS

Comprehension Check 15-1

1. a   2. d   3. b   4. c   5. d

Comprehension Check 15-2

6. a   7. b   8. c   9. a

Developing Your Supervisory Skills

GETTING TO KNOW YOURSELF

Before you can effectively supervise others, you must understand your present strengths and areas in need of development. To assist in this learning process, we encourage you to complete the following self-assessments from the Prentice Hall Self-Assessment Library 3.4.

1. Am I a Type A? (I. A. 3.)
2. How Creative Am I? (I. A. 5.)

3. How Well Do I Respond to Turbulent Change? (III. C. 1.)

After you complete the assessment, we suggest you retain the results and store them as part of your "portfolio of learning about yourself."

BUILDING A TEAM

AN EXPERIENTIAL EXERCISE: THE SPACE COWBOYS COMPANY

Objectives

1. To illustrate how forces for change and stability must be addressed in organizations.

2. To illustrate the effects of alternative change techniques on the relative strength of forces for change and forces for stability.

The Situation

The marketing division of the Space Cowboys Company (SCC) has gone through two major reorganizations in the past seven years. Initially, the structure changed from a functional to a matrix form. But the matrix form did not satisfy some functional area supervisors, and neither did it lead to organizational improvements. They complained that the structure confused the authority and responsibility relationships. In reaction to these complaints, senior management revised the structure back to the functional form. This "new" structure maintained market and project teams, which were managed by project supervisors with a few general staff personnel. But no functional specialists were assigned to these groups.

After the change, some problems began to surface. Project supervisors complained that they could not obtain necessary assistance from functional staffs. It not only took more time to obtain necessary assistance but also created problems in establishing stable relationships with functional staff members. Because these problems affected their services to customers, project supervisors demanded a change in the organizational structure. Faced with these complaints

and demands from project supervisors, senior management is pondering yet another reorganization for the division. They have requested an outside consultant (you) to help them in their reorganization plan—one that will provide some stability in the structure, address their issues, and help the organization succeed in achieving its strategic goals.

1. Divide into groups of five to seven and take the role of consultants.
2. Each group should identify the forces necessitating the change and the resistance to that change found in the company.
3. Each group should develop a set of strategies for dealing with the resistance to change and for implementing those strategies.
4. Reassemble the class and hear each group's recommendations and explanations.
5. After each group has presented, probing questions should be posed by other "consulting groups" about the presenting group's recommendations.

➤ Internet: Web Activity

Go to http://www.pearsonhighered.com/robbins/. Find *Supervision Today!* 7th Ed. and click Companion Website.

➤ Communicating Effectively

1. Describe a significant change event you experienced (going from high school to college, changing jobs, etc.). How did you prepare for the change? What fears did you encounter and how did you overcome those fears? Knowing what you know now about the change, what would you do differently today that you didn't do then? How can you apply these "should haves" to changes you'll face in the future?

2. Business programs have traditionally focused on developing rationality. They haven't emphasized creativity. That may be a mistake. In two to three pages, describe how you would change the business curriculum to promote student creativity. Specify the kinds of courses or activities that you think should be included in business school classes that would foster creativity and innovation.

THINKING CRITICALLY

➤ Case 15-A: Technology Drives Change

The Crystal Company is a software developer with products in the payroll and personnel records areas. Joshua and Alyson Bennett started the company fifteen years ago. The Bennetts both have significant experience in programming and accounting. Alyson wrote the company's initial programs when her daughter was an infant. At the time, Joshua was a manager at a public accounting firm and heavily involved with clients' record-keeping activities. Their products, named Crystal Payroll and Crystal Personnel, have been mainstay products for approximately three hundred companies who use the software to compute and process their payroll and maintain all the personnel records. At the time the Crystal products were developed, they were one of the only software products that integrated both personnel records and payroll processing.

The company employs approximately twelve customer service reps, who spend all their time helping clients use the systems and problem-solve all types of issues. A sales staff of ten calls on small and medium-sized companies by phone and in person all across the United States. The Crystal Company is known for excellent customer service and their close ties with the Association of Personnel Management. Alyson and Joshua are frequent speakers at association meetings held at different times around the country. This combination of a good product, excellent customer service, and ties to the association has made Crystal a very successful company.

At the beginning of this year, some dramatic changes in payroll tax rules occurred. In addition, competitive companies have introduced a new software product written in an easy-to-revise database format that has taken a significant amount of business away from the Crystal Company. These new products are being offered at much lower prices and give greater flexibility to the users. The Bennetts would like to start a project immediately to find a way to convert or rewrite their products into a new format that might bring some of the same benefits as the new competitive products. This project will require the focus of the entire company and great effort. And the project will be extremely expensive. It may be expensive enough to put the company out of business if it is not successful.

RESPONDING TO THE CASE

1. What are some of the reasons people at Crystal may resist this change?

2. What actions might you suggest for helping the Crystal Company deal with the changes in a positive manner?

3. How might this new product development be turned into a case of innovation?

➤ Case 15-B: Moving Changes for Introl Systems, Inc.

Nearly from its beginning, Introl Systems, Inc. (the company that produces computer chips used in desktop and notebook computers), was located in Englewood Cliffs, New Jersey. This location was convenient for a wide range of employees. Those who lived in New York City had only a twenty-minute commute to work. Those who preferred to live in the suburban areas had more than a dozen small New Jersey communities from which to choose. Even those who preferred a rural lifestyle could find it within a forty-five-minute commute to work.

In 2003, however, company officials determined that the organization had outgrown its facility in Englewood Cliffs. Attempts to obtain permits from local government offices to expand the facility met with resistance. As a result, the company bought the former headquarters of Eastern Union in Morris Plains, New Jersey. After some remodeling to fit company needs, Introl Systems began operating in Morris Plains in June 2003.

The biggest issue facing supervisors concerning the move was the realization that hiring and retaining employees might be affected—especially in the engineering and design departments. That's because many of these employees lived in New York City. What was once a twenty-minute commute from the city would now take nearly an hour each way. Further compounding this change was the realization that no public transportation was available. Going to work now required employees to have access to automobiles.

Kathy Wilson supervised a small group at Introl Systems that worked exclusively on designing computer chips. All six of her employees lived in New York City. When Kathy learned of the move to Morris Plains, she immediately informed her employees. Initially, news of the move appeared to have little effect. But as the date of the move drew nearer, rumors were rampant that almost all of her staff were looking for jobs in New York City.

RESPONDING TO THE CASE

1. Why do you believe most of Kathy Wilson's employees were resistant to the move? Describe the factors leading to this resistance.

2. Assume that you are Kathy Wilson and it is spring 2003. You don't want to lose any of the skilled and talented people you have on your staff. What specific steps will you take to ensure that your employees remain at Introl Systems?

3. Do you believe that company officials could have avoided some of the resistance to change—especially for those employees who lived in New York City? Explain.

16

CHAPTER

Supervision and Labor

Key Concepts

After completing this chapter, you will be able to define these supervisory terms:

- agency shop
- authorization cards
- collective bargaining
- dues checkoff
- economic strike
- fact-finding
- Federal Mediation and Conciliation Service (FMCS)
- grievance procedures
- grievance (rights) arbitration
- interest arbitration
- labor relations
- Landrum-Griffin Act
- lockout
- maintenance of membership

- National Labor Relations Board (NLRB)
- open shop
- Racketeering Influenced and Corrupt Organizations Act (RICO)
- representation certification (RC) election
- representation decertification (RD) election
- secondary boycott
- Taft-Hartley Act
- union
- union shop
- Wagner Act
- wildcat strike

Chapter Outcomes

After reading this chapter, you will be able to:

1. Define *union*.

2. Discuss the effect the Wagner and Taft-Hartley acts had on labor–management relations.

3. Describe the union-organizing process.

4. Describe the components of collective bargaining.

5. Identify the steps in the collective bargaining process.

6. Explain the various types of union security arrangements.

7. Describe the role of a grievance procedure in collective bargaining.

8. Identify the various impasse resolution techniques.

Responding to a Supervisory Dilemma

Inherent in collective bargaining negotiations is an opportunity for either side to generate a power base that may sway negotiations in its favor. For example, when labor shortages exist, or when inventories are in short supply, a strike by the union could have serious ramifications for the company. Likewise, when the situation is reversed, the company has the upper hand and could easily lock out the union to achieve its negotiation goals. In fact, two primary labor–management pieces of legislation attempted to make the playing field as level as possible by requiring both sides to negotiate in good faith and permit impasses if they should be warranted.

For decades, this scenario played itself out over and over again. Timing of a contract's expiration proved critical for both sides. For example, in the coal industry, having a contract expire just before the winter months—when coal is needed in greater supply for heating and electricity—worked to the union's advantage, unless the coal companies stockpiled enough coal to carry them through a lengthy winter strike. This game, although serious to both sides, never appeared to be anything more than a bargaining strategy—one that could show how serious both sides were. And even though a Supreme Court case from 1938, *NLRB v. MacKay Radio*, gave employers the right to hire replacement workers for those engaged in an economic strike, seldom was that used. In fact, to settle a strike, and for the organization to get back its skilled workforce, one stipulation would often be that all replacement workers be let go.

But in the early 1980s, the situation began to change. When then-President Ronald Reagan fired striking air traffic controllers and hired their replacements, businesses began to realize the weapon they had at their disposal. As their union-busting attempts succeeded, some organizations, such as Caterpillar, the National Football League, and John Deere, realized that using replacement workers could be to their advantage. The union members either came back to work on company officials' terms, or they lost their jobs—period.

Undoubtedly, in any strike situation, a company has the right to keep its doors open and to keep producing what it sells. Often that may mean using supervisory personnel in place of striking workers or in some cases bringing in replacements. But does a law that permits replacement workers undermine the intent of national labor laws? Does it create an unfair advantage for companies, who can play hardball just to break the union? Should a striker replacement bill (which would prevent permanent replacement workers from being hired) be passed? Should striking workers' jobs be protected while they exercise their rights under federal law? What's your opinion?

In this chapter, we discuss the unique supervisory elements that exist when a labor union is present. We look at what unions are, the laws regulating this process, why employees join unions, and the unique role supervisors play in the labor relations process.

What Is Labor Relations?

labor relations
All activities within a company that involve dealing with a union and its members.

Labor relations is a term used to include all activities within a company that involve dealing with a union and its membership.[1] The key component in this definition is a union.

---

[1]Material in this chapter is adapted from D. A. DeCenzo and S. P. Robbins, *Human Resource Management*, 8th ed. (Hoboken, NJ: John Wiley & Sons, 2005), Chapter 16.

A union is an organization of workers, acting collectively, seeking to promote and protect its mutual interests through collective bargaining. However, before we can examine the activities surrounding the collective bargaining process, it is important to understand the laws that govern the labor–management process, what unions are, and how employees unionize. Although it is true that just under 12 percent of the private-sector workforce is unionized, the successes and failures of organized labor's activities affect most segments of the workforce in two important ways. First, because major industries in the United States—such as automobile, steel, and electrical manufacturers, as well as all branches of transportation—are unionized, unions have a major effect on some of the important sectors of the economy (see Exhibit 16-1). Second, gains made by unions often spill over into other nonunionized sectors of the economy. So, the wages, hours, and working conditions of nonunion employees at a Linden, New Jersey, lumberyard may be affected by collective bargaining between the United Auto Workers and General Motors at one of the latter's North American assembly plants.

In 2010, the union membership rate, the percent of wage and salary workers who were members of a union, reported by the U.S. Bureau of Labor Statistics, was 11.9 percent, down from 12.3 percent a year earlier. The number of wage and salary workers belonging to unions declined by 612,000 to 14.7 million. In 1983, the first year for which comparable union data are available, the union membership rate was 20.1 percent, and there were 17.7 million union workers.

According to the 2010 data the union membership rate for public sector workers (36.2 percent) was substantially higher than the rate for private sector workers (6.9 percent). Workers in education, training, and library occupations had the highest unionization rate at 37.1 percent. Black workers were more likely to be union members than were white, Asian, or Hispanic workers. Among states, New York had the highest union membership rate (24.2 percent) and North Carolina had the lowest rate (3.2 percent).[2]

For many supervisors, activities in a unionized organization consist chiefly of following procedures and policies laid out in the labor contract. This labor contract was agreed to by both management and the labor union, stipulating, among other things, the wage rate, the hours of work, and the terms and conditions of employment for those covered by the negotiated agreement. Decisions about how to select and compensate employees, employee benefits offered, procedures for overtime, and so on are no longer unilateral prerogatives of management for jobs that fall under the union's jurisdiction. Such decisions are generally made at the time the labor contract is negotiated.

The concept of labor relations and the collective bargaining process may mean different things to different individuals depending on their experience, background, and so on. One means of providing some focus in these areas is to understand why people join unions and the laws that serve as the foundation of labor–management relationships.

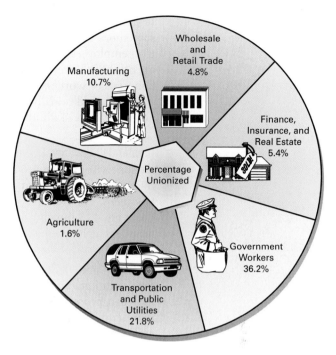

Exhibit 16-1

Union membership by industry concentration.

Source: Adapted from Bureau of labor Statistics, "Table 3. Union Affiliation of Employed Wage and Salary Workers by Occupation and Industry," *January 21, 2011, http://www.bls.gov/news.release/union2.t03.htm (accessed May 27, 2011).*

union

An organization that represents workers and seeks to protect their interests through collective bargaining.

WHY DO EMPLOYEES JOIN UNIONS?

The reasons people join unions are as diverse as the people themselves. Just what are they seeking to gain when they join a union? The answer to this question varies with the individual and the union contract, but the following discussion captures the most common reasons.

[2]United States Department of Labor, U.S. Bureau of Labor Statistics, Division of Labor Force Statistics, "Union Members Summary," *Economic News Release*, January 21, 2011, http://www.bls.gov/news.release/union2.nr0.htm (accessed May 27, 2011).

Higher Wages and Benefits There are power and strength in numbers. As a result, unions sometimes are able to obtain higher wages and benefits packages for their members than employees would be able to negotiate individually.[3] One or two employees walking off the job over a wage dispute is unlikely to significantly affect most businesses, but hundreds of workers going out on strike can temporarily disrupt or even close down a company. Additionally, professional bargainers employed by the union may be able to negotiate more skillfully than any individual could on his or her own behalf.

Greater Job Security Unions provide their members with a sense of independence from the supervisor's power to arbitrarily hire, promote, or fire. The collective bargaining contract stipulates rules that apply to all members, thus providing fairer and more uniform treatment. For example, after a lengthy strike involving the Teamsters union and the Giant Food Company, the parties reached an agreement that guarantees Teamsters union members lifelong job security—regardless of external factors affecting the company.

Influence on Work Rules Where a union exists, workers can participate in determining the conditions under which they work and have an effective channel through which they can protest conditions that they believe are unfair. Therefore, a union not only represents the worker but also provides rules that define channels in which complaints and concerns of workers can be registered. Grievance procedures and rights to third-party arbitration of disputes are examples of practices that are typically defined and regulated as a result of union efforts.

Compulsory Membership Many labor agreements contain statements that are commonly referred to as *union security clauses*. When one considers the importance of security arrangements to unions—importance brought about in terms of numbers and guaranteed income—it is no wonder that such emphasis is placed on achieving a union security arrangement that best suits their goals. Such arrangements range from compulsory membership in the union to giving employees the freedom in choosing to join the union. The various types of union security arrangements—the union shop, the agency shop, and the right-to-work shop, as well as some special provisions under the realm of union security arrangements—are briefly discussed in this section and summarized in Exhibit 16-2.

The most powerful relationship legally available (not legally available in right-to-work states[4]) to a union is a union shop. This arrangement stipulates that employers, although free to hire whomever they choose, may retain only union members. That is, all employees hired into positions covered under the terms of a collective bargaining agreement must, after a specified probationary period of typically thirty to sixty days, join the union or forfeit their jobs.

An agreement that requires nonunion employees to pay the union a sum of money equal to union fees and dues as a condition of continuing employment is referred to as an agency shop. This arrangement was designed as a compromise between the union's desire to eliminate the "free rider" and the organization's desire to make union membership voluntary. In such a case, if for whatever reason workers decide not to join the union (religious beliefs, values, etc.), they still must pay dues. Because workers will receive the benefits negotiated by the union, they must pay their fair share. However, in a 1988 Supreme Court decision involving union dues, the Court ruled that a union may be violating rights of nonmembers who are required to pay "agency fees" for union representation if it uses those fees for political and other activities not directly related to collective bargaining.

union shop
An arrangement that stipulates that employers, although free to hire whomever they choose, may retain only union members.

agency shop
An agreement that requires nonunion employees to pay the union a sum of money equal to union fees and dues as a condition of continuing employment.

---

[3] Find out more at AFL-CIO, available online at www.aflcio.org/joinaunion/.
[4] Currently, twenty-two states are right-to-work states: Alabama, Arizona, Arkansas, Florida, Georgia, Idaho, Iowa, Kansas, Louisiana, Mississippi, Nebraska, Nevada, North Carolina, North Dakota, Oklahoma, South Carolina, South Dakota, Tennessee, Texas, Utah, Virginia, and Wyoming. See National Right to Work Legal Defense Foundation, Inc., *Right to Work States*, 2005, www.nrtw.org.

Union Shop	*Strongest of the union security arrangements.* Mandates that employees join the union within a specified period of time–or forfeit their jobs. Union shops are illegal in right-to-work states.
Agency Shop	Union membership is not compulsory, but non-union workers in the bargaining unit must still pay union dues. These workers do have the right to demand that their monies be used for collective bargaining purposes only. Like the union shop, the agency shop is illegal in right-to-work states.
Open Shop	The weakest form of union security. Workers are free to choose to join the union or not. Those who do join must pay union dues. Those who do not join do not have to pay dues. Leaving the union typically can occur only during an escape period at the expiration of a contract. In right-to-work states, the open shop is the only permissible union security arrangement.
Maintenance of Membership	In an open shop, membership is required for the duration of an existing contract.
Dues Checkoff	Involves the employer deducting union dues directly from a union member's paycheck. The employer collects the money and forwards a check to the union treasurer. Management typically offers this service free of charge to the union.

Exhibit 16-2
Union security arrangements (and related elements).

The least desirable form of union security from a union perspective is the open shop. This is an arrangement in which joining a union is totally voluntary. Those who do not join are not required to pay union dues or any associated fees. For workers who do join, there is typically a maintenance-of-membership clause in the existing contract that dictates certain provisions. Specifically, a maintenance-of-membership agreement states that should employees join the union, they are compelled to remain in the union for the duration of the existing contract. When the contract expires, most maintenance-of-membership agreements provide an escape clause—a short interval of time, usually ten days to two weeks—in which employees may choose to withdraw their membership from the union without penalty.

A common provision in union security arrangements is a process called the dues checkoff. A dues checkoff occurs when the employer withholds union dues from the members' paychecks. Similar to other pay withholdings, the employer collects the dues money and sends it to the union. There are a number of reasons employers provide this service, and a reason the union would permit them to do so. Collecting dues takes time, so a dues checkoff reduces the "downtime" by eliminating the need for the shop steward to go around to collect dues. Furthermore, recognizing that union dues are the primary source of income for the union, knowing how much money is in the union treasury can tell the company whether a union is financially strong enough to endure a strike. Given these facts, why would a union agree to such a procedure? Simply, the answer lies in guaranteed revenues! By letting the company deduct dues from a member's paycheck, the union is assured of receiving its monies. Excuses from members that they don't have their money, or will pay next week, are eliminated.

Being Upset with the Supervisor One of the many reasons employees join a union appears to be management, especially the first-line supervisor. If employees are upset with the

open shop
An arrangement in which joining a union is totally voluntary.

maintenance of membership
An agreement that should employees join the union, they are compelled to remain in the union for the duration of the existing contract. Such an agreement often provides an escape clause when the contract expires in which employees may choose to withdraw their membership from the union without penalty.

dues checkoff
A provision that often exists in union security arrangements whereby an employer withholds union dues from members' paychecks.

way their supervisor handles problems, upset over how a coworker has been disciplined, and so on, they are likely to seek help from a union. In fact, it is reasonable to believe that when employees vote to unionize, it's often a vote against their immediate supervisor rather than a vote in support of a particular union.[5]

Labor Legislation

The legal framework for labor–management relationships has played a crucial role in their development. In this section, therefore, major developments in labor law are discussed. An exhaustive analysis of these laws and their legal and practical repercussions is not possible within the scope of this book. However, we focus our discussion on two important laws that have shaped much of the labor relations process. We then briefly summarize other laws that have helped shape labor–management activities.

THE WAGNER ACT

Wagner Act
Also known as the National Labor Relations Act, this act gave employees the legitimate right to form and join unions and to engage in collective bargaining.

The National Labor Relations Act of 1935, commonly referred to as the Wagner Act, is the basic "bill of rights" for unions. This law guarantees workers the right to organize and join unions, to bargain collectively, and to act in concert to pursue their objectives. In terms of labor relations, the Wagner Act specifically requires employers to bargain in good faith over mandatory bargaining issues—wages, hours, and terms and conditions of employment.

The Wagner Act is cited as shifting the pendulum of power to favor unions for the first time in U.S. labor history. This was achieved, in part, through the establishment of the National Labor Relations Board (NLRB). This administrative body, consisting of five members appointed by the president of the United States, was given the responsibility for determining appropriate bargaining units, conducting elections to determine union representation, and preventing or correcting employer actions that can lead to unfair labor practice charges. The NLRB, however, has only remedial and no punitive powers.

National Labor Relations Board (NLRB)
A group that has primary responsibility for conducting elections to determine union representation and to interpret and apply the law against unfair labor practices.

Unfair labor practices (Section 8[a] of the Wagner Act) include any employer tactics that

- interfere with, restrain, or coerce employees in the exercise of the rights to join unions and to bargain collectively;
- dominate or interfere with the formation or administration of any labor organization;
- discriminate against anyone because of union activity;
- discharge or otherwise discriminate against any employee because he or she filed or gave testimony under the act; or
- refuse to bargain collectively with the representatives chosen by the employees.

Although the Wagner Act provided the legal recognition of unions as legitimate interest groups in American society, many employers opposed its purposes. Some employers, too, failed to live up to the requirements of its provisions. That's because employers recognized that the Wagner Act didn't provide protection for them from unfair union labor practices. Thus, the belief that the balance of power had swung too far to labor's side, and the public outcry stemming from post–World War II strikes, led to the passage of the Taft-Hartley Act (Labor–Management Relations Act) in 1947.

---

[5]See, for instance, M. Romano, "Hospital Accused of Iron-Fist Tactics," *Modern Hospital*, January 8, 2001, 16.

THE TAFT-HARTLEY ACT

The major purpose of the Taft-Hartley Act was to amend the Wagner Act by addressing employers' concerns in terms of specifying unfair union labor practices. Under Section 8(b), Taft-Hartley states that it is an unfair labor practice for unions to

- restrain or coerce employees in joining the union, or coerce the employer in selecting bargaining or grievance representatives;
- discriminate against an employee to whom union membership has been denied, or cause an employer to discriminate against an employee;
- refuse to bargain collectively;
- engage in strikes and boycotts for purposes deemed illegal by the act;
- charge excessive or discriminatory fees or dues under union-shop contracts; or
- obtain compensation for services not performed or not to be performed.

In addition, Taft-Hartley declared illegal one type of union security arrangement: the closed shop. Until Taft-Hartley's passage, the closed shop was dominant in labor contracts. The closed shop was an arrangement where a union "controlled" the source of labor. Under this arrangement, an individual would join the union, be trained by the union, and sent to work for an employer by the union. In essence, the union acted as a clearinghouse of employees. When an employer needed a number of employees—for whatever duration—the employer would contact the union and request that these employees start work. When the job was completed and the employees were no longer needed on the job by the employer, they were sent back to the union.

By declaring the closed shop illegal, Taft-Hartley began to shift the pendulum of power away from unions. Furthermore, in doing so, the act enabled states to enact laws that would further reduce compulsory union membership. Taft-Hartley also included provisions that forbade secondary boycotts and gave the president of the United States the power to issue an eighty-day cooling-off period when labor–management disputes affect national security. A secondary boycott occurs when a union strikes against Employer A (a primary and legal strike), and then strikes and pickets against Employer B (an employer against which the union has no complaint) because of a relationship that exists between Employers A and B, such as Employer B handling goods made by Employer A. Taft-Hartley also set forth procedures for workers to decertify, or vote out, their union representatives.

Whereas the Wagner Act required only employers to bargain in good faith, Taft-Hartley imposed the same obligation on unions. Although the negotiation process is described later in this chapter, it is important to understand what is meant by the term *bargaining in good faith*. This does not mean that the parties must reach agreement, but rather that they must come to the bargaining table ready, willing, and able to meet and deal, open to proposals made by the other party, and with the intent to reach a mutually acceptable agreement.

Realizing that unions and employers might not reach agreement and that work stoppages might occur, Taft-Hartley also created the Federal Mediation and Conciliation Service (FMCS) as an independent agency separate from the Department of Labor. The FMCS's mission is to send a trained representative to assist in negotiations. Both employer and union are responsible for notifying the FMCS when other attempts to settle the dispute have failed or contract expiration is pending. An FMCS mediator is not empowered to force parties to reach an agreement, but he or she can use persuasion and other means of diplomacy to help them reach their own resolution of differences.

OTHER LAWS AFFECTING LABOR–MANAGEMENT RELATIONS

Whereas the Wagner and Taft-Hartley acts are the most important laws influencing labor–management relationships in the United States, some other items are pertinent to our discussion: the Landrum-Griffin Act of 1959 and the Racketeering Influenced and Corrupt Organizations Act of 1970. Let's briefly review the notable aspects of these two laws.

Taft-Hartley Act (Labor–Management Relations Act)
A law passed in 1947 that specified unfair union labor practices and declared the closed shop to be illegal.

secondary boycott
A union strikes against Employer A (a primary and legal strike), and then strikes and pickets against Employer B (an employer against which the union has no complaint) because of a relationship that exists between Employers A and B, such as Employer B handling goods made by Employer A.

Federal Mediation and Conciliation Service (FMCS)
A government agency that assists labor and management in settling their disputes.

Landrum-Griffin Act
Also known as the Labor and Management Reporting and Disclosure Act, this legislation protects union members from possible wrongdoing on the part of their unions. Its thrust is to require all unions to disclose their financial statements.

Landrum-Griffin Act The Landrum-Griffin Act of 1959 (Labor and Management Reporting and Disclosure Act) was passed to address the public outcry over misuse of union funds and corruption in the labor movement. This act, like Taft-Hartley, was an amendment to the Wagner Act.

The thrust of the Landrum-Griffin Act is to monitor internal union activity by making officials and those affiliated with unions (union members, trustees, etc.) accountable for union funds, elections, and other business and representational matters. Restrictions are also placed on trusteeships imposed by national or international unions, and conduct during a union election is regulated. Much of this act is part of an ongoing effort to prevent corrupt practices and to keep organized crime from gaining control of the labor movement. The mechanisms used to achieve this goal are requirements for unions and individuals employed by unions to file annual reports to the Department of Labor regarding administrative matters—reports such as their constitutions and bylaws, administrative policies, elected officials, and finances. This information, filed under forms L-M 2, L-M 3, or L-M 4[6] with the Department of Labor, is available to the public. Furthermore, Landrum-Griffin includes a provision that allows all members of a union to vote irrespective of their race, sex, national origin, and so forth. This provision gave union members certain rights that were not available to the general public for another five years until the passage of the Civil Rights Act of 1964. Landrum-Griffin also requires that all who vote on union matters do so in a secret ballot, especially when the vote concerns the election of union officers.

Racketeering Influenced and Corrupt Organizations Act (RICO)
Legislation whose primary emphasis with respect to labor unions is to eliminate any influence exerted on unions by members of organized crime.

Racketeering Influenced and Corrupt Organizations Act (RICO) Although this act has far-reaching implications, the Racketeering Influenced and Corrupt Organizations Act (RICO) of 1970 serves a vital purpose in labor relations. RICO's primary emphasis with respect to labor unions is to eliminate any influence exerted on unions by members of organized crime. Over the past decade, RICO has been used to oust a number of labor officials in unions who were alleged to have organized crime ties.

Comprehension Check 16-1

1. An organization of workers acting collectively, seeking to promote their mutual interests is called a
   a. workgroup
   b. work team
   c. union
   d. labor group

2. Approximately what percentage of the workforce is unionized?
   a. 12
   b. 16
   c. 17
   d. 21

3. Which one of the following is *not* a reason people join unions?
   a. Seeking increased wages and benefits
   b. Seeking an individual voice with employers
   c. Seeking to influence work rules
   d. Seeking to create greater job security

---

[6]L-M 2 reports are required of unions that have annual revenues of $200,000 or more and those in trusteeship. L-M 3 reports are a simplified annual report that may be filed by unions with total revenues of less than $200,000 if the union is not in trusteeship. L-M 4 is an abbreviated form and may be used by unions with less than $10,000 in total annual revenues if the union is not in trusteeship. These reports are due within ninety days after the end of the union's fiscal year.

4. A union shop

   a. requires nonunion employees to pay a sum of money equal to union dues

   b. stipulates that an employer may retain only union members

   c. makes union membership voluntary

   d. is illegal

5. Which labor act gives employees the legitimate right to join a union?

   a. Wagner Act

   b. Taft-Hartley Act

   c. Landrum-Griffin Act

   d. Labor–Management Relations Act

6. Which one of the following is *not* an unfair labor practice for unions?

   a. Restraining employees in joining the union

   b. Charging excessive union dues

   c. Refusing to bargain collectively with employee representatives

   d. None of the above

How Are Employees Unionized?

Employees are unionized after an extensive and sometimes lengthy process called the organizing campaign. Exhibit 16-3 contains a simple model of how the process typically flows in the private sector. Let's look at these elements.

Efforts to organize a group of employees may begin with employee representatives requesting a union to visit the employees' organization and solicit members; or the union itself might initiate the membership drive. In some cases, unions are using the Internet to promote their benefits to workers. Regardless of how, as established by the NLRB, the union must secure signed authorization cards from at least 30 percent of the employees it wishes to represent. Employees who sign the cards indicate that they wish the particular union to be their representative in negotiating with the employer.

Although at least 30 percent of the potential union members must sign the authorization card prior to an election, unions are seldom interested in bringing to vote situations in which they merely meet the NLRB minimum. Why? The answer is simply a matter of mathematics and business: To become the certified bargaining unit, the union must be accepted by a majority of those eligible voting workers. Acceptance in this case is determined by a secret-ballot election. This election held by the NLRB, called a representation certification (RC) election, can occur only once in a twelve-month period; thus, the more signatures on the authorization cards, the greater the chances for a victory.

authorization card
A card signed by prospective union members indicating that they are interested in having a union election held at their work site.

representation certification (RC) election
The election process whereby union members vote in a union as their representative.

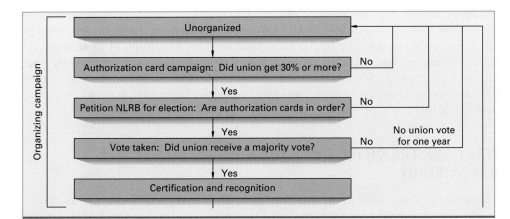

Exhibit 16-3
The labor relations process.

Even when a sizable proportion of the workers signs authorization cards, the victory is by no means guaranteed. The company often is not passive during the organization drive (see "News Flash! When the Union Arrives"). Although laws govern what supervisors can and cannot do, supervisors in the organization may attempt to persuade the potential members to vote no. Union organizers realize that some initial signers might be persuaded to vote no, and thus unions usually require a much higher percentage of authorization cards so that they can increase their odds of obtaining a majority.

When that majority vote is received, the NLRB certifies the union and recognizes it as the exclusive bargaining unit. Irrespective of whether the individual in the certified bargaining union voted for or against the union, each worker is covered by the negotiated contract and must abide by its governance. Once a union has been certified, is it there for life? Certainly not. On some occasions, union members may become so dissatisfied with the union's actions in representing them that they want to turn to another union or return to their nonunion status. In either case, the rank-and-file members petition the NLRB to conduct a representation decertification (RD) election. Once again, if a majority of the members vote the union out, it is gone. However, once the election has been held, no other action can occur for another twelve-month period. This grace period protects the employer from employees decertifying one union today and certifying another tomorrow.

representation decertification (RD) election
The election process whereby union members vote out their union as their representative.

Even more rare than an RD is a representation decertification election initiated by management, or RM. The guidelines for the RM are the same as for the RD, except that the employer is leading the drive. Although RDs and RMs are ways of decertifying unions, it should be pointed out that most labor agreements bar the use of either decertification election during the term of the contract.

Organizing drives may be unsuccessful, but when unions do achieve their goal to become the exclusive bargaining agent, the next step is to negotiate the contract. In the next section, we look at the specific issues surrounding collective bargaining.

Collective Bargaining

collective bargaining
A process for developing a union contract, which includes preparing to negotiate the contract, negotiating the contract, and administering the contract after it has been ratified.

The term collective bargaining typically refers to the negotiation, administration, and interpretation of a written agreement between two parties that covers a specific period of time. This agreement, or contract, lays out in specific terms the conditions of employment; that is, what is expected of employees and the limits in management's authority. In the following discussion, we take a somewhat larger perspective—we also consider the organizing, certification, and preparation efforts that precede actual negotiation.

Most of us hear or read about collective bargaining only when a contract is about to expire or when negotiations break down. When a railroad contract is about to expire, we may be aware that collective bargaining exists in the transportation industry. Similarly, teachers' strikes in Cleveland, workers striking against Verizon Communications, or baseball players striking against Major League Baseball owners remind us that organized labor deals with management collectively. In fact, collective bargaining agreements cover about half of all state and local government employees and one-ninth of employees in the private sector. The wages, hours, and working conditions of these unionized employees are negotiated for periods of usually two or three years at a time. Only when these contracts expire and company representatives and the union are unable to agree on a new contract are most of us aware that collective bargaining is a very important part of a supervisor's job.

WHAT ARE THE OBJECTIVE AND SCOPE OF COLLECTIVE BARGAINING?

The objective of collective bargaining is to agree on an acceptable contract—acceptable to management, union representatives, and the union membership. But what is covered in this contract? The final agreement reflects the problems of the particular workplace and industry in which the contract is negotiated.

Irrespective of the specific issues contained in various labor contracts, four issues appear consistently throughout all labor contracts. Three of the four are mandatory bargaining issues, which means that management and the union must negotiate in good faith over these issues. These mandatory issues were defined by the Wagner Act as wages, hours, and terms and conditions of employment. The fourth issue covered in almost all labor contracts is the grievance procedure, which is designed to permit the adjudication of complaints.

News Flash!

WHEN THE UNION ARRIVES

What can company representatives do when they learn that a union-organizing drive has begun in their organization? Under labor laws, although they are permitted to "defend" against the union campaign, they must do so properly. Here are some suggested guidelines for what to do and what not to do during the organizing drive.

- If your employees ask for your opinion on unionization, respond in a neutral manner. For example, "I really have no position on the issue. Do what you think is best."
- If contacted directly by a union representative, you should not look at any list of employees they may attempt to give you, or any cards or letters with names on them, or any papers employees may attempt to hand you.
- You can prohibit union-organizing activities in your workplace during work hours only if they interfere with work operations. This may apply to the organization's e-mail, too.
- You can prohibit outside union organizers from distributing union information in the workplace.
- Employees have the right to distribute union information to other employees during breaks and lunch periods.
- Don't discriminate against any employee who is involved in the unionization effort.
- Be on the lookout for efforts by the union to coerce employees to join its ranks. This activity by unions is an unfair labor practice. If you see this occurring, report it to your boss or to human resources. Your organization may also want to consider filing a complaint against the union with the NLRB.

- Supervisors should remember TIPS at all times. TIPS reminds supervisors not to do the following:
  T—**Threaten.** Don't make any threats that are related to the possibility of unionization—for example, "If this union effort succeeds, upper management is seriously thinking about closing down this plant. But if it's defeated, they may push through an immediate wage increase."
  I—**Interrogate.** Don't question employees publicly or privately about union-organizing activities—for example, "Are you planning to go to that union rally this weekend?" But if an employee freely tells you about the activities, you may listen.
  P—**Promise.** Don't promise incentives to any who refrain from joining the union or who may oppose organizing activities.
  S—**Spy.** Don't spy on employees' union activities—for example, by standing in the cafeteria to see who is distributing pro-union literature.

Sources: Adapted from M. K. Zachary, "Labor Law for Supervisors: Union Campaigns Prove Sensitive for Supervisory Employees," *Supervision*, May 2000, 23–26; S. Greenhouse, "A Potent, Illegal Weapon against Unions: Employers Know It Costs Them to Fire Organizers," *New York Times*, October 24, 2000, A-10; J. E. Lyncheski and L. D. Heller, "Cyber Speech Cops," *HR Magazine*, January 2001, 145–150; J. A. Mello, "Redefining the Rights of Union Organizers and Responsibilities of Employers in Union Organizing Drives," *SAM Advanced Management Journal*, Spring 1998, 4; and S. Quisenberry, "Union Awareness and Maintaining Union-Free Status," *SHRM white paper*, September 1997, www.shrm.org/hrresources/whitepapers_published/CMS_000223.asp (accessed June 25, 2008).

WHAT IS THE COLLECTIVE BARGAINING PROCESS?

Let's now consider the actual collective bargaining process. Exhibit 16-4 contains a simple model of how the process typically flows in the private sector—which includes preparing to negotiate, actual negotiations, and administering the contract after it has been ratified.

Preparing to Negotiate Once a union has been certified as the bargaining unit, both union and company representatives begin the ongoing activity of preparing for negotiations. We refer to this as an *ongoing* activity because ideally it should begin as soon as the previous contract is agreed upon or union certification is achieved. Realistically, it probably begins anywhere from one to six months before the current contract expires. We can consider the preparation for negotiation as composed of three activities: fact gathering, goal setting, and strategy development.

Information is acquired from both internal and external sources. Internal data include grievance and accident records; employee performance reports; overtime figures; and reports on transfers, turnover, and absenteeism. External information should include statistics on the current economy, both at local and national levels; economic forecasts for the short and intermediate terms; copies of recently negotiated contracts by the adversary union to determine which issues the union considers important; data on the communities in which the company operates (cost of living, changes in cost of living, terms of recently negotiated labor contracts, and statistics on the labor market); and industry labor statistics to see which terms other organizations, employing similar types of personnel, are negotiating.

With homework done, information in hand, and tentative goals established, both union and management must put together the most difficult part of the bargaining preparation activities—a strategy for negotiations. This includes assessing the other side's power and specific tactics.

Negotiating at the Bargaining Table Negotiation customarily begins with the union delivering to company officials a list of "demands." By presenting many demands, the union creates significant room for trading in later stages of the negotiation; it also disguises the union's real position, leaving management to determine which demands are adamantly sought, which are moderately sought, and which the union is prepared to quickly abandon. A long list of demands, too, often fulfills the internal political needs of

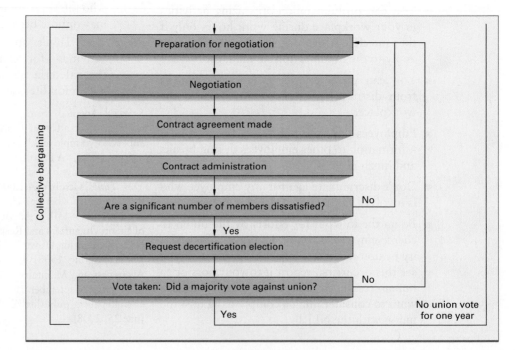

Exhibit 16-4
The collective bargaining process.

the union. By seeming to back numerous wishes of the union's members, union administrators appear to be satisfying the needs of the many factions within the membership.

Although both union and company representatives may publicly accentuate their differences, the real negotiations typically go on behind closed doors. Each party tries to assess the relative priorities of the other's demands, and each begins to combine proposals into viable packages. What takes place, then, is the attempt to get management's highest offer to approximate the lowest demands that the union is willing to accept. Hence, negotiation is a form of compromise. When an oral agreement is achieved, it is converted into a written contract. Negotiation finally concludes with the union representatives submitting the contract for ratification or approval from rank-and-file members. Unless the rank-and-file members vote to approve the contract, negotiations must resume.

Contract Administration Once a contract is agreed upon and ratified, it must be administered. Four stages of contract administration must be carried out: (1) getting the contract terms out to all union members and management personnel; (2) implementing the contract; (3) interpreting the contract and grievance resolution; and (4) monitoring activities during the contract period.[7]

When providing information to all concerned, both parties must ensure that changes in contract language are spelled out. For example, the most obvious would be hourly rate changes; company officials must make sure that the payroll system is adjusted to the new rates as set in the contract. But it goes beyond just pay: Changes in work rules, hours, and the like must be communicated. If both sides agree to mandatory overtime, something that was not in existence before, all must be informed of how it will work. Neither the union nor the company can simply hand a copy of the contract to each organization member and expect it to be understood. It is necessary to hold meetings to explain the new terms of the agreement.

The next stage of contract administration is ensuring that the agreement is implemented. All communicated changes now take effect, and both sides are expected to comply with the contract terms. One concept to recognize during this phase is *management rights*. Typically, management is guaranteed the right to allocate organizational resources in the most efficient manner; to create reasonable rules; to hire, promote, transfer, and discharge employees; to determine work methods and assign work; to create, eliminate, and classify jobs; to lay off employees when necessary; to close or relocate facilities with a sixty-day notice; and to institute technological changes.

Probably the most important element of contract administration relates to spelling out a procedure for handling contractual disputes. Almost all collective bargaining agreements contain formal procedures to be used in resolving grievances about the interpretation and application of the contract. These contracts have provisions for resolving specific, formally initiated grievances by employees concerning dissatisfaction with job-related issues.

Grievance procedures are typically designed to resolve grievances as quickly as possible and at the lowest level possible in the organization (see Exhibit 16-5).[8] The first step

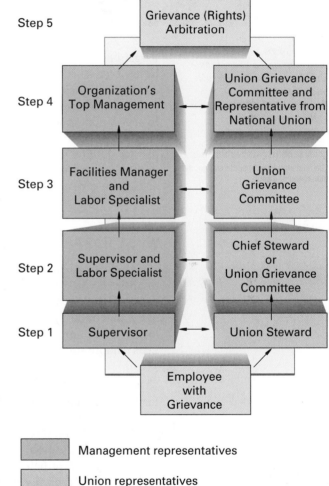

Exhibit 16-5
A typical grievance procedure.

grievance procedures
Procedures designed to resolve disputes as quickly as possible and at the lowest level possible in the organization.

[7]M. H. Bowers and D. A. DeCenzo, *Essentials of Labor Relations* (Upper Saddle River, NJ: Prentice Hall, 1992), 101.
[8]See also M. I. Lurie, "The 8 Essential Steps in Grievance Processing," *Dispute Resolution Journal* 54, no. 4 (November 1999), 61–65.

These workers are walking the picket line over a labor dispute. Unable to reach an agreement in contract negotiations, they decided to withhold their labor in the form of a strike.

grievance (rights) arbitration
The final step used to settle a labor and management dispute.

economic strike
An impasse that results from labor and management's inability to agree on the wages, hours, and terms and conditions of a new contract.

wildcat strike
An illegal strike in which employees refuse to work during the term of a binding contract, often as a result of ambiguities in the current contract.

almost always has the employee attempt to resolve the grievance with his or her immediate supervisor. If it cannot be resolved at this stage, it is typically discussed with the union steward and the supervisor. Failure at this stage usually brings in the individuals from the organization's industrial relations department and the chief union steward. If the grievance still cannot be resolved, the complaint passes to the facilities manager, who typically discusses it with the union grievance committee. Unsuccessful efforts at this level give way to the organization's senior management and typically a representative from the national union. Finally, if those efforts are unsuccessful in resolving the grievance, the final step is to go to arbitration—called grievance (rights) arbitration.

In practice, we find that almost all collective bargaining agreements provide for grievance (rights) arbitration as the final step to an impasse. Of course, in small organizations the five steps described tend to be condensed, possibly moving from discussing the grievance with the union steward to taking the grievance directly to the organization's senior executive or owner, and then to arbitration, if necessary.

Finally, in our discussion of preparation for negotiations, we stated that both company and union need to gather various data. One of the most bountiful databases for both sides is information kept on a current contract. By monitoring activities, company and union can assess how effective the current contract was, when problem areas or conflicts arose, and what changes might need to be made in subsequent negotiations.

WHAT HAPPENS WHEN AGREEMENT CANNOT BE REACHED?

Although the goal of contract negotiations is to achieve an agreement that is acceptable to all concerned parties, sometimes that goal is not achieved. Negotiations do break down, and an impasse occurs. Sometimes these events are triggered by internal issues in the union, the union's desire to strike against the company, the company's desire to lock out the union, or the company's knowledge that striking workers can be replaced. Let's explore some of these areas.

Strikes versus Lockouts Negotiations have only three possible preliminary outcomes. First, and obviously preferable, is agreement. The other alternatives, when no viable solution can be found to the parties' differences, is a strike or a lockout.

There are several types of strikes. The most relevant to contract negotiations is the economic strike. An economic strike occurs when the two parties cannot reach a satisfactory agreement before the contract expires. When that deadline passes, the union leadership will typically instruct its members not to work—thus leaving their jobs.[9] Although in today's legal climate, replacement workers can be hired, no disciplinary action can be taken against workers who participate in economic strike activities.

Another form of strike is the wildcat strike. A wildcat strike generally occurs when workers walk off the job because of something management has done. For example, if a union employee is disciplined for failure to call in sick according to provisions of the contract, fellow union members may walk off the job to demonstrate their dissatisfaction with management's action. It is important to note that these strikes happen while a contract is in force—an agreement that usually prohibits such union activity. Consequently, wildcat strikers can be severely disciplined or terminated. In the past, the most powerful

---

[9]To be accurate, a strike vote is generally held at the local union level, in which the members authorize their union leadership to call the strike.

weapon unions in the private sector had was the economic strike. By striking, the union was, in essence, withholding labor from the employer, thus causing the employer financial hardships.

After the strike is underway, a form of protest referred to as picketing usually begins in an attempt to prevent dissident members of the union, members of other unions, and nonunionized workers from crossing the picket line to work. Picketers congregate outside a place of work to draw public attention to their cause and pressure the company to meet their demands. The pressure comes from harm caused to the business through loss of customers and negative publicity that prevent it from operating normally.

A strikebreaker is someone who crosses the picket line and works despite the strike. Strikebreakers may also be referred to as scabs or rats and are usually individuals who are not employed by the company prior to the strike, but rather hired prior to or during the strike to keep production or services going. Strikebreakers must be willing to deal with taunts, threats, and even violence from strikers. The most effective union action is a strike, and strikebreakers render a strike useless. Employers focused on breaking the union consider strikebreakers as one of their best tools.

In contemporary times, we have witnessed an increase in company officials' use of the lockout. A lockout, as the name implies, occurs when the organization denies unionized workers access to their jobs during an impasse. A lockout, in some cases, is the company's predecessor to hiring replacement workers. In others, it's the company officials' effort to protect their facilities and machinery and other employees at the work site.

lockout
A company action equivalent to a strike; when management denies unionized employees access to their jobs.

In either case, the strategy is the same. Both sides are attempting to apply economic pressure on their "opponent" in an effort to sway negotiations in their direction. And when the strategy doesn't work, negotiations are said to have reached an impasse. When that happens, impasse resolution techniques are designed to help.

Impasse Resolution Techniques When labor and management in the private sector cannot reach a satisfactory agreement themselves, they may need the assistance of an objective third-party individual. This assistance comes in the form of *conciliation and mediation, fact-finding,* and *interest arbitration.*

Conciliation and mediation are two very closely related impasse resolution techniques in which a neutral third party attempts to get labor and management to resolve their differences. Under conciliation, however, the role of the third party is to keep the negotiations ongoing. In other words, this individual is a go-between—advocating a voluntary means through which both sides can continue negotiating. Mediation, on the other hand, goes one step further. The mediator attempts to pull together the common ground that exists and make settlement recommendations for overcoming the barriers that exist between the two sides. A mediator's suggestions, however, are only advisory. That means that the suggestions are not binding on either party.

Fact-finding is a technique whereby a neutral third-party individual conducts a hearing to gather evidence from both labor and management. The fact finder then renders a decision as to how he or she views an appropriate settlement. Similar to mediation, the fact finder's recommendations are only suggestions—they, too, are not binding on either party.

fact-finding
A technique whereby a neutral third-party individual conducts a hearing to gather evidence from both labor and management.

The final impasse resolution technique is called interest arbitration. Under interest arbitration, generally a panel of three individuals—one neutral and one each from the union and management—hears testimony from both sides. After the hearing, the panel renders a decision on how to settle the current contract negotiation dispute. If the three members of the panel are unanimous in their decision, that decision may be binding on both parties.

interest arbitration
Arbitration in which a panel of three individuals hears testimony from both sides and renders a decision on how to settle a contract negotiation dispute.

In public-sector impasse resolution techniques, some notable differences do exist. For instance, in many states that permit public-sector employee strikes, some form of arbitration is typically required. The decisions rendered through arbitration are binding on both parties. Moreover, in the public sector, a particular form of arbitration, called *final-offer arbitration,* is witnessed. Both sides present their recommendations, and the arbitrator is required to select one party's offer in its entirety over the other. There is no attempt in final-offer arbitration to seek compromise.

Something to Think About (and promote class discussion)

CAN BOEING SHIFT THE WORK?

Boeing Corporation, builder of some of the world's finest airliners, wants to build its newest commercial jet in South Carolina instead of Washington State. Boeing is planning to shift some production of its new 787 "Dreamliner" from its union-represented plant to the right-to-work (meaning workers can choose whether or not they want to be unionized) plant. These plans are polarizing Republicans and Democrats as well as union and right-to-work supporters over the issue of job creation.

The National Labor Relations Board filed suit claiming that Boeing's intent was to punish the International Association of Machinists (IAM) for the union's past strikes because Boeing allegedly moved to open the new factory after failing to win a nonstrike promise from the IAM union. Boeing insists that the 23,000 Machinist union members in Washington will not lose work to the 1,000 nonunion workers at the South Carolina plant. South Carolina is on line to build three of the ten 787 jets now being built each month while workers in Washington will be put to work on other aircraft. The first jet from the South Carolina plant is scheduled to roll off the line in the fall of 2012.

Boeing's position, expressed by spokesman Tim Neale, is that the Dreamliner is too important to risk interruptions from union disputes. Boeing needs to insure its production, and he points out that the IAM union, which struck against Boeing for fifty-eight days in 2008, is "… starting to give us a reputation as an unreliable supplier. We pay penalties to the customers when we're late delivering the planes." Boeing estimates losses from the 2008 strike at $1.8 billion. Neale stated that even if some of the Dreamliner production were shifted to South Carolina, hourly employment at the Washington plant is still on the rise. "We're in a hiring mode across the board," he said.

The International Association of Machinists general counsel Chris Corson has concerns that "Once that plant is up and running, our members in Puget Sound will be saying, 'That's what happens if we strike, if we negotiate hard at the bargaining table, they take our work away.' " He points out that starting pay at the South Carolina plant will be about $14 an hour compared to $15 an hour at the Washington plant, where a veteran worker can earn about $27 an hour, or about $56,000 a year before overtime.

The NLRB filed a complaint, charging that Boeing broke the law when it decided to shift production. "A worker's right to strike is a fundamental right," said NLRB acting general counsel Lafe Solomon when he issued the complaint. "We also recognize the rights of employers to make business decisions based on their economic interests, but they must do so within the law." The NLRB says it's not trying to prevent Boeing from opening the plant altogether, it just doesn't want Boeing to shift work away from the union-represented workers in Washington.

While both Boeing and the Machinist union express confidence they will prevail in the ultimate legal battle, the Machinist union is concerned that the union could win the legal fight and lose the public relations war. "Boeing is so far pretty successfully using this case to throw some red meat at the larger debate in this country about labor and capitalism," said Corson. "I think our message is getting out, but I don't think we have as much money and connections as Boeing does." The case is scheduled to go before an administrative law judge in June 2011 and will likely be followed by a decision from the full NLRB. Boeing and the IAM both vow they will appeal the case to a federal court if they lose before the bipartisan board.

What do you think? Do organizations have the right to locate manufacturing facilities where they feel they get the best deal? Should they be constrained to continue production where they originally located? Should the government intervene in the decisions of business? Do workers have the right to choose whether or not they want to be unionized?

Sources: C. Isidore, "A tug-of-war over middle-class jobs," *CNNMoney*, May 20, 2011, http://money.cnn.com/2011/05/20/news/companies/boeing_nlrb_jobs/?section=money_latest (accessed May 26, 2011); R. Lowry, "The Persecution of Boeing. The NLRB's Claims Are Laughable on Their Face," *National Review*, May 2011, http://www.freerepublic.com/focus/f-news/2719339/posts (accessed May 27, 2011); The New York Times, "Boeing and the N.L.R.B.," *The Opinion Pages*, April 25, 2011, http://www.nytimes.com/2011/04/26/opinion/26tue2.html (accessed May 27, 2011); R. Lowry, "Boeing faces NLRB persecution," *The Columbia Daily Tribune*, May 26, 2011, http://www.columbiatribune.com/news/2011/may/26/boeing-faces-nlrb-persecution/ (accessed May 27, 2011).

Comprehension Check 16-2

7. The labor act that attempted to address the public outcry over the misuse of union funds was the

   a. Wagner Act
   b. Taft-Hartley Act
   c. Landrum-Griffin Act
   d. RICO Act

8. The election process whereby union members vote in a union is called a

   a. representation decertification election
   b. representation certification election
   c. representation verification election
   d. representation NLRB election

9. The first step in contract negotiations for labor management is

   a. contract agreement
   b. negotiations
   c. contract ratification
   d. none of the above

10. The process to settle an employee complaint is called

    a. grievance (rights) arbitration
    b. contract administration
    c. interest arbitration
    d. labor–management cooperation

11. An illegal strike in which employees refuse to work during the term of a binding contract is called

    a. an economic strike
    b. a wildcat strike
    c. a secondary boycott
    d. a lockout

12. A technique whereby a neutral third-party individual conducts a hearing to gather evidence from both labor and management is called

    a. interest arbitration
    b. fact-finding
    c. rights arbitration
    d. grievance arbitration

Enhancing Understanding

SUMMARY

After reading this chapter, I can:

1. **Define** *union*. A union is an organization of workers, acting collectively, seeking to promote and protect its mutual interests through collective bargaining.

2. **Discuss the effect the Wagner and Taft-Hartley acts had on labor–management relations.** The Wagner (National Labor Relations) Act of 1935 and the Taft-Hartley (Labor–Management Relations) Act of 1947 represent the most direct legislation affecting collective bargaining. The Wagner Act gave unions the freedom to exist and identified unfair employer labor practices. The Taft-Hartley Act balanced the power between unions and management by identifying unfair union labor practices.

3. **Describe the union-organizing process.** The union-organizing process officially begins with the completion of an authorization. If the required percentage of potential union members show their intent to vote on a union by signing the authorization card, the NLRB will hold an election. If 50 percent plus one of those voting vote for the union, the union is certified to be the bargaining unit.

4. **Describe the components of collective bargaining.** Collective bargaining typically refers to the negotiation, administration, and interpretation of a written agreement between two parties that covers a specific period of time.

5. **Identify the steps in the collective bargaining process.** The collective bargaining process comprises the following steps: preparation for negotiations, negotiations, and contract administration.

6. **Explain the various types of union security arrangements.** The various union security arrangements are the closed shop (made illegal by the Taft-Hartley Act); the union shop, which requires compulsory union membership; the agency shop, which requires compulsory union dues; and the open shop, which enforces workers' freedom of choice to select union membership or not.

7. **Describe the role of a grievance procedure in collective bargaining.** The role of the grievance procedure is to provide a formal mechanism in labor contracts for resolving issues over the interpretation and application of a contract.

8. **Identify the various impasse resolution techniques.** The most popular impasse resolution techniques include conciliation and mediation (a neutral third party informally attempts to get the parties to reach an agreement); fact-finding (a neutral third party conducts a hearing to gather evidence from both sides); and interest arbitration (a panel of individuals hears testimony from both sides and renders a decision).

COMPREHENSION: Review and Discussion Questions

1. What three pieces of legislation have been most important in defining the rights of management and unions? Provide the highlights of each.

2. Explain the appeal of unions to employees.

3. What is the process for establishing a union as the legal collective bargaining representative for employees?

4. "All that is required for successful labor–management relations is common sense, sound business judgment, and good listening skills." Do you agree or disagree with this statement? Explain.

5. How do union shops and agency shops differ?

6. Given your career aspirations, might you join a union? Why or why not? Explain.

7. What is collective bargaining? How widely is it practiced?

8. Describe the collective bargaining process.

9. What is the objective of collective bargaining?

10. "An employer might not want to stifle a union-organizing effort. In fact, an employer might want to encourage employees to join a union." Do you agree or disagree with this statement? Explain your position.

KEY CONCEPT CROSSWORDS

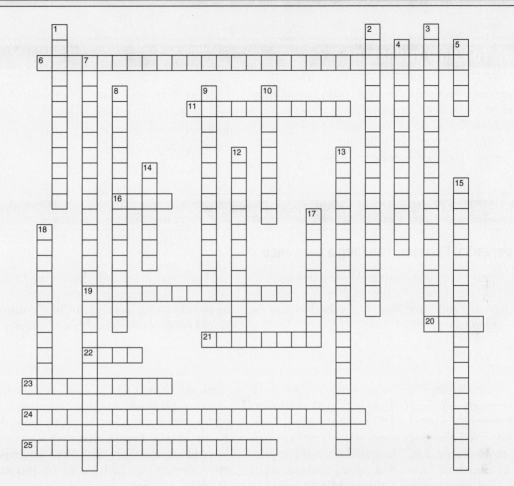

ACROSS

6. the election process whereby union members vote out their union as their representative
11. an act passed in 1947 that specified unfair union labor practices
16. legislation whose primary emphasis with respect to labor unions is to eliminate any influence exerted on unions by organized crime
19. an impasse that results from labor and management's inability to agree to a contract
20. a group that has the primary responsibility for conducting elections and applying laws against unfair labor practices
21. an arrangement in which joining a union is totally voluntary
22. a govt. agency that assists labor and management in settling their disputes
23. an agreement that requires nonunion employees to pay a sum of money equal to union dues
24. an agreement that employees who join a union are compelled to remain in the union for the duration of the existing contract
25. a signed document by prospective union members indicating that they are interested in holding a union election

DOWN

1. a provision in a labor contract in which the employer withholds union dues from members' paychecks
2. steps designed to resolve labor–management disputes as quickly as possible and at the lowest levels in the organization
3. the final step used to settle a labor and management dispute
4. an act that was passed to address the misuse of union funds and corruption in the labor movement
5. an organization that represents workers' interests through collective bargaining
7. the election process whereby union members elect a union as their representative
8. a union strike against another employer because the employer has a relationship with an employer with whom the union has a disagreement
9. all activities within a company that involve dealing with a union
10. this act gave employees the legitimate right to form and join a union
12. an illegal strike whereby employees refuse to work during the term of a binding contract
13. a process for developing a union contract, from negotiation to administration
14. a company action equivalent to a strike when management denies unionized employees access to their jobs
15. a three-member panel that hears labor–management testimony and renders a decision on how to settle a dispute
17. an arrangement that stipulates that employers may retain only union members
18. a technique whereby a neutral third-party individual conducts a hearing to gather evidence from both labor and management

ANSWERS TO COMPREHENSION CHECKS

Comprehension Check 16-1

1. c   2. a   3. b   4. b   5. a   6. C

Comprehension Check 16-2

7. c   8. b   9. d (preparation for negotiations)
10. a   11. b   12. B

Developing Your Supervisory Skills

GETTING TO KNOW YOURSELF

Before you can effectively supervise others, you must understand your current strengths and areas in need of development. To assist in this learning process, we encourage you to complete the following self-assessment from the Prentice Hall Self-Assessment Library 3.4.

1. How Well Do I Handle Ambiguity? (I. A. 4.)

After you complete the assessment, we suggest you retain the results and store them as part of your "portfolio of learning about yourself."

BUILDING A TEAM

➤ An Experiential Exercise: Handling a Grievance

Break into teams of three. This role-play requires one person to play the role of the HR director (Chris), another to play the role of the employee (Pat), and a third to play the role of the union steward (C. J.).

Each team member should read the following scenario and the excerpt from the union contract. Then, you are to role-play a meeting in Chris's office. This role-play should take no more than fifteen minutes.

Scenario

The head of security for your company has recently been focusing attention on the removal of illegal substances from the company's workplace. One morning last week, a guard suspected the possession of a controlled substance by an employee, Pat. The guard noticed Pat placing a bag in a personal locker and subsequently searched the locker. The guard found a variety of pills, some of which he thought were nonprescription types. As Pat was leaving work for the day, the security guard stopped Pat and asked to see the contents of Pat's bag. Pat was not told why the request was being made. Pat refused to honor the request and stormed out the door, leaving the company premises. Pat was terminated the next morning for refusing to obey the legitimate order of a building security guard. Feeling that they were unable to address the issue satisfactorily with Pat's supervisor, Pat and the union steward, C. J., have set up this meeting with the HR director, Chris.

Chris wishes to enforce the supervisor's decision to terminate Pat and justify the reason for it. C. J. and Pat, on the other hand, claim that this action is a violation of the union contract.

Relevant Contract Language

The following is excerpted from the labor agreement:

An employee who fails to maintain proper standards of conduct at all times, or who violates any of the following rules, shall be subject to disciplinary action.

Rule 4: Bringing illegal substances, firearms, or intoxicating liquors onto company premises, using or possessing these on company property, or reporting to work under the influence of a substance is strictly prohibited.

Rule 11: Refusal to follow supervisory orders, or acting in any way insubordinate to any company agent, is strictly prohibited.

Role for Chris

To handle this grievance, listen to the employee's complaint, investigate the facts as best you can, and make your decision and explain it clearly.

➤ Internet: Web Activity

Go to http://www.pearsonhighered.com/robbins/. Find *Supervision Today!* 7th Ed. and click Companion Website.

RESOLVING A GRIEVANCE

As the first person involved in a dispute, you can take certain actions to help resolve the problem.

STEPS IN PRACTICING THE SKILL

STEP 1: Listen to the employee's complaint. Don't be defensive and don't take the complaint personally. Employees regularly have grievances, and you're the first contact point in the process that represents the organization. Calmly listen to the employee's complaint. Keep an open mind. It is very important at this stage not to argue with the employee. You want to gain understanding.

STEP 2: Investigate to get the facts. You want to separate facts from opinions. Is the situation as presented by the employee complete and factual? Interview any key people who may be able to verify the employee's claims. Review all pertinent documents. Go over the clauses in the labor contract that apply to the employee's complaint. If you're unsure about the contract's language or how a relevant clause should be interpreted, get counsel from a labor specialist in your human resource department. Getting assistance isn't a sign of ignorance. You're not a legal specialist, so don't pretend to be one.

STEP 3: Make your decision and explain it clearly. You need to complete your investigation promptly so that you can reach your decision in a relatively short period of time. Why? Because most labor agreements specify a definite time period within which a grievance must be answered. If you determine that the grievance is unfounded, verbally give the employee and union steward your interpretation. Be sure to back up your decision with specific reasons

for denying the grievance, citing evidence from your investigation and/or language from the contract. You should then follow up the verbal answer with a written response. If the grievance has merit, provide a written response to the employee and union steward stating this fact. Additionally, you should describe the corrective action you plan to take. Before you write this response, be sure that your remedy is consistent with established practices, doesn't set any new precedents, and is within your authority. When in doubt, get approval from your boss or a manager in human resources. You want to be very careful about making individual exceptions to past practices. This might seem like an easy way to make the grievance disappear, but you could end up setting a precedent that might seriously hurt the organization in future contract negotiations or in future arbitration decisions.

STEP 4: Keep records and documents. It's important to document everything you do relating to a grievance. Remember that the labor agreement is a binding legal contract. As such, formality is important. You have to follow the language of the contract. To protect yourself and the organization against charges that you have not followed the contract as intended, you must keep all the records that you've accumulated on every grievance.

STEP 5: Be prepared for appeals. If you rule against the employee, you should expect the employee or the union steward to appeal your decision to a higher level. Be prepared to be questioned by union officials and various labor specialists from your organization's human resource group. Don't let this shake you, and don't let an employee's or union representative's threat of appeal influence your decision.

➤ Communicating Effectively

1. In a two- to three-page report, discuss the pros, cons, and class perceptions of what it would be like to work in a unionized environment. Would you consider working in such an environment? Why or why not?

2. Visit the AFL-CIO's website (www.aflcio.org). Research and summarize two current union issues the AFL-CIO is working on/supporting legislation for. End your report with your support for or against the union perspective.

THINKING CRITICALLY

➤ Case 16-A: Texaco Provides Labor–Management Training

Mike Leonard works at Texaco, Inc., where a significant reorganization has recently taken place. A large number of employees took reassignments, some even in other parts of the world. The numerous changes that have been made in the operations of this oil and gas giant have created the need for more training, especially labor–management relations training for supervisors.

Mike is the director of labor relations and has helped to develop and administer the policies of the organization. He is particularly adept at warding off and defusing employee grievances as well as negotiating contracts that will benefit management and employees alike. He frequently gives workshops to unit supervisors about changes in labor legislation, about how such laws affect Texaco's employees and company officials, and about promoting effective labor–management relations for the good of the organization.

In less than a month, Mike will begin a training session for several new Texaco supervisors. Mike has provided each supervisor with the basic labor relations policies and procedures manuals for the company. Janet, Tom, and Ginny are three Texaco supervisors who will receive training. Each has recently been promoted from within the company. They all have several common concerns, two of which are the increased concern by company officials with raising productivity and promoting an atmosphere to avoid employee grievances.

RESPONDING TO THE CASE

1. What do these new supervisors need to know about labor relations and the collective bargaining process?

2. Describe the various roles a supervisor may have in labor matters (e.g., organizing drives, negotiations, contract administration).

➤ Case 16-B: Faragut Services Faces a Union Challenge

Ari Ainge is the manufacturing supervisor for Faragut Services, an eight-year-old company that produces memory chips for the digital camera industry. The company has grown from eight employees working on a government contract to a 150-person company that is a leading supplier to two of the industry leaders in the digital camera world. Faragut's product is known to be high quality and exceptionally well engineered. Ari has been with the company for six years, and one hundred employees work for him on two manufacturing shifts. Ari has introduced most of the manufacturing systems and controls. He has always considered himself a people person and values his relationship with employees.

In the past eighteen months the company has been driven to meet the demand from its two major customers. To do this, the company has increased the manufacturing shifts from forty hours per week to an average of forty-eight hours per week. Three times in the last quarter the manufacturing department created a third shift filled with experienced people from the other two shifts and temporary workers. In all cases the workers have been paid overtime and received performance bonuses that averaged an extra week's pay. Ari has prided himself on the way the manufacturing department has been able to produce extraordinary amounts of product.

Ari has heard some mild complaining about the increase in hours and the need to work the third shift from some of the employees. He considers this to be normal and usually tries to remind people how exciting it is to work in a growing company with the opportunity for overtime and bonuses.

In June the company president tells Ari that a local union affiliate will be conducting an organizing campaign at Faragut starting in two weeks. Ari is shocked!

RESPONDING TO THE CASE

1. What are some of the reasons that a union is attempting to organize at Faragut Services?

2. What things might Faragut Services do to prepare for the organizing effort?

3. If you were a supervisor at Faragut Services, what would you do? Explain.

Postscript: Personal Development

Introduction

Career development is important to us all. We know that people sometimes have difficulty achieving their career goals. This reflects the new and unexpected complexities that supervisors must now confront in their efforts to mobilize and supervise their employees, and themselves. The historical beliefs that anyone would jump at the chance for a promotion, that competent people will somehow emerge within the organization to fill arising vacancies, and that a valuable employee will always be a valuable employee are no longer true. Lifestyles, too, are changing. We are becoming increasingly aware of our different needs and aspirations.

Some drastic changes have occurred over the past thirty years. Years ago career development programs in organizations were designed to help employees advance in their work lives by giving them the information and assessments they needed to realize their career goals. Career development was also a way for an organization to attract and retain highly talented personnel. But those days are all but disappearing in today's dynamic work environment—and so, too, are jobs as we have known them for the past several decades.[1] Downsizing, restructuring, work process engineering, globalization, contingent workers, and so forth have drawn us to one significant conclusion about managing careers: You, the individual, are responsible for your career.[2] It's not the organization's obligation! Sadly, millions of employees have learned this the hard way over the past few years.[3] Therefore, you must be prepared to do whatever is necessary to advance your career.

What, if any, responsibility does the organization have for career development under the "new rules" in today's contemporary organization? Basically the organization's responsibility is to build employee self-reliance and to help employees maintain their marketability through continual learning.[4] The essence of a contemporary career

---

[1]L. T. Eby, M. Butts, and A. Lockwood, "Predictors of Success in the Era of the Boundaryless Career," *Journal of Organizational Behavior* 24 (September 2003), 689–709.

[2]D. C. Feldman and C. R. Leana, "What Ever Happened to Laid-Off Executives?: A Study of Re-employment Challanges After Downsizing." *Organizational Dynamics* 29, no. 1 (Summer 2000), 64–75.

[3]K. Heim, "With Layoffs Up and Stock Prices Down at High-Tech Firms, Unions Step Up Their Quest for Power in the New Economy," *San Jose Mercury News* (December 28, 2000), A-1.

[4]See "Career Development Ranks Among the Most Demanded Content Areas Across Industries Worldwide," *Training and Development* (September 2003), 18.

development program is providing support so employees can continually add to their skills, abilities, and knowledge. This support includes the following:

- *Communicating clearly the organization's goals and future strategies.* When people know where the organization is headed, they're better able to develop a personal plan to share in that future.
- *Creating growth opportunities.* Employees should have access to new, interesting, and professionally challenging work experiences.
- *Offering financial assistance.* The organization should offer tuition reimbursement to help employees keep current.
- *Providing the time for employees to learn.* Organizations should be generous in providing paid time off from work for off-the-job training. Additionally, work-loads should not be so demanding that they preclude employees from having the time to develop new skills, abilities, and knowledge.

What Is a Career?

The term *career* has a number of meanings. In popular usage it can mean advancement ("He's moving up in his career"), a profession ("She has chosen a career in medicine"), or stability over time (career military).[5] For our purposes, we will define career as "the pattern of work-related experiences that span the course of a person's life."[6] Using this definition, it is apparent that we all have or will have careers. The concept is as relevant to transient, unskilled laborers as it is to engineers and physicians. For our purposes, therefore, any work, paid or unpaid, pursued over an extended period of time can constitute a career. In addition to formal work on the job, careers can include school-work, homemaking, and volunteer work. Furthermore, career success is defined not only objectively, in terms of promotion, but also subjectively, in terms of satisfaction.

Effective career development is also important for each individual. Because the definitions of *career* and what constitutes success have changed, the value of individual career development programs has expanded. Career success may no longer be measured merely by your income or hierarchical level in an organization. Career success may now include using your skills and abilities to face expanded challenges, or having greater responsibilities and increased autonomy in your chosen profession. Intrinsic career development, or "psychic income," is desired by many contemporary workers who are seeking more than salary and security from their jobs. Contemporary workers seek interesting and meaningful work; such interest and meaning are often derived from a sense of being the architect of their own careers.

HOW DO I MAKE A CAREER DECISION?

The best career choice is the choice that offers the best match between what you want and what you need. Good career choice outcomes for any of us should result in a series of positions that give us an opportunity for good performance, make us want to maintain our commitment to the field, and give us high work satisfaction. A good career match, then, is one in which we are able to develop a positive self-concept and to do work that we think is important.[7]

---

[5]D. T. Hall, *Careers in Organizations* (Santa Monica, CA: Goodyear Publishing, 1976); and J Van Maanen and E. H. Schein, "Career Development," in J. R. Hackman and J. L. Suttle (eds.), *Improving Life at Work: Behavioral Sciences Approaches to Organizational Change* (Santa Monica, CA: Goodyear Publishing, 1977), pp. 341–355.
[6]J. H. Greenhaus, *Career Management* (New York: Dryden Press, 1987), 6.
[7]D. E. Super, "A Life-Span Life Space Approach to Career Development," *Journal of Vocational Behavior* 16 (Spring 1980), 282–298.

Career planning is designed to assist you in becoming more knowledgeable about your needs, values, and personal goals. This knowledge can be achieved through a three-step self-assessment process.[8]

- *Identify and organize your skills, interests, work-related needs, and values.* The best place to begin is by drawing up a profile of your educational record. List each school you attended from high school on. What courses do you remember liking most and least? In what courses did you score highest and lowest? In what extra-curricular activities did you participate? Did you acquire any specific skills? Did you gain proficiency in other skills? Next, assess your occupational experience. List each job you have held, the organization you worked for, your overall level of satisfaction, what you liked most and least about the job, and why you left. It's important to be honest in covering each of these points.

- *Convert this information into general career fields and specific job goals.* Step 1 should have provided some insights into your interests and abilities. Now you need to look at how they can be converted into the kind of organizational setting or field of endeavor that will be a good match for you. Then you can become specific and identify distinct job goals. What fields are available? In business? In government? In nonprofit organizations? Your answer can be broken down further into areas such as education, financial, manufacturing, social services, or health services. Identifying areas of interest is usually far easier than pinpointing specific occupations. When you are able to identify a limited set of occupations that interest you, you can start to align them with your abilities and skills. Will certain jobs require you to move? If so, would the location be compatible with your geographic preferences? Do you have the educational requirements necessary for the job? If not, what additional schooling will you need? Does the job offer the status and earning potential to which you aspire? What is the long-term outlook for jobs in this field? Does the field suffer from cyclical employment? Because no job is without its drawbacks, have you seriously considered all of the negative aspects? When you have fully answered questions such as these, you should have a relatively short list of specific job goals.

- *Test your career possibilities against the realities of the organization or the job market by talking with knowledgeable people in the fields, organizations, or jobs you desire.* These informational interviews should provide reliable feedback as to the accuracy of your self-assessment and the opportunities available in the fields and jobs that interest you.

CAN I INCREASE MY CHANCES FOR GETTING INTO THE ORGANIZATION?

In Chapter 5 we briefly introduced the recruiting process in organizations. When recruiters make a decision to hire employees, information is often sent out announcing the job in some format. When you see such an announcement and feel that there's a potential match between what you can offer and what the organization wants, you need to throw your hat into the "hiring ring."

One of the most stressful situations you will face happens when you apply for a job. This occurs because generally there are no specific guidelines to follow to guarantee success. However, several tips may increase your chances of finding employment. Even though getting a job interview should be one of your major goals in the hiring process, procuring an interview requires hard work. You should view getting a job as your job of the moment.

---

[8]I. R. Schwartz, "Self-Assessment and Career Planning: Matching Individuals and Organizational Goals," *Personnel* (January–February 1979), 48.

WHERE CAN I FIND JOBS ADVERTISED ON THE INTERNET?

Newspaper advertisements and employment agencies may be on their way to extinction as primary sources of information about job openings and finding job candidates. The reason: Internet recruiting. Nearly four out of five companies currently use the Internet to recruit new employees by adding a recruitment section to their websites.[9] Large organizations or those planning to do a lot of Internet recruiting often develop sites specifically designed for recruitment. They have the typical information you might find in an employment advertisement—qualifications sought, experience required, benefits provided. But they also allow the organization to showcase its products, services, corporate philosophy, and mission statement. This information increases the quality of applicants because those whose values don't mesh with those of the organization tend to self-select out. The best designed of those websites include an online response form so applicants don't need to send a separate résumé by mail, e-mail, or fax. Applicants need only fill in a résumé page and hit the "Submit" button. Facilitating the growth of Internet recruitment are commercial job-posting services that essentially provide electronic classified ads.[10]

Preparing a Résumé

All job applicants need to circulate information that reflects positively on their strengths. That information needs to be sent to prospective employers in a format that is understandable and consistent with the organization's hiring practices. In most instances, this is done through the résumé.

No matter who you are or where you are in your career, you should have a current résumé. Your résumé is typically the primary information source that a recruiter will use in determining whether to grant you an interview. Therefore, your résumé must be a sales tool; it must give key information that supports your candidacy, highlights your strengths, and differentiates you from other job applicants. Anything positive that distinguishes you from other applicants should be included. For example, things such as volunteer or community service show that you are well rounded, committed to your community, and willing to help others.

It's important to pinpoint a few key themes regarding résumés that may seem like common sense but are frequently ignored. First, if you are making a paper copy of your résumé, it must be printed on a quality printer. The style of font should be easy to read (e.g., Courier or Times New Roman type fonts). Avoid any style that may be hard on the eyes, such as a script or italic font. A recruiter who must review one hundred or more résumés a day is not going to look favorably on difficult-to-read résumés.

Many companies today are relying on computer software for making the first pass through résumés. Each résumé is scanned for specific information such as key job elements, experience, work history, education, or technical expertise. This has created two important aspects of résumé writing that you need to be aware of. The computer matches key words in a job description. Thus, in creating a résumé, you should use standard job description phraseology. Second, the font should be easily read by the scanner; if it isn't, your résumé may be put in the rejection file. Your résumé should be copied on good-quality white or off-white paper (no off-the-wall colors). In certain

---

[9]M. N. Martinez, "Get Job Seekers to Come to You," *HR Magazine* (August 2000), 42–52.

[10]See, for example, B. Leonard, "Online and Overwhelmed," *HR Magazine* (August 2000), 37–42; P. Curry, "Log on for Recruits," *Industry Week* (October 16, 2000), 46–54; R. E. Silverman, "Your Career Matters: Raiding Talent Via the Web—Personal Pages, Firms' Sites Are Troves of Information for Shrewd Headhunters," *Wall Street Journal* (October 3, 2000), B1; and M. N. Martinez, "Get Job Seekers to Come to You," *HR Magazine* (August 2000), 45–52.

types of jobs—such as a creative artist position—this suggestion may be inappropriate, but these are the exceptions. You can't go wrong using a twenty-weight bond paper that has some cotton content (about 20 percent). By all means, don't send standard duplicating paper—it may look as though you are mass-mailing résumés (even if you are).

Much of what we stated in the last few paragraphs also holds true if you are producing an electronic résumé. Whether the electronic résumé is required will often be designated in the advertisement you've read, or provided as direction on the Internet recruiting site where you saw the job opening. Many aggressive job candidates are setting up their own Web pages to "sell" their job candidacy—they're called websumés. When they learn of a possible job opening, they encourage potential employers to "check me out at my website." There, applicants have standard résumé information, supporting documentation, and sometimes a video in which they introduce themselves to potential employers.

Finally, regardless of whether your résumé is electronic or on paper, be sure to proofread it carefully. Because the résumé is the only representation of you the recruiter has, a sloppy résumé can be deadly. If it contains misspelled words or is grammatically incorrect, your chances for an interview will be significantly reduced. Proofread your résumé several times and, if possible, let others proofread it.

Excelling at the Interview

Interviews play a critical role in determining whether you will get the job. Up to now, all the recruiter has seen is your well-polished cover letter and résumé. Remember, however, that very few people, if any, get a job without an interview. No matter how qualified you are for a position, if you perform poorly in the interview, you're not likely to be hired!

The reason interviews are so popular is that they help the recruiter determine whether you are a "good fit" for the organization, in terms of your level of motivation and interpersonal skills. The following suggestions can help make your interview experience successful.

First, do some homework. Do a search for the company on the Internet (or visit your library) and get as much information as possible on the organization. Develop a solid grounding in the company, its history, markets, financial situation—and the industry in which it competes.

The night before the interview, get a good night's rest. As you prepare for the interview, keep in mind that your appearance is going to be the first impression you make. Dress appropriately. Incorrect attire can result in a negative impression. Arrive at the interview location about fifteen minutes ahead of your scheduled interview. It's better to have to wait than to contend with something unexpected, such as a traffic jam, that could make you late. Arriving early also gives you an opportunity to survey the office environment and gather clues about the organization. Pay attention to the layout of the waiting room, the formality of the receptionist, and anything else that can give you insights into what the organization may be like.

When you meet the recruiter, give him or her a firm handshake. Make good eye contact and maintain it throughout the interview. Remember, your body language may be giving away secrets about you that you don't want an interviewer to pick up. Sit erect and maintain good posture. Although you'll undoubtedly be nervous, try your best to relax. Recruiters know that you'll be anxious, and a good one will try to put you at ease. Being prepared for an interview can also help build your confidence and reduce the nervousness. You can start building that confidence by reviewing a set of questions most frequently asked by interviewers. You can usually get a copy of these from the career center at your college. Develop rough responses to these questions beforehand. This will lessen the likelihood that you'll be asked a question that catches you off guard. But our best advice is to be yourself. Don't go into an interview with a prepared text and recite it from memory. Have an idea of what you would like to say, but don't rely on rehearsed responses. Experienced interviewers will see through this "overpreparedness" and are likely to downgrade you on their evaluation.

If possible, go through several "practice" interviews. Universities often have career days on campus, when recruiters from companies are on site to interview students. Take advantage of them. Even if a job doesn't match what you want, the practice will help you become more skilled at dealing with interviews. You can also practice with family, friends, career counselors, student groups, or your faculty adviser.

When the interview ends, thank the interviewer for his or her time and for giving you the opportunity to talk about your qualifications. But don't think that "selling" yourself has stopped there. As soon as you get home, send a thank-you letter to the recruiter for taking the time to interview you and giving you the opportunity to discuss your job candidacy. This little act of courtesy has a positive effect—use it to your advantage.

Some Suggestions for Developing a Successful Career

What can you do to improve your chances for career success? You're already doing the *most* important thing: You're getting a college education! It's the surest way to increase your lifetime earnings. Currently, the average high school graduate earns $27,915 a year. His or her counterpart with a college degree earns $51,206. College graduates earn, on average, $800,000 more than high school graduates over their working career. Investing in your education and training is one of the best investments you'll make in your lifetime. What *else* can you do? Here are some suggestions based on extensive research into career management:

Assess Your Personal Strengths and Weaknesses Where do your natural talents lie? What can you do, relative to others, that gives you a competitive advantage? Are you particularly good with numbers? Have strong people skills? Good with your hands? Write better than most people? Everyone has some things that they do better than others and some things where they're weak. Play to your strengths.

Identify Market Opportunities Where are tomorrow's job opportunities? Regardless of your strengths, certain job categories are likely to decline in the coming decades—for instance, bank tellers, small farmers, movie projectionists, travel agents, and secretaries. In contrast, there are likely to be abundant opportunities created by an increasingly aging society, continued emphasis on technology, increased spending on education and training, and concern with personal security. This is likely to create excellent opportunities for jobs in gerontological counseling, network administration, training consultants, and security-alarm installers.

Take Responsibility for Managing Your Own Career Historically, companies tended to assume responsibility for their employees' careers. Today, this is the exception rather than the rule. Employees are increasingly expected to take responsibility for their own careers.

Think of your careers as your business and you're its CEO. To survive, you have to monitor market forces, head off competitors, and be ready to quickly take advantage of opportunities when they surface. You have to protect your career from harm and position yourself to benefit from changes in the environment.

Develop Your Interpersonal Skills Interpersonal skills, especially the ability to communicate, top the list of almost every employer's "must have" skills. Whether it's getting a new job or a promotion, strong interpersonal skills are likely to give you a competitive edge.

Practice Makes Perfect There's an increasing amount of evidence indicating that super-high achievers aren't fundamentally different from the rest of us. They just work harder and smarter. It's been found, based on studies of world-class performers in music, sports, chess, science, and business, that people like Tiger Woods, Mozart, and Bill Gates put in about 10,000 hours (or ten years at 1,000 hours a year) of persistent, focused training and experience before they hit their peak performance level. If you want to excel in any field, you should expect to have to put in a lot of deliberate practice—consistently engaging in repeated activity specifically designed to improve performance beyond your current comfort and ability level.

Stay Up-to-Date In today's dynamic world, skills can become obsolete quickly. To keep your career on track, you need to make learning a lifetime commitment. You should be continually "going to school"—if not taking formal courses, then reading books and journals to ensure that you don't get caught with obsolete skills.

Network Networking refers to creating and maintaining beneficial relationships with others in order to accomplish your goals. It helps to have friends in high places. It also helps to have contacts who can keep you informed of changes that are going on in your organization and in your industry. Go to conferences. Maintain contact with former college friends and alumni. Get involved in community activities. Cultivate a broad set of relationships. And in today's increasingly interconnected world, join online business networking groups like LinkedIn, Spoke, and Talkbiznow.

Stay Visible Networking can increase your visibility. So, too, can writing articles in your professional journals, teaching classes or giving talks in your area of expertise, attending conferences and professional meetings, and making sure your accomplishments are properly promoted. You increase your mobility and value in the marketplace by keeping visible.

Seek a Mentor Employees with mentors are likely to have enhanced mobility, increased knowledge of the organization's inside workings, greater access to senior executives, increased satisfaction, and increased visibility. For women and minorities, having mentors has been shown to be particularly helpful in promoting career advancement and success.

Leverage Your Competitive Advantage Develop skills that will give you a competitive advantage in the marketplace. Especially focus on skills that are important to employers, skills that are scarce, and areas where you have limited competition. Try to avoid a worst-case scenario: You have a job that anyone can learn in thirty minutes. Remember that the harder it is for you to learn and develop a highly prized skill, the harder it'll also be for others to acquire it. Generally speaking, the more training necessary to do a job and the fewer people who have that training, the greater your security and influence.

Here's an insight from many years as a student and a professor: To succeed in school, you have to be a generalist and excel at everything. For instance, to earn a 4.0 GPA, you need to be a star in English, math, science, geography, languages, and so on. The "real world," on the other hand, rewards specialization. You don't have to be good at everything. You just need to be good at something that others aren't and that society values. You can be lousy in math or science and still be a very successful opera singer, artist, salesperson, or writer. You don't have to excel in English to be a computer programmer or electrician. The secret to life success is identifying your comparative advantage and then developing it. And, as we've noted previously, you need to invest approximately 10,000 hours in honing your skills to achieve optimum proficiency.

Don't Shun Risks Don't be afraid to take risks, especially when you're young and you don't have much to lose. Going back to school, moving to a new state or country, or quitting a job to start your own business can be the decision that will set your life in a completely new direction. Great accomplishments almost always require taking the path less traveled; and the road to nowhere is paved with fears of the unknown.

It's OK to Change Jobs Past generations often believed "you don't leave a good job." That advice no longer applies. In today's fast-changing job market, staying put often only means that you're staying behind. Employers no longer expect long-term loyalty. And to keep your skills fresh, your income increasing, and your job tasks interesting, it will be increasingly likely that you'll need to change employers.

Opportunities, Preparation, and Luck = Success Successful people are typically ambitious, intelligent, and hardworking. But they are also lucky. It's not by happenchance that many of the biggest technology success stories—Bill Gates and Paul Allen at Microsoft, Steve Jobs at Apple, Scott McNealy at Sun Microsystems, and Eric Schmidt at Novell and Goggle—were born in a narrow three-year period between June 1953 and March 1956. They were smart. They were interested in computers and technology. But they were also lucky. They reached their teens and early 20s in 1975—at the dawn of the personal computer age. Those people with similar interests and talents but born in the mid-1940s were likely to have joined a firm like IBM out of college and been enamored with mainframe computers. Had they been born in the early 1960s, they would have missed getting in on the ground floor of the revolution.

A Final Word

Success is a matter of matching up opportunities with preparation. It's been suggested that few of us get more than a couple of special opportunities in our lifetime. If you're proactive, you will recognize those opportunities, have made the proper preparations, and then act on them.

You can't control when you were born, where you were born, your parents' finances, or the like. But what you can control is your preparation and willingness to act when opportunity knocks.

Succeeding in tomorrow's organizations needn't be a hopeless cause. You must recognize that yesterday's career paths don't exist everywhere. But with proper preparation and a positive mindset, you can open doors to career growth. Now, however, it will be solely your responsibility.

Good luck, and we hope that some of the material we presented in this book helps you reach your career goals.

Additional Sources: "Managing Your Career Module" based on: J. H. Greenhaus, V. M. Godstalk, and G. A. Callahan, *Career Management*, 3rd ed. (Cincinnati, OH: South–Western, 2000); K. A. Ericsson, "Deliberate Practice and the Modifiability of Body and Mind," *International Journal of Sports Psychology* 38 (January–March 2007), 4–34; J. P. Newport, "Mastery, Just 10,000 Hours Away," *Wall Street Journal*, March 14–15, 2009, W6; "Capital One Survey Highlights What Today's College Graduates Want from Employers," http://www.businesswire.com (June 10, 2008); M. Gladwell, *Outliers: The Story of Success* (New York: Little, Brown, 2008); R. N. Boles, *What Color Is Your Parachute? 2009: A Practical Manual for Job-Hunters and Career-Changers* (Berkeley, CA: Ten Speed Press, 2009); D. E. Super and D. T. Hall, "Career Development: Exploration and Planning," in M. R. Rosenzweig and L.W. Porter (eds.), *Annual Review of Psychology* 29 (Palo Alto, CA: Annual Reviews, 1978), 334; and M. B. Arthur and D. M. Rousseau, *The Boundaryless Career: A New Employment Principle for a New Organizational Era* (New York: Oxford University Press, 1996).

Glossary

360-degree appraisal   Performance feedback provided by supervisors, employees, peers, and possibly others.

A

accommodation   A method of maintaining harmonious relationships by placing others' needs and concerns above one's own.

active listening   A technique that requires an individual to "get inside" a speaker's mind to understand the communication from the speaker's point of view.

activities   The time or resources required to progress from one event to another.

adjective rating scale   A method of appraisal that uses a scale or continuum that best describes the employee using factors such as quantity and quality of work, job knowledge, cooperation, loyalty, dependability, attendance, honesty, integrity, attitudes, and initiative.

affirmative action   An active effort to recruit, select, train, and promote members of protected groups.

agency shop   An agreement that requires nonunion employees to pay the union a sum of money equal to union fees and dues as a condition of continuing employment.

appraisal process   The elements of a performance appraisal as defined by the organization; may involve self-evaluation and peer evaluation in addition to a supervisor's input.

assertiveness training   A technique designed to make people more open and self-expressive, saying what they mean without being rude or thoughtless.

attitudes   Evaluative statements or judgments concerning objects, people, or events.

authority   Rights inherent in a supervisory position to give orders and expect those orders to be obeyed.

authorization card   A card signed by prospective union members indicating that they are interested in having a union election held at their work site.

autocratic leader   A taskmaster who leaves no doubt as to who's in charge, and who has the authority and power in the group.

availability heuristic   The tendency of people to base their judgments on information that is readily available to them.

avoidance   Withdrawing from a conflict or ignoring it.

B

baby boomers   The largest group in the workforce; they are regarded as the career climbers—at the right place at the right time. Mature workers view them as unrealistic in their views and workaholics.

basic corrective action   Action that gets to the source of a deviation and seeks to adjust the differences permanently.

behaviorally anchored rating scale (BARS)   A scale that helps a supervisor rate an employee based on items along a continuum; points are examples of actual behavior on a given job rather than general descriptions or traits.

benchmarking   The search for the best practices among competitors or noncompetitors that lead to their superior performance.

body language   Gestures, facial configurations, and other movements of the body that communicate emotions or temperaments such as aggression, fear, shyness, arrogance, joy, and anger.

boundaryless organization   An organization that is not defined or limited by boundaries or categories imposed by traditional structures.

brainstorming   A technique for overcoming pressures for conformity that retard the development of creative alternatives; an idea-generating process that specifically encourages alternatives while withholding criticism of those alternatives.

budget   A numerical plan that expresses anticipated results in dollar terms for a specific time period; used as a planning guide as well as a control device.

business plan   A document that identifies the business founder's vision and describes the strategy and operations of that business.

C

carpal tunnel syndrome   A repetitive stress injury of the wrist.

cause-effect diagram   A depiction of the causes of a problem that groups the causes according to common categories such as machinery, methods, personnel, finances, or management.

central tendency error   Appraisers' tendency to avoid the "excellent" category as well as the "unacceptable" category and assign all ratings around the "average" or midpoint range.

centralization   Decision-making responsibility in the hands of top management.

chain of command   The continuous line of authority in an organization.

change   An alteration of an organization's environment, structure, technology, or people.

change agent   A person who acts as a catalyst and assumes the responsibility for overseeing the change process.

change process   A model that allows for successful change by requiring unfreezing of the status quo (equilibrium state), changing to a new state, and refreezing the new change to make it permanent. Unfreezing the equilibrium state is achieved by (1) increasing driving forces, (2) decreasing restraining forces, or (3) combining these two approaches.

channel   The medium by which a message travels.

charismatic leader   An individual with a compelling vision or sense of purpose, an ability to communicate that vision in clear terms that followers can understand, a demonstrated consistency and focus in pursuit of the vision, and an understanding of his or her own strengths.

checklist   A list of behavioral descriptions that are checked off when they apply to an employee.

code of ethics   A formal document that states an organization's primary values and the ethical rules it expects employees to follow.

cohesiveness   The degree to which group members are attracted to each other and are motivated to stay in the group.

collaboration   An approach to conflict in which all parties seek to satisfy their interests.

collective bargaining   A process for developing a union contract, which includes preparing to negotiate the contract, negotiating the contract, and administering the contract after it has been ratified.

collectivism   A view holding that the group above the individual in terms of politics, society, and economic issues trumps the claim of any individual. This view stresses interdependence over independence.

communication   The transference and understanding of meaning.

compensation administration   The process of determining a cost-effective pay structure that will attract and retain competent employees, provide an incentive for them to work hard, and ensure that pay levels will be perceived as fair.

competency-based compensation   Payments and rewards to employees on the basis of skills, knowledge, and behaviors.

compromise   An approach to conflict that requires each party to give up something of value.

conceptual competence   The mental ability to analyze and diagnose complex situations.

concurrent control   A type of control that takes place while an activity is in progress.

conflict   A process in which one party consciously interferes in the goal-achieving efforts of another party.

conflict management   The application of resolution and stimulation techniques to achieve the optimal level of departmental conflict.

consultative-participative leadership   The leadership style of an individual who seeks input and hears the concerns and issues of followers, but makes the final decision using input as an information-seeking exercise.

continuous improvement   Activities in an organization that enhance processes that result in the improved quality of goods and services produced.

control by exception   A system that ensures that one is not overwhelmed by information on variations from standard.

control chart   A statistical technique used to measure variation in a system to produce an average standard with statistically determined upper and lower limits.

control process   A three-step process that consists of (1) measuring actual performance, (2) comparing results with standards, and (3) taking corrective action.

controlling   Monitoring an organization's performance and comparing performance with previously set goals. If significant deviations exist, getting the organization back on track.

corrective control   A type of control that provides feedback after an activity is finished to prevent future deviations.

creativity   The ability to combine ideas in a unique way or to make unusual associations between ideas.

credibility   Honesty, competence, and the ability to inspire.

critical incidents   Incidents that focus attention on employee behaviors that are key in making the difference between executing a job effectively and executing it ineffectively.

critical path   The longest or most time-consuming sequence of events and activities in a PERT chart.

cultural environments   Values, morals, customs, and laws of countries.

culture   A set of unwritten norms that members of the organization accept and understand, and that guide their actions.

customer departmentalization   Grouping activities around common customer categories.

cyberloafing   Lost productivity time as a result of an employee using the Internet at work for personal reasons.

D

decentralization   The pushing down of decision-making authority to those closest to the problems.

decision tree   A diagram that analyzes hiring, marketing, investment, equipment purchases, pricing, and similar decisions that involve a progression of decisions. Decision trees assign probabilities to each possible outcome and calculate payoffs for each decision path.

decision-making process   A seven-step process that provides a rational and analytical way of looking at decisions. The steps include identification of the problem, collection of relevant information, development of alternatives, evaluation of alternatives, selection of the best alternative, implementation of the decision, and follow-up and evaluation.

decoding   A receiver's translation of a sender's message.

delegation   Allocation of duties, assignment of authority, assignment of responsibility, and creation of accountability.

democratic-participative leadership   A leadership behavior whereby the leader offers followers a say in what is decided; decisions are made by the group.

departmentalization   Grouping departments based on work functions, product or service, target customer or client, geographic territory, or the process used to turn inputs into outputs.

devil's advocate   A person who purposely presents arguments that run counter to those proposed by the majority or against current practices.

discipline   Actions taken by supervisors to enforce an organization's standards and regulations.

dismissal   Termination of employment.

distributive bargaining   A negotiating process that operates under zero-sum conditions; any gain made is at the expense of the other person, and vice versa.

divisional structure   An organization made up of self-contained units.

downsizing   A reduction in workforce and reshaping of operations to create "lean and mean" organizations. The goals of organizational downsizing are greater efficiency and reduced costs.

dues checkoff   A provision that often exists in union security arrangements whereby an employer withholds union dues from members' paychecks.

E

e-business   A comprehensive term describing the way an organization does its work by using electronic linkages with its key constituents to achieve its goals efficiently and effectively.

e-commerce   The online buying and selling of products or services.

economic strike   An impasse that results from labor and management's inability to agree on the wages, hours, and terms and conditions of a new contract.

effectiveness   Doing the right task; goal attainment.

efficiency   Doing a task right; also refers to the relationship between inputs and outputs.

electronic meeting   A group decision-making technique in which participants are positioned in front of computer terminals as issues are presented. Participants type responses onto computer screens as their anonymous comments, and aggregate votes are displayed on the projection screen in the room.

emergent leader   A leader who emerges within a workgroup without having formal authority in the organization.

employee assistance program (EAP)   A program designed to act as a first stop for individuals seeking help with the goal of getting productive employees back on the job as swiftly as possible.

employee benefits   Nonfinancial rewards designed to enrich employees' lives.

employee counseling   An emphasis on encouraging training and development efforts in a situation in which an employee's unwillingness or inability to perform his or her job satisfactorily is either voluntary or involuntary.

employee stock ownership plan (ESOP)   A compensation program that allows employees to become part owners of an organization by receiving stock as a performance incentive.

employee training   Changing the skills, knowledge, attitudes, or behavior of employees. Determination of training needs is made by supervisors.

employment planning   Assessing current human resources and future human resource needs; developing a program to meet future human resource needs.

employment-at-will   A legal doctrine that defines an employer's rights to discipline or discharge an employee.

empowerment   An increase in the decision-making discretion of workers.

encoding   The conversion of a message into symbolic form.

entrepreneurship   The process of initiating a business venture, organizing the necessary resources, and assuming the risks and rewards.

equity theory   The concept that employees perceive what they can get from a job situation (outcomes) in relation to what they put into it (inputs), and then compare their input–outcome ratio with the input–outcome ratio of others.

escalation of commitment   An increased commitment to a previous decision despite negative information.

ethics   Rules or principles that define right and wrong conduct.

events   Endpoints that represent completion of major activities.

expectancy theory   A theory that individuals analyze effort–performance, performance–rewards, and rewards–personal goals relationships, and their level of effort depends on the strengths of their expectations that these relationships can be achieved.

expected value analysis   A procedure that permits decision makers to place a monetary value on various consequences likely to result from the selection of a particular course of action.

extrinsic feedback   Feedback provided to an employee by an outside source. *See also* performance feedback.

F

Fact-finding   A technique whereby a neutral third-party individual conducts a hearing to gather evidence from both labor and management.

Federal Mediation and Conciliation Service (FMCS)   A government agency that assists labor and management in settling their disputes.

feedback loop   Information received by the sender from a receiver regarding a message that was sent.

first-level managers   Managers who represent the first level in the management hierarchy. *See also* supervisors.

flowchart   Visual representation of the sequence of events for a particular process that clarifies how things are being done so that inefficiencies can be identified and the process can be improved.

forcing   Attempting to satisfy one's own needs at the expense of the other party.

formal communication   Communication that addresses task-related issues and tends to follow the organization's authority chain.

formal group   A workgroup established by the organization and given designated work assignments and established tasks.

free-rein leader   An individual who gives employees total autonomy to make decisions that will affect them.

functional authority   Control over individuals outside one's own direct areas of responsibility.

functional departmentalization   Grouping activities into independent units based on functions performed.

functional structure   An organization in which similar and related occupational specialties are grouped together.

G

Gantt chart   A bar chart with time on the horizontal axis and activities to be scheduled on the vertical axis; shows when tasks are supposed to be done and compares actual progress on each task.

geographic departmentalization   Grouping activities into independent units based on geography or territory.

goal setting   A system by which employees jointly determine specific performance goals with their supervisors. Progress toward goals is periodically reviewed, and rewards are allocated on the basis of this progress.

grapevine   The means of communication by which most operative employees first hear about important changes introduced by organizational leaders; the rumor mill.

grievance (rights) arbitration   The final step used to settle a labor and management dispute.

grievance procedures   Procedures designed to resolve disputes as quickly as possible and at the lowest level possible in the organization.

group   Two or more interacting and interdependent individuals who come together to achieve particular objectives.

group-order ranking   Placing employees into classifications, such as "top one-fifth" or "second one-fifth." This method prevents a supervisor from inflating or equalizing employee evaluations.

groupthink   Withholding of differing views by group members to appear to be in agreement.

H

halo error   A tendency to rate an individual high or low on all factors as a result of the impression of a high or low rating on some specific factor.

hierarchy-of-needs theory   A theory of Abraham Maslow that states that a satisfied need no longer creates tension and therefore doesn't motivate. Maslow believed that the key to motivation is to determine where an individual is along the needs hierarchy and to focus motivation efforts at the point where needs become essentially unfulfilled.

"hot stove" rule   A set of principles for effectively disciplining an employee that demonstrates the analogy between touching a hot stove and receiving discipline.

human resource inventory   A database listing name, education, training, prior employer, languages spoken, and other information for each employee in the organization.

human resource management   The process of finding, hiring, training, and keeping employees in the organization.

hygiene factors   Herzberg's term for factors, such as working conditions and salary, that, when adequate, may eliminate job dissatisfaction but do not necessarily increase job satisfaction.

I

ill-structured problems   New problems about which information is ambiguous or incomplete.

immediate corrective action   Action that adjusts something right now and gets things back on track.

imminent danger   A condition under which an accident is about to occur.

incidence rate   A measure of the number of injuries, illnesses, or lost workdays as it relates to a common base rate of 100 full-time employees.

individual ranking   A method that requires supervisors to list all employees in order from the highest to lowest performer.

individualism   A view holding the individual above the group with the expectation that individuals will stand up for themselves and choose their own affiliations rather than blindly obeying external forces of politics, society, and economic issues. This view stresses independence over interdependence.

informal communication   Communication that moves in any direction, skips authority levels, and is as likely to satisfy social needs as it is to facilitate task accomplishments.

informal group   A social group that forms naturally in the work environment in response to the need for social contact.

innovation   The process of turning a creative idea into a useful product, service, or method of operation.

integrative bargaining   A negotiating process that operates under the assumption that there is at least one settlement that can create a win–win solution.

interest arbitration   Arbitration in which a panel of three individuals hears testimony from both sides and renders a decision on how to settle a contract negotiation dispute.

intermediate-term plan   A plan that covers a period of one to five years.

interpersonal competence   The ability to work with, understand, communicate with, and motivate other people, both individually and in groups.

intrinsic feedback   Self-generated feedback. *See also* performance feedback.

ISO 9000 series   Standards designed by the International Organization for Standardization that reflect a process whereby independent auditors attest that a company's factory, laboratory, or office has met quality management standards.

J

job description   A written statement of job duties, working conditions, and operating responsibilities.

job design   Combining tasks to form complete jobs.

job enrichment   The degree to which a worker controls the planning, execution, and evaluation of his or her work.

justice view of ethics   A view that requires individuals to impose and enforce rules fairly and impartially so that there is an equitable distribution of benefits and costs.

just-in-time (JIT) inventory systems   A system in which inventory items arrive when they are needed in the production process instead of being stored in stock. *See also kanban.*

K

kaizen   Japanese term for an organization committed to continuous improvement.

kanban   In Japanese, a "card" or "sign." Shipped in a container, a *kanban* is returned to the supplier when the container is opened, initiating the shipment of a second container that arrives just as the first container is emptied.

karoshi   A Japanese term for sudden death caused by overwork.

L

labor relations   All activities within a company that involve dealing with a union and its members.

Landrum-Griffin Act   Also known as the Labor and Management Reporting and Disclosure Act, this legislation protects union members from possible wrongdoing on the part of their unions. Its thrust is to require all unions to disclose their financial statements.

layoff-survivor sickness   A set of attitudes, perceptions, and behaviors of employees who survive involuntary staff reductions.

leadership   The ability an individual demonstrates to influence others to act in a particular way through direction, encouragement, sensitivity, consideration, and support.

leadership traits   Qualities such as intelligence, charm, decisiveness, enthusiasm, strength, bravery, integrity, and self-confidence.

leading   Motivating employees, directing activities of others, selecting the most effective communication channel, and resolving conflicts among members.

learning organization   An organization that has developed the capacity to adapt and change continuously.

leniency error   Positive or negative leniency that overstates or understates performance, giving an individual a higher or lower appraisal than deserved.

line authority   The authority that entitles a supervisor to direct the work of his or her employees and to make certain decisions without consulting others.

lockout   A company action equivalent to a strike; when management denies unionized employees access to their jobs.

locus of control   The source of control over an individual's behavior.

long-term plan   A plan that covers a period in excess of five years.

M

Machiavellianism   Manipulative behavior based on the belief that the ends can justify the means.

maintenance of membership   An agreement that should employees join the union, they are compelled to remain in the union for the duration of the existing contract. Such an agreement often provides an escape clause when the contract expires in which employees may choose to withdraw their membership from the union without penalty.

management   The process of getting things done, effectively and efficiently, through and with other people.

management functions   Planning, organizing, leading, and controlling.

marginal analysis   A method that helps decision makers optimize returns or minimize costs by dealing with the additional cost in a particular decision, rather than the average cost.

matrix   A structure that weaves together elements of functional and product departmentalization, creating a dual chain of command.

message   Information that is sent.

middle managers   All employees below the top management level who manage other managers; responsible for establishing and meeting specific departmental or unit goals set by top management.

motivation   The willingness to do something conditioned upon the action's ability to satisfy some need for the individual.

motivation-hygiene theory   A theory of Frederick Herzberg that the opposite of satisfaction is not "dissatisfaction" but "no satisfaction" and the opposite of dissatisfaction is not "satisfaction" but "no dissatisfaction."

musculoskeletal disorders (MSDs)   Continuous-motion disorders caused by repetitive stress injuries.

N

National Institute for Occupational Safety and Health (NIOSH)   The government agency that researches and sets OSHA standards.

National Labor Relations Board (NLRB)   A group that has primary responsibility for conducting elections to determine union representation and to interpret and apply the law against unfair labor practices.

need   A physiological or psychological deficiency that makes certain outcomes seem attractive.

need for achievement   A compelling drive to succeed; an intrinsic motivation to do something better or more efficiently than it has been done before.

negotiation   A process in which two or more parties who have different preferences and priorities must make a joint decision and come to an agreement.

nominal group technique   A technique that restricts discussion during the decision-making process.

nonprogrammed decision   A decision that must be custom-made to solve a unique and nonrecurring problem.

nonverbal communication Communication that is not spoken, written, or transmitted on a computer.

O

Occupational Safety and Health Act A law that enforces, through standards and regulations, healthful working conditions and preservation of human resources.

open shop An arrangement in which joining a union is totally voluntary.

operative employees Employees who physically produce an organization's goods and services by working on specific tasks.

organization A systematic grouping of people brought together to accomplish some specific purpose.

organization development (OD) The process of making systematic change in an organization.

organizing Arranging and grouping jobs, allocating resources, and assigning work so that activities can be accomplished as planned; determining which tasks are to be done, who is to do them, how the tasks are to be grouped, who reports to whom, and when decisions are to be made.

orientation An expansion on information a new employee obtained during the recruitment and selection stages; an attempt to familiarize new employees with the job, the work unit, and the organization as a whole.

P

parochialism Seeing things solely through one's own eyes and from one's own perspective; believing that one's own way is the best.

participative leadership The leadership style of an individual who actively seeks input from followers for many of the activities in the organization.

pay-for-performance programs Compensation plans that pay employees on the basis of some performance measure.

people-centered leader An individual who emphasizes interpersonal relations with those he or she leads.

performance appraisal A review of past performance that emphasizes positive accomplishments as well as deficiencies; a means for helping employees improve future performance.

performance feedback Information that lets an employee know how well he or she is performing a job; may be intrinsic (provided by the work itself) or extrinsic (provided by a supervisor or some other source).

performance-simulation tests Selection devices based on actual job behaviors, work sampling, and assessment centers.

PERT chart A diagram that depicts the sequence of activities needed to complete a project and the time or costs associated with each activity.

planning Defining an organization's goals, establishing an overall strategy for achieving these goals, and developing a comprehensive hierarchy of plans to integrate and coordinate activities.

policies Broad guidelines for supervisory action.

political competence A supervisor's ability to enhance his or her power, build a power base, and establish the "right" connections in the organization.

politicking The actions one can take to influence, or attempt to influence, the distribution of advantages and disadvantages within an organization.

power distance Extent to which the less powerful members of institutions and organizations expect and accept the idea that power is distributed unequally. Belief in small power distance results in expectance of power relations that are more consultative or democratic, with people relating to one another more as equal regardless of terminal positions. Belief in large power distance results in the less powerful accepting power relations that are more autocratic and paternalistic, wherein subordinates acknowledge the power of others based simply on their position in certain formal hierarchical positions.

preventive control A type of control that anticipates and prevents undesirable outcomes.

problem A discrepancy between an existing and a desired state of affairs.

procedure A standardized way of responding to repetitive problems; a definition of the limits within which supervisors must stay as decisions are made.

process The primary activities supervisors perform.

process departmentalization Grouping activities around a process; this method provides a basis for the homogeneous categorizing of activities.

product departmentalization Grouping activities into independent units based on problems or issues relating to a product.

productivity Output per labor hour, best expressed by the formula Productivity = Output/(Labor + Capital + Materials). Productivity measures can be applied to the individual, the group, and the total organization.

program   A single-use set of plans for a specific major undertaking within an organization's overall goals. Programs may be designed and overseen by top management or supervisors.

programmed decision   A repetitive decision that can be handled by a routine approach.

progressive discipline   Action that begins with a verbal warning, and then proceeds through written reprimands, suspension, and finally, in the most serious cases, dismissal.

Q

quality control   Identification of mistakes that may have occurred; monitoring quality to ensure that (it) meets some preestablished standard.

quality of life   Belief that places more value on relationships and overall worth of one's life in society.

quantity of life   Belief that values competitiveness, assertiveness, ambition, and the accumulation of wealth and material possessions.

R

Racketeering Influenced and Corrupt Organizations Act (RICO)   Legislation whose primary emphasis with respect to labor unions is to eliminate any influence exerted on unions by members of organized crime.

range of variation   Variation in performance that can be expected in all activities.

readiness   The ability and willingness of an employee to complete a task.

realistic job preview   A job interview that provides both positive and negative information about the job and the company.

recency error   An error that occurs when appraisers recall and give greater importance to employee job behaviors that have occurred near the end of the performance-measuring period.

recruitment   The process of locating, identifying, and attracting capable applicants.

reliability   An indication of whether a test or device measures the same thing consistently.

repetitive stress injuries   Injuries sustained by continuous and repetitive movements of a body part.

representation certification (RC) election   The election process whereby union members vote in a union as their representative.

representation decertification (RD) election   The election process whereby union members vote out their union as their representative.

representative heuristic   The tendency of people to match the likelihood of an occurrence with something they are familiar with.

responsibility   Supervisory obligations such as achieving a unit's goals, keeping costs within budget, following organizational policies, and motivating employees.

richness of information   A measure of the amount of information that is transmitted based on multiple information cues (words, posture, facial expressions, gestures, intonations), immediate feedback, and the personal touch.

rights view of ethics   A view that calls on individuals to make decisions consistent with fundamental liberties and privileges as set forth in documents such as the Bill of Rights.

ringisei   In Japanese organizations, consensus-forming decision-making groups.

risk propensity   A willingness to take chances, characterized by rapid decision making with the use of less information.

roles   Behavior patterns that correspond to the positions individuals occupy in an organization.

rule   An explicit statement that tells employees what they ought or ought not to do.

S

scatter diagram   An illustration of the relationship between two variables that shows correlations and possible cause and effect.

scheduling   Detailed planning of activities to be done, the order in which they are to be done, who is to do each activity, and when the activities are to be completed.

secondary boycott   A union strikes against Employer A (a primary and legal strike), and then strikes and pickets against Employer B (an employer against which the union has no complaint) because of a relationship that exists between Employers A and B, such as Employer B handling goods made by Employer A.

selection process   The hiring process, designed to expand the organization's knowledge about an applicant's background, abilities, and motivation.

self-esteem   The degree to which an individual likes or dislikes himself or herself.

self-monitoring   The ability to adjust behavior to external situational factors. High self-monitors adapt easily and are capable of presenting striking contradictions between public personas and private selves; low self-monitors tend to display their true feelings and beliefs in almost every situation.

sexual harassment   Anything of a sexual nature that is required for getting a job, has an employment consequence, or creates an offensive or hostile environment, including sexually suggestive remarks, unwanted touching, sexual advances, requests for sexual favors, and other verbal and physical conduct of a sexual nature.

short-term plan   A plan that covers a period of less than one year.

sick building   An unhealthy work environment.

similarity error   Rating others in a way that gives special consideration to qualities that appraisers perceive in themselves.

simple structure   A nonelaborate structure, low in complexity, with little formalization, and with authority centralized in a single person; a "flat" organization with only two or three levels.

single-use plan   A detailed course of action used once or only occasionally to deal with a problem that doesn't occur repeatedly.

situational leadership   Adjustment of a leadership style to specific situations to reflect employee needs.

six sigma   A philosophy and measurement process that attempts to "design in" quality as a product is being made.

skill   The ability to demonstrate a system and sequence of behavior that is functionally related to attaining a performance goal.

social loafing   Becoming a free-rider in a group because individual contributions to the group effort cannot be identified. As a result, the overall team's performance suffers.

social obligation   The foundation of a business's social involvement. An organization's social obligation is fulfilled when it meets its economic and legal responsibilities.

social responsibility   An obligation that organizations have to pursue long-term goals that are good for society.

social responsiveness   A process guided by social norms that requires businesses to determine what is right or wrong and thus seek fundamental truths; an attempt to do those things that make society better and not to do those things that could make it worse.

span of control   The number of employees a supervisor can efficiently and effectively direct.

staff authority   A limited authority that supports line authority by advising, servicing, and assisting.

standing plan   A plan that can be used over and over again by managers faced with recurring situations.

status   A social rank or the importance one has in a group.

strategic planning   Organizational planning that includes the establishment of overall goals and positioning an organization's products or services against the competition.

stress   Something an individual feels when faced with opportunities, constraints, or demands perceived to be both uncertain and important. Stress can show itself in both positive and negative ways.

stressors   Conditions that cause stress in an individual.

supervisors   Part of an organization's management team, supervisors oversee the work of operative employees and are the only managers who don't manage other managers. *See also* first-level managers.

supervisory competencies   Conceptual, interpersonal, technical, and political competencies.

supply chain management   An internally oriented process that focuses on the efficient flow of incoming materials to the organization.

suspension   Time off without pay; this step is usually taken only if neither verbal nor written warnings have achieved desired results.

T

tactical planning   Organizational planning that provides specific details on how overall goals are to be achieved.

Taft-Hartley Act (Labor–Management Relations Act)   A law passed in 1947 that specified unfair union labor practices and declared the closed shop to be illegal.

task-centered leader   An individual with a strong tendency to emphasize the technical or task aspects of a job.

team   A workgroup whose members are committed to a common purpose, have a set of specific performance goals, and hold themselves mutually accountable for the team's results.

team-based structure   An organization that consists entirely of workgroups, or teams.

technical competence   The ability to apply specialized knowledge or expertise.

technology   Any equipment, tool, or operating method designed to make work more efficient.

telecommuting   Linking a worker's remote computer and modem with those of coworkers and management at an office.

Theory X–Theory Y   A theory of Douglas McGregor that a supervisor's view of human nature is based on a certain grouping of assumptions and that he or she tends to mold behavior toward subordinates according to those assumptions.

top management   A group of people responsible for establishing an organization's overall objectives and developing the policies to achieve those objectives.

transactional leader   A leader who guides or motivates employees in the direction of established goals by clarifying role and task requirements.

transformational leader   A leader who inspires followers to transcend self-interests for the good of the organization and who is capable of having a profound and extraordinary effect on followers.

trust   The belief in the integrity, character, and ability of a leader.

U

uncertainty avoidance   The extent to which members of a society attempt to cope with anxiety by minimizing ambiguity. Cultures with high uncertainty avoidance prefer rules and structured circumstances, whereas low uncertainty avoidance cultures operate effectively in the absence of clear-cut rules, policies, and procedures.

union   An organization that represents workers and seeks to protect their interests through collective bargaining.

union shop   An arrangement that stipulates that employers, although free to hire whomever they choose, may retain only union members.

unity of command   A principle that states that an employee should have one and only one supervisor to whom he or she is directly responsible.

utilitarian view of ethics   A view in which decisions are made solely on the basis of their outcomes or consequences.

V

validity   A proven relationship between a selection device and some relevant criterion.

value chain management   The process of managing the entire sequence of integrated activities and information about product flows from start to finish—when the product is in the hands of the ultimate user.

verbal intonation   The emphasis an individual gives to words or phrases through speech.

verbal warning   A reprimand, a temporary record of which is kept by the supervisor.

visionary leadership   The ability to create and articulate a realistic, credible, attractive vision of the future that grows out of, and improves upon, the present.

W

Wagner Act   Also known as the National Labor Relations Act, this act gave employees the legitimate right to form and join unions and to engage in collective bargaining.

websumé   A web page used as a résumé.

wellness program   Any type of program that is designed to keep employees healthy, focusing on such things as smoking cessation, weight control, stress management, physical fitness, nutrition education, blood pressure control, and so on.

well-structured problems   Straightforward, familiar, easily defined problems.

wildcat strike   An illegal strike in which employees refuse to work during the term of a binding contract, often as a result of ambiguities in the current contract.

work process engineering   Radical or quantum change in an organization.

work specialization   The process of breaking down a job into a number of steps, with each step being completed by a different individual.

workforce diversity   The composition of the workforce to include men, women, whites, blacks, Hispanics, Asians, Native Americans, people with disabilities, people with diverse sexual preferences, the elderly, and so on.

written essay   A written narrative describing an employee's strengths, weaknesses, past performance, potential, and suggestions for improvement.

written warning   The first formal stage of the disciplinary procedure; the warning becomes part of an employee's official personnel file.

wrongful discharge   Improper or unjust termination of an employee.

Solutions

➤ **CHAPTER 1**

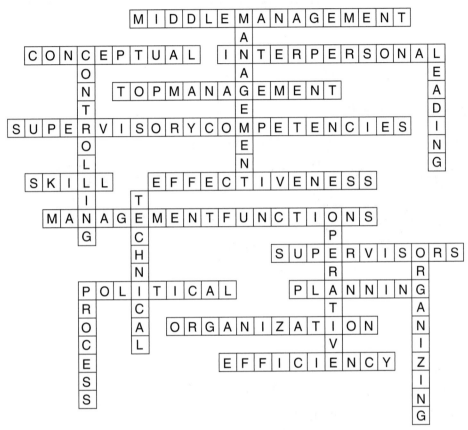

➤ **CHAPTER 2**

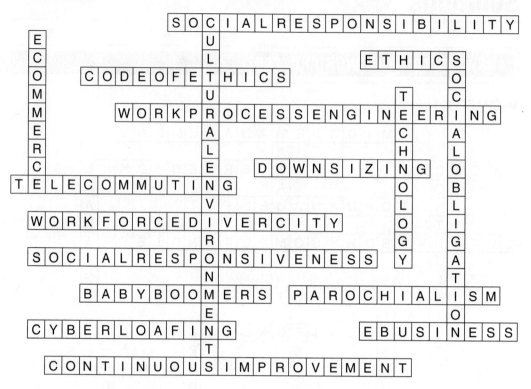

➤ **CHAPTER 3**

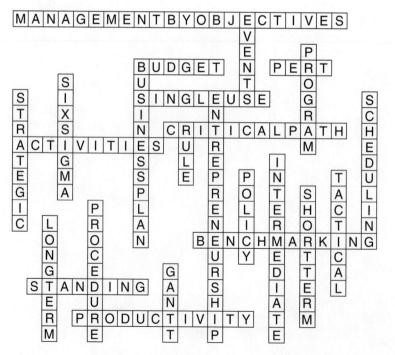

➤ CHAPTER 4

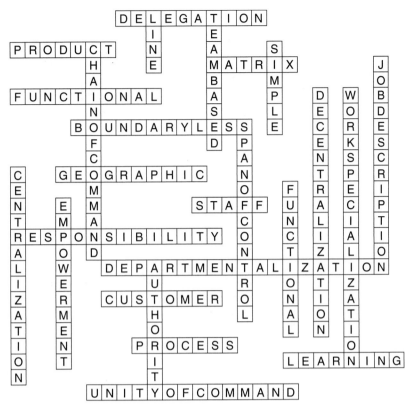

➤ CHAPTER 5

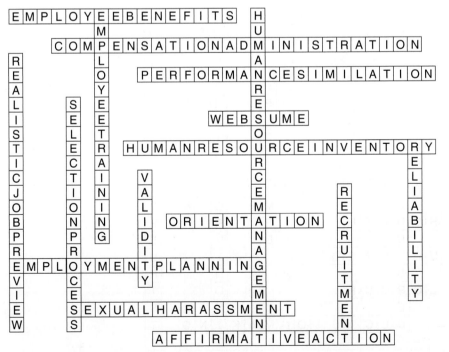

➤ **CHAPTER 6**

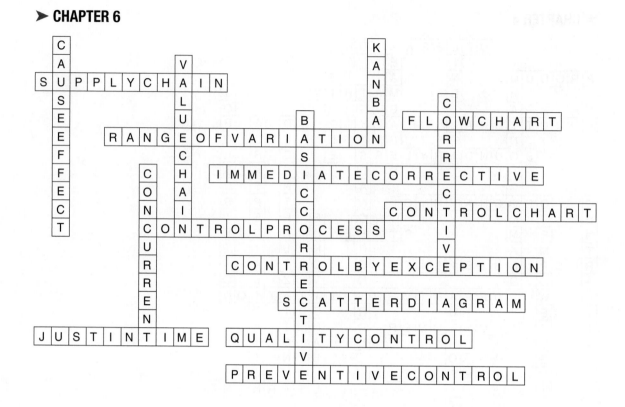

➤ **CHAPTER 7**

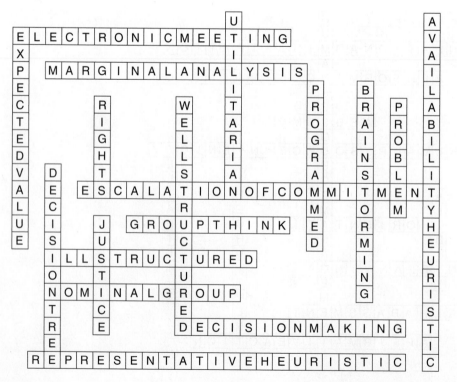

> **CHAPTER 8**

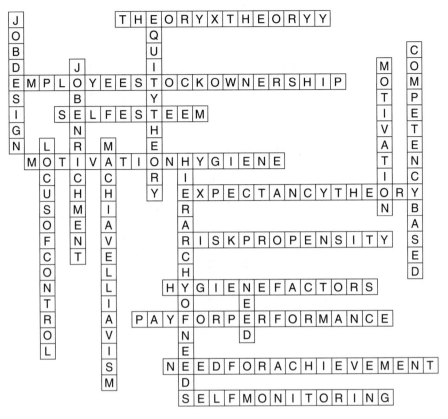

> **CHAPTER 9**

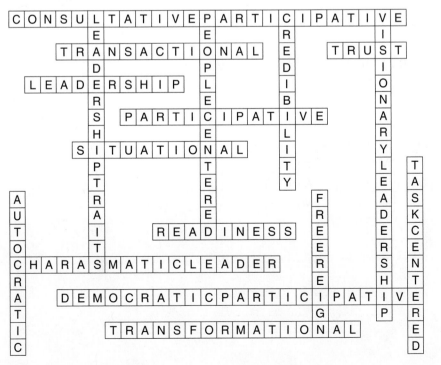

➤ **CHAPTER 10**

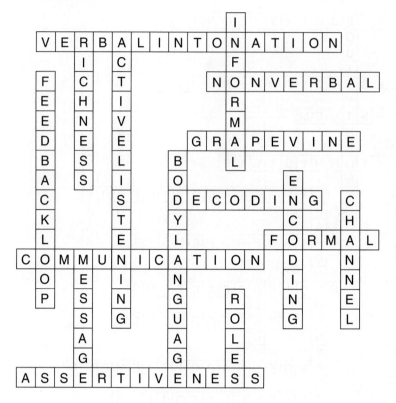

➤ **CHAPTER 11**

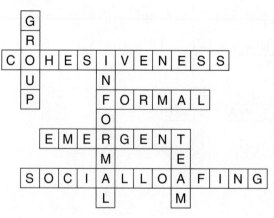

➤ CHAPTER 12

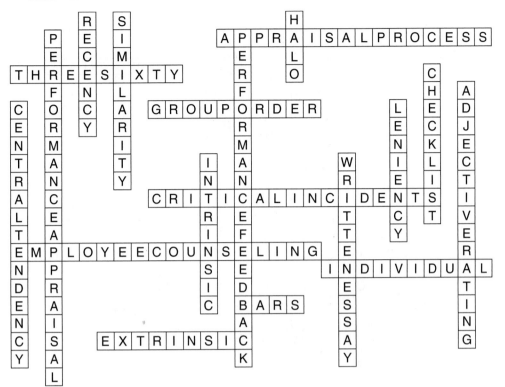

➤ CHAPTER 13

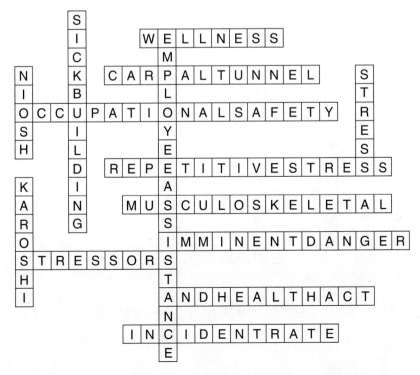

➤ **CHAPTER 14**

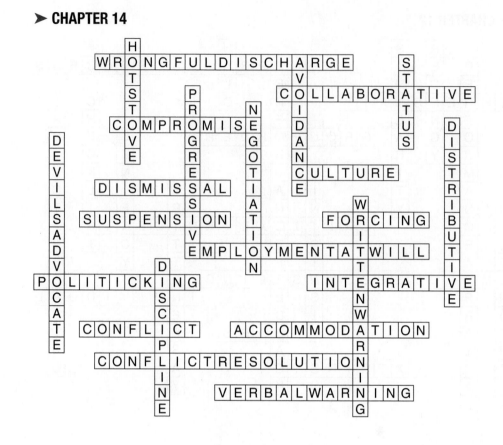

➤ **CHAPTER 15**

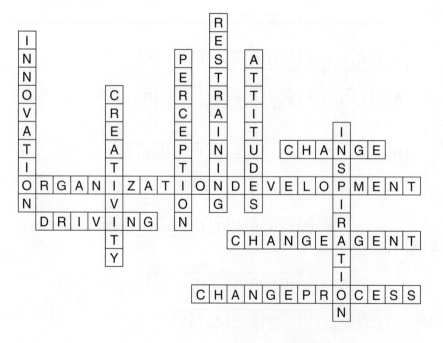

➤ CHAPTER 16

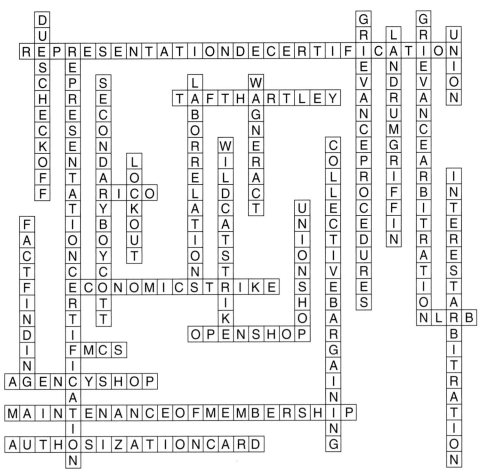

Index

Note: The locators followed by 'ex' denotes 'exhibits' cited in the text.

Photo Credits

p. 3: Fredrik Renander/Alamy

p. 4: Sebastian Czapnik/Dreamstime

p. 10: Mark Cowan/UPI/Newscom

p. 11: Robbins/DeCenzo/Wolter/ Getty Images USA, Inc.

p. 27: Jacob Wackerhausen/iStockphoto

p. 28: Dorling Kindersley

p. 34: Prism68/Shutterstock

p. 35: Mambo/Alamy

p. 39: Andrew J. DuBrin, 2011, Human Relations for Career and Personal Success: Concepts, Applications, and Skills, 9th edition, page 126, Prentice Hall, Upper Saddle River

p. 48: Janine Wiedel Photolibrary/Alamy

p. 59: Roger Bradley/Alamy

p. 60: Corbis/PhotoLibrary

p. 68: Richard Levine/Alamy

p. 87: Blend Images/Alamy

p. 88: James Woodson/Thinkstock

p. 103: AP Photo/Kathy Willens

p. 115: Ryan McVay/Photodisc/Thinkstock

p. 116: Robbins/DeCenzo/Wolter/Dorling Kindersley Limited

p. 130: Dick Luria/Photo Researchers, Inc.

p. 134: Image Source; Robbins/DeCenzo/Wolter/ Getty Images USA, Inc.

p. 144: Darrin Klimek/Thinkstock

p. 158: James Lauritz ; Robbins/DeCenzo/Wolter/Getty Images USA, Inc.

p. 171: Comstock Images/Thinkstock

p. 172: Jim Wileman/Alamy

p. 173: 1983 by Pat Brady. Reprinted with Permission

p. 180: Bryan Yablonsky/Sports Chrome/Newscom

p. 199: Blend Images/Alamy

p. 200: Jason Smith/Dreamstime

p. 215: Colin McConnell/Toronto Star/ZUMA Press/ Newscom

p. 227: JUPITERIMAGES/Brand X/Alamy

p. 228: Steve Gorton; Robbins/DeCenzo/Wolter/Dorling Kindersley Limited

p. 229: Mitchell Gerber/Corbis

p. 253: Adrian Sherratt/Alamy

p. 254, p. 266: Robbins/DeCenzo/Wolter/Dorling Kindersley Limited

p. 282: Dorling Kindersley/Dorling Kindersley Limited

p. 307: Michal Heron; Robbins/DeCenzo/Wolter/Pearson Education

p. 308: Robbins/DeCenzo/Wolter/Dorling Kindersley Limited

p. 324: AGStockUSA/Alamy

p. 335: Blend Images/Alamy

p. 336: Robbins/DeCenzo/Wolter/Dorling Kindersley Limited

p. 350: Siri Stafford/Thinkstock

p. 361: © allesalltag/Alamy

p. 362: Newscom

p. 364: Alan Williams; Robbins/DeCenzo/Wolter/Dorling Kindersley Limited

p. 393: Jim West/Alamy

p. 394: Jose Luis Pelaez/Corbis

p. 395: Alan Briere; Robbins/DeCenzo/Wolter; Dorling Kindersley Limited

p .404: ImageSource/AgeFotostock

p. 413: Corbis/AgeFotostock

p. 414: David Joel/Getty Images

p. 426: Joe Dunne/Getty Images